Islands in the Lake

Now notorious for its aridity and air pollution, Mexico City was once part of a flourishing lake environment. In nearby Xochimilco, Native Americans modified the lakes to fashion a distinctive and remarkably abundant aquatic society, one that provided a degree of ecological autonomy for local residents, enabling them to protect their communities' integrity, maintain their way of life, and preserve many aspects of their cultural heritage. While the area's ecology allowed for a wide array of socioeconomic and cultural continuities during colonial rule, demographic change came to affect the ecological basis of the lakes; pastoralism and new ways of using and modifying the lakes began to make a mark on the watery landscape and on the surrounding communities. In this fascinating study, Conway explores Xochimilco using native-language documents, which serve as a hallmark of this continuity and a means to trace patterns of change.

Richard M. Conway is Associate Professor of History at Montclair State University. A historian of colonial Latin America, his research focuses on the social and environmental history of Mexico.

CAMBRIDGE LATIN AMERICAN STUDIES

General Editors
KRIS LANE, Tulane University
MATTHEW RESTALL, Pennsylvania State University

Editor Emeritus
HERBERT S. KLEIN
Gouverneur Morris Emeritus Professor of History, Columbia University and Hoover
Research Fellow, Stanford University

Other Books in the Series

(*Continued after the Index*)

Islands in the Lake

Environment and Ethnohistory in Xochimilco,
New Spain

RICHARD M. CONWAY
Montclair State University

CAMBRIDGE
UNIVERSITY PRESS

CAMBRIDGE
UNIVERSITY PRESS

University Printing House, Cambridge CB2 8BS, United Kingdom

One Liberty Plaza, 20th Floor, New York, NY 10006, USA

477 Williamstown Road, Port Melbourne, VIC 3207, Australia

314–321, 3rd Floor, Plot 3, Splendor Forum, Jasola District Centre,
New Delhi – 110025, India

103 Penang Road, #05–06/07, Visioncrest Commercial, Singapore 238467

Cambridge University Press is part of the University of Cambridge.

It furthers the University's mission by disseminating knowledge in the pursuit of
education, learning, and research at the highest international levels of excellence.

www.cambridge.org
Information on this title: www.cambridge.org/9781316518892
DOI: 10.1017/9781009003957

First published 2021

A catalogue record for this publication is available from the British Library.

Library of Congress Cataloging-in-Publication Data
NAMES: Conway, Richard M., author.
TITLE: Islands in the lake : environment and ethnohistory in Xochimilco,
New Spain / Richard M. Conway, Montclair State University, New Jersey.
DESCRIPTION: Cambridge, UK ; New York, NY : Cambridge University Press, 2021. | Series:
Cambridge Latin American studies ; 124 | Includes bibliographical references and index.
IDENTIFIERS: LCCN 2021025421 (print) | LCCN 2021025422 (ebook) | ISBN
9781316518892 (hardback) | ISBN 9781009003957 (epub)
SUBJECTS: LCSH: Horticulture – Mexico – Mexico City – History. | Traditional farming –
Environmental aspects – Mexico – Mexico City – History. | Xochimilco (Mexico City,
Mexico) | BISAC: HISTORY / Latin America / General
CLASSIFICATION: LCC SB319.3.M6 C66 2021 (print) | LCC SB319.3.M6 (ebook) | DDC
630.972/53–dc23
LC record available at https://lccn.loc.gov/2021025421
LC ebook record available at https://lccn.loc.gov/2021025422

ISBN 978-1-316-51889-2 Hardback

Material in the introduction and Chapter 3 was originally published in "Lakes, Canoes, and
the Aquatic Communities of Xochimilco and Chalco, New Spain," *Ethnohistory*, vol. 59,
no. 3, pp. 541–568. (c) 2021, the American Society for Ethnohistory. All rights reserved.
Republished by permission of the copyright holder, and the present publisher, Duke
University Press. www.dukeupress.edu.

To Susan Schroeder

Contents

Illustrations

TABLES

Preface

In 1987, some ten centuries after its founding on the shore of a freshwater lake, Xochimilco became a World Heritage Site. The UNESCO award recognized the remarkable, historic achievement of the city's residents in fashioning an abundant system of wetland agriculture from the lake. Using extensive engineering works and soil dredged from the shallow waters, Native peoples created thousands of incredibly fertile, raised gardens, surrounded by an intricate network of canals, that supported first the rise of Tenochtitlan and the Aztec Triple Alliance and then, after its defeat by Spaniards and their Native American allies, Mexico City. By 1987, at a time when the region was gaining notoriety for its air pollution and aridity – and when many feared the final desiccation of what little was left of the old lakes – Xochimilco remained one of the last vestiges of the old aquatic world of the Aztecs.

To this day, Xochimilco (pronounced "so-chi-MIL-co") retains an identity of its own, one that remains distinct from that of Mexico City, much as it had through three centuries of colonialism. Even though it was located just to the south of the epicenter of Spanish rule in North America, surprisingly, Xochimilco resembled some of the more distant, peripheral regions of New Spain: Spanish intrusion remained limited, particularly when it came to the ownership of land; the modified lake environment served as a kind of aquatic barrier against outside intervention and disruption; relatively few Spaniards and other non-Native outsiders settled in the area; and the indigenous inhabitants of the city successfully preserved much of their cultural heritage, especially as it was set down in documents written in their language, Nahuatl, many of which are still extant in the archives today. These and other colonial-era sources show us how Xochimilco maintained so much of its distinctive character over the course of a thousand years.

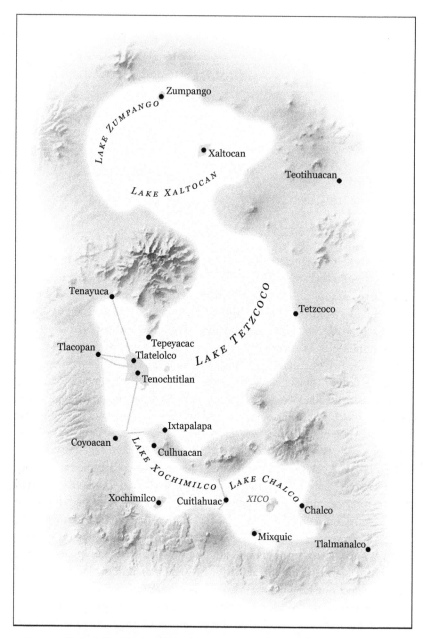

MAP O.1 The Basin of Mexico, 1519. Map by Geoffrey Wallace. Causeway, lake, and island features after Vanegas (Mundy, 2015), Gibson (1964), and Horn (1997). Additional data from INEGI and USGS.

Acknowledgments

Without the guidance and generous assistance of many people, I could not have written this book. First, I would like to thank Susan Schroeder, who has taught me so much. Her kindness and graciousness are matched only by her patience and generosity. Thank you. I would also like to express my gratitude to the other members of my dissertation committee: Colin MacLachlan, for his humor and advice, and James Boyden, for all his enthusiasm and encouragement. At Cambridge University Press, I thank Cecelia Cancellaro for her support of this book. I owe tremendous debts of gratitude to Kris Lane and to Matthew Restall.

I am most grateful to the institutions that provided research support. Financial assistance was received through Tulane University when I was a student there, including the Department of History, the Lurcy Fund, and the Stone Center for Latin American Studies. The Tinker Foundation also financed preliminary research. I would like to thank the Program for Cultural Cooperation between Spain's Ministry of Culture and United States Universities for enabling me to conduct research in Spain. The Newberry Library and its staff also deserve special thanks for making it possible for me to consult materials in the Ayer Collection, and I thank Sarah Austin and John Aubrey for their kind consideration. I am grateful to Montclair State University for funding that made possible two summer research trips, and I thank the current and former chairs of the department – Michael Whelan, Esperanza Brizuela-García, Robert Cray, and Jeff Strickland – for their advice and encouragement. I owe a particular debt of gratitude to Jeff and to James Woodard. I would also like to thank Shannan Clark, Megan Moran, and Susan Goscinski.

It is a pleasure to thank the many archivists and staff of Mexican repositories who have been so helpful and welcoming. The late Roberto Beristáin of the Archivo General de la Nación kindly shared his knowledge of the collections and introduced me to the archive's rich and abundant sources. I would also thank the staff of gallery four for being so patient with my requests for documents. I very much appreciate the assistance of the archivists and librarians of the Archivo Histórico of the Instituto Nacional de Antropología e Historia, the Biblioteca Nacional of the Universidad Nacional Autónoma de México, and the Archivo General de Notarías. Linda Arnold deserves special recognition for having generously shared her vast knowledge of Mexico City's archival collections. The archivists of Spain's Archivo General de las Indias and the Archivo Histórico Nacional also provided invaluable assistance. At Tulane's Latin American Library, I thank the director, Hortensia Calvo, as well as Verónica Sánchez, María Dolores Espinosa, and Sean Knowlton. David Dressing, the library's curator of manuscripts, was especially kind over the years and patiently taught me paleography. I am also grateful to the staff of the New York Public Library and to Jay Barksdale, in particular. The opportunity to use the Wertheim Study in the Stephen A. Schwarzman Building is much appreciated.

Faculty members and staff from my time at Tulane University have been very supportive. I thank Donna Denneen, Liz McMahon, Randy Sparks, and Justin Wolfe. The faculty and staff of the Stone Center and the Murphy Institute also offered me many opportunities and much vital assistance. Beyond Tulane, I am most grateful to James Lockhart for his interest in Xochimilco and for his indispensable wisdom. I very much appreciate his help in translating and understanding the Nahuatl documents from Xochimilco; all mistakes of transcription and translation are mine alone. I also thank Vera Candiani for encouraging me to consider the question of Xochimilco's ecological autonomy and Gregory Luna Golya for kindly sharing his dissertation with me. Barbara Mundy has also been most generous in sharing her knowledge of the history of water in central Mexico. Sonya Lipsett-Rivera passed along citations for some fascinating sources, and Jerry Offner and Sarah Cline were so kind as to send me reproductions of an excellent set of documents. Geoff Wallace considerably improved the book by making a couple of beautiful maps. Many other scholars deserve special thanks for their support and for sharing their knowledge, among them Ida Altman, William Beezley, Arne Bialuschewski, Elizabeth Boone, Louise Burkhart, John Chuchiak, Susan Deeds, Jake Frederick, William French, Kevin

Gosner, Jonathan Graham, Robert Haskett, María Hernández-Ojeda, Susan Kellogg, W. George Lovell, James Maffie, J. Gabriel Martinez-Serna, Martin Nesvig, Michel Oudijk, Justyna Olko, Alisa Plant, Stafford Poole, John Schwaller, Amara Solari, Lisa Sousa, John Sullivan, David Tavárez, Kevin Terraciano, Camilla Townsend, Stephanie Wood, and Yanna Yannakakis. I would also like to thank the reviewers of the book manuscript for their astute criticisms and excellent recommendations.

Many colleagues and friends should be mentioned, too, especially Gregg Bocketti, Mark Lentz, and Jonathan Truitt. I am also grateful to Erika Hosselkus, Bradley Benton, Mark Christensen, Spencer Delbridge, Owen Jones, Sarah Osten, Robert Schwaller, Lisa Singleton, Tatiana Seijas, Margarita Vargas-Betancourt, Dana Velasco Murillo, Peter Villella, and Ken Ward. I owe immeasurable thanks to Guillermo Náñez Falcón and William Wallace as well as to Michael Polushin and Wendy Kasinec. Michael introduced me to Latin American history and set me on the path to studying Mexico's past. He and Wendy did so very much to help me get here. Finally, I thank my family, Colin Conway, Patricia Valerie Conway, and Jessica Ambler. I will forever be grateful for your love and support.

Introduction

On Tuesday, March 24, 1579, a Spanish magistrate arrived at the lake-shore. Acting on an order from the viceroy, he set out in a canoe for the small island community of Santa María Magdalena Michcalco, located near the great causeway dividing Lakes Xochimilco and Chalco. The short journey took him from the deeper pool at the dock facilities into a maze of narrow canals. The waterways traversed dozens of rectangular artificial gardens that rose above the lake's shallow waters. Local, indigenous farmers cultivated these horticultural plots all year round, and if not preparing maize for one of their half dozen annual harvests, they would have been tending to their crops of chiles, squash, tomatoes, and other vegetables. Stretching into the distance with the many gardens were water willows whose root systems, partially visible from the canoe, held together the edges of the aquatic gardens. From the small canals, the magistrate, propelled along by an oarsman, would have passed into larger routes, including perhaps the main royal canal, before Michcalco came into view in the watery distance.[1]

Two days earlier, on the Sunday morning, the magistrate's notary and scribe had paid a visit to the imposing church in the village's parish seat, another island town, named San Pedro Cuitlahuac, where the indigenous community had just celebrated mass with the Dominican friar. Congregated there were the governor, other Native American officials, and the citizens of the parish's communities. It was to these assembled individuals that the scribe, speaking through the interpreter, delivered the

[1] Archivo General de la Nación (henceforth AGN), Mexico City, Ramo Tierras, volume 2681, expediente 6, folios 65–84v.

news that a Spanish resident, Bernardino Arias de Ávila, wanted to acquire two parcels of land and a house lot in Michcalco. On the following Tuesday, the officials announced, the magistrate would conduct an inspection to determine if the village's lands had indeed fallen vacant, as Bernardino had claimed.

The news would have been met with immediate consternation. Cuitlahuac (also known as Tlahuac; see Map o.2) and the villages like Michcalco in its jurisdiction were suffering the third year of what would become, by its end two years later, one of the most devastating epidemics in the history of the Americas. With innumerable people succumbing to disease, lands across Mexico had fallen vacant and remained uncultivated. Under medieval Castilian law, such unused land became the property of the crown. The monarch, or his representative – in this case the viceroy of New Spain – could then redistribute the land to those who would put it to productive use. Before redistributing the plots in Michcalco, though, the government had to ensure that the lands were indeed vacant and that their reallocation would not prove prejudicial to the community – hence the magistrate's inspection scheduled for the following Tuesday.

The Nahua officials quickly set about preparing a defense. As stipulated in the viceroy's order, they summoned five individuals who could provide testimonies. They also produced a map that could help the colonial authorities identify the lands in question and better understand their situation. The map was included in the papers of the report (see Map o.3). It depicted territory in the lake that was bounded on all sides by canals. Within the canals were dozens of the long, narrow raised garden plots of land. These gardens were lined up together in compact clusters, some of them parallel to one another, others arranged perpendicularly. The territory also encompassed six islands, shown as irregularly shaped ovals, of which the four that had structures drawn on them were Native communities. Santa María Magdalena Michcalco appeared on the left-hand side (the Nahuatl toponym, "the place of the fish house," is indicated by the glyphs for house and fish). The lands in question were located immediately to the right of the village, in the area full of wavy reeds and between glyphs that signified units of measurement. An alphabetic gloss, added by a scribe, indicated that these were the plots of land to be inspected.

While the map itself would have constituted valuable evidence, it was the Nahuas' depositions that proved crucial to the outcome of the case. The witnesses all hailed from the nearby city of Xochimilco and one of its subordinate villages. These individuals, like those from nearby Michcalco and San Pedro Cuitlahuac, were Nahuas, which is to say the speakers of

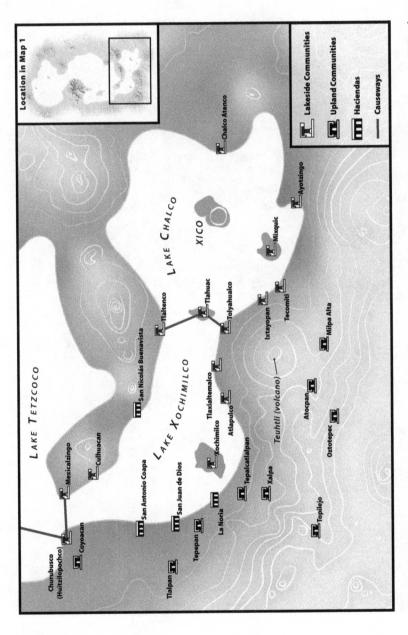

MAP 0.2 Lakes Xochimilco and Chalco. Map by Geoffrey Wallace. Causeway, lake, island features after Vanegas (Mundy, 2015), Gibson (1964), and Horn (1997). Additional data from INEGI and USGS.

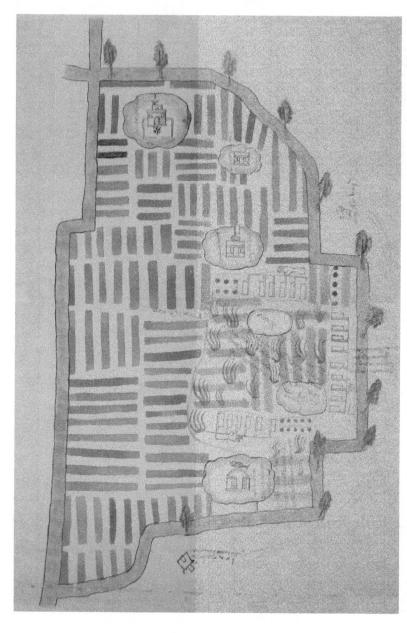

MAP 0.3 Map of Santa María Magdalena Michcalco, 1579. By permission of the Archivo General de la Nación, Mexico City, Tierras, vol. 2681, exp. 6, f. 2.

the Nahuatl language of central Mexico (commonly referred to as the Aztecs). The five men were all familiar with the lands in question, they declared under oath, and they knew that residents of the village had long sown and cultivated the lands peacefully and productively – or at least that had been the case until three years earlier when the *cocoliztli* epidemic broke out. Meaning sickness in Nahuatl, cocoliztli could refer to several diseases, although here it probably referred to typhus or a kind of hemorrhagic fever.[2] Such was the severe and ongoing loss of life, the Nahua witnesses noted, that the community had yet to reallocate the lands to the survivors. To redistribute them to Bernardino would be prejudicial and harmful, they averred. It would only add to the residents' misery.

A key element in the defense of Michcalco's lands had to do with their particular characteristics. As the Nahuas emphasized, the plots were not just any old parcels of land. Rather, as one witness testified, they were a kind of land known as a *chinamitl*.[3] The Nahuatl word meant "enclosure." It was used to refer specifically to the thousands of aquatic gardens that rose out of Lakes Xochimilco and Chalco (these were gardens that were enclosed by the roots of the water willows). A derivative of this word, *chinampa*, is the one that has entered into common usage today.

The chinampas were a defining feature of the landscape and history of Xochimilco and its neighboring communities. (They can be seen in the geometrically ordered, thick gray lines on the map produced in this case). The chinampas not only represented a creative adaptation by Nahuas to the lake environment but they were also tremendously fertile and productive. The witnesses argued that the gardens had to remain in the hands of Michcalco because they were essential community resources. The making of the gardens took a great deal of time – one that spanned multiple generations, as Juan Damián noted. The witnesses further explained that

---

[2] James Lockhart, *Nahuatl as Written: Lessons in Older Written Nahuatl, with Copious Examples and Texts* (Stanford: Stanford University Press and UCLA Latin American Center, 2001), 215; Elsa Malvido and Carlos Viesca, "La epidemia de cocoliztli de 1576," *Historias*, vol. 11 (1985), 27–33; Noble David Cook, *Born to Die: Disease and New World Conquest, 1492–1650* (New York: Cambridge University Press, 1998), 121; Hanns J. Prem, "Disease Outbreaks in Central Mexico during the Sixteenth Century," in Noble David Cook and W. George Lovell, eds., *"Secret Judgments of God": Old World Disease in Colonial Spanish America* (Norman: University of Oklahoma Press, 1991), 38–42; Rodolfo Acuna-Soto, David W. Stahle, Matthew D. Therrell, Richard D. Griffin, and Malcolm K. Cleaveland, "When Half the Population Died: The Epidemic of Hemorrhagic Fevers of 1576 in Mexico," *FEMS Microbiology Letters*, vol. 240, no. 1 (November 2004), 1–5.

[3] AGN, Tierras, vol. 2681, exp. 6, ff. 9–9v.

the process of constructing the chinampas was time consuming and laborious because farmers first had to dredge and haul mud from elsewhere and then pile it on top of the new plot of land. They then had to build up the gardens by adding alternating layers of mud and what were called *céspedes*, beds made out of aquatic plants. Thanks to the nutrients from these plants, the productive chinampas enabled Nahua farmers to grow a great deal of maize and chiles and other crops. The chinampas, then, were a specific and distinctive kind of land, and the residents ought to be able to continue to benefit from their considerable investment. In effect, the witnesses concluded, giving the chinampas to Bernardino would be to squander them.[4]

It is possible that the witnesses thought Bernardino Arias de Ávila might waste the land because he was an outsider and a Spaniard. One witness suggested as much.[5] Bernardino's identity, though, may have been beside the point. If anything, Bernardino was actually fairly well integrated into life in the predominantly Nahua region. He was identified as a permanent resident of Cuitlahuac and he had apparently lived in the area long enough to have established social connections with other residents, be they Nahuas or individuals of Spanish and mixed ancestries. Some of these acquaintances testified on his behalf. More importantly, and in a pattern that emerged among many of the Spaniards who took up residence in the lake areas, Bernardino was particularly well versed in Nahua culture, so much so, in fact, that he knew Nahuatl. Remarkably, Bernardino penned a petition in Nahuatl, in his own distinctive hand, which he submitted to the Native officials of Cuitlahuac about his request for the lands.[6] In other words, Bernardino's identity and relationship with the community may not have been the overriding issue. Rather, the specific, explicitly stated concern was that he intended to use the vacant chinampas for a purpose other than the ones for which they were intended. He preferred to raise goats and sheep on them. Bernardino himself acknowledged this. The problem was thus one of adhering to proper land use as practiced in the lake areas. The chinampas were gardens for growing vegetables and cereals, the argument ran. They were most certainly not for raising animals. To keep livestock on the lands would risk damage to nearby chinampas, the defendants and their

---

[4] AGN, Tierras, vol. 2681, exp. 6, ff. 9v–10v.
[5] Baltasar de San Martin stated that any Spaniard taking over the lands would cause much damage and harm to the Native people, AGN, Tierras, vol. 2681, exp. 6, f. 9v.
[6] AGN, Tierras, vol. 2681, exp. 6, f. 14.

witnesses pointed out, since the animals would either devour their crops or trample all over them. On a more fundamental level, though, the implication was that horticultural lands should not be used as pastoral ones. To do so would be to undermine local agricultural traditions – indeed, to undercut a key element of the lake area's patrimony – and it would also undermine the hard work that had gone into the making of the chinampas in the first place. In the end, these arguments prevailed. On July 14, the viceroy upheld the defense of Michcalco's lands and denied Bernardino's application.[7]

The case of Michcalco's chinampas takes us to the main issues explored in this book. As an environmental history and an ethnohistory of the chinampa districts with the city of Xochimilco at their heart, *Islands in the Lake* argues that the complex interplay between lake-area residents and their natural surroundings – which themselves had been transformed through extensive, centuries-long human interventions – profoundly shaped the fortunes of Native peoples in their cross-cultural encounters and exchanges with ethnic outsiders under Spanish rule. Dynamic human relations with the lake environment were central to the post-conquest fortunes of Native peoples. The highly engineered lacustrine landscape and the uses to which it was put played vital roles in enabling Nahuas to protect their communities' integrity, maintain their way of life, and preserve many aspects of their cultural heritage. The resilience of the Nahuatl language serves simultaneously as a hallmark of this continuity and as a means, thanks to the survival of an abundance of the native-language sources, for us to identify and trace patterns of change. At the same time as the chinampa districts' ecology allowed for a wide array of economic continuities, demographic decline proved devastating. Ultimately, factors of demography came to affect the ecological basis of the lakes. By the end of the colonial period pastoralism and, by extension, new ways of using and modifying the lakes, had begun to make a mark on the watery landscape.

***

The contested ownership of Michcalco's chinampas took place in one of the most distinctive and fascinating landscapes in the Americas. While the Basin of Mexico consisted of five interconnected lakes, the two southern ones, Lakes Xochimilco and Chalco, had long been important agricultural centers thanks both to their fresh waters and to the ingenuity and expertise

---

[7] AGN, Tierras, vol. 2681, exp. 6, ff. 9–12v, 14, 17, and 19–19v.

of local residents. Far from existing in a pristine natural state, since ancient times Native peoples had modified these two shallow lakes with irrigation works so as to realize the twin goals of reducing the risk of crop failures and increasing the size of their harvests. In their turn, the modified lakes brought changes to Native communities since irrigation relied upon and encouraged yet more complicated forms of sociopolitical organization. As communities gradually converted the natural setting into an aquatic, agricultural land-scape by digging ditches and constructing miles of dams and dikes, so the population grew in size and density, thereby encouraging and making possible yet more alterations to the lakes.[8] Eventually, the water manage-ment system came to affect all parts of the area's hydrology, from the entrance of water into the lake system through precipitation, creeks, rivers, and natural springs to its exit via a narrow channel into Lake Tetzcoco, which lay to the north and at a lower elevation. At all points between its entry and egress, Native peoples had stored, redirected, and channeled water, ultimately regulating it so that, by the time of the founding of the Aztec Triple Alliance, in 1428, the peoples of Xochimilco, Cuitlahuac, Mixquic, and other lakeshore communities had converted much of the water into thousands of the artificial islands like the ones Bernardino Arias de Ávila coveted. The lakes, according to historians, geographers, and archaeologists, thus came to be a highly engineered landscape.[9]

While chinampas existed elsewhere in the Basin of Mexico they were most prolific in Lakes Xochimilco and Chalco. There the local residents became so closely associated with the aquatic gardens that the Nahua annalist and historian don Domingo de San Antón Muñón Chimalpahin Quautlehuanitzin referred to them as the *chinampaneca*, or the chinampa people.[10] The term was common enough to appear in other accounts such

---

[8] William T. Sanders, Jeffrey R. Parsons, and Robert S. Santley, *The Basin of Mexico: Ecological Processes in the Evolution of a Civilization* (New York: Academic Press, 1979).

[9] Matthew Vitz, *A City on a Lake: Urban Political Ecology and the Growth of Mexico City* (Durham: Duke University Press, 2018), 137; Gregory Luna Golya, "Modeling the Aztec Agricultural Waterscape of Lake Xochimilco: A GIS Analysis of Lakebed Chinampas and Settlement," PhD dissertation, Pennsylvania State University, 2014, 173–175; Vera Candiani, *Dreaming of Dry Land: Environmental Transformation in Colonial Mexico City* (Stanford: Stanford University Press, 2014); Teresa Rojas Rabiela, R. Strauss, and J. Lameiras, *Nuevas noticias sobre las obras hidráulicas prehispánicas y coloniales en el Valle de México* (Mexico City: Instituto Nacional de Antropología e Historia, 1974); Ángel Palerm, *Obras hidráulicas prehispánicas en el sistema lacustre del Valle de México* (Mexico City: Instituto Nacional de Antropología e Historia, 1973).

[10] Don Domingo de San Antón Muñón Chimalpahin Quautlehuanitzin, *Annals of His Time*, James Lockhart, Susan Schroeder, and Doris Namala, eds. and trans. (Stanford: Stanford University Press, 2006), 42n2.

as the *Florentine Codex*.[11] This label was not just one imposed by an outsider; in a variant form, the Nahuatl-speaking inhabitants of the area called themselves the *chinampatlaca* (*tlaca* also meant "people").[12] While the residents of the southern lakes had an identity as chinampa cultivators, they also viewed themselves to be the distinct people of their own, autonomous city-states, or *altepetl*. These foundational units of social and political organization in central Mexico were typically the homes to specific ethnic groups, for which reason historians often refer to them as ethnic states rather than city-states. The residents of Xochimilco – which meant "the place of the flower fields" – thus identified themselves, in their Nahuatl-language sources, as the Xochimilca (as in "the people of the place of the flower fields").[13] Similarly the inhabitants of Cuitlahuac were the Cuitlahuaca; of Chalco, the Chalca, and Mixquic, the Mixquica. These kinds of specific ethnic identity – deeply rooted as they were to their own communities – were common across Mesoamerica. It is notable, then, that the proclivity toward such micropatriotism among the Native inhabitants of the southern lakes overlapped with their wider identification with their famously bountiful system of agriculture.

The abundant harvests generated a great deal of wealth in and around the southern lakes. The chinampa districts were affluent and, unsurprisingly, became home to large, dense populations. By the time of the conquest – or, more accurately, the Spanish–Mexica War of 1519–1521 – the largest of the lakeside communities, the city of Xochimilco, was itself home to some 30,000 residents. (To put that into perspective, Castile's most populous contemporary city, Seville, had 55,000 inhabitants).[14] Such was its prosperity that Xochimilco had impressive

[11] Fray Bernardino de Sahagún, *Florentine Codex: General History of the Things of New Spain: Book 12 – The Conquest of Mexico*, Charles E. Dibble and Arthur J. O. Anderson, eds. and trans. (Santa Fe: School of American Research/University of Utah, 1975), 37 and 95.

[12] "Titulos de la congregación de San Gregorio Atlapulco, 1603," in appendix 2, Juan Manuel Pérez Zevallos, *Xochimilco Ayer*, vol. 2 (Mexico City: Instituto Mora, Gobierno del Distrito Federal, Delegación Xochimilco, 2003), 150; Juan Manuel Pérez Zevallos and Luis Reyes García, eds., *La fundación de San Luis Tlaxialtemalco según los títulos primordiales de San Gregorio Atlapulco, 1519–1606* (Mexico City: Instituto Mora, 2003).

[13] AGN, Criminal, vol. 138, exp. 10, ff. 138–138v and AGN, Vínculos y Mayorazgos, vol. 179, exp. 1, ff. 6–7.

[14] Population figures are discussed at greater length in Chapter 4, but it should be noted here that the 30,000 figure is not conclusive. For the population figure for Seville, see Barbara E. Mundy, *The Death of Aztec Tenochtitlan, the Life of Mexico City* (Austin: University of Texas Press, 2015), 1.

monumental architecture, its leading citizens owned opulent homes and had great stores of wealth, as Spanish conquistadors were quick to note, and Xochimilco's ruling dynasties, of which there were three principal lineages, were among the most prominent in the Nahua world.[15]

The impressive surpluses of the chinampa districts inevitably attracted the attention of the Aztec Empire. From its origins in the Triple Alliance between Tlacopan, Tetzcoco, and Tenochtitlan in and around Lake Tetzcoco, the Aztec Empire expanded to the south, making a concerted effort to conquer and subdue the chinampatlaca during the fifteenth century. As soon as the Aztecs incorporated the chinampa districts into their empire, they set about maximizing the food supply beyond simply extracting surpluses through tribute, significant though these riches were. The Aztecs also undertook an enormous land reclamation project in the southern lakes, as discussed in the first chapter. Their goal was to convert all of the lakes' waters into chinampas. No longer would the chinampas be confined to the areas close to the shoreline. Achieving this new goal required harnessing imperial resources, mobilizing thousands of laborers, and in a great feat of engineering, constructing mile after mile of hydraulic engineering works that enabled the artificial islands to be built throughout all of the southern lakes, even in places that had previously been their deepest points.[16] The extensive network of barriers and channels fundamentally transformed the lakes into a vast expanse of artificial islands. When completed, the chinampa districts provided sustenance for as many as 150,000 people. They supported the rise of Tenochtitlan as one of the greatest cities of the early modern world and provided the foundation for the far-flung expansion of the Aztec Empire.[17]

The collapse of the Triple Alliance and the defeat of Tenochtitlan during the Spanish–Mexica War did not mark a decline in the central significance of the chinampa districts to the region's economy. Warfare did, however, bring substantial dislocations to the southern lakes and their chinampas. During the fighting, the Spaniards and their allies

---

[15] Pedro Carrasco, "Los señores de Xochimilco en 1548," *Tlalocan*, vol. 7 (1977), 229–265; Bernal Díaz del Castillo, *The Discovery and Conquest of Mexico, 1517–1521*, A. P. Maudslay, trans. (New York: Farrar, Strauss, and Cudahy, 1956), 344–345.

[16] The phrase "hydraulic engineering" is borrowed from Candiani, *Dreaming of Dry Land*, 16.

[17] Jeffrey R. Parsons, "The Role of Chinampa Agriculture in the Food Supply of Aztec Tenochtitlan," in Charles E. Cleland, ed., *Cultural Change and Continuity: Essays in Honor of James Bennett Griffin* (New York: Academic Press, 1976), 242, 245; Luna, "Modeling the Aztec Agricultural Waterscape of Lake Xochimilco," iv, 148, 160.

breached the causeways and destroyed other features of the water management system, thereby inundating the new, Aztec-era chinampas in the middle of the lakes. The original chinampa zone, though, which was closer to the shore, survived. In a further shift, after the demise of the Aztec Empire's coordinated supervision of the lakes, under Spanish rule the maintenance of engineering works reverted to the altepetl level. The devolved authority for supervising and keeping up the dams and dikes and canals reflected one of the ways in which Nahuas enjoyed some measure of autonomy, at least when it came to controlling and preserving the lake environment.[18]

The chinampas, then, continued to provide essential supplies of maize and vegetables to Mexico City. Xochimilco went on to figure prominently in the new colonial order. In addition to provisioning the capital and providing sizable tribute revenues, the altepetl was awarded as an *encomienda*, a grant of tribute and labor, to Fernando Cortés's lieutenant, the conquistador Pedro de Alvarado. Xochimilco was the largest single encomienda in Mexico. Too great for any one individual, or so the crown worried, Xochimilco was swiftly escheated into the royal domain, whereupon it became an enduring single colonial jurisdiction and an important religious center for the Franciscans in their evangelizing efforts.[19] Reflecting its continued economic significance, in 1559 King Philip II granted Xochimilco the much-coveted and superior status of a city, making it one of the highest-ranking municipalities in Spain's emerging global empire. The only other cities in the region were the polities of the former Aztec Triple Alliance.[20]

For most of the colonial period, Xochimilco and the chinampa districts continued to flourish in many ways, notwithstanding the devastating loss of life from epidemic diseases. Because the colonial-era drainage project, the notorious *desagüe*, was designed to protect Mexico City from flooding by removing water from the northern part of the Basin of Mexico, the southern lakes retained their water levels. Nahuas could therefore preserve their hydraulic engineering works and continue to cultivate chinampas and use the lakes for transportation and commerce. Colonial-era observers themselves appreciated, at least to a certain extent, the ongoing,

---

[18] Mundy, *The Death of Aztec Tenochtitlan*, 72.
[19] Charles Gibson, *The Aztecs under Spanish Rule: A History of the Indians of the Valley of Mexico, 1519–1810* (Stanford: Stanford University Press, 1964), 61.
[20] *Colección de documentos inéditos, relativos al descubrimiento, conquista y organización de las antiguas posesiones españolas de ultramar*, vol. 22 (Madrid: Tipografía de Archivos, I. Olózaga, 1929), 103; Gibson, *The Aztecs under Spanish Rule*, 32.

albeit relative prosperity of the chinampa districts. In 1746, a Spanish treasury official named Joseph Antonio de Villaseñor y Sánchez enthused about the economic dynamism of Nahua communities in and around Lakes Xochimilco and Chalco.[21] He noted that the historically opulent city of Xochimilco still flourished thanks to the continued cultivation of chinampas. Xochimilco's heights of prosperity were further maintained by the many advantages afforded by canoe transportation, lively commerce, and vibrant craft traditions. Unlike other altepetl, a majority of the population remained employed as skilled artisans (or *oficiales*).[22] Xochimilco was hardly alone in its affluence. The nearby island town of Mixquic also had fertile lands, and many canoes passed through it carrying fruit, sugar, honey, and other foodstuffs. Ayotzingo, located further to the east, served as the main point of embarkation for grains coming from the province of Chalco, where everything needed to sustain life could be found. The Friday markets of Chalco Atenco attracted a great number of people from far and wide, and a multitude of canoes brought every kind of merchandise to customers. Villaseñor y Sánchez's laudatory descriptions of the southern lake areas suggest that the area enjoyed significant ecological, economic, and social continuities through the 1740s. These continuities stood in stark contrast with other communities, such as Tetzcoco, where the lakes had all but dried up. Villaseñor y Sánchez offered a somber characterization of that city, which had ceased to be populous and affluent, he claimed, because of a decline in commerce.[23]

As Villaseñor y Sánchez's description of ongoing vitality suggests, the history of Xochimilco should make us pause and reconsider the wider complexities and trajectories of change for Nahua communities in the colonial period. Indeed, the history of Xochimilco and the chinampa districts offers an opportunity to reconsider some of the fundamental assumptions that have followed from all too persistent stereotypes, engendered by conquest and colonialism, about European cultural superiority. As many decades of ethnohistorical scholarship have so powerfully shown us, and as recent advances in the revisionist literature on the history of science have further demonstrated, the flows of knowledge and innovation around the early modern world were multidirectional, often overlapping, sometimes mutually constitutive between Native peoples, Africans, Asians, and

[21] Joseph Antonio de Villaseñor y Sánchez, *Theatro americano: Descripción general de los Reynos y Provincias de la Nueva España y sus jurisdicciones* (Mexico City: Editorial Trillas, 1992), 103–106, 160–161.

[22] AGN, Padrones, vol. 29, f. 1.   [23] Villaseñor y Sánchez, *Theatro Americano*, 155.

Europeans.[24] The Spanish "conquest," for instance, is still essentially misunderstood by many as a victory of superior European technology; the recent historiographical innovations of the New Conquest History are still challenging and undermining the entrenched, old narratives.[25] The history of the chinampa districts is one that further subverts and fundamentally challenges these and other enduring fallacies.

Some colonial observers themselves were immediately aware of the vital intellectual, scientific, and technological accomplishments of Native Americans. The creole scientist, José Antonio de Alzate y Ramírez, for instance, found a great deal to admire in chinampa cultivation. In the 1790s Alzate published a highly laudatory and detailed account of aquatic garden agriculture. He argued that the chinampas were not only a source of patriotic pride but also a vindication of the achievements of Mexico's indigenous peoples. Alzate y Ramírez maintained that chinampa cultivation ought to be better known in other parts of the world because, if readers elsewhere were to adopt the novel and arguably superior farming techniques of the "Indians," they would be sure to suffer fewer failed harvests and enjoy larger yields and greater prosperity. It is worth dwelling on the significance of his words. Here was one of the most important intellectuals of the age extolling the virtues of indigenous people's inventiveness and industry at a time when Native peoples were commonly denigrated and dismissed for their supposedly inferior, backward technology. In contrast to the common idea of technological change being brought from Europe to the Americas, here was a Spaniard arguing that the rest of the world should harness indigenous expertise to alleviate hunger and prevent famine.[26]

---

[24] Jorge Cañizares-Esguerra, *How to Write the History of the New World: History, Epistemologies, and Identities in the Eighteenth-Century Atlantic World* (Stanford: Stanford University Press, 2002), 266–345; Cañizares-Esguerra, Nature, *Empire, and Nation: Explorations in the History of Science in the Iberian World* (Stanford: Stanford University Press, 2006).

[25] It is increasingly apparent that the conquest needs to be seen as a complex combination of violent conflicts – akin to a prolonged civil war waged over many years – that entangled and involved shifting alliances of many Native American groups, Spaniards, and individuals of African ancestry, and that the defeat of the Mexica owed much to indigenous allies and their many military, diplomatic, and logistical contributions. Matthew Restall, "The New Conquest History," *History Compass*, vol. 10, no. 2 (2012), 151–160; Matthew Restall, *When Montezuma Met Cortés: The True Story of the Meeting That Changed History* (New York: Ecco, 2018).

[26] Joseph Antonio de Alzate y Ramírez, "Memoria sobre agricultura," *Gacetas de literatura de México*, vol. 2 (Puebla: reimpresa en la oficina del Hospital de S. Pedro, 1831), 382–399, also published in Teresa Rojas Rabiela, ed., *La agricultura chinampera: Compilación histórica* (Mexico City: Universidad Autónoma Chapingo, 1993), 13–29;

Modern scholars have largely concurred with Alzate y Ramírez's assessment. The chinampas constitute one of the world's most innovative systems of wetland agriculture. Since the gardens were ideally irrigated and so very fertile, farmers enjoyed bumper crops. A single hectare of chinampas could provide an impressive annual harvest of some 3,000 kilograms of maize, enough for a single farmer to feed as many as fifteen people. With such vast surpluses, a few thousand agriculturalists could support cities numbering in the tens of thousands. Not for nothing, then, have archaeologists reckoned that chinampa agriculture was one of the most productive kinds of farming devised before the advent of modern agriculture with its fertilizers and pesticides.[27]

***

Just as the identity of the chinampatlaca – the chinampa people – cannot be separated from their unique and rich agricultural traditions, so the history of Xochimilco cannot be understood in isolation from its lacustrine environment or from its historical demography. Whereas the landscape and the ways people modified and used it provided a foundation for continuities in the colonial era, so catastrophic population collapse accounted for numerous discontinuities. For these reasons, *Islands in the Lake* seeks to provide an explanation for the contrasting experiences of continuity and ecological autonomy, on the one hand, and of crisis and upheaval, on the other.

To do this, the book offers the innovation of combining two historical approaches that have thus far remained distinct. The first is environmental history and the second, the New Philology, which is an important, revisionist branch of ethnohistory in which scholars analyze native-language sources to reveal the perspectives of Native peoples themselves, in their own words, about their experiences.[28] The merging of these approaches

see also Jorge Cañizares-Esguerra, "Introduction," and Fiona Clark, "'Read All about It': Science, Translation, Adaptation, and Confrontation in the *Gazeta de Literatura de México*, *1788–1795*," in Daniela Bleichmar, Paula De Vos, and Kristin Huffine, eds., *Science in the Spanish and Portuguese Empires, 1500–1800* (Stanford: Stanford University Press, 2009), 1–5 and 147–177.

[27] Luna Golya, "Modeling the Aztec Agricultural Waterscape of Lake Xochimilco," 61, 120, 153, and 156–157; Jeffrey R. Parsons, Mary H. Parsons, Virginia Popper, and Mary Taft, "Chinampa Agriculture and Aztec Urbanization in the Valley of Mexico," in I. S. Farrington, ed., *Prehistoric Intensive Agriculture*, vol. 1 (Oxford: BAR, 1985), 51; Parsons, "The Role of Chinampa Agriculture," 239, 242, and 245.

[28] Matthew Restall, "A History of the New Philology and the New Philology in History," *Latin American Research Review*, vol. 38, no. 1 (2003), 113–134.

represents a new departure in the scholarship, one that makes it possible to discern how the interplay between colonial encounters and changing human relations with the natural world created, in Xochimilco and the chinampa districts, a distinctive historical experience that diverges in some ways from the patterns observed in other parts of central Mexico.[29]

A key facet of Xochimilco's history, the book argues, is that the lakes, and the ways local residents modified and used them, acted as a buffer against the disruptions of Spanish rule. The Nahuas succeeded in maintaining their communities' economic vitality, social integrity, and cultural traditions insofar as they preserved lake conditions and protected their aquatic resources from the demands of colonial authorities. The buffer provided by local people's uses of the lakes amounted to a kind of ecological autonomy. This concept has been elucidated most comprehensively by the historian John Tutino. Tutino identified ecological autonomy as a foundation for the revolutionary capacity of insurgents in both 1810 and 1910, when Mexicans took up arms, respectively, against Spanish rule and the dictatorship of Porfirio Díaz. In this context, ecological autonomy allowed the insurgents to act independently of established economic or political structures by provisioning themselves with subsistence crops and livestock while also being able to turn the tools of daily life into the weapons of guerrilla warfare. Tutino explains that such ecological autonomy was neither absolute nor unchanging. Rather, he shows that there have been contrasting historical periods in which it was either undermined, as with the catastrophic demographic decline of the sixteenth century, or reconsolidated, as for instance in the period from 1550 to 1630 when the Spanish monarchy escheated encomiendas, asserted royal control, and incorporated Native Americans into the empire as vassals. Vassalage provided indigenous people with certain rights, such as to the ownership of their lands and to self-rule within their communities, which reinforced their autonomy.[30]

---

[29] Bradley Skopyk has combined a wide range of novel methodologies to examine the environmental history of watersheds in Teotihuacan and Tlaxcala and has made use of Nahuatl sources in his analysis. Bradley Skopyk, *Colonial Cataclysms: Climate, Landscape, and Memory in Mexico's Little Ice Age* (Tucson: University of Arizona Press, 2020). While not explicitly identified as a work of environmental history, Jonathan Amith has drawn extensively on Nahuatl sources, and while Mundy's work is, in part, an environmental history, she does use Nahuatl sources. Jonathan D. Amith, *The Möbius Strip: A Spatial History of Colonial Society in Guerrero, Mexico* (Stanford: Stanford University Press, 2005); Mundy, *The Death of Aztec Tenochtitlan.*

[30] John M. Tutino, "The Revolutionary Capacity of Rural Communities: Ecological Autonomy and Its Demise," *in Cycles of Conflict, Centuries of Change: Crisis, Reform,*

For Tutino, the resulting socioeconomic and political structures allowed for a modicum of ecological autonomy for rural communities. Indeed, this relative self-sufficiency has come to be seen as an essential feature of peasant societies, one that has made possible their resistance to destructive forces imposed by powerful outsiders. For Vera Candiani, such autonomy enabled indigenous communities in the northern lakes to push back against agents of the colonial administration who sought to drain Lakes Zumpango and Xaltocan and, as a result, undermine the integrity if not the viability of their communities. As Candiani notes, "religion, communal organization and integrity, town finances, cultural identity, and the entire fabric of social life were wrapped up in how lands, water, and the liminal space between them were used to meet food and subsistence needs."[31]

Following Candiani and Tutino, this book considers the history of Xochimilco and the southern lake areas in terms of their ecological autonomy. The foundations for such autonomy took various forms, both material and abstract. The material ones consisted of the chinampas themselves, the hydraulic infrastructure that controlled and regulated the lake waters, and also the tools and technology, including canoes, that made all this possible. The intellectual dimension of the Nahuas' autonomy encompassed their knowledge and skills – within a wider cultural matrix – that made possible the making and the maintenance of the engineering works, the cultivation of the chinampas, the manufacture of canoes, and the broader preservation of the distinctive, amphibious way of life.[32] Ecological autonomy also endured because Nahuas retained control over local decisions about managing water and soil and because community leaders could recruit and organize skilled workers who built and maintained the complex hydrological works while also undertaking the necessary, labor-intensive soil excavations.

Other factors augmented Xochimilco's ecological autonomy. The productivity of the chinampas and the value of canoe transportation proved important to a viceregal administration that was simultaneously

---

and Revolution in Mexico, Elisa Servín, Leticia Reina, and John Tutino, eds. (Durham: Duke University Press, 2007), 211–220.

[31] Candiani, *Dreaming of Dry Land*, 295; Candiani, "The Desagüe Reconsidered: Environmental Dimensions of Class Conflict in Colonial Mexico," *Hispanic American Historical Review*, vol. 92, no. 1 (2012), 5–39.

[32] Candiani and Tutino emphasize the significance of indigenous knowledge in their analyses; Candiani, "The Desagüe Reconsidered," 6; Tutino, "The Revolutionary Capacity of Rural Communities," 214.

eager to secure tribute income and anxious about the capital's food supply. The government thus showed a willingness to protect the chinampa system from Spanish intrusion for much of the colonial period. Only in the second half of the eighteenth century did this change. By then, the rise of large, landed estates known as *haciendas* – which came to dominate the provisioning of Mexico City – brought about a shift in government priorities. For the Hapsburg period of Xochimilco's history and for the early part of the Bourbon era, few Spaniards or other outsiders interfered in wetland agriculture, instead establishing farms in upland areas for dry-land agriculture and pastoralism.[33]

By contrast, several factors undermined, if only partially, Xochimilco's ecological autonomy. Principal among them was demographic collapse. The severe reduction of the population undermined the ability of communities to maintain the water management system. So much loss of life meant that lands and chinampas fell vacant.[34] At the same time, other severe disruptions followed from an unstable climate. Xochimilco, as with the Northern Hemisphere more broadly, experienced the deepening cold of the Little Ice Age, a period of global cooling during the long seventeenth century that brought wetter conditions and greater extremes of climate variability, including flooding. Added to these difficulties were others. The colonial government's demands for tribute and labor, at a time of demographic contraction and climatic upheaval, created hardships and tensions within communities. Xochimilco's political autonomy also went into decline as it faced closer scrutiny and intervention by outsiders. In the late Bourbon era, that intervention extended into the southern lakes' hydrology.[35]

The divergent and contrasting aspects of Xochimilco's ethnohistory – between the continuities in human relations with the landscape and the dislocations and transformations wrought by demographic upheaval –

---

[33] I thank one of the reviewers of the manuscript for kindly helping me to clarify and express these points.

[34] In a similar manner, Native peoples were less able to maintain agricultural terraces in other parts of central Mexico, as Aleksander Borejsza has shown in "Village and Field Abandonment in Post-conquest Tlaxcala: A Geoarchaeological Perspective," *Anthropocene*, vol. 3 (2013), 9–23.

[35] Vera Candiani has pointed out that the speed with which changes came to lake communities could have a profound effect on their ability to adapt to changing circumstances. The same can be said for Xochimilco, although in a different way: that the southern lakes were not subject to the full force of the desagüe project facilitated the process of adjustment. As a result of this, in part, Xochimilco's ecological autonomy proved enduring and Nahuas there had time to respond to new colonial pressures. Candiani, "The Desagüe Reconsidered," 33.

call on us to question and reconsider complexities in some of the wider patterns and structures of colonial Latin American history. The continuities, as research presented in this book demonstrates, were manifold and striking: most conspicuously, the lacustrine environment remained almost unchanged for centuries; Nahua communities enjoyed a good degree of ecological autonomy; they retained control of their landholdings; haciendas were not as disruptive here as elsewhere; water-borne commerce continued to thrive; Nahuas remained demographically ascendant; few Spaniards or other non-Native peoples settled in the area; the process of *mestizaje*, or biological and cultural mixing, took place slowly and on a limited basis, and, as though Native residents were seldom exposed to Hispanic influences, their Nahuatl-language sources retained many of the qualities of older forms of expression, exhibiting as they did far fewer intrusions from Spanish than would typically be seen at this time. If anything, as Bernardino Arias de Ávila's experience shows us, such cultural exchanges flowed in other directions, with Spanish settlers contending with Nahuas on the latter's terms, at least to a certain extent, and necessarily adapting to Nahua culture. Put another way, a surprisingly great deal of Xochimilco's heritage remained intact. As Charles Gibson concluded more than half a century ago, although Xochimilco was a large community, it nevertheless successfully "retained an Indian character."[36]

On the basis of all this, one might be forgiven for mistaking Xochimilco as somewhere remote and distant from the core areas of colonial rule when, in fact, it was but a dozen miles away from the viceregal capital, which is to say the administrative center and largest Spanish community in all of continental North America. Historians have long recognized a key distinction between core areas of colonial Latin America and their peripheries.[37] Xochimilco was clearly not located at the far reaches of the frontier. Nor did its history call into question this paradigm for understanding colonial Latin America's past. But its history did exhibit some striking anomalies for a place situated at the center – incongruities that merit close inspection. Indeed, Xochimilco's historical experience even stood out from other nearby communities in the Basin of Mexico. *Islands in the Lake* suggests that these discrepancies in historical experiences can be explained by the intricacy of shifting, intertwined, and mutually influential relationships between people and their lacustrine surroundings.

---

[36] Gibson, *The Aztecs under Spanish Rule*, 366.

[37] James Lockhart and Stuart B. Schwartz, *Early Latin America: A History of Colonial Spanish America and Brazil* (New York: Cambridge University Press, 1983).

On the other hand, there could be no ecological autonomy when it came to the arrival of foreign pathogens. The population trends of the chinampa districts closely tracked with those observed elsewhere in the Americas in the decades and centuries after the arrival of Europeans, Africans, and, to a smaller extent, Asians.[38] The loss of life from diseases to which Native peoples had not developed any kind of immunity was immediate, swift, and devastating. Xochimilco's population collapsed by about four-fifths within the first half century of contact with outsiders. Thereafter it continued to decline precipitously. The cocolitzli outbreak that had rendered the chinampas of Michcalco vacant may have been the last of the largest epidemics of the sixteenth century. But pestilence and any number of other viruses and bacteria continued to reduce the size of the Nahua communities until the middle decades of the seventeenth century, at which time they had been reduced to just a tenth of their original inhabitants.

The secondary effects of population collapse spread from the very viability of some communities to the reshaping of social structures in others. Across the lake areas, heightened conflicts over resources were deepened by demographic dislocations. The onerous demands of the colonial political economy – particularly in terms of tribute income, the provisioning of the capital, and levies of draft laborers – combined with population decline to upset local politics, undermine the ideological basis of Native authority, and destabilize the social hierarchy, aspects of which came to be fundamentally reconstituted. If people's relations with the engineered landscape of the lakes provided a degree of stability and secured a certain amount of separation from colonial pressures, demographic decline, by contrast, brought instability and precious little respite from colonial exactions. Demographic upheaval provoked, in certain fragile moments, violence and flight, as when the population reached its nadir in the mid-seventeenth century. As a result, Xochimilco and the chinampa districts were less like a periphery and more a kind of intermediate space, neither completely a zone of refuge, akin to those mountainous and forested places where peoples might flee, nor entirely a shatter zone, those places where the onslaught of conquest and colonialism brought violence, crisis, and complex reconfigurations of lived experiences, among them displacement, dispersal, and transformation, sometimes through ethnogenesis.[39]

---

[38] Cook, *Born to Die*.

[39] On zones of refuge, see Stuart B. Schwartz and Frank Salomon, "New Peoples and New Kinds of People: Adaptation, Adjustment, and Ethnogenesis in South American Indigenous Societies (Colonial Era)," in Stuart B. Schwartz and Frank Salomon, eds.,

In some respects, then, the colonial-era history of Xochimilco resembled the kinds of upheaval and transformation that historian Alfred Crosby described in his book *Ecological Imperialism*.[40] Crosby argued that European overseas expansion and settlement introduced a whole host of species to the Americas which undermined local ecosystems and remade parts of the Americas into "Neo-Europes," just as they did in other parts of the world where European settlers came to predominate, as in Australasia. In Crosby's telling, foreign species acted as advance parties of European colonization; that the foreign species thrived in the Americas, he argued, paved the way for European domination. To be sure, foreign biota and microbes brought fundamental changes to Xochimilco, most conspicuously in the case of epidemic diseases. But not all such introductions were necessarily deleterious or destructive, nor did they entail the wholesale substitution of native plants or animals. Rather, as Teresa Rojas Rabiela has noted, the introduction of European cultigens could instead serve to complement and enrich Nahua agriculture.[41] Similar processes of incorporation and adaptation, rather than substitution and displacement, can be observed in the introduction of livestock to Xochimilco, at least until the late colonial period when haciendas intruded ever further into the lakes in order to create cattle-ranching pastures. Accordingly, if one were to locate Xochimilco's historical experience on a spectrum of change, it would likely be somewhere in the middle, although closer to ecological autonomy than to Crosby's ecological imperialism. Xochimilco's history thus aligns with recent scholarship that has emphasized adaptation and perseverance over destruction and transformation, as with Bradley Skopyk's emphasis on Native people's ecological creativity, particularly when it came to agriculture.[42]

The Cambridge History of Native Peoples of the Americas (New York: Cambridge University Press, 1999), 443–502; James C. Scott, *The Art of Not Being Governed: An Anarchist History of Upland Southeast Asia* (New Haven: Yale University Press, 2009). On shatter zones, see Robbie Ethridge and Sheri M. Shuck-Hall, eds., *Mapping the Mississippian Shatter Zone: The Colonial Indian Slave Trade and Regional Instability in the American South* (Lincoln: University of Nebraska Press, 2009); Sami Lakomäki, *Gathering Together: The Shawnee People through Diaspora and Nationhood, 1600–1870* (New Haven: Yale University Press, 2014).

[40] Alfred W. Crosby, *Ecological Imperialism: The Biological Expansion of Europe, 900–1900* (New York: Cambridge University Press, 1986).

[41] Teresa Rojas Rabiela, "Ecological and Agricultural Changes in the Chinampas of Xochimilco-Chalco," in H. R. Harvey, ed., *Land and Politics in the Valley of Mexico: A Two Thousand Year Perspective* (Albuquerque: University of New Mexico Press, 1991), 281.

[42] Skopyk, *Colonial Cataclysms*, 19.

Perhaps Xochimilco and neighboring communities can best be understood as a particular kind of contact zone, one where cross-cultural interactions and exchanges took place in an aquatic environment that itself mediated and influenced the nature of colonial encounters. The lakes, swamps, chinampas, and waterways provided spaces where individuals of different ethnicities dealt with one another in a hybrid, modified landscape that tipped the balance of colonial power in multiple and unusual directions, some of which moved away from narratives of European domination and Native American dispossession and marginalization. In this way, the history of Xochimilco shared commonalities with the history of other aquatic territories, be they in the Amazon, Colombia's Pacific coast region, the Great Lakes, or along the coast of New York and southern New England.[43]

***

This book draws from several historiographical and methodological traditions. Its points of departure lie in the work of several pathbreaking historians. Charles Gibson, in his regional history of *The Aztecs Under Spanish Rule* – which covered the whole of the Basin of Mexico – identified some of the outlines of Xochimilco's distinctive past. He provided frequent references to Xochimilco, which, while brief and offered in passing, nevertheless afforded us with tantalizing glimpses into certain key trends, especially the endurance of chinampa agriculture, the negligible development of Spanish estates, and the correspondingly limited rates of Spanish settlement. Beyond the few specific details about Xochimilco, Gibson's landmark study advanced our appreciation for the environmental dimensions of the region's history, although he did not describe his work in these terms. Much of the book's treatment had to do with natural resources, and while he paid less direct and sustained attention to the landscape, Gibson did recognize the central importance of historical demography, a field that was gaining full traction at the time of his writing. The second scholar whose works have been essential to this book is Teresa Rojas Rabiela. Her studies stand out for having contributed to our knowledge of indigenous agriculture, chinampa

---

[43] Heather F. Roller, *Amazonian Routes: Indigenous Mobility and Colonial Communities in Northern Brazil* (Stanford: Stanford University Press, 2014); Ulrich Oslender, *The Geographies of Social Movements: Afro-Colombian Mobilization and the Aquatic Space* (Durham: Duke University Press, 2016); Richard White, *The Middle Ground: Indians, Empires, and Republics in the Great Lakes Region, 1650–1815* (New York: Cambridge University Press, 2010); Andrew Lipman, *The Saltwater Frontier: Indians and the Contest for the American Coast* (New Haven: Yale University Press, 2017).

cultivation, and some of the wider aspects of the indigenous economy. She also identified the eighteenth-century trend of haciendas expanding into the lakes, thereby upsetting the chinampa district's hydrology.[44] In many respects, *Islands in the Lake* aims to amplify and elaborate on the findings of these two historians.

Just as Gibson established the contours of several generations of scholarship on central Mexican ethnohistory, so James Lockhart advanced the literature further by founding the New Philology. This revisionist scholarship placed an emphasis on the historical and philological analysis of native-language sources in order to perceive how indigenous peoples themselves conceived of and wrote about their lives. This approach often made it possible to glean new insights into the past while also offering perspectives that complemented or contrasted with the evidence found in Spanish-language sources. Lockhart's methodology also provided a new means for identifying and charting key processes of linguistic and cultural change, showing how the Nahuatl language, for instance, incorporated, borrowed from, and adapted to Hispanic influences. In *The Nahuas after the Conquest*, Lockhart found much of interest in Xochimilco's sociopolitical organization and its Nahuatl sources.[45] He was less concerned about environmental history, however, and the focus of his work and that of subsequent new philologists, including his students, typically lay elsewhere.[46] For this reason, many of the key works on environmental history as it pertained to ethnohistory were descended from different scholarly lineages.

These lineages consisted of three traditions in environmental history. The first has to do with changes in populations over time; the second, the related subject of human interactions with landscapes, and the third, the

---

[44] Teresa Rojas Rabiela, *Las siembras de ayer: la agricultura indígena del siglo XVI* (Mexico City: Centro de Investigaciones y Estudios Superiores en Antropología Social, 1988); Rojas Rabiela, "Ecological and Agricultural Changes in the Chinampas of Xochimilco-Chalco," 275–290.

[45] James Lockhart, *The Nahuas after the Conquest: A Social and Cultural History of the Indians of Central Mexico, Sixteenth through Eighteenth Century* (Stanford: Stanford University Press, 1992).

[46] Some of their work, in addressing land and material culture, did consider ecological issues. S. L. Cline, *Colonial Culhuacan, 1580–1600: A Social History of an Aztec Town* (Albuquerque: University of New Mexico Press, 1986); Rebecca Horn, *Postconquest Coyoacan: Nahua-Spanish Relations in Central Mexico, 1519–1650* (Stanford: Stanford University Press, 1997); Matthew Restall, *The Maya World: Yucatec Culture and Society, 1550–1850* (Stanford: Stanford University Press, 1997); Kevin Terraciano, *The Mixtecs of Colonial Oaxaca: Ñudzahui History, Sixteenth through Eighteenth Centuries* (Stanford: Stanford University Press, 2001).

history of human responses and adaptations to changes in climate. The first two of these lines of inquiry can be traced back to historical geographers and demographers, led by Carl O. Sauer in the 1930s, at the University of California, Berkeley. Scholars there were among the first to attempt to calculate the size of pre-Columbian populations systematically and, from this basis, determine the scale of demographic decline of Native American societies after 1492.[47] The works of Sherburne F. Cook and Woodrow Borah came to define the field and set an agenda for subsequent studies in other regions.[48] Later studies also grew out of controversies about pre-contact population estimates, with some scholars arguing for more conservative, lower figures than Cook and Borah.[49] The study of demography remains ongoing, as does the scholarship on the role of epidemic diseases in the history of the Americas.[50]

Initial scholarship on demographic decline emphasized the singular importance of foreign diseases as well as the particular susceptibility of Native Americans to them. For many years, historians attributed the high rates of mortality to virgin soil epidemics, which is to say those bacteria and viruses to which Native peoples had not been exposed previously and, as a consequence, to which they had little or no immunological defense.

[47] Carl O. Sauer, *The Aboriginal Population of Northwestern Mexico* (Berkeley: University of California Press, 1935) and *Colima of New Spain in the Sixteenth Century* (Berkeley: University of California Press, 1948).

[48] Woodrow Borah and Sherburne F. Cook, *The Population of Central Mexico in 1548: An Analysis of the Suma de visitas de pueblos, Ibero-Americana 43* (Berkeley: University of California Press, 1960); Woodrow Borah and Sherburne F. Cook, *The Indian Population of Central Mexico, 1531–1610, Ibero-Americana 44* (Berkeley: University of California Press, 1960); Woodrow Borah and Sherburne F. Cook, *The Aboriginal Population of Central Mexico on the Eve of the Spanish Conquest, Ibero-Americana 45* (Berkeley: University of California Press, 1963), and Woodrow Borah and Sherburne F. Cook, *The Population of the Mixteca Alta, 1520–1960, Ibero-Americana 50* (Berkeley: University of California Press, 1968).

[49] For a summary of the debates, see the appendix to Suzanne Austin Alchon, *A Pest in the Land: New World Epidemics in a Global Perspective* (Albuquerque: University of New Mexico Press, 2003), 147–172; William M. Denevan, *The Native Population of the Americas in 1492* (Madison: University of Wisconsin Press, 1976); John D. Daniels, "The Indian Population of North America in 1492," *The William and Mary Quarterly*, vol. 49, no. 2 (1992): 298–320; David P. Henige, *Numbers from Nowhere: The American Indian Contact Population Debate* (Norman: University of Oklahoma Press,1998); W. George Lovell, Henry F. Dobyns, William M. Denevan, William I. Woods, and Charles C. Mann, "1491: In Search of Native America," *Journal of the Southwest*, vol. 46, no. 3 (2004), 441–461; Mann, *1491: New Revelations of the Americas before Columbus* (New York: Alfred A. Knopf, 2005).

[50] Juan Pedro Viqueira Albán and Tadashi Obara-Saeki, *El arte de contar tributarios: Provincia de Chiapas, 1560–1821* (Mexico City: El Colegio de México, 2017).

This explanation seemed highly plausible given the extraordinarily high mortality recorded in historical sources for many parts of the Americas (and for Xochimilco). Gradually, skepticism among scholars about Cook and Borah's population numbers – and, therefore, for the subsequent population decline – contributed to reappraisals of the virgin soil theory. Scholars noted that mortality rates from single epidemics in the Americas may not have differed much from those seen in other parts of the world.[51] Ultimately, it seems that what proved so devastating for Xochimilco, as elsewhere, was the sheer number and frequency of the epidemics: according to this interpretation, before societies could recover from one epidemic they succumbed to the next, and, over time, the cumulative effect of these disease outbreaks was demographic collapse.[52]

Revisionist scholarship has also contributed to the elaboration of new, more complex ideas about disease ecology that might further explain Xochimilco's population losses.[53] This approach considers the origins and courses of epidemics in their wider environmental and social contexts. As Linda Nash has explained, historians began to follow in the footsteps of medical and epidemiological experts who sought to uncover the contributing factors in the outbreak, spread, and severity of diseases. Poor sanitary conditions and warfare, for instance, are commonly understood to have surrounded typhus epidemics. Scholars from a variety of disciplines thus began to investigate how malnutrition, sanitation, crowding in urban areas, the flight of refugees, climate change, and the role of flora and fauna provided opportunities for etiological agents to produce epidemics.[54] Such factors are

---

[51] Some studies have continued to suggest that mortality rates were, on occasion, especially high, perhaps even above 50 percent, as with the outbreaks of what some have claimed were epidemics of hemorrhagic fever. Alchon, *A Pest in the Land*; Acuna-Soto et al., "When Half the Population Died," 1–5.

[52] Georgina H. Endfield, *Climate and Society in Colonial Mexico: A Study in Vulnerability* (London: Blackwell, 2008), 43; Thomas M. Whitmore, "A Simulation of Sixteenth Century Population Collapse in the Basin of Mexico," *Annals of the Association of American Geographers*, vol. 81, no. 4 (1991), 464–487.

[53] Linda Nash, "Beyond Virgin Soils: Disease as Environmental History," in Andrew C. Isenberg, ed., *The Oxford Handbook of Environmental History* (New York: Oxford University Press, 2014), 76–107.

[54] Jordan N. Burns, Rodolfo Acuna-Soto, and David W. Stahle, "Drought and Epidemic Typhus, Central Mexico, 1655–1918," *Emerging Infectious Diseases*, vol. 20, no. 3 (2014), 442–447; Acuna-Soto et al., "When Half the Population Died," 1–5; Thomas M. Whitmore, *Disease and Death in Early Colonial Mexico: Simulating Amerindian De-Population* (Boulder: Westview Press, 1992); Bradley Skopyk, "Undercurrents of Conquest: The Shifting Terrain of Indigenous Agriculture in Colonial Tlaxcala, Mexico," PhD dissertation, York University, 2010, 240–242.

harder to identify and trace in the sources from Xochimilco. Still, there are faint and scattered signs that colonial violence – for instance, of warfare and enslavement – may have contributed to the loss of life, as with other kinds of disruption, including famine.[55] Attention to disease ecology provides further clues as to why Native American populations did not recover after epidemics. A striking feature of Xochimilco's demographic history was the lack of a demographic rebound, which is perhaps attributable to persistently low birthrates.[56] To these many contributing factors other have been added, among them changes in climate and landscapes.

Having identified shifts in land use as a consequence of demographic decline – for instance, through soil erosion – members of the Berkeley school, among others, paved the way for the historical study of landscapes. The field gained momentum through the work of Alfred Crosby who argued that processes of change unleashed by the Columbian Exchange often undermined Mexico's ecosystems. Elinor Melville advanced this scholarship with her important examination of the Mezquital Valley, to the north of the Basin of Mexico. There she found that the introduction of sheep proved highly damaging to vegetation such that the landscape became drier, less biologically diverse, increasingly barren, and suitable for little else besides European livestock ranching.[57] While subsequent studies of ranching by Karl and Elisabeth Butzer and Andrew Sluyter, among others, have provided contrasting examples – showing stability or even the possibility of growth in vegetative cover – an emphasis on the degradation of landscapes remains a focus for environmental historians.[58]

---

[55] Alchon, *A Pest in the Land*.

[56] For a discussion of birthrates in relation to demographic decline in the Americas, see Massimo Livi Bacci, *Conquest: The Destruction of the American Indios* (Cambridge: Polity Press, 2008), and Livi Bacci, "The Demise of the American Indios," *Population and Development Review*, vol. 37, No. 1 (2011), 161–165.

[57] Elinor G. K. Melville, *A Plague of Sheep: Environmental Consequences of the Conquest of Mexico* (New York: Cambridge University Press, 1994).

[58] Skopyk, *Colonial Cataclysms*, 17–19; Terry G. Jordan, *North American Cattle-Ranching Frontiers: Origins, Diffusion, and Differentiation* (Albuquerque: University of New Mexico Press, 1993); Lucina Hernández, ed., *Historia ambiental de la ganadería en México* (Xalapa: Instituto de Ecologia, 2001); Andrew Sluyter, "From Archive to Map to Pastoral Landscape: A Spatial Perspective on the Livestock Ecology of Sixteenth-Century New Spain," *Environmental History*, vol. 3, no. 4 (1998), 508–528, and "The Ecological Origins and Consequences of Cattle Ranching in Sixteenth-Century New Spain," *Geographical Review*, vol. 86, no. 2 (1996), 161–177; Karl W. Butzer, "Cattle and Sheep from Old to New Spain: Historical Antecedents," *Annals of the Association of American Geographers*, vol. 78, no. 1 (1988): 29–56; Karl W. Butzer and Elisabeth K. Butzer, "Transfer of the Mediterranean Livestock Economy to New Spain: Adaptation and Ecological Consequences," in B. L. Turner, ed., *Global Land Use Change:*

The history of Xochimilco's landscape complicates this narrative since the changes, while attributable to ranching, had less to do with drought or desertification than with increasingly destructive floods in the late colonial period, when factors of climate variability were crucial.

Flooding serves as a strong reminder that Xochimilco's history stands apart from the well-known narrative of desiccation caused by the Basin of Mexico's drainage projects. The desagüe itself has long attracted attention from historians although only recently have there been dedicated environmental histories of it, as with Vera Candiani's studies.[59] Candiani's focus was on the agents of the desagüe – the scientists and administrators responsible for proposing and implementing the engineering works – as well as the propertied, upper class in Mexico City, which sought to control the environment by removing lake waters and opening up, at least theoretically, more land to generate wealth and, by extension, consolidate their position at the summit of the social order. At the same time, Candiani also contributed to long-standing scholarship on chinampas and the ways in which Native peoples harnessed and modified the watery landscape, as with the studies of Pedro Armillas and Rojas Rabiela.[60] Beyond these scholars, though, only a few have examined the colonial-era history of the chinampas, in part because archaeologists have been interested in the pre-Columbian past while other anthropologists have looked to present-day chinampa cultivation.[61]

A Perspective from the Columbian Encounter (Madrid: Consejo Superior de Investigaciones Científicas, 1995), 151–193.

[59] Candiani, *Dreaming of Dry Land*; Vitz, *A City on a Lake*; W. M. Mathes, "To Save a City: The Desagüe of Mexico-Huehuetoca, 1607," *The Americas*, vol. 26, no. 4 (1970), 419–438; Richard Boyer, *La gran inundación: vida y sociedad en México, 1629–1638* (Mexico City: Secretaria de Educación Pública, 1975); Louisa Schell Hoberman, "Technological Change in a Traditional Society," *Technology and Culture*, vol. 21, no. 3 (1980), 386–407.

[60] Mundy, *The Death of Aztec Tenochtitlan*; Exequiel Ezcurra, *De las chinampas a la megapolis: El medio ambiente en la cuenca de México* (Mexico City: Fondo de Cultura Económica, 1991), and Alejandro Tortolero Villaseñor, ed., *Tierra, agua y bosques: historia y medio ambiente en el México central* (Mexico City and Guadalajara: SEMCA, Instituto de Investigaciones Dr. José María Luis Mora, Universidad de Guadalajara, 1996); Rojas Rabiela et al., *Nuevas noticias sobre las obras hidráulicas prehispánicas y coloniales en el Valle de México*, and Palerm, *Obras hidráulicas prehispánicas en el sistema lacustre del Valle de México*.

[61] Pedro Armillas, "Gardens on Swamps," *Science*, vol. 174, no. 4010 (1971), 653–661; Teresa Rojas Rabiela, *Presente, pasado y futuro de las chinampas* (Mexico City: Centro de Investigaciones y Estudios Superiores en Antroplogía Social, 1995); and Rojas Rabiela, ed., *La agricultura chinampera: compilación histórica* (Mexico City: Universidad Autónoma Chapingo, 1993).

Water has long been an essential element in environmental histories, particularly in those arid regions where scarcity made it a precious resource.[62] Such scarcity also generated conflicts, as shown in Sonya Lipsett-Rivera's analysis of water rights in Puebla. There, she found, water was bound up with wider ecological and political processes. Changes in land use, for instance, contributed to ecological degradation: deforestation, the use of plows in farming, and the disintegration of terraces led to higher rates of soil erosion, which degraded agricultural lands and reduced some of them to the kind of infertile hardpan known as *tepetate*.[63] A variation on these processes took place in Xochimilco where soil erosion led to sediment being deposited into the lakes in the eighteenth century, which further heightened the risk of flooding. Xochimilco also had another historical trend in common with Puebla. Both places underwent shifts in the control of water. For Lipsett-Rivera, Puebla's history was initially characterized by a lack of centralized authority over water rights. That de-centralization persisted into the eighteenth century, when haciendas came to dominate the landscape and instituted a new irrigation regime. A similar trend applied to Xochimilco: the centralization of the Aztec Empire gave way to increased autonomy among individual altepetl until the late colonial period when haciendas and desagüe authorities asserted control over the area's hydrology.[64]

Unlike Puebla, though, the documents for Xochimilco do not emphasize eighteenth-century population growth, specifically, as having contributed substantially to increases in conflicts between Native communities,

---

[62] Cynthia Radding, *Wandering Peoples: Colonialism, Ethnic Spaces, and Ecological Frontiers in Northwestern Mexico, 1700–1850* (Durham: Duke University Press, 1997); Radding, *Landscapes of Power and Identity: Comparative Histories in the Sonoran Desert and the Forests of Amazonia from Colony to Republic* (Durham: Duke University Press, 2005); Radding, "The Children of Mayahuel: Agaves, Human Cultures, and Desert Landscapes in Northern Mexico," *Environmental History*, vol. 17, no. 1 (2012), 84–115; Susan M. Deeds, *Defiance and Deference in Mexico's Colonial North: Indians under Spanish Rule in Nueva Vizcaya* (Austin: University of Texas Press, 2003); Gabriel Martinez-Serna, "Jesuit Missionaries, Indian Polities, and Environmental Transformation in the Lagoon March of Northeastern New Spain," *Journal of Early American History*, vol. 3, no. 2–3 (2013), 207–234; Michael C. Meyer, *Water in the Hispanic Southwest: A Social and Legal History, 1550–1850* (Tucson: University of Arizona Press, 1996).

[63] Sonya Lipsett-Rivera, *To Defend Our Water with the Blood of Our Veins: The Struggle for Resources in Colonial Puebla* (Albuquerque: University of New Mexico Press, 1999), 49–52; Jack A. Licate, *Creation of a Mexican Landscape: Territorial Organization and Settlement in the Eastern Puebla Basin, 1520–1605* (Chicago: Department of Geography, University of Chicago, 1981).

[64] Lipsett-Rivera, *To Defend Our Water*, 39–43.

haciendas, and the colonial administration. For other parts of New Spain, such tensions grew out of sharper competition over and monopolization of water or land and eventually contributed to political violence and the insurrection against colonial rule led by the priest Miguel Hidalgo y Costilla in 1810.[65] For other scholars, though, including Georgina Endfield, eighteenth-century population growth exacerbated the vulnerability of certain regions and their inhabitants to the effects of climate changes.

Climate constitutes the third tradition within the field of environmental history that has influenced *Islands in the Lake*. With a growing appreciation of the role of climate changes in history, pioneering, recent work has shown that key trends in colonial Mexican history have been tied to people's adaptations and responses to changing conditions. This was particularly the case during the Little Ice Age, one of the coolest phases in the past 11,500 years in the Northern Hemisphere that took place during the long seventeenth century, with the period from 1570 to 1677 serving as its "peak," as Bradley Skopyk has noted. The trend toward a cooler, wetter climate can be attributed to a variety of factors, among them reduced solar radiation from fewer sunspots and atmospheric particles released through volcanic eruptions as well as to the El Niño–Southern Oscillation (ENSO) pattern.[66] The Little Ice Age did not simply lead to colder, wetter conditions, though. Skopyk identified the period from the 1550s as the "Colonial Mexican Pluvial," which stood out as a time when greater climate variability led to significant fluctuations in extremes between cold, drought, and dampness. The effects of these anomalous conditions were far-reaching and, at times, profound. Sam

---

[65] Arij Ouweneel, *Shadows over Anáhuac: An Ecological Interpretation of Crisis and Development in Central Mexico, 1770–1810* (Albuquerque: University of New Mexico Press, 1996); Georgina H. Endfield and Sarah L. O'Hara, "Degradation, Drought, and Dissent: An Environmental History of Colonial Michoacan, West Central Mexico," *Annals of the Association of American Geographers*, vol. 89, no. 3 (1999), 402–419. See also Michael C. Meyer, William L. Sherman, and Susan M. Deeds, *The Course of Mexican History*, 9th ed. (New York: Oxford University Press, 2011), 210–12; John M. Tutino, "Creole Mexico: Spanish Elites, Haciendas, and Indian Towns, 1750–1810," PhD dissertation, University of Texas at Austin, 1976; Susan Schroeder, ed., *Native Resistance and the Pax Colonial in New Spain* (Lincoln: University of Nebraska Press, 1998).

[66] On El Niño, see Geoffrey Parker, *Global Crisis: War, Climate Change and Catastrophe in the Seventeenth Century* (New Haven: Yale University Press, 2014), 14–17; see also Skopyk, *Colonial Cataclyms*, 12, who cites Raphael Neukom et al., "Inter-Hemispheric Temperature Variability over the Past Millennium," *Nature Climate Change*, vol. 4, no. 5 (2014), 362–367.

White has shown that they thwarted European imperial endeavors in North America, particularly in places like New Mexico, where the bone-chilling cold and drought led to dire food shortages.[67] For Skopyk, they played a vital part in the historical experiences of Native peoples in the river systems in Teotihuacan and Tlaxcala. In these areas, local residents suffered the twin cataclysms of climate extremes and then, from the late 1690s, a dramatic rise in fluvially deposited sediment, or alluvium, which obstructed river channels, filled in wetlands, and upset hydrological systems, leading to new patterns of flooding and the degradation of agricultural lands. To these cataclysms, Native peoples responded creatively, Skopyk argues, shifting their agricultural systems according to changing ecological and climatic circumstances.[68]

Climate fluctuations contributed significantly to Xochimilco's history even if some of the Little Ice Age's effects proved subtle and difficult to trace in the documentation. In the years from the 1610s through the early 1650s, for instance, Xochimilco and other nearby polities like Coyoacan fell behind in their tribute payments. They did so, arguably, because of persistent drought, cold, and the lower yields of harvests (at least in upland agriculture, if not in the lakes). While some climatic phenomena may be hard to detect in the historical sources and can only be inferred, thanks to the rich data provided in the Mexican Drought Atlas – a resource provided by the dendrochronologist David Stahle – patterns of moisture and dryness can be identified from tree rings. Evidence from these climate proxies shows that there were sharp spikes in moisture levels at certain moments: the timing of these spikes lined up almost exactly with instances of severe flooding in the lake areas during the early 1580s, the period from 1604 to 1607, and the 1810s.[69] In these disruptive moments, the climate undercut Xochimilco's ecological autonomy.

Beyond climate variations, human interventions in the lacustrine environment could also have a profound impact on the severity of flooding. As Georgina Endfield has shown, societies may take actions that are designed

---

[67] Sam White, *A Cold Welcome: The Little Ice Age and Europe's Encounter with North America* (Cambridge: Harvard University Press, 2017).

[68] Skopyk, *Colonial Cataclysms.*

[69] The data from this resource were taken for the grid point located at W 99.1°, N 19.26° for Lake Xochimilco from the online Mexican Drought Atlas at http://drought.memphis.edu /MXDA/Default.aspx (accessed January 18, 2021). For information about this resource, see Appendix A of Skopyk's *Colonial Cataclysms,* 213–245, and, more specifically, 217–222. For more on the atlas, see David W . Stahle et al., "The Mexican Drought Atlas: Tree-Ring Reconstructions of the Soil Moisture Balance during the Late Pre-Hispanic, Colonial, and Modern Eras," *Quaternary Science Reviews,* vol. 149 (2016), 34–60.

to militate against deleterious climate conditions even though they sometimes end up intensifying them, sometimes inadvertently. Noting that
floods, like droughts, are both social constructions as well as physical
phenomena, Endfield and her colleagues revealed that water management
programs, land use, and forms of conflict or cooperation, among other
dynamics, played pivotal roles in making societies more or less vulnerable
to climate extremes. In several case studies of the late colonial period,
Endfield showed how adaptability itself emerged as a key factor in medi-
ating and responding to adverse climate variations. While the southern
lake areas were not among Endfield's case studies, the situation there in
the late colonial period corresponds to her findings. The expansion of
haciendas into the lakes' waters combined with changing land use and
irrigation systems as well as the elaboration of competing engineering
works all served to render chinampas and low-lying communities especially susceptible to severe damage from inundations. The vulnerability of
Native American communities, moreover, was worsened by a shift in
government policies; with a desire to protect the capital's food supply,
the agents of the desagüe project determined that hacienda lands in the
lakes had to be protected. For this reason, and at the expense of lakeside
communities, the authorities ordered that sluice gates to the haciendas'
pastures be closed.[70]

While *Islands of the Lake* draws from and adds to these scholarly
literatures on climate, landscapes, demography, and disease ecology, it
also seeks to contribute to other recent trends in environmental history.
These include the study of animals, which most often meant fish or cattle
for Xochimilco, among other species, including sheep, goats, and locusts.
Minerals and vegetables also played a secondary role in the area's history.
These included saltpeter, limestone, and volcanic rocks as well as pine
forests, water willows, cedars, charcoal, and various kinds of grasses and
reeds, among them *tule* and *zacatl*, this latter being a kind of straw that
was used as fodder for horses and mules.

Beyond environmental history, the book also aims to contribute to the
literatures on agrarian and legal history, as well as the scholarship on
political economy. Mexican historians have furnished us with the best

---

[70] Endfield, *Climate and Society*; Endfield and O'Hara, "Degradation, Drought, and
Dissent"; Georgina H. Endfield and Sarah L. O'Hara, "Conflicts over Water in 'the
Little Drought Age' in Central México," *Environment and History*, vol. 3, no. 3 (1997),
255–272; Georgina H. Endfield, Isabel Fernández Tejedo, and Sarah L. O'Hara, "Conflict
and Cooperation: Water, Floods, and Social Response in Colonial Guanajuato, Mexico,"
Environmental History, vol. 9, no. 2 (2004), 221–247.

scholarship specifically about the altepetl of Xochimilco. In addition to Rojas Rabiela's work, Ludka de Gortari Krauss produced a useful study of tribute and labor in Xochimilco during the sixteenth century, one that was concerned with older debates about the move from feudalist to capitalist economic relations of production and distribution. Rebeca Ramos has also examined matters of sociopolitical organization, as has Juan Manuel Pérez Zevallos, who has delved into matters of local government.[71] Indeed, Pérez Zevallos has been the most productive chronicler of Xochimilco in his series of short but well-illustrated books. Largely written as a chronological narrative for a general audience, his volumes nevertheless identify historical themes and trends while also providing insightful and useful analysis.[72] His uncovering of many sources has been of inestimable value, and this book owes much to the work of Pérez Zevallos and other local historians.[73]

The book's geographical coverage is, for the most part, that of Xochimilco's colonial-era jurisdiction. This means the inclusion of villages in the lake areas, among them Santiago Tolyahualco and San Juan Ixtayopan, San Gregorio Atlapulco, and San Antonio Tecomitl, to name just a few. The jurisdiction also extended south into the piedmont and then the hills and finally the slopes of the Sierra de Ajusco range. In this upland region, which Spaniards called the *montes*, were large communities like Santa María de la Asunción Milpa Alta as well as the smaller villages of San Miguel Topilejo and San Pedro Atocpan, among others. While the book is concerned first and foremost with Xochimilco itself, information gathered from other lakeside communities such as San Pedro Cuitlahuac (later known simply as Tlahuac), San Andrés Mixquic, Santa Catarina Ayotzingo, and Chalco Atenco, has also been essential for understanding broader patterns of historical change. Each of these polities had much in common with Xochimilco. Some of them were once part of

---

[71] Rebeca Ramos, Ludka de Gortari Krauss, and Juan Manuel Pérez Zevallos, eds., *Xochimilco en el siglo XVI* (Mexico City: Cuadernos de la Casa Chata, 1981); Pérez Zevallos, "El Gobierno Indígena de Xochimilco (Siglo XVI)," *Historia Mexicana*, vol. 33, no. 4 (1984), 445–462.

[72] Juan Manuel Pérez Zevallos, *Xochimilco ayer*, vols. 1–3 (Mexico City: Instituto Mora, Gobierno del Distrito Federal, Delegación Xochimilco, 2002–2003).

[73] Teresa Rojas Rabiela and Juan Manuel Pérez Zevallos, eds., *Índice de documentos para la historia del antiguo señorío de Xochimilco* (Mexico City: Centro de Investigaciones y Estudios Superiores en Antropología Social, Cuadernos de la Casa Chata, 1981), and Pérez Zevallos and Reyes García, eds., *La fundación de San Luis Tlaxialtemalco*.

the Xochimilca territories. They were likewise located on the lakes, and their residents also practiced aquatic garden agriculture. Evidence from these communities provides a wider context in which to observe trends in Xochimilco and to draw conclusions. At times, their documentation helps to clarify certain points or to serve as a basis for comparison. Alas, insufficient documentary evidence survives for each of these communities on their own, which further explains their analysis in relation to Xochimilco in this book.

The specific geographical focus has allowed for the book's long chronological scope, from the 1540s to the early 1820s. These parameters also reflect the nature of the documentary sources. For the period before 1540, the records are too fragmentary to support comprehensive analysis, and the last of the documents produced before Mexican national independence date to the beginning of the 1820s. The coverage of such a long period of time is warranted by the simple observation that, until the eighteenth century, haciendas remained marginal to the environmental and ethnohistory of the area. In the 1700s, however, haciendas began to encroach into the lake areas more frequently and extensively. During that century, the estates expanded beyond the shore. In doing so, they not only ushered in new kinds of land use but they also intervened in and, at times, altered and destabilized the aquatic landscape. For these reasons a history of Xochimilco in the Hapsburg era was one that differed in significant ways from that of the Bourbon era. Whereas sources from the former era suggested continuity, those from the latter demonstrated significant change.

The book draws from several kinds of primary sources. Xochimilco is blessed with a sizable corpus of more than 120 discrete Nahuatl-language documents produced between 1548 and 1795. Of these, there is a substantial collection of more than fifty testaments. Other Nahuatl sources include "primordial titles," or community histories, and documents generated under the auspices of the ecclesiastical authorities, particularly the long runs of parish and confraternity records.[74] Although not enough to support a study based solely on them even if one were so inclined, especially for a history covering 300 years, the Nahuatl sources provide essential information not available in Spanish documents. Of

---

[74] Alas, documentation on the Franciscans is too scant and fragmentary to allow for a proper consideration of Xochimilco's religious history. Much as the Franciscans must have played a vital role in local affairs – glimpses of which do surface – details of their activities remain hidden.

these Spanish sources the book relies on a large number of administrative materials, particularly licenses, inspections, and numerous decrees about political and socioeconomic matters as well as the desagüe project, as it pertained to the southern lakes from the 1740s. Legal cases furnish some of the most extensive and abundant documentation. Of the extant lawsuits, Xochimilco is well represented in land disputes, civil litigation, and criminal records. There are also a few Inquisition cases. Information from administrative and legal sources has been further supplemented by contemporary chronicles and more mundane, quotidian documents such as notarial sources. Contractual documents, bills of sale, last wills and testaments, and other records of transactions were also written in Nahuatl.

***

The book consists of seven chapters. The first, on ecological and political landscapes, traces the intertwined rise from the distant pre-contact past of the modified lacustrine environment and lakeshore polities through the early Post-Classic period (ca. 900–1521 CE), when the Xochimilca, Cuitlahuaca, and Mixquica founded their altepetl on the lakeshore, until their incorporation into the Aztec Empire. Having synthesized the archaeological and ethnohistorical literatures for these early periods, the chapter moves on to cover the Spanish–Mexica War, which conquest accounts demonstrate as having had a vital hydraulic component. While the siege of Tenochtitlan has long been understood as a naval battle, in part, the analysis presented here follows the precedent of the New Conquest History in underscoring the vital contributions of Native participants to the conflict, particularly when it came to specialist knowledge of the Basin of Mexico's hydrology, as well as strategic efforts to defeat the enemies by turning the engineering works against them. The chapter concludes by tracing continuities in Xochimilco into the mid-sixteenth century, especially with the survival of the altepetl and its foundation for colonial-era jurisdictions and the municipal corporation, a Spanish innovation that Nahuas readily adopted and made their own. In so doing, they preserved the modified lake environment even as they adapted to new colonial realities.

The second chapter turns to the history of chinampas and the rise of rural estates. The chapter examines the chinampas' construction, cultivation, and distribution, particularly when it came to the marked dispersal of the holdings across the lake areas. As a result of these and other factors, the chapter observes the conspicuous absence of non-Native peoples as the owners of chinampas – and as parties in litigation over them – and establishes that, for the most part, the aquatic gardens remained firmly in the hands of Nahuas. That they remained Nahua property did not mean that chinampas remained free from controversies. Rather, they became a source of contestation within the indigenous community since claims of the communal, usufruct rights to chinampas rubbed up against efforts by the nobility to shore up their holdings through private ownership. In the sixteenth century, demographic decline and the competing demands of the colonial government, anxious about provisioning the capital during periods of scarcity, forced a restructuring of land tenure classifications. At the same time, Spaniards received grants to establish ranches away from the lakes where they and Nahuas both introduced livestock. As a consequence of all this, a distinctive historical geography came into being, with chinampas and intensive, small-scale horticulture in the lakes, and extensive pastoralism in the upland areas.

Similar, complementary spheres of activity also characterized the vibrant commercial sector of the economy as well as the busy transportation network that supported it. The third chapter, on transportation and commerce, demonstrates how canoes, navigating the region's waterways, and pack animals, crossing its roads, enabled artisans and traders to reach local and distant markets. The transportation infrastructure also contributed to the ongoing vitality of exchanges in lake-area marketplaces. Crucial to the provisioning of Mexico City, canoes and the dock facilities of lakeshore communities became key resources in the wider political economy of the region even as haciendas increasingly replaced Nahua communities as the main source of the capital's food supply by the early eighteenth century.

The next two chapters of the book move from the landscapes of the lakes and the *tierra firme*, or mainland, to their demography. The fourth chapter reconstructs the population history of the Nahua community in Xochimilco for the entirety of the colonial period. Having established the timing, rate, and extent of demographic change, the chapter traces the implications of population decline for social relations. The chapter argues that epidemics and subsequent interventions by the government in the tribute system, incomplete and unsuccessful though they were, represented an assertion of royal authority, one that provided opportunities for Nahua nobles and commoners to contest and renegotiate their relationships with each other and with the colonial administration. These changes proved to be especially threatening to the nobility. In response, the dynastic rulers sought to reassert their own political power within the altepetl, although their success owed much to the efforts of noblewomen in securing and harnessing economic assets to their families' advantage. They also contracted valuable strategic marriage alliances that bolstered, if only temporarily, their families' positions in the face of so much loss of life.

The ability of the nobility to shore up its position in the face of enduring demographic decline reached its limits in the mid-seventeenth century. At that time, Xochimilco's ongoing financial troubles, which had their twin origins in population loss and the dislocations brought by climate extremes of the Little Ice Age, further destabilized relations across class lines, as did the depredations and rampant criminality of a ruling class that had become estranged from the old collective and reciprocal bonds of the community. Chapter 5, on crime and crisis in the seventeenth century, presents a microhistory of malfeasance and political violence to explain the passing of the old order in Xochimilco. The upheavals may have represented a local variation in what Geoffrey Parker has termed a "fatal synergy," which is to say the unfortunate combination of climatic extremes and poor political decisions that exacerbated hardships in what was part of a wider, global crisis of the seventeenth century.[75] With the passing of the dynastic rulers, a new basis for political authority came into being. By the century's end, a new cohort of officeholders came to dominate local government. Their ability to retain office increasingly came to depend on their good stewardship of the city's finances and resources. Now that these new criteria determined the legitimacy of officeholders, lineage and ethnicity ceased to be key factors in local politics, which opened the way for non-Native peoples to assume positions of power and influence at a time when the city's demographic composition became more ethnically complex.

The final couple of chapters explore the two dominant countervailing forces at play in the eighteenth century. On the one hand, significant changes came to the lacustrine environment in the eighteenth century. The sixth chapter examines how Native communities and haciendas adopted livestock rearing and, in particular, cattle ranching as a new economic activity within the lakes. Responding to the rise of the urban market for meat as well as the demographic decline within Native communities – which undermined the labor-intensive horticultural traditions of the lake areas – residents of the chinampa districts expanded into the waters of the lakes in new and destabilizing ways. Alongside the chinampas, many of

---

[75] Parker, *Global Crisis*.

which survived and retained their value, haciendas and Native communities now fashioned pastures from the swamps. As they pushed further into the lake, pastoralists instituted new environmental management practices and constructed new hydraulic engineering works of their own. At the same time, the colonial administration, responding to renewed fears of flooding in the capital, increasingly intervened in the southern lakes' hydrology. These new forces for change, when combined with higher rates of rainfall because of renewed climate extremes, undermined both the ecological autonomy and the flood defenses of the Nahua communities, portending of wholesale environmental transformation if not ruination on the eve of Mexico's Independence.

In contrast to that portrait of disruption and change, the book concludes by examining some striking cultural continuities. The final chapter reveals how Nahuatl documentary traditions retained much of their vitality and importance. The sources themselves underwent changes, in orthography and content, that amounted to departures from earlier forms of written expression. These changes reflected the autonomous local traditions of documentary production. At the same time, though, the sources from across Xochimilco's jurisdiction also exhibited a remarkable degree of resilience and stability in their lexical and grammatical structures. Surprisingly, even by the end of the eighteenth century, the sources exhibited few of the common signs of Hispanic influence in which, typically, Native speakers could now be expected to incorporate not only Spanish nouns as loanwords in Nahuatl but also verbs, calques, particles, and other grammatical elements. All of these innovations remained conspicuously absent from Xochimilco's Nahuatl records. Viewed from another perspective, Xochimilco not only remained a predominantly Nahua place at the end of the colonial period, in terms of demographic orientation, but it also successfully preserved many aspects of its rich and distinctive cultural heritage.

I

Ecological and Political Landscapes

Over the course of several millennia, the mutual influences between Native societies and their natural surroundings profoundly affected the history of communities in and around Lakes Xochimilco and Chalco.[1] Early agricultural societies intervened in the lacustrine environment through irrigation projects that, in turn, encouraged population growth and enabled the rise of complex societies. During these changing, interconnected ecological and sociopolitical processes, the Xochimilca, Cuitlahuaca, and Mixquica and other ethnic groups settled in the southern lake areas. There they adopted chinampa cultivation and contributed to dramatic demographic growth and urbanization in the late Post-Classic period (ca. 1350–1521 CE), which culminated in the rise of Tenochtitlan and, with it, the Aztec Triple Alliance.

The imperial organization of the Aztecs made possible yet further modifications of the lake environment. Whereas previously the chinampa districts had been confined to the waters close to the lakeshore, in the fifteenth century the Aztecs deployed a great many resources, including a large labor force, in a coordinated effort to convert the entire southern lakes into a vast zone of abundant wetland agriculture. Tens of thousands of horticulturalists took up residence on the thousands of new, artificial islands rising above the shallow lake waters. The arrival of Spaniards and their subsequent war with their indigenous allies against the Mexica

---

[1] Elinor Melville has offered us the succinct definition of environmental history as "the mutual influences of social and natural processes" on the Conference on Latin American History's website, http://clah.h-net.org/?page_id=195 and http://clah.h-net.org/?page_id=114 (accessed January 18, 2021).

resulted in the destruction of many of the key engineering works that had protected the chinampa districts. The resulting flooding and the reversion of parts of the southern lakes to free-flowing waters meant that, by the second half of the sixteenth century, many of the recent chinampas had been washed away. The modified environment more or less returned to its earlier state, before the wholesale interventions of the Aztecs. Thereafter, the waters of the lakes and the chinampa agriculture within them survived through and beyond the colonial period. The colonial-era fortunes of Xochimilco need to be understood in this broad historical context.

Just as the lakes and the chinampas proved to be enduring, essential features of the ecological landscape, so Nahua polities long served as the mainstays of the political landscape. The altepetl, or ethnic state, lay at the heart of both precontact and colonial-era sociopolitical organization. Xochimilco's altepetl remained intact for the duration of Spanish rule. It provided the foundation for all of the central civil and ecclesiastical jurisdictions of the colonial administration. The persistence of Xochimilco's altepetl and, with it, the political landscape proved to be crucial for Nahuas as they adapted to the rapidly changing world of the early colonial period.

A WATERY LANDSCAPE

In awarding world heritage status in 1987, UNESCO explained that Xochimilco's history "testifies to the efforts of the Aztec people to build a habitat in the midst of an unfavourable environment."[2] This single-sentence explanation works well enough, conveying the point about Native peoples successfully adapting to the environment. But the claim is also slightly strange given the common images of Xochimilco's lush, fertile landscape. The Spanish-language phrasing makes the contradiction even more apparent. It describes the environment as being "hostil al hombre," as though it were the Atacama desert or the Arctic, whereas, in fact, the area was home to some of the earliest agricultural communities in Mesoamerica and, by extension, some of its first and most impressive complex societies. The environmental situation of Xochimilco was a good deal more hospitable and complicated than UNESCO's brief online description would seem to suggest.

---

[2] UNESCO, "Historic Centre of Mexico City and Xochimilco," https://whc.unesco.org/en/list/412 (accessed January 18, 2021).

Probably an island, possibly a peninsula, and, depending on the season or environmental conditions, perhaps just land that jutted out into the lake from the shore, Xochimilco was situated at the southwestern corner of the twin lakes of Xochimilco and Chalco. These were the two southernmost lakes of the Basin of Mexico. The Basin of Mexico itself was located at the southern edge of the Mexican *meseta central*, or highland plateau, which was created during the Paleogene (65.5 million to 23 million years ago), at which time volcanic activity and geological movements elevated the highlands and produced tall mountain ranges, which came to wall in the basin on its western, southern, and eastern sides (to the north, the basin is bounded by a series of hills). Gradually, with all the volcanic activity, deposits of lava and ash sealed up what had been the only natural outlet of the region, transforming it from a valley into a basin (today, the Basin of Mexico is still often and inaccurately referred to as the Valley of Mexico).[3] Having been sealed off, the basin came to take its present shape, an oval depression that resembles a great plain, stretching some seventy-five miles in length from north to south and approximately forty miles in width.[4] After the outlet was sealed, the basin became a closed hydrographic area of some 2,700 square miles (7,000 square kilometers), and it remained so for millennia – until, that is, the vast, centuries-long drainage projects begun during the colonial period, which breached the basin's northern boundary.

Until these changes, the entire basin had functioned as a single great watershed. It received water from rainfall as well as meltwater from the famous pair of snow-capped volcanoes, Iztaccihuatl and Popocatepetl. Water flowed down into the basin from the mountains via runoff and through streams and rivers while also emerging from the ground at dozens of natural springs. All of these courses of water washed down alluvial detritus that had been eroded from the surrounding hills and mountains.[5] The water and its suspended sediment eventually pooled at the bottom of the basin, forming five lakes that, depending on the season and the amount of rainfall, could swell into a vast, single body of water.[6] It was from this lake environment that the Aztecs fashioned their remarkable aquatic society.

Plentiful supplies of water and rich soils meant that the Basin of Mexico was well suited to agriculture. Even though the region is located within the

---

[3] Sanders et al., *The Basin of Mexico*, 81.   [4] Gibson, *The Aztecs under Spanish Rule*, 1.
[5] Sanders et al., *The Basin of Mexico*, 81.
[6] Mundy, *The Death of Aztec Tenochtitlan*, 34–35.

tropics, its high elevation made for a cool climate with moderate rainfall. The lowest part of the basin, where the lakes were located, lay at some 2,200 meters. The mountain peaks, of course, rose even higher. In the southern limits of Xochimilco's jurisdiction, the Sierra de Ajusco range reached 3,400 meters.[7] As a result of elevation, topography, and location, the basin had two seasons: a dry, cool winter and a warm, wet summer. Across the region, rainfall levels varied considerably and could be highly localized because of the mountainous landscape. Drawing on data from the 1970s, the archaeologists William Sanders, Jeffrey Parsons, and Robert Santley observed that the northeastern part of the basin received the least rainfall, on average at 450 millimeters per annum, while the southwest, where Xochimilco was located, received an abundance of rain, some 1,500 millimeters. It should be noted, though, that these rainfall figures would not have been the same in the past. Such were the changes in global climate, especially during the Little Ice Age, that rainfall amounts would have varied considerably, often from one year to the next. Still, as with other parts of central Mexico, the vast majority of the annual precipitation – more than 80 percent, according to Sanders and his colleagues – occurred between the beginning of June and October, when the summer temperatures were best suited for growing maize.[8] The conditions were not quite ideal, though. For one thing, the summer monsoon season was often interrupted by a dry spell, known as the *canícula*, in July and August. Later, maturing crops might be lost to frosts. Frosts were a risk from November through February, and crop failures could follow from early cold snaps in October and or from late freezes in March. The threats of frosts, delayed monsoons, and droughts during the rainy season were the most perilous for dry-land farming, particularly as the elevation increased; the wetlands in the lake, by contrast, were less susceptible to these dangers.

Given the propitious conditions, small settlements of sedentary agriculturalists emerged at an early date in the Basin of Mexico. During the early Pre-Classic period, between approximately 1500 and 1300 BCE, half of the basin's population, the majority of whom were farmers, lived in the south. Archaeologists have identified several early lakeshore settlements. By 1300–1150 BCE, some of them had grown into larger villages, such as the one at Tolyahualco. The early demographic concentration in

[7] Peter Gerhard, *A Guide to the Historical Geography of New Spain*, rev. ed. (Norman: University of Oklahoma Press, 1993), 245.
[8] Sanders et al., *The Basin of Mexico*, 81–82, 116, and 187.

the south, thanks to ample rainfall, continued until approximately 100 BCE, when the major shift in settlement patterns took place with the rise of the city of Teotihuacan to the north. Before that demographic relocation, though, early agricultural communities in the southern area of the basin underwent several important changes, from increasing social differentiation to the rise of civic-ceremonial architecture and the creation of small-scale water-control technologies.[9] The adoption of irrigation systems, possibly including chinampas, may well have been spurred by long drought in the Pre-Classic period, which, some have suggested, may have provided a foundation for the expansion of agricultural production and greater economic dynamism during the Classic era (300–950 CE).[10]

The advantages of implementing hydraulic technologies were immediate and manifold given the sheer abundance of water in the basin. The lakes covered some 1,500 of the basin's 7,000–8,000 square kilometers – fully one-fifth of the basin's total area. While some of the water that entered the basin evaporated or was absorbed into the soil, the majority of it kept the five lakes full.[11] Of these, the largest, Lake Tetzcoco, lay at the lowest elevation. Lakes Zumpango and Xaltocan, to the north, and Lakes Xochimilco and Chalco, to the south, lay between one and three meters higher, which meant that water flowed to the center of the basin, just as water settles at the bottom of a bowl. (More specifically, Lakes Xochimilco and Chalco were 2.6 meters higher than Tetzcoco).[12] Since the southern lakes' catchment area was filled by runoff, rivers, and springs – and given their regular discharge into Lake Tetzcoco – the two southern bodies of water differed from the others by being freshwater lakes. During the rainy season, water typically flowed from Lake Chalco to the west, into Lake Xochimilco, and then north, into Lake Tetzcoco.[13]

The shallow lacustrine environment was almost always in a state of flux, ebbing and flowing according to the season or rainfall levels. Seldom, if ever, would the lake levels have been constant for long. As the flow of water advanced and receded, the muddy, swampy areas by the shoreline gradually expanded or contracted. Rarely were land and water entirely discrete entities, as the historian Vera Candiani noted of the basin's "fluid

---

[9] Sanders et al., *The Basin of Mexico*, 94–95, 98, 102.
[10] Gibson, *The Aztecs under Spanish Rule*, 5; William E. Doolittle, *Canal Irrigation in Prehistoric Mexico: The Sequence of Technological Change* (Austin: University of Texas Press, 1990).
[11] Candiani, *Dreaming of Dry Land*, 16–18.
[12] Luna Golya, "Modeling the Aztec Agricultural Waterscape," 41.
[13] Mundy, *The Death of Aztec Tenochtitlan*, 35.

landscape." In winter, for instance, wetlands lost moisture, and land became more viscous and firmer. In a few places near the shore, lake waters gradually came to resemble marshes, if not dry land. In particularly parched years, this process of desiccation extended from the shallower areas by the shore and ever farther into the lake areas to the point where the two lakes of Xochimilco and Chalco came to resemble a vast swamp.[14] In the rainy summer, by contrast, the ground became soggier and waterlogged, and lands that had once been hard loosened up and became more liquescent. In deeper waters away from the shore, water flowed more freely.

The environment of Lakes Xochimilco and Chalco, then, was not unchanging. Neither was it uniform. Differences in the qualities of the water and land could be found from one place to another. Such variations might stem from the local circumstances of elevation or the shifting and uneven depths of the lake bed. Gradient might also affect local ecosystems both within the lakes themselves and in the nearby upland slopes, particularly where proximity to water courses and springs might further alter environmental conditions at lower elevations. For all these reasons and more, dry land might soon turn into a swamp in one place that, in turn, might not be too distant from a deep pool. Making matters more complicated were the islands within the lakes, some of which were large enough to become home to sizable communities, as with settlements on the islands on Mixquic, Cuitlahuac, and Xico.

The wetland ecosystems of the lakes, which could vary so much between the two seasons, afforded many advantages to local residents, not the least of which were renewable and large amounts of biomass that could be harnessed for food, fiber, fuel, and food.[15] Beyond freshwater, the lakes were home to fish and other fauna, from fowl to frogs and salamanders; various kinds of aquatic plants, including reeds; and a kind of scum, *tecuitlatl*, that comprised water fly eggs.[16] Trees also grew in the lake areas, providing fuel and construction materials, and some of the aquatic flora and fauna could be put to other uses, including as medicines.[17] Most significant were the abundant soils that were regularly

---

[14] Candiani, *Dreaming of Dry Land*, Chapter 1; Armillas, "Gardens on Swamps," cited in Sanders et al., *The Basin of Mexico*, 280.

[15] Candiani, *Dreaming of Dry Land*, 15.

[16] Frances F. Berdan, *The Aztecs of Central Mexico: An Imperial Society* (New York: Holt, Rinehart, and Winston, 1982), 25.

[17] Emily Walcott Emmart, ed. and trans., *The Badianus Manuscript (Codex Barberini, Latin 241) Vatican Library: An Aztec Herbal of 1552* (Baltimore: Johns Hopkins University Press, 1940).

enriched with fresh supplies of water and made all the more fertile thanks to the decomposition of organic matter in the lakes. The soils could be farmed productively, especially when residents started intervening in nature by constructing complex water management systems.

Increasingly intensive agriculture, made possible by irrigation, involved alterations of the environment that, over time, became ever more sophisticated and substantial.[18] The origins of chinampa cultivation remain unclear. Some scholars have argued that the earliest kinds of raised gardens can be traced to 1000 BCE, although others have expressed skepticism about this date. At the site of El Terremote in Lake Xochimilco, archaeologists have found layered platforms of soil and vegetation that were housed within enclosures and thus resembled chinampas.[19] Scholars have also argued that it would have been unlikely that certain population centers located in the lakes, such as the one on the island of Xico, would have been sustained without some sort of wetland agriculture.[20]

During the Pre-Classic period, farmers devised two types of irrigated field at the lakeshore ecotone.[21] The first of these fields were a kind of chinampa that Ángel Palerm named "de tierra adentro," that is, land-bound gardens. They had sufficiently high water tables, termed *tierra de*

---

[18] William E. Doolittle, "Agricultural Change as an Incremental Process," *Annals of the Association of American Geographers*, vol. 74, no. 1 (1984), 124–137; Rojas Rabiela, *Las siembras de ayer*; Rojas Rabiela, *Agricultura indígena, pasado y presente* (Mexico City: Centro de Investigaciones y Estudios Superiores en Antropología Social, 1990).

[19] Rojas Rabiela, "Ecological and Agricultural Changes in the Chinampas of Xochimilco-Chalco," 276. The skeptics note that archaeological data might be ambiguous: ceramic artifacts found in the remnants of ancient plots, for instance, could have already been in the soil when ancient peoples constructed chinampas. Sanders et al., *The Basin of Mexico*, 281; Charles D. Frederick, "Chinampa Cultivation in the Basin of Mexico: Observations on the Evolution of Form and Function," in *Seeking a Richer Harvest: The Archaeology of Subsistence, Intensification, Innovation, and Change*, ed. Tina L. Thurston and Christopher T. Fisher (New York: Springer Science + Business Media, 2007), 120; Luna Golya, "Modeling the Aztec Agricultural Waterscape," 66; Earle C. Smith and Paul Tolstoy, "Vegetation and Man in the Basin of Mexico," *Economic Botany*, vol. 35, no. 4 (1981), 415–433; Paul Tolstoy, "Settlement and Population Trends in the Basin of Mexico (Ixtapaluca and Zacatenco Phases)," *Journal of Field Archaeology*, vol. 2, no. 4 (1975), 331–349; Richard Conway, "Rural Indians and Technological Innovation, from the Chinampas of Xochimilco and Beyond," *in Oxford Research Encyclopedia of Latin American History* (New York: Oxford University Press, 2018), published online, DOI:10.1093/acrefore/9780199366439.013.530.

[20] Sanders et al., *The Basin of Mexico*, 281.

[21] Luna Golya, "Modeling the Aztec Agricultural Waterscape," 63; Tolstoy, "Settlement and Population Trends in the Basin of Mexico," and Paul Tolstoy, Suzanne K. Fish, Martin W. Boksenbaum, and Kathryn Blair Vaughn, "Early Sedentary Communities of the Basin of Mexico," *Journal of Field Archaeology*, vol. 4, no. 1 (1977), 91–106.

humedad, to allow for successful cultivation.[22] The fields could only be constructed right at the fluctuating shoreline, where the lakes transitioned into dry land and where the soils were frequently inundated. Local residents built up these beds so that they rose above the water level. They did so by using soils gathered nearby, including earth that may have been excavated from farther inland, on the gently sloping tierra firme, where they could dig ditches to channel water to inland fields. The advantages of the land-bound gardens at the lakeshore stemmed from the fertility of their soils and abundant supplies of water; the downside, however, was that the fields were suitable for cultivation only on a seasonal basis and before the monsoon rains, when they might be inundated, or else during times of prolonged drought, when the waters of the lake might recede farther away from the shore. The crucial limitations for successful farming, then, were the fluctuations in the lake levels.

While with these types of fields the lakes themselves remained essentially unmodified over time, during the Post-Classic period, indigenous people also pushed ever farther into the lakes by creating artificial, raised gardens.[23] These raised gardens were entirely surrounded by water and were thus identified by Palerm as a second kind of chinampa, which he termed *de laguna adentro,* or "within the lake."[24] Their construction required that two preconditions be met: first, that the lakes be shallow, and second, that the water levels be regulated and kept constant – in other words, that the lake environment itself be altered. It was no coincidence that this more interventionist form of irrigated agriculture emerged in tandem with the rise of such lakeshore polities as Culhuacan, Xochimilco, Cuitlahuac, Mixquic, and Chalco Atenco, each of which came to have populations around 5,000 people during the early Post-Classic period. By the fourteenth century, Xochimilco had grown to an estimated 10,000 inhabitants.[25] The greater political centralization of

[22] Luna Golya, "Modeling the Aztec Agricultural Waterscape," 66, 7; Palerm, *Obras hidráulicas prehispánicas en el sistema lacustre del Valle de México*; Rojas Rabiela, "Ecological and Agricultural Changes in the Chinampas of Xochimilco-Chalco."

[23] Parsons et al., "Chinampa Agriculture and Aztec Urbanization in the Valley of Mexico"; Palerm, *Obras hidráulicas prehispánicas en el sistema lacustre del Valle de México*; Luna Golya, "Modeling the Aztec Agricultural Waterscape of Lake Xochimilco," 7, 49, and 63–66.

[24] Luna Golya, "Modeling the Aztec Agricultural Waterscape," 63, 67; Armillas, "Gardens on Swamps"; Parsons et al., "Chinampa Agriculture and Aztec Urbanization in the Valley of Mexico"; Frederick, "Chinampa Cultivation in the Basin of Mexico"; Raul Avila López, *Chinampas de Iztapalapa, D. F.* (Mexico: Instituto Nacional de Antropología e Historia, 1991).

[25] Sanders et al., *The Basin of Mexico,* 151, 154.

these regional centers and the expanding population provided the labor and the organizational capacity necessary for undertaking large-scale engineering projects.[26]

At first, the water management programs consisted of canals, embankments, dikes, and sluicegates. The dikes, called *tlaltenamitl* by Nahuas, encircled a small section of the lake, creating a pool, or *lagunilla*, which functioned like a hydraulic compartment in which the lake waters could be regulated.[27] These compartments solved the problem of seasonal fluctuations in water levels (the map of Santa María Magdalena Michcalco's lands, Map 0.3, depicts one of these compartments).[28] In addition to being closely regulated, the water levels in these hydraulic compartments were typically kept slightly above the surrounding lake, so as to reduce the risk of damage from inundation during the rainy season. Conversely, in dry spells, water could be directed from springs and streams into the pools rather than being lost in the lake.[29] The pools spread out from the lakeshore, particularly at bays and inlets, and indigenous people gradually constructed successive rings of these lagoons farther into the lakes. The dike at the end of one pool thus served as the first barrier for the next. For the most part, though, these sets of engineering works were confined to the territorial waters near island or lakeshore polities. They were typically created and maintained by autonomous local polities, a tendency that changed with the rise of the Aztec Empire.

EMPIRE AND WATERSCAPE

The decline of Teotihuacan from 650 CE brought a shift in the balance of power in central Mexico to the rising city-states of Cholula and Tula. This latter city is often seen as having been the mythic or real home (or one of the homes) of the Toltecs, the migratory group that settled in the region and

---

[26] It should be noted that chinampas were cultivated elsewhere across the Basin of Mexico and that their creation was likewise tied to the growth of political communities. Christopher Morehart, for instance, makes the case that the largest chinampa system before the Aztec era was to be found at the northern, independent polity of Xaltocan. Christopher T. Morehart, "Mapping Ancient Chinampa Landscapes in the Basin of Mexico: A Remote Sensing and GIS Approach," *Journal of Archaeological Science*, vol. 39, no. 7 (2012), 2548–2549.

[27] Mundy, *The Death of Aztec Tenochtitlan*, 217n27.

[28] Parsons et al., "Chinampa Agriculture and Aztec Urbanization in the Valley of Mexico," 88.

[29] Luna Golya, "Modeling the Aztec Agricultural Waterscape," 70; Mary G. Hodge, "Lord and Lordship in the Valley of Mexico: The Politics of Aztec Provincial Administration," in Harvey, *Land and Politics in the Valley of Mexico*, 113–139.

integrated its peoples into a new cultural system during the early Post-Classic period (900–1250 CE). The Toltecs were but one of several nonsedentary ethnic groups to have migrated and settled in central Mexico. The others, most notably the seven "Chichimec" tribes who set out from the legendary ancestral home of Chicomoztoc (Seven Caves), included the Mexica as well as Chalca, who came to occupy the territory to the east of the Cuitlahuaca and the Mixquica, two of the southern lake area's ethnic groups. The Xochimilca had been one of these principal migratory groups.[30] They set out from Chicomoztoc under the leadership of a ruler called Huetzalin during the tenth century CE, if not earlier. After a long peregrination, they settled in central Mexico and established their home on the shore of the lake.[31] Thereafter, they expanded their territory through military conquest and by settling distant communities to the south and to the east. As the Xochimilca waged war against regional rivals and, as they gained greater power, they came to dominate, albeit only temporarily, the Cuitlahuaca and the Mixquica.

The Xochimilca founded communities far and wide. Some were located in the jurisdiction of Quautla Amilpas (today in Morelos) and Tochimilco (or Ocopetlayuca, Puebla), as well as Totolapa and Tlayacapan (later in Chalco). Their domains extended to the southern edge of the Chalca realm and, to the east, to just below the summit of Popocatepetl.[32] As a powerful group, the Xochimilca had at one time come to dominate the southern lakeside polities. Accordingly, the historian Charles Gibson remarked, "There can be small doubt that the Xochimilca were once an influential and formidable people."[33]

The Xochimilca, ultimately, were unable to maintain their regional dominance. From the twelfth century, decline set in. A series of wars gradually eroded the extent of the Xochimilca realm. Totolapa and

---

[30] Elizabeth Hill Boone, *Stories in Red and Black: Pictorial Histories of the Aztecs and Mixtecs* (Austin: University of Texas Press, 2000), 163; Berdan, *The Aztecs of Central Mexico*, 3.

[31] Fray Juan de Torquemada, *Monarquía indiana*, vol. 1 (Mexico City: J. Porrúa, 1969), 78; Fernando de Alva Ixtlilxochitl, *Obras históricas*, ed. Edmundo O'Gorman, vol. 1 (Mexico City: Universidad Nacional Autónoma de México, Instituto de Investigaciones Históricas, 1975), 411–412. Chimalpahin suggests that the Xochimilca arrived earlier. In his annals entry for 1608, Chimalpahin writes that "it has now been 940 years since the ancient Chichimeca who were Colhuaque came and settled here in Colhuacan; they found the Xochimilca already there living in their homes." Chimalpahin, *Annals of His Time*, 117.

[32] Fray Diego Durán, *Historia de las indias de Nueva España e islas de la tierra firme* (Mexico City: J. Porrúa, 1984), 22–23.

[33] Gibson, *The Aztecs under Spanish Rule*, 13.

Tlayacapan succumbed to attacks from Huexotzinco, Tlaxcala, and Cholula, and then wars and conquests by rival groups from the thirteenth through fifteenth centuries, including the Culhua, Tepaneca, and the combined forces of the Acolhuaque (of Tetzcoco) and the Mexica, finally reduced Xochimilco to a smaller area, one that eventually fell to the Aztec Triple Alliance. The Aztecs conquered Xochimilco during the reign of the Mexica emperor Itzcoatl (r. 1427–1440). Thereafter, the Aztecs launched military campaigns against other lakeside polities, ultimately defeating the Chalca during the reign of emperor Moteucçcoma I (r. 1440–1468), who had made this regional consolidation his priority.[34] By 1519, the Xochimilca domains were confined by the Sierra de Ajusco mountains to the south and reached across from the rocky ground known as the Pedregal in the west to Cuitlahuac in the east.[35]

Unsurprisingly, the prodigious output of the chinampa districts held a particular appeal to the rulers of the Aztec Triple Alliance. The Mexica were particularly attentive to the chinampas' abundance for the simple reason that they inhabited an island and, therefore, had only a limited amount of land from which to feed themselves. While some chinampas came to be built around the perimeter of Tenochtitlan, after engineering works were completed in Lake Tetzcoco to fashion the freshwater Laguna de México, the capital's population could not have grown without an expansion of the area of land under cultivation. Yet there was little land that had not been cultivated already. Archaeological evidence shows that, with an expanding population, farmers increasingly turned to the cultivation of thinner soils higher in the piedmont zones. By the late Post-Classic period, most of the basin's slopes had been terraced.[36] Without being able to open up more dry land for cultivation the Mexica identified the southern lakes as an ideal place to reclaim more land for agriculture.

The southern lakes, then, became the focus for a colossal state-sponsored project to convert watery swamps into prime agricultural land.[37] At once

[34] Mundy, *The Death of Aztec Tenochtitlan*, 35.
[35] Don Domingo de San Antón Muñón Chimalpahin Quauhtlehuanitzin, *Codex Chimalpahin: Society and Politics in Mexico Tenochtitlan, Tlatelolco, Texcoco, Culhuacan, and Other Nahua Altepetl in Central Mexico*, vol. 1, ed. and trans. Arthur J. O. Anderson and Susan Schroeder (Norman: University of Oklahoma Press, 1997), 205 and 227–233; Torquemada, *Monarquía indiana*, vol. 1, 89; Durán, *Historia de las indias*, 105–112; Pérez Zevallos, *Xochimilco Ayer*, vol. 1, 19–20.
[36] Sanders et al., *The Basin of Mexico*, 177, 383.
[37] Morehart, "Mapping Ancient Chinampa Landscapes in the Basin of Mexico," 2541–2551; Morehart and Daniel T. A. Eisenberg, "Prosperity, Power, and Change: Modeling Maize at Postclassic Xaltocan, Mexico," *Journal of Anthropological Archaeology*, vol. 29

a vast land reclamation project and an enormous engineering program, the transformation of the southern lakes into an agricultural landscape required a centrally planned and concerted effort. Indeed, the state-planned engineering program had to confront the hydrology of the Basin of Mexico as a whole. The new irrigation system was designed to manage the natural flow of water that, as we have seen, would otherwise ebb and flow according to the season; lake levels themselves also varied considerably, and in Lake Xochimilco the movement of water was especially complicated. Since the lake lay at a higher elevation than its neighbors, water typically flowed west and north, toward Lake Tetzcoco during the monsoon season; in the dry season, though, its flow reversed, and the water flowed to the east and into Lake Chalco. In both of these scenarios, engineering works were needed to restrict the flow of water and to stabilize the lakes' levels. The variations of lake levels across the lakes, which political fragmentation had done little to overcome, inhibited the expansion of chinampa cultivation. And farmers faced an additional problem: flooding and excessive waters that could submerge the chinampas.

To remedy all these problems, in the fifteenth century the Aztec administration drew on the expertise of specialist, imperial engineers, and recruited tens of thousands of workers to build mile after mile of embankments, dikes, bridges, sluicegates, locks, ditches, canals, and aqueducts across the entire lake system. Key features of the engineering works were the causeways traversing the lakes. These *calzadas* were impressive feats of engineering, especially the long ones in Lake Tetzcoco. Built with large wooden pylons to secure their sides, they were filled with stone hauled from beyond the lakes. Given their very size, which were some seven meters in width and many kilometers in length, the Mexica relied on labor levies from conquered polities to build them. The expansion of the hydraulic engineering works thus took place

(2010), 94–112; Sanders et al., *The Basin of Mexico*, 280; Palerm, *Obras hidráulicas prehispánicas*; Armillas, "Gardens on Swamps," 660. The scale of this project inspired Karl Wittfogel to include the Aztecs in his theories about hydraulic societies and "Oriental despotism." Karl Wittfogel, *Oriental Despotism: A Comparative Study of Total Power* (New Haven: Yale University Press, 1957); Wittfogel, "Developmental Aspects of Hydraulic Societies," in J. Steward, ed., *Irrigation Civilizations: A Comparative Study – A Symposium on Method and Result in Cross-Cultural Regularities* (Washington, DC: Pan American Union Social Science Monographs 1, 1955), 28–42. See also Ángel Palerm, *Agua y agricultura: Ángel Palerm, la discusión con Karl Wittfogel sobre el modo asiático de producción y la construcción de un modelo para el estudio de Mesoamérica* (Mexico City: Universidad Iberoamericana and Agencia Española de Cooperación Internacional, Dirección General de Relaciones Culturales y Científicas, 2007).

in tandem with imperial expansion.[38] In addition to being raised roads over the lakes, the causeways served as barriers to protect Tenochtitlan from flooding. Lengthy dikes, including the one named after the ruler of Tetzcoco, the Nezahualcoyotl Dike, also served this purpose.[39] Such flood protections were also located in the southern lakes, where two causeways were constructed. The first, erected in the 1420s, was a three-kilometer barrier across the narrow point between Huitzilopochco (later known as Churubusco), on the western Pedregal, and Mexicalzingo, to the east, at the foot of rising slope of the Cerro de la Estrella (a hill previously named Huixachtlan). Typically, water flowed through the bottleneck between these places and northward out of Lake Xochimilco and into the lower, saline Lake Tetzcoco. The second barrier, which ran either side of the island town of Cuitlahuac, was designed to limit the east-west flow of water from Lake Chalco into Lake Xochimilco. During the colonial period it came to be known as the calzada de Tlahuac. Besides protecting Tenochtitlan, these two raised roads also regulated the water levels across the southern lakes.[40]

The swift conversion of the southern lakes, under the direction of the Aztecs, into a vast zone of wetland agriculture required careful, centralized planning that had previously been lacking.[41] The results of their carefully coordinated and synchronized efforts during the late fifteenth

[38] Mundy, *The Death of Aztec Tenochtitlan*, 27, 35, 37; Margarita Carballal Staedtler and María Flores Hernández, "Las calzadas prehispanicas de la isla de México," *Arqueologia*, vol. 1 (1989), 71–80; Palerm, *Obras hidráulicas prehispánicas en el sistema lacustre del Valle de México*; Luis González Aparicio, *Plano reconstructivo de la región de Tenochtitlan* (Mexico City: Instituto Nacional de Antropología e Historia, 1973).

[39] Mundy cites a sixteenth-century codex that referred to 50,000 soldiers working on Nezahualcoyotl's dike. Mundy, *The Death of Aztec Tenochtitlan*, 34–39; Margarita Carballal Staedtler and María Flores Hernández, "Hydraulic Features of the Mexico-Texcoco Lakes during the Postclassic Period," in L. J. Lucero and B. W. Fash, eds., *Precolumbian Water Management* (Tucson: University of Arizona Press, 2006), 155–170; Luna Golya, "Modeling the Aztec Agricultural Waterscape of Lake Xochimilco," 41, 63; Coe, "The Chinampas of Mexico," 92–93 and 98; Gene C. Wilken, "A Note on Buoyancy and Other Dubious Characteristics of the 'Floating' Chinampas of Mexico," in I. S. Farrington, ed., *Prehistoric Intensive Agriculture in the Tropics*, vol. 1 (Oxford: BAR, 1985), 39; Parsons et al., "Chinampa Agriculture and Aztec Urbanization in the Valley of Mexico," 88.

[40] Mundy, *The Death of Aztec Tenochtitlan*, 35.

[41] Lee J. Arco and Elliot M. Abrams, "An Essay on Energetics: The Construction of the Aztec Chinampa System," *Antiquity*, vol. 80, no. 310 (2006), 906–918; Luna Golya, "Modeling the Aztec Agricultural Waterscape of Lake Xochimilco," 55–56; Edward E. Calnek, "Settlement Pattern and Chinampa Agriculture at Tenochtitlan," *American Antiquity*, vol. 37, no. 1 (1972), 104–115.

and early sixteenth centuries were astonishing. In the place of the old lacustrine environment with their waters and swamps, now there were thousands of artificial islands rising out of the lakes. In one survey of relic beds, within 1,000 hectares of lake area there were some 23,000 chinampas. The chinampas came to cover at least 10,000 hectares (some estimates place this figure higher, at 16,000 hectares).[42] To put that figure in perspective, the chinampa districts were the equivalent size of more than 15,500 association football (soccer) pitches.[43] A significant proportion of that space still consisted of pools and canals. But, taken together, within what had once been lakes were now so many raised gardens that scholars reckon there could have been a 1:1 ratio of land to water. Put another way, half of the surface area of the lakes was now land. In effect then, as Gregory Luna Golya concludes, the lake areas became an "agricultural waterscape."[44]

So, large were the chinampa districts that Nahuas took up residence on artificial islands in the middle of the lake. Archaeological surveys of the lake bed show a distinctive settlement pattern in the Aztec-era chinampa districts. Sanders and his colleagues identified these settlements as "dispersed radial" villages, in which clusters of chinampas surrounded single houses, indicating that individual households cultivated their own immediate sets of lands.[45] This was the scene that greeted Spaniards when they arrived in the region. As one Spaniard writing in the sixteenth century observed, "A large number of Indians dwell inside the lagoon; they make staked enclosures and fill these with earth to some height above the water, and built their houses on top."[46] The lake became home to innumerable households and hamlets. When counting shoreline settlements as well as towns and cities like Cuitlahuac and Xochimilco – which were situated on islands in the lake – there may have been tens of thousands of residents in

---

[42] Luna Golya, "Modeling the Aztec Agricultural Waterscape of Lake Xochimilco," 154, 177.

[43] This figure is calculated according to the official minimum lengths of the pitch used in international matches (100 m for the touchline, 64 m for the goal line). Since the pitch would be a minimum of 6,400 m² and with a hectare equaling 10,000 m², 10,000 hectares is the equivalent of 15,625 football pitches. Conway, "Rural Indians and Technological Innovation."

[44] Parsons estimated a 3:1 ratio of fields to water to support his assertion that the chinampa districts were the grain basket of the Aztec Empire. Parsons, "The Role of Chinampa Agriculture in the Food Supply of Aztec Tenochtitlan," cited in Luna Golya, "Modeling the Aztec Agricultural Waterscape of Lake Xochimilco," 154, 4.

[45] Sanders et al., *The Basin of Mexico*, 168–171.

[46] The quotation is by Bernardo de Vargas Machuca, cited in Armillas, "Gardens on Swamps," 660.

the chinampa zone on the eve of the Spanish conquest. Perhaps as many as 30,000 people lived on reclaimed land within the lakes.

Those residents and their chinampas contributed to food surpluses that allowed for the dramatic rise in the region's population. During the late Post-Classic period, from 1350 to 1519 CE, the population of the basin increased from 175,000 to as many as 1,200,000 people.[47] By the sixteenth century, according to one conservative calculation, the chinampa farmers could have grown enough food to feed not just the 30,000 residents of the lakes but also another 50,000 people elsewhere. Using a different methodology to compute the carrying capacity of the chinampa districts, another scholar reckoned that 12,700 farmers could have generated annual harvests of 28.5 million kilos of maize. That abundance would have been enough to feed some 140,000 people. It is no exaggeration to suggest that the chinampa districts made possible the rise of Tenochtitlan as one of the most impressive and populous cities of the early modern world.[48]

AQUATIC WARFARE

The extraordinary panorama of the chinampa districts was one of the first sights to greet Spaniards when they entered the Basin of Mexico in late October 1519. They marveled at the scene filled with so many islands, buildings, and cities rising out of the water. In one of the most famous passages of the *Discovery and Conquest of New Spain*, the conquistador Bernal Díaz del Castillo expressed a sense of wonder at the sight, writing that "when we saw so many cities and villages built in the water and other great towns on dry land and that straight and level causeway going to Mexico, we were amazed and said it was like the enchantments they tell of in the legends of Amadis, on account of the great towers and cues and buildings rising from the water." Historians frequently quote this passage to point out the grandeur of the Nahua world and the Spaniards' astonishment at it. What is often overlooked, though, is the specific context of the elderly conquistador's recollections: in his mind's eye, Bernal Díaz recalled this sight precisely at the point where the Spaniards and their allies had crossed over the Cuitlahuac causeway at the heart of the

---

[47] Sanders et al., *The Basin of Mexico*, 184.
[48] Parsons, "The Role of Chinampa Agriculture in the Food Supply of Aztec Tenochtitlan," 242, 245; Luna Golya, "Modeling the Aztec Agricultural Waterscape of Lake Xochimilco," iv, 148, 160.

southern lake districts.[49] Having taken in more of the view, he added: "with such wonderful sights to gaze on we did not know what to say, or if this was real. ... On the land side there were great cities, and on the lake many more. The lake was crowded with canoes."[50]

Fernando Cortés was no less impressed by the sight of the southern lake communities. Writing of Mixquic, which he estimated as having between 1,000 and 2,000 inhabitants, Cortés noted that it was "constructed entirely on the water and with many towers and no place to enter, or so it seemed from a distance." The use of the word "constructed" is telling insofar as it hints at the artificial, manufactured quality of the landscape. Moving on to the causeway into the middle of the lake, Cortés observed that Cuitlahuac, with another 2,000 residents, "was the most beautiful we had seen, both in regard to the well-built houses and towers and in the skill and foundations, for it is raised on the water." Mexicalzingo was likewise "built on the water," and Huitzilopochco, while being on the shore had many houses "on the water."[51]

These passages are worth noting for another reason: Spaniards like Cortés and Bernal Díaz were quick to observe the location of communities *within* the lakes themselves. Cortés related in his letters to the Spanish crown the "sight of a pleasant city called Suchimilco, which is built on the freshwater lake." Elsewhere in his letter, Cortés repeated the observation that Xochimilco "is on the water."[52] Bernal Díaz similarly wrote that Xochimilco was "a great city where nearly all the houses are built in a freshwater lake," adding that the "houses stood in the freshwater lake."[53] It should be pointed out that the emphasis on the location of cities in the lake is neither an accident of translation nor the result of any vagueness of prepositions. Rather, Bernal Díaz wrote, "por las grandes torres y cues y edifiçios que tenían *dentro en el agua*" (emphasis added). Similarly Cortés wrote that Xochimilco "está edificada en la laguna" and "está en el agua."[54] Indeed, such phrasing became a common refrain in conquest accounts.

---

[49] Parsons et al., "Chinampa Agriculture and Aztec Urbanization in the Valley of Mexico," 52; Luna Golya, "Modeling the Aztec Agricultural Waterscape of Lake Xochimilco," iv and 148; Hernán Cortés, *Letters from Mexico*, ed. and trans. Anthony Pagden (New Haven: Yale University Press, 1986), 190, 198–199; Díaz del Castillo, *The Discovery and Conquest of Mexico*, 192 and 377.

[50] Díaz del Castillo, *Discovery of New Spain*, 216.

[51] Cortés, *Letters from Mexico*, 82–83.   [52] Cortés, *Letters from Mexico*, 198–199, 221.

[53] Díaz del Castillo, *The Discovery and Conquest of Mexico*, 377, 384.

[54] Díaz del Castillo, *Historia verdadera de la conquista de la Nueva España*, ed. José Antonio Borbón Rodríguez (Mexico City: El Colegio de México, 2005), 435, and for other

Spaniards were equally impressed by the ways in which the Nahuas used and modified the watery landscape.[55] Cortés, for instance, described in detail the outlet between Lake Xochimilco and Lake Tetzcoco at Mexicalzingo, explaining that "a small chain of very high hills" separated these two lakes such that the channel where the waters met was narrow, "no wider than a bowshot" at the point where "these hills and the mountains join the lakes." There in the channel, Cortés continued, Nahuas "travel between one lake and the other and between the different settlements which are on the lakes in their canoes without needing to go by land." He was also perceptive in noting that "as the salt lake rises and falls with its tides as does the sea, whenever it rises, the salt water flows into the fresh as swiftly as a powerful river, and on the ebb the fresh water passes to the salt." Cortés and others in his party came to appreciate the dangers posed by the lakes and the hydraulic engineering works. Both these features of the landscape could put to strategic use against the conquistadors. The Spaniards' first experience of this aquatic danger came with their flight from Tenochtitlan after fighting broke out. Then, the Mexica dismantled the causeways, thereby preventing the escape of the Spaniards and their Tlaxcalan allies, as Cortés noted, "except over the water."[56] The next taste of peril, which nearly proved disastrous, came a few months later in Iztapalapa, not far from the channel between Lakes Tetzcoco and Xochimilco that Cortés had noted so carefully.

In the weeks before the final siege of Tenochtitlan, and to bolster the allied forces, the Tlaxcalans, Tetzcoca, Spaniards, and others pursued diplomatic missions that doubled up as reconnaissance trips around (and beyond) the Basin of Mexico. Early in 1521, the Spanish-Tlaxcalan forces entered Iztapalapa, having been lured into the center of the town by the enemy. Cortés acknowledged the ploy as such when he called the enemies' actions a "subterfuge." Bernal Díaz agreed, describing it as a "preconcerted stratagem." Oblivious to the danger, the Spaniards entered the section of the town that was fully on the water, where they enjoyed "the spoils of victory and [made] themselves comfortable in homes, it now being after dark." The Mexica scheme was to breach the causeway, "which served as a dike between the salt and fresh-water lakes," as Cortés noted, and to do so at the most advantageous moment

---

examples, 441 and 460; Hernán Cortés, *Cartas y documentos*, ed. Mario Hernández Sánchez-Borbón (Mexico City: J. Porrúa, 1963), 218, 143, and 160.

[55] On the causeways, see Díaz del Castillo, *The Conquest of New Spain*, 216, 235.

[56] Cortés, *Letters from Mexico*, 102, 135.

when the Spaniards had let down their guard. As a result, "the salt water began to flow into the fresh with tremendous force" such that the Spaniards in the town were nearly drowned, only escaping with their lives thanks to the warning by their Tetzcocan allies. Bernal Díaz recalled, "such a flood of water swept through the town that if the chiefs we had brought from Texcoco had not shouted to us to get out of the houses as quickly as we could and make for dry land, we should all have been drowned." Writing several decades later, the Tetzcocan chronicler don Fernando de Alva Ixtlilxochitl remarked that had the Spaniards not hurried, "they would have all drowned there."[57]

Bernal Díaz was humbled by the experience. He recalled returning to "Texcoco, somewhat ashamed of having been taken in by their trick with the water." Cortés, in typical fashion, remembered things differently, emphasizing the wisdom he had recently acquired from the earlier flight across Tenochtitlan's causeway: "it seemed that Our Lord inspired me and brought to my memory that causeway or dike we had seen broken, and revealed to me the great danger we were in." Such wisdom or clairvoyance aside, Cortés wrote to "assure Your Majesty that if that night we had not crossed the water, or had waited but three hours more, none of us would have escaped." At daybreak the Spaniards "saw that the water from the one lake was level with that of the other and flowed no more; the salt lake was full of warriors in canoes expecting to seize us there." The Spaniards fled to the safety of Tetzcoco.[58]

If the Spaniards had come to appreciate the strategic advantages afforded by hydrological knowledge, they were also deeply concerned by the threat of water-borne attacks by flotillas of canoes. To this end, and to enable reinforcements for the troops that assaulted Tenochtitlan by causeway, the Spaniards and their allies built thirteen sailing vessels – called variously sloops, launches, and brigantines in conquest accounts – that could be deployed on the lake and, if the winds were favorable, maneuvered swiftly during naval battles. The boats also had the singular advantage, or so Spanish accounts suggested, of being able to overwhelm enemy canoes by the crude expedient of ramming them. The imperative of being able to contend with attacks by canoes, moreover, was a lesson that had been

---

[57] Fernando de Alva Ixtlilxochitl, *The Native Conquistador: Alva Ixtlilxochitl's Account of the Conquest of New Spain*, trans. and ed. Amber Brian, Bradley Benton, and Pablo García Loaeza (University Park: Pennsylvania State University Press, 2015), 30.

[58] Díaz del Castillo, *The Conquest of New Spain*, 317–318; Cortés, *Letters from Mexico*, 174.

reinforced for Spaniards some ten days before they launched the brigantines. In mid-April 1521, the Spaniards first encountered the Xochimilca and suffered a significant defeat in the battle that followed. In advance of the fighting, the Xochimilca, as allies of the Mexica, had prepared by raising all the bridges leading into their home town – including those on a causeway that connected it to the mainland – and by building earthworks, digging ditches, and opening up the canals.[59] Initial skirmishes prompted the Xochimilca to withdraw in their canoes along the waterways, whereupon the Spaniards moved into the center of the altepetl. Some of the Spaniards climbed a tall structure "in which the Xochimilca kept their idols," to gain a sense of the lay of the land and, more importantly, the lake, where they saw thousands of canoes assembling for an assault. Finding themselves surrounded by water, the Spaniards remained in the city throughout the night and on guard against attack. Recognizing the danger of being encircled, Cortés ordered the bridges to be filled up "with stones and adobes which were at hand, so that the horses might enter and leave the city without hindrance." The Spaniards then set up a watch, particularly "at the landing-places and along the canals" where Xochimilca and Mexica canoes "might disembark."

The assault came early the next morning via land and water with 2,000 canoes, some approaching "with muffled paddles to disembark at the landing-place," and all of them carrying "more than twelve thousand warriors." The fighting was fierce, taking place over the course of several days and spreading from the city center to a hill on the southern outskirts of the city and back again. All the while, Xochimilca and Mexica canoes broke off from the main fleet to pursue probing attacks in different places, including along some of the deeper canals. Facing defeat, the Spaniards and their allies fled, but not before looting and pillaging. Bernal Díaz recalled the city having "many rich men" who had "very large houses full of cloaks and cloth and Indian shirts, all of cotton and feather-work and many other things," including gold ornaments. Before fleeing, though, Cortés ordered that everything in Xochimilco be set on fire: "in the end we left it burnt and ruined, and it was a notable sight, for there had been many houses and towers for their idols all built of stone and mason."[60]

[59] Díaz del Castillo, *The Conquest of New Spain*, 344; Cortés, *Letters from Mexico*, 201. On opening up the canals and tearing down the bridges, see Alva Ixtlilxochitl, *The Native Conquistador*, 35.

[60] Díaz del Castillo, *The Conquest of New Spain*, 344–345; Cortés, *Letters from Mexico*, 200–202; Alva Ixtlilxochitl, *The Native Conquistador*, 35.

Soon after the battle of Xochimilco warfare broke out across the southern lake areas. Much of the fighting grew out of the immediate shifts in the balance of power in the region. The Chalca, having been the most recent to succumb to Mexica conquest in the late fifteenth century, were among the first to ally themselves with the forces of the Spaniards, Tetzcocans, and Tlaxcalans (this last group having previously been their other regional rivals to the east). The Mexica and their Xochimilca allies thus launched naval attacks against the Chalca at the far end of the lakes. Accounts that were attentive to the Native perspective, such as Alva Ixtlilxochitl's, observed the spiraling violence among indigenous polities. This violence took on local meanings that may have been separate from – or at least parallel to – the fighting of the Spaniards against the Mexica. While Cortés construed the Chalca offensive against neighboring lakeshore towns like Cuitlahuac and Mixquic as having been part of an effort to spread the Mexica forces thin, and thereby offer some reprieve to the Spaniards, Alva Ixtlilxochitl wrote that "all the cities, towns, and places around Xochimilco, Cuitlahuac, Mizquic, Coyoacan, Culhuacan, Iztapalapan, Mexicatzinco, and the others allied with Mexico gathered more than 60,000 warriors and attacked again to see if they could finally defeat Chalco." As the war progressed, some of these polities shifted their allegiance. They did so not because of the imminent defeat of Tenochtitlan, necessarily, but because the combined forces of Tetzcoco and Chalco were proving unbreakable. Alva Ixtlilxochitl explained that "the people of Cuitlahuac, Mizquic, Culhuacan, Mexicatzinco, and Huitzilopochco came to join Cortés" because of the losses they had sustained from the Spaniards' allies. The representatives of the lake towns asked that the Chalca now stop harassing them "because every day they plundered their houses."[61]

The switching of allegiances of the southern lake communities contributed to the momentum gathering against the Mexica. The first polity to change sides, according to Bernal Díaz, was Mixquic, whose residents "had never been on good terms with the Mexicans and heartily loathed them." The new alliance was forged even before the final siege of Tenochtitlan had begun, and the Spaniards were "all very pleased at this people's coming, because of their position on the water, and because through them we hoped to be able to approach their neighbours further along the lake."[62] Clearly the Mixquica alliance offered a vital, aquatic

[61] Cortés, *Letters from Mexico*, 230–231; Alva Ixtlilxochitl, *The Native Conquistador*, 33, 48.
[62] Díaz del Castillo, *The Conquest of New Spain*, 318.

advantage. Spaniards further recounted being overjoyed at having secured assistance from additional polities. The chinampa districts had functioned as a staging ground for the Mexica, thereby forcing the Cortés and his lieutenants to devote thousands of warriors to defending their rear bases at the entrance to the causeways. Cristóbal de Olid apparently relied on 15,000 Tetzcocan soldiers to protect the southern entryway to the causeway at Culhuacan "so that the Mexica would not receive aid from Xochimilco and other places."[63] The former enemies had also previously supplied food to the Mexica capital.[64] Now with Cuitlahuac and other polities aligned with them, the Spaniards and Tlaxcalans benefited from receiving these valuable provisions at precisely the same time that shortages grew more acute in the capital. The Spaniards also gained more warriors and auxiliaries. Additionally, as Cortés readily acknowledged, the new allies' canoes proved to be especially useful. Keenly aware that they would "encounter the greatest dangers and risks on the water," Cortés specifically required in negotiations with new allies that they commit to making ready as many warriors in canoes as possible.[65]

Only when the siege of Tenochtitlan was well under way – and the probability of Mexica defeat seemed ever more likely – did the Xochimilca throw their support behind the Spaniards and Tlaxcalans.[66] The Nahuas who collaborated with fray Bernardino de Sahagún in the *Florentine Codex*'s account of the conquest wrote of the treachery of the Xochimilca and the Cuitlahuaca in turning against the Mexica and their neighbors, the Tlatelolca. Having first feigned to offer their support, in an act of sudden and shocking duplicity the Xochimilca and Cuitlahuaca switched sides and launched a surprise attack. While many warriors were captured by both sides, as the Tlatelolca recalled bitterly, the marine forces of the new enemies enforced the blockage of the island capital, thereby inflicting great suffering of its peoples. The warriors from the southern lakes also provided a significant advantage to the Spaniards and the Tlaxcalans, who were able to press their advantage along the roads into capital because the Mexica and Tlatelolca warriors were simultaneously trying to fend off

[63] Alva Ixtlilxochitl, *The Native Conquistador*, 42.

[64] Cortés, *Letters from Mexico*, 217; Díaz del Castillo, *The Conquest of New Spain*, 375.

[65] Cortés, *Letters from Mexico*, 230.

[66] The Xochimilca had long remained loyal to the Mexica, fighting with them and even providing fresh drinking water after the pipes in the aqueduct from the lakeshore had been destroyed at the beginning of the siege. Alva Ixtlilxochitl, *The Native Conquistador*, 46; Díaz del Castillo, *The Conquest of New Spain*, 395; Cortés, *Letters from Mexico*, 209, 231; Mundy, *The Death of Aztec Tenochtitlan*, 72.

attacks from the water.[67] Nahua nobles from Xochimilco later recalled that 12,000 of its citizens had fought in the Spanish-Mexica War.[68]

Just as the final stages of the conflict took the form of a naval battle, as well as a multipronged assault along the causeways, so the hydraulic infrastructure continued to be utilized – or, in some cases, destroyed – in the service of military objectives. The destruction of Tenochtitlan went hand in glove with the destruction of the engineering works that surrounded it. In a repeating sequence, the Mexica broke the causeways leading into the capital so as to fend off attack, and then the Spaniards and their allies filled in the gap in order to resume the offensive.[69] It was not just the causeways that were damaged, though. In some of the most consequential acts of strategic demolition, the dikes were also breached. In order for the Spaniards to encircle the capital, provide naval support for infantry on the causeways, and attack Tenochtitlan from many directions at once, they and their allies smashed apart sections of the Nezahualcoyotl Dike. The breaches were large enough to allow passage of the brigantines as well as thousands of allied canoes.[70] The Mexica used similar tactics. They destroyed much of the causeway between Iztapalapa and Coyoacan to prevent the Spaniards from crossing it. This barrier was, apparently, the one crossing the narrow channel between Lake Tetzcoco and Lake Xochimilco and hence one of the most important points in the overall water management system.[71] Its destruction upset the hydrology of the southern lakes, which had profound implications for the chinampa districts.

The effects of warfare on the environmental situation of Xochimilco and the chinampa districts were severe. Archaeologists have argued that the destruction of key parts of the wider system of water management during the Spanish-Mexica War ushered in a period of fairly swift environmental change. The breaches in the dikes and causeways during the

---

[67] Sahagún, *Florentine Codex, Book 12 – The Conquest of Mexico*, 95–97, 103–104, and 109–111.

[68] AGI, Patronato, leg. 184, ramo 50; see also Restall et al., eds., *Mesoamerican Voices*, 67.

[69] Cortés, *Letters from Mexico*, 233; Díaz del Castillo, *The Conquest of New Spain*, 297. The laborious – and not to mention, perilous – work was done by thousands of native allies. Alva Ixtlilxochitl claimed at one point that 50,000 Tetzcocans were recruited for this task. Elsewhere he put the figure at 20,000. Regardless of his mathematical precision, large numbers of individuals would have been needed. Alva Ixtlilxochitl, *The Native Conquistador*, 37, 47.

[70] Cortés, *Letters from Mexico*, 232, 215; Alva Ixtlilxochitl, *The Native Conquistador*, 40–41.

[71] Cortés, *Letters from Mexico*, 215.

fighting allowed for the free flow of water to and from Lakes Xochimilco and Chalco, which in effect inundated and swept away the Aztec-era lake bed chinampas.[72] The chinampa districts were thus reduced in size. They came to be confined to the areas surrounding the islands and shores of Lakes Xochimilco and Chalco. In other words, the watery landscape reverted to its earlier appearance, before the rise of the Aztec Triple Alliance. The ancient chinampa districts proved to be more resilient than their Aztec-era counterparts.[73]

The collapse of the Aztec imperial state and demographic decline also played important roles in these environmental changes. Gone were the system-wide policies, large-scale labor levies, and centralized supervision necessary for the upkeep of the old waterworks. Some parts of the old monumental hydraulic projects of the Aztecs survived in a few areas. Archaeologists consider them to be examples of *landesque* capital, a term that refers to the enduring dividends from previous investments of resources that could be harnessed and enjoyed by subsequent generations.[74] As Vera Candiani has observed, some of the hydraulic infrastructure "remained in place, doing its job by inertia."[75] But with no single, overarching supervision of the entire system, the control measures that had once regulated the water levels disappeared, at least for a while.

In spite of all these changes, Lakes Xochimilco and Chalco survived. While the conquest era had coincided with a period of drier climate, from the 1550s, the period of higher humidity that Bradley Skopyk has called the "Colonial Mexican Pluvial" ensured that the southern lakes remained well stocked with water.[76] The higher water levels, in turn, helped ensure the persistence of chinampa cultivation in the areas close to the lakeshore. At the turn of the seventeenth century, this watery landscape still retained many of the characteristics described by archaeologists for earlier periods, including the presence of many small, dispersed settlements on the artificial islands. During an inspection of the chinampa districts of Mexicalzingo, a Spanish official, don Lope de Ulloa y Lemos, described the scene. Traveling by canoe, he observed that residents lived in homes made of adobe and wood that were scattered ("desparramadas") between the many canals. These homes were adjacent to those chinampa plots

---

[72] This trend contrasts with the lowering of the water levels in Lake Tetzcoco, which Barbara Mundy notes, and which stemmed from drought during the first two post-conquest decades. Mundy, *The Death of Aztec Tenochtitlan*, 72.

[73] Luna Golya, "Modeling the Aztec Agricultural Waterscape," 25.

[74] Luna Golya, "Modeling the Aztec Agricultural Waterscape," 26, 77–78, 173–175.

[75] Candiani, *Dreaming of Dry Land*, 16.　　[76] Skopyk, *Colonial Cataclysms*, 11.

cultivated by the households. The chinampas themselves constituted the only land under cultivation. In a few communities such as Huitzilopochco and Culhuacan, the entirety of the tierra firme was taken up by parish churches.[77]

The chinampas, the island settlements, and the hydraulic infrastructure – which also included the nearby great canal to Xochimilco and Chalco as well as the causeways – all survived as vital elements of the area's landesque capital. Because they remained intact, for many generations the residents of the lake areas were able benefit from the investments of their ancestors. The engineering works did not need to be rebuilt from scratch; instead, Nahuas could maintain them even as their ability to do so diminished with dramatic demographic decline. While some parts of the irrigation system gradually fell into disrepair during the colonial period, they could be repaired and restored. In this way, the canals, causeways, chinampas, dams, and dikes were reminiscent of the examples of landesque capital that the geo-archaeologist Aleksander Borejsza has studied for colonial-era Tlaxcala. While agricultural terraces there fell into a state of disrepair following population loss, he notes that they later served as a foundation for rehabilitating vacant lands and restoring them to agricultural use.[78] In Xochimilco, the survival of key features of the water management system also made it possible for Nahuas to preserve the economic vitality of the lake-area altepetl. It now fell to these communities to maintain the lake area's aquatic gardens and engineering works, just as they had in the days before the rise of the Aztec Empire.[79]

POST-CONQUEST ALTERATIONS AND ADAPTATIONS

As with the lakes and chinampa cultivation, the lake-area polities of the Nahuas survived the Spanish–Mexica War. Native political structures and jurisdictions proved indispensable for the nascent Spanish government and, thanks to their enduring quality and value, they remained firmly in place long into the colonial period. None of these structures was more important than the altepetl. The ethnic state initially served as the main venue for interactions between Nahuas and Spaniards, and it underlay all

---

[77] AGN, Civil, vol. 1271, exp. 1, f. 43.

[78] Borejsza, "Village and Field Abandonment in Post-conquest."

[79] Luna Golya, "Modeling the Aztec Agricultural Waterscape," 25, 74, 173–174; Gibson, *The Aztecs under Spanish Rule*, 276; Candiani, *Dreaming of Dry Land*, 16; Mundy, *The Death of Aztec Tenochtitlan*, 37, 196, and 199.

of the principal jurisdictions of the colonial system.[80] It also provided the essential basis for stability and continuity for Nahuas.[81] In itself and in its nomenclature, an altepetl was something both tangible and abstract. In terms of etymology, it comprised the words for water (*atl*) and mountain (*tepetl*), which served as a metaphor for the key natural features required to sustain and preserve life. Beyond this conception, the altepetl was also a physical space and a well-defined territory. Each altepetl had a nucleated core, a marketplace, a temple for the worship of a particular deity, and a *tecpan*, or "palace," for its dynastic ruler. An altepetl was at once the domain of this ruler and the home to a people whose identity was tied to their altepetl, as with the Xochimilca.

In part because of its intertwined abstract and physical dimensions – as a place, people, and sociopolitical entity – the material manifestation of an altepetl can be hard to locate, particularly in the case of Xochimilco, for which there is no single document that clearly delineates the altepetl's entire territory or that identifies all of its constituent parts. Adding to this complexity, the altepetl itself comprised smaller units, known as *calpolli*, which were clusters of kin groups and associations, and the cellular organization of these and the larger entities could change over time. Additionally, Xochimilco was also an example of a "complex" or "composite" altepetl, which meant that it comprised three distinct ruling dynasties and their separate domains.[82] Furthermore, the altepetl had outlying satellite settlements that despite being at a distance from the nucleated center were nonetheless integral parts of it.

The best single representation we have of the territorial and political contours of Xochimilco is shown in a map included in the Codex Cozcatzin, a pictorial document that presents several subjects, including a history of the Aztec emperors (hence the appearance of Moteucçoma in the upper left of the image; see Map 1.1).[83] The map depicts the altepetl of

[80] Horn, *Postconquest Coyoacan*, 1.

[81] Lockhart, *The Nahuas after the Conquest*; Susan Schroeder, *Chimalpahin and the Kingdoms of Chalco* (Tucson: University of Arizona Press, 1991); Cline, *Colonial Culhuacan*.

[82] Lockhart, *The Nahuas after the Conquest*, 20–28, and James Lockhart, "Complex Municipalities: Tlaxcala and Tulancingo in the Sixteenth Century," in *Nahuas and Spaniards: Postconquest Central Mexican History and Philology* (Stanford: Stanford University Press and UCLA Latin American Center, 1991), 23–38.

[83] Ana Rita Valero de García Lascuráin and Rafael Tena, eds., *Códice Cozcatzin* (Mexico City: Instituto Nacional de Antropología e Historia, 1994); María Castañeda de la Paz, "Un plano de tierras en el *Códice Cozcatzin*: Adaptaciones y transformaciones de la cartografía prehispánica," *Anales de Antropología*, vol. 40, no. 2 (2006), 41–73.

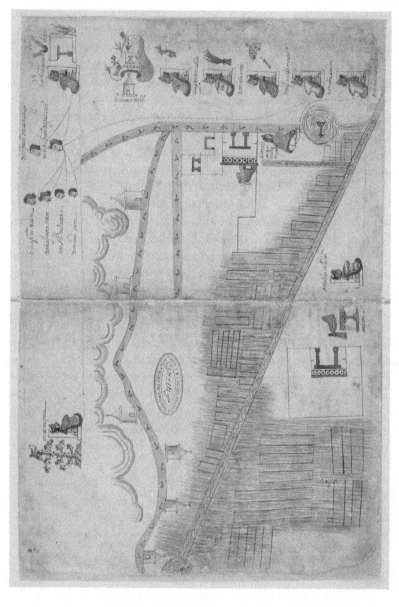

MAP 1.1 Map of Xochimilco in the Codex Cozcatzin. Bibliothèque Nationale de France (Paris), Département des Manuscrits, Mexicain 41–45.

Xochimilco, which is identified through the bell-shaped glyph on the upper right-hand side. The flowers emerging from it refer to the toponym, "the place of the flower fields," and the name "Xochimilco" has been added as a gloss in Roman alphabet. At the center of the map are dozens of rectangular chinampas, some perpendicular to others, within shading that could represent reeds or the lacustrine landscape (or both). The chinampas are located next to a canal which in turn is connected, at either end, to swirls of water, suggesting either pools or, more likely, springs. Surrounding the chinampas are roads and, at the top, representations of hilly terrain like the contour lines on a modern map.

To this physical space, the unknown mapmaker added emblems of political and religious organization. In addition to the chapels along the roads, there are the symbols of three palaces of Xochimilco's rulers: these are the square structures; two of them, one at the bottom center and the other at the center right of the map, have doorways with a row of circular (or doughnut) shapes next to them that are all facing upward; the third one is in the upper right-hand corner and is shown in profile.[84] The three palaces also served as focal points on the map for the altepetl's three constituent districts: each of them was under the control of a dynastic ruler, or *tlatoani*, who appears seated on a throne. These rulers are depicted alongside their relatives, past and present. Thus, shown vertically on the right-hand side, is the generational lineage of rulers for the district named Tepetenchi, whose names are provided in alphabetic glosses. The first, Xiuhtemocatzin, had been the ruler in the conquest era; he was followed by don Martín Cortés, then don Pedro de Sotomayor, don Martín Cerón ("Serom"), and finally, in faded ink, another don Martín Cerón, this one being the younger. It is worth pointing out that his wife, doña Joana de Los Ángeles, is seated outside the palace of Tepetenchi; also worth noting is that by the time of this last ruler, as discussed later, the three ruling dynasties had become intertwined through marriage alliances, which explains why lines extend from the figure of the younger don Martín Cerón to don Hernando de Santa María, at the bottom, and doña Francisca de Guzmán, at the top, who was the spouse of don Francisco.

Although there is a degree of abstraction to the map, and a lack of clarity as to the exact geographical situation of Xochimilco, it does give some sense of the altepetl's territoriality. There is no indication as to whether Xochimilco was located on an island or not. (By the seventeenth

---

[84] Mundy, *The Death of Aztec Tenochtitlan*, 89.

century, with changes to water levels in the lakes, Xochimilco may have ceased to be on an island). Nor is the central plaza depicted on it. But the three palaces and dynastic lineages do seem to occupy separate spaces on the map. In fact, the domains of the three rulerships, named Tepetenchi, Tecpan, and Olac, were distinct parts of the altepetl both in terms of politics and territory. Each of them surrounded the chinampa districts and each extended beyond the lakeshore and up in the mainland.

Besides having a territorial orientation that encompassed both land and water, Xochimilco stood out from other polities in central Mexico because of its distinctive tripartite sociopolitical configuration. Most of the complex altepetl – for instance, Tlalmanalco, Amecameca, Coyoacan, Huexotzinco, and Tlaxcala – typically consisted of a symmetrical, numerical arrangement of two, four, six, or eight internal parts. Cuitlahuac was organized this way.[85] Xochimilco represents an alternative case of how the Nahuas arranged their world. Importantly, the altepetl's distinctive orientation also proved to be especially resilient, escaping the perils of disintegration and enduring long after the conquest, as the map in the Codex Cozcatzin itself shows. Some complex altepetl, by contrast, were reorganized by Spanish authorities.[86] In a few instances, Spaniards sought to divide complex altepetl into separate jurisdictions, with a dynastic ruler remaining in place for each, although as historian James Lockhart notes, they usually did so in a way that reflected preexisting indigenous organization. On other occasions, Nahua preferences for local identities underpinned the movement toward fragmentation.[87] Alternatively, Spaniards promoted one of the rulers at the expense of the others, creating a single *cabecera*, or head town of the jurisdiction.[88]

None of these scenarios played out in Xochimilco. Although the three subunits had corresponding sets of dynastic rulers, the altepetl remained a single, complex entity. The three ruling dynasties kept their formal titles,

---

[85] Lockhart, *The Nahuas after the Conquest*, 16.

[86] See, by contrast, the conflicts over the status of Zumpango in Gibson, *The Aztecs under Spanish Rule*, 68.

[87] Lockhart, *The Nahuas after the Conquest*, 27–28.

[88] Lockhart, *The Nahuas after the Conquest*, 31; Horn, *Postconquest Coyoacan*, 23. Xochimilco was large enough to merit division into separate juridical entities, like Tulancingo, but presumably its high level of nucleation, consistent with an urban orientation, may have precluded this. Early descriptions by Spaniards refer to the urban form of Xochimilco, and each of the three tlaxilacalli was home to chinampas, meaning that they all reached the waterfront, further suggesting nucleation. See Díaz del Castillo, *The Discovery and Conquest of Mexico*, 377. On the division of Tulancingo, see Lockhart, "Complex Municipalities," 26–27.

if not their actual political offices (to be discussed in the next section). The subdivisions thus conform to what the Nahua historian Chimalpahin called *tlayacatl*, namely, constituent parts of a composite altepetl.[89] Chimalpahin called Xochimilco's subunits *tlayacatl*, although that term does not appear in Nahuatl sources from Xochimilco.[90] In its place we find the term *tlaxilacalli*. In a 1657 Nahuatl document, Joseph de la Cruz and his wife, Nicolasa Orsova, described themselves as residents of the tlaxilacalli of Tepetenchi.[91]

In preserving the original altepetl structure, the Spaniards designated the three subdivisions of Tepetenchi, Tecpan, and Olac individual cabeceras, thereby perpetuating the integrity of the whole polity.[92] (The Spanish documentation also occasionally referred to the sections of the city as *parcialidades*, *partes*, and sometimes *barrios*).[93] In fact, the term *cabecera* entered into Nahuatl vocabulary as a loanword referring to the three subdivisions. It can be seen in the records of gubernatorial salaries and in the 1588 testament of the tlatoani don Martín Cerón y Alvarado the Elder. Don Martín stated that he hailed from the "cabezera tepetenchi."[94] Several generations later, the last member of the family to hold the title of tlatoani, also named don Martín Cerón y Alvarado, used the term in his 1650 testament:

yn nehuatl niquitohua ca nican nichane yn ipan ciudad Xochimilco nitlatohuani notoca don mīn ceron Alvarado auh nipohui nicavecera ynipan tlaxilacalli tepetenchi.

I state that I am a resident here in the city of Xochimilco, I am its dynastic ruler, and my name is don Martín Cerón y Alvarado. I belong in the cabecera and tlaxilacalli of Tepetenchi.[95]

---

[89] Schroeder, *Chimalpahin and the Kingdoms of Chalco*, 131–136.

[90] Schroeder, *Chimalpahin and the Kingdoms of Chalco*, 135. Lockhart also uses tlayacatl when referring to Xochimilco's three districts. Lockhart, *The Nahuas after the Conquest*, 21 and 29.

[91] The Nahuatl reads: "yn nehuatl notoca Jusephe de la Cruz yhuan ynonamic nicolasa orsova nican tichanneque ypan ciudad Xuchimilco totlaxilacal tepetenchi." AGN, Ramo Civil, vol. 1823, f. 16.

[92] AGN, General de Parte, vol. 1, exp. 604, f. 124v.

[93] Lockhart observes this tendency in *The Nahuas after the Conquest*, 21; Pérez Zevallos, "Organización del señorío de Xochimilco"; AGN, Indios, vol. 3, exp. 380, f. 87v; vol. 5, exp. 265, f. 149v; exp. 548, f. 221v; vol. 6, 2a pte., exp. 1040, f. 280; AGN, Tierras, vol. 1525, exp. 3, f. 3, and exp. 5, f. 30.

[94] For the salary records, see AGN, Vínculos y Mayorazgos, vol. 279, exp. 1, ff. 69–70, 72, and the testament, f. 6.

[95] AGN, Vínculos y Mayorazgos, vol. 279, exp. 1, f. 10. This testament also provides another example of the simultaneous use of ciudad and altepetl. It closes with the following phrase "ymixpan testigos españoles nican chaneque ypan inin altepetl ciudad xochimilco" (f. 10v). Doña María de Guzmán, daughter of the tlatoani of Olac, don Francisco

Even though they were a different numerical arrangement, Xochimilco's three constituent tlaxilacalli districts adhered to the principles of sociopolitical organization seen in other complex altepetl in central Mexico. Political organization for the altepetl rested at the tlaxilacalli level. The districts had their own distinct identities, too, reflected, for instance, in the predominance of certain craft specializations. As elsewhere, rotational practices were also integral features of the three districts; the cellular structure of altepetl depended upon regular, sequential rotations in political representation and the performance of draft labor, which included the upkeep of the altepetl's hydraulic infrastructure.[96] The rotations usually followed the order of seniority of the constituent parts. While we lack the details of the foundation of the three units in Xochimilco, they were always referred to in the same order, with Tepetenchi first and then Tecpan and Olac. This order, as Juan Manuel Pérez Zevallos has noted, also reflected the size of each district.[97] Based on the official number of calpolli they contained, Tepetenchi, with twelve, was the largest and most populous.[98] Tecpan and Olac, in turn, were smaller, each containing seven calpolli. The perquisites of status accorded the nobles of the divisions, and the number of political offices apportioned to each, as listed in a 1548 document, also show that Tepetenchi was the most important of the three.[99]

In Xochimilco, the numerous, smaller calpolli units were commonly called tlaxilacalli, too, just like the three larger subdivisions of which they formed a part.[100] Nahuatl documentation surmounted this potential confusion by describing both entities together as a doublet or pair.[101] Doña Ana de Guzmán described her citizenship in terms of the noble city of Xochimilco and then, more specifically, "tepetenchi notlaxillacalpan tlachtonco," or "Tepetenchi, in my tlaxilacalli of Tlachtonco."[102] The

---

de Guzmán, refers to that subdivision as a cabecera too. AGN, Vínculos y Mayorazgos, vol. 279, exp. 1, f. 82. See also a 1600 bill of sale on f. 31.

[96] AGN, General de Parte, vol. 1, exp. 604, f. 124v.

[97] Pérez Zevallos, *Xochimilco Ayer*, vol. 1, 49.

[98] The number of calpolli climbs drastically, into the dozens, when counted in parish records. Rebecca Horn also notes a disparity between the number of official barrios in Coyoacan and the numbers seen in documentation. Horn, *Postconquest Coyoacan*, 22.

[99] Library of Congress, Krauss Collection, ms. 140, ff. 436–451v.

[100] I have found no instances of the term *calpolli* being used in Nahuatl sources from Xochimilco, which accords with Lockhart's observation that the term played only a small role in Nahuatl documentation. Lockhart, *The Nahuas after the Conquest*, 16.

[101] This was the common convention in parish records of baptisms and marriages. See, for example, AGN, Genealogía, vols. 1855–1857 and 1793–1797.

[102] AGN, Vínculos y Mayorazgos, vol. 279, exp. 1, f. 19. Sometimes the barrios had two names. Catalena Magdalena and her father, Joan Lázaro, came from Tepetenchi Tecpan

sources demonstrate several variations to this phrasing. In 1653, Martina Luisa listed them in the same sequential order, expressed as "my tlaxilacalli Tepetenchi Acatitlan."[103] Others distinguished between the two more clearly. In her 1566 testament, Ana Tiacapan wrote that she was a resident "of the city of Xochimilco, belonging to Tepetenchi, and Tlalnepantla is my tlaxilacalli."[104] On a few occasions, the sequence appeared in reverse order.[105] Regardless of the details of actual phrasing, though, the Nahuatl conventions of naming sociopolitical entities continued through the eighteenth century, as, for instance, in a testament from 1769.[106]

If the enduring usage of Nahuatl terminology and the long survival through the colonial period of the altepetl's complex, internal organization, was distinctive, so too was another particular characteristic of the polity's sociopolitical orientation: intriguingly, other altepetl that had been established by the Xochimilca exhibited the same tripartite division as the original polity, suggesting that the composition of such states owed much to the preferences of the ethnic groups that founded them.[107] Several other communities in colonial-era Xochimilca territories were

Colhuacantzinco. The original is as follows: "yn nehuatl catalena madalena nichpochnemi yhuan yn motatzin joan lazaro nican tichaneque ciudad xochimilco tipohui tepetenchi totlaxilacalpan tecpan colhuacantzinco." AGN, Vínculos y Mayorazgos, vol. 279, exp. 1, f. 47.

[103] AGN, Intestados, vol. 301, ff. 214–214v.

[104] The original reads: "nehuatl ana teacapā nicā nichane ciudad xuchimilco tepetenchi nipohui tlalnepātla notlaxilacalpā." AGN, Tierras, vol. 35, exp. 6, ff. 236–237.

[105] Doña Magdalena de Guzmán wrote, "My tlaxilacalli is Tlachtonco and I belong to Tepetenchi," or "notlaxillacalpā tlachtonco tepetenchi nipohui." AGN, Vínculos y Mayorazgos, vol. 279, exp. 1, f. 115. Testimony presented in 1580 provides another example: "Nehuatl Brº de la cruz nicā nichane ynipā noble ciudad xuchimilco notlaxillacalpa tlalnepātla macuihuaca tepetenchi nipohui." AGN, Tierras, vol. 95, exp. 6, f. 6.

[106] AGN, Tierras, vol. 2669, exp. 8, f. 8.

[107] Rebecca Horn suggested that Xochimilco may originally have consisted of four internal parts and that the reallocation of San Agustín de las Cuevas to Coyoacan reduced this number to just three. Horn, *Postconquest Coyoacan*, 33. Only one document, originating from the viceregal court in 1590, states that don Hernando de Santa María came from one of Xochimilco's *four* unidentified cabeceras. AGN, Indios, vol. 4, exp. 645, ff. 184–184v. This is the only instance in which four subdivisions were described. Having been written at the remove of the viceregal government, one must wonder if it was simply a mistake, especially as the internal structure of the altepetl was not a topic relevant to the case at hand. The notion that there were four districts contradicts the abundant documentation stating otherwise, as well as contemporary sources like the Codex Cozcatzin and chroniclers such as Chimalpahin. While the possibility that Xochimilco once had four subunits cannot be disproved, it seems highly unlikely. On the same division of other outlying Xochimilca polities, see Juan Manuel Pérez Zevallos, "El Gobierno Indígena de Xochimilco (Siglo XVI)," *Historia Mexicana*, vol. 33, no. 4 (1984), 448.

described as altepetl. San Miguel Topilejo and Santa María de la Asunción Milpa Alta both appeared in eighteenth-century Nahuatl documentation as such.[108] Milpa Alta also appeared as one in the seventeenth century, as did Santiago Tepalcatlalpan.[109] Many of these polities contained internal subdivisions that were described as tlaxilacalli, which shared the same names as Xochimilco's constituent parts.[110] Indeed, as the study by Rebeca Ramos of parish records has shown, all the communities within Xochimilco's jurisdiction contained districts named Tepetenchi, Tecpan, or Olac.[111] Thus in San Pedro Atocpan, for instance, Gabriel de San Antonio described himself in 1602 as a resident of Tepetenchi, while in her 1766 testament, doña María Pascuala identified with her tlaxilacalli of Tecpan, which she also called a barrio.[112]

Tlayacapan is the best documented example of a former Xochimilca polity that shared Xochimilco's sociopolitical organization. Tlayacapan had been one of the distant settler communities of the Xochimilca in the pre-contact period. For the colonial period, several sources provide the names of Tlayacapan's internal units. In 1656, officials from the district of Tepetenchi petitioned the viceroy to assist them because rivals from Tecpan had tried to seize the town's archive, held in the government offices. The Nahuas of Tepetenchi argued that from time immemorial and according to custom their community had housed the archive. They further argued – rather imaginatively, given the request for government assistance – that in spite of the threat of seizure, only their district could provide the necessary security for the town's papers.[113]

A separate political dispute from 1642 provides the clearest indication of Tlayacapan's organization. Spanish authorities and the town's friars had apparently blocked the annual election of political officers.[114] The resulting investigation by the General Indian Court noted that for more than fifty years, Nahuas from the two parcialidades and barrios of Tecpan and

---

[108] The document for Topilejo dates to 1768 and Milpa Alta, 1737. AGN, Criminal, vol. 24, exp. 1, 1a. tramite, ff. 50–50v; AGN, Ramo Civil, vol. 1230, exp. 7, ff. 2–2v.

[109] AGN, Tierras, vol. 1750, exp. 1, f. 24; AGN, Criminal, vol. 233, exp. 10, ff. 279–280.

[110] AGN, Ramo Civil, vol. 1230, exp. 7, ff. 2–2v.

[111] Rebeca Ramos, "Posibilidades analíticas de un archivo parroquial: el caso de San Bernardino de Sena, Xochimilco," in Ramos, Gortari Krauss, and Pérez Zevallos, eds., *Xochimilco en el siglo XVI*, 34–37.

[112] AGN, Tierras, vol. 1741, exp. 6, ff. 4–5; vol. 2429, exp. 3, f. 14.

[113] AGN, Indios, vol. 11, exp. 365, f. 298v; vol. 20, exp. 182, f. 133v (132v old foliation).

[114] AGN, Indios, vol. 14, exp. 42, ff. 46v–47v (301v–302v old foliation); exp. 43, ff. 47v–48v (302v–303v old foliation). This was not the first such intervention by friars. See also a case from 1591, AGN, Indios, vol. 5, exp. 1042, f. 267.

Tepetenchi were eligible for office as governor and *alcaldes* (officers of the town council). Apparently, according to tradition, the two districts had alternated in staffing these positions. Olac, by contrast, in having fewer than thirty residents, could only elect a subordinate *regidor* (councilman). The dispute had arisen when don Nicolás de Tolentino, then regidor and "a delinquent and unruly Indian," tried to usurp the governorship.[115] As this example shows, while the features of political representation differed from Xochimilco, Tlayacapan nevertheless had the same internal organization.

The enduring complexity in sociopolitical organization and the prolonged use of Nahuatl terms for sociopolitical entities, from the altepetl down to the tlaxilacalli levels, serve as compelling reminders that key elements of Xochimilco's precontact past continued to find a place in Nahua society after the arrival of the Spaniards. Indeed, continuity in the structure of the altepetl, and the enduring articulation and use of its organizational principles likely helped Nahuas as they adjusted to new colonial jurisdictions. In 1541, after the demise of encomendero Pedro de Alvarado (who was crushed under his horse during the Mixton War) and following the death of his widow, doña Beatriz de la Cueva, soon afterward, the Spanish government quickly moved to escheat Xochimilco and incorporate it into the royal domain.[116] Surely the haste – at a time when the power of encomenderos was a cause for crown concern – lay in the singular value of Xochimilco.[117] Xochimilco had been central Mexico's largest single encomienda, with some 20,000 tributaries.[118] Its attraction for treasury officials, of course, mirrored its appeal to prospective encomenderos, namely, the potential for substantial tribute income. Certainly Xochimilco was much coveted by those aware of its size and value. Conquistadors vied for control the encomienda. In the 1530s, Alvarado became embroiled in a dispute over the altepetl with adelantado Francisco de Montejo. Its control does not seem to have changed hands other than through a possible, temporary transfer to Alvarado's brother, Jorge.[119] At

---

[115] AGN, Indios, vol. 14, exp. 44, ff. 48v–49 (303v–304).

[116] *El libro de las tasaciones*, 304.

[117] The establishment of the corregimiento took place just prior to the New Laws of 1542, designed to consolidate crown authority against the pretensions of colonial subjects. See C. H. Haring, *The Spanish Empire in America* (New York: Harcourt Brace Jovanovich, 1975), 51–53.

[118] Gibson, *The Aztecs under Spanish Rule*, 61.

[119] AGI, Justicia, leg. 134, ramo 3, John F. Chuchiak IV, "Forgotten Allies: The Origins and Roles of Native Mesoamerican Auxiliaries and Indios Conquistadores in the Conquest of Yucatan, 1526–1550," in Laura E. Matthew and Michel R. Oudijk, eds., *Indian Conquistadors: Indigenous Allies in the Conquest of Mesoamerica* (Norman:

another, albeit unspecified point in the past – probably also in the 1530s – a brother-in-law of the Marqués de Mondéjar had allegedly offered to pay the enormous sum of 50,000 *ducados* for Xochimilco.[120] Having assumed direct control of Xochimilco, the Spanish crown created a new jurisdictional entity that rested on the altepetl. This was a *corregimiento*, which is to say the jurisdiction of a *corregidor*, or magistrate, based on Castilian precedent. In Xochimilco, the establishment of the corregimiento entailed little alteration of the altepetl.[121] According to Gibson, all that was required to bring about the change in jurisdiction was the appointment of a corregidor, "whereupon a complete and well-defined corregimiento was immediately at hand."[122] Corregimiento survived in this form until the establishment of the intendancy system by the reformist Bourbon monarchs in 1787.[123] Previously, the *congregación* programs (to consolidate scattered populations) of the early seventeenth century seem to have brought only minor adjustments, merely affecting one of the internal parts of Xochimilco.[124]

That Xochimilco was well suited to colonial jurisdictions was also reflected in the ecclesiastical domain. Parish organization under the Franciscans similarly followed that of corregimiento in its conformity with the altepetl. Some time between 1525 and 1535, Nahuas began construction of the friary of San Bernardino de Siena.[125] At this time

---

University of Oklahoma Press, 2007), 184; Gerhard, *A Guide to the Historical Geography of New Spain*, 245; William L. Sherman, "A Conqueror's Wealth: Notes on the Estate of Don Pedro de Alvarado," *The Americas*, vol. 26 (1969), 199–213.

[120] The date of this proposal is unclear. The prospective buyer, one "Martín Dircio," is mentioned in correspondence with King Philip II from Pedro de Logroño, Clerigo Presbitero of Guadalajara, in a letter dated 1567. The letter mentions previous events as far back as 1532. Archivo Histórico Nacional, Madrid, Diversos Colecciones, R. 24, n. 76, ff. 1–2. A ducado was the equivalent of 375 maravedís; 34 maravedís commonly equaled, according to Gibson, one real, or an eighth of a peso. Thus the 50,000 ducado offer, if correct, amounted to a huge sum (the exact figure remains difficult to calculate, given fluctuations in value). Gibson, *The Aztecs under Spanish Rule*, 604.

[121] Lockhart, *The Nahuas after the Conquest*, 46–47.

[122] Gibson, *The Aztecs under Spanish Rule*, 86. See also AGN, Mercedes, vol. 7, ff. 207v–208, and vol. 9, ff. 135v–136. An *alcalde mayor*, another kind of magistrate, one similar to a corregidor, was appointed in 1576. AGN, General de Parte, vol. 1, ff. 196–196v. See also Gibson, *The Aztecs under Spanish Rule*, 87.

[123] Gerhard, *A Guide to the Historical Geography of New Spain*, 246.

[124] AGN, Congregaciones, vol. 1, exp. 81, f. 57. A congregación was also proposed for San Gregorio Atlapulco but, on encountering opposition from Nahuas living in the hills, the plan seems to have been abandoned. AGN, Mercedes, vol. 5–6, 1a pte., ff. 138–138v.

[125] Gerhard, *A Guide to the Historical Geography of New Spain*, 246. The friary is also named as San Bernardino de Jesús in Nahuatl documentation.

fray Martín de Valencia had initiated the process of evangelization and fray Bernardino de Sahagún took up residence in Xochimilco.[126] Xochimilco's friary soon became an important Franciscan religious center. In 1538, fray Toribio de Benavente (Motolinia) enthused that more than 10,000 Xochimilca assembled to complain about having an insufficient number of friars to administer to their needs.[127] Numerous councils were held there and many of the most famous friars – including fray Gerónimo de Mendieta, fray Alonso de Escalona, fray Juan de Torquemada, and fray Agustín de Vetancurt – were either posted to the friary or served as its guardian.[128]

Because of the jurisdiction's large population, the Franciscans established friaries in several other parish seats (known as *cabeceras de doctrina*). The parish was essentially divided when the Franciscans founded a friary at Santa María de la Asunción Milpa Alta in the 1560s. And then other friaries were built in San Antonio Tecomitl (1581), San Gregorio Atlalpulco (by 1600), and Santa María Tepepan (1646). Otherwise the parish framework remained largely unchanged until secularization in 1786.[129]

Because the establishment of encomienda, corregimiento, and doctrina all proceeded with little disruption to the altepetl, its integrity lasted throughout the colonial period – albeit with one important exception. This was the loss of an altepetl, San Agustín de las Cuevas, that had been under Xochimilco's control before the arrival of the Spaniards. San Agustín (now Tlalpan) lay between Xochimilco and Coyoacan and in the 1520s had been acquired by the latter altepetl as part of the encomienda of Cortés. Subsequently, the Xochimilca managed to temporarily overturn the loss via the courts, but during the 1540s Coyoacan's claim once again prevailed.[130] In a 1563 letter to King Philip II, Xochimilco's nobles petitioned for the return of San Agustín as well as a few smaller communities that had been ceded during the conquest period.[131] Having

[126] Pérez Zevallos, *Xochimilco Ayer*, vol. 1, 125.

[127] Motolinia wrote that "in Xochimilco two priests baptized on one day more than fifteen thousand Indians." Toribio de Benavente (Motolinia), *Motolinia's History of the Indians of New Spain*, trans. Francis Steck (Washington, DC: Academy of American Franciscan History, 1951), 174, 211, and 245.

[128] On the Franciscan councils, see Chimalpahin, *Annals of His Time*, 53 and 77. See also Pérez Zevallos, *Xochimilco Ayer*, vol. 2, 20.

[129] AGN, Congregaciones, vol. 1, exp. 18, ff. 11–11v; Gibson, *The Aztecs under Spanish Rule*, 106–107; Gerhard, *A Guide to the Historical Geography of New Spain*, 246.

[130] Rebecca Horn ascribes Coyoacan's successful case to the political clout of the Cortés estate. Horn, *Postconquest Coyoacan*, 32.

[131] Restall et al., eds., *Mesoamerican Voices*, 67–68.

enumerated their many services to the crown – and invoking the precedent of Tlaxcala, which received "great boons and privileges" – the nobles argued that San Agustín should be given back to Xochimilco.[132] In spite of this plea, San Agustín de las Cuevas remained part of Coyoacan.[133]

Apart from the loss of San Agustín de las Cuevas, impressive continuity characterized the establishment of both encomienda and corregimiento. Thanks to the survival of the altepetl and its organizing principles, Nahuas were able to contend with other political changes from a position of relative strength.[134] None of these changes was as significant as the introduction of new forms of Spanish municipal government.

THE CHANGING POLITICAL LANDSCAPE

If continuity long characterized the sociopolitical organization of the Xochimilca realm, matters of local government were subject to more immediate and significant modification. In the 1540s, following the creation of the corregimiento, the Spanish government sought to incorporate Xochimilco more thoroughly into the royal domain by introducing the Spanish system of municipal government. At the center of this imported system of local administration was the town council, or *cabildo*, through which *vecinos* (citizens) – or in the case of Native societies, members of the nobility – elected from among themselves representatives who then assumed a variety of government positions under the supervision of the Spanish corregidor. If the particular details of cabildo administration were new to Nahuas – the laws, procedures, and offices – they nevertheless had cognates to the older Nahua political system, not the least of which were the dynastic rulers' courts, held in their tecpan, through which the tlatoque had governed and upheld justice.

At the summit of this new imported municipal administration was the governor, or *gobernador*, whose overlapping political and judicial

---

[132] The communities included Totollan, Quauhmilpan, Chalchiuhtepec, Cuentepec, Atonco, Metepec, Nepopohualco, and Ahuatlan. Restall et al., eds., *Mesoamerican Voices*, 68. Pérez Zevallos identified the communities as being located in Morelos. Juan Manuel Pérez Zevallos, "Organización del señorío de Xochimilco," in Ramos et al., eds., *Xochimilco en el siglo XVI*, 152.

[133] Restall et al., eds., *Mesoamerican Voices*, 67.

[134] When seen in light of the losses suffered in the precontact period, Gibson concluded, "the later territorial history of Xochimilco, under corregimiento, offers a contrasting and impressive continuity." Gibson, *The Aztecs under Spanish Rule*, 86. Gibson also notes that Xochimilco "remained a well-defined political entity throughout the colonial period" (28).

responsibilities mirrored those of the dynastic rulers in pre-contact times.[135] In fact, in the early colonial years, governors were typically the same individuals as the dynastic rulers. Essentially, then, the institutional structure of government changed in appearance while the ruling dynasties, who retained control, remained the same. Hence in 1542, a dispute over land between two tlatoque identified both these leading figures as governors, indicating that Xochimilco continued to be led by the rulers of the altepetl's constituent tlaxilacalli. Over time, though, the standard pattern for central Mexico – once the cabildo had taken root – was for the Spanish regime to promote other individuals to the highest position of local authority in place of the tlatoani, thereby undermining potentially powerful rivals who, at a time when Spanish control was tenuous and the power of the old guard was far from enfeebled, could pose a risk to royal authority. From having three tlatoque Xochimilco came to have just one governor.

On one level, then, the introduction of Spanish municipal government involved a significant disruption to the pre-contact political system and a severe loss of authority for its rulers. On another level, though, members of the Nahua nobility sought to capitalize on the changes, which complicates the story, even suggesting, at times, that local rivalries played a part in curbing the influence of the tlatoque. If divested of high office, the tlatoque nevertheless retained considerable power informally, and their demotion proved to be far from complete or permanent. Additionally, members of the Nahua nobility seized new opportunities afforded by the cabildo to protect the community and to provide much-needed political stability as part of promoting their altepetl's interests at a time of rapid change, some of which were catastrophically destructive, as with the epidemics sweeping through Mexico.

The introduction of municipal government to Nahua communities took place gradually. Spaniards first brought new municipal government to the most sizable and important Nahua polities during the mid-1530s, in many cases to key allies of the conquest era.[136] Among them, famously, was Tlaxcala, which produced wonderfully rich Nahuatl documentation about day-to-day matters of administration and justice. Xochimilco was among these early municipal corporations. Xochimilca holding Spanish

---

[135] The governor might also be called a "juez gobernador," a title that originally attached to outsiders who were sent to administer other altepetl. By the late sixteenth century and thereafter, governors were often styled judge-governors. Lockhart, *The Nahuas after the Conquest*, 34–35.

[136] Pérez Zevallos, *Xochimilco Ayer*, vol. 1, 41.

offices such as alcalde and regidor began appearing in the documentary record from 1542, a mere year after incorporation of the altepetl into the royal domain as a corregimiento.[137] The position of governor, in the person of the tlatoani, also dates to that time.[138] Given the alacrity with which the Xochimilca adopted the new institutions, the altepetl furnished many of the leaders who went on to administer other altepetl and to take with them their newly acquired expertise. The first viceroy, don Antonio de Mendoza, Conde de Tendilla (r. 1535–1550), appointed Esteban de Tejeda, an alcalde, to conduct a series of investigations in other jurisdictions on behalf of the Spanish government. That he was entrusted with several commissions and to investigate matters of land and water rights shows that Esteban had already gained some experience in Spanish legal and political practices and could be counted on to export them to new areas. Esteban's responsibilities took him to several different communities across central Mexico.[139] Esteban was the first in a line of itinerant judges who hailed from Xochimilco and went on to govern elsewhere. The most famous of them was don Esteban de Guzmán, who, after serving in government offices in Xochimilco, including a stint as governor in 1553, went on to pursue a career as an administrator in the capital, serving next as governor of Santiago Tlatelolco and lastly as governor of Tenochtitlan.[140]

Such appointments also worked in reverse, though, and outsiders might be brought in to resolve local disputes or exert power by proxy for the colonial administration. Thus, in Xochimilco the viceroy appointed a noble from Otumba named don Pedro de Suero to investigate disputes between the altepetl and its barrios over tribute and then to

[137] AGN, Mercedes, vol. 1, exp. 449, f. 210v, vol. 2, exp. 126, ff. 48v–49, and exp. 571, f. 232v.

[138] AGN, Mercedes, vol. 1, exp. 449, f. 210v. Later and dubious documentation points toward the early 1520s as the date when a governor first displaced the tlatoani. As Pérez Zevallos has noted, in 1609 Diego Cristóbal Cortés tried to lay claim to the rights of a cacicazgo in Xochimilco. In support of his lawsuit, Diego and his witnesses argued that his grandfather, Diego Tello Cortés Maçelotzin, had served as governor during the 1520s. The claim seems dubious at best: the plaintiff supplied documentation purporting to be a declaration of rights to the cacicazgo signed by Cortés in 1519. AGN, Vínculos y Mayorazgos, vol. 240, exp. 10, f. 7. See Gibson, *The Aztecs under Spanish Rule*, 162.

[139] AGN, Mercedes, vol. 1, exp. 82, ff. 44v–45, exp. 266, ff. 125v–126, exp. 414, f. 193v, and vol. 2, exp. 247, ff. 95–95v.

[140] AGN, Mercedes, vol. 3, exp. 91, f. 44; vol. 4, exp. 118, f. 35v; AGN, Mercedes, vol. 5–6, 1a pte., ff. 134–134v; *Códice Osuna*, f. 38, published as Luis Chávez Orozco, ed., *Códice Osuna*, facsimile ed. (Mexico City: Ediciones del Instituto Indigenista Interamericano, 1947), 257; Chimalpahin, *Codex Chimalpahin*, vol. 1, 177; Chimalpahin, *Codex Chimalpahin*, vol. 2, 41.

convene a *residencia* into the conduct of council members. The 1542 order shows that Nahuas had already begun to occupy Spanish-style offices and, given the possibility that the residencia was inspired by misconduct of some sort, the Nahuas may have begun to modify offices to suit their own purposes.[141] Don Pedro de Suero's mandate, however, was renewed again during the course of the 1540s so as to bring further changes to Xochimilco's municipal organization followed the catastrophic epidemic of 1545–1548.

The three tlatoque retained their positions as simultaneous gobernadores through 1548. Not long after, though, they were divested of their lifetime political positions; instead, they were replaced by a single, elected governor.[142] Demotion to occasional service as governors meant that the tlatoque now had to rotate with one another and lesser nobles, according to the outcome of annual elections. The dynastic rulers retained some access to the cabildo. But henceforth the term *tlatoani* came to connote social rank and not political office.[143] The changes introduced by Spaniards to local government thus entailed a transfer of power from the upper echelon of Xochimilco's rulers to lower ranking nobles (*principales* or, in Nahuatl, *pipiltin*).

During this process, the staffing of the cabildo expanded and grew more elaborate. As Lockhart has shown for central Mexico generally, the higher offices came into being first, with lower ones following later.[144] After 1548, when the tlatoque were last recorded as jointly occupying superior positions of authority, the rise of cabildo positions at the expense of the tlatoque became evident in Xochimilco. As shown in Table 1.1, Spanish-style political offices in Xochimilco developed quickly between 1548 and 1563.

---

[141] AGN, Mercedes, vol. 1, exp. 449, f. 210v, vol. 2, exp. 126, ff. 48v–49, and exp. 571, f. 232v.

[142] AGN, Vínculos y Mayorazgos, vol. 279, exp. 1, ff. 64, 65, and 104–110; on Nahua government and the rise of new political offices, see Robert Haskett, *Indigenous Rulers: An Ethnohistory of Town Government in Colonial Cuernavaca* (Albuquerque: University of New Mexico Press, 1991).

[143] In a few rare instances, other lords were sometimes described as tlatoque. Juan Manuel Pérez Zevallos argues that on these occasions, the term referred to those lords who ascended as heads of their respective houses within their tlaxilacalli. He gives as examples don Esteban de Guzmán, Juan de Santiago, and Miguel Damián, all in Tepetenchi. Pérez Zevallos, *Xochimilco Ayer*, vol. 1, 51. See also France V. Scholes and Eleanor B. Adams, eds., *Sobre el modo de tributar los indios de Nueva España a Su Majestad, 1561–1564* (Mexico City: J. Porrúa, 1958), 105.

[144] Lockhart, *The Nahuas after the Conquest*, 30.

Table 1.1 also shows that in 1548 Nahuas still used their own terminology to describe political offices. The subsequent inclusion of Spanish terms, however, did not reflect a departure from the use of their Nahuatl equivalents.[145] A 1582 document spelled out many of the same, earlier Nahuatl positions.[146] Nahuas also incorporated the new positions as loanwords. Hence one official wrote of *talcaldesme*, meaning "we alcaldes."[147] Alcaldes and regidores as well as notaries and interpreters soon appeared on the cabildo's staff. These posts were customarily filled through elections.[148] Cabildo positions like that of jailer may not have been elected, and lower ranking posts likely grew out of precontact equivalents, as was also the case with *topileque* and *calpixque*, or tax collectors.[149] Neither of these latter positions necessarily involved membership of the council. Other minor functionaries also came into being in the second half of the sixteenth century. *Mandones* served as officials who, in Xochimilco at least, provided supplementary assistance in the internal administration of the three tlaxilacalli.[150]

Table 1.1 also shows that by 1553 governors had supplanted tlatoque at the top of the cabildo hierarchy. The documentation from which this information comes also attests to ongoing struggles between nobles and

[145] The language catered to the intended audience. The 1553 records were sent to the viceroy, and the letter of 1563, as noted, was dispatched to the king.

[146] AGN, Vínculos y Mayorazgos, vol. 279, exp. 1, f. 76.

[147] AGN, Vínculos y Mayorazgos, vol. 279, exp. 1, f. 106.

[148] Restall et al., *Mesoamerican Voices*, 70. For examples of election results submitted for viceregal ratification, see AGN, Indios, vol. 6, 2a pte., exp. 273, f. 61, exp. 850, f. 207v; vol. 9, exp. 19, ff. 12v–13, and exp. 198, ff. 95v–96. The cabildo had its own interpreter, as did the city's Spanish governing apparatus. The separate interpreter "of the court" (*del juzgado*) was appointed by the viceroy and served the corregidor and his lieutenant (*teniente*). At times these latter interpreters were either individuals of mixed ancestry or perhaps even Spaniards. In 1576, Pedro Serrano was appointed interpreter. That he was described as a *residente* suggests that he may not have been a Nahua (who would customarily have been called a *natural* or *indio*), and that he may have come from somewhere else since the term *residente* often connoted status as a temporary town dweller. AGN, General de Parte, vol. 1, exp. 1043, ff. 196–196v; vol. 2, exp. 704, f. 143 (164 old foliation); AGN, Indios, vol. 9, exp. 29, ff. 18–18v.

[149] AGN, Intestados, vol. 301, ff. 219 and 223; AGN, Indios, vol. 3, exp. 380, ff. 88v–89.

[150] On the minor officials, see Lockhart, "Complex Municipalities," 34. Even though they lay at the bottom of the municipal hierarchy, mandones were not without influence. In 1590, Juan Populiloc and Felipe Chapul as well as two other, unnamed "consorts" had fomented unrest in the barrio of Tocalpan and as a result, were labeled "ynquietos y rreboltosos." The mandones had persuaded local residents to claim that they were free from personal service obligations. Failure to obey the tlaxilacalli's demand for labor on public works projects had prompted a standoff that ultimately required the intervention of the corregidor and the viceroy. AGN, Indios, vol. 4, exp. 563, f. 165.

TABLE 1.1 *Political offices in Xochimilco's cabildo, 1548–1563*

1548[a]		
Tepetenchi	Tecpan	Olac
Tlatoani	Tlatoani	Tlatoani
Tepetenchicalqui (or Tepetenchicalcatl teuctli)	Tecpanecatl	Tlacochcalcatl teuctli
Tlacateuctli	Tlacochcalcatl teuctli	Ticonauacatl
Tlacochcalcatl teuctli	Tlacateuctli	Quauhnochtli
Ticoquiyauacatl	Tziuhcuacatl teuctli	
	Mayordomo	

1553[b]		
Governor		
Alcalde	Alcalde	Alcalde
Cacique[c]	Cacique	Cacique
Six regidores, a notary, and, presumably, a jailer[d]		

1563[e]		
Governor		
Alcalde	Alcalde	Alcalde
Cacique	Cacique	Cacique
Seven regidores, two high constables, several notaries,[f] a jailer, and an interpreter		

[a] Carrasco, "Los señores de Xochimilco en 1548," *Tlalocan*, vol. 7 (1977), 230–231; Library of Congress, Krauss Collection, Ms. 140, ff. 436–451v. [b] Newberry Library, Chicago, Ayer Collection, ms. 1121, ff. 348–352. [c] The caciques could be present at cabildo meetings with the approval of the governor. [d] The document mentions a jail in Xochimilco. [e] AGI, Patronato, leg. 184, ramo 50; Restall et al., eds., *Mesoamerican Voices*, 70. [f] The document mentions six notaries, but this would have been an unusually large number.

tlatoque while revealing the ambiguous place of dynastic rulers in local government.[151] Though divested of formal power, dynastic rulers still exerted influence behind the scenes.[152] The regulations, which were set down by Nahuas under don Esteban de Guzmán provide insights into the operations of the town council in its formative years. They also convey a sense of the political culture of the time, one that in spite of articulating

[151] Newberry Library, Ayer Collection, Ms. 1121, ff. 348–352.
[152] Lockhart, *The Nahuas after the Conquest*, 32.

an idealized vision, still offers a glimpse into routine matters of government that had a distinctly Nahua quality to them.[153]

Many of the regulations addressed procedural issues and set down expectations for proper conduct in office. First, the new rules established the hours of cabildo business, including when and how often officers could take holidays. Failure to attend meetings would result in a fine and those malingerers who routinely failed to make an appearance would be sent into exile for as many months as the number of days they missed. The governor and alcaldes were to take charge of the government's books and pictorial records (*pinturas*) and keep them safe. Upon election, the governor and his family were to move into government accommodation, the "casa real," where they had to reside until the end of his tenure in office. The regulations enjoined governors never to eat in the home of any Spaniard or Nahua while on business in Mexico City because of potential conflicts of interest and so that they might set a good example. Furthermore, the regulations stated they should drink neither Castilian wine nor *pulque* (an alcoholic beverage made from maguey, referred to as *vino de la tierra*). If a Spaniard should happen to be eating in the home of the governor, he could drink wine, but the governor could not. The rules also explicitly stated that governors must not offer or receive gifts. Government business, furthermore, could only be conducted in the council office, except when homicides, assault, or other serious crimes occurred, in which case the governor and alcaldes were to venture outside to gather information from witnesses in the presence of the notary and then apprehend the culprit. No one could be arrested until officials had first obtained evidence, unless, of course, the perpetrator happened to be caught in the act.

The regulations demonstrated the importance of legal matters in the cabildo's business. The many civil, criminal, and land papers preserved in the archives show that the city council played a vital legal role as the court of first instance for Nahuas in the jurisdiction.[154] Regulations and other extant lawsuits further reveal that Nahua officials often went to the *audiencia* (high court) or later the General Indian Court when necessary. Accordingly, the documents assumed an important place, and Xochimilco had a municipal archive. The officials kept all current and pending litigation that did not require outside adjudication as well as tribute and financial records.[155] In common with other altepetl, Xochimilco also

---

[153] Pérez Zevallos, "El Gobierno Indígena de Xochimilco," 445–462.
[154] See also Horn, *Postconquest Coyoacan*, 20.
[155] AGN, General de Parte, vol. 1, exp. 1105, ff. 209–209v.

had a community chest in which funds were kept. The documentation from 1548 showed that cabildo members shared the three keys to the chest. A Nahua described as a mayordomo kept a key, too, thereby further reducing the risk of wrongdoing.[156]

The new provisions of 1553 also sought to limit and regulate interactions between officials and dynastic rulers. As such, they afford an insight into political influence behind the scenes, if only obliquely. The rules stated that the governor, alcaldes, and regidores were to meet in the cabildo. The presence of caciques and other nobles would be allowed only with the consent of the governor. Nobles and caciques had to obey the governor in all things. Those who disobeyed faced a fine and two days' incarceration in the city's jail. The nobles and caciques, moreover, were prohibited from involving themselves in matters of justice or administration. Likewise no governor could communicate with any nobles or caciques, nor could he eat at their houses or even maintain friendships with them, because "in order to have justice, it is proper to be free of such things." If caciques or principales wanted to discuss something with a governor, they had to do so in the presence of one or two alcaldes. Somewhat paradoxically, though, the regulations specified that on religious holidays, they should meet at the home of the governor and accompany him to and from church. Nobles also received a few rights in return. They could bring problems to the attention of cabildo officers, or lodge complaints against them, so long as they did so before the notary.

After the Nahuas submitted the new rules, Viceroy don Luis de Velasco the Elder, Conde de Santiago (r. 1550–1564), accepted them and ordered that they be implemented immediately. In so doing, he ostensibly approved of the subordination of the tlatoque to the cabildo. Whether the desire to curb the power of the tlatoque came from within Xochimilco or from above is impossible to tell, but given other documentation from that period (discussed in Chapter 4), there were certainly power struggles being waged by members of the lesser nobility within the altepetl, and in this the adoption of the cabildo may have served the interests of the arrivistes who sought an alliance with the viceroy to acquire greater influence. The regulations seem to have had some success in limiting the power of Xochimilco's erstwhile leaders, at least in the first few years after the promulgation of the cabildo's regulations.[157]

---

[156] Library of Congress, Krauss Collection, Ms. 140, f. 9v.
[157] Pérez Zevallos, *Xochimilco Ayer*, vol. 1, 61.

In spite of shifts in the locus of political authority away from the tlatoque, the cabildo pursued a wider reform campaign to bolster Xochimilco's position at a time of far-reaching upheavals following the recent epidemic of 1545–1548. The reforms dated to the early 1550s and were thus bound up with the drafting of the new cabildo regulations. The changes dealt with matters of local administration, issues of urban orientation, and the use of public space. Xochimilco's municipal leaders transformed the spatial orientation altepetl's urban center for a political reason: to unify the polity after the upheavals of the conquest era and thereby to shore up the nobles' power.

A key element of the reforms was the reconfiguration of the altepetl's nucleated core. In 1550, the altepetl's officials appeared before New Spain's first viceroy, don Antonio de Mendoza, to submit a report in which they explained that the altepetl "no esta traçado" – in other words, that its center had not been fashioned according to a grid layout.[158] Besides lacking a *traza*, the petitioners also pointed out that the market was held beyond the altepetl, which made for all kinds of inconvenience and disorder. Before 1550, Xochimilco's residents had held their public market outside the altepetl.[159] This location was unusual. Marketplaces were typically found at the heart of Nahua polities. Indeed, the presence of a marketplace is often understood to have been one of the defining features of an altepetl.[160] Now the nobles argued that a new, central marketplace would put an end to various troubles and nuisances while promoting public order and the common good. To accommodate a new marketplace, the governor and his fellow officials asked for permission to open up the streets, demolish any houses that were in the way, and create a central plaza. To show how all this would happen, they presented the viceroy with a pictorial document of their plans. Viceroy Mendoza, apparently impressed with the proposal, granted the Nahuas' request, and the plaza was soon established. Writing many years later, the Spanish friar Juan de Torquemada described Xochimilco's marketplace as especially large and spacious.[161]

After relocating the market, laying out the traza, and setting down Xochimilco's cabildo ordinances, the altepetl's leaders campaigned vigorously for the addition of further markers of prestigious municipal status.

---

[158] AGN, Mercedes, vol. 3, exp. 397, f. 144 (167 old foliation).
[159] Cortés, *Letters from Mexico*, 202.
[160] Lockhart, *The Nahuas after the Conquest*, 185.
[161] Torquemada, *Monarquía indiana*, vol. 2, 554–555.

On March 4, 1559, King Philip II of Spain conferred on Xochimilco the much-coveted and superior rank of a city.[162] The award was incredibly prestigious, the only other polities in the Basin of Mexico to be designated as cities having been the three pillars of the former Aztec Triple Alliance.[163] After the royal decree was issued, and in a display of micro-patriotism that would become common over the years, Nahuatl-language sources now opened with a variant of the phrase, "Here in the altepetl city of Xochimilco." One enthusiastic notary began a document by writing, "Here in the great altepetl and noble city of Xochimilco."[164] With its status and reputation newly burnished, Xochimilco also received a coat of arms. The attractive design incorporated pre-contact glyphic conventions, including the flowers used to identify Xochimilco as "the place of the flower fields."[165] These privileges reflected Xochimilco's eminence and economic importance as one of Mesoamerica's most opulent and populous polities. When they campaigned for the award of city status, the Xochimilca had been at pains to point out their many contributions to the royal exchequer.

The award of city status paved the way for further efforts to modify the altepetl's core. Government officers asked if they could construct a fountain in the public plaza, with water to be carried to other parts of the altepetl. In addition, they asked for walls to be erected along the four streets surrounding the friary. And besides asking for laborers to be assigned to these duties, they also asked for permission to build new government offices, including a community meeting place and a jail.[166] The new building work can be seen as part of the wider effort to centralize authority in the altepetl. These efforts were also reflected in the cabildo ordinances from 1553. At that date Xochimilco's nobles agreed to set up

---

[162] *Colección de documentos inéditos, relativos al descubrimiento, conquista y organización de las antiguas posesiones españolas de ultramar,* vol. 22 (Madrid: Tipografía de Archivos, I. Olózaga, 1929), 103.

[163] Gibson, *The Aztecs under Spanish Rule,* 32.

[164] AGN, Tierras, vol. 1525, exp. 3, f. 3, exp. 5, f. 6; AGN, Intestados, vol. 301, ff. 219–220v; AGN, Vínculos y Mayorazgos, vol. 279, exp. 1, f. 45; AGN, Tierras, vol. 2669, exp. 9, ff. 4 and 7.

[165] The coat of arms depicts a hill rising above the waves of the lake, and a cross appears on top of the hill. The combination of water and hill presumably symbolized the altepetl. For a description and reproduction of it, see María Castañeda de la Paz, "Central Mexican Indigenous Coats of Arms and the Conquest of Mesoamerica," *Ethnohistory,* vol. 56, no. 1 (2009), 138–140.

[166] It is unclear if these were to be a single or multiple structures. The wording is "unas casas rreales y de audiencia comunydad y carcel." AGN, Mercedes, vol. 5–6, 1ª parte, f. 287 (f. 312 old foliation); Gibson, *The Aztecs under Spanish Rule,* 191, 516n142.

the council offices in a single building, named *la casa real de cabildo*.[167] In what appears to have been a separate building – named *la casa del gobernador* – local authorities also established an official residence for the governor and his family, who were obliged to live there until the end of the governor's tenure in office.[168]

In effect, the town council wanted to create a single administrative center for the altepetl – one that had not existed previously. Previously the tlatoque had governed Xochimilco at their respective palaces, as shown in the map in the Codex Cozcatzin. As such, there had been three diffuse bases of authority, distributed across the three constituent parts of the altepetl. Now, and in the face of challenges to their political positions from the new office of the governor, the rulers sought to consolidate their power by creating a single administrative center, one that was located opposite the friary and on the very same public plaza that had recently been built at the behest of Xochimilco's rulers.[169]

CONCLUSION

The plaza, its surrounding traza, and the grid layout of streets have all been seen as common features of the urban landscape across Spanish America. Historians once saw these features as distinctly Spanish arrangements of public space, ones that could serve as mechanisms of order and control. Revisionist scholarship has complicated that perspective, pointing out that central plazas were not necessarily imported from Spain; instead, they may have been American innovations.[170] The reconfiguration of Xochimilco's urban center in the 1550s adds another dimension to this revisionist scholarship. It shows that the impetus for change came from Xochimilco's Nahua nobles. They may have been influenced

---

[167] Library of Congress, Krauss Collection, Ms. 140, f. 9v; AGN, General de Parte, vol. 1, exp. 1105, ff. 209–209v.

[168] Newberry Library, Ayer Collection, Ms. 1121, ff. 348–352.

[169] The palaces did not disappear with the 1553 regulations, of course. Later documentation shows that the tecpan remained the property of the tlatoque, although one *tecpancalli* had fallen into a state of such disrepair by 1650 that a tlatoani ordered its demolition. AGN, Vínculos y Mayorazgos, vol. 279, exp. 1, ff. 10–10v and 12–13v, 65–68, and 88; S. L. Cline, "A Cacicazgo in the Seventeenth Century: The Case of Xochimilco," H. R. Harvey, ed., *Land and Politics in the Valley of Mexico: A Two-Thousand Year Perspective* (Albuquerque: University of New Mexico Press, 1991), 269.

[170] Valerie Fraser, *The Architecture of Conquest: Building in the Viceroyalty of Peru, 1535–1635* (New York: Cambridge University Press, 2009); Lockhart and Schwartz, *Early Latin America*, 66–69; Matthew Restall and Kris Lane, *Latin America in Colonial Times* (New York: Cambridge University Press), 212.

by Spanish practices, especially by the Franciscans whose friary came to be located on the side of the plaza, but the reorganization of the center of the altepetl clearly reflected and suited their interests. Rather than just making Xochimilco conform with a standard template of Spanish urban planning, then, the changes to public space went hand in hand with reforms of local government. The alterations to the city's orientation further helped to shore up the political power of the dynastic rulers and the other Nahua leaders at a time of upheaval and worrying change. Changes in the political landscape thus became bound up with those of the urban landscape.

Even though the locus of political power shifted with the demotion of the tlatoque – a trend that, as seen in the fourth chapter, proved only temporary – the Xochimilca readily adapted to the new landscape of the Spanish municipal system. The cabildo may have been an imported, foreign institution. But, as in other parts of the Americas, Native peoples harnessed it to protect their communities and pursue their interests. They arguably made it their own. For the next few centuries the cabildo and its officers actively shaped the lives of their altepetl's citizens. They also contributed to the organization and upkeep of the irrigation and engineering works. As subsequent chapters show, the cabildo arranged, funded, and supervised the maintenance and repairs of the hydraulic infrastructure. With the new political arrangements Nahuas thus continued to intervene in and preserve the lacustrine landscape that simultaneously provided an ecological foundation for the altepetl and made possible the cultivation of the chinampas.

2

Land

While the establishment of Spanish rule brought innovations to Xochimilco's municipal government, it had a much less profound effect on Nahua land-holdings. Unlike other central Mexican altepetl, to a remarkable extent Xochimilco and neighboring lakeside communities escaped the full force of Spanish land alienation. The striking resilience of Nahua landownership, which played a vital role in guiding cross-cultural encounters in the colonial period, can be attributed to a variety of factors, primary among them having been environmental influences and chinampa cultivation itself.

The central importance of chinampas to the rise of complex societies and, later, of Tenochtitlan, has meant that they have attracted consider-able attention from scholars. Archaeologists, though, have tended to been less inclined to study chinampas during the colonial period.[1] Historians, meanwhile, have focused on subjects other than chinampas, examining instead the impact of Spanish settlement on indigenous patterns of land-ownership and, in particular, the alienation of valuable properties in those places where newcomers established haciendas.[2] As William Taylor noted, outside of the mining regions and centers of trade, "land was the main economic foundation of the social order."[3] Following François

---

[1] Gregory Luna Golya and Raul Avila López are two important exceptions.

[2] Gibson, *The Aztecs under Spanish Rule*, 257–299 and 406–409; James Lockhart, "Encomienda and Hacienda: The Evolution of the Great Estate in the Spanish Indies," *Hispanic American Historical Review*, vol. 49, no. 3 (1969), 411–429; Magnus Mörner, "The Spanish American Hacienda: A Survey of Recent Research and Debate," *Hispanic American Historical Review*, vol. 53, no. 2 (1973), 183–216.

[3] William B. Taylor, *Landlord and Peasant in Colonial Oaxaca* (Stanford: Stanford University Press, 1972), vii, 195.

Chevalier, historians considered landed estates in terms of the rise of a creole Spanish landholding class (i.e., one born in the Americas) at the expense of indigenous communities.[4] For a while, historians came to understand the estates as having brought wholesale socioeconomic changes to indigenous peoples by disrupting their holdings and altering labor arrangements such that Nahuas, no longer owning sufficient land for subsistence, had to turn to Spanish estates for employment.[5] The rise of haciendas, so it was once understood, thus accounted for fragmentation and decline in indigenous communities. Later, revisionist studies, however, demonstrated that there had been considerable variation and complexity not only in the kinds of estates that were established – their size, labor force, and profitability – but also in their influence on indigenous societies.[6] Taylor, for instance, observed little Spanish disruption to indigenous holdings in Oaxaca. The same pattern applies for Xochimilco, at least until the late eighteenth century.

While scholars' interest in haciendas subsequently waned, ethnohistorians retained an interest in the subject of land in indigenous societies. Their interest stemmed, in part, from the question of whether communities, by being able to retain land, could resist the encroachment of haciendas and maintain their economic independence, thus accounting for the continuity scholars observed in Nahua social and cultural forms.[7] The resulting literature has demonstrated the importance of land as part of a constellation of factors that shaped patterns of accommodation, resistance, and cultural change in the years after the Spanish–Mexican War.[8] In her study of Coyoacan, for instance, Rebecca Horn devoted three of eight

---

[4] François Chevalier, *La formation des grandes domains au Mexique, terre et société aux XVIe–XVIIe siècles* (Paris: Université de Paris, 1952).

[5] Murdo J. MacLeod, *Spanish Central America: A Socioeconomic History, 1520–1720* (Austin: University of Texas Press, 2008).

[6] Eric Van Young, "Mexican Rural History since Chevalier: The Historiography of the Colonial Hacienda," *Latin American Research Review*, vol. 18, no. 3 (1983), 5–61; Enrique Florescano, *Estructuras y problemas agrarios de México, 1500–1821* (Mexico City: Secretaría de Educación Pública, 1971); Tutino, "Creole Mexico, and Eric Van Young, *Hacienda and Market in Eighteenth-Century Mexico: The Rural Economy of the Guadalajara Region, 1675–1820* (Berkeley: University of California Press, 1981).

[7] As Eric van Young noted, many of the monographs produced by scholars associated with the New School of Philology included chapters on land. Eric Van Young, "Two Decades of Anglophone Historical Writing on Colonial Mexico: Continuity and Change since 1980," *Mexican Studies/Estudios Mexicanos*, vol. 20, no. 2 (2004), 280, 325.

[8] Cline, *Colonial Culhuacan*, 125–159; Lockhart, *The Nahuas after the Conquest*, 141–202; Terraciano, *The Mixtecs of Colonial Oaxaca*, 198–251.

chapters to the subject and demonstrated the pivotal place of land in informing socioeconomic relationships between Nahuas and Spaniards.[9] Still, ethnohistorical studies have usually considered chinampa agriculture only in passing. Indeed, few historians have systematically examined chinampa agriculture in the colonial period. Most prominent among those who have is Teresa Rojas Rabiela whose research on irrigation, technology, indigenous agriculture, and cultivation techniques provides a font of information about the chinampas, one that is unlikely to be surpassed.[10] Her studies, though, have paid less attention to patterns of ownership and tenure as they pertained to chinampas under Spanish rule.

This chapter elaborates on some of the brief, passing observations by Charles Gibson about the landholdings in the southern lake areas. On an essential level, he noted that Nahuas retained ownership of chinampas. He argued that chinampas "were among the most conservative and durable types of Indian agricultural holdings." But he provided little by way of explanation for this, for instance, arguing that the persistence of chinampa agriculture could be attributed to the urban market for vegetable food-stuffs, or else "a Spanish willingness to retain chinampa agriculture as an Indian specialty." Gibson further observed that while the neighboring province of Chalco attracted powerful hacienda owners and felt extreme land pressures, Xochimilco, "by a coincidence of circumstances" – which he did not elaborate upon – "maintained its craft economy and chinampa agriculture throughout the colonial period."[11] This chapter identifies and explains these circumstances.

AQUATIC GARDENS

Much as conquistadors expressed astonishment at the sight of cities rising out of the lakes, so chinampas elicited wondrous descriptions. The Jesuit philosopher, historian, and naturalist José de Acosta wrote of chinampas in fabulous terms, choosing to ascribe the origins of chinampa agriculture to legend. According to his influential *Natural and Moral History of the Indies*, published in Seville in 1590, prior to the rise of the Aztec Empire, the ruler of Azcapotzalco not only ordered greater tribute payments from the Mexica ruler, Acamapichtli, but he also asked the impossible – demanding that the

---

[9] Horn, *Postconquest Coyoacan*, 111–200.
[10] Rojas Rabiela, *Las siembras de ayer*, and Rabiela, ed., *Presente, pasado y futuro de las chinampas*.
[11] Gibson, *The Aztecs under Spanish Rule*, 321, 409.

Mexica create fields in the water so as to grow vegetables. Despairing at the apparent hopelessness of their task, and fearful of retribution lest they fail, the Mexica were only saved by the intercession of Huitzilopochtli. Acosta wrote:

Thus it was that when the time for tribute came the Mexicans brought the trees that had been demanded of them and also the field planted on the water and borne on the water, in which there was a great deal of maize (which is their wheat) already in ear; there were chiles, or *ají*, amaranth, tomatoes, beans, sage, squash, and many other things, all well grown and ready to harvest.

Those who have not seen the fields that they make in the lake of Mexico, in the midst of the water itself, will think that what I am describing here is an invention or at most will believe that it was a spell cast by the devil whom these people adored. But in truth it is a very practical thing and has often been done to make a movable seedbed in the water; for they put earth atop the reeds and grasses in such a way that the water does not dissolve it, and they sow and cultivate there, and the crop grows and ripens and can be moved from one place to another.[12]

Whereas Acosta turned to legends in tracing the origins of aquatic garden agriculture – and apparently confused chinampas with the floating seed-beds used in their cultivation – archaeologists and historians have provided more prosaic but reliable explanations.[13] Thanks to their studies, we know much about their construction and cultivation.

Nahuas followed several steps in building the raised garden plots. First, prospective farmers searched for a foundation, or *cimiento*, in the lake where the water was sufficiently shallow.[14] Most plots were of a standard shape and size, rectangular, and typically 3–10 meters in width and 10–200 meters in length, although smaller chinampas have been identified in Mixquic.[15] These dimensions can be identified from the archaeological record, although colonial-era sources do provide some measurements of the chinampas. Several Nahuatl terms were used for measurements. The standard unit of measurement for land was the *quahuitl*. Literally meaning

---

[12] José de Acosta, *Natural and Moral History of the Indies*, ed. Jane E. Mangan, trans. Frances M. López-Morillas (Durham: Duke University Press, 2002), 397–398.

[13] Scholars have noted that in his description lies the origin of the enduring but erroneous notion that chinampas were floating gardens. See Coe, "The Chinampas of Mexico," 90; Gibson, *The Aztecs under Spanish Rule*, 320. Gene Wilken noted that Acosta's description was later repeated by Alexander von Humboldt. Wilken, "A Note of Buoyancy and Other Dubious Characteristics of the 'Floating' Chinampas of Mexico," 34, 37.

[14] Thomas Outerbridge, "The Disappearing Chinampas of Xochimilco," *The Ecologist*, vol. 17, no. 2/3 (1987), 76–83.

[15] Sanders et al., *The Basin of Mexico*, 51; Wilken, "A Note on Buoyancy and Other Dubious Characteristics of the 'Floating' Chinampas of Mexico," 34–35.

"stick," a quahuitl was typically some seven to ten feet in length.[16] In a distinctive Xochimilca tradition, Nahuas made use of an equivalent, alternative term, the *nehuitzan*.[17] This latter measurement might have been used either for chinampas or other kinds of irrigated land.[18]

The use of the different measurements for both chinampas and other kinds of land makes it difficult to determine from the documentary records whether the size of chinampas changed over time. Archaeological excavations, though, such as those conducted by Raul Avila López in Iztapalapa, have revealed that colonial-era plots tended to be larger than they had been previously. Some documentary sources also confirm that, over time, the chinampas did come to vary appreciably in size. In 1566, Ana Tiacapan set down a testament in Nahuatl in which she bequeathed ten rows of chinampas, as well as other land, to her daughters and a granddaughter. She also bequeathed some of them to two women who were identified as dependents. Notably, the chinampas were of different sizes. Some consisted of twenty-five furrows, others of sixty furrows. The latter's larger size might be explained by its recent modification. Ana stated, "To my daughter Tlaco I give two rows of chinampas that are at Tetlacatzinco, 60 furrows each; recently the person who works it [i.e., who does duty there] filled it in and it is all together. This is truly my patrimonial land; Luis is working it."[19] Variations in the

---

[16] Lockhart, *The Nahuas after the Conquest*, 144–145, 610.

[17] This term seems to be a local variation on the *nehuitzanalli* or *nehuitzanantli*, which refers to a measure from the foot to the hand. Attestations for this measurement elsewhere were rare and seem to be confined to Tlaxcala when not appearing in sources from Xochimilco. AGN, Tribunal Superior de Justicia del Distrito Federal (TSJDF), Alcalde del Crimen, caja 2B, exp. 43, ff. 5–6; see the online Nahuatl dictionary's entry for nehuitzantli: https://nahuatl.uoregon.edu/content/nehuitzantli (accessed January 18, 2021), and AGN, Tierras, vol. 1525, exp. 5, ff. 5, 6, and 28.

[18] The two terms *quahuitl* and *nehuitzan* could be used interchangeably, as in Martina Luisa's 1653 testament. In another example, doña María de Guzmán's testament gave a sense of the unit's size. She referred to a single nehuitzan as being the same as twenty brazas. Thanks to the translator of the don Martín Cerón Cortés y Alvarado's codicil of 1650, we know that each nehuitzan was three and a half varas in length. Interestingly, the translator converted the word to *negüichales* in Spanish (in its plural form), as though it were a Nahuatl loanword for which there was no Spanish counterpart. In this document, *nehuitzan* appeared alongside *quahuitl*, further indicating that the two units were used interchangeably. AGN, Intestados, vol. 301, exp. 2, ff. 214–214v; AGN, Vínculos y Mayorazgos, vol. 279, exp. 1, ff. 12–13v; AGN, Vínculos y Mayorazgos, vol. 279, exp. 1, ff. 82–83v; AGN, TSJDF, Alcalde del Crimen, caja 2B, exp. 43, ff. 5–6; AGN, Vínculos y Mayorazgos, vol. 279, exp. 1, ff. 12–13v.

[19] AGN, Tierras, vol. 35, exp. 6, ff. 236–237v.

chinampas' size such as these were also recorded for the late colonial period. In a 1769 Nahuatl testament from Xochimilco, Rosa María gave to her "daughter named Paula María a little chinampa" and to her "female child named Juliana María a large chinampa."[20]

For Iztapalapa, Avila López argues that in the absence of central planning, individual farmers departed from earlier precedents.[21] Such an argument is supported by a growing tendency during the colonial period for Nahuas to depart from the regular, geometric orientation of chinampas, suggesting either ad hoc organization by individual farmers or the reversion, in the absence of Aztec supervision, to community-level direction.[22] Such local autonomy when it came to planning and managing the layout of chinampas had been the norm for much of the southern lake area's history. Only in the late fifteenth and early sixteenth centuries, with the Aztec Empire's coordinated construction efforts, was there a partial divergence from this trend. Before the Aztecs intervened, each altepetl had overseen its own set of hydraulic compartments and the clusters of chinampas within them. Under imperial auspices, by contrast, the efforts were synchronized: in order to maximize the available space, many of the new chinampas were arranged in a neat, symmetrical, and regular order, much like modern city blocks, with canals serving as the equivalents of streets; the longest of these new chinampas and their adjacent canals were laid out in a common orientation, rotated to a few degrees east of true north, and, intriguingly, this orientation mirrored that of the streets of Teotihuacan. Some have speculated that this alignment was chosen for astrological reasons. It may have also served as a mechanism for water management. As Luna Golya argues, the long beds of the chinampas could well have been laid out perpendicularly to the natural, northerly flow of the water, thereby providing an additional flood control measure.[23]

In spite of the apparent regularity of the newly constructed gardens further into the lakes, local residents were nevertheless granted a good deal of latitude by Aztec supervisors in laying out and constructing the

---

[20] AGN, Tierras, vol. 2669, exp. 9, ff. 8–8v.

[21] Avila López, *Chinampas de Iztapalapa;* Rojas Rabiela, "Aspectos tecnológicos de las obras hydráulicas coloniales," 44–55.

[22] Frederick, "Chinampa Cultivation in the Basin of Mexico," 117–124; Wilken, "A Note of Buoyancy and Other Dubious Characteristics of the 'Floating' Chinampas of Mexico," 42; Calnek, "Settlement Patterns and Chinampa Agriculture at Tenochtitlan," 104–115.

[23] Mundy, *The Death of Aztec Tenochtitlan,* 78; Coe, "The Chinampas of Mexico," 96–97; Armillas, "Gardens on Swamps," 658–660; Luna Golya, "Modeling the Aztec Agricultural Waterscape of Lake Xochimilco," 56.

raised fields. The project was not simply a matter of subordinate, conquered peoples complying with top-down designs and demands, as Luna Golya notes. Rather, the expertise of the chinampatlaca was harnessed by the Aztec imperial government. As a result of this decentralized administration – at the community level, at least – some of the chinampas might have different shapes or be lined up in irregular formations according to local knowledge, preferences, and geographical circumstances. For instance, some of the raised gardens apparently followed the meandering course of natural channels within the lakes. Additionally, there were local variations in the construction methods of the chinampas, as shown in the different layers of soil sediments and organic matter found by archaeologists. All of this suggests some degree of improvisation and decision making within communities beyond the broader directives coming out of Tenochtitlan.[24] This local autonomy in laying out the chinampas continued, and perhaps increased, in the years after the Aztec Empire's demise.

Having created the hydraulic compartments and determined the layout of the chinampas, Nahuas then constructed the raised gardens. In the initial stages, water had to be removed from the hydraulic compartment to make the work easier. Lower water levels also enabled Nahuas to identify the foundations of the chinampas and ensure their dimensions were correct. To these ends the farmers placed reed stakes around the perimeters to delineate the plots. Next they dredged soil using a *zoquimaitl* (a pole with a bag on its end).[25] As they scooped soil on to the plot, the farmers also created ditches or canals around the field's edges, which separated the chinampas and provided irrigation.[26] Having partially raised the plot, the Nahuas then prepared a *césped*, a bed of vegetation made from aquatic plants, and placed the bed on the small field. One of the witnesses for the Nahuas of Santa María Magdalena Michcalco, who sought to defend the villages holdings from alienation, explained some of ways in which the chinampas were painstakingly prepared, as with the use of these beds.[27] On top of the césped more soil was then

---

[24] Luna Golya, "Modeling the Aztec Agricultural Waterscape of Lake Xochimilco," 14–15, 125.

[25] Sometimes the soils of old chinampas were reused. The majority of the following description of the making of chinampas comes from Rojas Rabiela, "Ecological and Agricultural Changes in the Chinampas of Xochimilco-Chalco," 281.

[26] Ross Hassig, *Trade, Tribute, and Transportation: The Sixteenth-Century Political Economy of the Valley of Mexico* (Norman: University of Oklahoma Press, 1985), 47.

[27] AGN, Tierras, vol. 2681, exp. 6, f. 9.

deposited, sometimes with the process being repeated until the plot had risen sufficiently above the water level.[28] Around the plots' edges, *ahuejotes* (water willows) were planted, with their roots reinforcing the sides and preventing subsidence.[29] Then fertilizers were applied. Prior to the arrival of Spaniards, fertilizers had consisted of human waste and bat droppings (specifically for growing chiles) but afterward, farmers increasingly favored the use of manure from cattle, sheep, and poultry. Only after applying fertilizer did the chinampa become ready for planting.[30]

It should be noted that all this work was time consuming. Each step involved a considerable investment of labor – work that would often have to be done by several individuals at once, suggesting that kin or community bonds were essential for agriculturalists. In addition, the work could not be finished quickly since some time had to be allowed for the soils to settle and for the root systems of the water willows to take hold before the rising gardens could be built up further. In other words, only when the previous layer had compacted and stabilized could the next one be added. This work might be done gradually. In documentation from 1647, a young woman was called on by the authorities to explain her whereabouts at the time when a crime had been committed. Melchora de los Reyes lived in San Juan Ixtayopan and was identified a *mulata* (a woman of mixed African and Spanish ancestry), making her one of the very few non-Native peoples to have been recorded as a chinampa cultivator. Under questioning, she explained that she had been spreading mud on top of a chinampa as part of its preparation.[31]

The very making of chinampas, then, involved a considerable investment of labor – estimated at eight days for a group of four to six people – as well as competence in a series of skills.[32] Familiarity with irrigation techniques was essential. Archaeologists note that the dimensions of chinampas, being long and thin, were ideally suited to allow for the seepage and retention of water from the lake. The chinampa plots, moreover, had to rise to the correct height above the lake's water level. If the roots of some crops remained submerged in water they would perish; thus the roots had to stay above the lake level to allow for the upward capillary movement of water, but not at such a height that this would fail to

---

[28] Sanders et al., *The Basin of Mexico*, 277.
[29] Outerbridge, "The Disappearing Chinampas of Xochimilco," 76–83.
[30] Rojas Rabiela, "Ecological and Agricultural Changes in the Chinampas of Xochimilco-Chalco," 280.
[31] AGN, Criminal, vol. 232, exp. 14, ff. 338–338v.
[32] Hassig, *Trade, Tribute, and Transportation*, 47.

happen.[33] The determination of the correct height would have required considerable expertise, not least because of fluctuations in water levels according to season and rainfall and, as several archaeologists have noted, because water levels within the lake varied according to the different hydraulic compartments created by embankments and dikes.[34]

The cultivation of chinampas was similarly complex. After soils had been weeded and prepared, seeds were planted either by hand, directly into the chinampas, or on nurseries. The seedbed nurseries were sometimes raised on rafts, although they were also nurtured at the side of the chinampa. (It should be noted that Spaniards were not unfamiliar with the use of seedbeds; they called them *almácigos*, and this term, with its derivation from Arabic, suggests that there had been comparable cultivation practices in Spain).[35] To make the seedbeds, chinampa farmers combined mud with aquatic vegetation and, after several days of drying, they cut the mud into blocks known as *chapines*. Farmers made a hole in each of the blocks, into which they deposited the seed, and then added fertilizer. The chapines were gathered together and covered with corn stalks or straw to protect seedlings from the elements, especially hail, frost, or prolonged exposure to sunlight. Once the seeds had sprouted, farmers selected healthy ones and transplanted them from the nurseries to the chinampas.[36] If laborious, the use of seedbeds conferred many advantages. Seedbeds saved space, as Pedro Armillas argued, because seedlings could be planted in a small corner of the plot or away from the chinampas, perhaps on marginal lands elsewhere. Furthermore, because only healthy sprigs were transplanted, farmers could improve crop yields. And the use of nurseries meant that farmers could transplant seedlings immediately after the previous harvest, thus maintaining continuous, intensive cycles of cultivation.[37]

Farmers also perfected techniques of multiple cropping and rotation. They had to ensure that nutrients depleted by one cultigen were replaced

---

[33] Wilken, "A Note of Buoyancy and Other Dubious Characteristics of the 'Floating' Chinampas of Mexico," 35–39.

[34] Parsons et al., "Chinampa Agriculture and Aztec Urbanization in the Valley of Mexico," 88.

[35] On the term *almácigo*, see Gibson, *The Aztecs under Spanish Rule*, 321. For Iberian agriculture, see Joseph F. O'Callaghan, *A History of Medieval Spain* (Ithaca: Cornell University Press, 1975), 154–155, and Thomas F. Glick, *Irrigation and Society in Medieval Valencia* (Cambridge: Harvard University Press, 1970).

[36] Coe, "The Chinampas of Mexico," 95; Rojas Rabiela, "Ecological and Agricultural Changes in the Chinampas of Xochimilco-Chalco," 285.

[37] Armillas, "Gardens on Swamps," 654.

by others. A common cycle involved the successive planting of maize, chile, and tomatoes. With continuous cultivation, chinampas usually produced five to seven harvests per year, with two of them typically including maize.[38] Today five varieties of maize are still grown, and colonial records show the growing of beans, chile, tomatoes (including green ones), squash, two kinds of amaranth, and European vegetables such as broad beans and peas, many of which were suited to high levels of moisture, including carrots, lettuce, cabbage, radishes, beets, and onions. In addition, farmers raised flowers, among them marigolds, broom, larkspurs, dahlias, carnations, roses, and lilies. By the late colonial period, the naturalist Alexander von Humboldt recorded the cultivation of potatoes, artichokes, cauliflowers, and "an infinity of some other vegetables" in the chinampa districts.[39] Nahuas, then, continued to harvest their old crops even as they incorporated foreign species. Rojas Rabiela argued that the very diversity of plants raised by chinampa cultivators prior to the conquest assisted in the adoption of exotic species. She concluded that rather than signifying a process of substitution or displacement, imported species instead complemented and enriched chinampa cultivation.[40] They also presented Nahuas with opportunities to engage in commerce locally and in Mexico City. This would explain why chinampa cultivators even raised wheat and barley, for which there was considerable demand.[41]

Lake-area communities and their residents remained willing to commit to the considerable effort of modifying the aquatic landscape and constructing chinampas during the colonial period, as previously, because of their many, great advantages. The location of the gardens in the lakes and their continual immersion in a regulated water supply meant that they were ideally irrigated and were less susceptible to water shortages in times of drought or when the summer canícula was particularly severe.[42] In addition to the seepage of lake water into the porous soil (known as subirrigation), chinampa farmers could ensure that their crops remained properly hydrated with splash and scoop techniques. The regular, consistent watering of the plots was a tremendous

[38] Parsons et al., "Chinampa Agriculture and Aztec Urbanization in the Valley of Mexico," 51–52.

[39] Fray Agustín de Vetancurt, *Teatro mexicano* (Mexico City: J. Porrúa, 1971), 41, 56; Rojas Rabiela, "Ecological and Agricultural Changes in the Chinampas of Xochimilco-Chalco," 282–283.

[40] Rojas Rabiela, "Ecological and Agricultural Changes in the Chinampas of Xochimilco-Chalco," 281.

[41] Rojas Rabiela, "Ecological and Agricultural Changes in the Chinampas of Xochimilco-Chalco," 282–283.

[42] Luna Golya, "Modeling the Aztec Agricultural Waterscape," iii.

boon given the variability in rainfall. The aquatic gardens offered yet more advantages. The threat of frost, for instance, was reduced since the water helped to raise air and crop temperatures by a few degrees; in the evenings, the cooling air and the heat transfer of the relatively warm water in the canals allowed for a rise in humidity, which protected the plants. The raised gardens were for these and other reasons exceptionally productive. One hectare of intensively cultivated chinampas could yield 3,000 kilograms of maize. This amount would be enough support between fifteen and twenty people at a subsistence level, if one were to allow for an average consumption of 160 kilos of maize per year for the dietary needs of a single person (according to modern dietary requirements for rural inhabitants of central Mexico). A single farmer could cultivate 0.75 hectares of chinampa lands in each annual cycle. In other words, a single farmer could support eleven to fifteen people. The chinampas, then, provided a great deal of wealth for the lake-shore communities.[43]

Given their abundance, one might imagine that Spanish settlers would eagerly seek to obtain chinampas. But this did not happen. It is probably that the time-consuming, labor-intensive investments required to construct, maintain, and cultivate the raised aquatic gardens – which at key moments would have relied on the assistance of kin or corporate associations – and the mastery of intricate and complex cultivation techniques dissuaded outsiders from adopting chinampa agriculture. The vast majority of the extant sources about chinampas demonstrate a clear trend: non-Native peoples remained conspicuously absent from the lake areas as the owners of chinampas. The documentation shows that land disputes over chinampas involved Nahuas as both plaintiffs and defendants; Spaniards such as Bernardino Arias seldom appeared in these legal and administrative papers. Spaniards and other non-Native peoples also tended not to purchase, inherit, or bequeath chinampas, as notarial documents demonstrate. In Nahuatl-language notarial sources, the owners of neighboring or adjacent parcels of land do not often appear to have been Spaniards, although such evidence is, at best, ambiguous since markers of ethnic identity were not common in the Nahuatl sources, especially in the late colonial period. The point is worth emphasizing: in hundreds of surviving documents, and across thousands of manuscript folios, there were fewer

---

[43] Parsons, "The Role of Chinampa Agriculture in the Food Supply of Aztec Tenochtitlan," 242, 245; Luna Golya, "Modeling the Aztec Agricultural Waterscape of Lake Xochimilco," 61, 120, 153, and 156–157; Parsons et al., "Chinampa Agriculture and Aztec Urbanization in the Valley of Mexico," 51.

than a score of non-Native people – perhaps even fewer than a dozen individuals – who were recorded as owning or cultivating chinampas. Only a few more individuals sought to raise livestock in the lakes.

For the most part, then, the aquatic gardens seem to have remained firmly and overwhelmingly in the hands of Nahuas. Precisely why this was the case is difficult to determine, not least methodologically (since Spaniards and other outsiders did not obtain chinampas, we do not have primary sources explaining their absence). In other words, in many instances the reasons why Spaniards did not take control of chinampas cannot be observed but instead have to be surmised. It should be noted that it was not simply the case that Spaniards were unfamiliar with such a highly interventionist form of wetland agriculture. If anything, because of their centuries-long familiarity with irrigation technologies in Spain, thanks in no small part to the contributions of their Muslim neighbors, Spaniards were among those Europeans who were arguably the best prepared for such a distinctive agricultural system as chinampa cultivation.[44] What mattered more were such factors as membership in corporate organizations that could help maintain irrigation networks and construct the raised gardens and, even more importantly, the labor-intensive demands of their cultivation.

Those non-Native peoples who did come to own chinampas typically had several key characteristics in common with one another. They tended to be long-term residents of the area. They were well accustomed to living in the aquatic world of Lakes Xochimilco and Chalco. They maintained close familial, social, and economic ties with Nahuas, and they were conversant with indigenous ways, to the point where many of them could speak Nahuatl. These characteristics applied to Bernardino Arias de Ávila, who sought the rights to the chinampas in Michcalco. They also applied to Melchora de los Reyes, who testified that she had been preparing a chinampa before being involved in the commission of a crime. Others who obtained chinampas did so because of their close connections with Nahuas. In 1577, an illegitimate son of Xochimilco's dynastic ruler, who was explicitly identified as a Spaniard, inherited five chinampas. He received them through the last will and testament of his mother-in-law, doña Ana de Guzmán, who, by contrast, bequeathed hundreds of chinampas to fellow Nahuas.[45] In another rare example from 1695, doña

---

[44] Callaghan, *A History of Medieval Spain*; Glick, *Irrigation and Society in Medieval Valencia*.

[45] AGN, Vínculos y Mayorazgos, vol. 279, exp. 1, ff. 19–25v; see also Cline, "A Cacicazgo in the Seventeenth Century," 268.

Antonia Monsalve and her husband, a captain named don Diego Mejía, sold six chinampas in San Juan Ixtayopan (the same village where Melchora had lived) to a Spaniard named Miguel Betancurt. The purchaser identified himself as a Spaniard – and was identified as such by others – and he was a long-term resident of Xochimilco. The seller, doña Antonia, had inherited the chinampas from her parents who, in turn, had purchased them from a Nahua named Juan Miguel. Clearly all parties to the transaction were long-standing members of the community and were closely integrated into life in the southern lake areas.[46]

The labor-intensive demands of chinampa cultivation also seem to have been central to patterns of colonial-era land use and ownership. Demographic decline in the lake areas held implications for the ways in which Nahuas managed and used their many chinampas. With the Nahua population having been so drastically reduced in size, lands fell vacant, as had been the case in Michcalco. Additionally, Nahuas put the chinampas to other uses besides intensive horticulture. Thus in Michcalco, as elsewhere, local residents allowed tule and zacatl – respectively, reeds and a kind of straw – to grow naturally on the chinampas. These grasses required minimal effort to flourish as they were indigenous to the lake areas and did not rely on human intervention to reproduce. Once harvested, they also found a ready and reasonably lucrative market locally and in the capital. Tule was used in making mats as well as in decorations for homes and the church, and zacatl could be readily sold for a profit since it served as fodder for the growing population of mules and horses. The Mexico City market was particularly profitable if one were to judge from the demands of the colonial government for its provision and from that same government's unsuccessful campaigns to crack down on unlicensed resellers.[47] The grasses thus amounted to a valuable alternative use for chinampas. In the three years the lands of Michcalco had been vacant, Nahuas had put them to productive use, witnesses stated, since tule and zacatl had been grown on them.[48] Centuries later, in 1762, Nahuas such as Cristóbal Santos could still be seen setting aside land in the lake to raise zacatl.[49]

---

[46] Archivo General de Notarías del Departamento del Distrito Federal (hereinafter AGNM), Mexico City, Sección Juzgados de Primera Instancia, Serie Xochimilco (henceforth listed simply as Xochimilco), vol. 1, 33–34v.

[47] AGN, Indios, vol. 6, exp. 1196, f. 327; AGN, Mercedes, vol. 7, ff. 282–282v (317–317v old foliation). For more on this, see the next chapter.

[48] AGN, Tierras, vol. 2681, exp. 6, ff. 15–16.

[49] AGN, TSJDF, Corregidores, caja 31B, exp. 80, ff. 1–1v.

Shifting uses of the chinampas reflected the need to adopt less intensive kinds of farming at a time of demographic decline. This trend may have explained the adoption of foreign vegetables as new kinds of produce for the chinampas. More often, though, chinampas came to serve as pastures for raising livestock. It was precisely to this end that Spaniards and other outsiders sought to put the chinampas on many of the occasions when they did obtain them. This had been the motivation of Bernardino Arias de Ávila in 1579, when he petitioned for the rights to the land in Michcalco. While the Nahuas opposed his request on this occasion – and did so on the grounds that he was going to introduce livestock – by the seventeenth century, Nahuas themselves had turned to grazing animals on the vacant gardens. In the early 1600s, Nahuas were recorded as having introduced oxen into the wetlands of Mexicalzingo, and by the eighteenth century, it would not have been exceptional to see sheep, goats, cattle, and mules on lands located in the lake.[50] In a criminal investigation from 1713, the brothers Felipe and Nicolás Vásquez, who were also known as "Los Japones," were suspected of having kidnapped and falsely imprisoned a woman in their home in San Juan Ixtayopan. Were it not for a Franciscan friar, the authorities might not have discovered her. In the course of the investigation, the constable of the Santa Hermandad, a brotherhood tasked with policing duties, uncovered a long history of criminality involving both men. Felipe, for instance, was both a muleteer and a mule rustler. Previously, Joseph García, a Spanish farmer in Ayotzingo, had managed to have Felipe arrested for stealing several of his mules while, separately, Antonio López, who was identified as a rancher of African ancestry in Tolyahualco, had also had several mules stolen. López further informed the authorities that Felipe was hiding lots of stolen mules in the lake ("dentro de la laguna"). Acting on this tipoff, the constable recovered several of the mules on lands in the lake.[51]

While it made some degree of sense for individuals to turn to pastoralism as a way of utilizing chinampas that had fallen vacant because of demographic decline, the chinampa plots were far from ideal as pastures. Each of the fairly small, narrow plots could not accommodate sizable herds of livestock. The fact that the chinampas were surrounded by lake waters did not help matters. Traversing the canals would have made the task of relocating livestock from one plot to the next fairly inconvenient.

---

[50] AGN, Civil, vol. 1271, exp. 1, f. 44v.
[51] AGN, TSJDF, Corregidores, caja 32B, exp. 53, ff. 1–7.

(On the other hand, one wonders about the ability of goats to jump from one chinampa to the next). For these reasons, presumably, there were few, if any recorded instances in which local residents – Nahua and Spanish alike – reared livestock on the chinampas in any great number. What remains unclear is the documentary silence surrounding swine: there are precious few references to *ganado menor*, which is to say sheep and goats, being reared on chinampas, and none whatsoever about pigs. And yet, as Bradley Skopyk has noted for other parts of central Mexico, Native peoples raised Asian pigs in riverine and palustrine wetlands.[52] Perhaps the lake waters of Xochimilco and Chalco were less well suited to rearing them? While the documentary silence prevents us from understanding this absence of pigs, what is clear from the sources is that when local residents did engage in pastoralism on the chinampas, they did so with mules and cattle. Perhaps tellingly, when cattle ranching did become more common in the eighteenth century, as discussed in Chapter 6, the farmers sought to convert and consolidate the many individual chinampa plots into single, larger pastures.

Given that Spaniards typically favored extensive agriculture, from wheat farming to raising livestock – and eschewed intensive, small-scale, irrigated cultivation – they usually refrained from obtaining chinampas. Instead, they engaged in precisely these extensive kinds of agriculture. They did so by making use of the lands away from the lakes, in the piedmont areas of the tierra firme. As a result, Nahuas in the lake areas avoided the kinds of land alienation seen elsewhere in central Mexico. They retained chinampa cultivation as an indigenous specialization. The enduring significance of chinampas in lake-area communities was reflected in their appearance in Nahuatl-language sources from the late colonial period.

The raised gardens continued to be essential assets, ones that Nahuas took care to pass on to their heirs. In 1742, for instance, Cristóbal de Santiago bequeathed two chinampas to his wife.[53] Another Nahua sold one chinampa and set aside some others to support his daughters. That they came with a house suggests that the family lived in the lakes, just as their predecessors may have done centuries earlier.[54] In other instances Nahuas continued to cultivate chinampas even as they kept lands on the tierra firme.[55] As late as 1769, Rosa María, who described herself as

[52] Skopyk, *Colonial Cataclysms*, 73–77.   [53] AGN, Tierras, vol. 2427, exp. 3, ff. 17–17v.
[54] AGN, TSJDF, Corregidores, caja 31B, exp. 80, ff. 1–1v. For another example of a house being bequeathed with chinampas, see AGN, TSJDF, Alcalde del Crimen, caja 2B, exp. 43, ff. 5–6.
[55] AGN, Vínculos y Mayorazgos, vol. 279, exp. 1, ff. 6–7.

"a very poor person" still had half a dozen chinampas.[56] By this late date the Nahuatl terminology used to identify the chinampas had gradually changed. Several terms were originally used to identify the aquatic gardens – chinamitl and chinampa, as we have seen – along with a couple of others. The first was *atoctlalli*, which simply meant irrigated land, and which in Xochimilco could be synonymous with chinampa.[57] The second term, *chinantlalli*, came to be used as an alternative for chinampa. Also spelled *chinantlali* or *chinatlale*, its attestations are only seen in sources produced after 1650, as though it were a late colonial departure from the original term, chinamitl.[58] It combines *china* with *tlalli*, the latter term being the word for "earth," "soil," and "land." During the eighteenth century, chinamitl seems to disappear from usage, with chinantlalli taking its place.[59] The evolution of the terminology through the late colonial period reflected the ongoing importance of chinampas for daily life in the lake areas.

LAND TENURE AND OWNERSHIP

Even though Spaniards were disinclined to cultivate chinampas, landownership and its system of tenure in Xochimilco did not remain unchanged after the conquest. Demographic decline and ensuing viceregal policies upset the status quo and provided new opportunities for Nahuas to contest current ownership and, in so doing, to obtain new properties. Conflicts over land revealed tensions within the community; at times, these tensions cut across class lines, pitting commoners against nobles; land disputes further involved communities disputing the limits of their territory, and neighbors and family members quarreled over who controlled household property. As lands passed to different owners, so patterns of tenure underwent modification.

Nahuas recognized several civil categories of land before the arrival of Spaniards. Not all these categories survived into the postconquest period. Some underwent modification through Spanish intervention and Nahua litigation. The earliest extant documentation about land in Xochimilco dates to the 1540s, by which time two types of Aztec land holdings had

---

[56] AGN, Tierras, vol. 2669, exp. 9, ff. 8–8v.
[57] AGN, Tierras, vol. 35, exp. 6, ff. 240–240v.
[58] AGN, Vínculos y Mayorazgos, vol. 279, exp. 1, ff. 12–13v. See also the Nahuatl bills of sale in AGN, Tierras, vol. 2669, exp. 10, ff. 4–5 and 7–9.
[59] AGN, Tierras, vol. 2427, exp. 3, ff. 17–17v; AGN, TSJDF, Corregidores, caja 31B, exp. 80, ff. 1–1v.

fallen out of use: *teotlalli*, or land belonging to temples, and *tecpantlalli*, land attached to lordly palaces. As historians have noted, it would seem likely that both were absorbed into other categories, that of *altepetlalli* or *calpollalli*, or communally held lands (i.e., of the altepetl or calpolli, respectively), and nobles' lands (*tlatocatlalli* in the case of dynastic rulers, *pillalli* for lesser nobles). Evidence from other parts of central Mexico suggests that another category of land tenure – that of private ownership – existed prior to the Spanish conquest.[60] Of these, private property gradually assumed greater importance during the colonial period while calpollalli remained an important facet of corporate organization.

Community lands bore a general similarity to the commons of early modern Europe, although significant qualifications attach to their status and use in Mexico. In theory, these holdings belonged to the community as a whole. Calpollalli plots were distributed by local officials among individual households, who in turn cultivated them and used income generated from harvests to pay community expenses. In the mid to late seventeenth century, community leaders also set aside certain properties – among them urban properties, including shops, as well as a livestock ranch – for rentals to Spaniards.[61] Ordinarily, though, officials allocated community property to Nahuas. The recipients retained usufruct so long as they continued to cultivate their land and meet their tax obligations. They could use the land as they wished, even bequeathing it to heirs, but they could not alienate it or sell it as private property. Failure to cultivate the plots or to meet community obligations meant forfeiture, and the land in question was then escheated back to the community for reallocation.[62] Technically the administration of land remained under the purview of Nahua officials, although this did not prevent Spanish officials like the corregidor from involving themselves in decisions about its allotment.[63] Even with Spanish interference, the system of calpollalli remained remarkably resilient during the colonial period, although some residents sought to convert community lands into private property, or *tlalcohualli*.

[60] Lockhart, *The Nahuas after the Conquest*, 141–163.
[61] The shops were located on the public plaza and rental income was set aside to cover tribute. The rental properties also included a livestock corral used in the provision of meat for the city. AGN, Indios, vol. 12, 2a parte, exp. 123, ff. 242–242v (240–240v old foliation), vol. 30, exp. 240, ff. 226v–227, vol. 32, exp. 282, f. 244v, and exp. 369, ff. 319v–320.
[62] Gibson, *The Aztecs under Spanish Rule*, 256–264.
[63] AGN, General de Parte, vol. 1, exp. 153, ff. 31–v; vol. 2, exp. 1071, f. 239 (261 old foliation).

Community lands, and by extension those of households, shared some characteristics. Plots of similar size tended to be allocated to households, a pattern that was likely reinforced by the consistent regularity of chinampa dimensions. Nahua authorities also allocated different kinds of land to households, which further varied according to their quality. A household could expect to receive several valuable chinampas along with land away from the lake, including marginal plots best used for raising maguey cacti. Accordingly, households did not receive usufruct rights to contiguous plots; rather, the holdings were often scattered, a tendency that as Rebecca Horn has suggested, presumably reduced risk in times of adverse environmental conditions.[64]

Xochimilco and the chinampa towns resembled other Nahua communities in the scattered pattern of land holding. In 1602, Gabriel de San Antonio, a Nahua of the village San Pedro Atocpan, bequeathed twenty-five plots of land to his heirs. All of them appear to have been inland – he used the Nahuatl term *tlalmilli*, while most contemporary Nahuatl sources clearly distinguished ordinary land from chinamitl. The location of Gabriel's lands varied considerably; the twenty-five plots were scattered among eighteen different locales.[65] Such dispersal may have been especially pronounced in the case of chinampas because, as Sarah Cline has calculated for Culhuacan, seven chinampas were needed to support the food needs for one person per year.[66] In Xochimilco, authorities generally distributed enough chinampas to provide for households, and as such, they usually received numerous plots. The exact numbers are hard to determine because people might also have their own private lands. Also, inheritance within the extended family could significantly alter the composition of any one household's property. Thus, in her testament of 1569, María Xocoyotl bequeathed to three different heirs plots of land in three locations, of which two were chinampas.[67]

The complexity of landownership is revealed in the 1566 testament of Ana Tiacapan. Upon her death, Ana stipulated that plots of land were to be distributed among several family members: her daughter, María Tiacapan, received four chinampas in the neighborhood of Ocotitlan, and a further two chinampas, located in Tetelacatzinco, went to another daughter. A granddaughter named Clara received two more in Tlaxoloztoc; another María received two chinampas in Analco Tlachtonco, and a further plot of

[64] Horn, *Postconquest Coyoacan*, 116–120.
[65] AGN, Tierras, vol. 1741, exp. 6, ff. 1–12. [66] Cline, *Colonial Culhuacan*, 88.
[67] AGN, Tierras, vol. 35, exp. 6, f. 240v.

land, not described as a chinampa, went to another grandchild, Juan. Thus before her death, Ana had owned eleven plots of land, of which ten were chinampas. The plots were located in five different places and some were held under different forms of tenure: a pair of chinampas was distinguished by the term *nohuehuetlal*, indicating that these, at least, constituted her private property. After her death, the eleven plots were distributed among five heirs, further complicating the distribution of land.[68]

It thus proves hard to determine with any accuracy how many plots each household controlled. The impression is that any one household would have had access to several chinampas, perhaps at least a half dozen, but in a few cases, especially those involving nobles, Nahuas owned many more. For instance, after having dealt with matters of pious bequests and the inheritance of the Cerón y Alvarado family's estate, the noblewoman doña Ana de Guzmán disbursed nearly 400 chinampas to distant relatives and friends. Chinampas constituted a large proportion of the bequests made by doña Ana, excluding those made to the Franciscan friary and her immediate family. All 400 or so chinampas had been located in the Xochimilco barrio of Atizapan. Thus prior to her last will and testament, a great abundance of chinampas belonged to the family in a single place. After her death, a dozen individuals inherited the many chinampas.[69]

The highly diffuse nature of land holding in Xochimilco thus had a mosaic-like quality. Any one household could have cultivated plots of land located in several places. Or, viewed from another perspective, in any single location chinampas could be owned by many different households. This is clearly shown in the few surviving pictorial land records from Xochimilco. One cadastral showed fifteen chinampas (see Figure 2.1). Glyphs of heads, which appeared in profile, indicated the five owners, two of whom were women. Color further distinguished the plots, either reflecting ownership or, more likely, different kinds of land tenure. Three plots were each painted yellow and red, a further six were green, and the remaining three were left uncolored. Thus five people shared fifteen chinampas that could have been held under four kinds of tenure.[70]

The scattered character of land holding held several implications. The ownership of the plots could be a source of confusion, if not contention.

---

[68] AGN, Tierras, vol. 35, exp. 6, ff. 236–237.

[69] AGN, Vínculos y Mayorazgos, vol. 279, exp. 1, ff. 19–25v.

[70] AGN, Tierras, vol. 1525, exp. 5, f. 3. Cadastrals from the Cerón y Alvarado estate also show the same, interspersed pattern of ownership. AGN, Vínculos y Mayorazgos, vol. 279, exp. 1, ff. 48 and 77v.

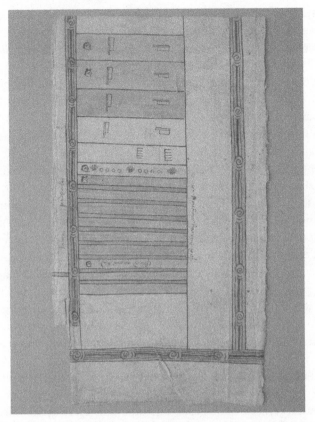

FIGURE 2.1 Pictorial document of chinampas in Xochimilco, 1568–1569. By permission of the Archivo General de la Nación, Tierras, vol. 1525, exp. 5, f. 3.

This applied as much to communities as it did to individuals. In 1595, Cuitlahuac and Xochimilco fought over the ownership of chinampas on the borders of their jurisdictions.[71] Such disputes often escalated to the point of requiring outside adjudication. Residents of the chinampa districts sought to obviate these potential conflicts when they gave names to individual plots of land. In a dispute over land belonging to another Nahua named Ana Tiacapan, Viceroy don Luis de Velasco the Younger was able to cite in his ruling the names of the contested plots.[72] On some

---

[71] AGN, Indios, vol. 6, 2a pte., exp. 1055, f. 286v.
[72] Their names were Quauhchilamal, Yzlapacolipan, Quauhtlapehualco, and Cacapola Xalcan. AGN, Indios, vol. 3, exp. 294, f. 69v (68v old foliation). In a separate case,

occasions, when controversies over land appeared before Xochimilca authorities, a group of community elders were entrusted with identifying the owners of lands. The presence of these elders, known as *tlalhuehuet-que* (land elders), likely reflected complexity in the city's system of land distribution.[73] And perhaps most significantly, the mosaic-like quality of landownership may have further deterred Spaniards from obtaining chinampas.

The comparative absence of Spanish disruption does not mean that Nahua landholding in Xochimilco remained unchanged or unchallenged during the colonial period. Rather, the changes took place within the Nahua community. Lands were transferred from one type of tenure to another, and residents sought to obtain new holdings. Population decline and Spanish colonial reforms of central Mexico's political economy provided opportunities to contest ownership. Concerns about food shortages and the delivery of tribute in grains, in the wake of epidemics, also meant that government reforms extended into the realms of land use and agricultural production. In 1558, the viceroy appointed don Francisco Jiménez, a Nahua from Tecamachalco, to serve as Xochimilco's governor and to conduct a thoroughgoing inspection of the land system. On the basis of that inspection, Jiménez instituted a program of land redistribution, known as a *repartimiento de tierras*.[74] The redistribution was substantial if one were to judge from the length of its records, which ran to at least ninety-three folios bound together in a single volume.[75] The repartimiento had several components to it. Don Francisco issued confirmations of titles to lands that were being cultivated and that were owned legitimately. He also supervised the reallocations of lands that lacked proper title or had fallen vacant. Since vacant plots, known as *tierras baldías* or *tierras realengas*, became the nominal property of the crown, they could be reallocated by royal officials. This had been the case with Martín Iuctli, who successfully petitioned Jiménez for the rights to six abandoned chinampas in a part of Xochimilco called Pilicac.[76] The cabildo also assumed

Juan de San Gabriel named his plots Tezcalatlaco, Acautla, Pequentla, Quauçalaqua, and Quentla Tequepayucan. AGN, Indios, vol. 3, exp. 770, f. 181.

[73] Lockhart, *The Nahuas after the Conquest*, 144.

[74] In 1555, for instance, Agustín de Osorio from Huexotzinco became governor in order to intercede in a dispute among Xochimilco's three tlatoque. He was possibly a replacement for don Esteban de Guzmán, whose term as residencia in Tenochtitlan began in 1554. Gibson, *The Aztecs under Spanish Rule*, 169, 188–189; AGN, Vínculos y Mayorazgos, vol. 279, exp. 1, ff. 99 and 106–112.

[75] AGN, Indios, vol. 3, exp. 286, f. 67v. Alas, the book has not survived.

[76] AGN, Tierras, vol. 1525, exp. 5, ff. 1–1v.

responsibility for implementing some of the changes. In November 1558, an alcalde named don Francisco de Galicia issued titles to several plots, including a chinampa, to Juana Tiacapan. The lands had previously been communal holdings – altepetlalli – but they had apparently fallen vacant. The alcalde reclassified them as private property, perhaps as a favor to Juana as the offspring of a fellow nobleman, don Luis Ihuitlmacoc.[77]

Jiménez's inspection afforded an opportunity for individuals to settle any questions about their legitimate ownership of property. In August 1558, three Nahua commoners appeared before the governor because two sons, Martín de Guzmán and Tomás Cortés, were uncertain about whether they would be secure in inheriting a chinampa from their mother, Agustina Teicui, who accompanied them to help clarify matters. Agustina explained that she had been given the land, in a place called Tequixquiapan, a decade earlier, when the judge's predecessor, don Pedro de Suero, conducted a similar program of land redistribution. At that time a chinampa that had been assigned communally to the dynastic ruler – the type of tenure had been tlatocatlalli – was not only reallocated to Agustina, a commoner, but it was also converted into private property.[78] The question of the chinampa's status was again an issue in 1558 because the sons apparently feared interference when inheriting it. Don Francisco upheld the earlier transfer.[79]

Members of the Nahua nobility, and not just commoners, benefited from the 1558 repartimiento. Don Esteban de Guzmán, for instance, secured confirmations of his title to lands, among them chinampas in Atizapan.[80] His wife, acting separately, obtained some more titles. Doña Madalena de Guzmán received confirmations of ownership for some chinampas in a place called Tlalnechpan, among other plots scattered across several locations.[81] Notably, these titles specified that the lands were held privately; they were not altepetl lands that were set aside for the nobility's use. The records are not definitive about the previous status but Jiménez could have allowed for the lands to be reclassified from

---

[77] AGN, Vínculos y Mayorazgos, vol. 279, exp. 1, ff. 106–107v.

[78] Or so the Nahuatl would seem to suggest. The operative phrasing is "don Pedro . . . yxiptla mochiuh ynin huehuetlal atemohuayan mani tlatocatlalli omochiuh auh"; AGN, Vínculos y Mayorazgos, vol. 279, exp. 1, f. 98. The Spanish translation reads, "don Pedro de Suero . . . entregue de otras tierras antiguas que tenia en el pago llamado atemohuayan que alli estan que fueron para el señorio las tierras i a ella solo sele dan para ella" (f. 99).

[79] AGN, Vínculos y Mayorazgos, vol. 279, exp. 1, ff. 98, 99.

[80] AGN, Vínculos y Mayorazgos, vol. 279, exp. 1, f. 110.

[81] AGN, Vínculos y Mayorazgos, vol. 279, exp. 1, f. 104.

communal to private holdings, which had the advantage of giving their owners greater freedom to dispose of them as they saw fit. A precedent for this may have been set during don Pedro de Suero's investigation a decade earlier. Then, some of the tlatoque had received confirmations of their patrimonial rights to land at the same time that their privileges were curtailed. Perhaps the reclassification of land served as a form of compensation for the loss of tribute support (discussed in Chapter 4). Either way, one of the 1548 Nahuatl orders confirmed that some of don Martín Cerón y Alvarado's lands in Tepetenchi were part of his ancestral estate (hueuhetlal). Other plots, in a place named Atonco, belonged to don Esteban de Guzmán.[82]

The 1558 repartimiento, though, was not solely (if at all) concerned about political negotiations. Don Francisco Jiménez's mandate specifically called for an inspection of the nobility's holdings to determine if they were too large and, if so, to require that they be redistributed to commoners. The overriding issue, it seemed, was the question of whether there were sufficient plots of *tequimilli*, or tribute land, for raising maize at a time of shortage.[83] This issue became a source of controversy between nobles and commoners, some of which proved to be long-lasting.[84] A decade later, in 1568, Martín Iuctli, who had been the recipient of six chinampas in the 1558 repartimiento, faced concerted opposition and a campaign of intimidation from a Nahua noblewoman who contested his rights to the plots. Doña María de Mendoza, who was the granddaughter of the tlatoani of Tecpan, don Hernando de Santa María, arranged for powerful allies to assist her. The governor, Juan de los Ángeles, issued a ruling in her favor, accusing Martín Iuctli of trespassing. Meanwhile the corregidor's lieutenant, Damián García Franco, had him imprisoned. Confronted by unified local opposition, Martín responded with a lawsuit submitted to the high court.[85] Other disputes surfaced

---

[82] AGN, Vínculos y Mayorazgos, vol. 279, exp. 1, f. 64.

[83] AGN, Vínculos y Mayorazgos, vol. 279, exp. 1, f. 104.

[84] If the Nahuatl admonitions against contravening the repartimiento were representative of official concerns, the nobles might be seen as having been unwilling to accept the reforms: "If any person goes against this order and is a nobleman or a lord, he will be shorn in the marketplace, be given a hundred lashes, and be disgraced; if he is a commoner he will not be punished." Such a statement, though, might well have been contemporary boilerplate for land titles. The original wording is "intlaaca texixicoliztica quicuiliznequiz intlapilli anoço tecuhtli iniuhqui quichivaz yc nitlanahoatia tianquizco ximaloz ihuan macuilpovalpa mecahuitecoz ihuan ic quicahoaz inimahuiço intlamaviztlacatl." AGN, Vínculos y Mayorazgos, vol. 279, exp. 1, f. 104.

[85] AGN, Tierras, vol. 1525, exp. 5.

years later. In 1591, the authorities needed to consult the book of don Francisco Jiménez's repartimiento records, and on doing so, the viceroy confirmed titles to the land that had been reassigned more than three decades earlier.[86]

Conflicts over land involving nobles became common as the sixteenth century wore on. In 1590, doña Polonia Cortés had to fend off challenges to land and a house she had inherited.[87] As with a cacica named Antonia Luisa, doña Polonia sought a protective order from the viceroy to frustrate the threats of her rivals.[88] Such threats also confronted members of Tepetenchi's ruling dynasty. In 1565, an agent for the family in Santa María Asunción Milpa Alta succeeded in fending off an attempt by Domingo Ceçeh, Juana Tiacapan, Gabriel Quauhtemoc, Juan Huizttecol, and Francisco Yohuallatonac to take over six plots of land that formed part of don Martín Cortés's estate. The agent, Agustín Hueicancalqui, had Xochimilco's cabildo issue Nahuatl titles confirming the family's legitimate rights to the plots. Three years later, don Martín Cerón, the tlatoani's nephew, had to fend off a second challenge. That the lands were classified as being assigned to the dynastic ruler (tlatocatlalli) suggested the depth of the commoners' audacity.[89]

Among other challenges to noble holdings, a series of disputes in a place called Xaxalpan revealed the depth of animosity across lines of social class in the 1580s.[90] Xochimilco's neighborhood of Xaxalpan was the site of more than 400 chinampas. A significant number of them had long been shared by two nobles, don Esteban de Guzmán and don Pedro de Sotomayor. Both had been prominent figures in Nahua society, serving on Xochimilco's cabildo and holding the post of governor.[91] Because of their political commitments, don Pedro and don Esteban did not actually cultivate their fields themselves. Rather, as part of the privileges accorded the nobility – and because the lands were distributed to them via usufruct rights – the two men employed *terrazgueros*, who were a subordinate class of dependent laborers assigned to the nobility, to work the chinampas for them. This arrangement continued after don Esteban's demise. At that point the chinampas passed to the control of don Pedro de Sotomayor and his wife, doña Juana de Guzmán. A few years later, though, don Pedro

[86] AGN, Indios, vol. 3, exp. 286, f. 67v.   [87] AGN, Indios, vol. 4, exp. 239, f. 72v.
[88] AGN, Indios, vol. 6, 2a pte., exp. 156, f. 37.
[89] AGN, Vínculos y Mayorazgos, vol. 279, exp. 1, ff. 79–81v.
[90] AGN, Vínculos y Mayorazgos, vol. 279, exp. 1, ff. 114–116v, 130–131.
[91] Newberry Library, Ayer Ms. 1121, ff. 211–211v.

died without having written a testament. His demise provided an opportunity for the terrazgueros to contest the control of the chinampas.
Defying doña Juana's claims, they seized the chinampas, in effect staging
a land invasion.[92]

Thanks to their political clout and the assistance of Franciscan friars, in
1582, the tlatoani don Martín Cerón y Alvarado and his son, don Martín
Cerón Villafañez, managed to evict the terrazgueros who had taken over
the chinampas. The dynastic ruler and his son were successful in removing
the trespassers because the chinampas were classified as communal lands
(altepetlalli) and, as the governor of the altepetl – having recently recovered
control of this political office – the elder don Martín had the authority,
with the agreement of the cabildo over which he presided, to expropriate
and redistribute the land.[93] In this case the circumstances of land tenure
and political power overrode the problem of the intestate demise. Don
Pedro's widow, doña Juana de Guzmán, took over the rights to some, but
not all, of the chinampas. The Cerón y Alvarado family also acquired some
of them, and they did so through an agreement with the church.

The church was involved because doña Juana had decided that her
estate should generate income for pious works. Doña Juana set aside some
of the chinampas in Xaxalpan for rental, with the income payable to
Xochimilco's friars. Don Martín Cerón rented some of her chinampas
from the friary. But the annulment of her testament now threw the status
of the land into confusion. To resolve the quandary, don Martín
approached the Franciscans. Finding a solution acceptable to both parties,
the tlatoani convened a meeting of the cabildo members during which don
Martín and fray Alonso Jiménez entered into a contractual agreement,
with the councilmen as witnesses, through which don Martín purchased
the chinampas from the Franciscans. Once the Nahuatl bill of sale was
signed, don Martín took possession of the chinampas. And by doing so
through a contractually binding and notarized instrument, which had
been witnessed and approved by the cabildo members, don Martín successfully switched the chinampas' class of tenure to private property,
which meant that he could incorporate them into his family's estate and,
in 1588, when he wrote his last will and testament, bequeath them as part
of his patrimony to his son.[94] The lands were depicted in a pictorial
document, as shown in Figure 2.2.

---

[92] AGN, Vínculos y Mayorazgos, vol. 279, exp. 1, ff. 91–95.
[93] AGN, Vínculos y Mayorazgos, vol. 279, exp. 1, ff. 76–78v.
[94] AGN, Vínculos y Mayorazgos, vol. 279, exp. 1, ff. 6–7 and 8–9v.

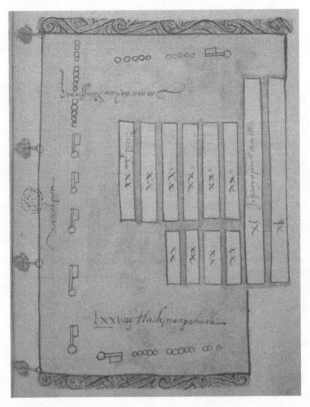

FIGURE 2.2 Chinampas of don Martín Cerón Villafañez. By permission of the Archivo General de la Nación, Vínculos y Mayorazgos, vol. 279, exp. 1, f. 77v.

The middle decades of the sixteenth century, then, witnessed dual threats to noble property. In part pressure was exerted from above. Crown authorities encouraged the redistribution of land by promising to shore up the remaining holdings as private property. This designation presumably afforded several advantages: it was no longer subject to oversight by the municipal council and could be rented or sold as the owner saw fit. Despite these advantages, challenges also came from below, with Nahua commoners contesting the ownership of noble lands at a time when they also proved less willing to meet their tribute and labor obligations.

Not all conflicts over land took place between nobles and commoners, and neighbors, family members, and rivals disputed one another's ownership of land. Transfers of property through sale and inheritance provided

an opportunity to contest landownership. The moment when land passed
from one owner to the next could be fraught with controversy. Given the
circumstances of population decline, disputes over inheritance may have
been especially contentious. After having married for a second time, Josefa
María came into conflict with a son from her first marriage over the
disposition of property.[95] The adjudication of a significant number of
these disputes passed beyond the Nahua municipal government regularly
appeared before Spanish courts through the sixteenth and seventeenth
centuries.[96]

An inheritance case from 1575 attests to the severity and intractable
nature of such conflicts. Juliana Tlaco approached community officials to
help recover chinampas and a house, along with its contents, claimed by
her daughter-in-law, Petronila Francisca. Petronila had assumed usufruct
rights to the properties upon the death of her immediate family. As the last
surviving member of the household, Petronila claimed the lands as hers.
But her mother-in-law, Juliana, disputed the claim. She argued that control of the chinampas should revert to her. The town council deliberated
on the matter, summoning the land elders to offer advice. But in availing
herself of the right to appeal, Juliana circumvented the cabildo and
brought the matter before Mexico City's high court. The dispute became
extraordinarily complex, and with further appeals the lawsuit passed
through the Spanish legal system all the way to the king. Philip II ultimately ruled in favor of Juliana.[97]

Inheritance may have been subject to contention because wills did not
always guarantee property rights. The circumstances of their authorship
and doubts about intent could stir acrimony. In some instances, plaintiffs
questioned their very legality. In 1586, the municipal council tried to
nullify the will of doña Juana de Guzmán, the widow of a nobleman,
don Pedro de Sotomayor. The council sought to overturn the decedent's
will on the basis that she had made subsequent revisions. Once again the
matter was adjudicated beyond the city's jurisdiction and the widow's

---

[95] AGN, Tierras, vol. 2959, exp. 109, ff. 275–276.

[96] AGN, Indios, vol. 3, exp. 323, f. 75v (74v old foliation), exp. 782, ff. 184–184v, exp. 970,
f. 235v, vol. 4, exp. 239, f. 72v, vol. 5, exp. 564, f. 156v (226v old foliation), exp. 582,
f. 161v (230v old foliation), exp. 663, ff. 182–182v, exp. 749, ff. 200v–201 (269v–270 old
foliation), vol. 6, 2a parte, exp. 61, f. 14v, exp. 156, f. 37, exp. 507, f. 111v, and for later
cases, vol. 20, exp. 149, ff. 107–107v, vol. 29, exp. 166, ff. 139v–140, and exp. 176, ff.
146v–147.

[97] AGN, Tierras, vol. 1525, exp. 3, ff. 2–9ff. (The folios are numbered only as far as 68, and
another thirty-odd folios follow after that. The royal judgment can be found among the
latter, unnumbered folios).

brother, don Juan de Guzmán, supplied remarkable testimony, including a recounting of conversations between him and the late testator about changes that had been made on his recommendation.[98]

As with inheritance, so sales could also provide an opportunity for Nahuas to advance claims to land.[99] Nahuas, and occasionally Spaniards, asked the viceroy or the General Indian Court to confirm their transactions.[100] In others, they did so in anticipation of potential challenges. Dionisio de San Juan, who purchased a house and land from his sister and brother-in-law, solicited confirmation of his title in order to forestall litigation.[101] Some confirmations required a determination of land tenure status. In 1591, a woman identified only as doña Paula received confirmation that several chinampas were hers and that they formed a part of her private estate (*patrimonio*) and not community land.[102]

In the latter half of the sixteenth century, then, a variety of factors contributed to a degree of flux in patterns of land tenure and ownership. Demographic changes and government interference enabled Nahuas to contest ownership, as did transfers of property through sale and inheritance. Population movements and corresponding reallocations of land further contributed to fluidity in landownership. Nahuas routinely relocated their residence. Sometimes they did so when they married. On other occasions they moved to obtain new properties.[103] In 1582, for instance, Agustín de San Miguel, originally a resident of the tlaxilacalli of Tepetenchi, moved to Tecpan where he had purchased a house and land. The officials of Tepetenchi blocked his relocation, though, arguing

[98] AGN, Vínculos y Mayorazgos, vol. 279, exp. 1, ff. 126–127v. For the translation of don Juan's testimony and details of the case, see James Lockhart, "The Testimony of don Juan" in *Nahuas and Spaniards: Postconquest Central Mexican History and Philology* (Stanford: Stanford University Press and UCLA Latin American Center, 1991), 75–87.

[99] The presentation of Nahuatl bills of sale and other documentation proved valuable to the success of litigants' claims. AGN, Indios, vol. 3, exp. 287, f. 68 (67 old foliation).

[100] In 1634, two Spaniards, Hipólita de Torres and Luis Carrasco, came into conflict over the latter's ownership of urban property. Having presented Nahuatl bills of sale and testimony to back up his claim, Carrasco prevailed. AGN, Tierras, vol. 95, 1a pte., exp. 1, ff. 1–46v.

[101] AGN, Indios, vol. 3, exp. 79, f. 20v (19v old foliation). See also vol. 5, exp. 968, ff. 249–249v (319–319v old foliation), vol. 6, 2a pte., exp. 665, f. 153, and vol. 11, exp. 178, ff. 148–148v.

[102] AGN, Indios, vol. 5, exp. 1121, f. 284v (354v old foliation).

[103] This happened with Francisco and Bernardino de San Luis, residents of San Gregorio Atlapulco, who inherited land and other property elsewhere. AGN, Indios, vol. 2, exp. 202, f. 51v, vol. 6, 2a pte., exp. 42, ff. 11v–12. See also the experience of Juan de San Francisco in his move from Tecpan to Olac in 1591, AGN, Indios, vol. 5, exp. 265, f. 71v (140v in old foliation).

that according to the latest tribute records, he owed contributions to them. Viceroy don Lorenzo Suárez de Mendoza intervened in the dispute and decreed that Agustín be allowed to move without having to fulfill obligations to his former tlaxilacalli. As with Agustín, so the relocation of other citizens could prompt opposition from Nahua officials charged with collecting tribute.

The movement of Nahuas made questions of inheritance and land-ownership all the more complicated. In a 1575, lawsuit originating in Mexico City, Nahua residents don Francisco Velázquez, don Hernando Tecon, and Pablo de Tapia claimed that a woman from Xochimilco called Ana Nenahuatl had usurped their lands, including chinampas, in the district of San Pablo. They argued that they had inherited their plots and that ownership could be demonstrated to have extended back 150 years to a common ancestor named Ixquauhtli. Ana countered their claims, arguing instead that she had inherited the lands and that the litigants had exploited the opportunity of her absence, while in Xochimilco, to appropriate them.[104] Similarly, a dispute over a house and fields of maguey cacti and fruit trees in Santa María de la Asunción Milpa Alta required several years to resolve; ultimately the case came to the crown for a ruling. The lawsuit, which took place between 1691 and 1695, involved a dispute between Miguel López and two other residents of the town. López argued that while away in Otumba, Juan Diego and his wife Sebastiana María had taken over his property. The defendants responded by arguing that they had proper legal title to the land. The litigation thus hinged on proof of owner-ship, and Nahuatl bills of sale and reports were gathered from as far back as 1645. The crux of the case lay in determining if the initial stipulations of the sale had been met; the original owner had sold the property on the basis that proceeds would pay for her burial and prayers for her soul.[105]

Residual claims by Nahuas who had moved elsewhere further compli-cated determinations of landownership. In the seventeenth century, liti-gants who claimed to belong to one of Xochimilco's dynastic families presented papers allegedly signed by Cortés in 1519 that, they claimed, upheld their rights to an estate.[106] In one instance, the Cerón y Alvarado

---

[104] The high court found in her favor. AGN, Tierras, vol. 32, exp. 1, ff. 1–25v. For their respective claims, see ff. 1 and 5. For another lawsuit involving plaintiffs in Mexico City, dating to 1574, which involved questions about inheritance and residents from Xochimilco, see AGN, Tierras, vol. 35, exp. 6, ff. 230–322.

[105] AGN, Tierras, vol. 1750, exp. 1, ff. 1–46.

[106] AGN, Vínculos y Mayorazgos, vol. 240, exp. 10, ff. 71ff; Gibson, *The Aztec under Spanish Rule*, 162.

family came into possession of lands that had been allocated to the Mexica at the time of Xochimilco's incorporation into the Aztec Empire. Presumably, the Spanish conquest afforded Xochimilco's dynastic rulers an opportunity to seize the lands. The shift in ownership was matched by a change in classification, from *mexicatlalli* (or land of the Mexica), to private property.[107]

The fate of the Cerón y Alvarado family's estate represents the broader trajectory of postconquest changes in Nahua landownership while also reflecting an overall pattern of continuity. The earliest will found in the estate's papers, dating to 1588, carefully elucidated the line of succession. It was less specific about the actual extent of the family's holdings. Because the estate would be passed on in its entirety, and because there were so many plots of land, the testator, don Martín Cortés Cerón y Alvarado opted not to enumerate them. His subsequent heirs took care to forbid the sale of lands to Spaniards and the estate seems to have remained intact, for the most part, until at least 1650 when don Martín's last direct heir set down his testament. In the intervening sixty years, the status of lands changed slightly. Some tlatocatlalli plots became private holdings. Most conspicuously, communal lands that were once cultivated by commoners had been converted for rental purposes.[108] Apparently population decline had rendered the ownership of land less valuable; after all, land required labor in order to generate income, and rentals provided an alternative source of income to offset declining labor service. This motive may also help explain the decision by the last ruler to establish a *capellanía*, or chaplaincy, for the family. The lands transferred to Xochimilco's Franciscan friary were then rented, with income set aside to pay for masses on behalf of family members' souls. In 1650, the family still owned land in more than fifty different locations, and in many of these places, they owned numerous plots. The demise of the estate came not from Spanish usurpation but instead through mortality. By the 1680s, only a few, distant relatives remained alive to claim the estate.[109] While the Cerón y Alvarado family's experience is exceptional – by virtue of its members'

---

[107] In this case, some of the patrimonial land was called *cihuatlalli*. *Cihuatlalli* directly translates as "woman land," but as Cline notes, it may have been a type of land acquired through dowry. AGN, Vínculos y Mayorazgos, vol. 279, exp. 1, ff. 82v, 86v; Cline, *Colonial Culhuacan*, 150, 235.

[108] The performance of personal service had become a contentious issue for the family. See AGN, Indios, vol. 2, exp. 830, ff. 188–188v.

[109] AGN, Vínculos y Mayorazgos, vol. 279, exp. 1, ff. 6–18v, 86–90v; Cline, "A Cacicazgo in the Seventeenth Century," 268–271.

noble status and political influence – it serves as a strong reminder that modifications in land tenure took place within an overall pattern of impressive continuity in Nahua ownership.[110]

Of course, the lacustrine environment was not the only place suitable for agriculture in Xochimilco; the territorial limits of lakeshore polities also included upland areas, where other kinds of irrigated land were to be found. The kinds of irrigation and agriculture practiced in these upland areas were determined by the quality and depth of the soil as well as the gradient and elevation. Throughout the Basin of Mexico the lakes were ringed by a band of what the archaeologists Sanders, Parsons, and Santley called the deep soil alluvium and which, for them, constituted a distinct ecological zone. These soils were especially rich and fertile, having been created both by deposits of clay and silt from floodwaters from the lakes as well as deposits of sediment washed down from the sierras over millions of years. The deep soil alluvium, which was located at elevations between 2,240 and 2,300 meters, was typically characterized by being relatively flat and by having soils that were often four or more meters in depth.[111]

While constituting markedly different ecological zones, both the lakes and the deep soil alluvium were crucial locations for agricultural coloniization in ancient times, and they long remained important zones for farming through the colonial period and beyond. With the abundant rains of the southern end of the basin, the deep soil alluvium was well suited to intensive cultivation, and with modest investments in hydraulic engineering, residents were able to secure bountiful harvests. To create agricultural fields in this dry-land zone, early farmers dug trenches that were perpendicular to the shoreline and extended into the water. The irrigation ditches allowed for drainage into the lake when there was ample rainfall; conversely, during dry months, water could be scooped from the trenches and sprinkled onto the fields. Ideally, of course, these irrigated fields were located on lands with a gentle gradient. This was especially true in the area to the east of Lake Chalco, where some of the

[110] Nobles were not above using coercion to press their claims. See, for instance, the case in which a governor from San Pedro Atocpan imprisoned a Nahua woman who had tried to prevent him from taking over lands to which she claimed rights. AGN, 1741, exp. 6, ff. 1–12.

[111] Sanders et al., *The Basin of Mexico*, 95, 98, 116, and 192. See also the supplementary map of the ecological zones.

irrigation channels could extend hundreds of meters beyond the edge of the lake.[112]

The extent of the deep soil alluvium zone varied according to topography at different places around the lakes. In certain areas it was a few kilometers wide, notably along the eastern shore of Lake Tetzcoco, the watershed of the Rio de Teotihuacan to the northeast, and to the west of Lake Zumpango. Another important location of the deep soil alluvium lay to the east of Lake Chalco. To the south of Lakes Chalco and Xochimilco the zone was, by comparison, quite narrow, and seldom more than a kilometer wide. This prime agricultural land became the site of many haciendas around the basin's lakes. And its narrowness helps to explain the limited development of haciendas in the south, which is to say in Xochimilco's jurisdiction.[113]

While the lakes and the deep soil alluvium constituted two of several distinct ecological zones, for Sanders and his colleagues, other such zones extended out from the deep soil alluvium and up the slopes of the Sierra de Ajusco's hills and mountains. The piedmont itself consisted of three zones. The lower piedmont, with a shallow gradient, rose to the 2,350 meters and was seldom wider than a kilometer because of the steep rise of the Sierra de Ajusco's escarpment. The sandy soils of this zone were suitable for maize cultivation, particularly with the greater rainfall levels found at higher altitudes. The lower piedmont was susceptible to erosion and, unsurprisingly, local residents turned to terracing to protect soils and control water supplies. In some locations, the terraces remained visible well into the twentieth century, before urban sprawl extended to the southern hills. In Acalpixca, for instance, terraces from the upland areas reached down almost as far as the lakeshore (although the proximity of chinampas and terraces was unusually close in Acalpixca, given the rapidly rising slopes).[114] As the gradient increased, so too did the risk of erosion. In many parts of the piedmont, exposed hardpan soils (tepetate) were to be found. Similar characteristics define the middle piedmont, which had a higher gradient and lay between 2,350 and 2,500 meters, as well as the upper piedmont, which reached up to the sierras at 2,700 meters, where the soils grew thin to the point of being almost nonexistent such that the possibilities for agriculture petered out and forests, especially of conifers, came to predominate.

[112] Luna Golya, "Modeling the Aztec Agricultural Waterscape," 64.
[113] This is discussed at greater length in the final chapter.
[114] Sanders et al., *The Basin of Mexico*, 86–87, 279.

Further affecting the opportunities for agriculture were the increased likelihood – and severity – of frosts at higher elevations, especially over 2,500 meters. In Xochimilco, in particular, the middle and upper pied-mont areas only had a tiny fraction of land that was cultivable; much of it was covered with volcanic rock.[115] Hence, following the arrival of non-Native peoples and foreign animal species, the upper reaches of the piedmont and the sierras became pasturelands, although these were often interspersed with difficult terrain, characterized by Sanders, Parsons, and Santley as "a chaotic mixture of great tongues of lava, young volcanos, masses of contorted rock, and small depressions."[116]

The proximity and the shifts between ecological zones, from the lake to the upper piedmont and finally the sierra, varied considerably according to the rugged topography. Extensive plains spread out to the east of Lake Chalco, allowing for a gradual gradient and, as noted, a wide band of deep alluvial soil. To the west of Lake Xochimilco there had also been a plain, although a volcanic eruption during the Pre-Classic period turned it into the rocky wasteland known as the Pedregal.[117] To the south, deep soils were confined to fairly narrow strips of land, and as at Acalpixca, with its terraces, in some areas the steeper slopes reached down as far as the lakeshore.

It was in these diverse, upland areas that Spanish colonists and Nahuas were issued land grants by the colonial administration. The earliest of these royal grants dated to 1542. It upheld Xochimilco's rights of access to hills in the south of the jurisdiction.[118] The confirmation set a precedent for many others that followed: it recognized the property interests of Nahua communities, in this case to woodland, but the community's rights were not exclusive; in the following months, Spaniards also received permission to cut timber in other, nearby areas. Timber was in high demand for the construction of houses and public buildings in Mexico City, and similar rights were established for Nahuas to obtain stone.[119]

The allocation of rights pertaining to an outlying area of the jurisdic-tion, away from the city itself, set another precedent. Subsequent grants to Spaniards, designed to establish livestock ranches, were awarded in the montes to the south of Xochimilco. In 1564, Francisco de Alambarri

---

[115] Sanders et al., *The Basin of Mexico*, 378.
[116] Sanders et al., *The Basin of Mexico*, 88, 188.
[117] Sanders et al., *The Basin of Mexico*, 188.
[118] AGN, Mercedes, vol. 1, exp. 48, f. 23. See also vol. 2, exp. 42, f. 19v.
[119] AGN, Mercedes, vol. 1, exp. 213, f. 101v; vol. 2, exp. 41, f. 19v, and exp. 356, f. 145v.

received rights to an *estancia*, or ranch, for 3,000 head of *ganado menor* (either goats or sheep).[120] To encourage Spanish settlement, numerous viceregal grants were awarded in quick succession, with more than a dozen in 1567 alone.[121] Some of these awards became the basis for the subsequent rise of rural estates.

A 1567 grant to Juan de Aguilar, a resident of Mexico City, is representative of many others. He received the standard amount of two *caballerías* of land, the equivalent of 210 acres, on the outskirts of the jurisdiction. Adjacent properties all belonged to fellow Spaniards, and the land was not especially valuable, having been described as located in poor country ("mal pays"). The corregidor's lieutenant, Damián García Franco, reported that Xochimilco's Nahua leaders had agreed to the grant, confirming that it would not trespass upon the rights of local residents. The land was more than six leagues from Xochimilco and located more than 900 yards (1,000 varas) away from the nearest Nahua settlement. The recipient was exhorted neither to infringe upon the Nahua settlement nor deny anyone access to woodlands.[122]

During the next thirty years, other grants followed, largely in the same format as Juan de Aguilar's.[123] They also shared another common feature with his grant: the lands he obtained were close to the *camino real*, or royal road, that passed through Xochimilco's jurisdiction and went south to Cuernavaca. Andrés García, for instance, obtained another two caballerías of land in the vicinity at this same time.[124] Apparently the government sought to cluster these grants in the area. Martín Abaruccia's grant, also from 1567, also consisted of two caballarías, and it specified that the land was next to the royal road and adjacent to other grants awarded to Juan de Velasco and (presumably the aforementioned) Andrés García.[125] Apparently these tracts of land near the road were all at a decent remove from Nahua communities. The nearest community to the newly awarded lands of Hernando Aragones was some 2,000 varas away.[126] Across from his property a widow named Ysabel Medina received her own tracts of land.[127]

---

[120] AGN, Mercedes, vol. 7, f. 246v (271v old foliation).
[121] AGN, Mercedes vol. 9, ff. 39v, 40, 81v, 84v, 85v, 86v, 87, 98, 127, 134, 135v, 182, 183, 194, and 194v.
[122] AGN, Mercedes, vol. 9, ff. 124v–125.
[123] A few of them confirmed Nahua holdings. AGN, Mercedes, vol. 11, f. 232, vol. 12, ff. 107, 186v, 197v, 199, 209v, vol. 15, ff. 33v, 87, and 182v.
[124] AGN, Mercedes, vol. 7, ff. 81v–82.   [125] AGN, Mercedes, vol. 7, ff. 127–127v.
[126] AGN, Mercedes, vol. 7, ff. 134–134v.   [127] AGN, Mercedes, vol. 7, ff. 135v–136.

As settlers established livestock ranches, so the population of goats, sheep, and cattle grew. Inevitably some animals strayed beyond their enclosures. The first recorded complaint about injury to Nahua agriculture in Xochimilco dates to 1561.[128] In 1586, the viceroy received reports of 250 head of cattle running amok in the city and, in addition to ordering an investigation, he threatened the incarceration of those responsible for letting the cattle loose.[129] Petitions inspired by damage to crops increased in number and frequency from the late 1570s. In 1579, Nahuas from Mixquic complained that mules and horses belonging to two *mestizos*, individuals of mixed European and indigenous ancestry, had eaten or trampled their crops.[130] A year later, residents of Xochimilco echoed Mixquic's petition, this time protesting about horses belonging to a Spaniard.[131]

Nahuas soon adapted to these new circumstances. In Cuitlahuac, Nahuas secured a grant to lands on which they forbade the rearing of livestock, as though seeking to limit the intrusion of unwanted animals.[132] But Nahuas did not pass up opportunities to profit from their lands and establish their own livestock ranches.[133] And Xochimilco even established its own hacienda, named Teuhtli, which generated valuable community income through rentals to Spaniards. As with Spanish pressure for land, though, so Teuhtli embroiled the city in a dispute during 1697 with the neighboring village of Santiago Tolyahualco.[134]

At the end of the sixteenth century Spanish ranches began to appear closer to Nahua villages. Occasionally some were established on the

---

[128] Gibson, *The Aztecs under Spanish Rule*, 278.

[129] AGN, General de Parte, vol. 3, exp. 9, ff. 5v–6 (4v–5 old foliation).

[130] AGN, General de Parte, vol. 2, exp. 279, f. 59v (80v old foliation).

[131] AGN, General de Parte, vol. 2, exp. 795, f. 165 (186 old foliation). Other cases involved goats in Cuitlahuac, AGN, Indios, vol. 6, 1a pte., exp. 6, f. 2v, goats and sheep in San Pablo, a village in Xochimilco's jurisdiction, vol. 6, 2a pte., exp. 361, f. 81. See also AGN, Ordenanzas, vol. 4, exp. 142, ff. 142v–145.

[132] AGN, Mercedes, vol. 12, f. 209v, vol. 15, f. 87–87v. See also the 1654 case involving Cuitlahuac and a Spaniard named don Francisco Brito over the rights to lakeside land and the question of livestock, AGN, Tierras, vol. 1631, exp. 1, cuad. 2, ff. 1–114v, discussed in Brian P. Owensby, *Empire of Law and Indian Justice in Colonial Mexico* (Stanford: Stanford University Press, 2008), 112–117.

[133] AGN, Mercedes, vol. 21, exp. 520 and 521, ff. 114–115v. See also the grant of rights to a livestock ranch in support of the city's hospital, vol. 21, exp. 533, f. 118v. For Mixquic see AGN, Indios, vol. 4, exp. 621, ff. 178v–179 (168v–169 old foliation) as well as AGN, Mercedes, vol. 12, f. 199, vol. 15, ff. 33v–34, vol. 18, exp. 730, ff. 222v–223. For Ayotzingo, see AGN, vol. 17, exp. 6, ff. 2–2v.

[134] AGN, Tierras, vol. 1802, exp. 6, ff. 1–33v.

outskirts of Xochimilco itself. In 1590, Diego Angulo received the first of these grants, which consisted of two caballerías at the edge of Xochimilco's district of Tecpan. Three more had followed by the end of 1592.[135] The awards signaled a shift in which Spanish properties gradually encroached upon Nahua agricultural lands, although not the chinampas, in large part because they had fallen vacant. By the early seventeenth century, a ranch of two caballerías for goats or sheep had been established in Cuitlahuac. On one side, the land abutted houses belonging to the village of San Pedro; on the other, it stretched to the lake shore.[136] Previous regulations against ranches being located near settlements seem no longer to have been enforced and several other grants soon followed.[137] By 1610, the size of the grants awarded in Cuitlahuac had grown, too. Diego Castro received three caballerías of land while Alonso Guajardo received four, and Juan Fernández de la Concha received six caballerías, the equivalent of 630 acres.[138]

The pattern of Spanish intrusion into the lake areas was more pronounced in the province of Chalco, home to Cuitlahuac, than in Xochimilco. There, as early as 1579 Spanish recipients of land grants came into conflict with Nahua communities. Cristóbal Pérez de Bocanegra received lakeside land between Mixquic and Ayotzingo. The communities brought litigation and managed to overturn the grant.[139] During the course of the seventeenth century, land disputes increasingly pitted communities against prospective hacendados.[140] Between 1675 and 1716, for instance, two generations of hacendados, Cristóbal Ramírez de Escovar and don Juan Félix Ramírez, sought to expand their holdings in the town of Chalco Atenco. Nahuas appealed to the audiencia for assistance, arguing that the lands in question fell within the 600 vara rule – the nearest distance which haciendas could come to towns.[141] During the seventeenth century, Chalco's haciendas extended all the way to the lake.[142]

As these examples show, on the tierra firme, the acquisition of land by outsiders and the rise of ranches engendered conflicts with Nahua

---

[135] AGN, Mercedes, vol. 16, f. 1, vol. 17, f. 170, vol. 18, ff. 104v and 193v.
[136] AGN, Mercedes, vol. 23, f. 154v.
[137] AGN, Mercedes, vol. 23, f. 213, vol. 24, f. 75, vol. 25, f. 436v.
[138] AGN, Mercedes, vol. 28, ff. 81v, 145, and 161v.
[139] AGN, Tierras, vol. 67, exp. 2, ff. 35–53v.
[140] See AGN, Tierras, vol. 2687, exp. 6, ff. 99–102.
[141] AGN, Tierras, vol. 1477, exp. 1, ff. 1–12, 35–177v, vol. 2771, exp. 11, ff. 1v–62.
[142] See the reports of haciendas during the high court's inspection of maize production from 1708. AGI, Escribania, vol. 194c and AGI, Audiencia de México, leg. 781.

communities and individuals. Such tensions stood in marked contrast to the lack of cross-cultural controversies surrounding the ownership of chinampas. The conflicts became more acute in the context of eighteenth-century Nahua population recovery and Spanish pressure for land. As a result, having the titles that proved landownership became all the more important. In 1709, Santa María de la Asunción Milpa Alta purchased land titles through crown *composiciones* proceedings, designed to provide title in exchange for fees to the royal treasury.[143] Between 1746 and 1759, facing challenges to community lands from Tecomitl and Xochimilco, Milpa Alta further sought confirmation of its lands. The protracted dispute continued until 1800.[144]

If conflicts over land in the deep soil alluvium zone and further upland became more frequent they did not necessarily represent a wholesale takeover of Nahua holdings. Instead, many Native peoples succeeded in retaining their lands. The members of Xochimilco's ruling Cerón y Alvarado family provide a conspicuous example of this. Their estate records consisted of the records of litigation over properties on the tierra firme as well as titles and, more notably, long lists of their holdings. These Nahuatl documents, called *memorias* in Spanish, ran to many manuscript folios. They identified dozens and dozens of extensive tracts of land spread out across the jurisdiction.[145] Communities themselves also kept such memorias. One such list itemized dozens more parcels of land owned by San Pablo, presumably a community in the montes named Oztotepec.[146] A good many of the tracts of land were substantial and Nahuas retained them through the colonial period. Doña María Pascuala, for example, set down her Nahuatl testament in San Pedro Atocpan in 1766. Her holdings included several dozen parcels of land that she bequeathed to her four offspring and their spouses. While it was the largest of her bequests, the inheritance of her son Martín Joseph nevertheless conveys a sense of the extent of her holdings:

To my third child named Martín Josef I have given and donated a field at Tlatempampa of two yokes. Second, I have given him a field of half a yoke at

[143] AGN, Tierras, vol. 2834, exp. 3, ff. 1–9.
[144] As early as 1657, the town had sought to shore up its land claims through primordial titles which covered the community's history to 1521. AGN, Tierras, vol. 3032, 1a pte., exp. 3 and 4, ff. 152–241v. Other *títulos primordiales* for the region include those of San Andrés Mixquic (in the same tierras volume and expedient) and San Gregorio Atlapulco, see Pérez Zevallos and Reyes García, eds., *La fundación de San Luis Tlaxialtemalco*.
[145] AGN, Vínculos y Mayorazgos, vol. 279, exp. 1, ff. 62–63v, 89–90v, 111–112v, and 117–118v.
[146] AGN, Vínculos y Mayorazgos, vol. 279, exp. 1, ff. 119–120v.

Tlalmantitlan. Third, I donated to him a field at Matlahuacalocan that is just little. I have given him a fourth piece of land that is just little at Tepeyacac. Fifth, I have donated to him a field at Tepetlatzintlan of one yoke. Sixth, I have left him another piece of land at Xaxalpan of half a yoke. Seventh I have given him a field at Hueicalpoltitlan of one yoke, and my son Martín on his own authority sold it to my son-in-law don Manuel, who gave him 9 pesos and 4 reales.[147]

Beyond the number of holdings, three characteristics of her bequests stand out. The first is that since her son had already sold one of the plots of land, she had apparently given away her land before setting down the testament; in other words, the testament confirmed what she had already in effect done. (The use of the past tense in the Nahuatl phrasing further suggests this). The second is the survival of Nahuatl names for the places where indigenous peoples had lands, which speaks further to the resilience of Nahua landholdings. The third is the use of the Spanish term *yunta*, or *yonta*, meaning "yoke," as a loanword and as a unit of measurement in place of quahuitl, nehuitzan, or the more common *mecatl*.[148] No direct evidence shows that this unit of measurement was ever used for chinampas, and while it was never defined in the sources, presumably these "yokes" suggest that the tracts of land were sizable: the unit was derived from the amount of a land a yoke of oxen could typically plow in a day.[149]

Such sizable holdings are unsurprising for a member of the Nahua nobility. Commoners also had significant property, though. Some of these lands were in prime agricultural locations, as with those of Pascuala de la Concepción. Some of her property was on the shore of the lake.[150] In 1689, another Nahua woman, María Ana, listed more than a dozen parcels of cultivated land in Santa Ana, up in the hills near Milpa Alta.[151] Similarly, in 1702, María Sebastiana bequeathed more than a dozen plots of land in Xochimilco. They were identified according to indigenous place names, and they were apparently located in the deep soil alluvium: her lands faced the lake to the north and the hills to the south.[152] A decade later Miguel Vicente

---

[147] AGN, Tierras, vol. 2429, exp. 3, ff. 14–15.

[148] AGN, TSJDF, Corregidores, Caja 31B, exp. 62, f. 7.

[149] For other examples of the use of the term *yonta*, see the testaments of Salvador Ylario from Atlapulco in 1788–1789. AGN, Tierras, vol. 2327, exp. 1, ff. 14–14v,15v, and 18–19 and Pascuala de la Concepción, also of Atlapulco, in 1786, AGN, TSJDF, Corregidores, caja 32A, exp. 29, ff. 3–3v and 5–5v.

[150] The Nahuatl expression identifying the location was *antentli*, a combination of *atl* for "water" and *tentli* for "lips" or, in this case, the edge or shore of the lake. AGN, TSJDF, Corregidores, caja 32A, exp. 29, ff. 3–3v and 5–5v.

[151] AGN, Tierras, vol. 1832, exp. 1, ff. 22–23.

[152] AGN, Tierras, vol. 1179, exp. 1, ff. 3–3v.

passed on enough land in San Pablo Oztotepec for his testament to cover
two and a half manuscript folios.[153] While many of the landholdings
consisted of *tlalmilli*, which is to say cultivated fields, others were specifically for raising livestock.[154] Diego López, for instance, bequeathed a corral
to his wife in Santa María de la Asunción Milpa Atzumpa.[155] María
Catalina of Tecomitl likewise passed on a corral to her heirs, and
Francisca María's corral was identified by the Nahuatl term
tecpancalli.[156] Other parcels of land were also on marginal lands, as with
some of those of don Marcos Antonio, from Tepepan, who had land near
the mouth of a cave and on a rocky outcrop, where he owned maguey
plants.[157] Besides having different kinds of land, with varying degrees of
value, so those individuals living in the montes had dispersed holdings,
much as those who owned chinampas did. Vicente de San Francisco, of San
Pablo Oztotepec, held lands in several different communities.[158]

The dispersed and diverse properties owned by nobles and commoners
alike speak to the endurance of Nahua landholdings on the tierra firme, as
in the lakes, through the colonial period. In other words, Nahuas
remained significant landholders. A significant proportion of the population thus retained some measure of autonomy and subsistence, and while
none of them was identified individually as an hacendado, some of their
estates were nonetheless extensive.

In Xochimilco, the numerous royal land grants did not translate into
a correspondingly large number of haciendas. Instead, haciendas remained
surprisingly few and far between. By the eighteenth century, only six
ranchos and five haciendas were in operation (and one of those belonged
to Nahuas). By contrast, there were more than thirty haciendas in
Chalco.[159] Haciendas in Xochimilco do not appear to have been large
enterprises. Only the nine residents of the hacienda La Noria appeared in
the 1792 census; the other estates presumably remained sufficiently small –
or with absentee owners – that they did not warrant inclusion.[160] We lack

[153] AGN, TSJDF, Corregidores, caja 31B, exp. 81, ff. 1–2.
[154] See the testament of Matías Miguel, AGN, Tierras, vol. 1179, exp. 1, ff. 6–6v.
[155] AGN, Tierras, vol. 1750, exp. 1, ff. 37–37v.
[156] AGN, Tierras, vol. 2326, exp. 10, ff. 5–5v; AGN, TSJDF, Corregidores, caja 31B, exp. 63, f. 3.
[157] AGN, Tierras, vol. 2669, exp. 7, f. 8.
[158] AGN, TSJDF, Corregidores, caja 31A, exp. 9, ff. 3–3v. For another example of dispersed
    holdings in the montes across different communities, see AGN, TSJDF, Alcalde del
    Crimen, caja 2B, exp. 43, ff. 5–6.
[159] AGN, Padrones, vol. 29, ff. 5–5v; Pérez Zevallos, *Xochimilco Ayer*, vol. 2, 50; Gibson,
    The Aztecs under Spanish Rule, 327.
[160] AGN, Padrones, vol. 29, f. 3v.

details of the foundation of these estates, presumably because of a lack of documentation from relatively few land disputes with Nahua communities. The earliest mention of haciendas in Xochimilco dates to 1626 with Santa Bárbara Coapa.[161] Hacienda La Noria began appearing in documentation as the property of don Francisco Velázquez de Robledo from the 1640s.[162] Other properties date to the second half of the seventeenth century, as with those of don José Olmedo y Lujan, which included the haciendas of San Juan de Dios, San Cristóbal, and San Juan Bautista, along with the rancho of San Buenaventura.[163] To judge from a lack of litigation, the rise of these estates does not appear to have been especially controversial. Several were located, like the earlier land grants, in the montes. Three others – La Noria, San Juan de Dios, and Santa Fé de las Ahuehuetes – were located in the vicinity of the lakes, although they occupied lands between, and at a slight remove from, Nahua villages.[164]

The limited impact of haciendas may have reflected the modest profits they generated. Juan de Aguilar's 1567 grant to land in poor country included the observation that Nahuas had only used the area for hunting. Similarly, in 1594 doña Marina de Mendoza and doña Catalina de Saldivar, nieces of the conquistador Captain Luis Marín, received rights to establish a livestock ranch on rocky ground (*pedregal*) located in "mal pays."[165] A grant issued to García de Canarias was likewise located among the many others in the vicinity of the royal road going to Cuernavaca. His new property, situated next to the lands of Martín Abarrucia, lay on the slopes of a mountain.[166]

The marginal quality of lands in the montes explains both their use for raising livestock and frequent transfers in ownership.[167] This seems to have been the case when Isabel García and the community of Santa Ana Tlatenco came into conflict in 1695 over the limits of her hacienda. The García family had owned the hacienda for many years – more than thirty, according to one witness – and Isabel assumed possession through inheritance from her

[161] AGN, Tierras, vol. 720, ff. 57–163v; Pérez Zevallos, *Xochimilco Ayer*, vol. 2, 49.
[162] AGN, Reales Cédulas Duplicadas, vol. 18, exp. 184, f. 131v; AGN, Criminal, vol. 138, exp. 10, f. 141.
[163] AGN, Tierras, vol. 3322, exp. 3 and 4, vol. 3208, exp. 1, ff. 1–675; AGNM, Xochimilco, vol. 1, ff. 266–266v.
[164] AGN, Censos, vol. 7, exp. 10, ff. 42–47.
[165] AGN, Mercedes, vol. 19, exp. 830, ff. 263–263v (with 263–263v listed in the foliation in red ink).
[166] AGN, Mercedes, vol. 9, ff. 194–194v.
[167] The hacienda named La Noria changed hands at least twice during the seventeenth century; see Chapters 5 and 6.

father. Relations between the family and the nearby village of Santa Ana do not appear to have been especially acrimonious during that time. But a few years prior to the lawsuit Isabel chose to rent part of the property to a fellow Spaniard named Miguel Betancurt (the individual mentioned above, who purchased chinampas). Some of the land appears to have been marginal at best, as shown not just by the decision to rent it, but also because the land was only used to raise a few livestock and obtain wood. Nevertheless, villagers protested the rental, arguing that it involved lands that did not belong to Isabel García. She in turn argued, unsuccessfully, that the villagers were encroaching upon her land.[168] The matter did not end there. After the lawsuit, Isabel bequeathed the hacienda to her son, Juan de Uriarte, who in turn sold some of its land to another Spaniard, Francisco de Zevallos. When the purchaser sought confirmation of title in 1708, the village of Santa Ana protested, this time with Nahuas from nearby Mixquic. Once again the Nahuas successfully defended their rights.[169]

The controversy between Santa Ana and Isabel García stemmed, in part, from questions about the rights of access to forest resources. These became common sources of controversy, not least because they often pitted communal rights of access against haciendas and ranchos. These conflicts also had explicit environmental dimensions, as shown in litigation from 1701. The Nahua governor of Xochimilco, don Hipólito de Alvarado, took a creative approach to the problem posed by the owners of an hacienda in the montes and on the outskirts of San Miguel Topilejo. He did so by provoking a lawsuit, albeit by doing so cleverly – and indirectly. What happened was that don Ramon Espiguel, one of the owners of Xoco, the estate, complained of trespassing by Nahuas on his hacienda's lands. Nahua woodsmen, including a wood splitter, had been caught cutting down trees on his property. They had been taking the wood, he argued, at the behest of don Hipólito, who opposed the don Ramon's plans to cut down the trunks of pine trees (specifically *ocotl* trees, the ones that were commonly used as torches). In this case the *ocotales* were going to be used to make charcoal, and don Hipólito vehemently opposed this plan because the entire removal of the trees would cause irreparable damage to the landscape. After the hacendado reported the incursion of the Nahuas, an initial investigation revealed that the trespassers in question had been paid by don Hipólito out of his own pocket to cut the wood. Don Hipólitio had then arranged for it to be delivered by canoe to the capital, as per the city's

---

[168] AGN, Tierras, vol. 1485, exp. 2, ff. 1–181v.
[169] AGN, Tierras, vol. 1485, exp. 3, ff. 182ff.

draft labor obligations. Don Hipólito's ruse seems to have succeeded: requested by the court to explain himself, the former governor explained that the land in question formed part of the commons of Topilejo and was not part of the hacienda property; the audiencia investigated and agreed, ruling in his favor.[170]

The marginal sources of revenue from upland areas and the frequent transfers of title suggest the limited profitability of haciendas.[171] During the seventeenth century, the Velázquez de Robledo family owned two haciendas in Xochimilco, La Noria and San Antonio Cuateclan, the latter having been located in the hills. By the turn of the eighteenth century, the family rented out both haciendas. The 1694 rental agreement by don Felipe Velázquez for his hacienda of San Antonio Cuateclan exposes its lack of profitability: the contract covered the hacienda property, house and land, as well as its forty steers and two mules, for the modest sum of 200 pesos per year.[172] The family likewise put La Noria up for rent in 1703.[173] Members of the Velázquez family also owned haciendas in Chalco and, from the 1710s, began to appear in notarial records as residents of Tlalmanalco, suggesting a shift in their priorities away from Xochimilco.[174] By the second half of the eighteenth century, a Mexico City merchant, don Juan García Trujillo, had come into possession of La Noria and a generation later, in 1785, the hacienda had been sold once again. Across the span of eighty years, then, La Noria had passed through the hands of at least three different families.[175] By 1792, the hacienda San Antonio Cuateclan had disappeared from a survey of Xochimilco's estates.[176]

CONCLUSION

The aquatic landscape of Xochimilco served as a kind of buffer against colonial intrusion, in part, because of its distinctive and abundant system

[170] AGN, Tierras, vol. 1769, exp. 4, ff. 1–12; for more papers of this litigation, see AGN, TSJDF, Corregidores, caja 32B, exp. 51.
[171] On this subject, see Van Young, *Hacienda and Market*, 114–138.
[172] AGNM, Xochimilco, vol. 1, ff. 31–32v.
[173] AGNM, Xochimilco, vol. 1, ff. 123v–124v.
[174] The Latin American Library (hereafter LAL), Tulane University, New Orleans, Viceregal and Ecclesiastical Mexican Collection (VEMC), leg. 46, exp. 8 (folder 1 of 2), no foliation (the document is a testament dated 1722), leg. 65, exp. 11, ff. 63v–65v, AGI, Audiencia de México, leg. 781, ff. 65, 66–66v.
[175] AGN, Tierras, vol. 2429, exp. 1, cuad. 1, f. 16, vol. 1119; Pérez Zevallos, *Xochimilco Ayer*, vol. 2, 48.
[176] AGN, Padrones, vol. 29, f. 3v.

of wetland agriculture. Spaniards and other non-Native peoples seldom engaged in chinampa cultivation. Instead, as Gibson noted, it remained a Nahua specialty. The intrinsic qualities of the chinampas themselves provide some clues about why this happened. Spaniards were at times reluctant to harness lake resources, including chinampas. Part of their reluctance stemmed from the very complexity of making and maintaining chinampas. The gardens' construction was painstaking, requiring a considerable investment of time and effort. Bountiful harvests also relied on specific skills, from the use of irrigation, mulching, and mucking to knowledge of fertilizers and familiarity with raising seedlings on separate nurseries. Because the fertile, well-irrigated chinampas were under almost constant cultivation – with the plots seldom being left fallow – abundant harvests depended upon farmers' knowledge of the proper cycles of planting.

Several other reasons explain the Spaniards' absence from chinampa agriculture. Nahuas ardently defended their lands, often doing so collectively and through the courts. As part of the common discourse surrounding vassalage – in which the king received tribute and labor in exchange for offering protections to Native Americans – the Nahuas in the lake areas used the sheer abundance of their harvests and their tribute payments as leverage in trying to defend their lands. The complexity of land tenure may have served as a further obstacle against Spanish land alienation. Communal holdings, as valued corporate assets, proved durable in the face of outside pressure, and the scattered pattern of landownership may have further hindered Spaniards in obtaining Nahua lands. Nahuas rarely owned plots of land that were grouped together in contiguous plots. Instead their lands were interspersed among each other's holdings. The distribution of ownership in a given location thus had a mosaic-like quality. The multiple forms of land tenure, and the scattered pattern of ownership, would have made it difficult for Spaniards to consolidate chinampas into the kinds of large, landed estates they favored. While any one of these factors may not have precluded Spanish interest, taken together they would have amounted to a formidable barrier against Spanish intrusion.

Moreover, chinampas did not suit the preferences of Spanish settlers, which tended toward the kinds of extensive farming associated with wheat cultivation and pastoralism. Spaniards engaged in precisely these kinds of agriculture, albeit away from the lakes. In the upland, piedmont areas, Spanish landholding was more conspicuous. Spanish policy under the first viceroy, don Antonio de Mendoza – concerned as it was about maintaining indigenous land holdings in order to secure tribute income and food for Mexico City – set a precedent for Spaniards establishing their rural estates in the outskirts of the jurisdiction. Marginal lands in the montes proved less valuable for horticulture and so Spaniards instead turned to raising livestock. While livestock estates began to disturb Nahua agriculture during the latter half of the sixteenth century, hacienda formation remained limited and only moderately profitable. Accordingly, in Xochimilco a distinct historical geography of landownership and use came into being. The lake areas remained the preserve of Nahuas; outsiders typically established ranches in the less densely populated outskirts of the jurisdiction. The environment, then, played a key role in influencing post-conquest patterns of landownership and the ongoing ecological autonomy of the lake districts. Just as the wetland environment was essential to chinampa agriculture, so the lacustrine landscape had a profound influence on cross-cultural exchanges when it came to water-borne commerce.

3

Canoes and Commerce

Much as the lakes and chinampas remained the realm of the Nahuas while Spaniards established their estates in the montes, so some of that same distinct historical geography applied to the transportation network. At the same time, that canoes, passing through canals, remained the preserve of Nahuas, so those who circumnavigated the lakes on overland routes reflected the wider ethnic complexity of the emerging colonial society. As with chinampas and haciendas, transportation and trade thus reflected two differentials of socioeconomic relations: the distinction between lake and upland areas was less pronounced in this case, though, than it was with land. Nahuas, who for centuries had traversed the terrain on foot as *tamemes*, or carriers, readily adopted beasts of burden, as did the famous long-distance merchants of old, the *pochteca*. Non-Native peoples, in turn, quickly turned to water-borne transportation routes for the benefits they afforded. But local knowledge, expertise with the waterways, and other factors provided a strategic advantage for Nahuas, making the lakes a particular kind of contact zone for colonial encounters, one that complicated relations of power between different historical actors.

The southern lakes served as a vital transportation and trading hub. The lakes proved important for distributing and exchanging goods, and not just producing them. As an effective and relatively inexpensive way of transporting goods in bulk, Nahuas long relied on canoes for a wide range of enterprises: lake-borne transportation provided employment for local residents; the manufacture of canoes was one of Xochimilco's main craft industries; farmers used canoes to make and cultivate their chinampas and deliver their crops to regional markets, and artisans and merchants reached their customers by canoe. The lakes facilitated the commercial integration of the region. Alongside the abundance afforded by chinampa cultivation, canoes underwrote the lake area's economic prosperity.[1] The Spanish monarchy came to appreciate the benefits of the water-borne transportation system. In 1575, agents of King Philip II sought to escheat the encomienda of Mixquic to the crown. To justifying the jurisdictional change, the government official was explicit in identifying the public interest: it was important precisely because of its location along the main canal leading to the capital.[2]

In the wider commercial scheme, the roads came to complement the water routes, the two catering to different needs but also, ultimately, integrating the southern lakes into a wider sphere of economic activity, one that made the markets of Mexico City, and beyond, readily accessible. Efficient transportation and lively commerce made it possible for a good many of Xochimilco's artisans to keep working, and Xochimilco stood out in the eighteenth century for still having a majority of its population employed in specialist trades. Environmental adaptations thus not only made canoe transportation viable for duration of colonial period but it also created a particular kind of aquatic space where commerce thrived and artisans preserved their specializations.

The benefits of water-borne transportation extended beyond the indigenous sector of the economy. Canoes helped supply Mexico City with essential goods and, as such, they were drawn into service for the viceregal political economy, transporting surprisingly hefty loads of freight.[3] The owners of haciendas also appreciated the benefits of canoes. They established *embarcaderos*, or wharves and dock facilities, on the shores of the lakes, and they hired rowers to deliver maize to Mexico City's main storehouse and granary. Canoes proved vital to the provisioning of the capital. Because of their value, canoes came to occupy a strategic place in the broader colonial enterprise. The rowers of canoes assumed a key, intermediary position in the transportation network. And as with merchants, so canoeists came into frequent and sustained contact with people of different ethnicities; they were thus at the forefront of cross-cultural encounters even as they retained control of water-borne transport. Nahuas deployed their control of canoes as a bargaining counter in negotiations with provincial and Spanish authorities, and were able, at

---

[1] On the integrating influence of bodies of water, see Fernand Braudel, *The Mediterranean and the Mediterranean World in the Age of Philip II*, 2 vols., trans. Sian Reynolds (New York: Harper and Row, 1966).
[2] AGI, Justicia, leg. 219, no. 1, ramo 2, f. 150.   [3] AGN, Indios, vol. 23, exp. 189, f. 180.

times, to wring concessions from them. The history of canoes, then, can tell us much about the role of the environment in the regional economy, cross-cultural encounters and exchanges, relations between Nahuas and colonial institutions, and the ability of Nahuas to advance their interests and preserve the relative economic prosperity that underpinned lakeside societies.

A NAVIGABLE LANDSCAPE

As a technological innovation, the canoe – or *acalli* in Nahuatl, literally "water-house" – was ideally suited to the large, interconnected lakes of the Basin of Mexico. From far into the pre-contact past and well into the twentieth century, canoes were unsurpassed as a swift and efficient form of transportation. The lasting significance of canoes was not simply because of an unchanging and abundant, watery environment – although the sufficiently high water levels of the southern lakes were, of course, essential to the canoes' success. Rather, canoes represented the complex interplay between human and environmental adaptations. Canoes were an essential part of what made it possible for people to modify the aquatic environment; the making and cultivation of chinampas; the creation of hydraulic compartments in which the chinampas could be constructed, and the building of embankments and dikes – all these and more depended on the use of canoes. This reliance on canoes extended to alterations of the lakes for purposes of transportation: since the lakes were often shallow – especially in the dry season – local residents had to dredge channels through which the canoes could pass. Nahuas also had to adapt features of the water management system, such as causeways and sluicegates, to allow for the passage of the canoes. At the same time, then, that canoes enabled people to alter the landscape so canoe transportation was made possible by those very same environmental modifications. Canoes were an adaptation to life in an aquatic setting; they were a means for making the landscape navigable.

Since the southern lakes were spared from the worst of the desagüe, canoe transportation long remained viable. The same could not be said for the northern lakes. As water slowly flowed out of the drainage ditch at Huehuetoca, Lakes Xaltocan and Zumpango gradually dried up. Lake Tetzcoco became increasingly shallow, and certain parts of it, at certain times of the year, might dry up altogether, making it ever more difficult for canoe transportation. With desiccation came a decline in canoe traffic. Attempts were made in the eighteenth century to dig a channel across Lake

Tetzcoco and to Mexico City, but the project was met with little success.[4] According to one observer, the once grand altepetl and city of Tetzcoco had ceased to be populous and affluent by the mid-eighteenth century because of a decline in commerce.[5] Eventually it all but disappeared.[6] By contrast, the southern lake areas retained their water levels and, with them, much of their prosperity.[7] If anything, communities there faced the opposite problem. At times of heavy rainfall, lakeside communities faced the prospect of flooding.[8] Even in the dry season Lakes Xochimilco and Chalco received enough water from springs as to support canoe transportation.[9]

In a hypothetically unchanged and natural state, Lakes Xochimilco and Chalco, while being abundantly supplied with water, would not necessarily have been perfectly suitable for canoe transportation. For one thing, the lakes could be quite shallow in places. For another, they could get clogged with vegetation, especially reeds known as tule. As a result, Nahuas fashioned various kinds of channel from the shallow waters. The smallest of these were the narrow ditches surrounding chinampas – as we have seen, the construction of chinampas involved scooping soil out of the lake and piling it onto the raised gardens; it was this process that produced the ditches. Around the clusters of chinampas were slightly wider and deeper passages, which could accommodate more canoes. And then there were the main boat routes, called *acalotli*, through which the most of the canoe traffic flowed. These avenues were of an impressive size. They had to be dredged to quite a significant depth, again with the removed soil being set aside to make chinampas elsewhere.[10] Typically, they were also fairly wide, usually measuring six, eight or fifteen varas across – in other words, between fifteen and forty feet. Their width meant that several canoes move alongside one another at once.[11] These channels are shown in several

---

[4] Gibson, *The Aztecs under Spanish Rule*, 362.

[5] Villaseñor y Sánchez, *Theatro Americano*, 155.

[6] Gibson, *The Aztecs under Spanish Rule*, 365.

[7] Fernando de Cepeda, *Relacion vniversal legitima, y verdadera del sitio en qve esta fvndada la muy noble, insigne, y muy leal ciudad de México, cabeça de las provincias de toda la Nueva España* (Mexico City: Imprenta de Francisco Salbago, 1637), 33–34.

[8] AGN, Indios, vol. 2, exp. 417, ff. 99–99v; AGN, Indios, exp. 584, ff. 134v–135; AGN, Indios, exp. 592, f. 137.

[9] Hernando Ojea, *Libro tercero de la Historia religiosa de la prouincia de México de la Orden de Sto. Domingo* (Mexico City: Museo Nacional de México, 1897), 2; Gibson, *The Aztecs under Spanish Rule*, 362.

[10] Alzate y Ramírez, "Memoria Sobre Agricultura," in *Gacetas de literatura*, vol. 2, 384.

[11] Ojea, *Libro tercero*, 2; Gibson, *The Aztecs under Spanish Rule*, 364.

Nahua maps and other pictorial documents. Maps from Cuitlahuac (see Maps 3.1 and 0.3) show the watercourses surrounding clusters of chinampas and zigzagging across the lake.[12] These routes became such an integral part of life in the region the term *acalote* was widely adopted by Spanish speakers as a loanword.[13]

Since these main waterways were also many miles long, they amounted to substantial feats of engineering. One of the major routes linked Chalco Atenco and Ayotzingo with Tlahuac before turning north toward Culhuacan. Its approximate length was fifteen miles. Another route extended from Xochimilco to the capital. As they funneled through the entrance to Lake Tetzcoco the channels joined the *acequia real*, or royal canal (also known as the *acalote real*), whence canoe traffic flowed into the heart of Mexico City.[14] The distance between Xochimilco and downtown Mexico City was some twelve miles.[15] As the canoes traveled along these routes they had to pass through a couple of sluicegates. The first formed part of the embankment and raised road (*calzada*) which bisected Lakes Xochimilco and Chalco and which connected Cuitlahuac to the northern and southern shores. The other sluicegate, or *compuerta*, was built into the flood defenses at Mexicalzingo, which restricted the amount of water flowing from the south and into Lake Tetzcoco.[16] Even though it was a fairly narrow bottleneck, as many as four channels passed next to Mexicalzingo.[17] Ideally, the channels were of a sufficient size not only to allow canoes to pass through them but also to keep the current of water flowing from the higher elevation of the southern lakes – except, ominously, when the capital was threatened by flooding.

The shallow waterways catered to all sizes of canoes, although smaller ones, which displaced less water, could be far more intrepid in their navigation around the chinampas. For the largest canoes, carrying bulky freight destined for Mexico City, the routes had to be cleared of debris and vegetation, usually reeds, to remain navigable. In 1635, vegetation had grown so thick that it slowed down traffic considerably: a single day's journey became an interminable four or five days.[18] Seasonal fluctuations in rainfall also affected accessibility. When passage became obstructed,

---

[12] AGN, Tierras, vol. 2681, exp. 6, f. 2l; AGN, Tierras, vol. 1631, cuad. 1, exp. 11, f. 96.
[13] AGN, Tierras, vol. 2429, exp. 1, f. 11v; AGN, Desagüe, vol. 43, exp. 5, f. 7.
[14] AGN, Desagüe, vol. 16, exp. 7, f. 35.
[15] These distances are calculated with the use of Google Maps.
[16] Fray Andrés de San Miguel, "Relación al Padre General," in Rojas Rabiela et al., *Nuevas noticias sobre las obras hidráulicas prehispánicas*, 48–49.
[17] Ojea, *Libro tercero*, 2.   [18] Gibson, *The Aztecs under Spanish Rule*, 364.

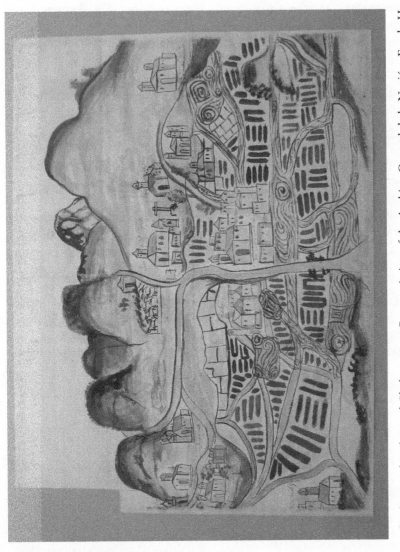

MAP 3.1 Map of Lakes Xochimilco and Chalco, 1653. By permission of the Archivo General de la Nación, Fondo Hermanos Mayo (Mapa 1155), Tierras vol. 1631, exp. 1, cuad. 11, f. 96.

Spanish authorities apportioned the task of clearing canals to Nahuas as part of their draft labor (*repartimiento*) duties.[19] Local officials also kept an eye on the condition of the waterways. In 1590, the town council of Tlahuac requested permission from the viceroy to open the channel to ease the passage of canoes through it. With its situation as an island, the unobstructed passage of canoes would have been essential to Cuitlahuac's sustenance, and the town councilmen explained that permission had been granted seventeen years earlier to widen the same channel.[20]

The investment of resources in the making and the maintenance of the canoe routes was invaluable to the transportation of goods and people. In central Mexico, as everywhere before the industrial revolution, moving goods by water was far more efficient than overland transportation.[21] The dynamics of momentum, friction, and inertia meant that ships, boats, and canoes faced less resistance to motion than did their overland counterparts. Those with no choice but to transport goods with carts, wagons, pack animals, or on their backs – as with the tamemes – faced more arduous journeys than canoeists. Canoes, mules, and tamemes traveled at a similar speed, but water-borne vessels could carry greater loads.[22] Canoes would also have been preferable given that ground transportation was ever more time consuming and expensive as distances increased and terrain became rugged and hilly.[23] For sixteenth-century Mexico, Ross Hassig calculated that while a porter could carry a twenty-four-kilogram load, a single canoeist could easily pole 920 kilograms at the same speed. Viewed from another angle, water-borne transport cost a tiny fraction of its overland equivalent.[24] Direct comparisons between the costs involved in moving freight by tamemes, mules, carts, and canoes are difficult to make.[25] Using figures supplied by the naturalist Alexander von Humboldt

[19] AGN, Indios, vol. 30, exp. 278, ff. 255v–256; Gibson, *The Aztecs under Spanish Rule*, 364.

[20] Newberry Library, Ayer Collection, ms. 1476, F IV.

[21] David R. Ringrose, "Transportation and Economic Stagnation in Eighteenth-Century Castile," *Journal of Economic History*, vol. 28, no. 1 (1968), 51–79.

[22] Ross Hassig calculated that in making journeys of a similar distance at the same speed, canoes could transport much more freight, and they therefore had an efficiency ratio of forty to one over porters. Hassig, *Trade, Tribute, and Transportation*, 133.

[23] Scott, *The Art of Not Being Governed*, 44–48.

[24] Ross Hassig, *Mexico and the Spanish Conquest* (London: Longman, 1994), 123–124.

[25] Coherent and comprehensive sets of quantitative data about transportation expenses do not exist. Figures from the 1560s indicate that canoe journeys cost between 0.21 and 0.83 *reales* per ton-league (a real was an eighth of a peso). But there are no comparable figures from this time period for tamemes or mules. Moreover, data sets are often too widely separated across time to make comparisons meaningful, as Ross Hassig noted. Also, the

for the early nineteenth century, Hassig calculated that the freight costs of canoes amounted to only 8.4 percent of those for mules. Similarly, a report from 1785 indicated that sixty or seventy canoes could replace 1,500 pack animals in transporting comparable amounts of maize or wheat.[26]

Canoes, then, were the most viable and affordable way of moving goods and people around the region and to Mexico City.[27] Environmental factors also favored the passage of canoes toward the capital. Lakes Xochimilco and Chalco lay at a higher level than Lake Tetzcoco, which meant that the rowers of canoes benefited from the assistance of the current. This flow of water made it easier to move canoes laden with cargo toward Mexico City. The journey from Ayoztinco to the capital took between six and eight hours when conditions were favorable.[28] Having delivered their goods, the lighter, return journey was less arduous for canoeists who propelled their craft by oars, paddles, and poles.[29] Many of these journeys took place at night. As historians have noted, nocturnal journeys avoided the heat of the day, better preserving perishable goods.[30] If they made daytime journeys, the rowers could unfurl canopies or awnings over their canoes to provide shade for

extant records seldom if ever provide all the relevant details of distances and cargo loads. Added to these concerns are other factors such as fluctuations in the value of money, especially in real terms. Moreover, the price of grain could affect the cost of using mules, as Clara Elena Suárez Argüello demonstrated. She calculated the costs of freight transportation by mule trains in 1800. She found that a ton-kilometer journey cost 11.85 *granos*, which was just less than a real (12 granos equaled a real). But it would be imprudent to compare this figure with the rate charged by canoers in the 1560s, not only because of the enormous gulf in time between the two sets of data but also because the measurement of a league could be imprecise, thereby frustrating conversion into kilometers. Hassig, *Trade, Tribute, and Transportation*, 216; Clara Elena Suárez Argüello, *Camino real y carrera larga: La arriería en la Nueva España durante el siglo XVIII* (Mexico City: El Centro de Investigaciones y Estudios Superiores en Antropología Social, 1997), 179; see also Roland Chardon, "The Elusive Spanish League: A Problem of Measurement in Sixteenth-Century New Spain," *Hispanic American Historical Review*, vol. 60, no. 2 (1980), 294–302.

[26] Canoe transportation cost 0.014 pence per pound as against 0.109 pence per pound for mules. Hassig, *Trade, Tribute, and Transportation*, 216–217.

[27] Canoes had the further advantage for the Aztec Empire of extending Tenochtitlan's reach into the hinterland: effectively, the friction of distance began only on the far side of the lakes and not at the island's edge. Hassig, *Mexico and the Spanish Conquest*, 123–124, and *Trade, Tribute, and Transportation*, 64–66.

[28] Gibson, *The Aztecs under Spanish Rule*, 364.

[29] Hassig, *Trade, Tribute, and Transportation*, 61.

[30] Gibson, *The Aztecs under Spanish Rule*, 362; Hassig, *Trade, Tribute, and Transportation*, 64; Chimalpahin, *Annals of His Time*, 96.

their produce.[31] But night-time trips were more convenient because they made it possible for crops, which had been harvested one day in Xochimilco's chinampa districts, to be delivered to Mexico City's markets in time for the next day's sunrise.[32]

The continued significance of canoes for the regional economy stemmed from their capacity to transport items in bulk. Nahuas fashioned the canoes from single trees that had been hollowed out. In the early colonial period, Nahuas preferred making canoes from spruce or hemlock trees, or *huiya-metl*, and their dimensions were constrained only by the size of the available trunks. Although the canoes were long, thin, and shallow – they had a broad stern, became narrower toward the bow, and both ends usually curved upward slightly – they were nevertheless capable of carrying substantial loads of cargo and numerous passengers.[33] When the last Aztec Emperor, Quauhtemoc (r. 1520–1521), fled from the ruins of Tenochtitlan, his canoe was sufficiently large as to have twenty oarsmen on board.[34] The greatest canoes, as Gibson and Hassig have noted, were typically fifty feet in length. These were big enough to transport such hefty freight as lumber and stone. They could carry three to three and a half tons of goods or as many as sixty passengers. Some sources mention massive, 100-foot-long canoes.[35] Smaller ones, by contrast, were usually fourteen feet long. Steered by a single rower, these vessels could still deliver more than a ton of maize to the capital per journey.[36] They became the preferred means of conveying maize for the owners of Spanish estates. During the eighteenth century, the smaller canoes, each capable of transporting thirty-five *cargas* (a load of usually two bushels), delivered maize to Mexico City's granary and storehouse.[37]

The very utility of canoes assured their use in great numbers. Spanish conquistadors had marveled at the sight of lakes crowded with canoes.[38] Reliable figures for the number of canoes at the time of the Spanish conquest

---

[31] AGN, Archivo Histórico de Hacienda, Temporalidades, leg. 106, exp. 7, f. 4.

[32] Gibson, *The Aztecs under Spanish Rule*, 364.

[33] C. Harvey Gardiner, *Naval Power in the Conquest of Mexico* (Austin: University of Texas Press, 1956), 55–56.

[34] Don Domingo de San Antón Muñón Chimalpahin Quauhtlehuanitzin, *Chimalpahin's Conquest: A Nahua Historian's Rewriting of Francisco López de Gómara's La conquista de México*, ed. and trans. Susan Schroeder, Anne J. Cruz, Cristián Roa-de-la-Carrera, and David E. Tavárez (Stanford: Stanford University Press, 2010), 333.

[35] Hassig, *Trade, Tribute, and Transportation*, 294n64; Gibson, *The Aztecs under Spanish Rule*, 362.

[36] Hassig, *Trade, Tribute, and Transportation*, 62.

[37] AGI, Audiencia de México, leg. 781, ff. 104, 222–223.

[38] Díaz del Castillo, *The Discovery and Conquest of Mexico*, 192.

are hard to come by, but since the Basin of Mexico was home to hundreds of thousands of people, there could have been tens of thousands of canoes on the lakes.[39] Early chroniclers suggested as much. Francisco Cervantes de Salazar put the number of canoes at more than 100,000.[40] Francisco López de Gómara, Cortés's secretary and biographer, offered an estimate of 200,000 canoes.[41] With demographic collapse the number of canoes declined correspondingly. In 1580, between 3,000 and 4,000 canoes a day passed Mexicalzingo on the way to the capital.[42] Seventeenth-century records show 1,000 canoes arriving in Mexico City every day.[43] In spite of reduced traffic, though, canoes remained a common sight well into the eighteenth century. In 1710, nearly 3,500 canoes transporting maize, which represented but a fraction of the total number of journeys, traveled between Chalco's haciendas and Mexico City.[44] And as late as 1777, more than 26,000 canoes still passed through the lakes each year.[45] The diminution in canoe traffic does not necessarily indicate that canoes ceased to be a practical means of transportation. Rather, other factors, from the desiccation of the northern lakes to the decline of the indigenous population, were involved.[46]

Canoes hardly became obsolete. Horses, mules, and carts did not entirely replace them even though Nahuas readily adopted these alternative means of transportation.[47] Constantino de San Felipe, for instance, whose Nahuatl last will and testament from 1572 provoked a legal dispute between his mother and widow, had been a successful merchant. Among his many belongings was a horse valued at ten pesos.[48] Nor did foreign

---

[39] Shawn William Miller, *An Environmental History of Latin America* (New York: Cambridge University Press, 2007), 10–11; Mundy, *The Death of Aztec Tenochtitlan*, 1; Susan Toby Evans, *Ancient Mexico and Central America* (New York: Thames and Hudson, 2013), 549.

[40] Cervantes de Salazar, *Crónica de la Nueva España*, vol. 1, 326.

[41] Francisco López de Gómara, *Historia de la conquista de México* (Mexico City: Editorial Pedro Robredo, 1943), vol. 1, 235; Gardiner, *Naval Power*, 54. See also Gibson, *The Aztecs under Spanish Rule*, 364. The Nahua historian Chimalpahin, who revised López de Gómara's account of the conquest, did not see fit to challenge his figures. Chimalpahin, *Chimalpahin's Conquest*, 205, 282.

[42] Hassig, *Trade, Tribute, and Transportation*, 62.

[43] Gibson, *The Aztecs under Spanish Rule*, 364.

[44] AGI, Audiencia de México, leg. 781, ff. 222–223, 231.

[45] AGI, Patronato, leg. 226, ramo 18, f. 4v.

[46] Hassig, *Trade, Tribute, and Transportation*, 265; Gibson, *The Aztecs under Spanish Rule*, 366.

[47] AGN, Indios, vol. 6, 2a pte., exp. 448, f. 100; AGN, General de Parte, vol. 1, exp. 45, f. 9; exp. 1201, f. 226v; AGN, Indios, vol. 3, exp. 856, ff. 206–206v.

[48] AGN, Tierras, vol. 1525, exp. 3. The document is included in Frances Karttunen and James Lockhart, eds., *Nahuatl in the Middle Years: Language Contact Phenomena in*

craft displace the canoes. Other kinds of vessel appeared on the lakes, but did so only rarely.[49] In the seventeenth century smaller craft were being assembled from different pieces of timber.[50] In 1607, the governor of Tetzcoco established a ferry service to Mexico City. Alas, the ship sank just six months after it had been built. A dozen passengers were lost, as was a cargo of cacao beans.[51] Canoes thus had few effective rivals and remained an unsurpassed form of lake transportation. Indeed, such was their efficiency that goods imported into Mexico City from beyond the lake areas, which made their initial journey by teams of mules, were then transferred to canoes at various embarcaderos on the lakeshore.[52]

Perhaps unexpectedly, the region's extensive road networks, while providing alternative means of transportation, also bolstered the canoe industry and commerce in the southern lake areas. They did so primarily by incorporating the chinampa districts into wider trade networks. Many local and long-distance roads crisscrossed the Basin of Mexico. Roads went around the shores of the southern lakes. One route traversed them, running on the top of the causeway that connected the island town of Cuitlahuac to the northern and southern shores. Beyond the local roads, the southerly *camino real*, or royal road, extended from Mexico City to Xochimilco and then on to Cuernavaca and eventually the Pacific coast port of Acapulco. Another major artery ran to the south of the lakes, in an east-west direction, connecting Tepepan and Xochimilco with Tolyahualco, Ayotzingo, and Chalco Atenco, where it divided into two, with one road going south to Oaxaca and the other continuing east to Cholula, Puebla, and the wheat-producing Valley of Atlixco. This route came to an end in Veracruz, thereby incorporating the lake areas into

---

Texts of the Colonial Period (Berkeley: University of California Press, 1976), 93–97, and is mentioned by Lockhart in his discussion of merchants; see *The Nahuas after the Conquest*, 193. For other merchants who owned horses and mules, see AGN, Indios, vol. 16, exp. 95, ff. 85v–86 (83v–84 old foliation).

[49] Evidence of the use of rafts, or *acapechtli*, for purposes of transporting goods on the lakes does not appear in any of the archival documentation I have seen. Apart from using rafts as seedbed nurseries in the cultivation of chinampas – which might account for the description of chinampas as floating gardens – the only reference to rafts I have found is in fray Diego Durán's account of the expansion of the Aztec Empire. Perhaps rafts were more commonly used on rivers, as is suggested in Durán's history: the rafts were mentioned in relation to the Mexica conquest of Tototepec and Quetzaltepec, and Durán remarked that the river of Quetzaltepec was "great and raging" (*grande y furioso*). Durán, *Historia de las indias de Nueva España*, vol. 2, 426, 428; Wilken, "A Note on Buoyancy and Other Dubious Characteristics of the 'Floating' Chinampas of Mexico," 34–37.

[50] AGN, Tierras, vol. 2913, exp. 8, f. 219v.   [51] Chimalpahin, *Annals of His Time*, 97.

[52] Hassig, *Trade, Tribute, and Transportation*, 219.

transatlantic as well as transpacific trade networks. Xochimilco, then, lay at the intersection of the two great transportation networks that integrated the early modern Iberian world. Unsurprisingly, travelers from far afield frequently passed through the city. In 1583, Spanish soldiers making their way to Acapulco were billeted there and made a nuisance of themselves by taking food supplies and stealing residents' possessions.[53] Besides soldiers, travelers and traders were a regular sight in the city; they appeared from time to time in parish records of burials, listed simply as "passengers," often of unknown identity or provenance.[54]

Even with proximity to overland transportation routes, canoes long remained a conspicuous and yet ordinary feature of daily life in the Basin of Mexico. They were common household possessions, so much so that by the eighteenth century Spaniards had come to refer to small canoes as *chalupas* (and in one case, a Spaniard referred to a larger one as a *chalupón*).[55] Families had canoes because their homes abutted the canals. And land might be more valuable if it came with access to canoe routes.[56] In 1715, a Spanish trader and resident of Xochimilco named don Manuel de Puente paid 650 pesos for a rancho in Santiago Tolyahualco. The land was bordered on its northern side by the main channel through which canoe traffic flowed between Ayotzingo and Mexico City (the Spanish-language bill of sale used the loan word acalote).[57] Canoes were also used in credit arrangements. In 1686, when a Spanish resident of San Juan Ixtayopan borrowed 200 pesos from the same don Manuel de Puente, he put up an embarcadero and seven canoes as collateral.[58]

As a practical adaptation to the lake environment, canoes served various ends. Spaniards and other non-Native groups quickly recognized their value for getting around the lake areas. Rowers were occasionally required by church authorities to ferry friars from one place to another.[59] Provincial authorities routinely rode in them. They sometimes did so to serve notice in person to communities or individuals of legal

---

[53] AGN, Indios, vol. 2, exp. 494, f. 115. For more on the billeting of troops and their disruption to communities, albeit for Castile, see David E. Vassberg, *The Village and the Outside World in Golden Age Castile: Mobility and Migration in Everyday Rural Life* (New York: Cambridge University Press, 1996), 105–108.

[54] AGN, Genealogía [microfilm], vol. 1855.

[55] AGN, Tierras, vol. 2252, exp. 8, f. 14v for the definition of chalupa as a small canoe; see AGN, Desagüe, vol. 43, exp. 5, ff. 7v and 9 for the big chalupa.

[56] AGNM, Xochimilco, vol. 2, ff. 69v–70v (second foliation).

[57] AGNM, Xochimilco, vol. 1, ff. 209v–211v.

[58] AGNM, Xochimilco, vol. 1, ff. 181v–182v.

[59] AGN, Indios, vol. 6, 1a pte., exp. 1160, ff. 318v–319.

actions (or to issue summonses).[60] Occasionally, they used canoes to transmit messages. In 1763, the governor of Mixquic hurried to Cuitlahuac to deliver an important announcement by a Spanish judge.[61] Ordinary administrative and legal tasks required the use of canoes, as with the ceremonies of possession of land in the lake areas. These customary acts required the traversing of the land's boundaries. This procedure was recorded in 1792, when don José Arteaga over took his father's hacienda of San Nicolás Buenavista. Accompanied by the Spanish authorities, witnesses, his father, the hacienda's administrator, and various other people, don José set out along the royal road as far as a neighborhood named Tomatlan, where a canoe had been prepared for them. They all boarded the canoe and then continued on their easterly route along the straight line of the *acequia real*, with the hacienda running to its north, before coming to the point where an acalote split off toward Xochimilco, which marked the hacienda's limit. There one of the formal acts of possession was done, and since no one spoke out against it, the party then pressed on in the canoe to continue the process at another point of the hacienda's perimeter, passing through swamps and such boundary markers as trees, and finally ending up at the border of the barrio of Zapotitlan in Tlahuac. On the other side of the water, the altepetl's officers had come out to witness the act of possession.[62]

While no one contested don José's ownership of the hacienda at this time, on other occasions canoes were called into service to survey lands that were subject to dispute. This was particularly the case with tours of inspection, or *vistas de ojos*, especially when the lands in question were chinampas that could only be reached by canoe. In these investigations, canoes enabled judges and plaintiffs to identify boundary markers, take measurements, and to bring experts and residents together to provide testimonies.[63] In 1800, eight years after taking possession of the hacienda, don José de Arteaga faced litigation from the Nahuas of Tlahuac over the ownership of an adjacent parcel of land named Tempilula. The parties involved surveyed the area in a chalupa, and so thick was the swamp that the judge remarked on the difficult passage of the vessel.[64] Beyond such land inspections, canoes also made it possible for the authorities to inspect the engineering works in the lakes and, at times, to identity the causes of

[60] AGN, Tierras, vol. 2681, exp. 6, ff. 65–84v.   [61] AGN, Desagüe, vol. 16, exp. 8, f. 60.
[62] AGN, Tierras, vol. 1930, exp. 2, ff. 40–41.
[63] AGN, Tierras, vol. 2681, exp. 6, ff. 65–84v.
[64] AGN, Tierras, vol. 1930, exp. 2, ff. 45–47.

flooding while also determining the severity of inundations and calculating the scale of the damage the high waters had inflicted.[65]

For Spanish officials in the lake areas, then, canoe transportation was indispensable. During an early seventeenth-century inspection of Mexicalzingo and its outlying neighborhoods, which was conducted to determine whether de-populated communities should be consolidated, several individuals gave evidence in which they highlighted the vital importance of aquatic and land-based transportation routes, particularly when it came to providing Mexico City's residents with food and its horses and mules with straw. The judge ultimately agreed, ruling against the consolidation, and he might well have reached this decision by having had to travel around the jurisdiction by canoe himself. During his tour, one of the witnesses he interviewed, a priest, explained that seemingly distant, outlying communities might not actually be all that far from Mexicalzingo's parish church when people traveled by canoe: Santa Marta, for instance, was just a quarter of a league away by canoe; over land, the same journey would require a circuitous trip of an entire league. The most direct route between two places might often be across water.[66]

Canoes were so integral to daily life that they were used in nefarious activities. In 1649, a Spaniard named Cristóbal Pérez faced a criminal investigation after Nahuas of the village of San Luis Tlaxialtemalco – located near Tolyahualco in Xochimilco's jurisdiction – brought a long list of charges before the authorities. The defendant lived in the village in contravention of royal orders, and had done so for a decade, during which time he had tyrannized locals, stolen plots of land, assaulted residents, and committed adultery even as he also lived with yet another woman, María Gerónima, outside of wedlock. María contributed to their upkeep by working as a trader. She rode a horse to local markets and poled a canoe to the capital. When Cristóbal found out that he was under investigation, he smuggled his lover into hiding in Mexico City in a canoe.[67]

In addition to illicit trade, canoes were also used in the commission of crimes. In 1644, Xochimilco's governor and other officials caught five Nahuas in the act of committing burglary. Under interrogation and facing the threat of the lash, the culprits confessed, and the authorities uncovered a prolonged and extensive criminal enterprise. Apparently the thieves

[65] AGN, Tierras, vol. 3708, exp. 1, ff. 14v–16; AGN, Desagüe, vol. 43, exp. 5, ff. 7v–11.
[66] AGN, Civil, vol. 1271, exp. 1, ff. 43, 44–44v.
[67] AGN, Criminal, vol. 49, exp. 19, f. 260.

were responsible for a spate of thefts. Having determined when residents were out of town, under the cover of darkness the gang quietly snuck up to the empty homes in a canoe. They broke inside, forced open chests, and stole their contents together with anything else lying within easy reach. They then made good their escape, loot in hand, on the lake.[68]

CANOES AND ECONOMIC SPECIALIZATION

Much as canoes formed an integral and routine part of daily life so they buttressed the indigenous sector of the economy. Countless Native residents of Xochimilco and nearby communities depended on lake transportation for their livelihoods. Some residents of the chinampa districts, from the makers of canoes to their rowers, made a living directly from their involvement in lake transportation. Others, among them fishermen, farmers, and artisans also relied on water-borne craft for their work.[69] Household income, trade, tribute, and town finance – all these and more benefited from the contributions of canoes to the local economy.

Unsurprisingly, given their prevalence in the southern lake areas, the manufacture of canoes was a prominent craft industry. The Franciscan friar Bernardino de Sahagún tells us that the Xochimilca were esteemed as master canoe makers.[70] Ordinarily it took a specialist craftsman a week to fashion one of the larger canoes from a single trunk. Once constructed, Nahua residents acquired canoes in several ways. As valuable and useful belongings, parents were careful to bequeath canoes to their offspring. In 1721, for instance, Blas de los Reyes set down a Nahuatl testament in which he divided his eight canoes among his children.[71] If they did not inherit them, Nahua residents would have obtained them either through private sales or from the market.[72] Or, in the early years, they would have received them through tribute provisions. In 1548, Nahuas supplied a set quota of canoes each year to the altepetl's lords. The dynastic rulers of two

---

[68] AGN, Criminal, vol. 49, exp. 1, ff. 1–44, especially the testimony on f. 9.

[69] Torquemada, *Monarquia indiana*, vol. 2, 556.

[70] Fray Bernardino de Sahagún, *Florentine Codex: General History of the Things of New Spain, Book 9 – The Merchants*, trans. Charles E. Dibble and Arthur J. O. Anderson (Salt Lake City: University of Utah/Museum of New Mexico, 1959), 80; Jacques Soustelle, *Daily Life of the Aztecs on the Eve of the Spanish Conquest*, trans. Patrick O'Brien (Stanford: Stanford University Press, 1961), 67; Berdan, *The Aztecs of Central Mexico*, 28.

[71] AGN, Civil, vol 2215, exp. 1, ff. 11–11v.

[72] AGN, Mercedes, vol. 3, exp. 714, ff. 277–277v; exp. 716, ff. 277v–278; exp. 717, ff. 278r–278v; exp. 806, ff. 318v–319, and exp. 809, f. 320, exp. 849, f. 335.

of Xochimilco's three subdivisions each received 240 canoes. Both retained a quarter for themselves. They distributed half to the leading nobles of their respective districts. The remaining canoes, sixty for each tlaxilacalli, were then passed on to residents in the chinampa districts. This distribution of the canoes provided a practical benefit. As small islands surrounded by water, the construction, maintenance, and cultivation of chinampas all relied on the use of canoes. The distribution of canoes promoted agriculture and enabled residents to meet their tribute obligations.[73]

The system of lake-borne transportation provided specific employment for residents. Embarcaderos had their own staff, with some Nahuas employed as stevedores. At the larger dock facilities, a few individuals were employed solely to launch canoes onto the lake.[74] For the most part, though, the rowers typically worked as freelancers and relied for their income on clients who hired them under wage labor terms.[75] In the late 1710s and early 1720s, the Jesuits relied on canoeists who worked as independent contractors for deliveries of timber (oak) and pine (for use as torches, probably), such staples as corn, wheat, and barley, as well as a few luxuries, among them sugar and honey. Some of these items came from Jesuit haciendas and all of them were loaded onto canoes at an embarcadero in Chalco. The surviving account books, which include the reconciliations and settlings of debts with the embarcadero's administrator, show that the rowers typically charged a standard rate for freight fees. The three pesos and four reales amount covered most commodities. A few heavier and more cumbersome items, such as lumber, cost more.[76] Canoeists, such as the ones who contracted for the Jesuits, were considered to be members of a distinct trade, or *oficio*. Some of them specialized in transporting certain types of freight, as was the case with one court witness who identified himself as a rower who transported timber.[77]

While the rowers transported items on behalf of others, artisans likewise relied on canoes. Artisans from Xochimilco had been esteemed since pre-contact times for their trade specializations. Don Fernando de Alva Ixtlilxochitl observed the Xochimilca as having been great masters of

---

[73] Library of Congress, Kraus Collection, ms. 140, ff. 436–451v.
[74] Hassig, *Trade, Tribute, and Transportation*, 62.
[75] AGN, General de Parte, vol. 4, exp. 19, f. 4v and AGN, Indios, vol. 5, exp. 950, ff. 244v–245.
[76] AGN, Archivo Histórico de Hacienda, Temporalidades, leg. 106, exp. 7, ff. 1–33.
[77] AGN, Criminal, vol. 138, exp. 17, ff. 343–344v.

architecture and carpentry.[78] In addition to making canoes, Sahagún tells us that Nahuas from Xochimilco were renowned for their lapidary arts and fishing.[79] Other, quotidian but no less specialized trades – which were common to communities across Mexico – catered to local needs, from pottery to the making of reed mats.[80] Not all of these crafts thrived after the conquest. But even in the late eighteenth century, Xochimilco, unlike other polities in the region, stood out for still being an important center for crafts production. Indeed, such was the strength of its manufacturing sector that the majority of the city's residents, uncommonly, were still classified as skilled artisans, or oficiales.[81] The resilience of Xochimilco's crafts traditions can be attributed, in part, to canoe transportation. Artisans gathered raw materials from the lake areas using their canoes and they ferried their finished products across the lakes for sale in the capital.[82]

While there were few Spaniards who worked as artisans in Xochimilco, outsiders did introduce crafts that had been previously unknown in indigenous communities before the conquest era.[83] Blacksmiths, locksmiths, saddlers, candle makers, and bakers – all would presumably have influenced production in Xochimilco; others, from tailors and cobblers to tanners, would have brought innovations to indigenous crafts with which they shared a general similarity. A few Spanish artisans did indeed establish themselves in the city, though they were typically tailors who maintained shops around Xochimilco's plaza, which they rented from members of the leading Cerón y Alvarado family.[84] Nahuas readily adopted imported trades. Nahua blacksmiths appeared on several occasions in the documentation.[85] Similarly, Nahuas appeared in litigation as bakers. In one case from 1591, the bakers Martín de Grado and Pedro de Zamora protested against having been threatened with forced labor in an

---

[78] Fernando de Alva Ixtlilxochitl, *Obras históricas*, ed. Edmundo O'Gorman (Mexico City: Universidad Nacional Autónoma de México, Instituto de Investigaciones Históricas, 1975), vol. 1, 411.

[79] Sahagún, *Florentine Codex: General History of the Things of New Spain, Book 9 – The Merchants*, 80. See also Vetancurt, *Teatro mexicano*, 56–58; Soustelle, *Daily Life of the Aztecs on the Eve of the Spanish Conquest*, 67; and Berdan, *The Aztecs of Central Mexico*, 28.

[80] Gibson, *The Aztecs under Spanish Rule*, 350.

[81] Gibson, *The Aztecs under Spanish Rule*, 351–352; AGN, Padrones, vol. 29, f. 1.

[82] Villaseñor y Sánchez, *Theatro americano*, 160–161.

[83] Rebecca Horn argues that the proximity to Mexico City accounts for a similar lack of Spanish crafts in Coyoacan. Horn, *Postconquest Coyoacan*, 212–216.

[84] AGN, Vínculos y Mayorazgos, vol. 279, exp. 1, ff. 61–61v.

[85] Villaseñor y Sánchez, *Theatro americano*, 165; *Sobre el modo de tributar*, 111.

obraje, or textile workshop.[86] On another occasion, from 1580, Nahua bakers complained that the public notary, Alonso Gutiérrez, among other Spaniards, had impeded their trade. In this case the bakers were clearly not making tortillas: rather, documentation specified that they had been selling *pan de castilla* (Spanish bread) in the market.[87]

Even as some Nahuas adopted Spanish craft techniques, their own traditions proved quite durable thanks to canoe transportation, lively regional markets, and the strength of their corporate organization. The Xochimilca lacked formal trade guilds. Only once, in passing, and in the context of uniting with the Franciscans in opposition to an unpopular governor, were Xochimilca artisans referred to as having a guild.[88] Instead they invested their corporate identity and interests in other community structures, much as their predecessors had in ancient times. The district of Tecpan was home to carpenters, blacksmiths, and potters. Artisans did not always reside in their own, exclusive neighborhoods, though, as carpenters were also to be found in Tepetenchi. Xochimilco's sculptors lived in Tepetenchi, too.[89] Within these neighborhoods, parents passed on their craft skills to children. In one instance a carpenter named Ambrosio de Santiago complained that local officials prevented him from instructing his boys, requiring instead that they perform labor duties even though, Ambrosio maintained, they were still children.[90]

The association between artisans and community was lasting, to judge from public festivities. In the 1720s, the Nahua carpenters of Tecpan held their own fiesta in honor of San Josef, the patron saint of carpenters, as did the carpenters of Tepetenchi, who participated in a mass followed by a procession.[91] Festivities consisted of elaborate performances that drew upon local traditions and gave expression to civic pride and religious piety. Artisans played a prominent part in them. The friar Agustín de Vetancurt described festivities held at the end of the seventeenth century, which included a major Corpus Christi celebration. Nahuas erected arches and decorated the plaza with flowers. Branches provided shade

---

[86] AGN, Indios, vol. 3, exp. 872, f. 211v (219v old foliation).
[87] AGN, General de Parte, vol. 2, exp. 843, ff. 176v–177 (197v–198 old foliation).
[88] AGN, Criminal, vol. 138, exp. 10, f. 137v.   [89] Vetancurt, *Teatro mexicano*, 56.
[90] AGN, Indios, vol. 3, exp. 109, f. 27. See also *Sobre el modo de tributar*, 107. On the vexed matter of age and adult majority, particularly in terms of tribute obligations, see Gibson, *The Aztecs under Spanish Rule*, 201–202.
[91] Instituto Nacional de Antropología e Historia (INAH), Archivo Histórico, Mexico City, Fondo Franciscano, vol. 48, ff. 5–5v.

from the sun.[92] The artisans participated in processions, each group representing their particular trade by wearing distinctive masks and their own elegant raiment. Each group of artisans played a set of musical instruments, and a drum provided an accompaniment for their many dances. Dancers dressed as eagles and lions and carried painted weapons. As part of the festivities, three or four elders sang songs of the histories of the Spanish–Mexica War and the subsequent arrival of the Franciscans. The evening's entertainment culminated with the Xochimilca reenacting an ancient battle in which they vanquished the Nahuas of Tepoztlan, winning as a trophy a drum that could be heard from a great distance.[93] The participation of artisans in these rituals attested to their conspicuous place in local society and also reflected their ongoing corporate identity.

The communal bonds that provided artisans with a degree of security were reinforced by the Spanish demands for skilled workers to contribute to public works projects and pay tribute. Craftsmen of all kinds were subject to their own, specific tribute levies, beyond those apportioned to the city's neighborhoods. As with merchants, they were required to cultivate their own fields; artisans living on the lakeshore were to be given community lands measuring five brazas in width and ten in length, which they cultivated exclusively for the crown, and those who lived in lake areas were likewise required to cultivate a chinampa; the intention was that these lands would yield a bushel of maize for each tributary per year. Presumably this measure was designed to secure a regular supply of tribute by providing artisans with a source of income separate from the sale of crafts.[94]

Much as artisans commanded higher salaries than unskilled workers, so the government taxed them at a higher rate.[95] The higher tribute schedule applied to a wide variety of artisans and, indeed, the specificity of viceregal orders demonstrates the lasting diversity of Xochimilco's crafts. Lumberjacks, carpenters, canoe makers, and masons appeared in tribute rolls from the 1560s. Each group had to appoint a representative to oversee its members' work and guarantee tribute collection. Other artisans mentioned in the regulations included blacksmiths, feather workers, painters, and tailors, all of whom were likewise instructed to cultivate tribute lands and to pay a higher rate of tribute. Other specialists included

---

[92] In another account, Torquemada described Xochimilco's flowers, used commonly in fiestas, as numerous and very pretty. Torquemada, *Monarchía indiana*, vol. 2, 60.
[93] Vetancurt, *Teatro mexicano*, 57–58.   [94] *Sobre el modo de tributar*, 106.
[95] Gibson, *The Aztecs under Spanish Rule*, 250.

fishermen, weavers, potters, cobblers, as well as the makers of reed mats.[96] Xochimilco also had a school teacher. Three assistants ensured that children were escorted to the friary at eight o'clock each morning for their lessons. Other sixteenth-century sources list sandal makers and metalworkers as artisans who performed personal service to Nahua nobles.[97] In 1591, a group of *voladores* – skilled performers who swung by rope around tall, vertical poles – still participated in festivities.[98]

In addition to tribute obligations, artisans also contributed to public works projects in the local community and for the viceregal government.[99] In the 1560s, labor drafts involved carpenters, locksmiths, masons, and others.[100] At times, demands were placed on artisans residing in certain barrios, as in 1576 with carpenters.[101] The viceregal government also conscripted Nahua woodsmen and carpenters into providing timber for building projects, in one case ordering a prominent Spanish resident, don Juan de Orozco, to desist from seizing their lumber.[102] When specific needs such as paving streets or making repairs to flood-damaged property arose, the government demanded the services of masons.[103] And the government called on the expertise of Nahuas from the southern lake districts when it came to water management projects in the capital. In 1592, residents of Tlahuac, Mixquic, Culhuacan, Iztapalapa, and Mexicalzingo were called on to open up a channel – described as a *zanja*, or ditch, and acequia – as part of the construction of Mexico City's Alameda out of the old plaza of San Hipólito.[104]

Over time, changes in the market for crafts affected Xochimilco's specialist, skilled laborers. Feather workers survived in documentation only until the 1560s; presumably the market for their skills diminished in tandem with the decline in the Nahua aristocracy's consumption of luxury

---

[96] Vetancurt, *Teatro mexicano*, 56; Gibson, *The Aztecs under Spanish Rule*, 250.

[97] AGI, Patronato, leg. 184, ramo 50.

[98] AGN, Indios, vol. 5, exp. 500, ff. 138–138v (207–207v old foliation).

[99] Local demand included the ornamentation of churches. AGN, General de Parte, vol. 1, exp. 634, f. 130v.

[100] *Sobre el modo de tributar*, 107.

[101] AGN, General de Parte, vol. 1, exp. 1140, f. 216v.

[102] AGN, General de Parte, vol. 4, exp. 20, ff. 4v–5; AGN, Indios, vol. 20, exp. 177, ff. 130v–131.

[103] AGN, General de Parte, vol. 3, exp. 128, ff. 63–63v.

[104] AGN, Indios, vol. 6, 2a pte., exp. 569, f. 125v. On the making of the Alameda and the relocation of the market of San Hipólito, see AGN, Indios, vol. 6, 1a pte., exp. 234, ff. 59v–60.

commodities.[105] Conversely, Nahua artisans who made essential goods long retained their specialties. The makers of reed mats, for instance, also benefited from other sources of demand, from decorations for festivities to the adornment of taverns. The reeds were also hung above the doors of churches and homes.[106] Other artisans found an outlet for their finished goods in Mexico City's Spanish market. In the eighteenth century, the Spanish treasury official Villaseñor y Sánchez noted that the Xochimilca were highly renowned for their furniture. (The proximity of forests in the sierras in the south of the jurisdiction probably explains, in part, the industry's prominence in Xochimilco). Nahuas from the city made doors, beds, benches, chairs, shelves, and cupboards. The manufacture of furniture, moreover, supported smiths who specialized in making locks for doors and chests, door knockers, and nails. Others made chains, latticework (or trellises, *celosias*), and balconies for houses. The finished products were then ferried to Mexico City for sale in its markets.[107]

In addition to reaching markets, artisans and other Nahuas also relied on water-borne vessels to gather local resources. Natural springs provided supplies of fresh drinking water, which carriers (*aguadores*) transported to urban residents via canoes.[108] The diverse and rich lake environment afforded further opportunities. Nahuas sold all manner of aquatic products in regional markets, from fish and insects to birds and aquatic plants.[109] Some residents made a living by collecting the reeds that were woven into mats or made into decorations.[110] More commonly, though, canoes were used in hunting and fishing. Nahuas captured ducks in nets or else they used spears to kill them. Enterprising swimmers, their heads concealed in hollowed-out pumpkins, slipped up on their unsuspecting prey.[111] Foreign methods of hunting were also introduced. In 1560 a group of Nahuas complained of the unfair advantage of rivals who had been blasting at ducks with a musket (*arcabuz*).[112]

Fishing also sustained several communities. The island towns of Mixquic and Cuitlahuac as well as San Luis Tlaxialtemalco were well

---

[105] Their perseverance, as Charles Gibson remarked, might be accounted for by the Spanish demand for quills. Gibson, *The Aztecs under Spanish Rule*, 342.

[106] Villaseñor, *Theatro americano*, 165–166.

[107] Villaseñor, *Theatro americano*, 164–165.

[108] AGN, Mercedes, vol. 8, f. 68v; Chimalpahin, *Chimalpahin's Conquest*, 203.

[109] Rojas Rabiela, *La cosecha del agua en la Cuenca de México*, 15; Gibson, *The Aztecs under Spanish Rule*, 337.

[110] Villaseñor, *Theatro americano*, 165–166.

[111] Gibson, *The Aztecs under Spanish Rule*, 342.

[112] AGN, Mercedes, vol. 5 (5–6, 1a parte), f. 179v; Gibson, *The Aztecs under Spanish rule*, 343.

known for fishing. Nahuas fished from canoes, often small ones called *chinchorros*, that might have been designed specifically for this purpose, and they used spears, rods, and nets.[113] In the early seventeenth century, the Dominican friar Hernando Ojea wrote about the abundance of two species of fish, which were like sardines; one of them being *amilotl*, or whitefish, which he noted were tasty; the others, known as *xihuiles* or *zoquimichi*, which he found less appealing. Ojea reported that demand was incredibly high: each year, he maintained, a million fish were taken from the lakes.[114]

Nahua residents thus jealously guarded their rights of access to fishing grounds and, at times, sought to exclude outsiders.[115] Nahuas accused interlopers of trespassing, as happened in a 1640 case that appeared before the viceroy. The municipal council of Tlahuac asserted that two Nahuas in the employ of a Spaniard named Francisco Luis had illegally crossed the town's limits while on the lake. On this basis, the town's officials had imprisoned the trespassers.[116] In litigation, Nahuas asserted that a portion of the lake belonged to their communities. According to the law, lake areas were considered analogous to land. Tlahuac rented out fishing grounds in the seventeenth century, and the courts even recognized and accepted communal ownership of water.[117]

In a 1694 lawsuit between a Spaniard named Juan de Castañeda and Tlahuac over fishing rights, the high court determined which part of the lake belonged to the town.[118] The court agreed that Tlahuac could legally claim rights to the lake within a half-league distance of its lakeshore. Accordingly, to find out if Castañeda had crossed this threshold, the court ordered the gathering of testimony. The lake was thus subject to the same demarcation and measurement as land. Witnesses identified the borders by reference to topographical features, from canals, swamps, and chinampas to poles and even a cross, which Nahuas had placed in the lake as boundary markers. The poles and the cross were even referred to in the same language – *mojones* – as markers of land. Indeed, such was the conformity between conceptions of land and lake as territorial property that, having

---

[113] Confusingly, *chinchorro* could refer to the small canoes or a kind of fishing net. AGN, Criminal, vol. 138, exp. 10, ff. 136, 139–139v, 143–144, 146v–147, 148–148v.

[114] Ojea, *Libro tercero de la Historia religiosa de la prouincia de México de la Orden de Sto. Domingo*, 2. See also Gibson, *The Aztecs under Spanish Rule*, 340.

[115] AGN, Indios, vol. 16, exp. 66, ff. 66v–67.

[116] AGN, Indios, vol. 12, 2a pte., exp. 43, f. 188v.

[117] Gibson, *The Aztecs under Spanish Rule*, 340–341.

[118] AGN, Tierras, vol. 1624, exp. 2, ff. 1–47v.

been dissatisfied by the witness testimonies, the high court ordered an inspection, or *visita de ojos* by don Miguel Ortiz, just as one would have in a dispute over land boundaries. An interpreter was present, as were *medidores*, surveyors appointed by the high court, along with the litigants, Juan de Castañeda and, representing Tlahuac, the governor don Diego Jacinto and councilman don Gregorio de la Cruz. In front of many residents, they embarked on the lake in a canoe. Using *cordeles*, or ropes, to take measurements, the group navigated around the perimeter of the lake claimed by the town. At one point, though, their passage was blocked by chinampas.[119] After completing the inspection and submitting its results, the high court upheld Tlahuac's territorial claim to the lake.[120] The judge further ruled that Castañeda had violated the town's watery limits. The matter did not end here, though. Attesting to the perceived value of fishing rights, Juan de Castañeda pursued yet more litigation. In 1702 he initiated a second lawsuit. The case took five years to resolve and passed through all levels of the legal system, eventually appearing before the crown.[121]

MARKETS AND MERCHANTS

Brisk commerce in the chinampa districts owed much to the transportation system, which extended beyond canoes to include the road network and inns, taverns, and shops catering to the needs of merchants. In 1552, Francisco Altamirano, a Nahua resident of Cuitlahuac, received a license to open a shop, which to judge from its inventory – paper and scissors as well as hats and shoes – catered to merchants and other mobile individuals.[122] In addition to shops, Nahuas also established inns. Mixquic's inn, like others, was held under communal ownership.[123] In Cuitlahuac, Nahuas rented theirs out to the highest bidder, using the income to fill community coffers.[124] Xochimilco's inn was similarly owned by the community. It was fully equipped for travelers' needs and provided stables for mules and horses. Presumably the inn received considerable use as it was in need of repair by 1579.[125]

---

[119] The records of the witness testimonies and the inspection appear on ff. 20–24v.
[120] See ff. 30–30v and, following appeals, 36v–37 and 44–44v.
[121] AGN, Tierras, vol. 1780, exp. 7, ff. 1–223v. For the king's verdict, in favor of Tlahuac, see ff. 131v–132.
[122] Newberry Library, Ayer MS. 1121, ff. 53–53v.
[123] AGN, Mercedes, vol. 15, ff. 195–195v.
[124] AGN, Indios, vol. 6, 2a pte., exp. 701, f. 162v.
[125] AGN, General de Parte, vol. 2, exp. 137, f. 29v.

Nothing was so important to ongoing commercial vitality as the lake area's richly provisioned and well-ordered markets. The markets were located in close proximity to roads and canals. Chalco Atenco was famous for its Friday markets, and the market apparently grew in importance over the years. According to one observer in the eighteenth century, the altepetl attracted a considerable number of customers from the neighboring juris-dictions and beyond. On Fridays, a multitude of canoes arrived in the town.[126] In 1771, a government investigation of sales tax revenues paid particular attention to large-scale purchases of comestibles in Chalco that were so large that they involved "fleets of canoes" delivering produce for resale in Mexico City.[127]

Xochimilco's market was just as bustling. The Spanish friar Juan de Torquemada described the city's marketplace as especially large and spacious.[128] The layout he admired had been a post-conquest innovation. As noted in the first chapter, before 1550, Xochimilco's residents had held their public market outside the altepetl, and as part of the early colonial refashioning of public space in the altepetl, the governor and other cabildo officials had it relocated.[129] The new marketplace became something of a commercial hub. It was – and still is – located within easy reach of Xochimilco's canals and embarcaderos. Properties around it were com-mercial and retail establishments. The altepetl's rulers together owned six shops on the plaza. All of the shops were rented out, and the income they generated was still sufficiently lucrative in the early seventeenth century for the tlatoque to go to court to protect them from the meddling of the Spanish magistrate. At that time, the six shops were still shared among the rulers: three belonged to don Martín Cerón, two others were owned by don Hernando de Santa María, and the final one formed part of the estate of the heirs of don Diego de San Francisco.[130] Some of the properties around the plaza were used by artisans as their workshops. In the mid-sixteenth century, the tlatoque rented shops on the corner of the plaza to Spanish tailors.[131]

The establishment of Xochimilco's central marketplace was soon fol-lowed by the promulgation of new regulations. Constables began to enforce compliance with new rules, which ranged from the ordering of

---

[126] Villaseñor, *Theatro americano*, 64; Gibson, *The Aztecs under Spanish Rule*, 363.
[127] AGI, Audiencia de México, leg. 2096, ff. 13–14v.
[128] Torquemada, *Monarchía indiana*, vol. 2, 554–555.
[129] Cortés, *Letters from Mexico*, 202; AGN, Mercedes, vol. 3, exp. 397, f. 144.
[130] AGN, Vínculos y Mayorazgos, vol. 279, exp. 1, ff. 61–61v.
[131] Cline, "A Cacicazgo in the Seventeenth Century," 266–267.

market days – to be held once a week, on Saturdays – to the use of coinage and standard weights and measures. To this end, in May 1550, the viceroy mandated that henceforth Nahua officials were to keep in the government offices samples of measurements – for half a fanega (or three-fourths of a bushel), one-twelfth of a fanega (or *almud*), and half an almud – for purposes of reference and evaluation. All beans, maize, and other crops were now to be sold in these amounts.[132] These requirements did not displace established commercial practices, though. Nahuas continued to favor their own vigesimal system of measurements and long relied on cacao as a means of exchange. Sometimes the two systems overlapped; in 1580 Nahuas from Mixquic valued a fanega of maize at a standard rate of ten cacao beans.[133] Not all traders adhered to the new rules, though. In 1580, a trader named Polonia, who had a license to carry a set of measures with which she sold fruit, chile, and other comestibles, complained of interference by market inspectors.[134] Subsequently, she was accused of having conned customers by misusing the new measurements.[135]

Reforms of commercial regulations also dovetailed with efforts by the viceregal government to regulate regional commerce in the interests of the capital, particularly in times of drought and scarcity. On March 4, 1551, Nahuas of Huitzilopochco (San Mateo Churubusco) received a confirmation of their rights to travel to Cuitlahuac, Mixquic, and Xochimilco to purchase fish, eggs, fruit, and other foodstuffs.[136] The very next day, though, Viceroy don Luis de Velasco effectively abrogated this license by banning indigenous markets within a ten-league radius of Mexico City. The new policy was designed to secure enough provisions for the capital in a time of shortage.[137] In response Xochimilco's governor and nobles successfully petitioned for a special dispensation to continue holding their market so long as they sold a variety of essential goods. These included foodstuffs such as tomatoes, salt, chiles, seeds (described as *pepitas*), and indigenous fruits. The market also stocked household wares such as wood, griddles (*comalli*), grinding stones, gourds (*xicalli*), digging sticks, pine torches, reed mats (*petlatl*), cotton, rabbit furs (*tocho-mitl*), needles (*agujas*), string or rope, and tumplines (*mecapalli*), as well as

---

[132] The measurements also included a quartillo, or one-fourth almud. AGN, Mercedes, vol. 3, exp. 131, f. 60.
[133] AGN, General de Parte, vol. 2, exp. 587, ff. 118–118v (139–139v old foliation).
[134] AGN, General de Parte, vol. 2, exp. 476, f. 95 (116 old foliation).
[135] AGN, General de Parte, vol. 2, exp. 522, ff. 103–103v (124–124v old foliation).
[136] AGN, Mercedes, vol. 3, exp. 716, ff. 277v–278.
[137] AGN, Mercedes, vol. 3, exp. 714, ff. 277–277v.

lime, tobacco, and small canoes.[138] In less straightened circumstances, lakeside markets sold a wider range of goods that reflected the full bounty of chinampa cultivation and artisanal production.

Women were particularly prominent as traders, as with Isabel and Ana from Tlahuac, who sold fish in Mexico City.[139] Similarly, a resident of the same altepetl, María de Espinosa, sold in Mexico City a kind of white fish (perhaps *iztacmichin* if not amillotl) as well as catfish, clams, and frogs.[140] The demand for these foods remained high, not least because of the prohibition against eating meat on Fridays, the very day María usually went to market via canoe.[141] The traders sold a wide range of foodstuffs. Francisca de Santa María's trading license specified that, among other things, she could deal in chickpeas, lentils, and various beans.[142] Others sold zacatl.[143] Juana Tiacapan and her daughter Cristina, who hailed from Xochimilco, visited Mexico City's markets of Santiago, San Juan, and San Hipólito to sell fruit and vegetables.[144] Some of the traders were widows who had no alternative source of support.[145] Others apparently enjoyed brisk trade. In 1561, the viceroy determined that widows from Xochimilco, who worked as regional merchants, should pay more tribute – at the same rate as noblewomen – because, he explained, "they are rich."[146]

In addition to female traders, others specialized in selling specific commodities. Nahuas from Chalco Atenco routinely ventured to Cuitlahuac and other communities and sold lime along with imported Castilian goods.[147] Similarly, Andrés Vásquez traveled from Xochimilco to sell cloth in neighboring communities. In 1591, he appeared in the documentary record because the alcalde mayor of Chalco seized his consignment.[148] Specialization in the buying and selling of certain items was not limited to those with canoes. Gregorio Jiménez received

---

[138] AGN, Mercedes, vol. 3, exp. 806, ff. 318v–319.

[139] AGN, Indios, vol. 2, exp. 600, f. 138.

[140] Chimalpahin, *Chimalpahin's Conquest*, 181.

[141] She also sold kingfish, which were referred to as "pexereyes". AGN, Indios, vol. 4, exp. 942, f. 242.

[142] AGN, Indios, vol. 2, exp. 294, f. 72v.

[143] AGN, Indios, vol. 4, exp. 466, ff. 133–133v; vol. 5, exp. 191, f. 53.

[144] AGN, Indios, vol. 2, exp. 408, f. 97.

[145] AGN, General de Parte, vol. 2, exp. 404, ff. 83v–84; AGN, Indios, vol. 6, 2a pte., exp. 170, ff. 39v–40.

[146] AGI, Patronato, leg. 182, ramo 2; *Sobre el modo de tributar*, 106.

[147] AGN, Indios, vol. 2, exp. 722, f. 165.

[148] AGN, Indios, vol. 6, 2a pte., exp. 85, ff. 18v–19.

a protective order from Viceroy Luis de Velasco the Younger in 1590 to secure his interests against Spanish interference. Jiménez ran a team of mules with younger assistants, transporting honey around the lakes.[149] These mercantile specializations sometimes grew into family enterprises. In 1651, Francisco de San Miguel trained his son, Miguel Álvarez, in business; the pair traveled the roads of central Mexico with ten mules laden with aquatic plants.[150]

Lucrative trade opportunities led to meddling, heightened competition, and no shortage of conflict. Interference in trade was a common concern of Nahua officials. Xochimilca officials remained alert to unlicensed traders. In 1576, Martín Tetel, one of Xochimilco's constables, prevented Nahua traders from Coyoacan from entering Xochimilco's market.[151] Preventative measures such as this sometimes involved appeals by Nahua officials for viceregal intervention. In 1564, the governor and councilmen of Culhuacan complained that outsiders had meddled in the sale of fruit and vegetables.[152] Similarly, individuals such as Juana Cécilia, who dealt in chile and vegetables, also appealed to viceregal authorities for judicial orders to protect their trade.[153] Traders often complained that outsiders either coerced Nahuas into selling their goods or simply stole them. Indeed, the sale of chinampa produce was sufficiently important that in 1641 Xochimilco's municipal council complained to Spanish authorities about the low prices merchants received for maize in Mexico City. Arguing that sales contributed to tribute income while also being of great benefit to the capital's citizens, they reminded the viceroy that trade had traditionally involved many Xochimilca and had been a very old custom.[154]

The movement of merchants around the lakes remained sufficiently common and robust that traditional commercial procedures lasted well into the seventeenth century. Traders usually paid fees to disembark in towns and villages. They gave gifts such as chickens to community officials in order to gain access to the market. Some of these practices had a ritual character, with negotiations taking place over cups of drinking chocolate, as was shown in 1650 when a group of Nahuas selling pulque approached the General Indian Court to complain of excessive demands

---

[149] AGN, Indios, vol. 3, exp. 856, ff. 206–206v (214–214v old foliation).
[150] AGN, Indios, vol. 16, exp. 95, ff. 85v–86.
[151] AGN, General de Parte, vol. 1, exp. 1156, f. 219, vol. 2, exp. 171, f. 35 (56 old foliation).
[152] AGN, Mercedes, vol. 7, f. 321v.   [153] AGN, Indios, vol. 5, exp. 114, ff. 30v–31.
[154] AGN, Indios, vol. 21, exp. 146, f. 137; vol. 13, exp. 349, ff. 310v–311 (288v–289 old foliation).

by Native officials who had insisted that the merchants stay the night in the town's inn and pay for their lodging, food, pillows, and bedclothes.[155]

Traders were drawn by the great abundance and diversity of items cultivated in the chinampa districts. Some customers came from far afield. María Teresa and a woman identified only as Juana regularly made the journey by canoe from Mexico City's district of San Juan Tenochtitlan to obtain items in Cuitlahuac.[156] Even a few pochteca, the special class of long-distance merchants, remained active during the sixteenth century despite seldom dealing in foodstuffs, preferring instead to trade less perishable and more valuable commodities. In 1563, a group of ten long-distance merchants from Tlatelolco sought a protective judicial order after having been harassed, even though they had the proper licenses to conduct trade via canoes.[157] Other merchants similarly took the precaution of obtaining licenses. In 1591, Pablo García, from San Juan Tenochtitlan, successfully petitioned for a trade license and he was allowed to use his canoe to deliver various items to the market.[158] Yet licensing did not prevent officials from interfering with traders. In 1564, a group of Nahuas who ordinarily sold fruit and other foodstuffs in Mexico City's public plaza, which they had previously purchased in surrounding towns, claimed that the cabildo of Ayotzingo had blocked their access to suppliers.[159]

The system of licensing shows that Nahua long-distance merchants remained important for sixteenth-century commerce. Not only did the Xochimilca continue to find work as pochteca but they also exploited the new opportunities of the post-conquest period. Don Pablo Hernández, for instance, adopted foreign beasts of burden for a variety of business ventures that included long-distance trade.[160] Others found new opportunities to benefit from the rise of silver mining. As early as 1543 Viceroy don Antonio de Mendoza, at the behest of Nahuas from Mexico City and Xochimilco, rescinded an earlier prohibition against trading in the silver mining town of Taxco.[161] The new policy was reinforced with a general license that allowed Nahuas to deliver foodstuffs, specifically maize and beans, to the mines.[162] The general order was subsequently followed by specific licenses to merchants from the chinampa towns of Xochimilco,

[155] AGN, Indios, vol. 13, exp. 110, ff. 112v–113.
[156] AGN, Indios, vol. 3, exp. 976, f. 236.   [157] AGN, Mercedes, vol. 6, ff. 428v–429.
[158] AGN Indios, vol. 3, exp. 194, ff. 45v–46.   [159] AGN Mercedes, vol. 7, f. 331.
[160] AGN, Indios, vol. 4, exp. 377, f. 122v; Lockhart, *The Nahuas after the Conquest*, 191–193.
[161] AGN, Mercedes, vol. 2, exp. 81, ff. 32–32v.
[162] AGN, Mercedes, vol. 2, exp. 80, ff. 31v–32.

Chalco, Iztapalapa, and Culhuacan.[163] Trade to the mines continued for the next half century. Miguel Constantino and Miguel Álvarez Constantino obtained licenses to sell Castilian and locally produced clothing in Zacatecas, Guanajuato, Nueva Galicia, and elsewhere. Their license specified that riding horses was further warranted because of the threat posed by "Chichimec Indians." Andrés García, whose license expressed the same concern about security in remote areas, conducted trade in the northern mining areas and to Guadalajara.[164]

Long-distance traders from Xochimilco could be found across the length and breadth of New Spain. A nobleman named Juan Mateo obtained a license to outfit himself in Spanish attire and carry a sword and dagger, "for the defense and ornamentation of his person," but he further received viceregal permission to saddle his horse and conduct trade in distant "Chichimec" areas of northern Mexico.[165] In 1580, Baltasar de San Francisco received permission from Viceroy don Martín Enríquez de Almanza to trade imported Castilian goods along with domestic merchandise to the Pacific coast, specifically to Acamalutlan, near Acapulco.[166] Long-distance trade remained sufficiently lucrative in 1590 that expatriate communities of Xochimilca could still be found living along trade routes. Nahuas from Xochimilco established a small community in Guamuchtitlan, located in what is now eastern Guerrero near the border with Oaxaca, where they provided merchants with lodging, food, hospitality, and momentary respite from the ardors of travel.[167]

While Nahuas sought the protection of licenses to conduct trade, viceregal administrations made use of them to ensure the ample provisioning of the capital at affordable prices. Unlicensed traders, especially those known as *regatones*, resellers (or middlemen), aroused considerable anxiety among Spanish authorities.[168] These illicit dealers allegedly purchased items in

[163] AGN, Mercedes, vol. 2, exp. 88 and 89, ff. 35, 35v.
[164] AGN, General de Parte, vol. 2, exp. 1258, f. 269 (291 old foliation), exp. 1318, f. 178 (300 old foliation).
[165] AGN, Indios, vol. 5, exp. 369, f. 99.
[166] AGN, General de Parte, vol. 2, exp. 628, f. 127v (148v old foliation); Gerhard, *A Guide to the Historical Geography of New Spain*, 39–40.
[167] Merchants from Xochimilco had complained to the viceroy that the governor of the town, don Gaspar, had prevented them from staying with their hosts and had instead insisted that they lodge at the town's inn. AGN, Indios, vol. 4, exp. 537, ff. 149v–150 (159v–160 old foliation); Gerhard, *A Guide to the Historical Geography*, 323.
[168] Gloria Artís Espriu, *Regatones y maquileros. El mercado de trigo en la ciudad de México (siglo xviii)* (Mexico City: Centro de Investigaciones y Estudios Superiores en Antropología Social, Ediciones de la Casa Chata,1986); Enrique Florescano, *Precios*

bulk, and thus at a discounted rate, with an eye to making profits from their subsequent individual resale at a higher price. Presumably this tactic could only have succeeded when demand was high or if there were many regatones purchasing large enough quantities as to be able to withhold foodstuffs from the market.[169] As early as 1542, the viceroy sought to clamp down on regatones because their sales of maize were seen as having artificially inflated prices.[170] Two years later, reports surfaced of the middlemen, among them Spaniards, black slaves, and Indian *naborias* (dependents of indigenous rulers or Spaniards) selling items away from its designated marketplace in Mexico City. The infraction was deemed sufficiently severe as to warrant a punishment of 100 lashes. Convictions seem to have been elusive, though. Seven years later, the problem still lingered, prompting the government to appoint Nahua constables to protect traders.[171] By 1550, sanctions were stiffened and the viceroy transferred trials of middlemen from local officials to the high court. Beyond these concerns, the new order explicitly stated that the fundamental problem posed by the middlemen lay in the sale of goods beyond regulated marketplaces, and thus in disregard of established price controls. Such concerns, obviously, became more acute in times of food shortages. The specter of shortages prompted the issuing of further restrictions.[172] The fraudulent tampering with weights and measures added to the government's worries, as did the mobility afforded by canoes. Regatones were accused of having sold goods in a clandestine, impromptu marketplace. Its location next to the royal canal in Mexico City was presumably chosen for easy access and escape.[173]

The middlemen also aroused concern among Nahuas, particularly when they competed against legitimate traders. In 1599, leaders from Xochimilco and Mixquic voiced concern over regatones who sold timber to the royal munitions works.[174] On other occasions, municipal councils sought to ban them altogether, as when officials in Ayotzingo tried to

---

del maíz y crisis agrícolas en México, 1708–1810 (Mexico City: El Colegio de México, 1969), 22, 156–158.

[169] Van Young, *Hacienda and Market in Eighteenth-Century Mexico*, 70, 92–934; AGN, General de Parte, vol. 2, exp. 587, ff. 118–118v; exp. 1042, f. 234; vol. 5, exp. 550, f. 122; AGN, Mercedes, vol. 7, f. 331.

[170] AGN, Mercedes, vol. 2, exp. 523, f. 212v.

[171] AGN, Mercedes, vol. 2, exp. 639, f. 257v; vol. 3, exp. 811, f. 320v (343v old foliation).

[172] AGN, Mercedes, vol. 3, exp. 227, f. 227v (250v old foliation). See also AGN, Mercedes, vol. 3, exp. 54, ff. 25v–26 (47v–48 old foliation).

[173] AGN, Mercedes, vol. 2, exp. 639, f. 257v; vol. 3, exp. 54, ff. 25v–26; exp. 627, f. 227v; and vol. 3, exp. 811, f. 320v.

[174] AGN, General de Parte, vol. 5, exp. 550, f. 122.

prevent regatones from entering the town.[175] As outsiders with a reputation for coercion and deceit, regatones aroused considerable suspicion. In 1580, the governor and nobles of Mixquic complained that Nahua regatones, who carried their own market measures, had engaged in fraud. The officials petitioned for the right to impound the measures.[176]

As with attempts to combat regatones and to license trade, the viceregal government regularly intervened in the food supply network, especially before the rise of haciendas, when Nahua towns supplied the capital with much of its food via tribute. The devastating epidemic of 1545–1548 had led to food shortages by the early 1550s, which prompted the viceroy to suspend regional markets so that, in theory, the capital would be better supplied. Similarly, the poor harvest of 1586 prompted the viceroy to resort to other extraordinary measures. He offered compensation to those individuals who could spare their horses and mules to transport maize to the city's granary.[177] The major embarcaderos of Ayotzingo, Chalco Atenco, and Xochimilco were also instructed to assist in the delivery of maize, and the order explicitly mentioned the need for canoes.[178]

To store grain for times of shortage, and to regulate food prices as a means of securing public order, the viceregal administration founded, in the late 1570s, the twin institutions of the *alhóndiga* and *pósito* (granary and storehouse) in Mexico City. These two facilities, one of them being used for storage purposes, the other as a grain market, were born out of that decade's food shortages, which had followed from a year of drought (1576), a year of continuous rains at the height of the growing season (1577), and then the outbreak of the ruinous cocoliztli epidemic, which killed millions and lasted beyond the end of the decade. Taken together, these devastating conditions had brought famine by 1579.[179]

The alhóndiga, as an institutional protection against dearth, was strategically located for ease of supply on the main canal leading into the city.[180] Its location both reflected and prolonged a reliance on canoes for the delivery of food to the capital. This reliance continued after haciendas replaced indigenous tribute as the leading source of grains. The foodstuffs

---

[175] AGN, Mercedes, vol. 7, f. 331 (366 old foliation).
[176] AGN, General de Parte, vol. 2, exp. 587, ff. 118–118v (139–139v old foliation).
[177] AGN, General de Parte, vol. 3, exp. 267, ff. 121–122.
[178] AGN, General de Parte, vol. 3, exp. 86, f. 41v.
[179] Gibson, *The Aztecs under Spanish Rule*, 449, 453.
[180] Gibson, *The Aztecs under Spanish Rule*, 397; AGI, Audiencia de México, leg. 781, ff. 1063v–1070v; Raymond L. Lee, "Grain Legislation in Colonial Mexico, 1575–1585," *Hispanic American Historical Review*, vol. 27, no. 4. (1947), 647–660.

that passed through the southern lakes came from the ever-expanding estates of the province of Chalco and the wheat haciendas further to the east – both of which were regions that came to be seen as the breadbaskets of central Mexico. Ayotzingo's embarcadero served as the main conduit for wheat from the jurisdiction of Puebla de los Ángeles.[181]

The grains from the south and the east were loaded onto canoes at numerous embarcaderos. According to the scholar Gregory Luna Golya, in 1769, there were thirty main embarcaderos between Chalco and Iztapalapa.[182] Some of them were substantial dock facilities. They had their own permanent staff, including managers and administrators. Some were run as independent enterprises which contracted with haciendas. The larger embarcaderos had their own storage facilities. The grain silos (*troxes*) of three embarcaderos in Chalco Atenco were examined during an inspection of the food supply system in 1711.[183] Together they were found to be holding 5,400 fanegas of shelled maize (a fanega being roughly the equivalent of 1.5 bushels). In other words, there were approximately 210 to 225 tons of maize being stored in the embarcaderos of just one altepetl.[184] Since single canoes typically carried between sixty-five and seventy fanegas of maize, the silos contained enough maize for seventy-seven to eighty-three canoe journeys.[185] An inspection of the grain silos in Chalco Atenco and other communities, including Ayotzingo, determined that more than 25,000 fanegas, or approximately 1,000 tons, of maize were being kept collectively at the embarcaderos.[186]

From the embarcaderos, vast supplies of corn, wheat, and barley flowed through the southern lakes via canoe and either to the alhóndiga or to Mexico City merchants. The embarcaderos were key ligatures in the food supply system. The high court judge, don Joseph Joachín de Uribe

---

[181] AGN, Indios, vol. 2, exp. 940, ff. 215–215v.

[182] Luna Golya, "Modeling the Aztec Agricultural Waterscape of Lake Xochimilco," 23.

[183] AGI, Audiencia de México, leg. 781, f. 73v.

[184] A US short ton is the equivalent of 2,000 pounds. A fanega was a unit of dry measure, roughly the equivalent of 1.5 US bushels. This means that the silos contained 8,100 bushels of maize. If a bushel were calculated to be between 52 and 56 pounds in weight, as the US government counts it – the amount varies, of course, according to the moisture in the grain – then the silos could well have been storing between roughly 420,000 and 450,000 pounds of maize, that is, somewhere around 210–225 tons. For the units of measure and their conversion into US bushels, see Gibson, *The Aztecs under Spanish Rule*, 551–552n39 and 552–553n48; Woodrow Borah and Sherburne F. Cook, *Price Trends of Some Basic Commodities in Central Mexico, 1531–1570, Ibero-Americana 40* (Berkeley: University of California Press, 1958), 11.

[185] Gibson, *The Aztecs under Spanish Rule*, 329.

[186] AGI, Audiencia de México, leg. 781, f. 226.

y Castejon, recognized this in his 1711 investigation of increasing maize prices, stating that the owners and administrators of the docks were the most experienced and best placed individuals to understand the delivery and sale of maize through the alhóndiga. Accordingly, he set out to Chalco to question the embarcaderos' administrators and examine their account books.[187]

The amount of maize delivered by canoes varied, of course, according to the size of the harvests. Charles Gibson found that 5,000 fanegas were sent during the harvest season each week in the late seventeenth century, enough for seventy canoe journeys. The numbers of canoes increased in proportion to rising supplies of grain, which in turn followed the expansion of Spanish estates. By 1709, 97,330 fanegas were delivered by 1,419 canoes. The figures rose to 155,120 fanegas and 3,463 canoes in 1710, although they dropped back down to 113,701 fanegas in 1741. The average harvests of 250,000 fanegas were reported for forty-six haciendas in Chalco in the middle of the eighteenth century. These figures excluded those for wheat harvests, which could number around 60,000 fanegas a year in the eighteenth century. As such, the supply of maize could require as many as 3,800 canoe journeys, approximately, each year, with nearly another thousand canoe journeys being used for the delivery of wheat.[188]

Beyond the provisioning of the capital, other facets of the colonial political economy required sustained attention to matters of transportation. Through repartimiento labor, the authorities required Nahuas to gather and deliver substantial quantities of raw materials for public works projects. That the canoes could transport significant quantities of cumbersome goods both cheaply and efficiently meant that they became closely bound up with the levies, so much so, in fact, that demands for essential items were measured in numbers of canoe loads. In 1597, a viceregal levy on chinampa towns for zacatl consisted of thirty canoes' worth each day, of which Xochimilco supplied fourteen.[189] By 1619, demand had grown so much that Xochimilco alone supplied fifty canoes' worth.[190]

The sustenance of horses in the capital, as well as of other beasts of burden, accounted for the great demand for zacatl. In fact, so great was

---

[187] AGI, Audiencia de México, leg. 781, ff. 97v–98. The examination of the embarcaderos can be found on ff. 98–166v.
[188] Gibson, *The Aztecs under Spanish Rule*, 328–329.
[189] AGN, Indios, vol. 6, exp. 1196, f. 327.
[190] AGN, Indios, vol. 9, exp. 113, ff. 59–59v, and exp. 172 and 173, ff. 82v–83; AGN, Reales Cédulas Duplicadas, vol. 5, exp. 800, f. 198.

the demand for straw that in 1564 the viceroy appointed a constable, a Nahua named Juan Fabián, to prevent people from selling to regatones the fodder they were supposed to be delivering for their repartimiento obligations. The viceroy also required that a town crier remind everyone of the rules by announcing them three times a day, for three days, at different points along the city's canals.[191] Apparently these precautions worked only temporarily. A few years later, Nahua traders, who brought zacatl into the city with canoes, had allegedly been charging extortionate prices. To make matters worse they had been engaging in fraud, selling straw in bundles that were well below the proper size. Alarmed, Spanish residents of the capital asked the city council for help. The cabildo in turn appealed to the viceroy, who agreed that price controls be established. On August 21, 1579, one of the city's public criers, Diego Hernández – who was standing on the bridge over the canal by the city's main plaza, next to the government offices – made the new ordinances known to residents. Henceforth, traders had to sell zacatl at the new, standard rate, and they had to keep a rope of the standard three-vara measure in their canoes for reference purposes. City officials were required to verify that the ropes were accurate, and breach of these rules would lead to the confiscations, fines, and fifty lashes. The viceroy's order showed that he was still concerned about regatones. He added a further stipulation that no one be allowed to purchase zacatl from Nahua traders out on the lakes or before they had brought their cargoes into the city. Sales, moreover, could only take place once the straw had been brought far enough into the city, and the order specified where this threshold was located.[192]

Canoes were capable of carrying even heavier items than fodder. The hills to the south of the lakes contained woods as well as quarries. Rowers frequently delivered lumber and stone into the heart of Mexico City via its main canal.[193] Nahuas were required to bring very large quantities, not least because of the ongoing construction of Mexico City's cathedral and the Hospital de los Naturales.[194] By the end of the sixteenth century, viceregal requirements for canoe deliveries had assumed a standardized quantity, usually twenty-five or fifty *brazas* (a linear measurement) of

---

[191] AGN, Mercedes, vol. 7, ff. 282–282v (317–317v old foliation).

[192] It was along the main canal, just past the home of the oidor, or high court judge, Vasco de Puga. AGN, Reales Cédulas Duplicadas, vol. 103, ff. 25–26.

[193] AGN, Indios, vol. 23, exp. 189, f. 180; AGN, General de Parte, vol. 3, exp. 201, ff. 92–92v.

[194] AGN, General de Parte, vol. 6, exp. 266, f. 80–80v, exp. 799, f. 290, and AGN, Indios, vol. 3, exp. 368, f. 86.

stone.[195] In 1587, to obtain stone for the building of the monastery of Nuestra Señora del Carmen in Mexico City, the viceroy ordered that fifty brazas be delivered from the chinampa towns, with Xochimilco alone providing half.[196] A month later, a further 100 brazas of stone were requested, and again Xochimilco provided half of the total.[197] Other examples include the demand for Tlahuac to supply stone via canoe for the friary of Santo Domingo in Mexico City.[198] Tlahuac and Xochimilco were further required to deliver yet more stone for the paving of streets and the upkeep of dikes.[199]

Canoes supplied Mexico City with food, they delivered the resources needed to build hospitals, churches, monasteries and convents, and they helped to maintain essential elements of the urban infrastructure. In a very material sense, then, canoes contributed to the construction of colonial rule. They were also of service to Spaniards in other, indirect ways. Canoes enabled many Nahuas to make a living and meet their tribute obligations. Nahuas keenly appreciated all this, and when circumstances were propitious, they used their influence over the transportation system to their advantage, seeking to secure better pay or other concessions. But the value of the canoes' cargo also attracted unwanted attention.

CONFRONTATION, NEGOTIATION, AND THE POLITICS OF LAKE TRANSPORTATION

Whereas the southern lakes remained the preserve of Nahua communities when it came to chinampa cultivation, in the context of canoe transportation and commercial exchanges the lakes and waterways functioned as a particular kind of contact zone, one where individuals of different ethnicities came into frequent, close, and sustained contact with one another. Some of those contacts were acrimonious, deriving as they did from competition over the lucrative commercial prospects of the lake areas. As early as 1550, rowers from Cuitlahuac complained to viceregal authorities of outsiders – among them Spaniards, blacks, and mestizos – meddling in their business.[200] Similarly, in 1583 Nahuas petitioned the viceroy for help in protecting them from Spaniards who had forced them,

---

[195] AGN, General de Parte, vol. 4, exp. 188, f. 55, vol. 5, exp. 342, f. 75v.
[196] AGN, General de Parte, vol. 3, exp. 201, ff. 92–92v.
[197] AGN, General de Parte, vol. 3, exp. 247, f. 112.
[198] AGN, General de Parte, vol. 3, exp. 277, ff. 126–126v.
[199] AGN, Indios, vol. 15, exp. 20, ff. 15v–17.
[200] AGN, Mercedes, vol. 3, exp. 620, ff. 218–218v.

without payment, to deliver freight to Mexico City.[201] This was a phenomenon common across the region, one that at times united rowers against officials, as shown in a 1658 case in which Spanish soldiers and ministers of justice were ordered to refrain from seizing rowers' goods.[202]

Fishermen faced similar challenges. On some occasions, fishermen were blocked from gaining access to markets.[203] On others they faced the threat of violence. As Charles Gibson noted, some mulatos armed with knives and garrotes forced fishermen out of Cuitlahuac's fishing grounds.[204] Alternatively, as they traveled to market fishermen might be set upon and robbed, even when still in their canoes.[205] These impediments were sufficiently common and troublesome that Nahuas hired legal representatives to defend their interests before the General Indian Court, seeking protective judicial orders.[206] Fishermen and rowers were also vulnerable to the demands of local authorities. In 1575, Nahuas from Cuitlahuac approached viceregal authorities for protection against the town's governor and other leaders, who had seized their catches.[207]

Abuse lay behind the unfortunate and picaresque case of don Miguel de la Cruz, who was the governor of the village of Tecomitl.[208] According to the records of a criminal investigation, on March 9, 1635, don Miguel had recruited two Nahua rowers, Juan Gaspar and Miguel de San Juan, to transport *michihuauhtli*, a type of amaranth, for sale in Mexico City.[209] All three of them embarked on the lake in the early hours of the morning when it was still dark outside. The journey began much as countless others would have, the rowers steering the canoe between chinampas and then into the main channels that ran through the lake. As dawn approached, though, and not far from the village of Tolyahualco, a great storm descended upon them. Waves pushed the canoe further away from land, and as they drifted in

---

[201] AGN, Indios, vol. 2, exp. 973, ff. 223–223v.
[202] AGN, Indios, vol. 23, exp. 189, f. 180.   [203] AGN, Indios, vol. 4, exp. 433, f. 136.
[204] Gibson, *The Aztecs under Spanish Rule*, 341.
[205] AGN, General de Parte, vol. 2, exp. 938, f. 201; AGN, Mercedes, vol. 5–6, 1a pte. (i.e., vol. 5), ff. 180–180v.
[206] AGN, Indios, vol. 17, exp. 49, ff. 74–74v.
[207] AGN, General de Parte, vol. 1, exp. 448, f. 98v.
[208] AGN, Criminal, vol. 233, exp. 11 and 12, ff. 192–225.
[209] AGN, Criminal, vol. 233, exp. 12, ff. 212–212v; Alonso de Molina defines *huahtli* as a kind of amaranth, or *bledos* in Spanish, in *Vocabulario en lengua castellana y mexicana y mexicana y castellana*, fascimile ed. (Mexico City: Biblioteca Porrúa, 2001), 20 (in the Castilian section) and 56 (in the Nahuatl section).

the swell, they came upon another stricken canoe, laden with a cargo of honey, rowed by two black men and a Nahua. The rowers brought their canoes together for safety as the waves grew in size, but as the wind picked up speed, both canoes capsized, plunging their terrified occupants into the lake. The two black men and don Miguel de la Cruz managed to scramble to the surface but after frantically calling out they could find no sign of the Nahuas. The three survivors clambered onto the overturned canoe and, exhausted, eventually drifted to shore at the village of San Lorenzo, on the other side of the lake in the jurisdiction of Culhuacan. Over the course of the next fortnight, the bodies of the Nahuas washed ashore and local residents buried them in the village's church.[210]

These were the tragic circumstances surrounding the men's deaths – or so don Miguel would have had a Mexico City judge believe. The matter was a good deal murkier than he suggested. Unusually, he gave this account as part of testimony in anticipation of a criminal inquiry. That he came forward in advance of a criminal complaint was itself peculiar; so too was the fact that he had also taken the precaution of bringing several supporters with him to give depositions. The judge, who was apparently not a little suspicious, decided to launch an investigation and, according to those who were interviewed – both for don Miguel and on behalf the drowned men's widows – there was no doubt about the severity of the storm. Nor was there any doubt about the storm having been strong enough to make waves that would capsize canoes. But some of the witnesses testified that don Miguel had a reputation for abusive behavior toward rowers. It emerged that instead of properly hiring the rowers, he had coerced them into working for him. He beat one of them with a stick and threatened the other with severe reprisals.

Don Miguel's behavior since the drownings, moreover, had also been suspicious. The court discovered that the defendant had stashed his belongings – to prevent them being impounded – with a Japanese trader named Juan Diego. Don Miguel must have trusted the Japanese man, who was a resident of nearby Tecomitl, where don Miguel served as a governor, and, indeed, there seems to have been something of a small Japanese community in the area who worked as traders. Juan Diego himself did business with his compatriots.[211] If hiding his belongings

---

[210] AGN, Criminal, vol. 233, exp. 11 and 12, ff. 193–196 and 213v–214v.
[211] AGN, Criminal, vol. 233, exp. 12, f. 206. For more on Juan Diego's activities as a merchant, see AGNM, Notary 4, Hernando Arauz, vol. 9, ff. 182v and 184ff. I would like to thank Tatiana Seijas for sharing these sources with me.

were not suspicious enough, in a further twist to the case, one of the victim's widows, Juana Petronila, claimed that don Miguel had offered her a bribe to drop the charges, which included culpability for the rowers' deaths.[212] There were even vague insinuations that the rowers may have been murdered for having crossed don Miguel in the past.[213] But the allegations proved groundless. Juana Petronila later recanted and confessed to having invented portions of her testimony at the behest of two Spaniards with whom don Miguel had been at odds. They had offered Juana certain promises and gifts so as to secure his conviction and therefore to prevent don Miguel from pursuing their expulsion from the village.[214] Ultimately, the court ruled don Miguel innocent of negligence in the deaths of the rowers but guilty of having mistreated them.[215]

If rowers were at times vulnerable to the depredations and excessive demands of others, they could also exploit their place in the transport network to their advantage. Given the government's concern for tribute income and regular flows of food into the capital, Nahua demands could be met with sympathy and favor. The rowers of canoes were sometimes strikingly bold in their demands. In 1689, officials from Tlahuac complained of "malicious" behavior by rowers. Clients hired and paid the rowers in advance to deliver wheat, maize, timber, and fruit to various customers in Mexico City. Having placed their trust in the rowers, they were dismayed to discover that they had been swindled. The rowers had allegedly made off with their cargoes and sold them in the villages of Ixtayopan and Tolyahualco.[216]

Rowers were not above exploiting their positions of influence in other ways. In 1711, Manuel de Peñafiel, the administrator of an embarcadero in Chalco, alleged that rowers employed various devious schemes to make extra money from delivering maize to the capital: they either tampered with weights and measures or they set aside some of the corn they were contracted to deliver and, to make up the difference in the weight of their cargo, so as to mask what they had done, they soaked the rest of the corn in water, thereby making it heavier. The leftover corn was then sold quietly and on the side. While it is hard to tell if there was any substance

---

[212] The bribe involved forgiveness of a debt owed by Juana's husband along with other payments. AGN, Criminal, vol. 233, exp. 12, ff. 203v–204.

[213] Juana Petronila reported that witnesses had seen suspicious bruises on the corpse of her husband.

[214] AGN, Criminal, vol. 233, exp. 12, ff. 210–210v.

[215] AGN, Criminal, vol. 233, exp. 12, ff. 200–204.

[216] AGN, Indios, vol. 30, exp. 301, ff. 275–276.

to Peñafiel's allegations, the administrators of Spanish institutions in the capital, who were provisioned by canoe and who kept accounts ledgers, did sometimes note the arrival of damp corn. In 1716, one of them refused to pay the full freight charge. He had the corn laid out in the sun to dry.[217] Because of such fraudulent practices, officials at the embarcaderos had arranged for guards to monitor the rowers' activities. Their efforts, though, had been thwarted by the rowers' ardent protests.[218] Guards were called in to monitor canoeists on other occasions. During times of shortages, guards could be stationed along the main canal into Mexico City. They were tasked with ensuring that the rowers did not get waylaid at pulquerias before making their deliveries.[219]

Rowers were accused of yet other extortionate practices. In 1563, Spanish farmers from the Valley of Atlixco complained of price gouging. According to the Spaniards' petition, rowers in Ayotzingo had refused to transport wheat to Mexico City unless the farmers paid exorbitant fees. By demanding sixteen *tomines* (i.e., two pesos), well above the usual rate of six tomines, the rowers had allegedly gone too far.[220] As a result, they maintained, food prices in the capital would necessarily increase. Unsurprisingly, the viceroy ordered the alcalde mayor of Chalco to enforce the original fees.[221] Such intervention proved only temporarily effective, though. Twenty years later the rowers were once more accused of extorting higher fees. In this 1582 case, Spanish farmers, again from Atlixco, claimed that after having loaded wheat and other foodstuffs on board the canoes the rowers then moved them out of reach in the middle of the lake. The rowers refused to proceed to Mexico City unless the farmers handed over more money. With their goods effectively stranded. Unwilling to submit to extortion, the farmers approached the authorities.[222] The same problem arose

---

[217] AGN, Archivo Histórico de Hacienda, Temporalidades, leg. 106, exp. 7, f. 4. A different administrator of an embarcadero corroborated the allegations about the adulteration of weights and measures. AGI, Audiencia de México, leg. 781, f. 107.

[218] AGI, Audiencia de México, leg. 781, f. 102v.

[219] Gibson, *The Aztecs under Spanish Rule*, 560n149; AGI, Patronato, leg. 226, ramo 20, f. 10.

[220] Tomines, a Nahuatl term, were equivalent to *reales*; hence, eight tomines equaled a peso. The document listed prices in tomines and pesos, and not reales. On the use of these terms, see Cline, *Colonial Culhuacan*, 237, and Anderson et al., eds., *Beyond the Codices: The Nahua View of Colonial Mexico* (Berkeley: University of California Press and the UCLA Latin American Center, 1976), 32–33.

[221] AGN, Mercedes, vol. 7, f. 113v.

[222] AGN, Indios, vol. 2, exp. 75, f. 18v, exp. 76, ff. 18v–19.

a year later, this time with the alcalde mayor having conspired with the rowers against the farmers.[223]

The belligerence of the rowers in demanding better pay could, at times, become protracted. Prolonged standoffs over fees sometimes resembled a kind of collective bargaining against Spanish institutions, in one case the Augustinian friary of Ayotzingo (1634) and, in another, the Hospital de San Hipólito in Mexico City (1637).[224] In the latter case, rowers in cahoots with staff of an embarcadero had refused to allow canoes to make their journeys. Concerned ecclesiastics claimed that the standoff jeopardized the hospital's food supply. Apparently this was a long-standing problem, one that had recurred intermittently over the previous four years.[225] Spanish institutions thus occasionally sought alternative ways of transporting material around the lakes, for instance, using slaves as the rowers of canoes. In 1583, an elderly black slave, who had been making the same journey by canoe for forty years, received a new license to deliver zacatl to Mexico City's Hospital de la Concepción.[226]

Disputes over freight fees took place at embarcaderos precisely because they were key junctures in the wider transportation network. The profitability of embarcaderos depended on such factors as their proximity to transportation routes. Thus towns connected to the royal road – for instance, Xochimilco, Chalco Atenco, and Ayotzingo – had sizable embarcaderos. Their wharves were important community assets. Controlled by municipal councils, they generated valuable rental income, either from leases of the embarcaderos themselves or through the rental of storage facilities, and this income bolstered town finances and could be quite lucrative, if one were to judge from the conflicts surrounding them.[227] Ayotzingo, as a point of entry for foodstuffs imported from the east, was a prime venue for disputes over transport. In 1673, a group of traders in honey, sugar, wheat, and maize brought litigation before the high court against Augustinian friars and Nahua officials. The traders accused locals of impeding access to Huitziltzinco, one of the altepetl's embarcaderos. The plaintiffs complained that the Augustinians and Nahuas, assisted by a magistrate's lieutenant, had demanded exorbitant fees even as they offered preferential treatment to others. They argued that such an

---

[223] AGN, Indios, vol. 2, exp. 940, ff. 215–215v.
[224] AGN, Tierras, vol. 2973, exp. 51, ff. 110–111.
[225] AGN, Tierras, vol. 3459, exp. 14, ff. 398–401.
[226] AGN, Indios, vol. 2, exp. 547, ff. 126–126v.
[227] AGNM, Xochimilco, vol. 2, ff. 46–47.

impediment proved contrary to the common good. To support their contention, the traders presented earlier rulings as precedents. Previous disputes had prompted the issuing of viceregal orders in 1614, 1635, and 1646.[228]

The strategic importance of embarcaderos as funnels through which cargo passed meant that they could be sufficiently profitable as to prompt Spaniards to establish their own wharves.[229] In 1643 a Spanish resident of Mixquic named Gerónimo de Echevaría, who traded in saltpeter and other commodities, owned a private embarcadero as well as seven canoes.[230] Prominent merchants, Nahuas and Spaniards alike, owned embarcaderos. In the late seventeenth century, a Nahua noble and merchant from Xochimilco, don Nicolás de Meza, owned several sizable canoes and an embarcadero. At the same time, a Spanish merchant named don Antonio de los Olivos owned an embarcadero along with two large canoes.[231] In addition to merchants, the owners of haciendas in Chalco also valued owning embarcaderos. They regularly established their own dock facilities. In 1711, three different hacendados owned embarcaderos in Chalco Atenco. Two others owned embarcaderos in Ayotzingo.[232] Such privately owned enterprises obviated the need to pay fees for docking and loading goods, presumably a boon given the attempts by Nahua rowers to extort higher rates from their customers. Private ownership also meant that hacendados could contract directly with rowers, thereby simplifying the process of transporting wheat and maize to Mexico City.

Sometime prior to 1586, Juan Alonso de Sosa, a Spanish official of the royal treasury, purchased lands in the Valley of Atlixco. He added to his purchase a lakeshore home, a shop, and an embarcadero, all of which he bought from Nahuas of Chalco Atenco. The property had the advantage of being located both by the lake and on the road connecting Mexico City to Puebla.[233] On his death in the 1580s, debts owed to the crown forced his heirs to sell the property. Thereafter the embarcadero passed through several hands – and was augmented by subsequent purchases of land, although it did suffer from occasional damage by flooding – until its

---

[228] AGN, Tierras, vol. 2877, exp. 11, ff. 1–11v.

[229] Gibson, *The Aztecs under Spanish Rule*, 364.

[230] AGN, Tierras, vol. 2913, exp. 8, ff. 218–224.

[231] AGNM, Xochimilco, vol. 1, ff. 295–296v, 304v–306, vol. 1 (second foliation), ff. 10v, 10v–11v, 21–22, 46–50v, and 59v–68v.

[232] AGI, Audiencia de México, leg. 781, ff. 98v–112v and 222–225.

[233] AGN, Tierras, vol. 3320, exp. 1, ff. 35–45.

ownership became the focus of a bitter dispute in the early eighteenth century. Those who tried to lay claim to the property included doña Catalina Rosel y Lugo, who owned haciendas in Chalco, the Nahuas of Chalco Atenco, and the local friary. The tripartite competition for its control implies that the embarcadero had become highly profitable.[234]

While Spaniards vied successfully for control over wharves, Nahuas long predominated as the rowers of canoes. Indeed, even as haciendas and Spanish government institutions came to dominate the food supply network, Nahua canoes remained an integral and vital element within it. The enduring reliance on canoes was shown in 1711 when viceregal authorities uncovered an elaborate plot to manipulate the supply of maize at Mexico City's storehouse and grain market.[235] Still acutely aware of the potential for disorder and violence in the event of food shortages and high prices – factors which the viceroy ascribed to the ruinous riot of 1692 – royal officials had been perturbed to discover a conspiracy at the alhóndiga to secretly hoard grain, limiting its release to the market and thereby artificially inflating prices until they rose to the point where the culprits could secure a handsome profit.[236] For all its deviousness the plot had relied on the complicity of several well-placed individuals. The many perpetrators of the crime included senior figures of the Spanish establishment, including Mexico City's corregidor and several administrators of the alhóndiga. Also involved were *trajineros*, factors who negotiated the delivery of maize from the embarcaderos, and, notably, Nahua rowers of canoes. By keeping quiet and acting as middlemen in the delivery of maize, the rowers had been essential to the plot's success.[237] That they were induced into participating in the conspiracy serves as a compelling reminder of the ongoing importance of canoes in the wider colonial economy.

CONCLUSION

Efficient and versatile, canoes were ideally suited to moving goods and people around the Basin of Mexico's lakes. They remained unsurpassed during the colonial period as the preferred means of transportation. Only

---

[234] AGN, Tierras, vol. 3320, exp. 1, ff. 1–103.
[235] AGI, Audiencia de México, leg. 781, ff. 282v–365v.
[236] AGI, Audiencia de México, leg. 781, ff. 80–83v.
[237] AGI, Audiencia de México, leg. 781, ff. 243–255.

in the nineteenth century, with renewed drainage projects and the coming of the railroads did the rowers of canoes face a fundamental challenge to their business. Yet even into the twentieth century residents of Xochimilco continued to use canoes in daily life, albeit with one difference: canoes were now made out of metal if not tree trunks. But modern technology still had not entirely supplanted the canoes.[238]

For those parts of the lake areas that escaped desiccation, and retained something of the "amphibious" character of the erstwhile Aztec world, canoes proved to be a remarkably enduring and successful technological adaptation to the environment.[239] Of course, Nahuas had long adapted to life in the lake areas even as they actively modified the environment by dredging channels through which canoes could pass and clearing them of vegetation. In staking out fishing grounds and maintaining passageways through the lakes, Nahuas continued to enjoy important benefits of water transport. Canoes kept rowers, artisans, farmers, fishermen, hunters, and traders in employment, and their income in turn supported innumerable households, contributed to the prosperity of regional markets, and bolstered town finances. The survival of the southern lakes, and the enduring use of canoes, meant that Nahuas successfully preserved a key foundation of the area's economy even if matters of distribution and exchange attracted a good deal of competition, if not outright conflict.

The commercial sector of the Nahua economy benefited considerably from Xochimilco's fortuitous situation. In addition to bountiful chinampa harvests and livestock, the jurisdiction was blessed with a wide range of natural resources: plentiful supplies of timber and stone could be found in the montes; the city had a limestone quarry and deposits of saltpeter; and the lake environment afforded an abundance of foodstuffs, including fish and other aquatic animals and plants that, along with chinampa produce, catered to a strong market, both locally and in Mexico City. Unsurprisingly, Xochimilco retained much of its commercial vitality at the same time that the majority of its citizens were employed in skilled trades.

Canoes, moreover, played an integral part in the political economy of Spanish colonialism in central Mexico. The example of lake-borne

---

[238] Magdalena A. García Sanchez, "El modo de vida lacustre en el valle de México, ¿mestizaje o proceso de aculturación?," in Enrique Florescano and Virginia García Acosta, eds., *Mestizajes tecnológicos y cambios culturales en México* (Mexico City: El Centro de Investigaciones y Estudios Superiores en Antropología Social, 2004), 36.

[239] Gibson, *The Aztecs under Spanish Rule*, 237.

transportation reminds us that the southern hinterlands were critical to the maintenance of New Spain's center of power. Canoes helped to keep Mexico City's residents provisioned with food. They contributed to the vitality of the market economy and helped Nahuas fulfill their tribute obligations to the colonial administration. The lakes and the canoes further facilitated the government's acquisition of valuable resources. Viceregal institutions relied on canoes for the delivery of the stone and timber needed for public works projects. Accordingly, colonial relationships between Nahuas and Spaniards, as well as between the capital and its hinterland, were influenced by environmental factors. For Lakes Xochimilco and Chalco, these interactions took place in the context of a complex ecological setting. The lacustrine environment and the use of canoes were bound up with the buoyancy of the colonial economy as well as the lasting vigor of Nahua communities. And thanks to their control of lake transportation, Nahuas could contend with Spanish institutions from a position of relative strength.

Spanish rule did not displace or submerge the indigenous sector of the economy. Rather, it continued to thrive in the lake areas to the south of Mexico City. Elements of the colonial and indigenous economies came to exist alongside one another. At times they came into contact, in some instances making for complex compounds of the two, as shown in the 1711 inspection of the food supply system: Nahuas and people of mixed and Spanish ancestries cultivated maize on Spanish estates; the maize was then taken to lakeside docks owned by Spaniards or Nahuas; there middlemen of various backgrounds made arrangements for its transportation by thousands of Nahua canoes, which in turn traversed the lakes and the old Aztec canals, delivering their cargo to a Spanish institution, the alhóndiga. This example indicates the importance of factors of distribution and exchange, which have often been overshadowed by attention to labor and land in ethnohistories of colonial Mexico.[240]

---

[240] These subjects have received attention from historians of the Andes: Luis Miguel Glave Testino, *Trajinantes: caminos indígenas en la sociedad colonial, siglos XVI/XVII* (Lima: Instituto de Apoyo Agrario, 1989); Jane A. Mangan, *Trading Roles: Gender, Ethnicity, and the Urban Economy in Colonial Potosí* (Durham: Duke University Press, 2005).

4

Demography and Society

If Xochimilco's colonial-era history was exceptional because of its watery landscape, which shielded it from some of the disruption faced by communities elsewhere, when it came to demographic change, it suffered from the same decline as the rest of the Americas. There was no buffer to protect Nahuas against the overwhelming loss of life. The Xochimilca suffered appallingly high mortality rates, as presumably did the Cuitlahuaca, Mixquica, and Chalca, although the few surviving sources for these latter three ethnic groups do not allow us to recreate their demographic history during the colonial period. As a larger altepetl and a single colonial jurisdiction, and one that was vital to the Spanish colonial administration, Xochimilco's changing population dynamics were better captured in the sources, especially in the tribute tallies produced from the second half of the sixteenth century. The sources show that Xochimilco suffered a swift and severe decline in its once large population. By the middle years of the seventeenth century, as elsewhere in central Mexico, it reached its nadir. Thereafter, recovery was only partial and fitful. At the end of the colonial period the population remained but a quarter of its original size.

Whereas the landscape provided foundations for continuity in certain key areas of life, demographic change brought wholesale disruption to others. This was especially the case when population loss intersected with the wider demands of the colonial political economy. In this the surviving tribute records provide both the quantitative basis for observing population trends and the historical context in which to see changing social relations taking place. The changing arrangements of extracting wealth via tribute and labor reflected and exacerbated the effects of population loss. The two together destabilized Nahua society and undermined some of the integrative structures of the altepetl, particularly when it came to the reciprocal ties between commoners and nobles. The consensus that was supposed to be at the heart of hierarchical relations broke down. As the colonial government meddled in municipal finances, it undermined position of the Nahua upper class. Commoners seized the opportunity to escape the burdensome exactions of their rulers or to renegotiate the terms of their vassalage. As a result, relations between lords and commoners became confrontational and the social hierarchy was destabilized.

DISEASE ECOLOGIES, COLONIAL DISLOCATIONS, AND DEMOGRAPHIC DECLINE

On July 11, 1572, Constantino de San Felipe, one of the merchants encountered in the last chapter, asked a messenger to go to Xochimilco's cabildo and notify the council officials that he "was at the very extremity of illness and desired to order his testament." Hearing this, the council officers dispatched a notary named Mateo Ceverino de Arellano – who had served as one of the aides to the famous friar, Bernardino de Sahagún – to go and take down the merchant's last will and testament.[1] Constantino's Nahuatl testament, among other documents that were bundled together in the papers of a subsequent lawsuit, leave us with a poignant, firsthand expression of people's anxieties at a time of appallingly high mortality rates.[2] The records of the litigation, which also include rare pictorial sources (Figures 4.1–4.3), among them a will as well as inventories of property and a genealogy, also provide a small, partial glimpse of the calamitous toll of epidemics on Native peoples.[3]

Constantino de San Felipe set down provisions for his three surviving family members, who are depicted in a genealogy (Figure 4.1). The image shows two lineages, those of Constantino and of his wife, Petronilla Teiuc. Petronilla is represented in profile, with her head at the top center of the image. She is identified in an alphabetic gloss and is shown alongside a speech scroll. Petronilla faces toward her husband across the dotted line that runs diagonally down to the right-hand side of the paper. Constantino likewise appears in profile, together with a speech scroll

---

[1] Lockhart, *The Nahuas after the Conquest*, 472.
[2] AGN, Tierras, vol. 1525, exp. 3; Karttunen and Lockhart, eds., *Nahuatl in the Middle Years*, 93–97.
[3] For an analysis of these sources, see Michel R. Oudijk and María Castañeda de la Paz, "Un testamento pictográfico de Xochimilco," *Revista Española de Antropología Americana*, vol. 36, no. 2 (2006), 111–123.

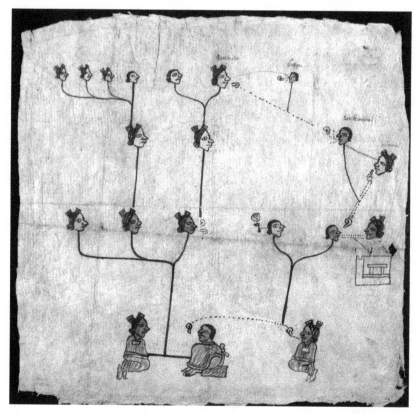

FIGURE 4.1 Genealogy of Constantino de San Felipe, 1576. Image courtesy of the Newberry Library, Chicago, Ayer Collection, MS 1902.

and an alphabetic gloss identifying him by name. Situated between husband and wife and above the dotted line connecting them is their son, Felipe. And behind Constantino, on the far right, is his mother, Juliana Tlaco.

It was to these three individuals – his wife, mother, and son – that Constantino bequeathed his property. The estate consisted of a cluster of chinampas, a house, and various other belongings, from digging sticks to grain bins, clay cups, as well as items that were crucial to his line of business, among them a horse and sixty blankets (see Figure 4.2).

Given the prevalence of disease and his own poor health, Constantino was cautious about how to dispose of this property: while passing on a part of his estate to his young son, he also set down a few conditions that, he hoped, would provide some security for his family and keep together those

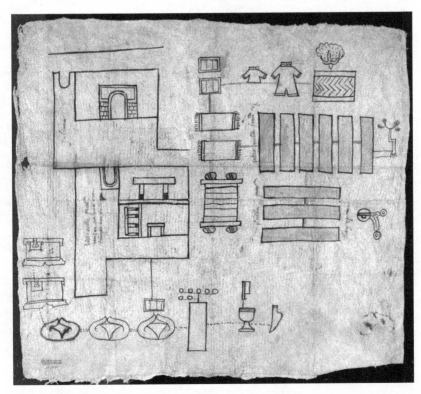

FIGURE 4.2 Property in the bequests of Constantino de San Felipe, 1576. Image courtesy of the Newberry Library, Ayer Collection, MS 1901.

who survived him. He specified that his wife would only inherit some items if she agreed to remain and look after his mother, who was herself a widow. Taking a further precaution, Constantino asked that "when our lord God brings about her end, if my spouse dies," the chinampas and grain bin would be "given to my precious child Felipe Constantino." Although he assigned them to his wife, "they are only for her to bring up my child, if he lives."[4] Unfortunately, the child did not live. Within a few years of his father's demise, Felipe also passed away, perhaps one of the early victims of the *cocoliztli* pandemic of 1576–1581 (cocoliztli translates as "sickness" or "pest" and could refer to several diseases, on this occasion either typhus or hemorrhagic fever).[5] In the span of four short years, then,

[4] AGN, Tierras, vol. 1525, exp. 3, ff. 3–4v.
[5] Lockhart, *Nahuatl as Written*, 215; Malvido and Viesca, "La epidemia de cocoliztli de 1576," 27–33; Cook, *Born to Die*, 121; Prem, "Disease Outbreaks in Central Mexico

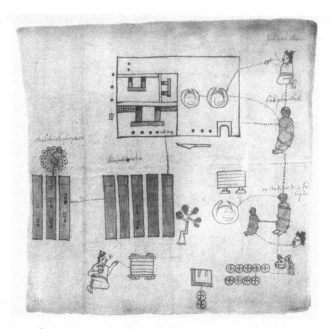

FIGURE 4.3 Juliana's property claims. Plate 33 in E. Eugène Goupil, *Documents pour servir à l'histoire du Mexique* (Paris: E. Leroux, 1891). Image courtesy of the Newberry Library (Ayer 507.B6 1891). Original image held by the Bibliothèque National de France.

Petronilla lost her husband and son. (In the genealogy, their faces have been shaded in, indicating that they had passed away). Constantino's mother also suffered from the losses. Juliana outlived her husband, son, grandson, and, as another pictorial document shows, yet another son. Her deceased relatives are shown in Figure 4.3, wrapped in burial shrouds.

The deaths endured by Constantino's family were part of a wider demographic collapse among Native peoples across the Americas in the years after the conquest. By the time Constantino de San Felipe and his son died in the 1570s, Xochimilco's population had already declined drastically. As the city's Nahua nobles reckoned the toll, for five decades new and recurring epidemics, among other factors, had reduced the city's Native population from approximately 30,000 to 6,000 people,

during the Sixteenth Century," 38–42; Acuna-Soto et al., "When Half the Population Died"; Rodolfo Acuna-Soto, David W. Stahle, Malcolm K. Cleaveland, and Matthew D. Therrell "Megadrought and Megadeath in 16th Century Mexico," *Emerging Infectious Diseases*, vol. 8, no. 4 (2002), 360–362.

if not fewer.[6] As many as four in five people may have perished across half a century. The devastating trend of demographic decline continued well into the seventeenth century. At its nadir in the 1640s, the city may have been reduced to fewer than 2,000 indigenous residents. The archbishop of Mexico conducted an inspection in 1646 and reported only 1,182 Nahuas confirmed in the Catholic faith.[7]

The demographic collapse can be attributed to a variety of factors. In the two decades following the Spanish-Mexica War, those individuals not lost to disease may have been killed in warfare or through enslavement. According to Xochimilco's nobles, the altepetl had contributed some 12,000 warriors to the conquest. While we lack details of the number who died in the fighting, it is likely that the city's population size declined to a certain extent. The possibility that warfare held significant demographic implications increases when factoring in the subsequent military campaigns after the defeat of the Mexica. In 1522, or thereabouts, and as a reward for his contributions to the conquest, the crown awarded Xochimilco as an encomienda to Pedro de Alvarado. For the duration of Xochimilco's encomienda period (1522–1541), Alvarado was absent, moving on to wage campaigns of conquest in Guatemala, Honduras, and elsewhere. Xochimilco contributed 2,500 warriors to Alvarado's conquests, as well as 500 soldiers to the Pánuco campaign and 600 more to Jalisco under Nuño Beltrán de Guzmán.[8] As Xochimilco's nobles later lamented, not one of their citizens ever returned from these military campaigns.[9]

Given the chaos of the immediate post-conquest period – for which there is but scant documentation – it is impossible to discern population changes. There may well have been something of a population recovery in the two decades after the smallpox epidemic of the early 1520s. But there is also the possibility that the population numbers may have remained lower. For one thing, the absence of more than 3,000 young men, in the prime of their lives, would have reduced the number of marriage partners

---

[6] The figures were provided by the nobles in 1563; at that time, they estimated, there were 6,000–7,000 residents of the city; since the population would have likely been lower a decade later, on the eve of the 1576 cocoliztli, I have opted for the nobles' lower figure. AGI, Patronato, leg. 184, ramo 50; see also Restall et al., eds., *Mesoamerican Voices*, 69.

[7] Newberry Library, Ayer Collection, ms. 1106, f. 1v.

[8] In his place, a certain Luis Delgado served as an administrator. *El libro de las tasaciones de pueblos de la Nueva España, siglo XVI* (Mexico City: Archivo General de la Nación, 1952), 304–307.

[9] AGI, Patronato, leg. 184, ramo 50; see also Restall et al., eds., *Mesoamerican Voices*, 67.

and therefore depressed birthrates.[10] The absence of several thousand individuals would have also reduced economic output to some extent – potentially reducing the number of chinampas under cultivation, for instance – thereby making for more straightened circumstances for those who remained. Colonial violence may explain demographic decline in one further way: any number of Xochimilca may have been enslaved in the years before Native American slavery was formally abolished 1542. The few surviving sources make it impossible to tell how many were enslaved but one small glimpse of this threat survives in the records. In December 1542, King Charles V issued a decree confirming that one Martín Zambrano, from Xochimilco, was a free man and that he should not be deprived of his liberty by those trying to enslave him.[11]

Given the absence of documentary evidence suggesting otherwise, disease appears to have been the largest single cause of high mortality in the early colonial period even as famine, flight, and other factors also contributed to demographic losses. Disease resulted in such high mortality for a variety of reasons. Native peoples had little to no resistance, at least initially, to a lethal combination of foreign pathogens. Virgin soil epidemics, meaning that their victims had not be exposed to the diseases previously, claimed many lives, much as they did in other parts of the world.[12] While historians once supposed that Native peoples of the Americas were more vulnerable to diseases than individuals in Africa or Europe and Asia, who had previously acquired some degree of immunity, recent research has suggested that comparable levels of morbidity and mortality followed from exposure to new viral or bacterial infections in the Americas as elsewhere. As Susan Alchon has noted, what distinguished the Americas for its high mortality – between 75 and 90 percent – were a combination of factors, including warfare, enslavement, colonial violence, and the terrible sequence of one outbreak of disease after another, at times in fairly quick succession.[13] Most common among the epidemic diseases were smallpox, measles, typhus, mumps, pneumonic plague, and perhaps hemorrhagic fever, this latter

---

[10] On the significance of natality as a factor of demographic change, see Skopyk, "Undercurrents of Conquest," 240–242; Thomas M. Whitmore, *Disease and Death in Early Colonial Mexico: Simulating Amerindian De-Population* (Boulder: Westview Press, 1992), and Livi Bacci, *Conquest*.

[11] AGI, Indiferente, leg. 423, ramo 20, ff. 565v–566.

[12] Woodrow Borah, "Introduction," in Cook and Lovell, eds., *"Secret Judgments of God,"* 7–10.

[13] Alchon, *A Pest in the Land*, 2–3; Nash, "Beyond Virgin Soils," 76–107.

possibly having been indigenous to the Americas. Epidemics spread far and wide, sometimes reaching pandemic proportions.[14]

In some cases, several diseases broke out simultaneously. These "compound epidemics," as the historian Woodrow Borah called them, were especially severe since the survivors of one disease were weakened and vulnerable to the next.[15] In these circumstances, it proves especially hard to determine which pathogenic agents were responsible for high death rates at any given moment. For one thing, compound epidemics make it difficult to single out specific diseases which were afflicting Native peoples. For another, medical knowledge of the time did not allow for reliable diagnoses, and similar and common symptoms, such as fever and vomiting, could be caused by different sicknesses. Hence documentary descriptions of skin rashes, commonly associated with measles, might be confused with symptoms of smallpox, which involved a progression from papules to vesicles and finally pustules.[16] Imprecise and inconsistent terms used in the records further complicate matters – as with *tabardillo*, which may have shifted over time in its meaning, becoming the common term for typhus later in the sixteenth century – as did issues of translation.[17] The Nahuatl term *zahuatl*, for instance, might refer to smallpox or measles, or, as Charles Gibson noted, it might refer to different intensities of the same disease.[18] Sources from Xochimilco seldom identified specific diseases; more often, Nahuas and Spaniards spoke of "epidemics" in vague or generic ways, as with the term *pestilence*, which did not necessarily mean bubonic plague.

Because of the relatively short distances between communities in the densely populated basin, and because of swift mobility by canoe or horse in and around the lakes, diseases observed elsewhere in the region likely spread to Xochimilco and its surrounding settlements. This was clearly the case with pandemics. The 1520–1521 smallpox pandemic, which figured so prominently in the Spanish-Mexica War, also ravaged Xochimilco.[19] Smallpox may have returned to central Mexico in 1531; this time the outbreak of smallpox may have coincided with one of measles, and both

---

[14] Acuna-Soto et al., "When Half the Population Died"; Cook, *Born to Die*, 132, 139; Prem, "Disease Outbreaks in Central Mexico during the Sixteenth Century," 48.
[15] Borah, "Introduction," 7.
[16] Cook and Lovell, "Unravelling the Web of Disease," in *"Secret Judgments of God,"* 217, 220.
[17] Prem, "Disease Outbreaks in Central Mexico during the Sixteenth Century," 40.
[18] Gibson, *The Aztecs under Spanish Rule*, 448.
[19] Cook, *Born to Die*, 65–66; Restall et al., eds., *Mesoamerican Voices*, 38.

diseases were recorded again in 1532 across the Basin of Mexico and specifically in Chalco.[20]

A series of epidemics responsible for the highest mortality in Mexican history, known as the great sickness or *huey cocoliztli*, broke out between 1545 and 1548.[21] Of the numerous pathogens, historians initially thought that typhus was the leading cause of death, with pulmonary plague also possibly afflicting the population.[22] Subsequently, scholars have proposed other maladies, including hemorrhagic fever and perhaps enteric fever brought on by a kind of salmonella bacterium.[23] With all these diseases, Nahuas suffered from a profusion of symptoms including nosebleeds, fever, and bleeding from the mucus membranes.[24] The historian David Noble Cook suggests that the 1552 medical text, *Libellus de medicinalibus indorum herbis*, one of the great works of Renaissance Mexico, likely described the symptoms of the illness of the mid-1540s. The book was compiled by an indigenous medical specialist, Martín de la Cruz, and was translated into Latin by Juan Badianus, a Nahua who hailed from Xochimilco. The text states:

The face of the feverish person takes on many aspects. At times it becomes red, sometimes black, and other times it becomes pallid. Blood is spit up. There is vomit. The body becomes agitated and moves to and fro. One sees little. The mouth senses at times, especially in the palette, bitterness, burning, and sometimes

---

[20] Alchon, it should be noted, questions the identification of these epidemics. She points out that the alleged smallpox epidemic struck a significant number of the elderly, who ought to have attained some degree of immunity from the outbreak a decade earlier. Conversely, the reported high mortality among children from measles seems surprising as it would, presumably, have affected all age groups since no one had been exposed to it previously. Alchon, *A Pest in the Land*, 69; Prem, "Disease Outbreaks in Central Mexico during the Sixteenth Century," 40; Gibson, *The Aztecs under Spanish Rule*, 448.

[21] The epidemics of the period between 1545 and 1548 are often seen as having been the most severe in Mexico's recorded history. Estimates for the total loss of life range from 5 to 15 million people. Acuna-Soto et al., "When Half the Population Died," 1–2; Alchon, *A Pest in the Land*, 69–70; Cook, *Born to Die*, 102–103; Robert McCaa, "Spanish and Nahuatl Views on Smallpox and Demographic Catastrophe in Mexico," *Journal of Interdisciplinary History*, vol. 25 (1995), 427–428. On the difficulties identifying the disease, and its association with a disease called *matlazahuatl*, see Skopyk, "Undercurrents of Conquest," 267.

[22] Gibson, *The Aztecs under Spanish Rule*, 448–449; Pérez Zevallos, *Xochimilco Ayer*, vol. 2, Appendix 1, 132.

[23] Åshild J. Vågene et al., "Salmonella Enterica Genomes from Victims of a Major Sixteenth-Century Epidemic in Mexico," *Nature Ecology and Evolution*, vol. 2, no. 3 (2018), 520–528; Acuna-Soto et al., "Megadrought and Megadeath in 16th Century Mexico," 360–362.

[24] Alchon, *A Pest in the Land*, 70.

sweetness. The stomach generally is very upset. If the danger is not dealt with when the urine is white, clear, or milkfish, it will be too late to prepare the medications.[25]

Other contemporary descriptions were less detailed and, as one would expect from a compound epidemic, they mentioned different symptoms. The entry for 1545 in the Nahuatl annals history of San Gregorio Atlapulco, a chinampa town in Xochimilco's jurisdiction, stated that "there was plague in which blood came out of the nose, from which there was death."[26] Mumps, or *quechpozahualiztli*, were then identified in Atlapulco's annals for 1548.[27]

The consequences of devastating loss of life in the late 1540s were far-reaching and enduring. By 1550, severe food shortages were being reported in the Basin of Mexico, which could have inhibited a demographic rebound.[28] Although there were significant fluctuations in climatic conditions and harvests, food insecurity continued well into the 1550s, if one were to judge from the variations in the price of maize. The colonial administration thus frequently altered the rules surrounding trade and the provisioning of cities. Indeed, the period from 1548 through the mid-1560s witnessed concerted efforts by the government to reform the tribute system, as discussed below. At the same time, the dislocations caused by the huey cocoliztli extended to increasingly strained social relations within Native communities. The emerging civil strife and disruptive political reforms of the period after 1548 may have reflected the kinds of damage to economic and political institutions that Susan Alchon identified as another explanation for the enduring decline of the Native population.[29]

Yet more instances of virulent diseases were recorded after the calamitous loss of life from 1545–1548. Pestilence was again seen in the Basin of Mexico in 1559.[30] On that occasion the disease may have been influenza or diphtheria.[31] Three years later, a scribe in Atlapulco made a note of an outbreak of measles by using the Castilian loanword "zarapio" for *sarampión* in the Nahuatl text.[32] A year after that, in 1563–1564, zahuatl,

---

[25] Cited in Cook, *Born to Die*, 101; see also Alfredo López Austin, *Textos de medicina Nahuatl* (Mexico City: UNAM, 1975), 40.

[26] The original tentatively reads as follows (with square brackets indicating uncertainty about the wording): "ynhua niquiac ye[ztli toacapan oquiz ic?] micoac." Pérez Zevallos, *Xochimilco Ayer*, vol. 2, Appendix 1, 130.

[27] Pérez Zevallos, *Xochimilco Ayer*, vol. 2, Appendix 1, 131.

[28] AGN, Mercedes, vol. 3, exp. 54, ff. 25v–26 (47v–48 old foliation).

[29] Alchon, *A Pest in the Land*, 3.   [30] Gibson, *The Aztecs under Spanish Rule*, 449.

[31] Alchon, *A Pest in the Land*, 69.

[32] Pérez Zevallos, *Xochimilco Ayer*, vol. 2, Appendix 1, 132.

measles, and perhaps typhus (*matlaltotonqui*) affected Huitzilopochco, across the lake from Xochimilco, as well as parts of Chalco, where, according to some sources, nearly half of the population died.[33] And then another cocoliztli pandemic flared from 1576 to 1581, which may have claimed the life of Constantino de San Felipe's son.

This latest pandemic proved to be the third most destructive outbreak of the sixteenth century and claimed many lives in Xochimilco, according to fray Gerónimo de Mendieta.[34] That the cocoliztli pandemic could have been of typhus or hemorrhagic fever speaks to the complex disease ecologies affecting colonial Mexico. Rather than simply being a case of deadly virgin soil epidemics, a variety of factors contributed to the outbreaks of certain diseases and to their high morbidity and mortality. Prominent among these were climatic conditions. As Bradley Skopyk has noted for Tlaxcala, diseases were far more likely to break out in periods of climatic stress.[35] While typhus, for instance, is notorious for having followed in the footsteps of war, famine, and poverty, drought also played a significant role in outbreaks, particularly in 1576.[36] A similar situation obtained with hemorrhagic fever, according to Rodolfo Acuna-Soto, David Stahle, and their colleagues, who observed that the disease apparently affected human populations as a result of complex interactions between altitude, climate, flora, and fauna. Long periods of drought, when followed by higher rates of precipitation, contributed to the initiation and then the rapid spread of the disease. These were precisely the conditions in Xochimilco, as elsewhere in central Mexico in both 1545 and 1576: during a long period of megadrought, in both these years there were abundant rains, and at the height of the rainy season of 1576, the disease suddenly became much more widespread, ultimately leading to the deaths of more than 50 percent of the population in some communities.[37]

Even after the 1576–1581 epidemic in Xochimilco, the recurrence of illness was seemingly relentless. In 1590, Atlapulco's residents were afflicted by an sickness that was simply identified as *tlatlaciztli*, or

---

[33] Gibson, *The Aztecs under Spanish Rule*, 449.

[34] Prem, "Disease Outbreaks in Central Mexico during the Sixteenth Century," 38–42; Cook, *Born to Die*, 120–121; Mendieta is cited in Pérez Zevallos, *Xochimilco Ayer*, vol. 1, 48.

[35] Skopyk, "Undercurrents of Conquest," 273.

[36] The correlation of drought and outbreaks of typhus, it should be noted, was observed for a later time period: Burns et al., "Drought and Epidemic Typhus, Central Mexico, 1655–1918," 442–447.

[37] Acuna-Soto et al., "When Half the Population Died," 1–5; Acuna-Soto et al., "Megadrought and Megadeath in 16th Century Mexico," 360–362.

cough.[38] Its identification by a single symptom fails to conveys a full sense of its severity: when the governor and nobles of Xochimilco asked the viceroy for relief from the usual labor drafts, they referred to the "sickness, calamitous mortality, and people having fled," all of which, they explained, had significantly reduced the population.[39] A decade later, another cocoliztli outbreak lasted eight months in Xochimilco, until June 1602.[40] It returned again in 1604–1607, 1613, 1629–1631, and 1641–1642 and was far from being the last epidemic to cause the deaths of many lake-area residents.[41] Over time, some of these diseases became endemic, although as Linda Nash has noted, natural selection may have worked in such a way that mutations of certain diseases may have increased their virulence.[42] It is worth noting that the population continued to drop even after the last of the sixteenth century's major epidemics.

POPULATION FIGURES

Quite how devastating each disease was remains hard to determine because we have only sporadic data about the population size of Xochimilco and the communities in its jurisdiction. No reliable census or tax records survive from before the 1560s. Indeed, before the 1560s we have no contemporaneous figures of any kind. Thereafter, fairly reliable quantitative data in the form of census and tax records began to be produced by the government and ecclesiastical authorities, allowing us to reconstruct the main outlines of Xochimilco's demographic history. Still, it should be emphasized that the small sample size and the inherent problems of the ways in which assessments were made, and the differing institutional prerogatives of those who conducted the counts, make for a good deal of imprecision and uncertainty in the recording of population sizes. Ecclesiastical records, for instance, recorded the population size as being markedly higher in 1588 than did New Spain's exchequer. In spite of such discrepancies, the data produced during and after the 1560s can be quite useful: it was common for government and ecclesiastical officials to count the number of tributaries, rather than individuals, which makes for

---

[38] Pérez Zevallos, *Xochimilco Ayer*, vol. 2, Appendix 1, 135.
[39] AGN, Indios, vol. 4, exp. 290, f. 87v (97v old foliation).
[40] AGN, General de Parte, vol. 6, exp. 147, f. 61 (156 old foliation).
[41] Gibson, *The Aztecs under Spanish Rule*, 449–450.
[42] Prem, "Disease Outbreaks in Central Mexico during the Sixteenth Century," 45–46; Nash, "Beyond Virgin Soils."

a relatively consistent frame of reference – given the especially high mortality rates for infants and the elderly, who were not counted as tributaries – and most of the assessments were for the corregimiento as a whole, thereby overcoming uncertainty about exactly which communities were included. Working against this, though, were deviations in the qualities of the reporting, shifts over time in birth and death rates, as well as the definition of tributary status, particularly when it came to determining at which age a youngster reached adult majority.

For all the inexactitude and ambiguity of the counts, a generally consistent pattern of demographic change can be discerned. From 1564 to 1643, the number of tributaries in Xochimilco fell rapidly and drastically. In 1564 there were 10,583 tributaries.[43] Six years later that number had declined by 19 percent to 8,577.[44] Figures from the 1580s were more susceptible to variation: a 1586 count had just 7,300 whereas another from two years later put the number at 9,019 tributaries.[45] On first glance, this number seems improbable, diverging as it does from the general trend of demographic decline. But perhaps it reflected instead a rebound in the population. As scholars have noted, there could be considerable turbulence in the population size of communities in central Mexico.[46] By 1592, when we next have a government assessment for tax purposes, there were 8,371 tributaries which suggests the possibility that the population might have recovered and perhaps even stabilized, at least temporarily.[47] From the 1590s, though, the decline resumed and, in certain moments, it did so at a higher rate. By 1619 and 1623, Xochimilco was down to 5,960 tributaries. The numbers continued to fall until 1643, when the lowest figures were recorded.[48] At that time there were just 2,686 tributaries remaining.

For the next half century, the population stayed more or less unchanged. In 1688, there were 2,734 tributaries.[49] In 1692, there were only a few more, 2,783.[50] And when fray Agustín de Vetancurt toured the

[43] *El libro de tasaciones*, 306.
[44] AGI, Audiencia de México, leg. 336, ff. 69v–70; Gibson, *The Aztecs under Spanish Rule*, 142–143; Gerhard, *A Guide to the Historical Geography of New Spain*, 246.
[45] AGI, Audiencia de México, leg. 287, f. 3 (there is no foliation); *Moderación de doctrinas de la Real Corona administradas por las ordenes mendicantes, 1623*, France V. Scholes and Eleanor B. Adams, eds. (Mexico City: J. Porrúa, 1959), 43.
[46] Skopyk, "Undercurrents of Conquest," 277.
[47] AGN, Indios, vol. 6/1a pte., exp. 482, ff. 129v–130.
[48] AGN, Indios, vol. 9, exp. 172 and 173, ff. 82v–83v; *Moderacion de doctrinas de la Real Corona administradas por las ordenes mendicantes, 1623*, 43.
[49] Gerhard, *A Guide to the Historical Geography of New Spain*, 246.
[50] Gibson, *The Aztecs under Spanish Rule*, 142–143.

jurisdiction in 1697 there may have been between 2,027 and 2,389 tributaries.[51] This pattern is striking: across a half century, the Nahua population remained close to its lowest recorded levels. Strikingly, no demographic rebound is recorded in the sources, although there are major gaps in the documentary record. One wonders if the depths of the Little Ice Age and depressed economic conditions inhibited recovery.

Only in the eighteenth century did the population begin to recover and even then it did so only slightly. The gradual and partial upswing in the number of indigenous residents took place fitfully, with sudden drops from further epidemics working against the general upward trend. In 1742 there were 3,440 tributaries.[52] Between 1763 and 1765, that figure had climbed to 4,314.[53] By the time of the comprehensive census of 1778, though, the tributary population had fallen once more. The census reported that 2,000 Indians had died in a recent epidemic, perhaps the one in 1772–1773 (the census did not specify which). The sudden and severe loss of life meant that the tributary population was reduced to around 4,000.[54] The numbers rose again afterward, but figures from the 1780s and 1790s are inconsistent. Charles Gibson determined from treasury records of the amount of tribute paid in 1782 that there were 4,730 tributaries in jurisdiction.[55] Between 1787 and 1794, according to a different calculation, there were 3,666.[56] And from 1797 to 1801, when we have more comprehensive and consistent data, there were some 4,278 to 4,282 tributaries.[57] In other words, by the turn of the nineteenth century the overall Native American tributary population had risen to approximately 4,300. All of this means that the eighteenth century's increase never reached the numbers of even the late sixteenth century, let alone the original population size of 1520.

---

[51] The tributary figures are calculated at the 2.8 and 3.3 conversion ratios of individuals to tributaries, as discussed below, and, working backward from the population figures. Included in the tally of the jurisdiction's communities were the city, including its fifteen barrios and its twelve outlying visitas, as well as Milpa Alta, Tecomitl, Tepepan, San Gregorio Atlapulco, and San Pedro Atocpan. Vetancurt, *Chronica*, 56, 65, 84, 86, 88–89.

[52] Villaseñor y Sánchez, *Theatro americano*, 103–106, 160–161; Gibson, *The Aztecs under Spanish Rule*, 142–143.

[53] AGN Tributos, vol. 2, exp. 1 and repeated in vol. 2 exp. 2; Gibson, *The Aztecs under Spanish Rule*, 142–143.

[54] The overall population totaled 18,049, and the number of tributaries, 4,000, was calculated by Peter Gerhard. AGN, Padrones, vol. 29, f. 4; Pérez Zevallos, *Xochimilco Ayer*, vol. 2, 78; Gerhard, *A Guide to the Historical Geography of New Spain*, 246.

[55] Gibson, *The Aztecs under Spanish Rule*, 142–143.

[56] AGN, Tributos, vol. 37, exp. 6; Gibson, *The Aztecs under Spanish Rule*, 142–143.

[57] AGN, Tributos, vol. 43, the last exp., ff. 4–4v; Gibson, *The Aztecs under Spanish Rule*, 142–143 and 146.

From the tributary counts it is possible to gain a sense of the overall population size for the jurisdiction. Doing so requires a calculation of the number of people who belonged to a single tributary's household. This calculation, in turn, depends on variations in birth and mortality rates as well as the definition of tributary status, which itself varied according to age or other factors such as disability or exemptions secured through service to the church, as with singers and sacristans. Taking these factors into consideration, the historical demographers Sherburne Cook and Woodrow Borah proposed conversion rates of between 2.8 and 3.3 individuals per tributary to determine the overall population for the sixteenth century.[58] Using these conversions for 1564, the earliest date for which we have reliable census data, Xochimilco's corregimiento was made up of 29,632 to 34,924 residents. In 1570, tax records stated that there were 8,577 tributaries for the jurisdiction, which gives us a population of between 24,016 and 28,304.[59] These figures would seem to be just outside the range of those furnished separately by Borah and Cook themselves for 1568, which used extrapolations from different data and which put the size of the jurisdiction at 23,166.[60]

From a range of 23,000 to 28,000 in 1570, Xochimilco's total population fell to 7,521–8,864 in the 1640s. Thereafter, the seventeenth-century demographic size of the jurisdiction remained consistently low. In 1697, Vetancurt reported 6,688 individuals, although his tally (of the total number of people, not just of tributaries) probably omitted some of the communities in the jurisdiction.[61] In the eighteenth century, with something of a recovery taking place, Gibson used data from Xochimilco to put forward a higher rate of 4.34 for converting the number of tributaries to the overall population.[62] This means that Xochimilco's corregimiento grew to 14,930 by 1742 and approximately 18,580 Native people by 1801.

These figures are for the entire jurisdiction; trying to infer the population size of Xochimilco as a city on the basis of the corregimiento's figures

---

[58] Their conversion rates were accepted and used by Gibson, *The Aztecs under Spanish Rule*, 140, 142–143, 501n26.

[59] *El libro de los tasaciones*, 306; AGI, Audiencia de México, leg. 336a, ff. 69v–70; Borah and Cook, *Population of Central Mexico in 1548*, 102; Borah and Cook, *The Indian Population of Central Mexico, 1531–1610*, 62, 68; Gerhard, *Guide*, 246.

[60] Borah and Cook, *The Indian Population of Central Mexico, 1531–1610*, 62, 68; Sherman, "A Conqueror's Wealth," 201n8.

[61] Vetancurt, *Chronica*, 56, 65, 84, 86, 88–89.

[62] Gibson, *The Aztecs under Spanish Rule*, 140, 501n26.

is problematic. In part this difficulty has to do with defining the city's limits: the documents do not tell us whether they were for the nucleated settlement itself or its outlying, subordinate settlements, some of which could be quite far-flung. In 1563, for instance, Xochimilco's nobles put the population of the city itself at 6,000–7,000 in their letter to the king. That figure may not have included sujetos. By contrast, a year later, in a separate letter to the king, the viceroy stated that there were 12,000–13,000 individuals in Xochimilco and all of its subject communities. Numbers from the entire corregimiento for 1564, meanwhile, show that there were between 29,632 and 34,924 inhabitants. Further complicating matters are changes over time in jurisdictions, which leads to a question about whether to include other altepetl, such as Santa María de la Asunción Milpa Alta or San Pedro Atocpan, which gained jurisdictional independence at various dates (discussed in the next chapter). In addition, on only three occasions do we have figures for both the city and the corregimiento, and among these sets of data are wide discrepancies in the numbers.[63]

It is no less difficult to calculate the entire corregimiento's population size at the time of the conquest. The one figure for the pre-contact population, mentioned previously, was furnished by the Nahua nobles in their 1563 letter to the king. The document's 30,000 figure seems to refer to the altepetl itself and not the jurisdiction, although there is no way to be sure about this (or indeed about the reliability of the number). There are a few good

---

[63] AGI, Patronato, leg. 182, ramo 2; *Sobre el modo de tributar*, 75. If we use the Nahua nobles' tally, the city's size, as a percentage of that of the corregimiento's, ranged from 17 to 24 percent (depending on whether a rate of 2.8 or 3.3 is used for converting the number of tributaries). If we use the viceroy's figure, on the other hand, the range is from 34 to 44 percent. These percentages can be compared with numbers supplied in 1692 by Vetancurt. He identified 2,500 Nahuas in Xochimilco's barrios and outlying visitas, with the overall corregimiento having 6,688 individuals. As such, the city may have accounted for as much as 37 percent of the corregimiento's population. Vetancurt, *Chronica*, 56, 65, 84, 86, 88, 89. The figures supplied by the friar and the viceroy thus essentially agree, putting the city's population at just over a third of the entire corregimiento's. But, as already noted, the numbers in Vetancurt may not have included all of the communities in the corregimiento. That the city comprised a smaller proportion of the corregimiento's overall size is further suggested in the data from the 1778 census. This tally gave the city's Native American population as 2,273, as compared with 18,049 for the entire jurisdiction, which indicates that the city was only 13 percent of the size of the corregimiento. (The lack of distinction between jurisdictions as a whole and their constituent communities makes it impossible to calculate the populations of Tlahuac, Mixquic, Ayotzingo, or Chalco Atenco, among other communities in Chalco's jurisdiction, since the counts were tallied with those for the larger polities of the province such as Tlalmanalco, Amecameca, and Chimalhuacan).

reasons to suppose, though, that the 30,000 figure did indeed refer specifically to what became the city. First, as we have seen, the census data from
1564 put the entire corregimiento at some 30,000–35,000 individuals.
Given the demographic losses between 1520 and 1564, including the vast
numbers of fatalities during the 1520–1521 and 1545–1548 pandemics, it is
implausible to suppose that the number of the jurisdiction's inhabitants
would have recovered to its original size.[64] Second, if the mortality rate for
Xochimilco followed that of the rest of central Mexico – at approximately
90 percent in the first century after initial contact – and if the number of
tributaries for the entire corregimiento at its lowest level was 2,686 – then it
might be reasonable to suppose that the original corregimiento's size could
have been around some 26,000 tributaries. This number would suggest an
overall population in 1520 of approximately 72,800 people.[65] In the end,
the best that can be said is that the 30,000 figure for 1520 was likely to refer
to the city's population. The population for the entire jurisdiction – and this
cannot be more than speculation – could have been ca. 70,000 residents.[66]
But, again, this cannot be established with any certainty from the available
sources. If this figure is correct, though, the overall population in 1801,
which was just 18,580, was perhaps only a quarter of that of the original
population at first contact.[67]

For all the indeterminacy of the population size from the 1520s to the
1560s, the basic demographic history of Xochimilco's indigenous society
otherwise corresponded with those of other communities across central
Mexico. From a substantial pre-Columbian population, rapid decline set
in. High mortality rates continued through the sixteenth and into the
seventeenth centuries. If there were sudden and severe losses of life
recorded for 1545–1548 and 1576–1581, the overall downward trend
continued, albeit with periods of partial and temporary recovery, until the
1640s when the population reached its lowest recorded level.
Xochimilco's population then stabilized but remained persistently low
for the remainder of the seventeenth century. Only in the eighteenth

---

[64] The 1570 tax records are consistent with those from 1564, putting the population of the
corregimiento at between ca. 24,000 and 28,000.

[65] Cook and Lovell, "Unraveling the Web of Disease," 190.

[66] In addition, if the Xochimilca did indeed contribute 12,000 warriors to the Spanish-
Mexica War, then the overall population might have been around 60,000, if one were
to use the standard ratio of 1 to 5 for that conversion. See Skopyk, "Undercurrents of
Conquest," 245; Charles Gibson, *Tlaxcala in the Sixteenth Century* (Stanford: Stanford
University Press, 1952), 139.

[67] If, that is, we estimate a 1520 population of ca. 70,000–78,000.

TABLE 4.1 *Population figures for Xochimilco, city and jurisdiction,*
1520s–1801

Date	City of Xochimilco	Xochimilco's jurisdiction
1520	[30,000?]	[70,000?]
1563	6,000–7,000	
1564	12,000–13,000	29,632
1570		24,016
1586	12,600	21,280
1588		25,253
1592		23,489
1608	7,000–8,000	
1619–1623	11,894	16,688
1643–1646	1,182[a]	7,521
1692		7,792
1742		14,930
1763–1765		18,723
1778	2,273	18,049
1782		20,528
1787–1794		15,910
1797–1801		18,580

[a] This is the archbishop's count of the number of confirmed individuals in Xochimilco, a figure that, in excluding children who were baptized but not confirmed in the faith, underrepresents the city's size.

century did it begin to recover. But that recovery was slow and partial, never approaching its previous heights. These trends can be seen in Table 4.1 and Figure 4.4, which provide numbers for the overall population, and not just tributaries, for the city and its corregimiento. With the exception of the entry for 1520, the numbers for the city in Table 4.1 are either provided by contemporary observers or, for the corregimiento as a whole, from documentary records of the tributary population, which have been converted using ratios of 2.8 tributaries to overall population for 1500s and 1600s and 4.34 after 1692.

The graph in Figure 4.4 is based on census and other recorded data from the 1560s until 1801, with the exception of the hypothetical figure of 68,000 for 1520 and, by extension, a speculative curve from that date and until the 1560s. It should further be noted that the flat horizontal line from the 1570s to the 1590s obscures the demographic turbulence during those

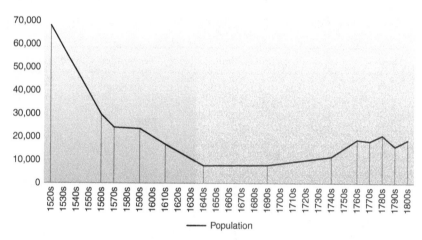

FIGURE 4.4 Population change in Xochimilco's jurisdiction, 1520s–1800s.

two decades: the cocoliztli of 1576–1581 would have reduced population numbers considerably; furthermore, there may have been something of a recovery in the subsequent decade.

CONGREGACIÓN AND COMMUNITY INTEGRITY

The drastic decline in Xochimilco's population generated any number of dislocations, from incomprehensible psychological trauma to terrible disruptions of family life. At times, the very existence of communities was called into question. This was especially the case when smaller sujetos faced the prospect of being relocated and consolidated under several *congregación* programs proposed by the government. The earliest of these programs recorded for Xochimilco's jurisdiction dated back to the 1560s and involved San Gregorio Atlapulco, although the changes do not seem to have been implemented.[68] Atlapulco was again supposed to be consolidated in the early seventeenth century. In 1603, the tlatoani of Xochimilco, don Martín Cerón y Alvarado – apparently acting at the behest of viceregal authorities – issued an order in Nahuatl that brought together several scattered and depopulated communities by the lakes. He required that the chinampa people, or *chinanpatlaca* as he called them, of San Juan Ahuehuetlitlan relocate to the shore of the lake in a place called Tlatotoca.[69] Similarly, those residents who were left

---

[68] AGN, Mercedes, vol. 5–6, 1a pte., ff. 138–138v.
[69] The term used here in the Nahuatl source for congregation was *hualmopachoquen*.

in San Sebastián Martir were moved to the lakeshore in Cihuatlalpan. In addition, the residents of settlements named Xochitepec and Jesús Nazareno were relocated to San Luis Tlaxialtemalco, while those of San Nicolás Cintatlalpan and San Marcos were also required to move elsewhere.[70] Some of the communities may have no longer been viable, at least according to the perspective of colonial authorities. With orders of congregation, a few of the communities may have disappeared entirely – although it was possible that residents might return later to their old homes. Alternatively, residents might have petitioned for the right to remain where they were, arguing that various inconveniences and dislocations caused by moving would prove overly prejudicial. One argument, put forward by the residents of San Pablo Oztotepec, had to do with proximity to their religious houses.[71] The accessibility of churches was a key element in the decisions of judges. In the case of Mexicalzingo, an inspector noted that outlying settlements might look as though they were distant when traveling along winding and indirect, overland routes but that, in fact, canoe transportation made them close enough for Nahuas to attend church easily.[72] Another common justification for remaining in the same place had to do with agricultural production and the provisioning of Mexico City. This line of reasoning typically ran as follows: the original communities had an abundance of land, given that many parcels had fallen vacant with population loss, and that the underutilized land was especially fertile, so much so that it would allow those who remained to produce food and support themselves. This was the position taken by the residents of Santa María Nativitas.[73]

The implications of the congregation programs could potentially be dire, not least because they threatened the essential survival of people's ancestral homes. In addition, they struck at the livelihoods of Nahuas and might portend a break from long-standing relations with the natural world. In the early seventeenth century, the judge of congregations in the province of Chalco proposed the relocation of several communities that were subordinate to Tlahuac. The communities of San Antonio, Santa Bárbara, Santa Ana, Santiago and la Exaltación de la Cruz all faced relocation away from the lakes and to a community called San Francisco, which was inland and

[70] "Titulos de la congregación de San Gregorio Acapulco, 1603," in Appendix 2 of Pérez Zevallos, *Xochimilco Ayer*, vol. 2, 150.
[71] AGN, Congregaciones, vol. 1, exp. 18, ff. 11–11v.
[72] AGN, Civil, vol. 1271, exp. 1, f. 43.
[73] AGN, Congregaciones, vol. 1, exp. 22, ff. 13–13v.

a good way up the side of a hill. San Francisco may not have been all that far
away as a simple measure of distance. But, at a higher elevation, it was
inconceivably far from residents' lives in their old aquatic communities. The
affected Nahuas ardently opposed the order, arguing that they made
a living from the cultivation of chinampas and from canoe transportation,
both of which helped to provision Mexico City. Access to embarcaderos
enabled them to meet their obligations to deliver straw and stone to the
capital. The appeal to such colonial interests was reinforced by a further,
desperate plea: they had no other forms of sustenance and would lose
everything. The petition was not simply about material concerns, existential
and dire though they were: the relocation also threatened something more
profound and fundamental to their sense of who they were. They explained
that their way of life – *modo de vivir* – was inextricably linked to the
environment they had fashioned from the lake.[74] For this reason, when it
became apparent that they had no choice but to move, the villagers proposed a compromise. They suggested that all of the communities be consolidated into Santiago, one of the communities on the lake. The viceroy
accepted their suggestion.[75]

In spite of demographic decline and the proposed congregations, many
smaller communities survived through the colonial period. In 1570,
Xochimilco had more than thirty sujetos in addition to the many barrios
within the city's limits. The number of sujetos dropped to twenty-nine in
1697, according to fray Agustín de Vetancurt. The 1778 census, by
contrast, listed thirty communities, and in 1791–1794 there were still
twenty-six pueblos, suggesting that a good many communities preserved
their integrity and remained viable across the colonial period.[76] Even so,
some communities shrank in physical size as their populations diminished;
lands that had emptied out eventually became ranches and larger, landed
estates. In the 1760s, for instance, litigation over the ownership of a ranch
called Huichiltepeque near Santiago Tepalcatlalpan included copies of
documents dating back more than two centuries. According to motions
submitted by the villagers, the five caballerías of land had been barrios of
the village since its foundation and through its congregación but, because
of epidemics, the barrios had ceased to be inhabited.[77] By the eighteenth

---

[74] The phrasing was "no teniendo ellos otras granjerías ni modo de vivir, lo perderan todo
y esta ciudad [i.e., Mexico City] el socorro que con ellas hacen."
[75] AGN, Congregaciones, vol. 1, exp. 53, ff. 36v–37.
[76] AGN, Padrones, vol. 29, f. 4; Vetancurt, *Chronica*, 56, 65, 84–89; Gerhard, *A Guide to
the Historical Geography of New Spain*, 246.
[77] AGN, Tierras, vol. 2670, exp. 1, ff. 14, 17, and 18–19v.

century, lands of several communities had been converted into haciendas. But the 1778 census did not indicate whether any communities themselves were absorbed into haciendas, although any resident Nahua laborers might have been kept unreported so that the hacendados would not be liable for their tribute obligations. The only hacienda with a resident population was, by official assessment, inhabited solely by Spaniards.[78]

If most sujetos survived intact, population loss also held implications for the sustainability of neighborhoods within Xochimilco. At one point, the viceroy proposed a congregation for one of the city's districts.[79] The proposal may have been prompted by diminished tribute payments. Problems paying tribute meant that communities frequently petitioned the authorities for temporary exemptions because of population loss, or, failing that, for new assessments to reflect the new demographic situation. On one occasion several residents of Xochimilco's barrio of Xuchiacan asked the corregidor for remission from providing labor. The corregidor forwarded the petition to the viceroy for deliberation because, as the plaintiffs explained, the lands had become barren and deserted through depopulation. Not only had the farmers died but so too had their offspring and heirs, leaving the land uncultivated.[80] Numerous petitions for relief from services, as well as investigations into failures to deliver tribute, attested to the magnitude of the problem.[81]

Residents themselves thus searched for ways to keep their neighborhoods sufficiently well inhabited to meet their tribute obligations. In some instances they did so by welcoming settlers displaced from elsewhere. Between 1579 and 1581, in the latter part of the cocoliztli pandemic, two groups of immigrants were incorporated into Xochimilco's sociopolitical structures. In this context, ninety immigrants from Tetzcoco, as well as Apaxco, Axacuba, and Tequizquiaque, who had moved to Xochimilco six years earlier, now formally established their own barrio in the city. The viceroy confirmed that they should contribute to Xochimilco's tribute and labor requirements. Previously, the settlers had contributed to the duties of those tributaries with whom they had stayed.[82]

---

[78] AGN, Padrones, vol. 29, f. 3v (f. 258 alternative foliation).
[79] AGN, Congregaciones, vol. 1, exp. 81, f. 57.
[80] AGN, General de Parte, vol. 2, exp. 1145, f. 252 (274 old foliation).
[81] AGN, General de Parte, vol. 1, exp. 766, f. 145, exp. 1140, f. 216v; AGN, Indios, vol. 3, exp. 286, f. 67, vol. 4, exp. 163, f. 52v, exp. 563, f. 165, exp. 760, f. 210v, and vol. 5, exp. 158, f. 45.
[82] AGN, General de Parte, vol. 2, exp. 73, f. 16v (37v old foliation).

Two years later, in 1581, another group of newcomers made Xochimilco their home. As Otomí from Tula, they were ostensibly ethnic outsiders. In spite of cultural differences they obtained land, built new homes, and established their own distinct barrio. In seeking confirmation of rights to land, the Otomí stated that community lands in Tepetenchi had become unoccupied and were liable for reallocation. Don Juan Enríquez, their leader, explained to the authorities that they had shared among themselves the vacant lots and could demonstrate their current use by having built houses. The government agreed and confirmed their titles. Both groups of immigrants, the Otomí and the Tetzcoca, among others, were accepted by the Xochimilca. They acquired formal recognition for their communities and, in so doing, they became incorporated into the preexisting urban fabric of Xochimilco. Crucially, they not only bolstered the city's population but also provided much-needed tribute and labor.[83]

DEMOGRAPHIC DECLINE, POLITICAL ECONOMY, AND SOCIAL CONFLICT

Of the many dislocations caused by demographic decline, problems with tribute and labor arrangements were among the most conspicuous and destabilizing. These colonial demands added to the burden of those who survived the epidemics. They also generated conflicts that upended social relations and jeopardized many forms of collective cohesion. In part these conflicts had to do with communities struggling to keep up with any number of exactions and obligations, from the payment of tribute in goods, including foodstuffs, as well as specie, to various forms of mandatory labor service, among them personal service to Nahua lords. Pressures on communities came from two directions at once – from outside and above, with the colonial administration intervening in Xochimilco's affairs – and from within and below, with overburdened commoners pushing back against the demands placed on them by their nobles. Outside intervention typically involved viceroys, audiencia judges, or their agents seeking to reform the ways in which labor, services, and goods were extracted from Native communities. These reforms essentially modified the former Aztec Empire's system of tribute, which Spaniards initially retained – and which, in Xochimilco, Pedro de Alvarado had kept for his encomienda – but which the government gradually adjusted because of demographic decline. At their most basic level, though, the

[83] AGN, General de Parte, vol. 2, exp. 1201, ff. 260–260v (282-v old foliation).

reforms were about simplifying and maximizing the collection of taxes and the recruitment of laborers. In this they consisted of redirecting personal service away from the Nahua upper class. The reforms culminated in the creation of the unitary tribute system of the 1560s, although frequent tinkering and revision continued long after that decade.[84]

The countervailing force, of commoners defying local and outside authorities, took many forms, from litigation to various strategies of resistance, including the application of political pressure – for instance, via appeals to the king for the protection of his vassals – as well as land invasions, absenteeism, and flight, this latter compounding the problem of population loss. In negotiations over the terms of tribute and labor, Nahua commoners, nobles, friars, and government officials formed shifting alliances. The controversies over central Mexico's political economy and population loss spilled over into the control and use of land, as discussed in Chapter 2, which provided yet another arena for the contestation of the conditions of vassalage and relations between rulers and commoners.

All of these issues came to weigh heavily on social relations in Xochimilco, much as they did for other communities in Mexico during the second half of the sixteenth century. Similar tensions were recorded in the famous pictorial document, the *Códice Osuna*, which on one level was a petition in which Nahuas of Tenochtitlan complained of changes to the capital's political economy.[85] Political strife over the terms of local government as well as tribute and labor exactions also plagued Tetzcoco and other altepetl.[86] In Xochimilco, the situation was particularly severe. At the same time that acrimony over land, labor, and tribute weakened communal bonds so growing controversies made for an estrangement between nobles and commoners, causing the foundations of the social hierarchy to degrade and become less stable. Disputes further strained societies by undermining reciprocal ties in which tribute revenues and labor service were understood to promote the common good. As a result, the ideology and the social practices that defined class relations shifted, gradually undermining – but not yet overturning – the old bases of Nahua

---

[84] The term *unitary tribute system* is from Borah and Cook, *Price Trends*, 2.

[85] Mundy, *The Death of Aztec Tenochtitlan*, 160–167; William F. Connell, *After Moctezuma: Indigenous Politics and Self-Government in Mexico City, 1524–1730* (Norman: University of Oklahoma Press, 2011), 22–89.

[86] Bradley Benton, *The Lords of Tetzcoco: The Transformation of Indigenous Rule in Postconquest Central Mexico* (New York: Cambridge University Press, 2019), 81–105; Horn, *Postconquest Coyoacan*, 86–108; for the persistence of the Nahua nobility in the face of challenges to their authority, see Haskett, *Indigenous Rulers*.

authority. Taken together, an unbroken if not straight line can be drawn from smallpox, measles, and typhus to struggles over political economy and, ultimately, manifestations of class conflict.

Tribute demands and the terms of noble privileges were the main sources of discord between Nahua commoners and their rulers. The earliest document to provide details of these privileges, which dates to 1548, shows how great the support for Xochimilco's lords had once been. The document was produced by a Nahua judge named don Pedro de Suero as part of a government inspection of tribute and town finance arrangements following the epidemic of 1545–1548. It listed a great many resources, either as raw materials, finished goods, or personal services that were provided by the populace. The arrangements reflected the size and prestige of Xochimilco's three constituent districts. The greatest amount of tribute and labor was provided by the residents of Tepetenchi, which with twelve barrios was the altepetl's largest constituent district. It had the greatest number of high-ranking lords to whom personal service and tribute were owed. All of these lords were of sufficiently high status as to warrant the honorific title "don." Tecpan had seven barrios and four noblemen who received tribute. One of the nobles was of lower social rank and was not identified by an honorific title. Olac also had seven barrios and four nobles. Only the tlatoani, don Francisco de Guzmán Omacatzin, merited the title "don."[87]

The support provided for these nobles varied according to their sociopolitical positions. The lesser nobles of Olac, Miguel Ticunabacatl and Juan Quaonochtl, each had four chinampas set aside for them, with only a portion of one chinampa to be cultivated by the community. The rest were to be cultivated at the expense of the nobles themselves or by *terrazgueros*, who were members of a subordinate, dependent class of commoners.[88] A third, higher-ranking nobleman, Agustín Maldonado, received a larger amount of support. In addition to more laborers for his greater number of lands, every year each of the district's tributaries gave him two pesos in coin, or *tepuzque* (a plural and variant form of the Nahuatl *tepoztli*, meaning "metal" but in this case probably referring to a coin made of a mixture of gold and copper). To put this tepuzque tribute in perspective, in 1548 cotton shirts made on indigenous looms cost thirteen pesos per *carga*, or load, which means that Agustín would have

---

[87] Library of Congress, Krauss Collection, ms. 140, ff. 436–451v.
[88] They were also known as *mayeque*. Lockhart, *The Nahuas after the Conquest*, 97, 112, 114.

been able to buy three shirts from the revenue provided by just a single tributary.[89] While it is not possible to calculate the number of tributaries in Olac in 1548, Agustín would have received payments from hundreds if not thousands of them. His tepuzque tribute alone would have made him uncommonly affluent.

These privileges were as nothing, though, compared to those assigned for the district's tlatoani, don Francisco.[90] Of his twenty privately held lands, of which nine were chinampas, commoners were to cultivate two (one of which was to be a chinampa). The same number were to be cultivated from among the twenty lands of his lordship (*señorio*), with the remainder to be worked at his expense or by terrazgueros. Every day, don Francisco could expect to receive two loads of wood and 100 cacao beans. Every Friday and Saturday he was given three baskets of fish, each of which contained twenty fish. Every week he was to be given a chicken, half a cake of salt, one small basket of pumpkin seeds, another of tomatoes, yet another of chile, and three bunches of incense. Every eighty days he would receive two valuable wooden chests or, in their place, the money to purchase them. And annually, every tributary was to give him twenty pesos.[91]

Olac was but the smallest of Xochimilco's three districts. The nobles of Tecpan and Tepetenchi thus received a much greater amount of tribute. The privileges due to don Esteban de Guzmán, of Tepetenchi, rivaled that of Olac's ruler even though don Esteban occupied the next rank below Olac's tlatoani. Don Esteban was nevertheless among the most eminent of Nahua nobles in central Mexico, having served a governor of Xochimilco, Tlatelolco, and Tenochtitlan.[92] Before reaching the summit of Nahua office-holding in the capital, though, don Esteban had been maintained as a lord of Xochimilco with a great many privileges.[93]

Don Esteban's privileges, though, were easily surpassed by the perquisites enjoyed by don Martín Cortés Cerón y Alvarado, tlatoani of Tepetenchi. Don Martín received the same kinds of support as don

[89] Borah and Cook calculated that the average price of cotton shirts and skirts, termed *ropa menuda*, was thirteen pesos per carga, with each carga containing twenty items. Borah and Cook, *Price Trends*, 23–24.

[90] Chimalpahin, *Codex Chimalpahin*, vol. 1, 151–153.

[91] Library of Congress, Krauss Collection, ms. 140, ff. 436–451v.

[92] See Chapter 1; Newberry Library, Ayer Collection, ms. 1121, ff. 348–352; AGN, Mercedes, vol. 3, exp. 91, f. 44; vol. 4, exp. 118, f. 35v; AGN, Mercedes, vol. 5–6, 1a pte., ff. 134–134v; Chávez Orozco, ed., *Códice Osuna*, 38, 257; Chimalpahin, *Codex Chimalpahin*, vol. 1, 177 and vol. 2, 41.

[93] Library of Congress, Krauss Collection, ms. 140, ff. 436–451v.

Esteban, only more so: ten of his forty-one plots of land were to be cultivated by commoners, four women were to make him tortillas, and four servants were to work in his home every day. Each day he received five loads of wood and 600 cacao beans. (His annual supply of cacao beans alone, at the standard sale price set by viceregal ordinances, would have generated a lucrative income of approximately 137 gold pesos).[94] What was more, every week don Martín would receive two chickens, 400 granos of chile, one cake of salt, a small basket of pumpkin seeds and another of tomatoes, and every fortnight ten loads of pine torches and ten loads of wood, as well as ten rabbits, four bunches of incense, and another braza of wood from canoe makers. Every year he would receive eighty canoes. Every tributary gave him fifty pesos a year. Since Tepetenchi was the altepetl's largest district, this monetary support alone would have made him a fortune. If don Martín were to have been the sole recipient of so much abundance – which, strictly speaking, he was not – he would have been extraordinarily wealthy.[95]

Don Martín clearly received tribute beyond the immediate needs of his family. The 1548 privileges were not designed exclusively for the nobility's support. Rather, much of the tribute was to be redistributed within the altepetl, compensating citizens for their public service. Hence the regulations specified that every year each household in Tepetenchi had to deliver to don Martín two blankets, measuring a braza in length and two spans (*palmos*) in width, so that he could pass them on to members of the lesser nobility, the tribute overseers (*tequitlatos*), and the custodians (*mayordomos*), carpenters, singers, and youngsters (*mozos*) who served in the church. The tribute allocations also functioned as a broader means of distribution to commoners. As the ethnohistorian Pedro Carrasco observed, market exchanges could be supplemented or sidestepped with this redistributive system. Doing so ensured that citizens would receive essential goods when needed, including manufactured goods.[96] In this manner, the altepetl's lords were able to maintain ties of patronage and use their largesse as a means for maintaining authority and promoting social cohesion.

Since the tribute provisions served to direct resources to benefit the community as a whole, they reinforced mutual bonds and obligations,

---

[94] A number of 600 cacao beans a day works out to roughly 219,000 per year. A carga of cacao consisted of 24,000 beans, so don Martín received just over nine cargas a year, with each carga being worth fifteen gold pesos at the rate set in 1550, resulting in a total of 136.88 pesos. Borah and Cook, *Price Trends*, 12, 36, and 77.

[95] Library of Congress, Krauss Collection, ms. 140, ff. 436–451v.

[96] Pedro Carrasco, "Los Señores de Xochimilco en 1548," 234.

with the nobles entrusted with the task of reallocation of goods. The three dynastic rulers, for instance, received nearly 500 canoes between them per year, some of which were for distribution to the residents of neighborhoods with chinampas, where the canoes were needed for water management projects. Further reinforcing the collective dimension of the tribute arrangements, the 1548 document acknowledged the hard work performed by macehualtin on altepetl lands and decreed that a portion of the harvests was to be channeled to the polity's administrative costs. As a collective contribution to the upkeep of the community, the nobles themselves were to contribute to the payments.

Beyond the material and practical applications of tribute, the mechanisms for distributing goods and sustaining the altepetl's rulers also had an ideological component. In upholding the social hierarchy while also promoting collective allegiances that bound together the altepetl's citizens, the tribute arrangements theoretically rested on some measure of consent. For this reason, the inspection which generated the 1548 documentation required consultation with residents. The Xochimilca were duly recorded by don Pedro de Suero as having agreed to pay tribute voluntarily; the wording of their statement involved a recognition of the lord's status and a confirmation that payment of tribute had been a customary practice, one provided to their current lords just as it had been to their fathers and forefathers.[97]

Impressive though the volume of all this tribute undoubtedly was, it is worth pausing to note that the privileges set down in 1548 were of an amount that had just been revised down according to reforms requested by the audiencia. While the inspection did not state whether the tribute to the nobles had been reduced, it would be hard to imagine a scenario in which the colonial administration would be willing to forego revenue in favor increasing the wealth of the Nahua nobility, especially in the aftermath of a pandemic. One can only wonder, then, how much tribute would have been received by the lords of Xochimilco before 1548.

The changes to noble privileges in 1548 not only reflected Xochimilco's smaller population but they also formed part of the government's wider reform program. The reforms were designed to accomplish several goals, although none of them were entirely or permanently realized since shifting circumstances dictated otherwise: first, the reforms were designed to replace the old delivery of tribute in a wide range of goods to a simpler system, with payments only in maize or coin; second, the reforms sought

[97] Library of Congress, Krauss Collection, ms. 140, f. 5v.

to "equalize" tribute, making the rates standard for each head of household, with the eventual – though unattained – aim of creating a uniform head tax; third, to bring the tribute levels into a realistic relation to the population size; and, finally, to redirect tribute away from the nobility and instead toward the treasury.[98]

The reforms had started after Xochimilco was incorporated into the royal domain in 1541. Initially, the crown retained Pedro de Alvarado's encomienda arrangements in which, every eighty days, the treasury was to receive fifty gold ingots (or bars, *tujuelos*), with each ingot weighing ten carats (*quilates*, which was also the equivalent to a weight of ten pesos). If that lucrative payment seemed straightforward it was complicated by the accompanying food allocations for the king and the corregidor.[99] The crown soon decided to extract more revenue from its newly escheated domain. In 1546, treasury officials adjusted Xochimilco's tribute rate in two ways. First, they commuted part of the gold the Nahuas had been obliged to give. At the same time, though, the tribute in foodstuffs was increased, and the overall balance amounted to an increase in royal income of 581¼ pesos.[100]

The desire to exact more revenue was thwarted, though, by the cocoliztli pandemic. By the time of don Pedro de Suero's 1548 inspection, demographic losses had required a reduction in tribute levies even as they also necessitated a return to partial payment in foodstuffs.[101] Payments in maize now proved essential given that food shortages followed in the wake of the pandemic. The first reports of scarcity came in 1550.[102] Shortages continued for most of 1551. As a result, between 1547 and 1551 the price of maize rose dramatically from one real to eight reales per fanega. A decent crop was gathered in fall 1551, bringing the price down to three reales. But it inched up again in 1554, to four or five reales. In response, the government instituted further changes to tribute. In 1554, the viceroy ordered that Native communities across central Mexico, and not just in Xochimilco, set aside land for communal plantings. These fields were to be cultivated solely for the purpose of delivering tribute in maize.[103] Two years later, the

[98] Gibson, *The Aztecs under Spanish Rule*, 198–199.
[99] *El libro de las tasaciones de pueblos de la Nueva España*, 304–307.
[100] *El libro de las tasaciones de pueblos de la Nueva España*, 304–305.
[101] Library of Congress, Krauss Collection, Ms. 140, ff. 9, 15, and 19.
[102] AGN, Mercedes, vol. 3, exp. 54, ff. 25v–26 (47v–48 old foliation).
[103] AGN, Mercedes, vol. 4, exp. 11, ff. 2v–3. Other, similar orders were issued in 1577 and 1587, see AGN, Reales Cédulas Duplicadas, vol. 46, exp. 65, ff. 151–152 and vol. 3, exp. 43, f. 20v.

viceroy modified his general order with another one specifically for Xochimilco: the altepetl now had to supplement its monetary tribute with 5,000 fanegas of maize.[104] This new requirement came just as the price of maize jumped to ten reales in 1557, when a plague of locusts struck. The locusts returned in 1558 and 1559, keeping maize at an elevated price of four to six reales per fanega.[105]

Concerns about food prices and the delivery of tribute in grains meant that government reforms extended into the realms of land use and agricultural production. In 1558, the viceroy appointed don Francisco Jiménez to institute a program of land redistribution which, as discussed in Chapter 2, contributed to tensions between Nahua nobles and commoners.[106] Another set of changes in that same year required that all commoners set aside a portion of their lands for the express purpose of growing maize solely for royal tribute. The new assessment of tribute was determined not on a predetermined amount of maize (or its equivalent value in gold) but according to the size of the parcel of land to be cultivated. The ruling made no distinction between chinampas or other lands, nor did it specify whether the rule applied only to lands distributed via usufruct, although this was implied; another stipulation required that those with private holdings farm a plot solely to pay their royal tribute. The rules also made allowances for other circumstances. Certain specialist craftsmen, especially blacksmiths, feather workers, painters, and tailors, were now to be given tribute land and taxed in the same manner as farmers because they "cannot be taxed according to what they make." Also, commoners who did not have any land of their own – or access to communal lands, it seems – were to rent plots from members of the nobility. The law stated that if any noble were to interfere in this, he or she would forfeit all rental income for three years, and the commoners would be allowed to cultivate the entire plot for themselves. Failure by the tributaries to cultivate their plots would lead to sentences of six days' incarceration. Further failure would result in a fortnight's imprisonment and "floggings until they obey."[107]

While the viceroy's regulations of 1558 were designed to promote agricultural production they also affected local finances. For municipal taxation, other kinds of payment besides maize were allowed. Some

[104] *El libro de las tasaciones*, 305.
[105] Gibson, *The Aztecs under Spanish Rule*, 452–453.
[106] Gibson, *The Aztecs under Spanish Rule*, 169, 188–189; AGN, Vínculos y Mayorazgos, vol. 279, exp. 1, ff. 99 and 106–112.
[107] *Sobre el modo de tributar*, 106, 109–111.

individuals, including nobles, were to pay in specie, according to their wealth, with the proceeds covering community expenses and the salaries of local officials. A graduated tax such as this was favored by King Philip II. The viceroy thus required that the Nahua lords don Joaquín and don Martín pay eight pesos a year while don Francisco, of Olac, pay half that amount. The lords of the next rank, among them don Esteban de Guzmán, had to pay two pesos; those immediately below them, such as don Pedro de Sotomayor, one peso, and members of the lesser nobility had to pay half a peso. In addition, there were further graduated rates of taxation for other wealthy individuals, among them widows and female merchants.[108]

If the viceroy's new regulations of 1558 added to the nobles' tax burden, they also marginalized the dynastic rulers' influence over local economic arrangements.[109] They did so by modifying how labor arrangements were used to generate local revenue. The viceroy ordered that henceforth Nahuas perform community service for one week on a rotational basis. Some duties were set aside for artisans. Carpenters, for instance, were to devote a week to their usual tasks, be they cutting wood and fashioning beams and boards or making canoes. The same arrangements applied to *tetlapanques*, or those who quarried or cut stone, as well as those who were tasked with delivering the stone to Mexico City and gardeners.[110] Other groups included in the rotational drafts were sawyers and basketmakers.[111] These specialists were to be compensated at the same rate as the income they earned each week from the sales of their goods. A notation to the document explained how this worked for canoe makers: each canoe was worth between eight or ten pesos, and so a carpenter who finished making a canoe in his week of service would be paid eight pesos. The community would now acquire valuable goods by employing local residents to make them, rather than have a set number delivered to specific nobles, as had been the case before. These items would then be given out to residents according to their needs, or they would be set aside for community projects. This process of redistribution would be entrusted to the cabildo – in other words, the system now excluded the tlatoque. In the decade since 1548, then, the rulers of Xochimilco were made to pay local taxes at a graduated rate even as they were also deprived of an economic dimension to their local authority.

---

[108] Gibson, *The Aztecs under Spanish Rule*, 201; *Sobre el modo de tributar*, 105.
[109] *Sobre el modo de tributar*, 106, 109–110.
[110] *Xuchimanques* may have been a variant of *xuchipixqui*, or *jardinero*. Molina, *Vocabulario* (Mexicana y Castellana), 161.
[111] From *acachiquihuitl*, or "reed basket."

The 1558 ordinances curtailed the dynastic rulers' privileges in further ways. The rulers' status was reduced, in part, when the viceroy ordered that the governor be granted some of the same benefits as them (at this time the tlatoque were not serving as governors). Previously the governor would have received only a salary. Now, though, he would also receive the personal service of four Nahuas, just as don Martín and don Joaquín did.[112] The rulers were allowed to retain their earlier allowances of fish, they still received deliveries of wood, and ten women were still assigned to make tortillas for them. But these privileges were now extended to the governor as well. Crucially, the tlatoque no longer received anything else. Gone were their bountiful supplies of cacao, cloaks, chickens, tomatoes, pumpkin seeds, canoes, wooden chests or other goods, as had been provided a decade earlier. The viceroy was explicit about this, stating directly that these items were no longer to be delivered to the rulers. As a result, all of the great many resources that had been channeled through the tlatoque for the upkeep of the community were now funneled through the cabildo. The lords' very great privileges had largely vanished.

The ordinances also undermined another basis for the dynastic rulers' authority by cutting some of their other reciprocal ties to the community. Whereas in 1548 the tlatoque were granted discretion in distributing the vast amount of tribute that remained within the community, in 1558 the viceroy spelled out how much support was to be allocated to the altepetl collectively. Cabildo officers (*merinos*) were now entrusted with supervising the deliveries.[113] In addition, the dynastic rulers no longer participated in community festivals. The viceroy reduced the number of festivals to six – for Christmas, Easter, Pentecost, and Epiphany, as well as the feasts of Saint Francis and Saint Bernardino – and then excluded the rulers from serving as the sponsors of feasts. Once again, the colonial administration determined how much tribute certain groups, such as artisans, would have to pay as well as how the proceeds should be disbursed. The feasts served to acknowledge and reward the public service of specific functionaries, instance, the sacristans and singers of the church as well as the captain and master of the chapel and the two constables who helped with marriage ceremonies. Finally, the dynastic rulers seem to have been

---

[112] Don Francisco, of the smaller district of Olac, had two individuals assigned to him.
[113] *Sobre el modo de tributar*, 105–112.

prohibited from partaking in the actual feasts themselves. They could only join in if they were cabildo officers.[114]

The changes from 1558 reflected a renewed momentum for increasing royal income, one that had been gathering pace since 1556, when King Philip II acceded to the throne and inherited a treasury unable to pay its debts. Forced to suspend payments, the new monarch sought to secure more revenue from his dominions.[115] In Mexico, this meant additional financial reforms from 1561 to 1564. As part of these efforts, audiencia judges conducted new inspections of the tribute system. The inspections generated controversy within Spanish officialdom. A few figures in the colonial administration, among them friars, argued that population decline and other burdens made further impositions unfeasible and unacceptable; others, such as the high court judge (*oidor*) Vasco de Puga, argued that Native peoples had not been paying enough tribute and that too much revenue was either kept in their communities, went to the clergy, or was squandered on extravagances like fiestas. Such views were not new. Controversies had developed following the tax assessments of Diego Ramírez in a visita from the 1550s, which had prompted some critics, including a treasurer, don Fernando de Portugal, to point out in a 1558 letter to the new king that earlier tax rates had been too low.[116]

Legitimately or not, the Nahua nobility came to be seen by the crown inspectors as an obstacle to securing the proper amounts of royal income. Vasco de Puga stated bluntly in August 1562 "that the Indians are worn out by their governors and lords who steal from them and subject them to the same tyranny of the days of their infidelity." Writing on another occasion to the king and the Council of the Indies, he also noted that while Indians from Xochimilco paid a lot of tribute, only some of it went to the royal treasury.[117] The implication was that Nahua nobles were

---

[114] The regulations specified that those who would eat together were "the governor, the alcaldes, regidores, merinos, other officials who serve the republic, and no one else." *Sobre el modo de tributar*, 110–112.

[115] Borah and Cook, *The Population of Central Mexico in 1548*, 1; Mauricio Drelichman and Hans-Joachim Voth, *Lending to the Borrower from Hell: Debt, Taxes, and Default in the Age of Philip II* (Princeton: Princeton University Press, 2014).

[116] AGI, Indiferente General, leg. 1093, *Cartas del licenciado Jerónimo Valderrama y otros documentos sobre su visita al gobierno de Nueva España, 1563–1565*. France V. Scholes and Eleanor B. Adams, eds. (Mexico City: J. Porrúa, 1961), 295; Ramírez also advocated for the preservation of the exemptions from tribute that had been long established in Native communities; Gibson, *The Aztecs under Spanish Rule*, 200.

[117] AGI, Patronato, leg. 182, ramo 2; AGI, Audiencia de México, leg. 68; *Sobre el modo de tributar*, 60–62.

gouging their subjects to enrich themselves and thereby reducing treasury receipts. Another common refrain among senior officials was that censuses had not adequately calculated the number of tributaries in major communities and that new counts were needed. For some the undercounting of tributaries amounted to little more than fraud – a term that was repeated over and over again in correspondence.[118] In a 1561 letter to the monarch, don Fernando de Portugal and others reckoned that a further 60,000 gold pesos could be paid each year without any harm to Indians. The viceroy did not entirely agree, noting in a letter to the king in 1562 that Nahuas were burdened by a range of other demands, particularly on public works projects. Furthermore, populations had dropped: Xochimilco and its sujetos had fallen below the 20,000 tributaries previously recorded, and yet the royal tribute remained at 5,000 fanegas of maize.[119]

While the investigations produced something of a consensus that tribute payments were too low, crown officials differed in their estimations of Xochimilco's size and appropriate tax rate. Writing in 1564, Viceroy Velasco noted that Xochimilco had a population of 12,000–13,000 Indians, including those living in its sujetos, down from 20,000 tributaries. The current population, he further maintained, could pay far above the previous amount of tribute. Similar figures for tribute and tributaries were supplied by others. In 1562, Vasco de Puga asked three individuals to give testimonies about revenues. While they reported different amounts of tribute paid by Xochimilco, they also noted that it was a very rich town and that it had more tributaries than the viceroy had suggested, at 18,000, who should collectively pay much more.[120]

Renewed attention to matters of taxation, and closer scrutiny of demographic and fiscal records, inspired the issuing of proposed changes even before the judges completed their investigations. In 1561, for instance, the viceroy revised his earlier ordenanzas for Xochimilco. These new rules were concerned with a variety of technical matters but two issues stood out as being especially important. The first had to do with the accounting of community expenses, primarily cabildo salaries, and the vast discrepancies between revenues that were supposedly collected and paid out.

---

[118] AGI, Patronato, leg. 182, ramo 2; *Sobre el modo de tributar*, 60, 64.

[119] *Sobre el modo de tributar*, 19–20, 23, 26–28.

[120] Why these individuals were summoned to express their opinions is not explained, nor is the basis for their expertise. *Sobre el modo de tributar*, 75, 91, 94, 97, 98, and 101.

Apparently the smoke billowing around Vasco de Puga's suspicions of fraud had not been entirely without fire: the governor's salary was set at 100 pesos; the overall salary burden amounted to 300 pesos; and yet the Nahua government had allegedly required that the total tribute collected from its citizens be more than 20,000 pesos. The viceroy was similarly concerned: while the city had paid the king 6,000 or 7,000 fanegas of maize, the remaining surplus was in excess of 10,000 fanegas.[121] Taken together, these surfeits suggested a trend: whereas in 1548 and 1558 the privileges of the Nahua nobility had been curtailed, now the nobles were allegedly taxing their citizens at inflated rates in order to bolster their own wealth.

The other issue dealt with in the 1561 revisions concerned labor, which seemed to the colonial authorities to be another resource that nobles were exploiting for personal gain. Recognizing that the city's residents were saddled with many duties, the viceroy ordered residents not to be made to work on projects other than the ones to which they had originally been assigned. This included personal service to nobles, which commoners now seemed to be reluctant to perform. Nor should there be excess levies of laborers beyond those stipulated by the law. In addition, the amount of work to be done had to be kept within the established limits. Among other examples, the viceroy ordered that canoes not be overloaded; there were water lines on their sides, and the canoes should not be so loaded down as to drop below those levels. Furthermore, payments to those who quarried and cut stone had to come from community funds, and the funds were supposed to be replenished from the sale of the stone in the capital. This latter provision grew out of the viceroy's concern that community revenues be adequately covered without dipping into the funds owed to the crown. In other words, the city's finances needed to work in such a way that tribute would not be generating vast surpluses while the crown's portion remained insufficient.

The renewed attention by the authorities to the mechanisms of local taxation provided an opening for Nahua commoners to seek redress for the excesses committed against them by their rulers. Commoners made full use of the opportunity to contest their tribute obligations. After having submitted many previous petitions, on March 6, 1562, a group of macehualtin from Xochimilco appeared before the viceroy to complain that their governors and alcaldes had, over the course of the past five years, caused them a great deal of harm by requiring them to deliver stone,

---

[121] *Sobre el modo de tributar,* 113–114; Gibson, *The Aztecs under Spanish Rule,* 517n14.

at their own expense, to Spaniards in Mexico City. When the commoners were unable to do as ordered, they were incarcerated and whipped. Some were still languishing in jail. Presenting a pictorial document and a copy of the 1561 rules, they asked that the governor, don Francisco de Luna, be required to appear before the audiencia, be shown the documentation, and made to comply with its stipulations.[122] The viceroy agreed to their requests. Xochimilco's cabildo was admonished not to commit any further abuses. The city's nobles, it now became clear, were facing political resistance from their subjects even as the colonial administration, under the inspection of Jerónimo Valderrama, was on the verge of imposing new tribute levies and further undermining the support the nobles had once enjoyed.

In response, Xochimilco's nobles bypassed the viceroy and appealed to directly to the crown. The governor, don Pedro de Santiago, along with alcaldes and other senior figures in local administration penned a remarkable letter to King Philip II. The 1563 letter was a model of epistolary supplication, one that deployed all the carefully honed tools of deference to appeal for royal favor. With many rhetorical flourishes and not without a little embellishment, the nobles identified themselves and elaborated on the many services they had performed for their monarch. Noting, not quite accurately, that they had never waged war against nor resisted Cortés and the "Christian army" at the time of conquest, they instead pointed to their contributions to Spanish victories in many battles and expeditions. They further pointed out that while the king bestowed great boons and privileges to Tlaxcala, "it is only fair that your majesty should show the same favors to us, who have served no less."[123]

Having established their exemplary record of service, Xochimilco's rulers explained their current plight. They were poor, having been dispossessed of many lands and jurisdictions that Cortés and other judges took away from them, "confident that we know little of litigation and cannot defend ourselves." After listing the towns and jurisdictions lost since the conquest – and the tribute from them which ought to be directed to Xochimilco again, and thence to the crown – the nobles turned to their immediate and pressing grievances, which are worth quoting at length:

Furthermore, we implore your majesty that because from time immemorial, when the Spaniards came and before, the caciques and noblemen of the said city of

---

[122] *Sobre el modo de tributar*, 103–104.
[123] AGI, Patronato, leg. 184, ramo 50, which is translated by Restall et al. in *Mesoamerican Voices*, 67.

Xochimilco by way of patrimony and lordship used the services of all the craftsmen –
carpenters, masons, woodcutters, metalworkers, fishermen, feather-workers, san-
dalmakers, and other craftsmen and people of the market – and other natives served
them by taking care of their fields and held them in high recognition, giving them
tokens of respect and presents, but now it is done no longer and they are dispossessed, and since it pertains to their patrimony and lordship, we implore your
majesty to order the abovementioned restored to us.

In addition, we advise your majesty that at the time when the Spaniards came
and since, assessments were made of what the macehuales were to give their
caciques and natural lords for their sustenance and by virtue of their lordship;
now the said macehuales, aided by some Spanish lawyers and attorneys, have
evaded it and do not want to pay or recognize their caciques, who are the caciques
of Tecpan, Tepetenchi, and Ollac, who are dying of hunger. In pagan times they
were great lords and the said Indians and macehuales served in their houses,
building adobe walls and performing other personal services, but now the caciques
are as beaten down as the macehuales, and all are equal. We implore your majesty
to decree and order that our lordship and patrimony be honored and our assessments fulfilled, and that the macehuales not be permitted to rise up against us nor
involve us in lawsuits, and that upon verifying the above-said we be restored in our
rights and sustained.[124]

The nobles went on to explain that problems with insubordinate commoners extended beyond the city itself. The residents of sujetos had tried
to gain jurisdictional independence and no longer obeyed their rulers
and went about agitating against them, for which reason the audiencia
had exiled some of the troublemakers. But the greatest challenge, the
nobles claimed, came from those who bypassed the court of first
instance – Xochimilco's cabildo – and brought lawsuits before the high
court.[125]

The commoners' lawsuits were primarily about matters of tribute and
labor. The situation regarding labor duties was especially urgent, the
nobles explained. The city provided 300 workers for service in Mexico
City, for building projects, as well as to cultivate lands or otherwise work
for Spaniards. The letter-writers complained of the excessive demands
these duties imposed on residents and asked for relief, explaining that "the
natives of the said city are diminishing rather than increasing" and that, as
"your vassals," they have to "pay tribute." In other words, the problems
of failing to deliver sufficient tribute were twofold – population decline
and the redirection and exploitation of laborers by Spaniards. The argument was essentially that if Nahuas were making Spanish citizens rich

[124] Restall et al., *Mesoamerican Voices*, 68.
[125] Restall et al., *Mesoamerican Voices*, 69–70.

then they were not contributing as much as they could to the royal treasury.[126]

Pressing their case further, the nobles asserted that they no longer enjoyed the exemption of paying tribute as one of the key benefits of their status. They thus asked that those thirty individuals who served in the church should be relieved of their tax obligations. Among them were the "singers and masters of the choir and of book-writing, and the musicians who play flutes, chirimías, and trumpets." Additionally, the cabildo officers wrote,

We say that in the said city there are about four hundred natives who are gentlemen, cavaliers, and free nobles of well-known houses who with their forebears from time immemorial have been exempt from paying duties, tributes, services, or taxes either royal or local, and even when Moteuczoma tyrannized this land he observed their noble privileges; but about ten years ago they imposed certain tributes on them for expenses of the community and local government, of which your majesty receives nothing. We humbly implore that their ancient privileges and nobility be ordered observed, that a verified list be made of the noble Indians, and that they be relieved of the said tribute.

Finally, the authors of the letter argued that the staff of the city's council received no benefits or fees from their offices, and the salaries they were granted by the viceroy were inadequate.[127]

The perspective of Xochimilco's commoners, predictably, was entirely different. In 1564, when Vasco de Puga conducted his visita of Xochimilco, the macehualtin found a receptive audience for their grievances. Notably, if not suspiciously, their agenda aligned almost perfectly with the interests of the judge. Here, in the commoners' complaints, was ample grist for an oidor looking to change tribute arrangements; for the commoners, the opportunity to testify before a high court judge allowed them to advance their quarrels with the nobility. Four Nahuas are recorded as having provided testimonies. On behalf of their fellow macehualtin, Juan de San Pablo, Agustín Díaz, Gabriel Quauhtli, and Miguel de Cáceres alleged that the nobles had been making excessive demands for labor, failing to pay them for their work or for the goods they produced, and forcing them to perform other personal services that were no longer sanctioned by law. Those affected each day numbered more than 200 commoners and, in addition to them, twenty woodsmen, ten stonecutters, twenty masons, forty

[126] Restall et al., *Mesoamerican Voices*, 69.   [127] Restall et al., *Mesoamerican Voices*, 70.

fishermen, four medical specialists, five sawyers, and an unknown number of makers of reed mats, silversmiths, feather workers, tailors, potters, and basketmakers were also made to produce their specialist goods without compensation. The witnesses' statements essentially confirmed Vasco de Puga's view that greater tribute revenue could be secured if Nahua lords were prevented from siphoning off commoners' labor.[128]

Further aligning their interests with those of the high court judge, the complainants also argued that land was essential to their ability to pay tribute. The four witnesses explained that they would be freed from the disturbances and personal service demands of their nobles if they were to be given land of their own. Not only did many commoners not have land but the nobles had taken away what had once been theirs. Further aggravating the situation was the fact that they had to work their nobles' land without pay and, worse still, that they were landless when so many plots had fallen vacant. If they could just have access to enough land, the four witnesses agreed, they would be perfectly able to produce a gold peso and a fanega of maize in tribute each year – an amount worth a good deal more than that currently paid by nobles.[129] To underscore the importance of land, Xochimilco's residents effectively went on strike: at the same time that Vasco de Puga conducted his visita, the Nahuas refused to cultivate those portions of the lands they were required to farm for tribute, as had been set down in the viceroy's 1558 ordinances.[130]

While widespread land reforms did not follow the reforms of the early 1560s, changes to tribute arrangements did. Previously, Xochimilco's cabildo had been assessing tax rates for residents according to their status or property holdings.[131] But in 1564, the high court ordered that each tributary in Xochimilco, as in other parts of Mexico more generally, should henceforth contribute an equal payment.[132] The distinction between noble and commoner for tax purposes had been erased; the gradual diminution of noble privileges, when it came to personal service and financial support was now complete, at least on paper.[133]

---

[128] *Sobre el modo de tributar*, 122–125.   [129] *Sobre el modo de tributar*, 124–125.
[130] AGN, Mercedes, vol. 6, ff. 207–207v; *El libro de las tasaciones*, 306.
[131] *Sobre el modo de tributar*, 95, 98, 102; Gibson, *The Aztecs under Spanish Rule*, 520n50.
[132] *El Libro de las tasaciones de pueblos*, 306.
[133] This was not, it seems, the first time that members of the lesser nobility had been classified as tributaries: in ca. 1553, 400 Nahua "hijosdalgos" were required to pay tribute to Xochimilco. In cases from other parts of the Basin of Mexico, as Gibson noted, even caciques were included on tribute rolls, although a 1572 royal order once again exempted them. *The Aztecs under Spanish Rule*, 200, 519n41, n43.

TLATOQUE, NOBLEWOMEN, AND THE PRESERVATION OF THE UPPER CLASS

In spite of the government reforms, opposition from commoners, and the destructiveness of high mortality rates, the upper echelon of the Nahua nobility succeeding in upholding its superior social position well into the seventeenth century. The enduring strength of the tlatoque can be explained, in part, in terms of politics: by the final quarter of the sixteenth century, the climate had apparently shifted enough, with the widespread consolidation of Spanish forms of municipal government, for the tlatoque to recover control of Xochimilco's governorship; apparently it was no longer imperative to keep the governorship and the tlatocayotl separate. Using their political influence and their close alliances with the Franciscans, noblemen were able to recoup many of their earlier losses. They did so by recovering land and by bolstering their income through gubernatorial salaries, which now served as an alternative to the earlier payments of tribute goods. But their successes were only partially attributable to politics. What also proved essential to their lasting prestige and prominence were the many contributions of Nahua noblewomen. Cacicas and other noblewomen played a vital role in navigating the changing circumstances of colonial rule and demographic decline.

In the last two decades of the sixteenth century, the tlatoque staged a remarkable political comeback, recovering much of their previous strength after having been in the political wilderness for decades. Between 1548 and 1580, the only dynastic ruler recorded as having served as governor was don Pedro de Sotomayor, from Tepetenchi, who held that office some time before 1577.[134] It was a significant turnaround, then, when don Martín Cerón y Alvarado assumed the governorship in 1580. He retained the office for the next three years. All the more remarkably, don Martín was not unseated when he ran afoul of royal officials for having illegally diverted twenty laborers to his own fields and those of other nobles.[135] Don Martín was far from the only cacique to commit this infraction. In 1591, don Diego de Francisco, of Olac, also interfered with labor recruitment.[136]

Other tlatoque besides don Martín secured the governorship in the 1580s. Don Alonso Constantino, the tlatoani of Olac, also shared in the resurgence of the dynastic rulers, serving for two terms beginning in

---

[134] AGN, Indios, vol. 1, exp. 121, f. 44v.
[135] AGN, Indios, vol. 2, exp. 830, ff. 188–188v.   [136] AGN, Indios, vol. 5, exp. 158, f. 45.

1585.[137] In a further sign that the dynastic rulers had regained their strength, after the death of don Martín Cerón in 1588, his son or nephew went on to become governor in 1590. The younger don Martín Cerón y Alvarado then dominated high office for much of the decade. He was either elected or appointed governor eight times. He served consecutively from 1590 through 1593 and then again from 1595 to the end of 1598.[138] And, as with his father or uncle, don Martín retained political office in spite of a severe transgression. In 1591, in one of the most perplexing and politically disruptive of late sixteenth-century disputes, Spanish authorities took the unusual step of dismissing Xochimilco's entire Nahua government. Usually such interference in local affairs only involved individuals and not the cabildo as a whole. But in this one rare instance, royal officials took a firmer stand because, much to their consternation and presumably to the ire of the Franciscans, the Nahua leaders had apparently tried to establish their own church.[139] The officials' timing could hardly have been worse – the decades-long construction of Xochimilco's friary had only just come to an end the year before.[140] Invoking the *patronato real* (or royal dominion over church affairs) the viceroy suspended all of Xochimilco's officials and exiled them for a year.[141] In place of the ousted officials, the viceroy ordered the corregidor to call and supervise a new election.[142]

Presumably this remedy failed. Soon afterward the viceroy intervened by appointing a noble from the San Juan district of Mexico City to come and govern Xochimilco.[143] This measure appears to have been no more successful than the previous effort at restoring order.[144] With turmoil in Xochimilco's politics continuing unabated, at the end of the year the viceroy repealed the order of exile and, on the return of the banished officials, called for a new election.[145] That next year, don Martín Cerón

---

[137] AGN, Vínculos y Mayorazgos, vol. 279, exp. 1, ff. 115 and 121–122v. See also AGN, Tierras, vol. 1525, exp. 3, f. 5, in which don Alonso Constantino appeared as an alcalde.

[138] AGN, Indios, vol. 5, exp. 79, f. 21 (90 old foliation); vol. 6, 1a pte., exp. 519, f. 139; vol. 6, 2a pte., exp. 668, f. 154, exp. 689, f. 158v, and exp. 1079, f. 294; see also vol. 6, 2a pte., exp. 850, f. 207v and vol. 6, 1a pte., exp. 927, f. 249.

[139] The wording of the viceregal order was frustratingly vague about what happened, referring only to the "excesso que el governador y alcaldes de la ciudad de Suchimilco cometieron en hacer y fundar una yglesia nueva."

[140] Pérez Zevallos, *Xochimilco Ayer*, vol. 1, 126.

[141] AGN, Indios, vol. 5, exp. 964, f. 248v (318v old foliation).

[142] AGN, Indios, vol. 5, exp. 965, f. 248v (318v old foliation).

[143] AGN, Indios, vol. 6, 2a pte, exp. 116, ff. 27v–28.

[144] AGN, Indios, vol. 6, 2a pte, exp. 276, f. 61v.

[145] AGN, Indios, vol. 6, 2a pte, exp. 199, ff. 45–45v and exp. 273, f. 61.

y Alvarado once again resumed his position as governor in spite of his earlier infraction.[146] Thus for the sake of peace, Spanish authorities exonerated the council members. Indeed, the exigencies of colonial rule combined with the maneuverings of Nahuas in local government to allow the dynastic rulers to recover some of their lost power. They continued to unite the title of tlatoani with governor well into the seventeenth century.[147]

The religious controversy of the 1590s contrasted markedly with the generally close and mutually beneficial relations of Xochimilco's nobles with the clergy. Of course, members of the nobility celebrated mass and other sacraments, as well as rites of passage and holy days, at the altepetl's Franciscan friary. In their last wills and testaments, they sought burial in the friary and to have masses sung on behalf of their departed souls. In some cases they established valuable chantries. But nobles and friars also developed strong personal relationships, including close associations of considerable trust, as with the younger don Martín Cerón, who appointed his confessor, a friar named Alonso de la Lima, as the executor of the estate.[148] Thanks to such ties, Nahua nobles turned to friars for assistance in resolving disputes. They also made use of their connections with Franciscans to pursue their agendas, taking full advantage of their newly recovered power to reassert their social standing and secure their estates, as seen with the recovery of the nobles' lands at Xaxalpan (discussed in Chapter 2), in which the friars had provided crucial assistance.

In addition to recovering land and augmenting their estates, the tlatoque also used their political positions to make up for some of the other losses they had sustained in the middle decades of the sixteenth century. From the late 1570s, the tlatoque were receiving income even though they did not occupy formal, political positions. Nahuatl-language receipts show that payments were made three times a year, following the traditional *tercios* (the three times per year when tribute was paid). The amounts they received varied and, in years of plenty, could be quite lucrative. Don Martín Cerón received a salary of 160 pesos in 1577. That compared favorably to salaries paid to cabildo officers in the small

---

[146] By 1598 don Martín had apparently had enough. He successfully petitioned the viceroy for permission to be excused from office. AGN, Indios, vol. 6, 2a pte, exp. 689, f. 158v; AGN, Indios, vol. 6, 2a pte., exp. 1010, f. 270.

[147] In 1614, for example, don Alonso de Valencia was "tlatoahuani" and "juez gobernador." AGN, Vínculos y Mayorazgos, vol. 279, exp. 1, f. 45v.

[148] AGN, Vínculos y Mayorazgos, vol. 279, exp. 1, ff. 10–10v.

town of Mixquic, where the governor earned thirty pesos.[149] That the amounts were tied to the surpluses from community tribute revenues would explain some of the gaps in the record and the significant fluctuations in payments. In 1578, during the cocoliztli pandemic, the amount paid to don Martín dropped to ninety-four pesos. In 1579, when the toll of disease had deepened, the amount fell to thirty pesos. Beyond what they received as tlatoque, however, the nobles recovered some of their predecessors' lost privileges through increasing official salaries.[150] When don Martín served in an official capacity, for instance during his three-year tenure as governor (1580–1582), he received more money than before, with payments coming from Tepetenchi, Tecpan, and Olac.[151] Over time, and in contrast to the complaint leveled in the 1563 letter to the crown, salaries for governors kept growing. Official income still came from tribute receipts, but from 100 pesos it rose to 200 and then 350 pesos by 1598.[152] In the seventeenth century, surprisingly, Xochimilco's governor earned more than many Spanish corregidores.[153]

The dynastic rulers' improved circumstances can also be explained in their careful management of their property and investments. In this inheritance assumed an important role, especially given the severity of frequent and recurring epidemics. For this reason in 1588 don Martín Cerón y Alvarado the Elder devoted a portion of his testament to listing the succession of his heirs. His son would inherit first but, in the event of his son's death, the entire estate would pass to the tlatoani's brother, don Tomás de Guzmán.[154] Spaniards typically favored lineal forms of inheritance, from parent to offspring, and over time the Nahuas, who in precontact times had practiced lateral inheritance (for instance, to siblings, nieces or nephews), increasingly adopted the foreign convention.[155] Both

---

[149] Each alcalde earned ten pesos, each regidor and mayordomo six, the scribe six, and the singers in the church each received two pesos. AGN, Indios, vol. 1, exp. 169, f. 62.

[150] Don Fernando de Santa María claimed the stipend of 250 pesos a year that his father had enjoyed. The viceroy was reluctant to allow it, citing diminutions in tribute. AGN, Indios, vol. 4, exp. 645, ff. 184–184v.

[151] AGN, Vínculos y Mayorazgos, vol. 279, exp. 1, ff. 69–70; Cline, "A Cacicazgo in the Seventeenth Century," 270.

[152] AGN, Indios, vol. 6, 1a pte., exp. 966, f. 262, 2a pte., exp. 933, ff. 240–240v. The gubernatorial salary of Tlahuac was eighty pesos; AGN, Indios, vol. 6, 1a pte., exp. 311, f. 84v and exp. 548, f. 145.

[153] Gibson, *The Aztecs under Spanish Rule*, 187.

[154] AGN, Vínculos y Mayorazgos, vol. 279, exp. 1, ff. 6–8v.

[155] Cline, "A Cacicazgo in the Seventeenth Century," 269, Pérez Zevallos, *Xochimilco Ayer*, vol. 1, 52. See also Susan Kellogg, *Law and the Transformation of Aztec Culture, 1500–1700* (Norman: University of Oklahoma Press, 1995), 121–212.

systems seem to have been operating here, and in at least two instances documented in the family's papers, daughters inherited property from both their mothers and fathers. In fact, women, and especially widows, proved crucial to transferring property from one generation to the next.

Such was the importance of their economic activities that Nahua noblewomen were vital to the preservation of family wealth and the maintenance of high social standing. If their husbands, fathers, or brothers took care of formal political matters, Nahua noblewomen assumed the responsibility for managing and preserving their estates. These complementary duties reflected well-established gender relations among Native peoples in central Mexico. While men are typically understood as having assumed prominent roles in public life, women were nonetheless active in ways that transcended the domestic sphere. Noblewomen were active in political and legal venues, from the cabildo to courts, even if they could not hold office, and they made full use of colonial institutions and practices to marshal family resources to generate income while also securing the integrity of the estate by contending with litigation, establishing rental agreements, obtaining loans, and buying and selling property. Of their many contributions to their families' fortunes, noblewomen's efforts at securing inheritance were crucial. The fate of the city's nobility depended in significant measure upon the acuity of noblewomen as they ensured the secure transmission of property from one generation to the next.

Not all their efforts were successful, of course, and the occasional, unfortunate transaction exposed the critical importance of noblewomen in economic affairs. In 1586, a series of property disputes erupted after doña Juana de Guzmán, the widow of don Pedro de Sotomayor, set down her testament. It was found to have several irregularities, having been drawn up without the presence of a notary or the usual witnesses.[156] The municipal council further sought to nullify the testament because its provisions had aroused antagonism among relatives.[157] Testimony provided by the late widow's brother, don Juan de Guzmán, shows the depth of his indignation at having been neglected. Don Juan recounted a conversation with doña Juana – which James Lockhart has translated – as he sat next to his ailing sister's bed. He said to her, "Oh my mistress, oh lady, I ask you, is it true that you have already made your testament?"

[156] AGN, Vínculos y Mayorazgos, vol. 279, exp. 1, ff. 121–126 and 132–138v; Cline, "A Cacicazgo in the Seventeenth Century," 273.

[157] AGN, Vínculos y Mayorazgos, vol. 279, exp. 1, ff. 65–68.

"Let me hear a bit just in your words how you have disposed the former palace of señor don Pedro de Sotomayor whom our lord God took, your dear late husband, what you have said and ordered in your testament."

And then she answered me and said, "Why do you ask?"

Then I said to her, "Just because I want to know if you have done something wrong about the ruler's house and all the ruler's lands, fields, and chinampas; let me hear a bit how it is."[158]

In reply, doña Juana explained that since no child of hers was alive, she had arranged for the sale of all the property, with the proceeds supporting masses for the souls of the deceased. On hearing this, don Juan rebuked her:

You have done very wrong; it is a bad thing you have done. Aren't there children, nephews, grandchildren, and won't they complain greatly of you when God has taken you, and curse you for it? Won't there be a great lawsuit after you are gone? Won't there be shouting, and discord among the nephews of the late señor don Pedro de Sotomayor, whom God took, your nephews as well, who are now alive? And because of this will they be able to pray to our lord God on your behalf? ... And what about me? ... You have greatly mistreated us too, it is as though you had scorned us.[159]

Don Juan's fear of a "great lawsuit" proved well founded. Although his sister subsequently altered her testament, its stipulations nevertheless generated controversy. In part, litigation followed from the complexity of donating and selling property through the Franciscan friary. Five years after the drafting of the testament, for instance, a singer named Diego Sánchez responded to a rival claim to property by showing that his title extended back through the friary to doña Juana's bequest.[160] The matter of doña Juana's will did not end there. Six decades later, in 1649, the younger don Martín Cerón continued to lay claim to land obtained by local residents.[161]

In Xochimilco, as elsewhere, widows assumed powerful positions in managing family resources. They took care of family properties, carefully preserving titles to property and the paperwork of transactions. Several bills of sale and certified listings of property, known as *memorias*, are preserved in the papers of the cacicazgo.[162] Even doña Juana appears less

---

[158] Lockhart, "The Testimony of don Juan," in *Nahuas and Spaniards*, 82.
[159] Lockhart, "The Testimony of don Juan," 83–84.
[160] AGN, Vínculos y Mayorazgos, vol. 279, exp. 1, ff. 130–131.
[161] AGN, Vínculos y Mayorazgos, vol. 279, exp. 1, ff. 138v–139.
[162] AGN, Vínculos y Mayorazgos, vol. 279, exp. 1, ff. 79, 80, 106–109v, 110–113v, 119–120v, and 126.

hapless than her aggrieved brother would have had us believe; she preserved the documentation of her late husband's debts, which she had repaid.[163] She was also adept at negotiating with colonial authorities. In 1577, doña Juana successfully petitioned for the right to receive the salary of her former husband, don Pedro de Sotomayor.[164]

Much as they looked after documentation, so Nahua noblewomen were cautious about how they disposed of their property. Several wills, including those of doña María de Guzmán and doña Juana de Guzmán, prohibited the sale of property to Spaniards in order to maintain the integrity of their estates.[165] Noblewomen also carefully identified their heirs. In her remarkably detailed testament from 1577, doña Ana de Guzmán not only named more than a dozen individuals but she also listed the properties to be sold or inherited.[166] Obviously much depended on the successful drafting of testaments, and noblewomen tried to ensure that their offspring were well looked after. In 1582, presumably to facilitate the implementation of her will, doña María de Guzmán passed on the majority of her estate to a daughter, doña Francisca. All the named parties and the nobles of the district of Olac, from which she hailed, subsequently appeared before the municipal council to state their satisfaction with the testament and attest to its legitimacy. Having secured the inheritance, doña Francisca then passed on some of her newly acquired property to her brother.[167]

Noblewomen such as doña Francisca were careful to secure their rights to inherited properties. Doña Francisca moved quickly to obtain confirmation of her titles and then performed the customary ceremonies of possession. In front of city officials, she entered her property and threw stones in the four cardinal directions. Presumably doña Francisca had learned the importance of such acts from her mother. In 1571, doña María de Guzmán had likewise recruited an official, this time the corregidor, to confirm title to property after the death of her husband. The corregidor also accompanied doña María as she performed the rituals of possession.

[163] AGN, Vínculos y Mayorazgos, vol. 279, exp. 1, ff. 132–138v. Similarly, in 1631, doña María Juana set aside three loads of chile in order to cover debts owed to five people. Universidad Nacional Autónoma de México (hereafter UNAM), Biblioteca Nacional, Fondo Reservado, Archivo Franciscano, caja 11, exp. 1531, f. 7v.

[164] AGN, Indios, vol. 1, exp. 121. ff. 44v–45.

[165] AGN, Vínculos y Mayorazgos, vol. 279, exp. 1, f. 87; Cline, "A Cacicazgo in the Seventeenth Century," 268.

[166] AGN, Vínculos y Mayorazgos, vol. 279, exp. 1, ff. 19–21v and 23–25v.

[167] AGN, Vínculos y Mayorazgos, vol. 279, exp. 1, ff. 82–90v.

At the same time, doña María diligently obtained documentation asserting the rights of her own children to her mother's estate. She thus managed to secure the smooth transfer of property across two generations.[168]

Xochimilca noblewomen obtained property from their parents as well as their deceased husbands. Doña Ana de Guzmán and doña María de Guzmán, while coming from different lineages, both inherited residences in Xochimilco and Mexico City from their respective parents.[169] Some women had enough resources of their own to buy land.[170] Doña Francisca, for instance, purchased property independently, in one case buying back a parcel of land that had previously been sold to commoners.[171] She was meticulous in arranging the details of such purchases, being careful to conform to contractual obligations and producing the requisite notarial records. That carefulness was more than merited given the complexities of prior ownership of property. In 1597, for instance, doña Francisca bought a plot of land that had previously belonged to no fewer than four other individuals.[172] On other occasions, married couples pooled their resources. Doña Francisca and her husband, don Martín Cerón y Alvarado, purchased two sets of houses and their lots as well as a shop. Joint ownership would have presumably afforded greater security in the context of epidemic disease.[173]

As the noblewomen's property dealings demonstrate, the family's estate did not remain an inert, untapped resource, one simply to be preserved. Rather, Nahua noblewomen devised ways of using their assets to generate income. Some used property as collateral to raise cash through loans.[174] Others proved especially skilled in exploiting resources; one entrepreneurial noblewoman even bought a sugar mill.[175] Another noblewoman named doña María Juana owned three houses which she rented out. One of the rentals involved a *censo*, or loan, in which a house was essentially mortgaged to the friary while simultaneously being rented by

---

[168] AGN, Vínculos y Mayorazgos, vol. 279, exp. 1, ff. 102–102v. On rituals of possession, see Terraciano, *The Mixtecs of Colonial Oaxaca*, 212. The individual confirmations appear in the estate records, AGN, Vínculos y Mayorazgos, vol. 279, exp. 1, ff. 102v–105v.

[169] AGN, Vínculos y Mayorazgos, vol. 279, exp. 1, ff. 19–25v and 87.

[170] AGN, Vínculos y Mayorazgos, vol. 279, exp. 1, ff. 10–11v and 40–41.

[171] Cline, "A Cacicazgo in the Seventeenth Century," 271.

[172] AGN, Vínculos y Mayorazgos, vol. 279, exp. 1, ff. 40–42.

[173] AGN, Vínculos y Mayorazgos, vol. 279, exp. 1, ff. 59–60v; Cline, "A Cacicazgo in the Seventeenth Century," 272–273.

[174] AGN, Vínculos y Mayorazgos, vol. 279, exp. 1, ff. 26–27v.

[175] AGN, Tierras, vol. 3018, exp. 1, ff. 1–3v and exps. 3 and 4, ff. 17v–31, exp. 2, ff. 4–17.

a third party, in this case a Spaniard named Francisco Pérez. His rent helped pay for religious festivals.[176] As with others, doña María Juana also rented houses to other Spaniards, among them a notary.[177]

Through their economic activities, and in taking care of the legal mechanisms that underpinned them, noblewomen came into regular contact with Spaniards and people of mixed ancestry whose presence in Xochimilco, given the shifting demographic profile of the city, was becoming more prominent. While doña Francisca purchased property from a mulata, doña Ana de Guzmán bequeathed a few chinampas to a Spaniard even as she quarreled with two others over debts.[178] One of doña María de Guzmán's tenants, a Spaniard named Juan López, had been sufficiently delinquent in paying rent that she ordered his eviction.[179] But Spaniards, especially Franciscan friars, could also be a boon to Nahua noblewomen. Fray Gerónimo de Mendieta, for instance, acted as an executor for doña Ana de Guzmán.[180] Friars also helped to arbitrate disputes. In 1574, two women, the daughter and the widow of don Esteban de Guzmán – respectively, doña Ana de Guzmán and doña Magdalena de Santa María – came into conflict over possession of his estate. Attesting to their skill in contending with legal and economic matters, both noblewomen appeared before the notary, Martín Pauper de Monte Alegre, to put into writing an agreement, or *concertado*, they had devised. Fray Alonso de Escalona witnessed its signing. The ladies agreed to resolve their differences by sharing the property. Doña Ana relinquished her claims to land and chinampas in several locations, and subsequently they performed the rituals of possession. Doña Magdalena then arranged the sale and donation of land to her son.[181] Thus doña Magdalena succeeded in resolving a conflict with a fellow noblewoman while also distributing property to her son. And in addition to dealing with local officials, she petitioned the viceroy for confirmation of her property titles.[182]

---

[176] The specific type of censo was not identified in the document, but its stipulations bear some similarity to the *censo consignativo* described by Kathryn Burns in *Colonial Habits: Convents and the Spiritual Economy of Cuzco, Peru* (Durham: Duke University Press, 1999), 64.

[177] UNAM, Fondo Reservado, Archivo Franciscano, caja 11, exp. 1531, f. 7v.

[178] AGN, Vínculos y Mayorazgos, vol. 279, exp. 1, ff. 19–25v, 60.

[179] AGN, Vínculos y Mayorazgos, vol. 279, exp. 1, ff. 82–90v.

[180] AGN, Vínculos y Mayorazgos, vol. 279, exp. 1, ff. 24; Cline, "A Cacicazgo in the Seventeenth Century," 267–268.

[181] AGN, Vínculos y Mayorazgos, vol. 279, exp. 1, ff. 102–105v.

[182] AGN, Vínculos y Mayorazgos, vol. 279, exp. 1, ff. 110–110v. Other noblewomen sometimes approached the viceroy for assistance. In 1590, doña Polonia Cortés asked the viceroy to issue an order of protection, this time for several plots of land she had inherited. A year later, a cacica named Antonia Luisa solicited protection for her two sons

Nahua noblewomen harnessed the wealth they so assiduously guarded to maintain the obligations and trappings of high social status. As was customary, they directed some of their prosperity to the church. Many testamentary bequests included payments for masses for the souls of the deceased. But women also made other donations. Doña Ana de Guzmán directed funds to several friaries in Xochimilco, Mexico City, and Tacuba, as well as to one of the capital's hospitals.[183] The Cerón y Alvarado family maintained a *capellanía*, a chantry whose chaplains said masses for departed members of the family.[184] Similarly, doña María Juana's family had a chapel in Xochimilco's friary dedicated to the veneration of Nuestra Señora del Pilar. Doña María donated the large sum of 3,000 pesos for its upkeep.[185] Her enthusiasm for the church extended to sponsorship of a confraternity, and she ensured that it was properly furnished with an insignia fit for display during Good Friday celebrations. Indeed, such was doña Juana's wealth that she owned black slaves, one of whom she manumitted while the other she sold.[186]

Nahua noblewomen shouldered a variety of social obligations made possible by their financial acuity. They acted as godmothers for members of the nobility and occasionally for commoners, thereby preserving some of the old social ties binding together Nahuas across the social hierarchy.[187] Children figured prominently in the uses to which they put their wealth. Doña María Juana set aside 200 pesos to support two children, one of whom lived in a convent.[188] And noblewomen often maintained ties to the wider community through testamentary bequests. Doña Ana de Guzmán devoted part of her testament to distributing chinampas to those who had "served us," among others. The Nahuatl terms *cuitlahuia* (to take care of) and *nemilia* (to provide sustenance) indicate a noble-dependent relationship.[189]

In addition to their many important socioeconomic roles, women also played a vital part in dynastic marriage strategies, continuing a tradition

---

(the document does not state exactly what they needed protection from). AGN, Indios, vol. 4, exp. 239, f. 72v; vol. 6, 2a pte, exp. 156, f. 37.

[183] AGN, Vínculos y Mayorazgos, vol. 279, exp. 1, ff. 19–21v.

[184] INAH, Fondo Franciscano, vol. 48, ff. 7, 19–19v.

[185] UNAM, Fondo Reservado, Archivo Franciscano, caja 11, exp. 1531, f. 4v.

[186] UNAM, Fondo Reservado, Archivo Franciscano, caja 11, exp. 1531, f. 7.

[187] See the parish registers of baptisms in AGN, Genealogía [microfilm], vol. 1793.

[188] UNAM, Fondo Reservado, Archivo Franciscano, caja 11, exp. 1531, f. 7v.

[189] That sense is reinforced in the contemporary Spanish translation of these terms by the local interpreter: "que me sirvia" or "que estaba con nosotros por lo bien que nos sirvio." AGN, Vínculos y Mayorazgos, vol. 279, exp. 1, ff. 19–21v.

that extended far back into the pre-contact past. The marriage strategies sought to secure and bolster noble lineages, which had long been a defining feature of high sociopolitical status.[190] Several Xochimilca ladies married into ruling lineages of other central Mexican altepetl. Both doña María Cerón and doña Leonor de Guzmán married into noble houses in Chalco (Tlalmanalco and Chimalhuacan). Others married and relocated to Cuernavaca.[191] Noblewomen from other altepetl also joined Xochimilca families. Doña Juana de Guzmán, whose testament had proved so controversial, came from Coyoacan. These strategic marriages across polities secured local lineages. In some cases the arrival of noblewomen from elsewhere enhanced the prestige of existing dynasties. In 1610, doña Francisca de Guzmán, whose maternal ancestry passed through Coyoacan's dynasty, incorporated the Cerón y Alvarado family into a prestigious lineage that extended back to the Mexica ruler Acamapichtli.[192]

Strategic marriages across altepetl also complemented internal ones among Xochimilco's subdivisions of Tepetenchi, Tecpan, and Olac. Facing colonial pressures and demographic collapse, over time the tlatoani lineages survived by becoming increasingly interconnected. At some point in the sixteenth century – the exact details remain obscure – the Santa María family of Tecpan combined with Tepetenchi through the marriage of doña Magdalena to don Esteban de Guzmán. Their daughter in turn married the Tepetenchi tlatoani don Martín Cerón y Alvarado the Elder.[193] In addition to these ties between Tecpan and Tepetenchi, other marriages incorporated nobles from Olac.[194] In the early seventeenth century, doña Francisca de Guzmán married the tlatoani of Tepetenchi, don Martín Cerón y Alvarado the Younger. Previously her mother, doña María de Guzmán, had married the ruler of Olac. Thus as a daughter and wife, doña Francisca united the lineages of Olac and Tepetenchi, further

---

[190] Haskett, *Indigenous Rulers*, 145; Susan Schroeder, "The Noblewomen of Chalco," *Estudios de Cultura Náhuatl*, vol. 22 (1992), 45–86.

[191] Chimalpahin, *Codex Chimalpahin*, vol. 2, 103, 117; Chimalpahin, *Annals of His Time*, 111; AGN, Vínculos y Mayorazgos, vol. 279, exp. 1, ff. 10–11v, 76.

[192] The family also became related, albeit indirectly, to the ruler of Tenochtitlan, Moteucçuma Xocoyotzin. Don Francisco de Guzmán Omacatzin, ruler of Olac Xochimilco, was the nephew of the Aztec emperor. Chimalpahin, *Codex Chimalpahin*, vol. 2, 97, 99. For her genealogy, see AGN, Vínculos y Mayorazgos, vol. 279, exp. 1, ff. 28–29; Luis Reyes García, "Genealogía de doña Francisca de Guzmán, Xochimilco 1610," *Tlalocan*, vol. 7 (1977), 31–35.

[193] AGN, Vínculos y Mayorazgos, vol. 279, exp. 1, ff. 23–25v, 91–96, and 97–98v.

[194] Cline, "A Cacicazgo in the Seventeenth Century," 272.

binding together the ruling families of Xochimilco. The connection between the two districts was underscored by the transfer of Olac's *tecpan*, or "palace," to ownership by the Tepetenchi family.[195] While distinctions between the lineages gradually blurred, alliances may have increased the likelihood of nobles retaining their resources within the expanded family: presumably because property could be passed on to a wider, interconnected pool of heirs, alliances within Xochimilco served to shore up the integrity of family lines while also consolidating their wealth.

Ultimately, though, marriage alliances and the efforts of Nahua noblewomen to protect their family's estates were undone by disease and high mortality rates. In 1650, when don Martín Cerón y Alvarado the Younger set down an initial version of his testament, all but one of his offspring had already passed away. The sole surviving heir was deemed unfit to inherit the estate, at least until the elderly tlatoani chose to revise his last wishes with a codicil. Initially, though, don Martín directed his bequests to the city's Franciscan friary.[196] His chantry generated revenue to pay for masses on behalf of the souls of his deceased relatives.[197]

CONCLUSION

Epidemics, warfare, enslavement, lower birthrates, and other factors all combined to reduce drastically the size of Nahua communities of the southern lake areas. While the greatest demographic shocks registered in 1520–1521, 1545–1548, and 1576–1581, those three epidemics did not account for all of the population collapse. Many other instances of epidemic were recorded in the sources, and such was their frequency through the late sixteenth and early seventeenth centuries that they proved destructive in their own frequent, persistent, and appalling way. Some of the diseases became endemic, perhaps serving to keep the population at low levels for a long time after it reached its nadir. The overall decline during the first century of the colonial period matches that observed elsewhere in the Americas. In Xochimilco, as with other places, there seems to have been only negligible recovery in the second half of the seventeenth century.

---

[195] AGN, Vínculos y Mayorazgos, vol. 279, exp. 1, f. 88.

[196] AGN, Indios, vol. 16, exp. 76, ff. 73–74 (71–72 old foliation); AGN, Reales Cédulas Duplicadas, vol. 15, exp. 171, f. 130v, exp. 179, f. 141v; AGN, Intestados, vol. 301, f. 214; UNAM, Biblioteca Nacional, Fondo Reservado, Archivo Franciscano, Caja. 112, exp 1531, ff. 1–8.

[197] INAH, Fondo Franciscano, vol. 48, ff. 7, 19–19v.

Such was the fragility of the recovery that it could be quickly undone by yet another outbreak of disease. This pattern continued into the eighteenth century. The significant fluctuations in the population figures of the 1760s through the early 1800s remind us of the persistence of high mortality rates and the ongoing precariousness of life.

High mortality rates life were reflected in the last wills and testaments set down by Nahuas. In a particularly distressing one from 1743, María Jacinta bequeathed two houses lots and a small plot of land between the road and the lakeshore, where she had several olive trees. María was an orphan. She stated that since her parents were in "heaven" (literally, the "sky") – where she herself expected to go soon – her father was now God and her mother was Nuestra Señora de los Dolores. María was young when she died, so young that the cabildo declared her testament null and void because she was a minor. One witness put her age at twelve. Other witnesses spoke of the epidemics that had claimed many lives in the community.[198]

Foreign pathogens cut through the ecological barrier afforded by the lakes. Where the landscape provided some degree of stability, the other, demographic dimension of Xochimilco's environmental history provided none. And yet, in spite of the demographic collapse, the vast majority of communities survived, albeit with greatly reduced numbers of people. Almost as many distinct communities appeared in records produced near the end of the colonial period as they had in earlier times. Many of them thus preserved their integrity and remained viable across the colonial period.

The repercussions of demographic collapse were widely felt and affected many areas of life. Primary among these were social relations within communities. Nahuas seized opportunities afforded by Spanish government's reforms of tribute arrangements to escape from onerous service to their lords or to secure the new legal protections afforded by colonial institutions. In a wider sense, demographic change entailed something of a reordering of society, one in which subordinate groups like terrazgueros and commoners sought to redefine their place in society even as members of the lesser nobility sought greater influence and the high Nahua aristocracy struggled to maintain its position. While the position of the nobility declined, it nevertheless held firm. For a while, the noble families managed to withstand demographic collapse. The tlatoque lineages did so by uniting their three families. Such strategic marriages were

[198] AGN, Tierras, vol. 2327, exp. 10, f. 2.

a necessary practical response to precarious circumstances. But they did involve an erosion of the old sociopolitical order in which the complex altepetl had been founded on the three ruling dynasties. Still, thanks to the economic and political acumen Nahua noblewomen, who alongside their male counterparts proved vital to their families' security and stability, the ruling lineages did preserve many of the foundations of the wealth that underpinned their high social standing.

Through the contestations between commoners and nobles, as well as the shifting alliances between these constituencies and the agents of the colonial administration – including the Franciscans – significant changes came to Nahua society during the sixteenth century. The ideology and the social practices that defined class relations shifted. They gradually undermined – but did not yet overturn – the old bases of Nahua authority.

5

Crisis in the Seventeenth Century

Xochimilco's governor and two of its dynastic rulers greeted the new year of 1607 from a jail cell in Mexico City. Don Francisco de Zapata Contreras, don Martín Cerón y Alvarado, and don Fernando de Santa María had been imprisoned for failing to pay tribute. By this time the colonial government had begun to hold Nahua rulers personally liable for their communities' tribute debts. Those who defaulted, as had Xochimilco's leaders, now faced criminal charges.[1] The three noblemen found themselves in a particularly precarious position: they had failed to pay tribute for the simple reason that there was nothing left for them to make payment with; severe flooding had ruined harvests and destroyed the city's chinampas. As a result, the aquatic gardens needed to be rebuilt and the irrigation system repaired before new crops could be grown, which meant that Xochimilco's debts to the treasury would not be paid anytime soon. Until that time, the three noblemen faced the unpleasant prospect of further incarceration as well as the dishonor of criminal sanction.

This difficult moment marked the start of nearly half a century's acute hardships for Xochimilco's residents. Environmental factors were at the forefront of these upheavals. Population collapse was prominent among them, and the city still faced decades of further demographic decline. Climate instability was also central to what happened. Central Mexico entered the coldest and dampest depths of the Little Ice Age from the late sixteenth century. A series of volcanic eruptions, first in Colima, Mexico in 1586, next in Colombia in 1595, and then at Huaynaputina in the

---

[1] AGI, Audiencia de México, leg. 227, no. 17, ff. 1, 3; Gibson, *The Aztecs under Spanish Rule*, 218.

Andes in 1600 all combined to bring much cooler, cloudier, and wetter conditions. The volcanoes sent dust and aerosols into the atmosphere which reduced solar radiation.[2] Further contributing to cooling temperatures were falling levels of atmospheric carbon dioxide and, as Bradley Skopyk notes, reduced solar output.[3] By 1601, temperatures in the Northern Hemisphere dipped by more than one degree Celsius below the millennium's average, producing what was possibly the coldest summer in the last 2,000 years.[4] Thereafter, Xochimilco as elsewhere in central Mexico, experienced a sustained period of climate extremes. The drought of the 1590s, for instance, gave way to sudden bursts of higher precipitation in the first years of the seventeenth century, which inundated the chinampa districts and made it impossible for Xochimilco's governors to meet their tribute obligations.

The trend toward increasing climate instability became more pronounced in the middle years of the seventeenth century. Between 1616 and 1621 drought returned to central Mexico. In 1629, though, high levels of precipitation led to inundations, this time submerging Mexico City for several years. From the late 1630s through 1644, another series volcanic eruptions – up to a dozen of them – further cooled the earth's atmosphere, as did a period of fewer sunspots, both of which provided yet more climate instability. As a result, Xochimilco experienced significantly lower temperatures in the early 1640s. For the Northern Hemisphere as a whole, 1641's summer was the third coldest in the past six centuries while the summer of 1642 was the twenty-eighth coldest and that of 1643 the tenth coldest. Barely any rain fell in the Basin of Mexico in 1640–1642. Such cold conditions returned again in the next decade, and the period from 1654 though 1667 was, on average, one degree Celsius cooler than in the late twentieth century.[5] The adverse conditions contributed to sudden shifts from flooding to drought and, by extension, failed harvests and food shortages. The impoverishment and hunger that followed prompted many citizens to flee, further compounding the difficulties faced by those who remained. As the population approached its lowest level, in the 1640s, so the ability of the city to meet its tribute and labor obligations became ever more difficult and burdensome.

Making matters worse were the depredations of several leading figures, including one particularly delinquent individual. Whereas in 1607 the Nahua rulers wound up in jail and faced the prospect of criminal charges

---

[2] White, *A Cold Welcome*, 76–77.   [3] Skopyk, *Colonial Cataclysms*, 12.
[4] White, *A Cold Welcome*, 77.   [5] Parker, *Global Crisis*, xxvii, xx, 14, and 64.

for what essentially had been a civil matter, by the 1630s a new cohort of leaders participated in a prolonged, far-reaching, and spectacularly profligate criminal conspiracy – one that if the complaints brought against them were to be believed, ran to bribery, embezzlement, extortion and fraud as well as theft and assault, among other crimes. These crimes amounted to departure from the occasional instances of abuse of office that had previously bedeviled Xochimilco's politics.[6] Prior to the seventeenth century, the potential for malfeasance in Nahua municipal government had been tempered by the practice of rotating office on an annual or biannual basis. Rotation acted as a check on any one person's designs on power and tended to set limits to any rivalry among nobles.[7] Brief tenure in office also limited the capacity of individual governors to cause too much mischief. Abuse of office, when it happened, had tended to be infrequent and short lived.[8] This situation changed in the 1630s. The criminal activities of the city's leaders became bound up with their prolonged retention of power. Abuse of office came to pervade political life. It represented a broader estrangement of municipal government from routine and acceptable administrative practices. A wide array of Spanish and Nahua officials in the city participated in illegal activities, from the corregidor at the summit of local power to minor officials such as tax collectors.[9] At the center of the criminal enterprise was the Nahua governor.

The offenses and abuses of office exacerbated the dire situation with municipal finances and created a profound crisis in the city – a crisis that shared much in common with the upheavals observed elsewhere in the world at that time. As Geoffrey Parker has noted of the wider, global crisis of the seventeenth century, a "fatal synergy" of poor climatic conditions and poor decisions by governments combined to generate widespread dislocations and turmoil. While central Mexico escaped many of the upheavals of the period, in Xochimilco there was very much a severe, prolonged crisis: the local government lost its legitimacy; the city went

---

[6] AGN, Indios, vol. 6, 1a pte., exp. 1023, ff. 276v–277, and AGN, Indios, vol. 3, exp. 260, ff. 60v–61 (59v–60 old foliation).

[7] Lockhart, *Nahuas after the Conquest*, 32; Haskett, *Indigenous Rulers*, 10, 12; Gibson, *The Aztecs under Spanish Rule*, 191; Gibson, "Rotation of Alcaldes in the Indian Cabildo of Mexico City," *Hispanic American Historical Review*, vol. 33, no. 2 (1953), 212–223.

[8] AGN, Indios vol. 11, exp. 1, f. 1; AGN, Indios, vol. 12, 1a pte., exp. 117, f. 79 (78 old foliation).

[9] AGN, Historía, vol. 36, exp. 2, ff. 95–196v; AGN, General de Parte, vol. 7, exp. 10, ff. 6v–7; vol. 7, exp. 37, ff. 23v–24, and vol. 7, exp. 42, f. 28v.

bankrupt; the municipal government fell into disarray, and citizens turned to flight or political violence.[10] By 1652, the old political order had collapsed. Gone was the long-standing tradition of tlatoani rule that extended back into the distant, pre-conquest past.[11]

INUNDATED, INSOLVENT, AND OVERWHELMED

Flooding was an infrequent but nonetheless severe threat to residents of the southern lake districts, just as it was for those who lived in the capital. Lakes Xochimilco and Chalco were prone to inundations because of the area's physical geography. While the two southern lakes were filled with fresh water from precipitation, natural springs, and runoff from the montes, the two lakes did not have much of an outlet; together they formed what was almost a smaller basin within the wider Basin of Mexico; the lakes were almost entirely surrounded by hills, the one exception to this encirclement being a narrow channel, with an embankment and sluicegates, at Mexicalzingo, behind which water levels might rise dramatically in times of heavy rainfall. That many communities were located in the lakes themselves, or on their shores, meant that they were especially vulnerable to inundations. Small differences in elevation could make them susceptible to even the slightest of increases in water levels. In 1640, low-lying San Pedro Tlahuac was flooded while nearby communities were spared. With no land remaining above water, the town's cabildo officers relocated and took up temporary residence in a nearby sujeto, Santa Catalina Tlahuac, which lay at a higher elevation and remained dry.[12]

Major floods, which is to say those affecting the southern lake areas in their entirety, were recorded on just a few occasions between 1520 and 1700 (further instances of flooding were also recorded in the eighteenth century, as discussed in Chapter 6). The first followed in the wake of the Spanish–Mexica War of 1519–1521: while not recorded in historical documents, archaeologists have observed that the destruction of the hydraulic engineering works during the conflict resulted in the loss of the many chinampas that had been constructed under the supervision of the Aztec government; with the unimpeded flow of water, once again,

---

[10] For the comparatively limited crisis in the Americas, see Parker, *Global Crisis*, 462–468.

[11] AGN, Indios, vol. 13, exp. 391, ff. 343–344 (321–322 old foliation), vol. 15, exp. 17, ff. 14–14v, and vol. 18, exp. 140, f. 106v.

[12] AGN, Indios, vol. 13, exp. 104, ff. 109v–110.

much of the engineered, agrarian landscape was transformed back into being a lake. On this occasion, high levels of precipitation were not responsible for the flooding; rather, the inundation followed from changes to the basin's drainage system.[13] In addition to this instance of flooding, two other the widespread, early floods took place in 1582 and, intermittently, between 1604 and 1607. Both of them were tied to high levels of rainfall, although the latter also had to do with closing the sluicegates at Mexicalzingo in order to protect the capital. The closing of these gates all but guaranteed the submersion of the chinampa districts behind them.

The vulnerability of the lake towns made it vital to keep the flood defenses properly maintained. In 1648, after an outbreak of disease in Tlahuac, which brought many deaths and prompted some of the survivors to flee, those who remained suffered from a flood and petitioned the government for exemptions from their assigned labor demands so that they could complete their work on the town's dike and floodgates. According to data provided by the dendrochronologist David Stahle through the Mexican Drought Atlas, the flooding must have stemmed from a spike in precipitation at that time.[14] The drought atlas allows for the analysis of soil moisture conditions according to a seven-point index, which ranges from –3 (for drier than normal conditions at a specific site) to 3 (much wetter than normal at the same site). The index is known as the Palmer Drought Severity Index (PDSI), which has become a standard tool for measuring drought.[15] In the case of Tlahuac in 1648, the data indicate a PDSI value of 2, which is to say a significant spike in wetter conditions (this value being observed for the grid point located at W 99.1°, N 19.26° for Lake Xochimilco).[16] The sudden increase in precipitation held significant implications for lake-area residents. In the resulting investigation, a Spanish justice reported that the town had been abandoned, having been ruined in the rising waters, and that its people were burdened by infinite labors. In no way could they perform yet more work. So severe had the flooding been, he continued to explain, that after the waters had crested,

---

[13] The years before the arrival of Spaniards and until the late 1530s were ones of persistent drought. Skopyk, *Colonial Cataclysms*, 11.

[14] See the online Mexican Drought Atlas at http://drought.memphis.edu/MXDA/Default .aspx (accessed January 18, 2021).

[15] See Appendix A, Skopyk, *Colonial Cataclysms*, 217–228; David W. Stahle, Edward R. Cook, Dorian J. Burnette et al., "The Mexican Drought Atlas: Tree-Ring Reconstructions of the Soil Moisture Balance during the Late Pre-Hispanic, Colonial, and Modern Eras," *Quaternary Science Reviews*, vol. 149 (2016), 34–60.

[16] The Mexican Drought Atlas at http://drought.memphis.edu/MXDA/Default.aspx (accessed January 18, 2021).

homes had to be demolished. A friar, Domingo de Amasa, also confirmed what had happened and reported that the town's church was falling down because of floods and earthquakes.[17]

Extensive inundations may also have occurred in spite of preventative measures. In 1582, Tlahuac and Mixquic were overwhelmed by flood waters. Again, the flooding was closely tied to higher rainfall amount that was similar to 1648's (an approximate value of two PDSI). The flooding also corresponded with the start of the thirty-year extreme wet-cold wave in 1580, which Skopyk has identified as one of the key characteristics of the Colonial Mexican Pluvial climate pattern.[18] In 1582, waterlogged chinampas were ruined and that year's harvest was lost. The distressed Nahuas of Mixquic explained to the viceroy that there was no more land to be cultivated since their town was "founded and situated in the middle of the lake and surrounded in every direction by water and canals."[19] Without other land besides chinampas to cultivate, residents were unable to plant the next maize crop.[20] Making matters worse, recovery would take a long time; months after the water had receded the chinampas were still spoiled.[21] As such, the leaders of the two towns asked for relief from their labor obligations so that they could devote themselves to rebuilding, which would require much time and effort: the chinampas, they explained, were "made by hand with much work and expense, because of flooding they are neither durable nor permanent, with only a small increase in water their crops will be lost, and with water remaining the fields cannot be farmed."[22]

In the aftermath of the subsequent floods, near the start of another wet and cold wave some thirty years later, in 1607 San Pedro Tlahuac submitted a similar request for labor exemptions. The governor, don Marcos de San Pedro, explained the situation in language that had much in common with the earlier petition: Tlahuac was a small island in the middle of the lake; the flooding had been ruinous; chinampas long remained submerged; harvests were lost; some residents had died, and others had been forced to

---

[17] AGN, Indios, vol. 15, exp. 20, ff. 15v–17.   [18] Skopyk, *Colonial Cataclysms*, 11.
[19] "Su pueblo esta fundado y asentado en medio de laguna y cercado por todas partes de agua y acequias." AGN, Indios, vol. 2, exp. 592, f. 137.
[20] AGN, Indios, vol. 2, exp. 417, ff. 99–99v.
[21] AGN, Indios, vol. 2, exp. 584, ff. 134v–135.
[22] "Camellones hechos a mano con mucho travajo y coste y que no duran ni son permanentes antes anegadicos y tales que por poco que creze el agua se les pierde el fruto por lo qual y por su mucha ocupacion y continua no pueden labrar ni benefiçiar las dichas sementeras de comun." AGN, Indios, vol. 2, exp. 592, f. 137.

leave. What differed this time, however, was the severity of the damage. Flooding had brought a great calamity, don Marcos told the viceroy, and with so many homes, fields, and haciendas destroyed the town had not had a single harvest over the past three years. No longer able to cope with labor demands, the governor asked Spanish authorities to forgive Nahua residents their obligations.[23]

Environmental dislocations such as these held profound implications for the region's political economy. The floods in 1582, which also followed the cocoliztli pandemic of the previous half-decade, forced the government to make changes to tribute arrangements. The authorities abandoned the system of calculating tribute payments that had been instituted in the 1560s – in which communal lands of a set size were reserved for the sole purpose of growing maize for tribute – and replaced it with a new, direct assessment for each tributary.[24] Tlahuac was to raise two reales per tributary. Chalco Atenco and Mixquic were required to set the rate at one and a half reales.[25] Similar changes were introduced in Xochimilco such that during the seventeenth century most of the city's tribute was collected in the form of monetary payments from individual tributaries. The viceregal government calculated the entire tax obligation in relation to the size of the tributary population and demanded payment in a bulk amount. In 1607, the total amount owed by the city was 8,000 pesos. Its nonpayment had landed the governor and the dynastic rulers in jail.[26]

The three noblemen protested their incarceration to the Inspector General of New Spain, Licentiate Diego de Lanieras y Velasco. They claimed that they should be released because of exceptional circumstances beyond their control. Not only had there been a recent cocoliztli epidemic but periodic inundations since 1604 had brought further suffering.[27] The floods had recurred frequently over the past three years and had brought about a disaster. (Their claims are borne out in the tree-ring data: those years witnessed a steeper spike in moisture levels: according to the

[23] AGI, Audiencia de México, leg. 126, ramo 4, item 33, f. 1.

[24] Those changes had placed increased burdens on communities, with deficits growing over the years; Tetzcoco and Tenochtitlan and Tlatelolco together owed some 29,000 pesos to the treasury in 1570. Gibson, *The Aztecs under Spanish Rule*, 217.

[25] AGN, General de Parte, vol. 2, ff. 295v–296 and 301v; AGN, Indios, vol. 2, ff. 100–100v, 133–133v, 135v–136, and 138; Gibson, *The Aztecs under Spanish Rule*, 211n118, 525.

[26] AGN, Hospital de Jesús, vol. 325, exp. 5, ff. 42ff.; Gibson, *The Aztecs under Spanish Rule*, 206, 211n118, 525.

[27] AGN, General de Parte, vol. 6, exp. 147, f. 61.

Mexican Drought Atlas, during the period leading up to and including 1607 the levels increased by a much higher three PDSI value, which was far higher than in 1582 or 1648 and the highest at any time during the colonial period with the possible exception of ca. 1550).[28] The nobles stated that rising water levels had ruined all of the crops. More than 600 houses were destroyed. With homes having collapsed or been rendered uninhabitable, their owners had fled and, in their continued absence, farming had all but come to a halt. The officials concluded that whereas once there had been abundance, now those Nahuas who remained went hungry. Recently impoverished residents, no longer able to pay tribute, were being treated poorly, and to make matters worse, without food or adequate shelter, they were becoming sick and dying. The situation was so bad, the officials lamented, that no more than 2,000 tribute payers remained. And "with widespread sickness, like an outbreak of pestilence," everyday another fifteen to twenty people died. The climate clearly had a profound effect not only on water levels but also on socioeconomic conditions and, more specifically, the city's population size.[29]

Don Francisco, don Martín, and don Fernando explained all of this as part of a forthright defense that consisted of several arguments. Given the calamitous nature of recent events, they explained, the residents of Xochimilco were in immediate and urgent need of compassion and clemency, especially since they were loyal vassals of the king. For another, they reminded the judge that the Xochimilca had only just assisted in helping to repair Mexico City, which had likewise sustained water damage. For this work the Nahuas had transported stone and wood, valued at 26,000 pesos, at their own expense. In light of their generous contribution, the noblemen averred, the Xochimilca should receive lenient treatment and be forgiven their debts. If they still had to make payment then they really should be given more time to do so. And, more importantly, the government should take a broader view of Xochimilco's great contributions to the Spanish government.

The nobles argued that the government should recognize that the city's singularly productive agriculture had not only provided vast amounts of tribute but had also supplied abundant foodstuffs for the capital's

---

[28] The value is again observed for the grid point located at W 99.1°, N 19.26° for Lake Xochimilco on the Mexican Drought Atlas, online at http://drought.memphis.edu/MXD A/Default.aspx (accessed January 18, 2021). Skopyk observed that the floods of these years were "tied to Mexico's entry into peak pluvial," *Colonial Cataclysms*, 63.

[29] AGI, Audiencia de México, leg. 227, n. 17, ff. 1–2.

residents. Faced with the destruction of the chinampas, the government now needed to give Nahuas the time and space, without sanctions or overbearing demands, to rebuild their abundant but fragile agricultural system. Only then would the flow of harvests and tribute resume. It was imperative, the three noblemen maintained, that the government remember they had always been scrupulous in paying tribute. Current circumstances, after all, stood in marked contrast to the usual prosperity of the chinampa districts. The city was one of the greatest suppliers of maize in all of New Spain. The nobles pointed out that abundant harvests were achieved thanks to the considerable diligence and labor of the city's chinampa farmers. They then provided details about chinampa cultivation, stressing that bountiful harvests also owed much to lake irrigation, which guaranteed good harvests "even when no rain fell from the sky." Thanks also to intensive cultivation, they concluded, every year Xochimilco supplied a vast amount of maize, more than 40,000 bushels, to the government. Even if we allow for some exaggeration – and Franciscan friars, who served as witnesses in the lawsuit, confirmed that the city was vital to the supply of food – the figures supplied by the Nahua officials represented an enormous amount of maize. By contrast, the annual maize supply in 1602 from the jurisdictions of Tacubaya and Chalco had been 11,124 and 16,091 bushels, respectively.[30] Xochimilco contributed more than maize, though, and the noblemen noted that the chinampas provided a large quantity of "chia, beans, and vegetables, including chiles, large and small tomatoes, lettuce, onions, and other crops with which Nahuas supported themselves, paid their tribute, and provisioned Mexico City." From this bounty, the Nahua nobles concluded, Xochimilco's residents had been "rich and prosperous, never before having fallen behind in their royal tribute of maize and money."[31]

The nobles continued to press their case by explaining that they were not culpable for the failure to pay tribute. The problem, unquestionably, had been flooding. But the inundation was not simply an act of God. Rather, it could also be attributed to the policies of the very same viceregal administration that had thrown them in jail. In an indignant complaint, the nobles argued that the chinampa districts had been sacrificed to save Mexico City. With flooding in the capital the government had ordered the barrier at Mexicalzingo to be closed. This was common knowledge, they averred, and Franciscan friars could attest to what had happened. Fray

[30] Gibson, *The Aztecs under Spanish Rule*, 324.
[31] AGI, Audiencia de México, leg. 227, n. 17, ff. 1–2.

Juan Mazora, of Xochimilco's friary of San Bernardino, confirmed the
noblemen's claims, as did fray Pedro de la Cruz.[32] Sources independent of
the investigation also corroborated the testimonies of the officials and
friars. The accounts of fray Juan de Torquemada, the Franciscan chronicler, also mentioned what had happened, as did Chimalpahin, the Nahua
historian.[33] He recorded in an entry for June 1607 that "all the chinampas
entirely disappeared and were flooded." Chimalpahin later wrote:

Then came the month of August, in which likewise there were very strong rains, so
that one saw that the waters greatly rose, filled everything up, spilled over, and
swelled so that the whole altepetl of Mexico Tenochtitlan was flooded everywhere,
so that again they went to close the dike at Mexicatzinco, which was open in
various places; they had [previously] opened it in three places, from where water
was coming out and coming toward Mexico here. The reason they made [the
water] diminish was that [everything] was about to be lost all over the chinampa
district, in all the said altepetl – Colhuacan, Xochimilco, Cuitlahuac, Mizquic –
which were greatly destroyed through the water having been closed off.[34]

The flooding proved all the more damaging because it destroyed chinampas. In the same terms used by petitioners in Tlahuac (in 1607 as in 1582),
the nobles from Xochimilco pointed out that the making and cultivation
of chinampas required great effort, and that the city also needed time to
rebuild. Since the chinampas had to be made again, it would take some
time before cultivation could resume.

The nobles' arguments were apparently persuasive. They secured their
release from jail. They successfully negotiated a new tribute payment schedule. And they secured a commitment that a new census would be taken.

In spite of these concessions, the floods of 1607 had a lasting impact on
the finances of the chinampa towns. For all their bounty the lakeside
communities did not recover quickly. In 1616, Xochimilco's cabildo, led
by the governor Alonso de Valencia, stated in a petition to the viceroy that
over the previous years, "more than two thousand Indians had forsaken
their homes and lands because of the great hunger they had suffered, and
for this reason, there have been major shortfalls in tribute and labor
service." As the tax burden increased, so the likelihood of flight grew,
making the burden on the remaining Nahuas even greater. The viceroy
ordered Nahua officials in the capital to identify and return the fugitive

---

[32] AGI, Audiencia de México, leg. 227, n. 17, ff. 8–8v, 17–17v.
[33] Torquemada, *Monarchia indiana*, tomo I, 728–730; Chimalpahin, *Annals of His Time*,
78–85, 93, 96–97.
[34] Chimalpahin, *Annals of His Time*, 97–99.

Xochimilca.[35] Xochimilco's governor, whom the viceroy supported for his dedication to paying back tribute, died later that year. The city's nobles elected don Juan Mateo as his replacement.[36] The new governor inherited the tribute problems of his predecessor, which remained intractable. In 1617, still with too few tributaries, the city still could not meet outstanding debts for years past let alone its current tribute payments. The viceroy thus extended the deadline for paying tribute on the outstanding sum. The temporary reprieve did not come without an additional price: beyond the regular tribute amounts, each resident had to make up an extra amount. By 1618, only a part of the debt had been recouped. By 1620, Xochimilco's cabildo could still not make payment and asked for another three years to make up the shortfall. Speaking to the ongoing dislocations of the earlier floods, the 1620 documentation specifically noted that the debts accrued by the city dated back to 1608–1609.[37]

Xochimilco was not the only community to sink into arrears after the inundations of 1604–1607. In the lakeside communities of Chalco the difficult situation brought political conflict. In 1614, the colonial administration installed don Buenaventura de los Reyes, a cacique from Tlaxcala, as the governor of Mixquic. He was charged with setting the town's finances in order to ensure the back payment of its outstanding tribute. Apparently, don Buenaventura was successful in this – paying off the arrears swiftly and overseeing the implementation of a new repartimiento schedule – and so in 1616, while remaining in charge of Mixquic, he was also appointed governor of nearby Tlahuac. By the end of that year, don Buenaventura explained that while he had made progress he needed more time to fulfill his mandate and the viceroy thus extended his governorship for another year. By 1618, though, don Buenaventura was complaining of the opposition being fomented against him by Tlahuac's friars.[38] Five months later, that opposition had hardened as the situation worsened. The Nahuas of Mixquic complained of don Buenaventura's abuses over the course of the previous four years. They brought criminal charges against him and, in retaliation, don Buenaventura allegedly attacked one of his accusers. To avoid further violence, the community received permission to hold an election for a new governor.[39]

---

[35] AGN, Indios vol. 7, exp. 84, ff. 41–41v.
[36] AGN, Indios, vol. 9, exp. 19, ff. 12v–13 and exp. 198, f. 212.
[37] AGN, Indios, vol. 9, exp. 212, ff. 102v–103.
[38] AGN, Indios, vol. 7, exp. 132, ff. 64v–65; AGN, Indios, vol. 7, exp. 291, ff. 144–144v.
[39] AGN, Indios, vol. 7, exp. 330, f. 194.

If don Buenaventura de los Reyes had managed to balance Mixquic's books, many other communities long remained saddled with debts. In part, this had to do with the compounding multiplication of arrears over the years and, during that same time, the continuing decline of the Native population. In the 1620s Xochimilco fell further behind on tribute payments. The coincidence of drought in five of the six years from 1616–1621 may also have been a factor in this; while the chinampas in the lakes may not have been as susceptible to drought, upland fields would have been.[40] In some moments the city owed as much as 10,000 pesos. Coyoacan owed a similar amount, and in 1628, the records of Mexico City's Spanish cabildo put the overall tribute debt for the region at 25,000 pesos.[41] Thereafter, Xochimilco's debt, which remained bound up with seesawing climatic conditions, remained a persistent issue in local politics. Decades later the pressures were still being felt, for instance, with local tax officials being strict if not overbearing in their demands for payment of tribute. In 1654 a widow complained that she was still being held liable for her deceased husband's tribute.[42] A year later, residents were recorded as having fled Milpa Alta, which then defaulted on its tribute payment.[43]

The ongoing demands for labor exacerbated the difficult situation. One of the most controversial issues in local politics during the middle decades of the seventeenth century, labor service took two forms: rotational local drafts, within the altepetl, which were known as *coatequitl*, and external levies required by the colonial administration. Just as Xochimilco encountered persistent difficulties in meeting its tribute levies, so both kinds of labor draft became ever more onerous. As numerous petitions attest, the assessments of tribute and labor quotas, which were calculated according to figures supplied by censuses or reviews of parish records, usually lagged behind precipitous death rates.[44] Communities that had been emptied by epidemics were unable to meet their obligations.[45] In such instances, they

[40] Parker, *Global Crisis*, xxvii.
[41] AGN, Hospital de Jesús, vol. 278, exp. 10, ff. 37v–38; *Actas de Cabildo del Ayuntamiento de la ciudad de Mexico, vol. 27: Actas Antiguas de cabildo*, Ignacio Bejarano, comp. (Mexico City: A. Carranza y Comp. Impresores, 1908), 69; Gibson, *The Aztecs under Spanish Rule*, 218 and 527n159.
[42] AGN, Indios, vol. 17, exp. 119, ff. 135v–136.
[43] AGN, Indios, vol. 18, exp. 140, f. 106v.
[44] AGI, Audiencia de México, leg. 126, ramo 4, item 33; Gibson, *The Aztecs under Spanish Rule*, 194–219 and especially 199.
[45] See Gibson, *The Aztecs under Spanish Rule*, 233–236; Horn, *Postconquest Coyoacan*, 230–231, and AGN, Indios, vol. 8, which covers repartimiento drafts for Chalco (and was used by Gibson).

petitioned authorities for new censuses, temporary exemptions from their duties, or revised assessments, as had been the case in 1607. In 1629, for instance, Xochimilco's governor, Joseph Bernal – who was later ousted for a multitude of offenses, from abuse of laborers to the contravention of political rules surrounding elections and the nonpayment of tribute – asked the government for relief from services performed by the Xochimilca in repairing the raised road of San Lázaro; the governor explained that he could not send enough workers because so many had fallen ill.[46]

Making matters worse were two further factors. First, an expanding and shifting range of labor services made for a great deal of confusion in the provision of laborers. That confusion, in turn, contributed to a propensity for officials to recruit laborers illegally. With preponderant control over the recruitment, supervision, and direction of the drafts, local officials had ample opportunities to divert laborers for their own enrichment. The officials' excesses risked placing an overwhelming burden upon an already stretched population, adding another volatile element to an already unstable situation, one that was primed for acts of political violence.[47]

Demands for laborers and ways of recruiting them had changed in line with wider economic adjustments since the mid-sixteenth century. Central to these changes were demographic decline and the rise of haciendas in the capital's hinterland, which meant that new kinds of labor arrangements came into being even as others gradually fell out of use. The expanding estates needed a reliable workforce and, from July 1550, the government had instituted a new kind of recruitment via *repartimiento*, a mandatory, rotational labor draft that replaced the old encomienda system.[48] Xochimilco was immediately included in the new drafts.[49] There were several kinds of repartimiento, among them one for agriculture and another for public works programs in the capital.[50] The residents of the southern lake districts (but not Chalco Atenco, which fell under a different jurisdiction) were exempt from the agricultural levies since there were few haciendas in the area and, more importantly, because residents were instead assigned to the Mexico City repartimiento, which meant that

---

[46] AGN, Indios, vol. 10, exp. 186, ff. 102v–103.
[47] On riots and rebellions stemming from abuses by local officials of labor and tribute, see William B. Taylor, *Drinking, Homicide, and Rebellion in Colonial Mexican Villages* (Stanford: Stanford University Press, 1979), 133–134.
[48] Gibson, *The Aztecs under Spanish Rule*, 225–226.   [49] AGN, Mercedes, vol. 3, f. 97v.
[50] A third repartimiento, for mining, did not affect Xochimilco.

their primary responsibilities were to work on construction projects and provide essential raw materials, typically straw and stone, for the capital's residents and institutions. With both kinds of repartimiento, the agricultural one and its counterpart for the capital, Nahuas were supposed to provide a week's labor service three or four times a year, for which they were to receive a small amount of monetary compensation.[51]

Over time, though, the agricultural levy proved insufficient to the needs of haciendas. Part of the problem was that laborers were needed at certain key moments – planting, weeding, harvesting – that might come into conflict with the Nahuas' own agricultural schedules. Conversely, fewer laborers were needed for long stretches of the growing season. The repartimiento drafts were not always flexible enough to accommodate these fluctuations. Nor were they reliable in supplying a sufficient number of laborers. Nahuas, facing deepening labor burdens, began to disregard the quotas and increasingly turned to absenteeism. So common were these absences that in 1619 and 1620 Chalco's Nahuas did not once provide the requisite number of laborers.[52] As a result, on several occasions during the seventeenth century, the colonial administration attempted without much success to reform or repeal the repartimientos, most notably in the formal abolition of the agricultural levy in 1632, ordered by the king and issued in New Spain by the viceroy. At the same time that farm hands became scarcer, Spanish estates enticed prospective workers with wages and other incentives. They also resorted to illegal methods of securing their workforce, either through peonage, coercion, or the redirection of laborers away from their officially assigned projects, this latter requiring the collusion of Nahua authorities.[53] On at least one occasion, those convicted of public drunkenness in Xochimilco were required to perform personal service for Spaniards.[54] If residents of Xochimilco seldom worked on the few estates of their own jurisdiction they might nevertheless be induced or compelled to work on haciendas in other parts of the Basin of Mexico.

Shortages of workers and the rise of wage labor generated competition among estate owners in Xochimilco. In a case from 1651, which involved one of Xochimilco's most prominent Spanish residents, the hacienda owner don Francisco Velázquez de Robledo complained to the viceroy about interference in hiring workers. He charged a prominent,

[51] Gibson, *The Aztecs under Spanish Rule*, 226–227 and 229.
[52] Gibson, *The Aztecs under Spanish Rule*, 233.
[53] AGN, Indios, vol. 7, exp. 464, ff. 221–221v; Gibson, *The Aztecs under Spanish Rule*.
[54] AGN, Indios, vol. 6, 1a pte., exp. 1026, f. 277v.

rival hacienda owner, Bernardo López de Haro, with obstructing the recruitment of laborers. Velázquez explained that he paid his entirely voluntary staff for their labor and, moreover, he had covered their tribute obligations, a common way of attracting prospective employees.[55] Demonstrating the acceptability of wage labor practices the viceroy upheld Velázquez's petition and, in promulgating the resulting decree, set fines for any interference of the right of hacienda owners and laborers to contract wage labor service.[56] This decree, among others like it, attested to ongoing labor shortages and conflicts between hacendados.[57] Three years later, don Francisco Velázquez still struggled to obtain enough laborers and was accused of coercing and abusing those Nahuas who worked on the estate.[58]

While formal agricultural drafts were gradually replaced by wage labor and then officially eliminated, the Mexico City repartimiento remained firmly in place. If anything, over time the demands for labor service in the capital grew, at least in relation to the population size, even as labor duties became more diverse. In part this diversification of duties stemmed from the 1629 catastrophic flooding in Mexico City, which brought a sudden redirection of labor away from fields.[59] Nahuas from Xochimilco and other communities were diverted from their usual labor tasks to make emergency repairs of the city's infrastructure (they were spared the grueling toil on the desagüe itself, though). Spanish authorities ordered Nahuas to clean roads and canals to improve drainage and to repair dikes and other features of the water management system.[60] All these labor obligations joined the many other tasks apportioned to Xochimilco's residents.

Nahua communities were supposed to provide a set quota of labor for public works projects. During the sixteenth century, two kinds of draft were established, the *sencilla* (for November through April), and the *dobla* (May through October). Until the 1580s, 2 percent of a community's population would be called up for work duties. As the population fell, that percentage rose, climbing to 5 percent for the sencilla and even 10 percent for the dobla in the late sixteenth century, thereby making labor duties even more arduous. In the early seventeenth century, the government usually assessed the quota for Xochimilco at a minimum of

[55] MacLeod, *Spanish Central America*, 226.
[56] AGN, Reales Cédulas Duplicadas, vol. 18, exp. 184, f. 131v.
[57] AGN, Ordenanzas, vol. 4, exp. 142, ff. 142v–145.
[58] AGN, Indios, vol. 17, exp. 140, ff. 148–148v.
[59] Gibson, *The Aztecs under Spanish Rule*, 233–243.
[60] AGN, Indios, vol. 10, exp. 156, ff. 87v–88.

4 percent of the population.[61] In 1616, for instance, officials determined that Xochimilco should contribute 4 percent of its tributary population to quarry stone and provide fifty canoes filled with fodder for livestock. The tasks were divided among residents according to residence in lake areas ("los de la parte de la laguna") or on the mainland (tierra firme).[62]

Of course, official demands for labor could exceed the usual stipulation of 4 percent. This was shown in viceregal orders for Tlahuac in the 1590s. According to parish records, in 1591, Tlahuac had a tributary population of 961 people. Of these, the presiding judge excluded 165 people deemed too old or infirm to perform labor duties, leaving a workforce of 796 residents who were to be divided among various tasks. Thirty-six of them, who made up the 4 percent, worked on the church of Santo Domingo in the capital, on building schools, as well as for the Discalced Franciscans friars and the Jesuits. Beyond these allocations, the judge stipulated that at the time of the harvest, residents would be recruited at a rate of 10 percent.[63]

Five years later, the levies had become yet more burdensome because the total tributary population had fallen. The loss of fifty-six tributaries, from 961 to 905, had made for a 5.8 percent decline in the town's size in just half a decade. Fewer people meant more work for those who remained: of the thirty-six who were assigned to jobs in the capital, including those destinations specified in 1591, two now worked for the Royal Indian Hospital and two others provided personal service in the home of Tlahuac's encomendero, Alonso de Cuevas; another thirty were sent to gather harvests on Tetzcoco's haciendas; twenty-four delivered stone to the capital, and another twenty-four delivered straw. An unspecified number of residents ferried passengers and friars around the lakes in their canoes. Having complained about these excessive burdens, the viceroy agreed that the levies were now too high and reduced them.[64]

A list of further tasks commonly assigned to residents of Xochimilco and other lakeside towns was sufficiently long and complex as to suggest why fraud could be perpetrated all too easily by unscrupulous overseers.[65]

---

[61] Gibson, *The Aztecs under Spanish Rule*, 226–233.

[62] AGN, Indios, vol. 9, exp. 172 and 173, ff. 82v–83v. The same apportioning of tasks between lake and mainland residents applied for coatequitl levies; AGN, Indios, vol. 4, exp. 1, f. 1.

[63] AGN, Indios, vol. 5, exp. 600, ff. 166–166v.

[64] AGN, Indios, vol. 6, 1a pte., exp. 1160, ff. 318v–319.

[65] As Gibson noted, "at the same time the competition among Spaniards for Indian workers became more intense, and the frequency and sophistication of malfeasance increased." Gibson, *The Aztecs under Spanish Rule*, 233.

The list included working on construction projects and delivering supplies of building materials.[66] Some Nahuas were to work on the maintenance of roads and the paving of streets.[67] Others were to repair government and ecclesiastical property.[68] A few Nahuas were called up to work in other areas, for instance, personal service to prominent Spaniards in the capital, such as government officials or, in one case from 1600, the daughter of a conquistador.[69] Some helped with preparations for Corpus Christi festivities.[70] Labor in munitions works was also common, as were requests for Nahuas, often from Mixquic and Tlahuac, to gather and deliver saltpeter.[71] Occasionally, residents fulfilled their duties by working in slaughterhouses.[72] While Nahuas from the lake areas were exempt from usual service in agriculture or in mining, occasional levies, at times of drastic labor shortages, were demanded.[73] In addition to all this, the rebuilding of Mexico City's cathedral routinely consumed the energies of many Xochimilca residents.[74] Indeed, during the seventeenth century, Xochimilco provided an annual supply of between 1,400 and 1,900 laborers for this project, perhaps more than any other community in central Mexico besides the capital's indigenous districts.[75] In addition to the levies mentioned above, Spanish authorities required the labor of skilled artisans, particularly carpenters and stone masons in church construction.[76] Alternatively, those with other skills were directed to

---

[66] AGN, Mercedes, vol. 7, ff. 75v–76; AGN, General de Parte, vol. 4 exp. 19, f. 4v and exp. 20, ff. 4v–5; AGN, General de Parte, vol. 6, exp. 107, f. 49v. See also AGN, Indios, vol. 3, exp. 368, f. 86.

[67] AGN, General de Parte, vol. 3, exp. 128, ff. 63–63v; AGN, Indios, vol. 28, exp. 248, ff. 211v–212, vol. 30, exp. 278, ff. 255v–256.

[68] AGN, Indios, vol. 2, exp. 701, ff. 158v–159; vol. 6, 1a pte., exp. 1102, f. 302.

[69] AGN, General de Parte, vol. 5, exp. 995, f. 207v.

[70] AGN, Reales Cédulas Duplicadas, vol. 14, exp. 3 bis, ff. 1–24v; vol. 14, exp. 17, f. 32v, exp. 18, f. 32v, exp. 28, f. 36v, exp. 34, f. 41v, exp. 63, f. 62v, exp. 62, ff. 62–v, exp. 68, f. 64v, among others in this volume; AGN, Indios, vol. 32, exp. 354, ff. 309v–310.

[71] AGN, General de Parte, vol. 5 exp. 1393, f. 299v; exp. 1394, ff. 299v–300, and exp. 1395, f. 300; AGN, Indios, vol. 5, exp. 404, ff. 108–108v; AGN, Indios, vol. 12, 1a pte., exp. 98 and 99, ff. 57v–58v.

[72] AGN, Reales Cédulas Duplicadas, vol. 20, exp. 324, ff. 167v–168; AGN, Indios, vol. 9, exp. 235, ff. 113v–114.

[73] AGN, Indios, vol. 15, cuad. 2, exp. 77, ff. 147v–149; AGN, General de Parte, vol. 3, exp. 486, ff. 228v–229; vol. 4, exp. 671, f. 183v; vol. 5, exp. 252, f. 55v; vol. 5, exp. 622, ff. 135–135v.

[74] AGN, Indios, vol. 5, exp. 549, ff. 152v–153, exp. 789, ff. 210v–211, and exp. 950, ff. 244v–245.

[75] AGN, Reales Cédulas Duplicadas, vol. 14, exp. 3bis, ff. 1–24v.

[76] AGN, Reales Cédulas Duplicadas, vol. 14, exp. 51, f. 56v; vol. 14, exp. 88, f. 80.

specific tasks, as with Juan Bautista, who was assigned to tend the sick in a hospital.[77] With such diversity in duties, requirements could easily exceed the established quotas, not least because dishonest government figures redirected labor illegally and applied arbitrary levies, a concern that lay behind inspections of Xochimilco's obrajes in 1628.[78] The number of laborers supplied for the construction of the cathedral alone exceeded the upper level of labor allocation.

Local officials arranged and supervised the recruitment of laborers. The drafts were to be shared on rotation among the Xochimilco's three districts, and then again among the districts' constituent tlaxilacalli, thereby spreading the duties so that no one neighborhood was overly burdened. That arrangement held less well for outlying villages in the corregimiento, sometimes generating tensions between cabeceras and their subordinate communities. The Spanish superimposition of this hierarchy of cabeceras and sujetos on indigenous forms of sociopolitical organization, which were not congruent, often deepened disputes about the delivery of labor.[79] In 1652, for instance, the villagers of San Pedro Atocpan petitioned the viceroy for relief from services required by the government of their head town of Milpa Alta.[80]

Conflicts over labor extended beyond jurisdictional arrangements and intruded into the internal organization of individual communities. Residents of Milpa Alta hired a lawyer to represent them against Mateo Constantino, a Nahua who served as the chief constable of the town's church (in charge of attendance at mass). Constantino, the plaintiffs alleged, obliged them to cultivate the church's orchard and fields beyond their usual requirements.[81] Similarly, in 1658, a sacristan of the chapel of Tepetenchi, together with the chapel's singers, brought a case before viceregal authorities. As functionaries of the church, they gained an exemption from performing labor services that had been disregarded by the governor, magistrates, and chief constable.[82] The cases attest not only to jurisdictional conflicts between civil and religious jurisdictions but also to the tensions between subordinate and dominant polities. That demands

---

[77] AGN, Indios, vol. 3, exp. 380, ff. 88v–89.

[78] AGN, Reales Cédulas Duplicadas, vol. 8, 2a pte., 431, f. 510.

[79] Lockhart, *The Nahuas after the Conquest*, 45–47, 52–58; for earlier cabecera-sujeto disputes over labor in Xochimilco's corregimiento, see AGN, General de Parte, vol. 2, exp. 715, ff. 145v–146; AGN, Indios, vol. 4, exp. 563, f. 165.

[80] AGN, Indios, vol. 18, exp. 51, ff. 43–43v; exp. 228, f. 168v.

[81] AGN, Indios, vol. 20, exp. 233, ff. 185v–186 (184v–185 old foliation).

[82] AGN, Indios, vol. 23, exp. 112, ff. 105–105v (104–104v old foliation).

for labor reached beyond those required by the larger sociopolitical structures like altepetl and tlaxilacalli, and instead fell on smaller configurations of community, meant that they gave substance and meaning to local forms of solidarity, as though reinforcing a sense of community from external pressure.

Labor service also promoted a sense of community solidarity and pride. Xochimilco's residents often sought to divert burdensome viceregal demands by petitioning for work on alternative, local projects. They pitched their requests for these duties in ways that would appeal to Spanish authorities. The petitions usually related to repairing essential infrastructure. In one instance, the parlous state of fresh drinking water provided an opportunity for residents to petition for an exemption from labor in Mexico City. In their submission to the viceroy, the Nahua governor and his retinue of officials were careful to state that the provision of drinking water would be of benefit to the entire community, Nahuas and Spaniards alike.[83] Other communities sought to improve sanitation and living conditions. In 1620, Nahuas of Milpa Alta were allowed to redirect repartimiento laborers to build a conduit into the town.[84] Most commonly, though, petitions focused on the need to repair Nahuas' neighborhood churches.[85]

There is little reason to doubt the genuine concern of parishioners for the preservation and good condition of their churches. As focal points for the community, and for other reasons, Nahuas frequently displayed remarkable enthusiasm and devotion to their houses of worship.[86] By the mid-seventeenth century, many of the churches first established in central Mexico were showing the signs of wear and tear. In instances where corregidores and friars were required to report on their condition, they concurred that the churches were in a poor state and needed attention. Some were urgent situations, too, and Spanish officials commented that without immediate action, there was a real risk of some churches collapsing. In one case, Xochimilco's corregidor, Sebastián de la Fuente Ayala, took the city's notary with him to inspect the state of a church. The

---

[83] AGN, Indios, vol. 9, exp. 303, ff. 150v–151.

[84] AGN, Indios, vol. 6, 1a pte., exp. 817, ff. 218–218v.

[85] AGN, Indios, vol. 12, 2a pte., exp. 121, ff. 240–240v.

[86] See, for example, studies of local religion in colonial Mexico, particularly the "Introduction" by Susan Schroeder and Stafford Poole to their edited volume *Religion in New Spain* (Albuquerque: University of New Mexico Press, 2007), 1–11, as well as various chapters of Martin A. Nesvig, ed., *Local Religion in Colonial Mexico* (Albuquerque: University of New Mexico Press, 2006).

toll of earthquakes and floods, it was determined, more than warranted the repairs. The petitioners secured a not inconsiderable two-year exemption from the usual labor requirements.[87]

Many churches needed to be repaired because of flooding. In 1603, even before the worst of the inundations of that decade, the Discalced Franciscan convent of Santa Catalina Churubusco (formerly Huitzilopochco), which was said to be one of the oldest churches in the region, had to be mended. Ten laborers from Xochimilco were redirected there. Their duties extended to reinforcing flood defenses.[88] In a telling sign of the severity of the damage done by the same floods, years later, in 1617, Tlahuac sought permission to repair its church, which was "one of the best in New Spain." So weakened had it become from the water damage that sections were on the brink of falling down, and there was a distinct risk, the petitioners explained, of parishioners being killed during mass.[89] Notably, the same church had been repaired only a decade before the inundations, back in 1592.[90] In another example, from 1673, the community of Santa Cruz, a village subordinate to Xochimilco, sought to escape demands for labor imposed by that city's Nahua government. In this case, the corregidor's lieutenant, don Juan Velázquez de Robledo (a relative of don Francisco, the hacienda owner of the same name), concurred with their petition. The petitioners explained that their church had sustained damage in a recent flood. They secured the exemption.[91]

Such requests were numerous and, judging from the extant documentation, remarkably successful. In some cases, petitioners gained extensions for original labor substitutions.[92] In others, residents even managed to escape tribute obligations in order to fund repairs. In the 1680s, the Nahuas of Tepepan obtained an exemption from tribute for two years. The viceroy extended the concession to two nearby villages. In the investigation prompted by the petitions, which initially requested four years' relief from labor and tribute, the high court determined that two years would suffice. The presiding Spanish officials noted that the population of the villages in question had been reduced to just 157 tributaries.[93]

---

[87] AGN, Indios, vol. 16, exp. 78, ff. 74v–76 (72v–74 old foliation).
[88] AGN, General de Parte, vol. 6, exp. 763, ff. 277v–278.
[89] AGN, Indios, vol. 7, exp. 199, ff. 98–98v.
[90] AGN, Indios, vol. 6, 1ª pte., exp. 307 and 1072, ff. 83, 291v–292.
[91] AGN, Indios, vol. 24, exp. 462, ff. 338v and 350.
[92] AGN, Indios, vol. 9, exp. 230, ff. 111–111v.
[93] AGN, Indios, vol. 27, exp. 339, ff. 228v–229v; vol. 28, exp. 24, ff. 23–23v; vol. 26, cuad. 2, exp. 196, ff. 183–184.

Exemptions to work on local projects were of considerable importance to Nahuas and were jealously guarded because they afforded many advantages. Beyond expressing community pride and reinforcing and affirming communal ties, with residents working together in their own neighborhoods, local service would have involved less of an imposition on Nahuas otherwise forced to travel away from their homes, sometimes for extended periods, to work on public projects for the benefit of other communities. Local labor service was likely seen as a more legitimate requirement. And while it might be going too far to infer from the petitions a subtext of resistance, certainly the petitioners were shrewd in presenting their cases to appeal to Spanish religious sensibilities. The residents of San Mateo Xalpa were careful to argue in their 1651 petition that the poor state of their church inhibited their ability to celebrate holy sacraments, divine works, and festivities with appropriate decency. Labor drafts, they avowed, prevented them from attending to the church's needs.[94] Their petition was upheld. The Nahuas of San Mateo Xalpa thus navigated successfully between the secular and religious realms of Spanish rule, finding space between the two to press for their own advantage. Their success represented a considerable achievement. Only a few years previously, the governor of Xochimilco had abrogated an earlier concession. Local residents had risen up against Xochimilco's officials. The local government only quelled the disturbance by resorting to violence.

CRIME AND THE MICROHISTORY OF A CRISIS

On Saturday April 9, 1633, during Xochimilco's weekly market, more than 200 men and women entered the public plaza carrying flowers and making a great commotion. At the front were two men, the brothers don Felipe and don Francisco de Santiago. A council officer, don Diego Juárez, witnessed what happened next. At one o'clock in the afternoon, don Diego later testified before Spanish authorities, don Felipe, don Francisco, and their followers approached the government offices.[95] There they confronted the city's officials. Don Felipe handed the governor, Joseph Bernal, a document written in Nahuatl which was, he announced, an order from none other

---

[94] AGN, Indios, vol. 16, exp. 35 and 78, ff. 35v and 74v–76 (72v–74 old foliation).
[95] AGN, Criminal, vol. 232, exp. 21, ff. 416v–418v (entire case is ff. 409–432v). Brian Owensby has analyzed this case and a few of the other lawsuits against don Diego Juárez. Specific observations and ideas that come from Owensby's analysis will be noted below. Owensby, *Empire of Law*, 242–246.

than the viceroy of New Spain which supposedly required the governor, magistrates, and councilmen of Xochimilco to put a halt to obligatory labor service performed by Nahuas in the city and its jurisdiction (the formal abolition of the agricultural repartimiento, it should be noted, had gone into effect not long before). The governor in turn passed the Nahuatl order to a Spanish lieutenant and a scribe, who were in attendance. Don Diego Juárez later testified that the document was clearly a forgery, penned in the unmistakable hand of don Felipe. But in these tense moments, with the local government considerably outnumbered, the Spanish officials prevaricated, announcing that they could not post the decree in the marketplace, as requested, without first consulting the city's corregidor.

On hearing this, the irate Nahuas began to shout in protest. Some called the officials thieves and demanded that they be arrested. Others accused them of acting illegally and threatened them with reprisals, shouting that the officials would pay for "the dirty trick" of "selling the Indians."[96] As tensions rose, the crowd demanded that don Felipe be installed as their governor to deliver them from the abuses of the current one, Joseph Bernal, whom they accused of unlawfully profiting from their labor. In the face of intransigence by officials, don Felipe threatened to go to the viceroy for help. As the protesters turned to leave the plaza, they came across a councilman leading a group of laborers to go work on their assigned repartimiento duties. Given the circumstances, the sight proved too much: violence broke out, government officials fled, but the rioters seized one of the councilmen and began shoving him and striking him with stones, shouting that they were going to send him to Mexico City to work on the very same projects they labored on. In the confusion of the moment, he somehow broke free and managed to escape. Otherwise, as don Diego Juárez testified, he would surely have been killed.

The events of that Saturday unsettled Xochimilco's governing nobles. Of particular concern was the threat posed by the Santiago brothers. Both don Felipe and don Francisco occupied an ambiguous place in society. They came from the subordinate community of San Mateo Xalpa, below Xochimilco in the hierarchy of municipalities, and yet they were stirring opposition against the cabecera. Don Felipe, moreover, professed himself to be a weaver, but as a noble he formed part of the ruling class he opposed.[97] If all of this were not unnerving enough in a general sense, of

---

[96] This translation is Owensby's in *Empire of Law*, 242.
[97] Lockhart suggests that the practice of crafts was not antithetical to Nahua concepts of nobility. Lockhart, *The Nahuas after the Conquest*, 486n106.

more pressing concern was the fact that don Felipe served as a figurehead for opposition and could rally more than 200 mutinous Nahuas to his cause. He was upheld by his supporters as an alternative to the actual governor, and, by presenting the forged order, he metaphorically assumed a position of authority, as if he were the viceroy overruling the municipal government. Xochimilco's leaders had further reasons to be anxious. Don Felipe was literate, bilingual, and, as subsequent events revealed, adept at contending with the legal system.[98] He and his brother could succeed in gaining the support of both Nahua residents and the viceroy, and they were also well attuned to the power of symbols in colonial politics. Hence the flowers. The protesters had carried the flowers into the plaza to point out their shared identity and, by extension, their unity of purpose: the flowers were a symbol of the altepetl; flowers formed part of the iconography of the Nahuatl pictorial glyph for Xochimilco, which was incorporated into the city's coat of arms, and the flowers further spoke to corporate identity for the simple reason that Xochimilco meant "the place of the flower fields."

The flowers were not the only symbol to be deployed in the Nahuas' protest. The forged Nahuatl order itself demonstrated the brothers' shrewdness: while the order was obviously a fake and had no practical or legal value, its symbolic force was greater. It reminded the councilmen that the legal apparatus could be arrayed against them. The forged document also served notice to the corrupt regime of its scant legitimacy in the eyes of the governed.[99] By presenting the order, don Felipe and don Francisco raised the specter of summoning royal authority. The message to the cabildo officers and their Spanish allies was clear: desist from abusive and illegal conduct, especially with regard to labor levies, or face the prospect of further disorder and outside intervention.

The city's officials reacted swiftly, initiating criminal proceedings against the brothers and prompting the Spanish authorities to order their incarceration in Santiago Tlatelolco's jail. There don Felipe and don Francisco languished for a couple of months before the case against them moved forward. The delay arose, in part, because of lingering doubts about what had happened. To counter the allegations against them, the

---

[98] On intermediaries as key figures in colonial societies, see Yanna Yannakakis, *The Art of Being In-Between: Native Intermediaries, Indian Identity, and Local Rule in Colonial Oaxaca* (Durham: Duke University Press, 2008).

[99] See in particular AGN, Criminal, vol. 232, exp. 21, f. 424, which is a petition from don Felipe without any mention of a legal agent. His signature appears on its own at the bottom of the page.

Santiago brothers appealed to the viceroy for assistance. They claimed that the charges were baseless and that they were being set up by a dishonest administration in Xochimilco.[100] In addition, their legal representative argued that the brothers had not deliberately instigated a riot; rather, they had merely made a legitimate request, that their demands be heard. The brothers further explained that they did not rouse the crowd. Those who entered the plaza with them had done so spontaneously and of their own free will.[101] After hearing their defense, the viceroy showed himself to be not entirely unsympathetic to the brothers' position. He ordered the corregidor to investigate charges of abuse and agreed to the release of the Santiagos, though not on any presumption of innocence but rather on bond.[102] And with allegations of malfeasance by Xochimilco's cabildo having come to his attention, the viceroy also ordered the corregidor to ensure that officials refrain from molesting don Felipe and don Francisco.[103]

The experience of incarceration does not seem to have deterred the Santiago brothers. Soon after gaining their freedom, they resumed their campaign against Xochimilco's government. Don Francisco began by visiting communities in the jurisdiction, soliciting support, including financial contributions, from Nahuas to help him pursue litigation against don Diego Juárez. Don Diego had been the councilman who arranged for the Santiagos to be arrested after the riot; now, a year later, he had just become Xochimilco's governor, and don Francisco filed a criminal complaint against him. In response, don Diego put forward a defense in which he maligned the character of his opponent, labeling don Francisco a rebel and troublemaker. Don Diego's supporters, brought before a judge to defend him, backed up the characterization of a rebellious don Francisco.[104] There were thus two pending criminal cases involving Xochimilco's rulers; the one against the Santiago brothers for inciting a riot, and the other in which the plaintiffs and defendants traded places. Over the next year, the fortunes of the Santiago brothers waxed while those of the Xochimilco's leaders waned. The governor at the time of the riot two years earlier, Joseph Bernal, had once enjoyed the favor of the viceroy, receiving his initial appointment as governor from him. In 1630, after having been reelected, he had also received permission to remain in

---

[100] AGN, Criminal, vol. 232,exp. 21, ff. 431–432v.   [101] Owensby, *Empire of Law*, 243.
[102] AGN, Indios, vol. 12, 1a pte., exp. 117, f. 79 (78 old foliation).
[103] AGN, Indios, vol., 12, 1a pte., exp. 96, f. 57 (56 old foliation).
[104] Owensby, *Empire of Law*, 243.

office even though he had already served two previous terms as governor.[105] But now in 1635, because of the criminal investigations, the viceroy decided to intervene in local affairs – just as don Felipe's forged order had foretold.

The intervention followed the news that Xochimilco's nobles had once again reelected Joseph Bernal to the governorship, this time succeeding don Diego Juárez. The viceroy now blocked Bernal's reappointment, citing his poor record and his "dimwittedness and poor governance." The investigations had revealed that Bernal had been responsible for the nonpayment of the vast sum of 9,000 pesos of tribute owed to the royal treasury. The suspicion was that Bernal and his cronies had spirited away some of the funds. Bernal's underhand dealings had also been revealed the year before, when he appointed don Diego to the governorship in violation of election protocols and in contravention of the rules about holding office since don Diego was said to be a mestizo and mestizos were technically prohibited from serving as cabildo officers. The situation had deteriorated so much that, as one commentator exclaimed, not without a little exaggeration, the reelection of Bernal would bring about "the total destruction of the city."[106] Now revealed as incompetent and crooked, Bernal was expelled from the governorship.[107] By contrast, don Felipe and don Francisco de Santiago apparently walked free, their stance against Xochimilco's leaders essentially vindicated.

Xochimilco's problems did not end with the removal of Bernal, however. As Bernal's successor the viceroy chose don Martín Cerón y Alvarado. This appointment was of considerable value because don Martín, as tlatoani, was the city's most eminent figure.[108] Presumably he was reappointed in the wake of recent upheavals to provide stability, his position being uncontroversial because of his commanding authority and his many years of service as governor. In 1635, though, the opportunity afforded by don Martín's appointment for resolving the crisis quickly passed. The aging nobleman did not long remain in power; presumably he went into retirement from public life. Don Martín was soon replaced by his son, don Diego Juárez, who now took up the position of governor for a second time – and he clung to this position for an unprecedented sixteen

---

[105] AGN, Indios, vol. 10, exp. 189, f. 104–104v.

[106] AGN, Indios, vol. 12, 1a pte., exp. 180, ff. 116–116v. See also Brian Owensby, *Empire of Law*, 242–246.

[107] AGN, Indios, vol. 12, 1a pte., exp. 180, ff. 116–116v.

[108] On the changing use of the term tlatoani, see Lockhart, *The Nahuas after the Conquest*, 31.

years, from 1635 to 1651. Over the course of his administration, don Diego was repeatedly brought before authorities on civil and criminal charges. His crimes plunged Xochimilco into a deep and transformative crisis – one in which the legal conflict between don Diego and the Santiago brothers had been but the opening salvo.[109]

When don Diego succeeded his father to the governorship, which happened some time before in 1635, he did not seem to command the same respect and authority as the old tlatoani; whereas his father's standing and reputation were unassailable, don Diego's status seemed uncertain.[110] Little information survives about his background other than that he was born soon after the turn of the seventeenth century, perhaps around 1605, that he came from the tlaxilacalli of Olac, and that he held lesser positions on the cabildo prior to becoming governor.[111] In 1631, for instance, he served as a notary, drafting the testament of a noblewoman, doña María Juana.[112] Don Diego's status may have been questionable for several reasons. He could conceivably have been illegitimate. Unlike the rest of his ancestors who were strongly tied to Xochimilco's district of Tepetenchi, he came from Olac, and his baptism did not appear in the parish records for legitimate children, for which we have a comprehensive and seemingly coherent set of records.[113] Alternatively, don Diego may have been adopted by the Cerón y Alvarado family, as might be suggested by his different surname, one that was not shared by any other member of the dynastic family.[114] And there were further signs of ambiguous status; in 1641 he obtained a license to ride a horse, wear Spanish dress, and carry arms, thus acquiring the trappings of elevated status several years after first becoming governor; intriguingly, he did not already enjoy these privileges when he assumed the governorship (and, forebodingly, the license allowed him to keep an

---

[109] AGN, Indios, vol. 16, exp. 137, ff. 129–130v (127–128v old foliation); AGN, Vínculos y Mayorazgos, vol. 279, exp. 1, f. 18.

[110] The uncertainty over the date derives from the absence of a viceregal confirmation for don Diego assuming office. The dates have to be inferred from later testimony in which plaintiffs in criminal cases testified about the length of time that don Diego had governed Xochimilco. In one instance from 1647, it amounted to fourteen years. AGN, Criminal, vol. 128, exp. 10, f. 139. In 1651, a petition stated that don Diego had served as governor for seventeen years. AGN, Indios, vol. 16, exp. 137, f. 129.

[111] AGN, Criminal, vol. 48, exp. 30, f. 517, and see his deposition in AGN, Criminal, vol. 232, exp. 21, ff. 409–432.

[112] UNAM, Fondo Reservado, Archivo Franciscano, caja 112, exp. 1531, ff. 1–8.

[113] AGN, Genealogía [microfilm], vols. 1793–1797.

[114] Furthermore, another of don Martín Cerón's offspring, doña Josepha Cortés Cerón y Alvarado, was illegitimate.

harquebus at home and carry other weapons with him when outdoors, ostensibly "because of the risk to his person when collecting tribute").[115] And only after he became governor did Nahuatl sources begin to refer to him as tlatoani (Spanish sources, on the other hand, identified him as a cacique).[116] Perhaps most telling of his uncertain status were the many times he was identified as a mestizo. The label may have pointed to his mixed ancestry, but it could also have simply been a way for rivals to accuse him of wrongfully holding office.[117] Regardless of his ancestry, whatever authority don Diego once had was undermined by his crimes; even if, at some point, he were to have been a legitimate tlatoani, his behavior came to be seen as inimical to holding office.

The first attempt to unseat don Diego and have him held to account for his crimes, by the Santiago brothers in 1634, came to nothing. The outcome of that criminal case has not survived in the archives but don Diego clearly retained control of the governorship because a second criminal complaint was brought against him in September 1640. That suit included the allegation that he had unlawfully clung to power for six years. It was brought by Nahuas of San Mateo Xalpa, the same village of don Francisco and don Felipe de Santiago came from. On this second occasion, and perhaps to protect themselves from being singled out for retribution, the complainants brought their charges collectively, on behalf of their community and those of other neighboring sujetos. The plaintiffs accused don Diego of more or less the same crimes that Nahuas had been protesting before the riot broke out, for instance, illegally coercing laborers, not paying them, sending them to work for hacendados in other jurisdictions, or extorting fees from them to avoid this illegal agricultural service.[118]

Don Diego apparently avoided prosecution once again because other Nahuas stepped forward to pursue criminal complaints against him three years later, in 1643. On this occasion San Mateo Xalpa resubmitted its charges that the governor made them perform illegal agricultural labor.[119] The extent of his criminality now reached further, though. Without the authority to do so, don Diego revoked the residents' license to perform

[115] AGN, Indios, vol. 13, exp. 249, ff. 214–214v.

[116] See, in particular, the petition in AGN, Criminal, vol. 138, exp. 10, ff. 138–138v, in which the complainants against don Diego only refer to him as governador, reserving the term tlatoani for the viceroy ("titohuey tlatocatzin S^r. eccelentissimo"). The exception can be found in AGN, Intestados, vol. 301, f. 214.

[117] AGN, Reales Cédulas Duplicadas, vol. 15, exp. 179, f. 141v.

[118] AGN, Criminal, vol. 41, exp. 38, ff. 524–525 and 527–527v.

[119] AGN, Criminal, vol. 48, exp. 30, ff. 500–502v.

work on San Mateo Xalpa's church, and when villagers put up a defense against his demands, don Diego turned to violence. At first he sent a Spanish constable and councilmen to arrest four local residents. Shortly afterward, around midnight on a Thursday evening, according to one of the alleged victims and the witnesses, don Diego came in person to the village, accompanied by Xochimilco's interpreter and presumably some constables, and seized several residents, bound their hands, and dragged them off to Xochimilco's jail. The plaintiffs explained that on don Diego's instructions, a guard struck the plaintiffs with 100 violent lashes. Mateo de San Juan was singled out and received a more severe beating, presumably in retribution for having testified against don Diego in an earlier criminal case. Mateo was whipped with such great force that he could no longer stand up and nearly died. The plaintiffs were then threatened with forced labor in an obraje if they failed to pay a hefty fine.[120]

Faced with mounting evidence of his crimes, the General Indian Court ordered that don Diego Juárez be arrested and called upon to provide a formal answer to the allegations against him. After putting forward his defense, and with a final determination pending, in summer 1644 the Nahuas' legal representative discovered that don Diego had missed a key deadline for filing paperwork, as the historian Brian Owensby has noted. That he had not filed a proof meant, theoretically, he would automatically lose the case. That would have happened were it not for a clever, evasive maneuver: don Diego avoided being served with the court's orders through the simple expedient of refusing to meet with his lawyer. He managed to get away with this for more than a year, after which time, in December 1645, the General Indian Court overturned don Diego's power of attorney and tried to serve him directly and in person. These efforts continued into 1646 but, again, were thwarted when the defendant went to ground and fled.[121]

In response, the Nahuas of San Mateo Xalpa campaigned for justice again a year later. By 1647, don Diego had returned and his malfeasance had grown even worse: stone masons were now being redirected from labor on the cathedral to repair Spaniards' homes in Mexico City; laborers had been forced to quarry stone; as before, they were sent to cut wood in the hills and work on haciendas in Chalco and elsewhere. Moreover, don Diego put women to work grinding chocolate and maize for sale in the market. The litigants also claimed that he compelled them to work at night

---

[120] AGN, Criminal, vol. 48, exp. 30, ff. 508–510v, 512.
[121] Owensby, *Empire of Law*, 244.

on the lake, either gathering reeds or fishing, and with exposure to cold water, they grew sick. The toil, the plaintiffs argued, led to the death of a local resident.[122] In addition, don Diego illegally demanded that an interpreter obtain bribes from market vendors and he also impounded goods that their owners relied on for sale in markets.[123] Don Diego's crimes also extended to outright theft. He stole crops, maguey plants, community funds, and local supplies of stone, which he then sold.[124] He also sold community land that did not belong to him. He commissioned sculptors and painters to make religious statues without paying them and stole money from lay religious brotherhoods as well as funds set aside for the expenses of feast days and Easter celebrations. And to tyrannize the population, using incarceration and the whip to compel compliance, he converted the local hospital into a jail, even imprisoning sick women. Fearing discovery when an inspection of the diocese by the archbishop of Mexico was imminent, don Diego then restored the hospital to its original function and seized pillows and other items to give it the appearance of proper use. Apparently the archbishop remained oblivious to don Diego's deception; he does not mention it in his *visita* (inspection) of 1646.[125]

In spite of all these alleged offenses, don Diego again managed to avoid conviction. In part he did so because of his talent for forging valuable contacts who could shield him. His adroitness in contending with the legal system also helped, as did his success in shielding his crimes from the view of Spanish authorities. Don Diego presented his actions as legitimate, and he deftly manipulated his image and appealed to the interests and expectations of the judges.[126] In one interrogation, don Diego denied having compelled laborers to work involuntarily, citing his compliance with government decrees to provide labor for Mexico City's cathedral and the gunpowder works, and he effectively rebutted charges that he had received bribes to exempt laborers from service. His defense emphasized that the laborers had already absented themselves and, before absconding, they had left 3½ pesos with their wives as payment for replacements.[127]

Don Diego also successfully defended himself against the charges of wrongfully imprisoning and ordering the beating the Nahuas of San

[122] AGN, Criminal, vol. 138, exp. 10, f. 143.

[123] AGN, Indios, vol. 13, exp. 349, ff. 310v–311 (288v–289 old foliation).

[124] AGN, Criminal, vol. 48, exp. 30, ff. 500–502v.

[125] The Newberry Library, Ayer Collection, Ms. 1106 D-1, ff. 1v–2.

[126] AGN, Indios, vol. 13, exp. 346, ff. 309–309v (287–287v old foliation); AGN, Criminal, vol. 48, exp. 30, ff. 517–517v.

[127] AGN, Criminal, vol. 48, exp. 30, ff. 517–517v.

Islands in the Lake

Mateo Xalpa and, in particular, the violence meted out against Mateo de San Juan. Don Diego asserted that on the day before the arrests, council-men of the village had sought to collect royal tribute and recruit laborers. His version of events explained that Mateo de San Juan had led residents into rebellion, pelting officials with rocks and trying to kill them.[128] On hearing news of the riot, don Diego informed the corregidor of Xochimilco, who then initiated legal proceedings against the rebels. To avoid further disturbances, don Diego went to the village to arrest the rebels himself and imprison them in Xochimilco's jail, thereby restoring public order and royal authority. He argued that his actions fell within the remit of his office and that he did not order the jailer to administer lashes. Xochimilco's notary and Spanish lieutenant confirmed don Diego's state-ments about arresting the rebels, affirming that he had previously notified and obtained support from the corregidor. Their testimonies raise the possibility that at the end of the legal proceedings, the presiding judge might have found reasonable doubt in favor of the defendant. They also suggest, moreover, that don Diego's corruption relied on complicity with Nahua and Spanish officials.[129] This was strikingly evident in criminal charges against don Diego that also implicated Luis de Valverde, a Spaniard who held the office of *amparador*, or protector, in Xochimilco. The viceroy had appointed Luis amparador because of alle-gations of abuse and to ensure that tribute be paid. That charges were lodged against Luis together with don Diego speaks to the extent of their collusion.[130] Don Diego was also able to assemble influential supporters before the courts, including elderly residents and fellow council officers.[131] Further connections with useful allies can be seen in don Diego's known associates, among them Spanish hacienda owners, both local and distant, the jailer, and numerous other people in positions of authority including the interpreter. Their allegiance could be invaluable: the corregidor, his lieutenant, and Xochimilco's scribe all provided exculpatory evidence before the court on behalf of don Diego.[132]

---

[128] Or rioted – the verb used was *motínar*.
[129] AGN, Criminal, vol. 48, exp. 30, ff. 517–519.
[130] AGN, Indios, vol. 15, exp. 115, f. 83, AGN, Criminal, vol. 138, exp. 10, ff. 136–144. I have not found a description for amparador in the historical literature. See the 1726 dictionary definition for amparador, Real Academia Española, *Diccionario de autori-dades, edición facsímil* (Madrid: Editorial Gredos, 1990), 275.
[131] AGN, Criminal, vol. 48, exp. 30, ff. 527, 528v–529, 531–531v, 534, 536v, and 538v–539.
[132] AGN, Reales Cédulas Duplicadas, vol. 15, exp. 179, f. 141v.

Despite the support he could muster, don Diego Juárez's position was not invulnerable. In 1641 he had apparently aroused the enmity of don Francisco Velázquez de Robledo, the Spanish hacienda owner previously encountered in his dispute over wage laborers.[133] A year later, apparently still concerned over access to labor and don Diego's control over it, Francisco Velázquez petitioned the viceroy to nullify the reelection of don Diego to the governorship. Invoking an order from the former viceroy, don Juan de Palafox y Mendoza, which forbade mestizos from holding office, Velázquez charged that don Diego should not have been elected.[134] The viceroy concurred and ordered don Diego's removal from office.[135] Local authorities did not comply with the order, though. Don Diego remained in power. In spite of this setback, failure did not deter the hacendado, and by 1645 he had secured access to testimony from the notary of the General Indian Court about pending charges against don Diego, seeking evidence that might further his claims in the ongoing confrontation with the governor.[136]

Finding common cause, Nahua residents joined with Velázquez in trying to oust the governor, also enlisting support from members of a Nahua guild and Franciscan friars.[137] The alliance with Velázquez was well calculated, if ultimately unsuccessful. Velázquez had achieved a significant measure of importance in the community. An advisor to the General Indian Court confirmed this, saying that he was a prominent figure.[138] He owned extensive properties including haciendas and benefited from connections to important viceregal officials. He secured, for instance, contracts to supply wood, an abundant commodity in the hills to the south of Xochimilco's jurisdiction, for the rebuilding of a Mexico City playhouse, the theater in the Royal Indian Hospital.[139] From his position of influence, Velázquez could bend legal practice to his own ends. After he had lodged formal allegations against don Diego, the embattled governor tried to discredit Velázquez by using his lawyer to complain of the familiarity between the hacienda owner and an official from the audiencia who

[133] AGN, Bienes Nacionales, vol. 416, exp. 23.
[134] For Palafox's order, see AGN, Reales Cédulas Duplicadas, vol. 15, exp. 171, f. 130v.
[135] AGN, Reales Cédulas Duplicadas, vol. 15, exp. 179, f. 141v.
[136] AGN, Criminal, vol. 48, exp. 30, f. 550v.
[137] AGN, Criminal, vol. 138, exp. 10, f. 137v.
[138] Robledo was described as a "vecino que tiene grande mano en esta jurisdicion." AGN, Indios, vol. 15, exp. 12, ff. 9–10.
[139] AGN, Historía, vol. 467, exp. 1, ff. 49–50, 52, 220, 224v. I would like to thank Jonathan Truitt for showing me this document.

had been sent to investigate a land case. The lawyer claimed that instead of pursuing his investigation, the investigator enjoyed lunch with Velázquez at La Noria, his hacienda.[140]

Even after facing opposition from Velázquez and criminal charges lodged by Nahuas, don Diego could rely upon sufficient, albeit shrinking, support to retain power. In 1648, an emerging, rival faction of Nahuas managed to defeat him in an election. Their candidate received enough votes to secure the governorship. That the electors chose him, as a Nahua noble who came from outside Xochimilco, is a telling indicator of the severity of the crisis. Yet don Diego's supporters managed to overturn the election result, arguing before the viceroy that the rival candidate, by not hailing from Xochimilco, was unqualified for office. The viceroy agreed and annulled the election result.[141] Presumably either unaware of don Diego's crimes or unfazed by them, the viceroy chose to reappoint don Diego, as he put it, in the interests of peace (the political situation surrounding the election having become quite tense).[142] Even though don Diego still clung to power, the rise of a rival faction demonstrated a weakening in his support and a breach in the alliance of collusion that had kept him in power.

What ultimately led to the governor's downfall, though, were Xochimilco's never-ending problems with tribute. By the time don Diego became governor the city had been indebted for decades, and in 1635, when he returned to the governorship, he inherited the 9,000 pesos of tribute arrears from his predecessor, Joseph Bernal.[143] But don Diego fared no better in resolving Xochimilco's revenue problems. Presumably his failures owed much to his malfeasance, although the difficult circumstances of demographic decline and prolonged drought surely made the task harder. As early as 1640, don Diego was accused of failing to deliver to the crown 9,500 pesos in tribute.[144] The situation grew worse over the course of the 1640s, not least because his illegal labor demands and other abuses prompted residents to flee and, at times, led to widespread absenteeism. (Given the frequent references to flight in the 1640s and 1650s, the difficult political and economic situation may have further prolonged the low population size and hindered any demographic recovery). In November 1641, Xochimilco's cabildo petitioned for relief from tribute

[140] AGN, Criminal, vol. 138, exp. 10, f. 141. For further litigation with don Francisco and don Diego, see AGN, Reales Cédulas Duplicadas, vol. 50, exp. 80, f. 70.
[141] AGN, Indios, vol. 15, cuad. 2, exp. 6, ff. 100–100v.
[142] AGN, Indios, vol. 15, exp. 12, ff. 9–10.
[143] AGN, Indios, vol. 12, 1a pte., exp. 180, ff. 116–116v.
[144] AGN, Criminal, vol. 41, exp. 38, ff. 524–524v.

demands, stating that a great number of tributaries had absconded, revenues were down significantly, and that it was not possible for those who remain to cover the shortfall, for which reason the city could not deliver tribute at the level required by the last tax assessment.[145]

The problem for don Diego Juárez and Xochimilco's cabildo officers was not simply that they had almost insurmountable difficulties, with the altepetl's population reaching its lowest level, in meeting paying their taxes. What proved crucial to their undoing was one particular facet of their tribute arrangements, namely, that Xochimilco also owed money to the Marquesado del Valle, the great estate of Fernando Cortés and his heirs. The vast domains of this fiefdom had originally included the port and town of Tehuantepec, in southern Mexico, which opened up trade to Central and South America. Given its strategic location, King Philip II and his advisors had been worried that private ownership of a port would be improper and contrary to the common good, potentially threatening the unimpeded movement of commodities and hindering commerce. As such it was agreed in 1560 that the port be turned over to the crown, with the formal transfer taking place three years later. In recompense to the estate of Cortés, a portion of the tribute revenues from various polities, among them the cities of Cholula, Huexotzinco, and several others in the province of Chalco, were now directed to the Marquesado del Valle.[146] The same arrangement applied to Xochimilco. What proved so troublesome for don Diego Juárez were the indefatigable efforts of the Marquesado's agents to get the money they were owed.

The same tribute shortfall caused by the absenteeism of residents in 1641 also meant that Xochimilco could not make good on its tribute obligations to the Marquesado. This proved to be a long-standing problem, one possibly related to the ongoing drought. On March 4, 1644, representatives of the estate demanded back payment of tribute from the prior three years in addition to the outstanding amount for the current one. A month later Xochimilco's cabildo admitted that it could not make the payments, offering as an excuse the unfortunate recent fluctuations in the price of maize.[147] (Since the beginning of the decade, the price of maize in Mexico City had quintupled).[148] A year later, with the situation having

---

[145] AGN, Indios, vol. 13, exp. 391, ff. 343–344 (321–322 old foliation).
[146] Gerhard, *A Guide to the Historical Geography of New Spain*, 265.
[147] AGN, Hospital de Jesús, vol. 325, exp. 5, ff. 39 and 48v–49.
[148] Parker, *Global Crisis*, 462; Virginia García Acosta, Juan Manuel Pérez Zevallos and América Molina de Villar, eds., *Desastres agrícolas en México: Catálogo histórico, vol. I:*

become untenable, Xochimilco's cabildo sought permission to alter the terms of its debts. The 1645 negotiations led the city to enter into what was, essentially, a loan with the Marquesado. The new conditions thus involved a restructuring of the debt and the creation of a new payment schedule, one in which a set amount of money was to be delivered every four months until it had all been paid back.[149]

Under renewed pressure to meet the altepetl's obligations – even as they apparently continued to embezzle funds for themselves – don Diego Juárez and his allies applied ever greater pressure on the city's residents. Don Diego demanded unauthorized tribute payments (*derramas*) from commoners, above and beyond the usual exactions, and once again resorted to illegal and coercive means to raise funds.[150] Besides collecting derramas, don Diego also tried to generate more tribute revenue by expanding the definition of tributary status, clearly pushing it beyond the legal limits by demanding that children as young as eight years of age be counted.[151] These unlawful practices continued for years. In 1647, don Diego also sought payments from deceased family members who should have been removed from the tribute rolls.[152]

For all these abuses and illegal exactions, Xochimilco's municipal revenues remained inadequate to the task of meeting tribute payments. By 1647, Xochimilco again defaulted on its obligations to the Marquesado del Valle. Various penalties attached to the nonpayment. In February the representatives of the estate, under the authority of the high court, commissioned a man named Juan Maestre to recover outstanding debts. This appointment proved to be decisive. Almost inevitably, Juan became don Diego's nemesis, not least because his commission made him something of a dangerous blend of a debt collector and a judicial agent, one who had a well-defined legal mandate, who carried a staff of office, and who could make legally binding decisions further to that mandate – for instance, the right to seize property.[153] Juan set about his task immediately and industriously. He departed quickly for the city. There he intended to announce his commission and demand immediate payment.[154] In the meantime, though, Xochimilco's cabildo officers had

Época prehispánica y colonial, 958–1822 (Mexico City: Fondo de Cultura Económica, 2003), 176–179.

[149] AGN, Hospital de Jesús, vol. 325, exp. 5, ff. 34–37.

[150] AGN, Criminal, vol. 41, exp. 38, f. 530.   [151] AGN, Criminal, vol. 41, exp. 38, f. 528.

[152] AGN, Criminal, vol. 138, exp. 10, f. 136.

[153] AGN, Hospital de Jesús, vol. 325, exp. 5, ff. 37v–38.

[154] AGN, Hospital de Jesús, vol. 325, exp. 5, ff. 40–41.

apparently received word about the latest developments, and thus when Juan arrived, the altepetl's officials were nowhere to be found.[155]

In their absence Juan Maestre set about inventorying and impounding property to cover the outstanding debts. Some of the property to be seized belonged to the Nahua officeholders, although don Diego had apparently had the foresight to spirit away most of his movable property. All that Juan could confiscate was a grain bin containing some twenty fanegas of corn, a table, and a Chinese wooden chest, which was locked and for which don Diego's servants said they did not have a key. The house itself, though, was liable to seizure, as were the houses and lands belonging to other councilmen. Much as these individuals' private property could be seized, so too could communal assets of the altepetl. Among the city's holdings identified by Juan for appropriation were storage facilities for grains – and their contents – along with a shop on the plaza, community lands, and plots of land in various locations, including one parcel of land opposite don Francisco Velázquez de Robledo's hacienda of La Noria, and, finally, the city's own hacienda of San Nicolás de Buenaventura, along with all of its tools and livestock (a herd of goats).[156]

After Juan Maestre finished identifying the property to be impounded and left the city, don Diego Juárez quietly returned. In January 1648, he petitioned the government for relief from the city's financial troubles, which had only grown worse in the previous few months, not least because many residents, following the example of their leaders, had once again fled the jurisdiction. Don Diego and the town council appealed to viceregal authorities for assistance in tracking down the fugitive Xochimilca. Giving scant mention of motives behind the residents' flight, for obvious reasons, the officials merely stated that the absent Nahuas had sought to evade their tribute obligations. To gain viceregal support in returning the residents, the petition noted that their absence was jeopardizing community finances and that the city faced falling yet further into debt. The viceroy, again apparently oblivious to the criminal charges leveled against the governor, responded to his request by ordering Spanish officials to find and return the absentee Nahuas to their homes.[157] The order made little difference in bolstering revenues. In 1649 and 1650, Juan Maestre extended the remit of his commission to

[155] AGN, Hospital de Jesús, vol. 325, exp. 5, ff. 41v–43v.
[156] AGN, Hospital de Jesús, vol. 325, ff. 42–43.
[157] AGN, Indios, vol. 15, exp. 17, ff. 14–14v.

cover the ongoing tribute deficits for these years and for 1648, which had also gone unpaid.[158]

In the face of worsening fortunes, and either as a desperate, last measure or a daring bid to outmaneuver their adversary, in October 1650, don Diego Juárez and his fellow council officers submitted to Xochimilco's corregidor a criminal complaint, set down in Nahuatl, against Juan Maestre. The cabildo accused Juan of several crimes, chief among them being that he had undervalued the maize to be sold for tribute revenue and had then forced the city to make its payments precisely when the prices were at their lowest. These underhand practices had been going on for years, the plaintiffs alleged. Making matters worse, at the height of the crisis in 1645, when the cabildo had been forced to renegotiate its debt obligations, Juan had had the cabildo officers apprehended and, during their incarceration, he had illegally seized their belongings and the city's maize supplies and sold everything. To support these allegations, don Diego lined up nine individuals to provide testimony. These witnesses provided further details, for instance, that Juan had seized tribute maize and had sold it himself, only subsequently notifying the cabildo of the prices he got for it. These reported prices, moreover, were fraudulent. All the more troublesome, though, had been the seizure and sale of a crop before it was harvested, as well as of its seeds, which meant that the next year's crops could not be sown, thereby guaranteeing the prolongation of yet more indebtedness. In subsequent investigations, witnesses further alleged that Juan illegally seized property belonging to residents, including two of the city's *escritorios*, or writing desks (bureaus), which contained any number of important papers, including receipts and bills of sale that, conveniently, could be used to support don Diego's case. The cumulative testimonies sufficed, for the viceroy, in justifying the order for Juan Maestre's arrest.[159]

After being placed in jail in January 1651, Juan requested copies of the case file and the evidence submitted in support of the charges. He then responded to the allegations. He refuted the charges, arguing that the corregidor, Sebastián de la Fuente Ayala, and don Diego Juárez had long been conspiring against him, and that the corregidor had provided don Diego with cover and protection for all these years. Together they were now bringing false accusations so that don Diego and Xochimilco

---

[158] AGN, Hospital de Jesús, vol. 325, exp. 5, ff. 58–61 and AGN, Hospital de Jesús, vol. 328, exp. 1, f. 6.

[159] AGN, Hospital de Jesús, vol. 325, exp. 5, ff. 11–22, 23v.

could escape their debts. To this end, they had lined up witnesses who gave false testimony in support of the spurious accusations. And against all this, Juan could provide actual tangible evidence – and not just a parade of unreliable witnesses – in the form of receipts and other documentation, including the legal papers of his commission. On this basis, Juan's prospects of acquittal looked sufficiently strong that in February 1651 he refused to respond to the specific charges brought against him.[160]

Two further developments in March 1651 drastically changed don Diego Juárez's fortunes. The first had to do with a lawsuit brought against him by residents of Xochimilco, which the viceroy ordered to be taken up and investigated by the audiencia. The Xochimilca had apparently been sufficiently emboldened by the governor's troubles as to campaign again for his removal.[161] The second blow came with another decision by the viceroy. This second ruling had to do with jurisdictional matters and whether the other case would be taken up by the General Indian Court or by a different judge whose special jurisdiction encompassed the Marquesado del Valle. One of the privileges of the administrators of Cortés's estate was the right to have legal matters adjudicated by a dedicated judge, or *juez privativo*, on the audiencia. In this case the judge just so happened to be both the high court's most senior justice and the very same judge from whom Juan Maestre had received his commission to collect Xochimilco's tribute arrears. Juan had asked that his case be heard by the oidor and the viceroy now agreed, dealing don Diego Juárez's criminal case a fatal blow.[162]

At some point in early 1651, probably by March at the latest, don Diego Juárez disappeared. He was never to be seen in public again.[163]

Xochimilco's municipal government was thrown into chaos. Some of its cabildo officers, including the governor himself, who had absconded previously, were now in absentia once again. With no effective leader, and with the local government operations having all but ceased to exist, the viceroy intervened in late spring, appointing a successor to the governorship.[164] The new governor was expressly charged with the duty of covering the tribute debt and delivering it directly to the royal treasury. The corregidor was enjoined to supervise all of this carefully. Even so,

---

[160] AGN, Hospital de Jesús, vol. 325, exp. 5, ff. 29–29v, 30–32v, and 50.

[161] AGN, Indios, vol. 16, exp. 76, ff. 73–74 (71–72 old foliation).

[162] AGN, Hospital de Jesús, vol. 325, exp. 5, ff. 53 and 57.

[163] At least not according to any subsequent sources.

[164] AGN, Indios, vol. 16, exp. 76, ff. 73–74 (71–72 old foliation).

compliance once again proved slack. In part this had to do with the
partisan and corrupt dealings of the corregidor, who was the same individual who had been allied with don Diego Juárez and who, for this
reason, had been in conflict with Juan Maestre (the latter had succeeded
in having the corregidor recused from his case).[165] The continuing failure
to deliver tribute also had much to do with the new governor's own
proclivity for peculations, and the viceroy soon issued yet another order,
this time requiring immediate compliance with tribute regulations. With
ongoing conflict, political rivals and residents of Xochimilco soon banded
together in opposition against the governor and don Diego's cronies, who
had clung on to positions of power. In November the viceroy ordered an
election and then the accession of an entirely new group of officials.[166]

The old, long-standing political order of don Diego Juárez and his
supporters, who had retained power for sixteen years, was overturned
in a matter of weeks. The accession of a new cohort of leaders was
consolidated in a few further developments at the end of the year. In
December, the new governor assumed his duties. So severe had the
situation been that the new governor hailed from outside Xochimilco.
Previously governors elected by Xochimilco's nobles had hailed from
the city's districts of Tepetenchi, Tecpan, and Olac. Don Francisco
Benites Inga, by contrast, came from Xochimilco's subject town
Nuestra Señora de la Asunción Milpa Alta. The election of this new
governor thus represented an inversion of hierarchy: a Nahua from
a town subordinate to Xochimilco became the city's governor.[167] In
the order confirming the new governor's election, the viceroy required
don Francisco to provide a guarantee in the form of a surety that
tribute would be paid and that the governor adhere to new and stricter
book keeping practices.[168]

Also in December the full extent of Xochimilco's financial troubles
became apparent. Don Diego Juárez, it was now determined, had presided
over the increase of the overall debt burden to an unprecedented 14,000
pesos. It further emerged that his successor had managed to add to the
arrears during his short time in office. Given the severity of these debts, the
new cabildo officers asked that they not be saddled with the tribute arrears
of their predecessors; they asked that only the previous officials be held

---

[165] AGN, Hospital de Jesús, vol. 325, exp. 5, ff. 51–51v.
[166] AGN, Indios, vol. 16, exp. 134, ff. 126–127 (124–125 old foliation).
[167] AGN, Indios, vol. 20, exp. 233, ff. 185v–186 (184v–185 old foliation).
[168] AGN, Indios, vol. 16, exp. 137, ff. 129–130v (127–128v old foliation).

liable.[169] These were especially pressing issues for the new cabildo officers because, in the same month the judge presiding over the criminal case against Juan Maestre reached a verdict. The judge found Juan to be innocent and dismissed all of the charges against him.[170] The Marquesado's agent was now free to pursue those responsible for Xochimilco's debts. Juan set out in search of Xochimilco's former officials. Some he tracked down and under the authority of the Marquesado's judicial representatives, he had don Diego's successor to the governorship as well as several alcaldes, regidores, and mayordomos arrested and imprisoned. As soon as they were jailed, Juan went to see them to identify and seize their property. He had still not completed his task of recovering the funds owed to the Marquesado in 1656, some five years later.[171]

Juan Maestre and other representative of the Marquesado had less luck in holding don Diego Juárez to account. For a while the Marquesado's legal documents listed him as a fugitive, "in flight because of the great amount of money he owed the estate and to His Majesty." Juan had searched in vain for the fugitive governor – at least until don Diego finally surfaced in Xochimilco's Franciscan friary in late 1651. There he had claimed sanctuary. Within the friary, don Diego was shielded from civil justice under canon law. Whether he had succeeded in escaping to the friary on his own, or whether he was sent into seclusion there by the viceroy in a case of summary justice and in lieu of a formal prosecution, remains unclear. But what was clear was that don Diego had evaded justice and escaped punishment, even though the viceroy called him out for having embezzled tribute funds and, as a result, for having contributed to Xochimilco's ruinous debts.[172] Safely ensconced in the friary, don Diego also remained beyond the reach of Juan Maestre who in 1652 was still trying to have him held to account. Several years later, at the end of 1655, Juan's successor Alonso de Mesa was still unable to get at the former governor. In a memorandum, Alonso wrote that don Diego "was still in retreat in the church and friary of this city."[173] And don Diego remained in the friary until the last time he appeared in the documentary record, in 1657, when he was listed as a fiscal in a Nahuatl testament.[174]

---

[169] AGN, Indios, vol. 16, exp. 137, ff. 129–130v (127–128v old foliation).
[170] AGN, Hospital de Jesús, vol. 325, exp. 5, f. 69.
[171] AGN, Hospital de Jesús, vol. 328, exp. 1, ff. 7, 55.
[172] AGN, Indios, vol. 16, exp. 137, ff. 129–130v (127–128v old foliation).
[173] AGN, Hospital de Jesús, vol. 328, exp. 1, ff. 7, 52–52v.
[174] AGN, Civil, vol. 1823, exp. 12, ff. 16–16v.

AFTERMATH: A NEW COLONIAL ORDER

The seclusion of don Diego Juárez in Xochimilco's friary did not bring an end to political discord. In 1652, a few months after taking office, the governor was replaced by an ally of the previous administration, who set about trying to secure the release of the imprisoned former officials.[175] If the old guard was trying to restore itself to power, its efforts were met with opposition. At the same time, and in an apparent decline in deference by commoners to their rulers, a councilman approached a local resident named Miguel de Zárate who had been remiss in paying tribute. Asked why he had not made payment, Miguel responded by seizing the man's staff of office and accusing him of being a despicable drunkard. As a further affront to the official's authority, Miguel denied that the councilman was a noble. The confrontation took place in front of government officials and, significantly, drew a crowd of Nahua men and women who then joined in the mockery, laughing at the councilman and his colleagues, and tugging their beards. Calm was finally restored when the corregidor intervened and sent Miguel to prison. Asked why Miguel refused to pay tribute, one witness replied it was because of his little respect for municipal government.[176] This was hardly an isolated case. In a separate incident, Spanish constables encountered not only a lack of respect but also violence. As in the above case, a crowd assembled at the scene and several Nahuas joined the fray, grabbing a constable's staff of office and smashing it, tearing his shirt, and then severely beating him.[177]

In the midst of these disorders, the viceregal government instituted a series of reforms to Xochimilco's government. Some of these changes reflected the priorities of the colonial administration; others were generated by pressure from Xochimilco's citizens and the residents of its subject communities. The reforms typically focused on three areas: the closer monitoring and enforcement of more stringent rules about tribute payment; the revamping and supervision of elections, and alterations to the jurisdiction through the granting of cabecera status to former sujetos. The jurisdictional changes were inspired, in part, by the abuses of the previous administration. Don Diego's excesses had engendered a good degree of solidarity within and among subject communities, with San Mateo Xalpa prominent among them. It had been at the forefront of pursuing the 1640

---

[175] AGN, Hospital de Jesús, vol. 328, exp. 1, ff. 30–31v.
[176] AGN, Criminal, vol. 132, exp. 10, ff. 553–560v.
[177] AGN, Criminal, vol. 138, exp. 17, ff. 336–362v, especially ff. 337–339.

criminal case against the governor, and in this it had been joined by the villages of Santiago, San Andrés, and Santa Cécilia. Four years later the subject towns of Xalpa and San Francisco Tlalnepantla banded together and then, in 1647, in a remarkable case of intercommunity solidarity, those who petitioned for criminal sanctions included the subject villages of Santiago Tepalcatlapan, San Mateo Xalpa, San Miguel Topilejo, San Francisco Tlalnepantla, San Salvador, Santa Cécilia, San Andrés, San Lucas, San Lorenzo, Santa María Nativitas, and Santa Cruz.[178] As soon as don Diego was removed from office, residents from some of these communities sought to be freed from the control of Xochimilco. Jurisdictional independence meant escaping the altepetl's demands for labor, assuming control over local administration, and dealing directly with the colonial government. Only by escaping from the altepetl's control could Nahuas in these communities be assured of avoiding future abuses by don Diego's successors.

In 1651, the Nahuas of Nuestra Señora de los Remedios Tepepan, a community under Xochimilco that had suffered from tribute and labor abuses, petitioned Spanish authorities for a prohibition against the city's officials entering their town. Not only did the viceroy grant this but, following an inspection, he also granted Tepepan jurisdictional independence from Xochimilco. Henceforth, Tepepan would no longer have to channel its tribute payments and labor levies through the city. The town's separation also meant that it could elect its own officials. This separation had the advantage for Spanish authorities of direct and – in the light of recent interruptions – more reliable delivery of tribute.[179] Soon afterward, the newly elected officials received their staffs of office.[180]

In another example, the town of Tolyahualco also secured independence from Xochimilco. In their initial request, the town's officers asked to be granted the separation because of the extortion they had suffered but also, and in conformity with requirements for independent administration, because they had their own church for the celebration of holy sacraments. Observing that the presence of a church provided Nahuas with an argument in favor of political independence, James Lockhart noted that much construction work was undertaken specifically for this reason.[181] Similarly, Ryan

---

[178] AGN, Criminal, vol. 138, exp. 10, ff. 136–144.
[179] AGN, Indios, vol. 16, exp. 124, ff. 116–117v (114–115v old foliation).
[180] AGN, Indios, vol. 17, exp. 17, ff. 29v–30v; see also AGN, Indios, vol. 18, exp. 51, ff. 43–43v and exp. 228, f. 168v.
[181] Lockhart, *The Nahuas after the Conquest*, 208–209.

Crewe has observed that sixteenth-century church construction provided Nahuas with opportunities to assert local sovereignty. In the case of sujetos which had been under the auspices of the Franciscans of Xochimilco, the building and repair works of the seventeenth century may well have formed part of deliberate strategies to gain autonomy by fragmenting larger sociopolitical entities, concentrate power locally, and even secure land that might be at risk of expropriation.[182] For Tolyahualco, the petitioners stressed their devotion and reminded the viceroy that they had just finished refurbishing and repairing their church. As had happened in the case of Tepepan, Xochimilco's government tried to obstruct the separation.[183] For Xochimilco, the independence of subject towns and villages threatened the integrity of the jurisdiction and represented an end to the valuable opportunity for obtaining tribute. In the years after the upheavals of mid-century, Xochimilco lost at least two of its constituent communities. The impressive century-long jurisdictional resilience, since the earlier loss of San Agustín de las Cuevas in the immediate aftermath of the Spanish conquest, had come to an end.[184]

Viceregal reforms also included the closer supervision of municipal elections. Closer oversight of elections provided new opportunities for factions to contest local power and brought a return to the earlier tradition of frequently rotating officials, which had prevented any single person from monopolizing office. In instances when incumbent authorities tried to retain power by bypassing elections or ignoring the results, their rivals sought viceregal intercession. In 1680, for instance, the governor Nicolás López tried to remain in office by rigging the outcome of elections. A rival group of electors and nobles petitioned the viceroy to withhold confirmation of the results.[185] The viceroy agreed but the matter did not end there. In holding a new election and contriving to have himself reelected, Nicolás prompted a second complaint by the rival faction. The petitioners successfully appealed against fraud and coercion: they argued that the election should be nullified, in part, because the interpreter had unduly swayed its outcome.[186]

---

[182] Ryan Crewe, "Building in the Shadow of Death: Monastery Construction and the Politics of Community Reconstitution in Sixteenth-Century Mexico," *The Americas*, vol. 75, no. 3 (2018), 502–512.

[183] AGN, Indios, vol. 30, exp. 13, ff. 9–9v; exp. 165, ff. 157v–158, and exp. 182, ff. 170v–171v.

[184] On the loss of San Agustín de las Cuevas, see Chapter 1 and Horn, *Postconquest Coyoacan*, 56.

[185] AGN, Indios, vol. 26, cuad. 1, exp. 1, ff. 2–2v (1–1v old foliation).

[186] AGN, Indios, vol. 26, cuad. 1, exp. 25, ff. 24–24v; exp. 26, ff. 24v–25 (23v–24 old foliation).

A decade later, and after he had returned to office again, Nicolás tried once again to retain office for a consecutive term. On this second occasion, Nicolás's rival candidate, don Joseph Bautista de Alvarado, challenged the election result. To do so, he alleged that Nicolás had contravened tribute requirements. While malfeasance apparently continued to trouble political relations, opponents now used the specter of failures to deliver tribute as a means to inspire outside intervention and to oust rivals. The allegations against Nicolás prompted the viceroy to order the suspension of officials, the seizure of their staffs of office, and the holding of a new election.[187] Adding to the allegations about fiscal and electoral impropriety, don Joseph claimed that Nicolás was ineligible for office because he was a mestizo.[188] In this instance, the accusation may have been effective because the viceroy barred Nicolás from candidacy in the new election, demanding that the new governor be a Nahua. Thereafter, Nicolás disappeared from administrative sources.[189] To find a replacement, Spanish officials brought together the electors and supervised the new election, which installed as governor don Francisco Nicolás de Mendoza Cortés. Don Francisco was apparently a compromise candidate, one acceptable to both factions – a significant number of nobles having remained opposed to don Joseph Bautista de Alvarado. Two months later, though, the new governor suddenly passed away. Presumably in order to avoid holding another controversial election, the viceroy appointed don Joseph as his replacement.[190]

The installation of don Joseph in 1689 marked a turning point in Xochimilco's politics, heralding a return to greater continuity in the staffing of the governorship. For the next few decades, local government was dominated by a handful of figures whose authority rested not on tradition and lineage, as with the tlatoque of old, but on their administrative abilities, rectitude, and their cross-cultural fluency, both in terms of language and dealings between peoples of different ethnicities as well as expertise in contending with the law and colonial institutions. Don Joseph and his son, don Hipólito, who later succeeded his father as governor, exemplified this trend. While both of them were identified as caciques there is no evidence to suggest that they were descended from any of the old tlatoque lineages. Rather, in 1687, when a noblewoman named doña

[187] AGN, Indios, vol. 30, exp. 219, ff. 205v–206; exp. 223, ff. 210v–211.
[188] AGN, Indios, vol. 30, exp. 241, ff. 227v–228v.
[189] AGN, Indios, vol. 30, exp. 248, ff. 232–232v.
[190] AGN, Indios, vol. 30, exp. 266, ff. 247–247v.

Josepha Cerón Cortés y Alvarado petitioned to inherit the estate of the erstwhile tlatoani of Tepentenchi, of whom don Diego Juárez had been the last in the line of succession, no mention was made in the deliberations about don Joseph or don Hipólito.[191] Indeed, there is surprisingly little documentary material about them before they entered government. If their ancestry is unknown, they clearly established for themselves and their descendants a position at the summit of the Nahua community; their sons and grandsons, who appear in land records through the 1760s, were all identified with the title "don" and retained control, in spite of recurring legal challenges, of the estate they inherited.[192] Don Joseph and his son proved themselves to be well qualified for office. In addition to serving as governor the Alvarados staffed the positions of scribe and interpreter, meaning that they were well versed in administrative practices and the law.[193] They both spoke Spanish and were literate, and among the Nahuatl documents they authored were bills of sale and rental agreements.[194] The two men forged close relations with prominent figures in the community, including the Orozco family, which was arguably the highest-ranking Spanish family in the city.[195] In later years the two men remained influential figures in the community, working informally to help residents, sometimes involving themselves formally in judicial matters, either hiring legal representatives on behalf of neighbors and communities or taking on powers of attorney to help others in legal matters.[196]

In 1689, don Joseph soon revealed himself to be an active and competent governor, one who sought to shore up Xochimilco's finances. He devised a few policies to build up the city's coffers. One method involved securing more land for the altepetl. In October 1691, don Joseph sought to have land that once belonged to a village named Santa Catarina, which had fallen vacant with population loss, reallocated to Xochimilco. Don Joseph made a point of setting aside the revenues generated from rentals of this land to pay for local expenses. Specifically, the income was used to complete various projects, among them the repairs of the cabildo offices and the

[191] AGN, Indios, vol. 29, exp. 249, ff. 201v–202v; AGN, Vínculos y Mayorazgos, vol. 279, exp. 1.
[192] AGN, Tierras, vol. 2670, exp. 1.
[193] AGN, TSJDF, Corregidores, caja 31B, exp. 61; AGN, TSJDF, Corregidores, caja 31B, exp. 62; AGN, TSJDF, Corregidores, caja 31B, exp. 86.
[194] AGN, TSJDF, Corregidores, caja 31B, exp. 60.
[195] AGN, Tierras, vol. 2670, exp. 1, f. 18 (second foliation).
[196] AGN, Tierras, vol. 1769, exp. 4, ff. 1–12; for more papers of this litigation, see AGN, TSJDF, Corregidores, caja 32B, exp. 51; see also AGNM, Xochimilco, vol. 1, ff. 135v–136 and 180–180v.

jail, both of which had fallen into disrepair.[197] Don Joseph also carefully managed the rental of other community property, including Xochimilco's hacienda, Teuhtli. In 1693, the estate was rented out at an annual rate of 150 pesos to a local Spaniard, Miguel Betancurt, for a period of six years.[198] Apparently that arrangement did not work out; two years later, don Joseph arranged a new rental agreement, one that was secured with a viceregal confirmation, and the hacienda now brought in 200 pesos of annual revenue from a Spaniard who held a license to supply the city with meat.[199] Proceeds from the hacienda's rental supported the local hospital, but in times of shortage, as in 1696, when residents fled because of widespread hunger – there having been drought conditions this year – the cabildo reserved the right to use the land for raising crops.[200] Don Joseph and don Hipólito even explored the possibility of selling off Teuhtli in order to guarantee adequate funding for the hospital.[201]

Don Joseph's efforts to generate community income proved highly successful. In 1689 the viceroy had appointed him governor, in part, because of his good standing in the delivery of tribute.[202] This held true for the next few years. Don Joseph and don Hipólito successfully negotiated with local officials and the audiencia in restructuring and eventually settling the tribute debts of subject communities. As part of sorting out the repayment schedule, they insisted on having a formal debt obligation written up and notarized, with well-known individuals serving as guarantors for what now, in effect, became a loan.[203] The Alvarados continued to enjoy support because of their fiscal prudence, so much so, in fact, that their experience marked something of a turning point: much as malfeasance could inspire protest and political upheaval, so, conversely, the irreproachable adherence to tribute requirements could help maintain governors in power. Don Joseph and don Hipólito, father and son, were granted a special dispensation to take alternating turns as governor, thereby sidestepping the rules against reelection.[204] By promptly supplying tribute, and doing so reliably, they managed to serve several consecutive terms, a feat not achieved since the days of don Diego Juárez. Their opponents brought litigation

---

[197] AGN, Indios, vol. 30, exp. 461, ff. 440v–441v.
[198] AGNM, Xochimilco, vol. 1, ff. 19–20v.   [199] AGN, Indios, vol. 32, exp. 282, f. 244v.
[200] Skopyk, *Colonial Cataclysms*, 9.
[201] AGN, Indios, vol. 32, exp. 369, ff. 319v–320; AGNM, Xochimilco, vol. 1, ff. 65–66v.
[202] AGN, Indios, vol. 30, exp. 266, ff. 247–247v.
[203] AGNM, Xochimilco, vol. 1, ff. 41–42v.
[204] AGN, Indios, vol. 30, exp. 475, ff. 457v–458.

before the high court in a bit to unseat the Alvarados. The plaintiffs alleged that the Alvarados had committed crimes in their excessive collection of tribute – an allegation that apparently little concerned the viceroy, who rejected the allegations and confirmed don Hipólito in his office.[205] The ensuing and protracted lawsuit passed all the way through the Spanish political hierarchy to Madrid. There the king ordered that the Alvarados be disqualified from office.[206]

At the distant remove of New Spain, though, the royal decree was ignored, perhaps because of the 1692 riot in the capital. A shaken administration perceived the conflagration's origins in food shortages following the failed harvests and the sudden, severe drought.[207] The audiencia allowed don Joseph to become governor in 1692 after Xochimilco's Nahuatl election report proved that he won a clear majority.[208] In addition, the audiencia and local Spanish officials recognized that the Alvarados enjoyed widespread popularity among Xochimilco's electors and the representatives of the altepetl's sujetos, who all made a show of strength in appearing together before Spanish authorities and putting their names to a petition in which they requested that don Joseph be kept on as governor, as per the election results.[209] In returning don Joseph de Alvarado to office once again in 1695, the viceroy explicitly affirmed that he had satisfied tribute requirements and, tellingly, had provided much-needed food. Even though don Joseph's opponent had received more votes in the election, the viceroy nevertheless favored the incumbent because he was more reliable in delivering tribute.[210]

Malfeasance over tribute had previously brought an end to the political careers of Joseph Bernal and don Diego Juárez. But at the end of the century, the Alvarados successfully negotiated their intermediary position between Nahua commoners and Spanish officialdom through the leverage of tribute, which enabled them to surmount the opposition of a rival faction. They translated their skill in contending with viceregal authorities

---

[205] AGN, Indios, vol. 30, exp. 475, ff. 457v–458.

[206] AGN, Civil, vol. 2182, exp. 14, ff. 1–4v.

[207] According to the Mexican Drought Atlas, the drought of 1692 registered at a value of almost –4 PDSI, the deepest level in the colonial period. See the online Mexican Drought Atlas at http://drought.memphis.edu/MXDA/Default.aspx (accessed January 18, 2021).

[208] AGN, Civil, vol. 2182, exp. 14, ff. 7v–8; for the food shortages being seen as a cause of the riot, see AGI, Audiencia de México, leg. 781 and R. Douglas Cope, *The Limits of Racial Domination: Plebeian Society in Colonial Mexico City, 1660–1720* (Madison: University of Wisconsin Press, 1994), 125–160.

[209] AGN, Civil, vol. 2182, exp. 14, ff. 19–19v.

[210] AGN, Indios, vol. 32, exp. 251, ff. 220–220v.

into a remarkable maintenance of power, it having become so common-place for them to alternate in office that documents referred them both as governors of Xochimilco, either as though they were serving together simultaneously or that it did not matter much which one was the actual governor at any given moment. The consecutive terms of don Joseph and don Hipólito paved the way for a partial return to continuity to the office of governor.

CONCLUSION

Whereas the landscape had served as a foundation for continuity in Xochimilco, demographic collapse and climate extremes – which produced both major inundations and damaging drought – brought a variety of changes that gained pace during the first half of the seventeenth century. Together with flooding and the substantial shortfalls in town finances that followed, demographic decline contributed to a severe a crisis, one that was deepened by the depredations of a ruling class that had become estranged from the old collective and reciprocal bonds of the community. The attenu-ation of authority and the rampant criminality of the cabildo officers coincided – and was connected to – both the nadir of the Nahua population and increasingly onerous demands for labor by haciendas and the govern-ment. Indeed, that Xochimilco's population size remained so low during and after the middle decades of the seventeenth century may have owed much to the combined economic and political crisis in the city. Civil strife prompted people to flee the jurisdiction; the crisis may also have contrib-uted to enduringly low birthrates, which would have inhibited a population recovery. Parish registers of baptisms, which serve as a useful if vague indicator of birthrates, show a distinct trend: between 1658, when the sources began, and 1671, the number of baptisms remained consistently low, at between 200 and 250 per annum. While there is a gap in the records for the next four years, the birthrate apparently increased in the latter part of the century, rising from 250 baptisms to almost 390 a year by 1688.[211] Perhaps tellingly, the Mexican Drought Atlas data for this latter period indicate a gradual departure away from the earlier pluvial conditions and a return to a warmer, drier climate.[212]

---

[211] AGN, Genealogía [microfilm], vols. 1794 and 1795.
[212] The value is once more observed for the grid point located at W 99.1°, N 19.26° for Lake Xochimilco on the Mexican Drought Atlas, online at http://drought.memphis.edu/MX DA/Default.aspx (accessed January 18, 2021).

The crisis of mid-century brought with it political violence, outside intervention, and the fall of the old ruling dynasties. The conflicts gave rise to a new political order in Xochimilco. For all the havoc wrought by don Diego Juárez and the others, though, the structures of municipal government held fast and survived intact. The one significant exception to this was the escape of several subject communities from Xochimilco's jurisdictional control. Viewed from the perspectives of Tepepan and Tolyahualco, though, independence was something to be welcomed as it reinforced the tendency among Nahuas to prefer local forms of association and representation. In the city itself (and what remained of its jurisdiction), the old order came to be replaced by a new cohort of leaders whose legitimacy now rested not on lineage but on administrative competence, financial prudence, and the marshaling of public resources in support of the common good. In achieving these goals and gaining the support of both citizens and the colonial administration, the Bautista de Alvarados achieved a degree of legitimacy not enjoyed since the days of the last tlatoani. Indeed, a returning vitality in elections after the 1650s and the ascendancy of these and other governors represented a returning vigor and credibility for the city's government.

6

Late Colonial Watersheds

Even though the political situation in Xochimilco began to stabilize in the later years of the 1600s, the crisis of that century highlighted the city's limited autonomy when it came to the implications of demographic decline, susceptibility to climate extremes, and the burdens of tribute and labor exactions by the colonial government. Whereas the viceregal administration and the audiencia had meddled extensively in local politics, the aquatic way of life in the chinampa districts and the underlying hydraulic engineering system had essentially been left alone. Thus the upheavals in demography and local politics stood in sharp contrast to continuities in the landscape, which had underpinned Xochimilco's ecological autonomy. Apart from intermittent floods, the landscape had scarcely been altered since the destruction of the Aztec-era chinampas in the wake of the Spanish–Mexica War. In the eighteenth century, though, the continuity in the landscape began to change. Several factors, which came to intersect over time, accounted for the shifts in the area's ecological autonomy.

The first and most conspicuous changes, at least insofar as they were discussed in the sources, had to do with the expansion of haciendas into the lake areas. Whereas previously haciendas had been confined, for the most part, to the upland areas away from the lakes, a handful of the more prominent and commercially viable estates now began to push into the lakes themselves. The haciendas encroached into the lake waters and converted chinampas and marshlands into pastures. In a few places, the lands of the lakes were becoming livestock ranches. Lake-area residents, Nahuas and Spaniards alike, had long taken to rearing livestock on chinampas on a limited, small-scale basis when chinampas fell vacant from demographic decline. Such livestock as there had been were few in number and hardly deserved to be called herds. By the end of the eighteenth century, by contrast, the cattle in newly created pastures came to number in their thousands.

Besides amounting to a significant change in land use – away from horticulture – the growth of grazing lands began to undermine the ecological autonomy Nahua communities had previously enjoyed. As local residents and colonial authorities readily acknowledged, the expansion of ever larger pastures where once there had been lakes and chinampas began to cause environmental dislocations, with more frequent and widespread flooding being the most conspicuous and deleterious example.[1] The southern lakes thus began to experience what Georgina Endfield and Sarah O'Hara have called "landscape instability" (although it should be noted that their observations pertained to the markedly different context of drought in Michoacán).[2] In Xochimilco and Chalco, where haciendas had once been negligible to the area's history, now they were becoming transformative: if the interrelated ecological and economic foundations of Xochimilco had, by and large, remained intact in 1700, by 1800 they no longer were.

The expansion of haciendas into the lakes was the most conspicuous reason for the increasingly frequent, large-scale and destructive floods that beset the lake areas from the late eighteenth century. Investigations of the inundations by colonial officials tended to confirm what Native peoples had suspected, namely, that by keeping their pastures sealed off from the lakes with dikes and embankments, the haciendas had reduced the volume of the basin and forced water to rise elsewhere. But the water levels themselves, though, would not have risen so significantly were it not for elevated levels of rainfall. Greater amounts of precipitation were seen in the final decades of the colonial era. As Bradley Skopyk has shown, from the second half of the seventeenth century and for much of the eighteenth century, the climate had become much more balanced. There were a similar number of wet and dry years, and central Mexico began to experience a gradual warming of temperatures and drier overall conditions.[3] Some of the surviving historical sources seem to support

---

[1] Rojas Rabiela, "Ecological and Agricultural Changes in the Chinampas of Xochimilco-Chalco," 289; Rojas Rabiela, "Aspectos tecnológicos de las obras hidráulicas coloniales," 56–57.
[2] Endfield and O'Hara, "Degradation, Drought, and Dissent," 402–419.
[3] Skopyk, *Colonial Cataclysms*, 7.

this trend, if only anecdotally; maps from the eighteenth century, for instance, show much more extensive areas of marshland, and less flowing water, than one might expect to see (see Map 6.3).[4] Written sources also increasingly referred to marshes and swamps rather than lakes, opening up the possibility that drier conditions had enabled hacendados to extend their holdings into the lakes. Later in the eighteenth century, though, the climate shifted once again.

From the 1780s, intermittent and severe droughts gave way to a period of sustained high humidity, which persisted for several decades. Between 1791 and 1818, as Skopyk has observed, 79 percent of the years were wetter than normal. The year 1816 was the second wettest on record, primarily because of the effects of the Tambora volcanic eruption the year before.[5] That eruption, which remains the largest in recorded history, combined with fewer sunspots to reduce temperatures between 1° and 2° Celsius (a decrease comparable to that of the depths of the Little Ice Age in the mid-seventeenth century).[6] The cooler, wetter conditions of the late eighteenth and early nineteenth centuries exacerbated the disruption already under way in the lakes. The climate also contributed significantly to undermining the resilience of the hydraulic system that had long served to regulate the lake waters. Because of modifications to the hydraulic system, in large part because of interventions by hacendados and agents of the desagüe project, Xochimilco and other lakeside communities became ever more vulnerable to the kinds of climatic upheaval that Georgina Endfield has described for other parts of Mexico. On occasions of high levels of precipitation, the flood defenses ceased to able to cope with the volume of water. The causeway at Tlahuac, for instance, exhibited clear signs of serious wear and tear, and in the nineteenth century, it was overtopped by floodwaters, rendering it almost ineffective.

Alterations to the hydraulic system served as the third factor that undermined Xochimilco's ecological autonomy. From the 1740s, the colonial administration renewed its efforts to pursue the desagüe project. Responding to growing fears of flooding in the capital – fears that, over time, became more acute as the climate shifted – desagüe authorities began to turn their attention to the southern lakes and not just to the engineering works at Huehuetoca in the north. Under the leadership of the superintendent of the desagüe, don Domingo de Trespalacios y Escandón, government officials increasingly intervened in the southern lakes' hydrology.

---

[4] AGN, Desagüe, vol. 18, exp. 3. [5] Skopyk, *Colonial Cataclysms*, 7–9.
[6] Parker, *Global Crisis*, 688.

Having conducted a survey of the drainage system there in the late 1740s, Trespalacios noted that the water management infrastructure, which the government had disregarded for so long, had fallen into a state of significant disrepair. In other words, the benefits of the centuries-old landesque capital had begun to yield fewer dividends. The poor condition of the causeway at Tlahuac served as a stark reminder of the degradation of the flood defenses. From the 1760s, further weaknesses in the engineering works became apparent, prompting more sustained government intervention. In revamping the flood defenses, the agents of the desagüe project came into conflict with hacendados, whose interests were not always aligned, and both of these groups also found themselves at odds with Nahua communities who, in turn, were concerned about the prospect of yet more destructive flooding and its implications for their way of life.

HACIENDAS, ENVIRONMENTAL INTERVENTION, AND LACUSTRINE PASTORALISM

As discussed in Chapter 2, hacienda development had been limited in the early colonial period. Most estates established in the sixteenth century had been located on poor, rocky soil up in the montes. There the owners of ranches typically confined themselves to rearing livestock. A few of the haciendas occupied better, lower-lying lands near the lake, but even these had encountered difficulties in generating wealth. That they were rented out or sold frequently suggests as much. While this pattern persisted well into the seventeenth century, the growth of haciendas around the lakes gradually gained pace. As the eighteenth century approached, haciendas began to extend down the slopes and to the shores of the lakes themselves. By the eighteenth century, a couple of estates in Xochimilco had come to occupy valuable waterfront property. Thereafter they continued to expand. Lacking space on the tierra firme in which to do so, the haciendas instead pushed ever further into the water – or what had previously been water. Much as the Mexica had sought to reclaim land from the southern lakes in the fifteenth century, now in the eighteenth, hacendados sought to realize the same goal, albeit with other kinds of land than chinampas; they began to fashion pastures from the lakes. Converting the lakes from a horticultural landscape into a pastoral one required significant interventions in the environment.

None of the estates in Xochimilco's jurisdiction were more prominent than the haciendas of La Noria and San Juan de Dios. (The main house of the former is famous today for being the site of the Museo Dolores Olmedo

Patiño). In the eighteenth century both haciendas stood out for being among the most substantial and influential estates in the southwest corner of the Basin of Mexico. In Charles Gibson's study of the Basin of Mexico's principal haciendas, only La Noria and San Juan de Dios made an appearance in Xochimilco's jurisdiction. Gibson observed that hacienda development was strikingly limited there, especially when compared with other areas, like Chalco and Tetzcoco. Conspicuously absent were haciendas across the southern shore of Lakes Xochimilco and Chalco.[7]

While the comparative absence of haciendas in Xochimilco can be explained by several factors, none of them was more significant than the geographical situation of Lake Xochimilco's littoral, which consisted of a narrow band of land between the lakes and the rising slopes of the Sierra de Ajusco (see Map 0.2 and, in particular, the concentration of the topographical lines to the south of the lakeshore). As Robert Santley has shown, this thin strip of gently sloping land was the site of one of the region's distinct ecological zones, the deep soil alluvium, which contained exceptionally rich soils. The land was also ideally located for irrigation. In the second half of the colonial era, this area provided the perfect place for the rise of haciendas, especially those cultivating grains – or, at least, it would have been an ideal location were it not for the fact that it was so narrow.[8] For this reason, only a few haciendas developed in Xochimilco. By contrast, hacienda development was concentrated in the wider, more extensive zones of the deep soil alluvium elsewhere in the Basin of Mexico. The most substantial estates around Lakes Xochimilco and Chalco, therefore, were clustered to the west of the lakes, around San Agustín de las Cuevas and Coyoacan, and to the east, in Chalco.[9] The presence of several rivers, as well as the extensive, gently sloping tracts of land, also meant that haciendas were far more numerous to the east of Lake Chalco than in Xochimilco.

In both Chalco and Xochimilco, as elsewhere, the few estates in these prime locations became ever more valuable in the late eighteenth century. They passed into the hands of influential colonial figures, including senior ecclesiastics and few members of New Spain's titled nobility – such as the Marqués de San Miguel de Arauyo y Santa Olaya – as well as the Jesuits and prominent members of Mexico City's merchant guild.[10] Indeed, the sale of Jesuit properties after their expulsion from New Spain in 1767 provided a further impetus to the intrusion of landed estates into the lakes.

---

[7] Gibson, *The Aztecs under Spanish Rule*, 291.
[8] Sanders et al., *The Bason of Mexico*, supplementary map materials, map 1.
[9] Tutino, "Creole Mexico." [10] AGN, Tierras, vol. 1618, exp. 1, cuad. 3, f. 2.

Following the promulgation of a royal decree concerning the sale of expropriated properties, for example, don Marcos de Arteaga purchased the hacienda of San Nicolás Buenavista, which was located to the north of Xochimilco and between Tlahuac and Mexicalzingo. Arteaga's investment included the lands, pastures, and waters of the estate, along with its houses, offices, and storehouses, among other structures, as well as its grains and livestock. All this amounted to a substantial investment of 63,677 pesos and six granos. Having made an initial payment, Arteaga secured credit from the government, at a rate of 5 percent over nine years, to pay for the outstanding sum of 29,000 pesos. And to make good on his investment, Arteaga sought to obtain more lands by expanding into the lakes. There he could convert swamps into pasture. The hacienda thus encroached into a swamp named Tempilula, which Nahuas of Santiago Zapotitlan and San Pedro Tlahuac claimed as their own, thereby provoking a lawsuit.[11]

The rise of haciendas involved various kinds of intervention in the lake area's hydrology. The earliest efforts by hacienda owners to modify the landscape date to the second half of the seventeenth century, in Chalco. There, hacendados sought to divert waters from rivers to their lands in the deep soil alluvium. In 1676, for instance, the government confirmed the permission granted first to don Diego de Villegas and then his son, don Fernando, to redirect water from the Rio de Amecameca into his fields. In this instance, the diversion of the water through two irrigation channels was merited on the grounds that the hacienda raised livestock and employed Nahua laborers. One important condition was attached to the grant, however: both men had to promise to close the channels during the rainy season so as to ease the flow of water and reduce the likelihood of flooding in the lakes. Not all efforts by hacendados to secure ample water for their estates succeeded. Three years later, the government summoned more than a dozen estate owners from Chalco to present their titles granting rights of access to water within fifteen days. Many of them had failed to do so, which prompted the government to ban them from taking water from the rivers on pain of a 500 peso fine.[12]

The hacendados' modifications of the landscape often took place at the point where the hills leveled off as they reached the deep soil alluvium. In the late seventeenth century, don José Olmedo y Lujan sought permission

---

[11] AGN, Tierras, vol. 1930, exp. 2, ff. 41–43v.
[12] AGN, Mercedes, vol. 58, ff. 123–123v; AGN, Mercedes, vol. 59, 2a pte., f. 280v (282v old foliation).

to relocate the royal road – which ran in a north-south direction to the west of Lake Xochimilco and through his hacienda of San Juan de Dios – because all the foot and hoof traffic had damaged his fields.[13] The new location, though, proved problematic. Olmedo reached an understanding with the government in which he could redirect the road so long as he built and maintained a bridge to span the San Agustín de las Cuevas River. This agreement had apparently been upheld during his time as the hacienda's proprietor.[14] In the first half of the eighteenth century, though, San Juan de Dios came into the possession of a new set of owners, the Gomendio family, who, unlike their predecessor, neglected to maintain the bridge. The problem was that the flow of water from the river running beneath it could become strong enough in the rainy season that it damaged the bridge (the high rate of discharge perhaps resulted from the increasingly common problem of soil erosion and deforestation in the hills above, although this was not entertained as a possibility at the time).[15] The bridge and the road both needed ongoing investments to keep them in good repair. In response, during the 1720s don Francisco de Aguirre Gomendio took to charging travelers a toll to use the bridge, the constant maintenance having proved to be so costly.[16] His exactions prompted a lawsuit before the audiencia that found in favor of the Nahuas of Xochimilco and Tepepan and that required Gomendio to shoulder the costs of repairs himself.[17] But the matter did not end there. The next owner, Gomendio's son, don Domingo de Gomendio Urrutia, was no less neglectful in his duty to maintain the roads. Not only did he continue to leave the bridge in a state of disrepair but he also closed off access to other paths across his estate. By 1753 things were so bad that Nahuas initiated another lawsuit. The bridge had now collapsed, itself becoming an obstacle to the flow of water from the river, the adjacent land thus flooded more severely. The royal road had become impassable.[18]

During the presentation of evidence for the 1753 lawsuit, it emerged that the problems with the bridge and the flooding were but a part of a wider manipulation of the flow of water down from the sierra. In a separate petition from 1736, for instance – which was entered into evidence in 1753 – don Domingo Gomendio blamed an upland estate,

---

[13] AGN, Tierras, vol. 3322, exp. 3 and 4; vol. 3208, exp. 1, ff. 1–675.
[14] AGN, Tierras, vol. 2429, exp. 1, cuad. 4, ff. 5–6.
[15] Gibson, *The Aztecs under Spanish Rule*, 303, 305.
[16] AGN, Tierras, vol. 2429, exp. 1, cuad. 4, ff. 4–4v, 8–8v, and 13v–15.
[17] AGN, Tierras, vol. 2429, exp. 1, cuad. 4, f. 8v.
[18] AGN, Tierras, vol. 2429, exp. 1, cuad. 4, ff. 1–22v.

the rancho named Ojo de Agua, for flooding his property and the village of Tepepan.[19] According to Gomendio, about six years earlier, the ranch had redirected the course of a creek that fed into the San Agustín de las Cuevas River. As a result, water had flowed a faster rate down to his estate, flooding its land, and putting passengers along the royal road in danger. Apparently, a Spaniard had drowned.[20] The court investigated these claims and determined that the water flowed down from the hill above Tepepan to a *caja*, a kind of storage tank. From this tank different groups sought to redirect the water for their own purposes. According to evidence gathered in the course of the investigation, Gomendio and the owner of the neighboring hacienda of La Noria had themselves been responsible for the flooding. Having allegedly conspired to change the flow of water – referred to as *avenidas de agua* – to prevent their lands from flooding, they had instead "foisted" the water onto the Nahuas of Tepepan. The Gomendios, one witness claimed, were to blame for the drowning of that unfortunate individual.[21]

Beyond manipulating rivers and creeks in the hills and creating irrigation works in the littoral, hacendados and their employees also altered the environment within the lakes themselves. Doing so was central to their efforts to extend their landholdings beyond the shore. The interventions involved demolishing chinampas and dredging soil from swamps, which in turn required the construction of various kinds of barriers in the lake. These barriers were called *albarradones* or, more often, *bordos*. Some of these earthen dams or levees may have been fairly substantial, made as they were with stone and concrete. But others were quite rudimentary. They consisted of soil and silt that had been built up and compacted and then held in place with twigs, sticks, and stakes. Crude though they may have been, they were nonetheless effective enough. They required little capital and minimal labor investments to build. These savings were of further value because some of the barriers were designed to be temporary. The purpose of the bordos was not to retain water within their limits, as had been the case with the hydraulic compartments of the chinampas. Rather, they were to keep the lake's waters out of the newly reclaimed lands. At the same time, they had to allow the new lands to drain into the lake, for which reason they had gates built into their sides. After an initial

---

[19] The ranch was located within the jurisdiction of San Agustín de las Cuevas. AGN, Tierras, vol. 1479, exp. 1, and vol. 2747, exp. 3.

[20] AGN, Tierras, vol. 2429, exp. 1, cuad. 3, f. 1.

[21] AGN, Tierras, vol. 2429, exp. 1, cuad. 4, ff. 4–9.

section of the lake had been successfully reclaimed – and once it had dried out sufficiently – the hacienda's staff would then push further into the lake and repeat the process by building another barrier, whereupon the old one could be dismantled. In this manner the haciendas pushed further into the lakes. In doing so, they disrupted drainage systems and engendered greater degrees of landscape instability.[22]

Most of these new lands were put to use as pastures. Of course, using lands in the lake for livestock was hardly a phenomenon new to the eighteenth century. In 1579, Bernardino Arias de Ávila had sought permission to obtain vacant chinampas in Michcalco to raise sheep and goats, and, as discussed in Chapter 2, Nahuas themselves introduced livestock of their own into the swamps, or *ciénegas*.[23] While the term *ciénega*, or *ciénaga*, had several meanings, in the eighteenth century it came to denote pastures in the lakes. Technically, a ciénega was a marsh or swamp – literally a place full of mud or silt (*cieno*) – but it came to be used more broadly as a wetland, which is to say as land distinct from the tierra firme but also not a chinampa. (A pasture, then, might be called a ciénega; also, it might have been made out of soil that had once been part of cluster of chinampas, but the ciénega itself was not a chinampa). One hacienda owner, don Domingo Gomendio, was simultaneously specific and ambiguous in identifying his ciénega. He stated that it was neither lake nor tierra firme.[24] This in-between quality owed much to the moisture of the land. The solidity or viscosity of a ciénega varied according to whether it was the rainy season or not. When the conditions were suitable, some communities and individuals cultivated maize and even wheat on them.

Native communities often had ciénegas of their own. They might generate useful rental income. In 1732, for instance, the governor of Xochimilco, don Nicolás de la Cruz, and his fellow cabildo officers negotiated the rental of a plot of swampy land ("tierra sienegoso") a caballería in size. Don Joseph Braceros, a Spaniard, agreed to drain the plot at his own expense because he wanted to grow wheat.[25] It was unusual for someone to go to the trouble of cultivating wheat on these ciénegas, though. Their more common use was as land for grazing

---

[22] This was a process that was not confined just to Lakes Xochimilco and Chalco. For Iztapalapa, see AGN, Tierras, vol. 2252, exp. 8, ff. 1, 15, 23v–24v.

[23] AGN, Tierras, vol. 2681, exp. 6, ff. 65–84v.

[24] AGN, Tierras, vol. 2429, exp. cuad. 2, ff. 1–2.

[25] AGNM, Xochimilco, vol. 1, ff. 122–123v.

livestock. The term *ciénega* often appeared interchangeably with pasture and paddock (*pasto* and *potrero*).[26]

If some of the ciénegas were naturally occurring, seasonal wetlands, located along the shore, others had been fashioned deliberately from the lakes, which explains the need for all the environmental engineering. Some even consisted of former chinampas. In the papers of one lawsuit, the ciénega in an area named Yxtepan, according to the governor of Tlahuac, don Pablo Juan, had once been the site of chinampas. The governor indicated that they had been converted into pastures to generate income.[27] Often such income came through rentals. Those entering into contracts with Xochimilco and other towns did so at their own risk: the danger was that the drained land might not always remain dry, as José del Castillo discovered to his dismay in the early 1780s, when he rented a ciénega from Xochimilco. He complained about his oxen and cows getting stuck in the mud. Clearly the land was less well suited to ranching in the rainy season.[28] Castillo, frustrated in his attempt to make money from rearing livestock in the watery lands, petitioned the authorities for permission to open up a drainage ditch, or *zanja*. The administrator of the neighboring hacienda of San Antonio Coapa opposed this proposal, though, arguing that it would be prejudicial to his estate's drainage system. Castillo's efforts were further thwarted by the awkward location of his proposed ditch at the dividing line between the jurisdictions of Xochimilco and Culhuacan. Faced with these obstacles, Castillo abandoned his lease, failed to pay rent, and left Xochimilco without valuable income for a number of years.[29] Because the rentals of pastures had provided significant income, the city campaigned for payment for two decades.[30]

---

[26] AGN, Tierras, vol. 1597, exp. 2, f. 41.   [27] AGN, Tierras, vol. 1597, exp. 2, ff. 30–30v.
[28] Alternatively, Castillo may have been unfortunate in his timing: he might have made a decision to raise livestock in the lakes on the basis of a drier climate only to find, in the 1780s, that wetter conditions prevailed. AGN, Tierras, vol. 1618, exp. 1, cuad. 3, f. 2.
[29] In response, the city's officials long campaigned for restitution. Their efforts were repeatedly thwarted. First, it proved difficult to have Castillo's property impounded because, as a priest, he claimed the ecclesiastic privilege of being beyond the jurisdiction of civil courts. The high court ruled against him, though. His appeal then dragged on for several more years, during which time he passed away, and so Xochimilco sought satisfaction from his guarantor, Captain don Francisco Ramos. When he in turn died without having settled the debt, Xochimilco's woes continued. His widow refused to make payment, arguing that the conditions of her dowry prevented her from incurring her husband's debts, and, besides, as the audiencia determined, she had slid into penury and was living in a miserable state in Mexico City. AGN, Tierras, vol. 1618, exp. 1, cuad. 1, ff. 1–75 and 93–98, and cuad. 3, ff. 1–9.
[30] In this case, the city was owed a total of 2,620 pesos and seven tomines. AGN, Tierras, vol. 1618, exp. 1, cuad. 1, f. 60.

Some of the lands leased by communities were explicitly set aside for livestock rearing. In 1729, the former corregidor of Xochimilco, don Bernardo de la Maza Riva – who returned to the jurisdiction as the new owner of the hacienda of La Noria – became embroiled in a dispute with the Nahua cabildo for failure to pay annual rent of 100 pesos for the ciénega named San Diego. As the governor Juan Luis Cortés explained, the rental of the ciénega included a slaughterhouse's *tajón*, which is to say the equipment used for butchering animals, in Xochimilco. The rental was specifically intended for those who had obtained the quasi-monopolistic right (*obligado*) to supply meat to the capital (the *abasto de carne*) from Mexico City's cabildo.[31] José del Castillo, the delinquent renter of Xochimilco's ciénega in the 1780s, had likewise held the abasto rights.[32]

The rentals could be sufficiently lucrative as to engender animosity between neighboring communities. The location of territorial limits served as a common source of controversy. This was the case in 1778. Ayotzingo claimed that portions of a ciénega fell within its territorial waters, specifically the places named La Tortuga, Piedras Coloradas, El Arbolito, and Acolocalco (interestingly, for such a late date, the parcels of land still retained their Nahuatl names, as with Yxtepan and Comalchic). A judge noted, though, that the swampy land's "inconstant identity" complicated the determination of its boundaries, a problem not helped by the communities' lack of titles. The inspection formed part of a wider set of disputes that ran until 1800 between Tlahuac, Mixquic, and Ayotzingo over two ciénegas. One of the disputes, over the ciénega of Nanahuizco, stemmed from competing claims over ownership. The land was used to raise livestock or to grow maize. The other one, named Santo Domingo, was rented out exclusively to the abasto holders, all of whom were Spaniards living nearby. Tlahuac and Mixquic fought over who should receive the proceeds of the annual rental income, for which Mixquic sought forty pesos and Tlahuac seventy. The papers of the lawsuits, including witness testimonies, specified that cattle were being

---

[31] AGN, Tierras, vol. 2252, exp. 13, f. 1. See also Ivonne Mijares, *Mestizo alimentario: El abasto de la ciudad de México en el siglo XVI* (Mexico City: UNAM, 1993); William H. Dusenberry, "The Regulation of Meat Supply in Sixteenth-Century Mexico City," *Hispanic American Historical Review*, vol. 28, no. 1 (1948), 38–52; Jeffrey M. Pilcher, *The Sausage Rebellion: Public Health, Private Enterprise, and Meat in Mexico City, 1890–1917* (Albuquerque: University of New Mexico Press, 2006), 25–27.

[32] AGN, Tierras, vol. 1618, exp. 1, cuad. 1, f. 9 and cuad. 3, ff. 2v, 12.

kept on pastures, and part of the dispute had to do with the great number of them and their straying onto different altepetl's lands.[33]

Such were the ciénegas' value that disputes over them not only set Native communities against one another but also dragged them into conflicts against expanding haciendas. In the early 1800s, Xochimilco's long-standing difficulties over the ciénega for which José del Castillo had failed to pay rent morphed into a more serious dispute with owners of the neighboring hacienda of San Antonio Coapa, which once again dragged on for many years. The origins of the dispute went far back into the eighteenth century, and it lasted until don Juan de Noriega took possession of the hacienda in 1809. Before the rental to Castillo, Xochimilco had held the ciénega under usufruct arrangements.[34] When Castillo forfeited the rental agreement and abandoned the land, these communal rights resumed. But during the transition, the rival hacendado had moved to claim the wetlands as his own. The hacienda's staff sought to take effective possession of the land by introducing cattle.[35] The maneuver was a shrewd one. The hacendado's lawyer could argue that the land had been vacant and that his client had therefore obtained legitimate possession through effective use. The hacendado's position seemed stronger, at least for a brief moment, when Xochimilco was unable to present title proving its ownership of the ciénega.

What followed next were a series of rebuttals by Xochimilco's cabildo officers and their legal representatives. The hacienda itself could not provide title to the land, they noted, and its claim to effective use rights were undermined by three important pieces of evidence. The first of these was the lawsuit against José del Castillo over the rental arrears. This in itself demonstrated prior use and ownership. Secondly, Xochimilco's residents had in fact resumed their use of the ciénega after Castillo abandoned it, and they did so in ways that were clearly demonstrable: they had reconverted the ciénega back into chinampas. Thirdly, the Nahuas called on witnesses who could testify that, in the distant past, the land had indeed been the property of the city. One of them, a lieutenant named don José Ortiz, a Spanish vecino of Xochimilco, recalled that many years ago the governors of the altepetl had themselves covered the rent of the ciénega, with the income going to the city's coffers. A second witness, who was

---

[33] AGN, Tierras, vol. 1597, exp. 2, ff. 1, 2v, 14, 16, 20v, 21v, 23, 24v, 30, and 47v.
[34] AGN, Tierras, vol. 1618, exp. 1, cuad. 1, ff. 2, 14.
[35] AGN, Tierras, vol. 1618, exp. 1, cuad. 3, ff. 21–21v; AGN, Tierras, vol. 1591, exp. 6, ff. 269–269v.

a fellow Spanish citizen of Xochimilco, corroborated this information and added that the rent had once been 700 pesos a year and that, since 1737, it had been covered by the governors, whom he remembered clearly as having been don Juan López and then don Sebastián Tepito and don Sebastián de la Cruz.[36]

In 1809, though, after Noriega had taken over the hacienda's ownership, the employees resorted to ever more aggressive tactics to seize land from Xochimilco. They introduced yet more cattle into the ciénega – this time 800 of them – and one of the hacienda's subalterns resorted to violence against Nahuas from the barrio of the Assumption, who had been gathering zacatl there. Xochimilco's governor warned the *subdelegado* (district officer) that he feared the local population might rise up against the hacienda. While the judge ordered that the new owner desist from fashioning ranches from the ciénega, tensions persisted, and the lawsuit remained unresolved at least as late as 1816, during which time violence against haciendas had broken out as part of the wider breakdown of law and order during the independence-era insurgency against Spanish rule.[37]

The severity of the dispute over the ciénega speaks to the extent to which ranching had become a crucial economic activity within the lakes, which themselves were becoming ever more ecologically oriented toward pastoralism. The sheer number of cattle introduced into the lake areas indicated this. Many head of cattle were recorded besides the 800 Noriega introduced into the ciénega in 1809. Back in the 1780s, Castillo had populated the same land with 1,600 cattle.[38] And before that, in 1762, some 2,000 cattle were ordered to be removed from Tlahuac in order for repairs to be made to the channels through the lakes.[39] So common had pastoralism become in the lake areas that a bridge was called "Las Vacas."[40] The bridge may have been erected specifically to allow the passage of the livestock; a raised road located within La Noria was labeled on a map as being the place where livestock entered the ciénega.[41]

The incursion of haciendas into the lakes, and the conversion of waters into swampy pastures by Nahuas and Spaniards, provided an additional

[36] AGN, Tierras, vol. 1618, exp. 1, cuad. 5, ff. 11–12, 15v, and 17v–18.

[37] AGN, Tierras, vol. 1618, exp. 1, cuad. 5, ff. 1, 2–2v, 4, and 10. For more on the lawsuit against Noriega in 1816, see AGN, Tierras, vol. 1591, exp. 6; for references to violence against haciendas, see AGN Tierras, vol. 3708.

[38] AGN, Tierras, vol. 1618, exp. 1, cuad. 1, f. 9.   [39] AGN, Desagüe, vol. 16, exp. 7, f. 55.

[40] AGN, Tierras, vol. 1618, exp. 1, cuad. 4, f. 3.

[41] See item 26 on the map found in AGN, Tierras, vol. 2429, exp. 1, cuad. 5, f. 21bis.

layer of complexity to human interactions with the lacustrine environment. Whereas previously Nahua communities might have been at odds with one another over the boundaries of their land or water, they nevertheless conceived of the uses and management of the lakes from a position of consensus, agreeing that water be regulated to enable chinampa cultivation and that flood protection measures be coordinated for the well-being of the region as a whole. The rise of lacustrine pastoralism upended this. Now there were divergent attitudes toward the lake resources as well as different conceptions of how the lakes could be harnessed and modified. The relations between the Nahuas of Tlahuac and the hacienda of San Nicolás Buenavista exemplify these competing perspectives. What connected the parties was the single large ciénega named Tempilula. On one level, the Nahua communities sought to defend their claims to the swamp against the owners of the former Jesuit hacienda, whose agents stood accused of moving or removing boundary markers – among them trees and tezontle boulders – in the months leading up to the litigation in 1799. The dispute also involved complaints by the Nahuas that, as a reprisal for having opposed the hacienda's trespasses, its staff had stolen fifteen cattle. On another level, though, the competing groups vied over access to the diverse resources afforded by the swamp. Nahuas had long enjoyed customary access to the reeds that proliferated there. The swamp was also home to several fishing grounds, which the Nahuas likewise claimed as their own. Now, with the hacienda encroaching into Tempilula, the diversity of the ciénega, with its pools, was under the threat of being reduced, via drainage to lands used solely for grazing goats and sheep.[42]

Disputes over the peculiar issue of which parts of the lake ought to remain watery became increasingly common in the second half of the eighteenth century. The lake area's hydrology also became increasingly difficult to manage given the competing interests and engineering works of Nahua communities and haciendas. In spite of the use of dams and gates around pastures, the fields might quickly rehydrate during the rainy season. The refilling of the ciénegas with water meant that hacendados had to open up networks of ditches, drains, and channels to redirect the flow of water around their land and into the lake. The works that proved advantageous to one hacienda or community might prove detrimental to another. Such complexities were revealed in a series of problems in Chalco Atenco in 1763.

[42] AGN, Tierras, vol. 1930, exp. 2, ff. 2–3v, 9–9v, 45–47, 69–69v, and 79.

The first years of the decade had seen unusually heavy rains during the monsoon seasons. Those who gave testimony in an investigation were clear about this, and the tree-ring data compiled by the Mexican Drought Atlas indicate a spike in moisture levels for those years.[43] By 1763, the waterlogged areas around the lake – which a judge described as a quagmire – began to overflow. Part of the problem was that the water flowing into the lake now did so at places that could not cope with the greater volume. The shifts in the discharge of water into the lake were caused by haciendas in the upland areas and along the shore. In the montes, two hacendados had altered the course of a river as it passed through some *barrancas* (ravines) on the way down to the lake. One of the hacendados diverted some of the water to create small reservoirs in a place called Nextipa, which he could then use to irrigate his lands. The lake-shore hacienda of San Joseph, meanwhile, which was owned and administered by the Jesuits, had opened up ditches to drain water out of some pastures. At the same time, the hacienda also redirecting some of the water from the Rio de Chalco by creating a canal, which passed under the royal road, to ensure the hacienda's embarcadero had enough water to remain operational.[44]

The unintended consequences of these three alterations were striking. For one thing, the water from the river now flowed along new courses and did so with enough force, as witnesses claimed, to wash away a bridge along the royal road. For another, the new outlet from the river combined with the new canal to cause flooding along the lakeshore and, more harmfully, in Chalco Atenco itself. So bad was the flooding there that the plaza, some 18,000 square varas in area, was submerged in half a vara of water. The repairs to both the bridge and to the plaza, which was to be raised a vara higher with the construction of a new terrace, proved costly.[45]

The circumstances of climate variation, local geography, and the competing demands of haciendas, Nahua communities, and the owners of embarcaderos also contributed to flooding a few years later in nearby Ayotzingo. In 1776, don Diego José Baquedano contacted the authorities to express his concern about silt being deposited from the river that flowed into the lake. Deforestation may again have been a contributing factor in

---

[43] See the online Mexican Drought Atlas at http://drought.memphis.edu/MXDA/Default.aspx (accessed January 18, 2021).
[44] AGN, Desagüe, vol. 16, exp. 8, ff. 2, 7, and 14–14v.
[45] AGN, Desagüe, vol. 16, exp. 8, ff. 9v, 27, 58v, 66, 76–80; AGN, Desagüe, vol. 16, exp. 10.

this although, as Bradley Skopyk has observed, climatic conditions, shifting land use, and hydraulic engineering projects contributed to rising amounts of sediment transportation.[46] Baquedano owned the embarcadero of Nuestra Señora de la Soledad at the entrance to the town. He had witnessed firsthand the silting of the pool at his docks. The docks would eventually need to be dredged if canoes were to continue to disembark there. The issue of the sedimentation, Baquedano suggested, came from the soil suspended in the discharge of water flowing through haciendas.[47] In the investigation that followed, government engineers identified further silting at the mouth of the river: the main channel divided into two courses, called *brazos*, as they approached the lake, and both of them were seen as being too narrow and shallow (precisely because of the silting) to accommodate the flow of water. For this reason, the river had topped its banks and the adjacent community of San Pablo had been inundated the year before. Notably, there had been a significant increase in rainfall at that time.[48] Making matters worse, the banks themselves were unstable, and without them being shored up with boards, erosion would continue to add to the problem of mud and soil filling up parts of the lake. The government inspector identified a further threat. An "albarradonsillo," or small dike, along the edge of another embarcadero was in need of repair, and if its owner, don Juan Francisco de Sotomayor did not fix it, Ayotzingo might flood.[49]

The government ordered Sotomayor and the hacendado to complete the construction works. The most substantial part of the project was designed to shore up the river's outlet so as to prevent flooding and ensure the unimpeded movement of people and goods through the lake area's transportation network. On the one hand, the canoes and the embarcaderos of Ayotzingo were important to the provisioning of Mexico City, particularly with the lucrative trade in sugar and honey from Quautla Amilpas. On the other, flooding along the shore would damage the royal road – a problem that was now becoming chronic around the lakes – and thereby obstruct overland transportation, especially when it came to the movement of livestock. Of particular concern was the lack of a bridge near the mouth of the river.[50] A year later, the government conducted an

---

[46] Skopyk, *Colonial Cataclysms*, 204.   [47] AGN, Desagüe, vol. 20, exp. 2, ff. 1–2.

[48] Mexican Drought Atlas at http://drought.memphis.edu/MXDA/Default.aspx (accessed January 18, 2021).

[49] AGN, Desagüe, vol. 20, exp. 2, ff. 11v–13v and 28–30.

[50] AGN, Desagüe, vol. 20, exp. 2, ff. 3, 25.

inspection of the engineering works it had requested. Not only had Sotomayor failed to repair the dike, the local landowners had also neglected to reinforce or widen the channels of the river. If anything, one of them had made matters worse: don José Fernández Paiba had rented land along the river from Ayotzingo, then took it upon himself to alter the irrigation system, doing so by dividing one of the two outlets of the river, which then channeled the flow of water toward Ayotzingo. As a result, the town's cemetery, church, embarcadero, and central plaza were submerged in floodwaters.[51]

Reflecting on the complexity of the situation, the owner of the embarcadero, Baquedano, made a particularly astute observation. He responded to the announcement of the proposed engineering works by pointing out that there was a distinct possibility that preventing flooding in one location near the river might only serve to make it more likely to happen somewhere else. His prescient note could have been applied to other parts of the lake and, by the nineteenth century, much of the southern lakes' overall hydrology.[52]

Central to the problems of flooding were the multiple overlapping, contradictory, and competing interests of the government, rival hacendados, and Nahua communities when it came to harnessing the lake environment. In the absence of centralized planning and coordination – as there had been with the Aztec Empire's conversion of the southern lakes into the chinampa districts – independent hydraulic works advanced by different groups ended up working against each other and exacerbating problems. The results included the accumulation of layer upon layer of ever more elaborate and conflicting local irrigation projects. Even as lake-area residents continued to rely on the old Aztec barriers and channels so they added to them in new and conflicting ways.

DESAGÜE AND A WATERLOGGED LANDSCAPE

The haciendas' effects on the lacustrine environment became a cause for concern for the government from the late 1740s because of fears of flooding in the capital. Those fears had been reawakened in 1747 after a prolonged period of unusually heavy rainfall.[53] The heightened sense of danger served as a powerful reminder that the centuries-long desagüe, to drain the northern lakes through the outlet at Huehuetoca, had only been

---

[51] AGN, Desagüe, vol. 20, exp. 2, ff. 33–34v.   [52] AGN, Desagüe, vol. 20, exp. 2, f. 15.
[53] AGN, Tierras, vol. 2429, exp. 1, cuad. 1, ff. 46–47.

of limited success. For all the expense and effort invested in the drainage works, the fundamental threat of inundation in the capital remained. As a result, the government deployed a cadre of experts and engineers – among them surveyors, impressively named *agrimensors*, "master architects," and *philo-matemáticos*, among others – to manage and extend the drainage projects and to marshal the resources necessary to protect Mexico City. The reinvigorated efforts were led by one particularly dedicated official, don Domingo de Trespalacios y Escandón. His supervision of the desagüe signaled a shift in Lakes Xochimilco and Chalco away from the neglect that had long characterized the government's attitude to the hydraulic system in the southern lakes.[54]

Just as the incursion of haciendas into the lakes and the conversion of swamps into pastures began to undermine the ecological autonomy of the chinampa districts, so the Nahuas' autonomy over matters of water management now also went into sharp decline. Whereas once the indigenous inhabitants of the region had provided expertise and instruction about the control of water – crucial intelligence that over the centuries had been coopted by outsiders – now they were marginalized by Trespalacios and his cohort of experts.[55] When the government solicited advice from local residents about the irrigation network, it increasingly did so by turning to Spaniards. Decisions about supervising repair works and deploying laborers were no longer devolved to Nahua cabildos. Instead, Trespalacios and his agents took charge.

For Trespalacios, the perceived threat of inundation in 1747 highlighted the general need for a *reconocimiento*, or survey, of the southern lake areas to determine how best to manage the water there. A second, more immediate and specific issue explained his 1748 survey. On March 23, don Domingo de Gomendio Urrutia, the owner of San Juan de Dios, filed a petition against an order issued by one of Trespalacios's subordinates in an ongoing dispute over the estate's irrigation system. At issue was the function of a bordo around a ciénega that Gomendio used as a pasture.[56] The government's representative had demanded that the hacendado remove the dam. Gomendio opposed this, arguing that to do it would be to risk flooding first his hacienda and then, more menacingly, Mexico City. This wider threat, Trespalacios and his colleagues determined, warranted a proper investigation of the water management

[54] Candiani, *Dreaming of Dry Land*, 16.
[55] Candiani, *Dreaming of Dry Land*, 150–151.
[56] AGN, Tierras, vol. 2429, exp. cuad. 2, ff. 1–2.

programs of the southern lakes within the overall hydrology of the Basin of Mexico. Valuable in and of itself, the reconocimiento also served to answer the specific question about the hacienda's dam. It so happened that this survey ended up serving as a template by which decisions about the desagüe in the southern lakes would be made for the next two decades.

The basic premise underpinning the survey was that the threat posed by the southern lakes to Mexico City was marginal in comparison with Lakes Tetzcoco, Zumpango, and Xaltocan (or what little remained of them). Moreover, no drainage outlet like that at Huehuetoca could be excavated in the south, given the surrounding mountains, which meant that the basic issue was one of regulating water levels through carefully managed drainage rather than the removal of the water altogether. Additionally, Trespalacios and his colleagues concluded that flooding in the southern lake areas served as a precursor to flooding in the capital. Essentially, if the waters were to build up in Lakes Xochimilco and Chalco too much, they might reach the point where they would surge northward and overwhelm Mexico City. Consequently, the government had to ensure that the engineering works allowed for water to enter the lakes from its points of origin – primarily from the surrounding springs and the rivers – and then pass freely through the lakes themselves, via the acalotes and the royal canal, before draining at a gradual but gentle and manageable rate through the sluicegates at Mexicalzingo and into Lake Tetzcoco. Rather than rushing toward Mexico City, the flow would enter Lake Tetzcoco gently and harmlessly. From there it could be directed toward the outlet at Huehuetoca.

To promote this goal, Trespalacios insisted that water courses through the southern lakes be made to flow as freely as possible. The movement of water might be blocked by vegetation or other debris, by silt clogging up the canals, or by the canals' sides collapsing through erosion. The heightened rainfall of the monsoon season posed a particular risk. For these reasons, Trespalacios was later adamant that the flooding in Chalco Atenco in 1763 be considered a sign of problems within the wider drainage system. The investigation into what happened at the altepetl led to the conclusion that the channels across the southern lakes were not flowing freely and that, as a result, they may have contributed to the localized flooding.[57] Accordingly, Trespalacios ordered that canals near and far be cleared of their impediments. The work was to done by Native residents under the supervision of their town council officers and at the overall

[57] AGN, Desagüe, vol. 16, exp. 8, f. 65.

direction of don Diego de Baena, one of the superintendent's staff members. Several weeks later Trespalacios wanted to verify that the channels were flowing again. He dispatched don Ildephonso de Iniesta Vejarano, master architect and agrimensor, to investigate. Iniesta set out on October 7 from Chalco and made for Ayotzingo, where he met with the Nahuas of that altepetl and of Mixquic and Tlahuac. They apprised him of the work done, and together they all passed through the lakes as far as Tlahuac. They found no remaining impediments.[58]

Just as the canals had to remain free of impediments to the flow of water, so haciendas also had to allow for the ready discharge of water into the royal canal, which now functioned as the main drainage channel for the southern lakes. At seemingly every estate Trespalacios visited – among them San Antonio Coapa, los Agueguetes, and San Juan de Dios – he determined that all gates and ditches be kept open or closed in such a way so as to ease the flow of water.[59] This goal was especially desirable in the rainy season, as Trespalacios noted of the Jesuit hacienda of San Joseph, which had been partly responsible for the flooding of Chalco Atenco.[60] The same priorities informed Trespalacio's approach to his dispute with don Domingo de Gomendio Urrutia, the owner of San Juan de Dios, who had opposed the order to remove the dam around the ciénega.[61] This controversy had provided the immediate occasion for Trespalacios to conduct his survey in 1748, and it remained an ongoing issue more than five years later when it became the subject of further litigation.

A new lawsuit of 1753 reflected the complexities of contestations between the desagüe authorities, the Native communities of Tepepan and Xochimilco, and the owners of the rival haciendas of San Juan de Dios and La Noria. The case consisted of two main parts. The first had to do with the ways in which water from the natural springs in the hills entered into Lake Xochimilco. Apparently dissatisfied by the earlier ruling, the new owner of San Juan de Dios, don Pedro Antonio de Quintela, lodged a new complaint against Tepepan for causing flooding on his hacienda. He alleged that the Nahuas had redirected water from the springs by constructing a dam and a ditch. Whereas once the water flowed to Xochimilco's ciénega to the east, now it inundated his lands. He

[58] AGN, Desagüe, vol. 16, exp. 8, ff. 61–62.
[59] AGN, Tierras, vol. 2429, exp. 1, cuad. 4, f. 43v.
[60] AGN, Desagüe, vol. 16, exp. 8, f. 54v.
[61] AGN, Tierras, vol. 2429, exp. cuad. 2, ff. 1–2.

invoked the specter of flooding in the capital. Taking the threat seriously, Trespalacios sent the master architect don Manuel Álvarez to investigate.[62] Since the fact of the flooding on the estate was incontestable, and since there were indeed new engineering works, Trespalacios ordered the Nahuas to remove them and rehabilitate the old ones. At this point in the proceedings, though, the Nahuas gained concessions of their own. These included a resolution to the long-standing problem with the royal road. Traffic along it had long been impeded by flooding and the poor state of the bridge across the river. By the 1750s, as noted previously, the bridge had collapsed. Now the Nahuas of Xochimilco and Tepepan successfully sued Quintela to pay for the rebuilding of this bridge, and they won a victory against him that other engineering works, from the 1730s, which redirected spring water, also be dismantled.[63]

The second part of the 1753 lawsuit had to do with changes to the ditches, canals, dams, and gates that regulated the flow of water into and around the ciénegas down in the lake. The underlying impetus for the alterations to the irrigation system there had to do with the creation of livestock ranches. The ciénegas were divided into four sections, those of Xochimilco, La Noria, Tepepan, and San Juan de Dios. Added to these four interested parties was a fifth: the desagüe authorities. While the government sought to impose its own conception of a coherent, overarching plan for the lake during the course of the lawsuit, it did so only after the Nahua communities and the hacendados had already constructed their own hydraulic works. These works did not necessarily serve the same ends as the government's. Furthermore, while a set of engineering works might prove advantageous to one group, they might simultaneously be prejudicial to the others, which meant that rivals responded by adding new hydraulic works of their own. The results of these competing visions and interests took the form, on the ground, of a chaotic mix of old and new engineering works that modified the natural features of the landscape, among them the natural springs and streams (*veneros*) that issued from the hill at Tepepan, the pastures and swamps below them and then, further away, the royal canal and the chinampa districts of Xochimilco. All these things were set down on a map, from 1754, that formed an essential part of the lawsuit (Map 6.1).

---

[62] AGN, Tierras, vol. 2429, exp. 1, cuad. 1, ff. 1–2.
[63] AGN, Tierras, vol. 2429, exp. 1, cuad. 3, ff. 4–9; cuad. 1, ff. 4–4v.

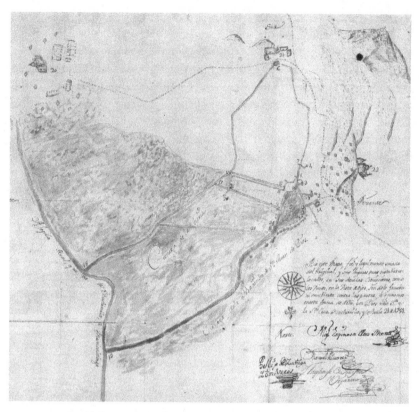

MAP 6.1 Map of the Ciénega and the Haciendas La Noria and San Juan de Dios.
By permission of the Archivo General de la Nación, Tierras, vol. 2429, exp. 1,
cuad. 5, f. 21bis.

Since the map is oriented with north at the bottom, Xochimilco is
located at the top left (labeled number 20). In the center were the
ciénegas and chinampas of Xochimilco, below them the ciénega of la
Noria – divided by two channels – and then the ciénega of San Juan de
Dios. Tepepan appears to the right, which is to say the west (number 22).
The acequia real appears on the far left, fed in two places by acalotes
running either side of La Noria (18 and 19). The lower channel, the
Acalote of San Bartolomé, was one of the key issues addressed in the
litigation. This channel and other hydraulic works can be seen in the detail
from Map 6.2.

In addition to the Acalote de San Bartolomé, the lawsuit also closely
considered the function of the dam (number 12), which bordered San Juan

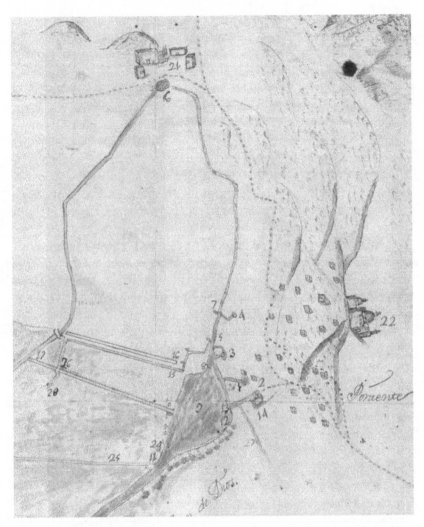

MAP 6.2 Detail from map of the Ciénega and the Haciendas La Noria and San Juan de Dios. By permission of the Archivo General de la Nación, Tierras, vol. 2429, exp. 1, cuad. 5, f. 21bis.

de Dios, and the gate across the ditch that entered La Noria (number ten, which is just to the left of number 9).

Since Quintela, the owner of San Juan de Dios, had already successfully defended his rights to having a dam for his ciénega (12), Trespalacios instead required that the water flowing down from the springs and into Tepepan's ciénega be released elsewhere. With San Juan de Dios now closed off, Trespalacios ordered the gate across the drainage ditch (10) on the other side be opened. Any excess water would henceforth drain into the ciénega of La Noria. The estate's owner, don Juan García Trujillo, vigorously opposed this decision for precisely the same reason that Quintela had. As with Quintela, Trujillo claimed that the redirection of the drainage to his pastures would go on to pose a threat to capital, albeit via a different route.[64] At its very core, then, the lawsuit boiled down to a seemingly straightforward, binary choice: release water through either a dam into San Juan de Dios or through the gate and ditch into La Noria. The fact of the matter was that both haciendas could not simultaneously be free from the risk of flooding and that to guarantee the security of one against the threat of being submerged would be to condemn the other to inundation. In effect, it was a zero-sum game.

The apparent simplicity of the options, however, was belied by a long series of secondary considerations. Among them was the question of how the Acalote of San Bartolomé interacted with the ciénegas and the drainage patterns. Could it cope with the flow of water from the hills? Would its flow into the acequia release too much water at once and put Mexico City in danger? These questions, and others, formed the heart of a second inspection in response to Trujillo's opposition to Trespalacios's order.[65] The answers to these questions quickly became very complicated. They depended on a series of variables, among them the length of the acalotes, the direction in which the water flowed, the rate of flow through the channels, and the pressure of the water, which in turn involved figuring out the dimensions of the channels, including their depth. The elevation and gradient of different parts of the landscape also needed to be understood properly in order to predict the water's flow into and beyond the ciénegas. If all this were not complicated enough, Trespalacios's experts had to calculate the variable merits of different combinations of the engineering works. For this there were innumerable permutations. How would each part interact with another, and then how would the entire system work together? A key factor in this determination was the age of the engineering works: which barriers or ditches were old or new? What did these works do? When had they done it, and to what effect?[66]

---

[64] AGN, Tierras, vol. 2429, exp. 1, cuad. 1, ff. 10–10v
[65] AGN, Tierras, vol. 2429, exp. 1, cuad. 1, ff. 11–11v.
[66] The results of this inquiry can be found in AGN, Tierras, vol. 2429, exp. 1, cuad. 1, ff. 23–51v. The inquiry itself forms the material in AGN, Tierras, vol. 2429, exp. 1, cuad. 5, ff. 13–37 and then 37v–50v.

In other words, a host of questions swirled around the issue of historical precedent. The owner of La Noria, Trujillo, maintained that his land should not be inundated because the original hydraulic works had not included an opening into his estate. In early 1754, the audiencia agreed that the very antiquity of the dams and dikes surrounding Trujillo's property, which he had scarcely altered, shored up his position.[67] The investigation, as such, ended up trying to uncover the earlier layers of the irrigation network. And yet for all the experts' interest in looking back into the landscape's past, their point of view remained strangely myopic: no one pointed out that the original hydraulic works would have served to protect chinampas, not the pastures that had recently been fashioned from the lake. Even so, the government agents were clear in recognizing that the ciénegas were not simply a pristine environment. One even referred specifically to the "environment's artificial land."[68] In any case, the audiencia eventually ruled in June 1755 that the new gate to Trujillo's pasture be kept sealed and that Trespalacios's earlier order be revoked. The deciding issue, for all the complexity of the case, was the overriding one of how best to protect Mexico City from flooding. The implications of this for Quintela, Tepepan, Xochimilco, or for that matter, Trujillo, were of secondary and marginal interest.[69]

The same priority of protecting Mexico City informed other decisions by Trespalacios and the desagüe authorities elsewhere in the southern lakes.[70] Central to this overriding issue was the causeway across Tlahuac. This key defensive barrier, which also served as a road and as a portal through which canoes passed, was widely recognized for its great value in regulating the southern lakes' waters. Don Antonio de Leca, for instance, who was charged with supervising its maintenance, understood that the raised road had been important since the pre-conquest period.[71] In November 1763, when Trespalacions turned his attention to rehabilitating the calzada, he was acutely aware of the flooding just a few months earlier in Chalco Atenco and, two years before that, in Churubusco. These floods had spurred the government

---

[67] AGN, Tierras, vol. 2429, exp. 1, cuad. 1, ff. 15–21, 23v, 26v, and 37.

[68] The original phrasing was "el ambito de la artificiosa tierra," AGN, Tierras, vol. 2429, exp. 1, cuad. 4, f. 45.

[69] AGN, Tierras, vol. 2429, exp. 1, cuad 4, ff. 51–51v.

[70] The heavy rains over three consecutive years at the beginning of the 1760s, for instance, emphasized the persistent danger of flooding for the capital and once again called attention to inadequate flood defenses. AGN, Desagüe, vol. 16, exp. 9, f. 1.

[71] AGN, Desagüe, vol. 20, exp. 4, f. 14.

to renew its efforts to clean the canals.[72] More than routine maintenance was now called for, Trespalacios concluded. He had previously earmarked the calzada for repairs, having seen its ruined state, after so many years of abandonment, during his reconocimiento of 1748. The causeway's value, as an ancient and substantial structure – which is to say as a key element in the area's landesque capital – had begun to diminish even as the waters were rising. In 1763, Trespalacios commissioned a new survey, conducted by Iniesta, who estimated that the work to be done would cost some 24,000 pesos (along with an additional 6,000 pesos if the calzada's top were to be paved). This substantial investment, Iniesta averred, was needed because the calzada was in such a poor state that several sections of its 106-cordel (i.e., 5,200-vara) span were fully submerged.[73] The reconstruction would entail building it higher – using earth and stone – and making it wider and therefore more resilient. Three of the gates passing through it, moreover, needed to be repaired. Two of them were located at the far ends of the calzada, in Tolyahualco and San Francisco Tlaltenco (on the northern shore), and the third was to be adjacent to the town of Tlahuac. Iniesta further recommended that, in order to gain the maximum benefit from the reconstruction work, other projects in adjacent areas would also be needed. Among these were repairs of the barrier across the exit of Lake Xochimilco from Mexicalzingo and over to Churubusco. Additionally, Inieista called for the excavation of a ditch from Culhuacan to Iztapalapa and the removal of several dikes on the western side of Lake Xochimilco, which began at the Acalote of San Bartolomé (apparently the same canal dividing La Noria and San Juan de Dios).[74]

As was so often the case with the desagüe, the proposed repairs were only partially realized. On this occasion, bureaucratic inertia and lack of funds did not fully explain the delays. In 1764 heavy rains had destroyed more of the calzada, placing the capital at further risk, and then later, in 1775, further precipitation had brought yet more damage, with breaches opening up in the embankment's side; some of the trees used to reinforce it had also perished.[75] In addition, a 300-vara stretch of the superstructure was ruined, and more such damage could be expected because the calzada was no longer high enough to avoid being overtopped by floodwaters. Because of its poor condition, the drainage in the surrounding area had

---

[72] AGN, Desagüe, vol. 16, exp. 8; AGN, Desagüe, vol. 16, exp. 9, f. 2.
[73] For the vara measurement, see AGN, Desagüe, vol. 20, exp. 4, f. 5.
[74] AGN, Desagüe, vol. 16, exp. 9, ff. 3v–8.
[75] AGN, Desagüe, vol. 20, exp. 4, ff. 1v and 7.

ceased to be effective, and much of what should have been free-flowing waters were now swampy. For all these reasons, the holes in the embankment were to be patched, the sluicegates through which the canoes passed were to be reinforced and vaulted, both to the tune of 2,000 pesos, and, ideally, the road on the top of the embankment was to be raised by three-fourths of a vara at yet more additional cost. It also needed to be widened, so as to accommodate the passage of pack animals, for which the superintendent weighed up the merits of adding a layer of tezontle stone covered with céspedes (in this case plots of turf held together by the grass's roots that would provide a further layer of protection). Over thirteen years, the costs had spiraled to some 44,000 pesos.[76]

Bothered by the expenses, especially of the road leading over the calzada, the desagüe's officials decided that their investment ought to be protected properly. Since, as Iniesta argued, the damage done to the embankment owed almost as much to livestock as it did to flood waters – or, at the very least, this could be said for the surface of the road – the government attached a condition to the repair work. Henceforth, no cattle or pack animals would be allowed to cross the raised road. The Nahuas of Tlahuac, Tlaltenco, and Tolyahualco were charged with enforcement, and a new *guarda volante* – or flying squad – was established to check on the state of the dams and the raised roads of Tlahuac and Culhuacan every Monday and Thursday.[77]

PASTURES, CLIMATE EXTREMES, AND INUNDATIONS

The concerns about the damage done by animals were shared widely among the desagüe's experts. The introduction of livestock into the lake areas, Iniesta and others argued, had contributed to the undermining of the hydraulic infrastructure. Others agreed. In November 1762, the owners of embarcaderos in Chalco approached don Diego Baena, the teniente in Ayotzingo, to complain about the grave harm brought by the indigenous communities of Mixquic, Ixtayopan, Tolyahualco, and Tlahuac renting out their pastures to those who introduced livestock along the royal canal. As a result, they maintained, the sides of the canoe-routes were collapsing. With soil being dislodged from all the hooves trampling the edge of the pastures, the canals were silting up. So badly clogged were the canals that canoes were finding it difficult to make

[76] AGN, Desagüe, vol. 20, exp. 4, ff. 2–4, 5v, 14–19v, and 35v–36.
[77] AGN, Desagüe, vol. 20, exp. 4, ff. 31v–34 and 41.

progress. A journey to the capital that once took a few hours now dragged on for three interminable days.[78]

The government agreed that this had become a significant issue. It further acknowledged that ranching was indeed to blame. As Vera Candiani has noted, the desagüe authorities were concerned about subsidence and siltation in other parts of the Basin of Mexico and instituted prohibitions against livestock grazing within fifty varas of riverbanks or the shores of the lakes.[79] In Xochimilco and Chalco, the Nahuas were ordered to remove livestock from the lake areas and to repair the canals. Failure to relocate the animals would result in their slaughter wherever they happened to be found. The Nahuas balked at these new rules. Don Felipe de Santiago, the governor of Mixquic, notified Trespalacios that an ongoing epidemic had made it impossible for the town to complete the rehabilitation of the channels in the stipulated three days. Too many of his citizens had died for the town to be able to do the repairs, he stated, and too many of those who had survived were sick and unable to work. As a consequence of this, the authorities looked to the renters of the pastures, the owners of the embarcaderos, and the *cofradías* that usually shouldered the responsibility of maintaining the channels, to contribute to the repairs. Finally, Trespalacios ordered 2,000 cattle be removed from the lake areas and taken to higher ground in Tolyahualco, Milpa Alta, and Xochimilco. Alas, and not without some irony, the relocation of the animals itself caused a significant amount of damage to the royal canal. Tlahuac thus demanded compensation.[80]

Beyond the issue of the watery arteries becoming clogged with soil, many people saw the expansion of the pastures into the lakes as the essential cause of flooding.[81] On this issue Trespalacios was forthright:

It is known that the problem stems from the reduced capacity of the basins of Lakes Chalco, Xochimilco, Mexicalzingo, and Tetzcoco, which is caused by all the owners of estates and the farms on the shores of these lakes, as well as by the native people's towns, which together have extended their pastures and the land under cultivation beyond the shore by constructing dikes, ditches, and dams such that they have been able to create entire haciendas in the lakes where previously there had been water, and it is recognized these days that this brings flooding that will be the ruin of the capital of this kingdom.[82]

---

[78] AGN, Desagüe, vol. 16, exp. 7, ff. 1–1v.

[79] Candiani, "The Desagüe Reconsidered," 33; Candiani, *Dreaming of Dry Land*, 299.

[80] AGN, Desagüe, vol. 16, exp. 7, ff. 2, 5v–12, 14–23v, and 55.

[81] AGN, Desagüe, vol. 20, exp. 4, ff. 35v–36.

[82] The original reads "en Ynteligencia de que esta causa prosede de las estreches de los basos de las lagunas de Chalco, Suchimilco, Mexicalzingo, y Tescuco, causada de que todos los

Trespalacios was not alone in calling out the lake-area haciendas for being responsible for the increasingly frequent and severe flooding. A few years later, Native communities themselves echoed his observation. The capital may not have been ruined but the lakeside communities were facing devastation on an unprecedented scale, they explained, because of the conversion of the old lacustrine landscape into pastures. The scale of this change in the lakes is suggested in a map (Map 6.3) attributed to Iniesta that dates to 1769, in which the majority of the lakes now looked like swamps as opposed to the free flowing waters represented by wavy lines.

By the end of the century, flooding still affected the same low-lying areas where it had been a problem before. Now the scale of the problem had grown in tandem with a shift in the climate toward greater humidity: between 1790 and 1820, Xochimilco's climate had become predominantly wet. With elevated rainfall levels, many places became chronically prone to flooding. Among those places susceptible to being submerged were the lands next to the royal roads, as with the one traversing San Juan de Dios. This was the same road that had been at the center of previous disputes, in 1753, between the Nahuas of Xochimilco and Tepepan against that hacienda. By the 1790s, the situation had deteriorated so much that the audiencia seriously considered the possibility of constructing an entirely new road, although it proved difficult to compel the current owners of the estate to fund the construction work since the first owner, don Manuel de la Borda, passed away while the matter was under investigation and his heirs were still minors. The bold proposal to build an entirely new road partly reflected the influence of powerful interest groups and the severity of the situation. Pressing for a solution was a group of thirty prominent Spanish merchants resident in Xochimilco. The deterioration of the road was so bad that the ruined bridge remained an issue – indeed, there were now two of them that could not be crossed – and the royal road was again impassable. A stretch of it remained completely under water. Clearly, the land surrounding the road did not drain properly, as in previous decades. Making matters worse was a further worrisome issue: runoff from the mountains during the rainy season had created new channels of water. Witnesses stated that the torrent of

dueños de haziendas y tierras laborias de las orillas de dhas lagunas y pueblos de naturales, por acresentar tierras para siembras, y potreros han dejado en lamar las orillas de estos vasos valiendose de construir Albarradones, sanjas, contra sanjas, y estacadas, de manera que han conseguido formar haziendas enteras en el cuerpo de los basos donde antes se estendian las aguas y oy se reconocen finas quantiosas seguras de que se les ynunden acosta de la ruina de la capital del reino." AGN, Desagüe, vol. 16, exp. 9, f. 1v.

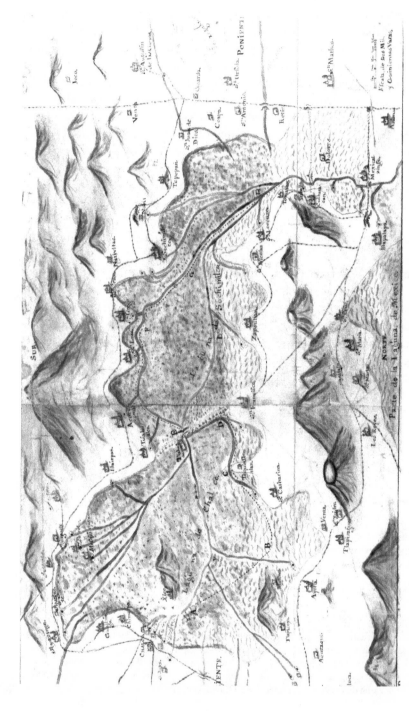

MAP 6.3 Map of Lake Chalco, 1769, by Ildefonso Iniesta Vejarano. By permission of the Archivo General de la Nación, Desagüe, vol. 18, exp. 3.

water cascading down toward the lake was unlike anything they had ever been seen before. Apparently the witnesses were describing the effects of climate extremes: the overall levels of moisture were now at levels not seen since the mid-seventeenth century.[83]

The flooding of the royal road was as nothing, though, compared to the widespread and disastrous inundations of wide swathes of the southern lakes around 1806–1807, when the data from the Mexican Drought Atlas provide a PDSI value of 2, indicating a significant spike in wetter conditions.[84] In 1807, Nahuas from Tlahuac approached the viceroy to express their concern about rising water levels. They explained that flooding had followed in the wake of the hacienda of San Nicolás Buenaventura's expansion into the lake. This hacienda, located next to Tlahuac but technically in the jurisdiction of Mexicalzingo, had long been embroiled in conflicts with nearby Nahua communities. This was the former Jesuit estate that the Arteaga family had purchased in installments from the government following the expropriation (the one whose new owners had tried to claim the ciénega of Tempilula from the village of Santiago Zapotitlan and Tlahuac).[85] By 1807, the hacienda had pressed further into the lake and had built up its flood defenses around pastures to the point where they displaced significant amounts of water.[86] In other words, the hacienda's protections worked against those of Tlahuac, rendering the latter more vulnerable to the threat of flooding. And the problem had become all the more acute because of the unusually damp conditions.

Awareness of the problem was not confined to Tlahuac. Reflecting the increasingly far-reaching ramifications of shifting water levels, the Xochimilca paid close attention to the situation across the lake.[87] The shifts in climate, in other words, were now being felt far and wide. Increasingly, landscape instability followed heavy rains and the encroachment of haciendas into the lakes. For Tlahuac, the government's intervention provided immediate relief. The viceroy ordered the gates of the hacienda's pastures to be opened so as to allow the water to enter. When this happened, the speed at which the water levels declined suggests how much the hacienda had destabilized the lake's hydrology: within

---

[83] AGN, Tierras, vol. 2426, exp. 1, ff. 57, 64, 106, and 110–115.

[84] See the online Mexican Drought Atlas at http://drought.memphis.edu/MXDA/Default .aspx (accessed January 18, 2021).

[85] AGN, Tierras, vol. 1930, exp. 2, ff. 41–43v.   [86] AGN, Tierras, vol. 3708, ff. 1–1v.

[87] AGN, Desagüe, vol. 43, exp. 5, f. 2.

twenty-four hours, Tlahuac's cabildo officers observed a decline in local water levels of three-fourths of a vara; within the hacienda's pastures a sizable lake formed that was deep enough for canoes to traverse it. As the floodwaters abated in Tlahuac, its citizens could "breathe easily" once again.[88]

The respite proved only temporary. The flooding returned in the mid-1810s and was catastrophic. The increasing humidity of those years was such that on several occasions, the PDSI values were frequently in excess of 2, and in 1816 rose above 3, making it the wettest year of the past two centuries in Xochimilco and the third wettest year of the entire colonial period (the others having been back in the 1550s and in 1607). This uncommonly high level of moisture followed the 1815 eruption of Mount Tambora. Exceptional though this event was, the dramatic surge in floodwaters in 1816 only compounded the preexisting problems with inundations. Vast areas had been submerged for unprecedented amounts of time. When Xochimilco pleaded with the government for help in 1816, the area had already suffered three years of inundations, and the flooding over those years had spread so far and wide that Xochimilco's cabildo officers were joined by the alcaldes of Nativitas, San Gregorio Atlapulco, Santa Cruz, San Luis Tlaxialtemalco, Tolyahualco, and San Juan Ixtayopan in seeking assistance. Possibly unaware of the effects of a volcanic eruption in distant Indonesia, the Nahuas presented a furious but also distressing petition in which they laid the blame for their woes on various haciendas, among them San Nicolás Buenavista, as before, along with San Antonio Coapa and the pastures of Azuluacan and Barbuena, all in the jurisdiction of Mexicalzingo. To give a sense of the scale of the flooding, these estates were up to fifteen miles away from the submerged Nahua communities. Some of the communities were on the far side of the calzada de Tlahuac. The causeway had failed to halt the flooding.[89]

The Nahuas began their petition by stating in no uncertain terms that the "greed of the hacendados is the main source of our calamity." The hacendados had placed their own particular, private interests above those of the rest of society by erecting barriers around their pastures in what had been, since the distant pre-contact past, the basin of the lake. As a result of this intrusion, the Nahuas had been buried under their collapsed homes.

---

[88] "los havitantes de nuestro pueblo pudieramos respirar con suelo." AGN, Tierras, vol. 3708, f. 1v.

[89] This calculation is based on Google Maps, with points plotted for Ixtayopan and Mexicalzingo (rather than the defunct haciendas) today.

The Nahuas could only escape, they claimed, with the help of his majesty's government. Since the haciendas refused to allow any water to drain into their holdings, the Nahuas' lands, houses, and fields had flooded, depriving them of the basis of their livelihoods – and the foundation of their service to the king (*servidumbre*). This ruination was similar to that of 1807, they reminded the government, when the viceroy had come to the aid of Tlahuac.[90]

In a powerful reminder of the persistence of the communities' historical memory, the Nahuas continued to explain that the undermining of their dams went all the way back to the conquest. Now the costs of this harm extended to the total submersion of their pueblos. So bad was the damage done by the flooding that it not only impeded Nahuas' ability to work but it also prevented them from supporting their families, worshiping in church, providing for their communities' expenses and tribute, and – significantly, given the current context of the powerful insurgency against Spanish rule that had been raging since 1810 – their ability to make their contributions to the military effort. In a sign of the wider crisis, the communities were no longer able to help the sick. Some individuals were dying without being able to confess their sins. Finally, in a common discursive strategy that had been deployed for hundreds of years – and just over 200 years since the last widespread floods in 1604–1607 – the Nahuas reminded the colonial administration that Xochimilco and the other lakeside communities were essential to the provisioning of the capital with vegetables and grains. They concluded by asking for the same assistance they had received in 1807.[91]

The government responded by launching an investigation. The inspectors set out early one morning and found abundant evidence in support of the Nahuas' claims for the severity of recent years' flooding. If anything the latest flooding had been worse than ever. The immediate signs of this included the large sections of masonry that had been loosened, if not dislodged, from the engineering works. Xochimilco's barrio of la Asunción was indistinguishable from the lake. The chapel had sustained so much damage that the priest had cancelled the previous year's Easter procession. In the afternoon, the master architect, don Joaquín de Heredia, and his colleagues resumed their tour of inspection and set out by canoe along the canals, which Heredia observed had been kept free of reeds and other impediments. Innumerable chinampas had been submerged.[92]

[90] AGN, Desagüe, vol. 43, exp. 5, ff. 1–2.   [91] AGN, Desagüe, vol. 43, exp. 5, ff. 2–4v.
[92] AGN, Desagüe, vol. 43, exp. 5, ff. 6v–7v.

The next day, the inspection proceeded on to San Gregorio Atlapulco. All along the way the water had crested over the shore. The chinampas again were all submerged. The group took measurements of the depth of water in various places around the lake, calculating the highest reaches of the floodwaters, at times observing or marking them against the sides of buildings like community chapels. At the calzada of Tlahuac they found further evidence of the severity of the inundations. The waters had risen so high that Lakes Xochimilco and Chalco had not been kept separate. The only structures that had remained above the water were the church, the elevated road in front of it, and the stairs leading up to the home of the priest.[93] Concerned about the danger of the flooding spreading to the capital, the last stops of the inspection took Heredia and the others to Mexicalzingo, where they saw the gates that had prevented water entering into the pastures of the hacienda of San Antonio Coapa. Because of this, the desagüe authorities reported that water levels at the barrier to the entrance of Lake Tetzcoco had risen to worrying levels. The government thus ordered the barriers protecting Mexico City to be checked.[94]

The hardships of the lakeside communities did not end in 1816. Four years later Tlahuac's town council again petitioned the authorities for assistance from flooding. Altogether, flooding was recorded for the years 1807, 1813–1817, and 1820. Whereas flooding had once been rare, now it was becoming an increasingly regular occurrence, one that aligned with the climate extremes of the age. In 1820, as before, the Nahuas raised many of the same points about the loss of livelihoods and homes, and of the importance of the chinampas to the wider food supply network. They emphasized the damage done to their church as well as the failure of the calzada to keep the waters of Xochimilco and Chalco apart. In spite of all this, water had not entered the hacienda of San Nicolás Buenaventura. Instead, the rising waters threatened the capital, just as it had a few years earlier. In other words, the Nahuas now wielded the old argument that the interests of Mexico City and the Native countryside were one and the same. Tellingly, they stood in opposition to the private interests of the haciendas. The gates to the estates' pastures had to be opened. To bolster their position, the Nahuas invoked the survey of 1748, in which Trespalacios had called for the opening or removal of the haciendas' barriers. His warning, the Nahuas averred, had been prescient.[95]

[93] AGN, Desagüe, vol. 43, exp. 5, ff. 7v–9v.
[94] AGN, Desagüe, vol. 43, exp. 5, ff. 10v–12v.   [95] AGN, Tierras, vol. 3708, ff. 1–6.

After lengthy investigations, the government sided with the haciendas, just as it had when it overruled Trespalacios decades earlier. Tlahuac was too far away, Heredia reckoned, for the closure of the gates to the hacienda's pastures to affect the water level there. Why Tlahuac was being flooded so much and so often remained unexplained. Furthermore, given the high price of food and the value of haciendas for provisioning the capital, the hacienda's pastures had to be protected.[96] Perhaps an observation by the man who rented its pastures provided a further explanation for the government's position: don Domingo Trueba pointed out that the fields should be protected since the owner of the estate had already "suffered a great deal because of the unfortunate circumstances of the rebellion."[97]

CONCLUSION

In 1700, much of Xochimilco's ecological autonomy had remained intact notwithstanding drastic demographic decline. While relations across the social hierarchy had been upset, with the crisis of the seventeenth century having exacerbated grievances and conflict in local politics, the wider landscape had proven resilient. Nahuas had continued to enjoy some degree of space and separation from the demands of the colonial system, thanks in part to the aquatic buffer of the lakes: the lakes' waters remained well regulated, Nahuas continued to cultivate their chinampas, and the local economy continued to benefit from the advantages of canoe transportation. Whereas Spanish estates became increasingly intrusive and disruptive forces for altepetl in Coyoacan and Chalco, such haciendas as had been established in Xochimilco were few in number and tended to be located in the hills.[98] When they did reach down from the montes into the deep soil alluvium, they remained at a distance from Nahua communities and their chinampas.

By 1800, the distinct historical geography of the jurisdiction, in which the intensive horticulture of the lake areas contrasted against the extensive

---

[96] AGN, Tierras, vol. 3708, ff. 20v–21v. The reasoning behind this decision appears in ff. 16–17v.

[97] AGN, Tierras, vol. 3708, f. 12v.

[98] Horn argues that haciendas had come to predominate in Coyoacan around 1650. Haciendas became prominent features of the landscape in Chalco during the seventeenth century as well. Horn, *Postconquest Coyoacan*; Tutino, "Creole Mexico"; Tutino, "Hacienda Social Relations in Mexico: The Chalco Region in the Era of Independence," *Hispanic American Historical Review*, vol. 55, no. 3 (1975), 496–528.

pastoralism of the hills, had blurred. A handful of haciendas – La Noria, San Juan de Dios, San Antonio Coapa, and San Nicolás Buenavista – had grown in size and influence. They expanded into the lake waters, churning up chinampas and converting them into pastures for ranching, all the while displacing water and generating conflicts. Whereas once Nahuas had enjoyed a degree of independence in creating and maintaining dikes, embankments, canals, and other features of the water management system, now the employees of haciendas interfered in the flow of water, building their own dams and installing their own sluicegates around the lacustrine pastures they sought to drain. As a result, the landscape came to be covered and modified by new layers of competing, irregular, and increasingly contradictory and chaotic engineering works. Conflicts also became more severe and complex. Hacendados and their agents fought against each other. They also fought with Nahua communities whose territorial waters, hydrological systems, and aquatic resources were being disrupted. By the end of the colonial period, Nahuas had come to blame their deteriorating fortunes, which were bound up with severely curtailed ecological autonomy, on the haciendas. The superintendent of the desagüe project, Trespalacios y Escandón, agreed with them. At the same time, though, other figures in the colonial government now sided with the haciendas. Previously the government had sought to protect chinampa cultivation in order to safeguard the provisioning of Mexico City; now it sided with the haciendas that had come to be seen as the mainstays of the food supply system.

While Trespalacios and the Nahuas of Xochimilco and Tlahuac, among other communities, blamed the destructive flooding on haciendas, a variety of complex environmental factors were at play. These included heightened levels of rainfall, the redirection of rivers, altered drainage, and the clogging of canals from increases in siltation – all of which, in turn, were affected by significant shifts in the climate. In the final few decades before independence, the lake areas were subjected once again to cooler, wetter conditions, much as they had been in the peak of the Colonial Mexican Pluvial many decades earlier. In the late eighteenth century, the southern lake areas had become increasingly vulnerable to the threat posed by higher levels of precipitation. Now that the basin itself had been reduced in volume by the expansion of pastures into the lakes' waters – pastures belonging both to haciendas and to Nahua communities – and now that the drainage system had become muddled and inconsistent, flooding, when it came, proved to be all the more severe and damaging. This was most conspicuously the case in the climatic fallout from the Tambora eruption of 1815. On this occasion, as on others, not only did floods become more frequent but they also came to submerge greater swathes of territory. In the 1810s they even overtopped the ancient causeway at Tlahuac. At their worst, the rising waters were said to have inundated communities and their chinampas over a vast distance, with Nahuas claiming that the closure of sluicegates to pastures in one location brought devastation many miles away. Such ecological autonomy as Nahua communities in the lake areas had once enjoyed now went into steep decline. At the same time, though, such disruptions had yet to make themselves felt on Nahua cultural forms, at least insofar as can be traced in the Native-language sources.

7

Nahuatl Sources from Xochimilco

Even though the eighteenth century's changes in land use and water management undermined Xochimilco's ecological autonomy and brought significant dislocations, many aspects of life in the lake areas continued much as they had before. The ecological and economic foundations of communities remained intact, at least in those years when there were no major floods, and Nahuas continued to cultivate their chinampas and transport their harvests and other goods to regional markets with their canoes. A majority of the population remained skilled artisans. Nahuas still constituted the vast majority of the population. Local institutions such as the town council served the interests of residents notwithstanding the occasional dispute, for instance, over the identity of its members, which continued to be an issue as the cabildo's membership diversified in line with the greater ethnic complexity of the city.[1] The altepetl's internal organization also remained resilient and long reflected the

---

[1] See, for instance, the case of don Antonio Abad Galicia, whose election to the governorship in 1788–1789 engendered a dispute over his eligibility for office since some rivals identified him as a black or mulato. The dispute seems to have been only temporary; don Antonio had been identified as a cacique a decade earlier, and he later appeared in sources as the governor and defending Xochimilco in lawsuits against the encroachments of haciendas, including San Juan de Dios. AGN, Civil, vol. 1344, exp. 1 and 2; AGN, TSJDF, Corregidores, caja 31A, exp. 40; AGN, TSJDF, Corregidores, caja 32B, exp. 42. For the earlier example of don Antonio de los Olivos, who served as the Nahua republic's governor on multiple occasions in the first decades of the eighteenth century, and who did so apparently with the support of the city's citizens, even though he identified himself as a creole, see Conway, "Spaniards in the Nahua City of Xochimilco: Colonial Society and Cultural Change in Central Mexico, 1650–1725," *The Americas*, vol. 71, no. 1 (2014), 9–35.

centuries-old structures that had been in place.[2] Most conspicuously, many aspects of Nahua culture continued to thrive, none more so than in linguistic expression, for which we have a good amount of Nahuatl documentation. Nearly fifty Nahuatl sources are extant from the eighteenth century alone. Of these, thirty-four (or ca. 70 percent) are last wills and testaments; the remaining fourteen include bills of sale, receipts, confraternity records, and other materials. Not only does the continued production of Native-language sources speak to the resilience of Nahua culture but so too do the kinds of linguistic expression found in these rich and invaluable sources.

Nahuatl expression proved to be remarkably resilient in Xochimilco. Whereas the Nahuatl of other communities of central Mexico often exhibited many borrowings from Spanish after 1650, among them verbs and prepositions – as well as the nouns that had already been adopted as loanwords – Xochimilco's Nahuatl seemed far less susceptible to such Hispanic influences. The relative absence of Spanish-language intrusions perhaps owed something to the small non-Native population size, at least when compared with other communities in central Mexico. Arguably, the ecological autonomy of Xochimilco had also acted as a buffer against outsiders settling in the altepetl in significant numbers. Accordingly, a variety of lexical and grammatical structures retained many of their older characteristics, and local writing traditions proved long-lasting even as they did undergo some changes. Such changes as can be traced in the Nahuatl sources had to do less with Hispanic influences and more with micropatriotism and local forms of expression.

Even in the late colonial period Nahuas set great store by their documentary traditions. Important economic transactions such as the sale of property and urgent matters, such as the setting down of last wishes, continued to be recorded by Nahuas in their own language. And the language they used retained many of the characteristics of earlier times. It was as though there had been a lag between changes in other areas of life – for instance, in the rise of lacustrine pastoralism – and those exhibited in the Nahuatl documents; arguably the declining ecological autonomy had yet to be fully registered when the last surviving Native-language document from the colonial period was set down in 1798. Key aspects of

---

[2] The litigation over the election of don Antonio Abad Galicia includes rich details of Xochimilco's organization, including records of elections going back to the 1760s, and the altepetl continued to comprise its tripartite division into tlaxilacalli. AGN, Civil, vol. 1344, exp. 1 and 2.

Xochimilco's cultural heritage thus retained their vitality and importance for Nahuas. As Charles Gibson noted, the area retained much of its distinctive indigenous character.

DEMOGRAPHIC CHANGES AND CROSS-CULTURAL
ENCOUNTERS

The relative lack of Hispanic influences on Xochimilco's Nahuatl documents may have owed much to the light presence of native-Spanish speakers, at least as compared with other central Mexican communities. While the Nahua population declined precipitously, the numbers of Spaniards, creoles, or individuals of mixed ancestry only gradually came to account for a significant proportion of the population. In the late eighteenth century, such individuals were still very much in the minority even in the city itself. Their numbers were smaller in outlying villages across the jurisdiction. This demographic orientation held significant implications for patterns of cultural change; Nahuas would have had relatively few occasions in which they encountered Spanish speakers, which, in turn, contributed to the resilience of older forms of Nahuatl expression.

For the sixteenth and early seventeenth centuries, a lack of reliable demographic data prevents us from accurately gauging the size of the Spanish community. Government agents, interested primarily in revenues from tribute, paid scant attention to the Spanish population and instead counted the number of Nahuas more assiduously.[3] It seems reasonably clear, though, that during the first half of the colonial period Spaniards were something of a rarity in Xochimilco. In the absence of reliable census materials until the second half of the eighteenth century, parish registers of baptisms, marriages, and burials supply the best information about the relative size of the Spanish and Nahua communities. The earliest of these parish records date to the late 1590s and between that decade and 1656 Franciscan friars had recorded the details of baptisms, marriages, and burials exclusively in Nahuatl in a single set of parish registers. This in itself testified to the small scale of Spanish society in the city.[4] The Franciscan friar in charge of the records was clear about this: he pointed

---

[3] AGI, Patronato, leg. 182, ramo 22; AGI, Indiferente, leg. 1529n2 and 3; AGI, Audiencia de México, leg. 256; *Cartas del licenciado Jerónimo Valderrama*, 196; *Sobre el modo de tributar*, 105.
[4] AGN, Genealogía [microfilm], vol. 1794.

out that separate entries for Spaniards had not been needed previously because there were so few of them.

Thereafter friars included separate records for Spanish and for residents of mixed ancestries (*castas*), which makes general comparisons between the numbers for both these groups and Nahuas possible.[5] In the first entry for Spaniards in 1657, the Franciscans noted just half a dozen baptisms and, a year later, just eight more, in contrast to more than 200 baptisms for Nahuas (no casta baptisms were recorded for that year).[6] There are fairly coherent and complete runs of the baptismal records for the next three decades. They provide a general sense of the proportion of the Nahua and Spanish populations, if only because of the considerable disparity in the numbers of their respective baptisms and burials: between 1658 and 1688, for instance, there were approximately 200 to 400 baptisms for Nahuas in any single year. By contrast, for Spaniards, there were between five and thirty-five baptisms each year. In both cases, the higher figures came from the final decade in the sample, suggesting an increase in birthrates, one that corresponded with a period of warmer and drier conditions as Xochimilco emerged from the coolest period of the Little Ice Age.[7] The demographic distance between Nahuas and Spaniards can also be seen in burial records. The number of burials recorded between 1708 and 1727 for Nahuas ranged from 110 to 190. For Spaniards, the figures were between five and thirty.[8]

The parish records thus suggest that until the latter half of the seventeenth century, there were comparatively few Spaniards in Xochimilco, and that even as the population grew during the seventeenth and eighteenth centuries – during which time the gulf in numbers between Nahuas and Spaniards gradually narrowed – Spaniards still remained very much in the minority. Other sources indicate the same pattern. In 1697, fray

---

[5] On the limitations of using parish registers to gain a sense of social composition, see Cope, *The Limits of Racial Domination*, 24–25, 51–57, 69; Conway, "Spaniards in the Nahua City of Xochimilco," 9–35. It should be noted that birth and death rates may have varied according to a variety of factors including the proportion of the population who were very young or elderly; some residents of Xochimilco, moreover, may have been more susceptible to diseases than others according to ethnicity, and birth and death rates may have varied further across divisions of class, thus making it harder to determine the proportion of non-Native peoples to the overall population. In 1718, for instance, parish records for Nahuas listed 112 children among 176 burials. By comparison, in the same year, Spanish and casta children accounted for just six of twenty-six burials. AGN, Genealogía [microfilm], vol. 1855.

[6] AGN, Genealogía [microfilm], vol. 1794.

[7] AGN, Genealogía [microfilm], vols. 1794 and 1795.

[8] AGN, Genealogía [microfilm], vol. 1855.

Agustín de Vetancurt estimated that there were 300 non-Native individuals in the city, as compared with 2,500 Nahuas.[9] If these figures were accurate, then Spaniards and castas together accounted for about 12 percent of the city's population. That small proportion had grown by the second half of the eighteenth century. In 1778, when we have more comprehensive census materials (see Table 7.1), the Spanish and casta population had more than doubled (to be specific, it had increased 2.58 times). Of a total population of 3,047 individuals, there were now 2,273 Nahuas, 591 Spaniards, and 183 castas. Of the castas, 134 were listed as mestizos.[10] The proportion of Spaniards and castas had thus grown to approximately a quarter of the city's overall population. In other words, over the course of eighty years, Spaniards and castas had gone from being from just over one in ten members of the population to one in four.

The proportion of non-Native peoples remained a good deal smaller in the communities of Xochimilco's countryside. For the entire jurisdiction in 1778, the combined number of Spaniards, castizos, mestizos, and mulatos was 1,874 (a notation in the records stated that no blacks lived in the corregimiento). That figure of 1,874 stood in marked contrast to the 17,935 indigenous peoples, which means that the non-Native population accounted for just under 10 percent of the jurisdiction's total.

The ethnic composition of Xochimilco thus differs from other major central Mexican polities. As an urban center, Xochimilco had comparatively few non-Indian residents. Whereas Spaniards and castas came to account for just over a quarter of the population of the city, in Cuernavaca, non-Indians had become the majority of the population by the late colonial period.[11] Similarly, the cabecera of Tulancingo had twice as many Spaniards and castas as indigenous peoples in 1792. Likewise, more than half of Toluca's population consisted of Spaniards in 1791. Five years earlier, the city of Tetzcoco had 571 Indian and 541 non-Indian families.[12]

Out in Tetzcoco's jurisdiction, the proportion of non-Indian families to Nahua ones fell significantly, just as it did in Xochimilco. For Xochimilco, non-Indian peoples accounted for 10 percent of the total corregimiento's population in the years between 1790 and 1804. This compared with

---

[9] Vetancurt, *Chronica*, 56; Newberry Library, Ayer Collection, ms. 1106, f. 1v; Gerhard, *A Guide to the Historical Geography of New Spain*, 246.

[10] AGN, Padrones, vol. 29, f. 258.

[11] Horn, *Postconquest Coyoacan*, 2; Haskett, *Indigenous Rulers*, 17.

[12] Gerhard, *A Guide to the Historical Geography of New Spain*, 331, 337; Gibson, *The Aztecs under Spanish Rule*, 501n32.

TABLE 7.1 *Census of Xochimilco, 1778*

Place	Native peoples	Spaniards	Castizos[a]	Mestizos	Mulatos[b]	Total
Xochimilco	2,273	591	20	134	29	3,047
Hacienda de la Noria		9				9
Tepepan	508					508
Xochitepec	166					166
Xicalco	108					108
Santiago	1,301	3				1,304
San Mateo Xalpa	232					232
San Lucas	148	18				166
San Francisco	427					427
Milpa Alta	2,527	21				2,548
San Pablo	869	16		23		908
San Lorenzo Tlacoyuca	582					582
San Francisco Tecoxpan	325					325
San Gerónimo	187					187
San Pedro Actopan	1,592					1,592
San Bartolomé	269					269
San Lorenzo Atemoaya	17					17
San Salvador	365					365
Tecomitl	709	37	21	40		807
Tolyahualco	797	227	67	145	38	1,274
Ixtayopan	294	171	53	151	8	677
Santa Ana	825	5				830
Tepenahuac	150					150
Topilejo	774					774
Bar° de dho Pueblo	483					483
Pueblo de Santa Cruz	662					662
Nativitas	426	47				473
San Gregorio	399					399

TABLE 7.1 *(continued)*

Place	Native peoples	Spaniards	Castizos[a]	Mestizos	Mulatos[b]	Total
San Luis	255					255
Santa Cécilia	93					93
San Andrés	172					172
Total	17,935	1,145	161	493	75	19,809

Note: From AGN, Padrones, vol. 29.
[a] Individuals of mixed Spanish and mestizo ancestry. [b] The census specified that there were no blacks.

20 percent for nearby Coyoacan, 22 percent for Citlaltepec, and 24 percent for Otumba. For Cuauhtitlan and Tetzcoco the percentages were 16 and 15, respectively.[13]

These differences held profound implications for the nature, frequency, and extent of cross-cultural relations across central Mexican polities. In Xochimilco, there were fewer non-Indian peoples as a proportion of the overall population than other altepetl. This simple fact goes a long way toward explaining how the city successfully preserved its indigenous character and how the Nahuatl documents exhibited fewer Hispanic influences than those produced elsewhere in central Mexico.

The faint presence of non-Native peoples was reflected in the Nahuatl documentation. Seldom did individuals who were readily identifiable as Spaniards or castas appear in the native-language sources, although it must be stressed that trying to identify ethnicity on the basis of naming patterns is difficult, if not perilous, not least because the pattern of Nahua commoners typically having two first names could be shared by mulatos, mestizos, and individuals of ambiguous or unclear ancestries (in contrast to members of the Nahua nobility and Spaniards, who were more likely to have surnames). In addition, the Nahuatl from Xochimilco rarely included markers of ethnic identity. Thus, in general terms, Nahuas seldom seemed to bequeath or sell property to Spaniards in their testaments and bills of sale. Spaniards were more likely to appear in the sources as neighbors, owning plots of land that were adjacent to those being transferred in notarial documents. This was the case with Gabriel de San

[13] Gibson, *The Aztecs under Spanish Rule*, 146; Gerhard, *A Guide to the Historical Geography of New Spain*, 101, 208, and 313.

Antonio, who lived in San Pedro Atocpan, where neighbors included Andrés de Ramos and Joachín de Rosas.[14] In Xochimilco itself, Juan de San Bernardino passed on some land to his heirs that was next to the road to the capital and adjacent to land belonging to a Spaniard, don Francisco Santare.[15] Neither of these sources dated to the eighteenth century; rather, they were set down much earlier, in the 1600s and 1610s. Significantly, in both of these examples, the lands in question were located in places, such as the piedmont town of Atocpan, where Spaniards were most likely to have established ranches and kept livestock.

NAHUATL SOURCES IN THE COLONIAL ERA

At the same time that fundamental changes were taking place in the eighteenth century, including the rise of the non-Native population, many facets of Nahua culture proved surprisingly stable. Nowhere were these cultural continuities more enduring than in linguistic expression. The Nahuatl language of Xochimilco remained remarkably constant over colonial period, exhibiting as it did relatively few Spanish-language intrusions after the changes it had undergone in the mid-sixteenth century. In several respects the Nahuatl from Xochimilco had something of a resilient quality.

This observation is based on an analysis of more than 120 Nahuatl documents produced in Xochimilco over two and a half centuries (between 1548 and 1798, to be precise). The sources have been examined in light of James Lockhart's model of linguistic change. Drawing on a corpus of Nahuatl-language sources from across central Mexico, Lockhart identified three stages of change: the first, which lasted briefly from the conquest until the 1540s involved Nahuas borrowing very few words from Spanish; the second, from 1550 through until ca. 1650, consisted of Nahuas incorporating only nouns as loanwords into their language; and the third stage, which extended from 1650 and to the present day, involved an ever greater number and range of loanwords entering into the Nahuatl language, including verbs and particles (mainly prepositions and conjunctions), as well as such further impositions as idioms and grammatical changes. While there is evidence for the persistence of some early stage 1 and 2 characteristics in Xochimilco at a later date than one might expect, it is with regard to the third stage that the sources depart from Lockhart's model in the most significant and striking

[14] AGN, Tierras, vol. 1741, exp. 6, ff. 4–4v.
[15] AGN, TSJDF, Alcalde del Crimen, caja 2B, exp. 43, ff. 5–6.

way: they exhibit almost no stage 3 phenomena.[16] The Nahuatl in documents from Xochimilco, unlike many other parts of central Mexico, thus shows comparatively little Spanish influence.

Whereas native-language documentation from elsewhere in central Mexico exhibited stage 3 characteristics as early as the 1620s and 1630s, and while Lockhart initially thought that the threshold for the third stage was around the midpoint of the seventeenth century, very few sources from Xochimilco showed signs of stage 3 linguistic changes even in the second half of the eighteenth century. This trend is apparent from a comparison between Xochimilco's sources and the broader pattern described by Lockhart in his wide-ranging, multiregional perspective, which encompassed the Basin of Mexico, the Toluca Valley, the Cuernavaca region, and regions to the east, among them Tlaxcala, Puebla, and Tulancingo, among other places. Since his foundational study, historians including Lockhart and Camilla Townsend have also paid particular attention regional and local variations in the Nahuatl preserved in the extant sources, as for instance, in Puebla and Tlaxcala.[17] Studies such as these have made it possible to compare Xochimilco's corpus of testaments with those from places like Toluca, which have been published and analyzed by historians such as Caterina Pizzigoni.[18]

The comparisons have been drawn from documents produced after 1650 in Xochimilco, when one would expect to start seeing stage 3 characteristics in the sources. For the purposes of this analysis, the

---

[16] I would like to thank James Lockhart for his kind assistance in translating and analyzing some of the Nahuatl sources; he, too, noted the lack of stage 3 phenomena among Xochimilco's sources (personal communication).

[17] Camilla Townsend, ed. and trans., *Here in This Year: Seventeenth-Century Nahuatl Annals of the Tlaxcala-Puebla Valley* (Stanford: Stanford University Press, 2010); see also Townsend, *Annals of Native America: How the Nahuas of Colonial Mexico Kept Their History Alive* (New York: Oxford University Press, 2019).

[18] Caterina Pizzigoni, *The Life Within: Local Indigenous Society in Mexico's Toluca Valley, 1650–1800* (Stanford: Stanford University Press, 2012), and Pizzigoni, *Testaments of Toluca* (Stanford: Stanford University Press, 2007); Miriam Melton-Villanueva and Caterina Pizzigoni, "Late Nahuatl Testaments from the Toluca Valley: Native-Language Ethnohistory in the Mexican Independence Period," *Ethnohistory*, vol. 55, no. 4 (2008), 361–391; Miriam Melton-Villanueva, *The Aztecs at Independence: Nahua Culture Makers in Central Mexico, 1799–1832* (Tucson: University of Arizona Press, 2016); see also Teresa Rojas Rabiela, Elsa Leticia Rea López, and Constantino Medina Lima, eds., *Vidas y bienes olvidados: Testamentos indígenas novohispanos*, 4 vols. (Mexico City: Centro de Investigaciones y Estudios Superiores en Antropología Social, Consejo Nacional de Ciencia y Tecnología, 1999–2002).

documentation from Xochimilco consists of two sets of sources: those that include testaments and codicils, on the one hand, and all other sources, on the other. Of the fifty-two Nahuatl testaments, twelve were written before 1650, which means that one might reasonably expect to see signs of stage 3 phenomena in the other forty testaments. This number compares to twenty-nine documents of other, diverse types produced after 1650: bills of sale, debt contracts, memorias, certifications and titles issued for property, legal agreements (*conciertos*, for instance, to divide or share property), petitions, election results, a parish census, lists of rental incomes, lists of church expenses, receipts of various kinds, as well as the accounting and other records of a Nahua confraternity. All of these sources, including the testaments and codicils, exhibit the same lack of stage 3 phenomena. The testaments, however, permit another, complementary perspective on patterns of language change that are not available with the other sources: testaments typically adhered to certain consistent conventions in structure and wording, especially in the formulaic phrases that often characterized their opening and closing statements.[19] These characteristics, which were originally based on a model testament, allow us to discern changes in expression over time. These alterations, it is worth noting, went beyond the issue of Hispanic influences and had to do with other linguistic trends. Given the diversity of the other kinds of Nahuatl sources, it is hard to pursue a similar philological analysis of them since they lack a common control by which to make comparisons (only bills of sale consistently followed a common formula – in terms of structure and wording – but there were only eight of them, which makes it harder to identify discrete trends over time).

Not only were there relatively few stage 3 characteristics in the post-1650 Nahuatl sources, but the specific signs of change they did exhibit were also few and far between. The vast majority of Xochimilco's Nahuatl sources remained firmly placed within the earlier, second stage of the linguistic tradition. This pattern of linguistic conservatism is shown clearly in the 1786 last will and testament Sebastiana María.[20] Beyond people's names, all of the loanwords in Sebastiana's relatively brief testament were nouns for foreign concepts or material items – among them the words for widow, memorandum, testament, God, holy church, candles, donkey – as well as such officials as the fiscal, alcalde, and notary.

[19] See, for instance, the examples in Melton-Villanueva's *The Aztecs at Independence*, 94–101.
[20] AGN, Tierras, vol. 1863, exp. 5, ff. 5–5v.

Accordingly, the document could have been written in the 1580s rather than the 1780s, at least when it came to vocabulary.

The early founding of Xochimilco's Franciscan friary, which became a major religious center in the sixteenth century, and the early establishment of the municipal government with its *tlacuilo* (scribe), likely proved important to the making of a strong writing tradition that underpinned the persistence of Nahuatl documentary production. Xochimilco's writing tradition began quite early. Early works included pictorial sources as well as combined pictorial and alphabetical texts, including the wonderful 1552 *Badianus Manuscript* (also known as the *Codex Barberini*). Juan Badianus, who co-wrote this beautiful Nahuatl and Latin illustrated herbal, hailed from Xochimilco, and he received his education from the Franciscans at the Colegio de Santa Cruz in Tlatelolco, which had been founded to teach the nobility and their children.[21]

The direct influence of the Franciscans on early writing systems in Xochimilco itself is readily apparent in the early Nahuatl sources. The Nahua notary Mateo Ceverino de Arellano, for instance, worked on the *Florentine Codex*. He was part of the team that copied it under the supervision of Sahagún.[22] Mateo Ceverino, moreover, set down the last will and testament of the merchant Constantino de San Felipe in 1572 (encountered previously in Chapter 4).[23] The document further indicates another vital Franciscan influence: it closely adhered to the model testament created by the philologian and friar Alonso de Molina, the author of the indispensable Spanish-Nahuatl dictionary. Molina's model testament, included in his confessional manual (first published in 1565), was designed to offer scribes a sample so as to facilitate the quick and consistent adoption of notarial and religious documentary conventions. These conventions, originating in Castilian practices but modified for and by Nahuas, included common sequences in the presentation of a testament's content as well as specific wording, for instance, in the testator invoking the trinity at the outset and then, in subsequent parts of the preamble, identifying him or herself, stating that the he or she was sound of mind but sick of body as death approaches, for which reason the final wishes were being set down. In this structure, according to Lockhart, Mateo Ceverino's testament followed Molina's in most respects, and while he

---

[21] Gibson, *The Aztecs under Spanish Rule*, 300, 382, and 404; *The Badianus Manuscript*.
[22] Lockhart, *The Nahuas after the Conquest*, 472.
[23] AGN, Tierras, vol. 1525, exp. 3, ff. 3–4v; Lockhart, eds., *Nahuatl in the Middle Years*, 93–97.

deviated from it from time to time with his own rhetorical additions and flourishes, he carefully returned to the model's main organization and phrasing for key points.[24]

It appears as though Mateo Ceverino played a significant part in developing an enduring tradition of Nahuatl documentary production. While his testament adopts the basic template of Molina's model, it also diverged in some ways that likely reflected Nahua preferences. For this reason, in place of stating the testator's parish, the Xochimilca long followed Mateo Ceverino's practice of referring to themselves as citizens of the altepetl (and city) and of their particular tlaxilacalli, which they then named. This and other distinctive characteristics of both his testament and Molina's model testament remained common in later documents, as shown in a comparison between the preambles of the testaments, in transcription and translation, that Mateo Ceverino produced along with those of another Nahua notary, Martín Pauper de Monte Alegre, who was writing almost a decade later.[25] Mateo Ceverino's testament begins as follows:

Yn ica ytocatçin tetçin tepiltçin yvā Espiritu santo ye nicpeoaltia yn notestam.to ma quimaticā yn isquichtin yn quittazque ynin amatl . ca yn nehoatl notoca Costantino de . s . phelippe nicā nichane yn ipā noble ciudad auh nipohui tepetenchi . notlaxillacalpā . tlalnepātla . maçivi yn cēca mococohoa nonacaio yeçe yn no yollo yn nanima yn notlacaquia yn notlalnamiq'liz yoā yn noçealiz . aᵒ . quen cah çā pactica . auh nicchistica yn miquiztli yn notçōquiçaliz . yn ayac vel yspanpa yehoa choloa . anoço quitlalcahuia . Auh yz catq' ye noconpehualtia .

v huel achtopa yehoatl yn nanima . ymactçinco nocō – cahoa nocō tlalia . nicnomaq' lia . yn tt.ᵒ d. yeica ca yascatçin ytlachioaltçin yoā oquimomaquistilli yca yn itlaçoeçotzin . auh çenca nicnotlatlauhtilia ynic nechmotlaocoliliz nechmopopolviliz ȳ notlatlacol yoā q'moviquiliz yn ichantzinco yn nanima yn ilvicatl yitic yn iq'c quitlalcaviz nonacaio –

v ynic ontlamātli niq'toa . yn nonacaio ytech nicpoa ytech niccauhtiuh yn tlali . yeica ca a.ᵒ tle ipā povi . atle ipā motta ca tlali ca tlaçolli . nicneq' ça çe tilmatli ynicmoq'miloz yn iquac motocaz yoan nicneq' ompa motocaz in tohueyteupan Sant Bernardino yitic altepetl çiudad xuchimilco . –

In the name of the father, the child, and the Holy Spirit I begin my testament. Let all those who see this document know that my name is Constantino de San Felipe, citizen here in the noble city and belonging to Tepetenchi in the tlaxilacalli of Tlalnepantla; although my body is very sick, yet nothing is wrong with my spirit, soul, understanding, memory, and will, but they are sound. I am awaiting my ending, death, which no one can flee from or avoid. Here is what I am now beginning with.

---

[24] Lockhart, *The Nahuas after the Conquest*, 468–474 and especially 473.
[25] AGN, Vínculos y Mayorazgos, vol. 279, exp. 1, ff. 82–83v.

v First of all I leave, place, and give my soul into the hands of our lord God, since it is his possession and creation, and he redeemed it with his precious blood. I pray urgently that he grant me pardon of my offenses and take my soul to his home in heaven when it takes leave of my body.

v Second, I declare that I assign and leave my body to the earth, since it counts for nothing and is held in no esteem, for it is earth and filth. I only want it to be wrapped in a blanket when it is buried, and I wish it to be buried in our great church of San Bernardino in the altepetl and city of Xochimilco. –

Martín Pauper de Monte Alegre started the testament for doña María de Guzmán with the following introductory statements:

<u>v</u> yn ica ytocatçin . santissima trinidad ȳ tetatçī . tepiltçī . Espu sāto ça çe nelli dios ye nicpehualtia . ȳ notestamento . ma quimomachitican . yn ixquichtin . quimottilizque ynin amatl . ca ȳ nehuatl notoca . doña maria . de guzmā . nichane ollac hueicā yn yn ipā yc Ey cabeçera . nicchihua . ȳ notestamēto . maçihui ȳ mococohua nonacayo . auh ȳ nanima . ȳ noçializ . ȳ notlalnamiquiliz . amo quē ca ça pactica yc nicchihua . ȳ notestamto . ȳ ça tlatçaca notlanequiliz . ynic mochipa yehuatl . mopiaz yn ayac quitlacoz –

huel achtopa yehuatl . ȳ nanima . ymactçinco nocōcahua ȳ tt.° dios . yehica . ca oquimochihuili . yhuā oquimomaquixtili yn ica ytlaçoEçotçī . çē ca nicnotlatlauhtilia . ynic nechmotlaocoliliz nechmopopolhuiliz . yn ixquich notlatlacol . yhuā quimohuiquiliz ȳ nanima yn itlatocachātçinco . yn ilhuicac . –

<u>v</u> ynic ōtlamantli ȳ nonacayo . ytech nicpohua . ȳ tlalticpactli yehica . ca itech oquiz . ca tlalli ca tlaçolli . ynic omochiuh . nicnequi ça çe tilmatli yehuatl . yn itilmatçin nr̄o señor . sā . fran^{co} ȳ abido . ynic moquimilloz nonacayo . yhuā . nicnequi . ompa motocaz . ȳ toteopan sā ber^{no} . ynic ōca teochihualoz . notlatatac –

<u>v</u> In the name of the most holy Trinity, father, child, and Holy Spirit, just one true God, I begin my testament. Know all who see this document that I named doña María de Guzmán, citizen in Ollac Hueican, in the third cabecera, make my testament. Although my body is sick, nothing is wrong with my soul, will, and memory, but they are sound, wherefore I make my testament, my last will so that it will always be observed and no one will violate it. –

First of all I deliver my soul into the hands of our lord God because he made it and redeemed it with his precious blood. I greatly pray him to favor me by pardoning me all my sins and taking my soul to his royal home in heaven. –

<u>v</u> Second, I assign my body to the earth because it came from it, for it is earth and made of filth. I want my body to be wrapped just in a cloak, the cloak of lord San Francisco, the habit, and I want it to be buried in our church of San Bernardino, so that my grave will be blessed there. –

The wonderfully lengthy, rich, and expressive wills of Xochimilco's ruling dynasty, such as the one above, shared much in common with the formulas of the 1573 will set down by Mateo Ceverino. These similarities can be seen in doña Ana de Guzmán's final wishes, written in 1577, and in those of her husband, don Martín Cerón y Alvarado (in 1588).[26] As late as 1616, the scribe who wrote Juan de San Bernardino's testament closely adhered to the earlier models and their rhetorical conventions.[27]

Intriguingly, the testament for the merchant, Constantino de San Felipe, which Mateo Ceverino wrote, forms part of a lawsuit that also included Nahua pictorial documents (see Chapter 4). These pictorials included a genealogy and two listings of property, and while the scribe who produced them is never identified, one wonders if he or she was a colleague of Mateo Ceverino's. Xochimilco's writing tradition included numerous pictorial documents, as we have seen, and at least one of them has been identified as a pictorial testament.[28] The pictorials continued to be produced well into the seventeenth century.[29]

That the great pictorial and alphabetic writing traditions in Xochimilco were established so thoroughly and so soon goes a long way to explaining their resilience. It was not just that stage 2 Nahuatl proved to be long-lasting. Some early, stage 1 writing also persisted beyond the typical 1550 threshold. In 1566, for instance, Ana Tiacapan asked to record her last wishes and bequeathed property to two daughters, whose names reflected very early conventions: both of them were named María but the two were identified separately with their Nahuatl names, Tiacapan and Tlaco. After the first mention of them, Ana proceeded to refer to her daughters by their Nahuatl names only. Additionally, the specific, detailed offerings for the sake of her soul in purgatory had something of an old-fashioned quality to them, in their specificity, that was not seen in later sources:

v Auh yn ipāpa naia yn ipalehuiloca ynic amo ōpa huecahuaz purgatorio ce missa niquitlani mocahuaz ȳ teopā huētçintli ce peso yoā ome to.ˢ yc mocohuaz vino yoā nahui to.ˢ yc mocohuaz castillan tlaxcalli yhuā no nahui to.ˢtica mocohuaz, candellas / auh nahui to.ˢ mocahuatiuh ospital ȳtech monequiz ȳ cocoxcatzitzintin yn ōcan mopatia –

v And concerning the help of my soul, so that it will not spend long in purgatory, I request a mass; as an offering one peso is to be delivered to the church, and two reales to buy wine, four reales to buy Spanish bread, and also four reales worth of candles are to be bought. And four reales are to be delivered to the hospital to be used for the poor sick people who are treated there. –

---

[26] AGN, Vínculos y Mayorazgos, vol. 279, exp. 1, ff. 19–21v and 12–13v.

[27] AGN, TSJDF, Alcalde del Crimen, caja 2B, exp. 43, ff. 5–6.

[28] See the will of don Miguel Damián, Newberry Library, Ayer Collection, ms. 1900. See also Oudijk and Castañeda de la Paz, "Un testamento pictográfico de Xochimilco," 111–123.

[29] See, for instance, those found in AGN, Vínculos y Mayorazgos, vol. 279, exp. 1.

Similar qualities are seen in the 1569 testament of María Xocoyotl. Several men, for instance, had indigenous names. Other features are reminiscent of some of the earliest extant writings. The scribe used the expression *onca* in place of the verb *pia*, which came to be used as the verb "to have." Thus María states "oncate nopilhuan yeintin," or "I have three children," and "onca ycal in inamic," "my spouse has a house." The scribe, Martín Cano, also followed an early convention for introducing new topics by using the phrase "iz catqui." He writes, for instance, "Auh Iz catqui niquitohua . nimaria xocoyotl nic ca yei pexus yc nopan missa mitoz," which translates as "And I María Xocoyotl say that here are 3 pesos with which a mass for me is to said." This introductory phrasing is also seen in the Cuernavaca census records from the 1530s and early 1540s. The testament shared further commonalities with the census, notably when it came to matters of orthography and the use of "tç" in place of "tz." Finally, Martín Cano's handwriting, with large letters and, in particular, the distinctive deep "v," resemble the characters of some of the very early colonial texts.[30]

Some of the early survivals proved quite consistent in their use. The "tç" spelling in place of "tz," for instance, was also seen in the 1582 testament of doña María de Guzmán, suggesting that it may not have been so much an archaic trait as a particular facet of the Xochimilco writing tradition. Additional signs of archaic Nahuatl can be found in the sources. These include the use of "Caxtillan" to refer to imported Spanish items, as with "Castilian colors" ("Caxtilla tlapalli"), for painting, in the set of cofradía records from 1610.[31] Other enduring characteristics of Xochimilco's documentation include the combination of Nahuatl plurals with Spanish loanwords, as with *padresme* for "fathers" (as in friars) in doña Ana de Guzmán's 1577 testament. Doña María Pascuala, whose testament was written nearly two centuries later, in 1766, referred to saints in the plural as *santome* and *santohme*, which at that late date was astonishingly old-fashioned, more so even than "santosme" much less *santos*, which had become the norm at that time in many places.[32] Although rare, indigenous naming conventions persisted as well. In

---

[30] AGN, Tierras, vol 35, exp. 6, ff. 236–27v (for Ana Tiacapan's testament) and 240–240v; S. L. Cline, ed. and trans., *The Book of Tributes: Early Sixteenth-Century Nahuatl Censuses from Morelos* (Los Angeles: UCLA Latin American Center Publications and the University of California, 1993).

[31] Lockhart, *The Nahuas after the Conquest*, 278; INAH, Fondo Franciscano, vol. 129, entries for March 1610.

[32] AGN, Tierras, vol. 2429, exp. 3, ff. 14–15.

1706, Micaela María identified her youngest child as *xocoyotl*, meaning the younger. In another document, from 1788, the testator referred to one Josef Chichintitla and Pedro Quaxohpa. In another will, this time a second, supplemental one for doña María Pascuala, individuals were identified by their first names and then, unusually, by reference to places, including toponyms. Hence we read about doña María Atlauhco as well as Pedro Techalotepec and don Manuel Acolpitenco. Elsewhere in the testament there is a specific place named Acolpitenco.[33]

If some of these examples were exceptional, potentially the quirks of the scribe who wrote the document, others were part of a writing style that was distinctive to Xochimilco. Some of this had to do with orthography, as with tç- in place of tz-. In a document produced at the behest of Micaela Isabel, for instance, the word nehuatl (meaning "I," as in the first person) was rendered "nehuatli," that is, with an additional letter "i." This idiosyncrasy seems to have been specific though not exclusively so, to Xochimilco.[34] Beyond orthography, some expressions appear to be uncommon. In the 1653 testament for Martina Luisa, the church notary included a few elaborations to the traditional opening statements (still reflecting the Molina model), as with the phrase "when my life on earth has ended" (the wider phrase in which this appears reads as follows: "I begin first of all with my soul; when my life on earth has ended, I place it very entirely in the hands of my precious father God"). Martina, or the scribe, also wrote unusually of the fire of purgatory (emphasis added): "Second, I say that when God has effaced me, so that my soul will be helped before God and not spend a long time in *the place where people are purified by fire*, purgatory."[35]

Some expressions can be understood in terms of the local geographical situation. In stage 3, sources one might expect to see the occasional word for a cardinal direction coming from the Spanish. Previously, Nahuas indicated directions according to the locations of major altepetl, such as Mexico or Quauhtla (to the south), or by reference to the places where the sun rises or sets.[36] In Xochimilco, no one used Spanish words for the cardinal directions, and in addition to the references to the sun, Nahuas oriented places with regard to the mountains (i.e., to the south) and the lake (the north).[37] Other distinctive terms had to do with land. Xochimilco seems to have had

---

[33] AGN, TSJDF, Corregidores, caja 31A, exp. 54, ff. 2–3; AGN, Tierras, vol. 2327, exp. 1, ff. 14–15v and 18–19; AGN, Tierras, vol. 2429, exp. 4, ff. 21–21v.

[34] AGN, Tierras, vol. 1863, exp. 2, f. 4.

[35] AGN, Intestados, vol. 301, exp. 2, ff. 214–214v.

[36] AGN, Tierras, vol. 2327, exp. 10, ff. 6–7v.

[37] AGN, TSJDF, caja 31B, exp. 62, ff. 3–6.

a distinctive vocabulary for units of measure when it came to different kinds of land. For dry land, up in the piedmont, Nahuas used *patlahuac* (for width) and *yunta* as measurements.[38] Yunta (or "yonta" in some renderings) seems to have referred to larger tracts of land, thereby distinguishing it from other commonly used measurements such as *quahuitl*.[39] The use of quahuitl was apparently confined to the tierra firme; for the chinampas, Nahuas used nehuitzan as an equivalent to a quahuitl. To these two other local terms can be added: *atoctlalli*, for irrigated land, which could be synonymous with chinampa, and later *chinantlalli*.[40]

Besides distinctive language for such physical things, some local expressions concerned abstract ideas. Nahuas in Xochimilco developed a distinctive tradition for expressing regret and humility when it came to matters of inheritance. This is seen in Sebastiana María's 1786 testament. At the end of the fourth clause of her testament, after she had bequeathed a little donkey and a grain bin to one of her daughters, Sebastiana added the poignant remark, "ma nechimotlapupulhuiliCa camo tlen nicpie Ca huel nicninotlaCatzintli ypatzinCo Di⁵," or "May they pardon me, for I have nothing and really a poor person before God." And she repeated this lament in the testament's next clause, for another daughter. In apologizing for not having more to give to her offspring, Sebastiana María was far from being alone. Micaela Isabel did so, too, in 1746. After passing on some property, including chinampas, she concluded, "That is all of the statement that I make. I have nothing; I am a very poor person. May god forgive me, and may my spouse forgive me" ("Ca san ixquich y niquitohua y notlatol Camo tli ninopilia Ca huel nicnotlaCatzitli ma nechmotlapopolhuili y Dios yhua nonamictzi ma nechmotlapopolhuili auh").[41] Other testaments, such as those of Micaela María (1706), doña Petrona Antonia (1759), Pascuala de la Concepción (1786), and Manuela Francisca (1795) included the same refrain.[42] There may have been something of a gendered dimension to this; the majority of the individuals who offered the apology were female, although Cristóbal de Santiago likewise asked for forgiveness. That the phrasing had assumed a figurative character, as though it were a trope, is suggested by Cristóbal's apparent prosperity; he bequeathed plenty of land, including eleven chinampas. Other

---

[38] Patlahuac appears in AGN, TSJDF, caja 31B, exp. 63, f. 3.
[39] AGN, Tierras, vol. 2429, exp. 3, ff. 14–15.
[40] AGN, Tierras, vol 35, exp. 6, ff. 240–240v.   [41] AGN, Tierras, vol. 1863, exp. 2, f. 4.
[42] AGN, Tierras, vol. 1863, exp. 5, ff. 5-5v; exp. 2, f. 4; AGN, TSJDF, Corregidores, caja 31A, exp. 54, ff. 2–3; AGN, Civil, vol. 1059, exp. 4, ff. 3–3v; AGN, TSJDF, Corregidores, caja 32A, exp. 29, ff. 3–3v and 5–5v; AGN, TSJDF, Corregidores, caja 32B, exp. 35, ff. 1–1v.

men expressed contrition – or at least admitted to being poor – as did Baltasar de San Nicólas in 1721. Baltasar, however, did not offer an apology. Neither did Agustín de los Ángeles, whose expression of humility appears in the documentary record at the early date of 1667.[43] The trend toward apologizing for the lack of property to pass on to heirs became more pronounced in the eighteenth century.

The eighteenth century witnessed two further changes in Xochimilco's Nahuatl. The first had to do with stage 3 phenomena, the second, to do with several gradual departures away from Xochimilco's earlier writing tradition. The first of these trends speaks to the resilience of the area's Nahuatl and its conservative qualities; the latter amounts to an alternative trajectory of linguistic change that did not involve acculturation through sustained, widespread encounters with Spanish speakers. Instead, the second set of changes seem to have developed internally (or auto-chthonously), and reflected the increasing autonomy of communities in producing their own local Nahuatl writing conventions.

STAGE 3 LINGUISTIC CHANGE IN XOCHIMILCO

Unlike other parts of central Mexico, Xochimilco's Nahuatl barely moved beyond the second stage of linguistic change. This is to say that loanwords from Spanish were, in the vast majority of cases, solely nouns and not verbs, prepositions, or conjunctions. Nor, indeed, were deeper structural changes in the language tied to Spanish influences, for instance, with the adoption of foreign grammatical conventions. Instead, eighteenth-century sources read in many ways like their seventeenth- and even their sixteenth-century prede-cessors. It should be noted that the sources did not remain the same and were unchanged over the centuries; rather, their orthography and forms of expres-sion did indeed evolve, although they did so beyond the impetus of Spanish-language intrusions. In other words, on first glance, Xochimilco's Nahuatl sources are unmistakably eighteenth-century in appearance – when it comes to handwriting and other characteristics – and they no longer have some of the elaborate phrasing of their predecessors, but they also lack many of the Spanish loanwords that had become common in stage 3. The last will and testament of María Sebastiana, for instance, which dates to 1702, could easily be mistaken for a testament written in the 1570s or 1580s – save for the handwriting and the omission of conventional statements such as being sick

---

[43] AGN, Tierras, vol. 2427, exp. 3, ff. 17–17v; AGN, Tierras, vol. 1863, exp. 2, ff. 2–2v; AGN, TSJDF, Corregidores, caja 31B, exp. 62, f. 7.

but sound of mind. Only a handful of Spanish influences can be detected, and even then, they are just nouns.[44]

It is hard to overstate the paucity of the stage 3 examples of linguistic change. While the stage 3 convention of beginning testaments by invoking "Jesus, Mary, and Joseph" was common among the testaments from Xochimilco, other tendencies were conspicuously absent. Unlike in Toluca, for instance, Nahuas from Xochimilco did not make use of Spanish terms for close blood relatives, such as brother or sister (*hermano* or *hermana*).[45] Thirty-seven out of a total of forty surviving testaments written after 1650 did not contain any Spanish loanwords that were not nouns. Doña María Pascuala's testament of 1766, for example, contained neither stage 3 loanwords nor calques. Similarly, Sebastiana María's 1786 testament contained just ten loanwords that were not proper nouns, and all ten of those terms were nouns.[46] The latest testament, dating to 1795, for Manuela Francisca, likewise had surprisingly few loanwords. None of them were stage 3 ones.[47] Even when the sources did exhibit signs of stage 3 phenomena, they did so infrequently and sparingly. It is worth recalling that only three of forty testaments exhibited these changes; in other words, just 7.5 percent of them. In 1769, for instance, Rosa María bequeathed to one of her offspring a chinampa as well as a house and its patio. She described the limits of the patio and, in doing so, used the preposition "asta" (*hasta*, "as far as").[48] This first attribution of the term in Xochimilco dated to 1769; its first appearance in Toluca, by contrast, was in 1654. Another "asta" can be found in the 1786 testament of Pascuala de la Concepción. The third example of a stage 3 loanword appears in doña Petrona Antonia's testament from 1759. Her testament is unusual in divulging details of her wayward son's behavior, which resulted in his punishment in their hometown, San Pedro Atocpan. Several loanwords – *alcalde, pena* (penalty), obraje – appear in Petrona's account, as does *corten*, from the verb *cortar* (to cut). These three examples make up the sum total of the stage 3 examples from Xochimilco's testaments: one preposition, *hasta*, and one verb, *corten*.[49]

A few other stage 3 loanwords can be found in Nahuatl sources other than testaments. The latest colonial-era Nahuatl document to be produced in Xochimilco' jurisdiction, in 1798, was a contract by which several

[44] AGN, Tierras, vol. 1179, exp. 1, ff. 3–3v.   [45] Pizzigoni, *Testaments of Toluca*, 9, 33.
[46] AGN, Tierras, vol. 2429, exp. 3, ff. 14–15; AGN, Tierras, vol. 1863, exp. 5, ff. 5–5v.
[47] AGN, TSJDF, Corregidores, caja 32B, exp. 35, ff. 1–1v.
[48] AGN, Tierras, vol. 2669, exp. 9, ff. 8–8v.
[49] AGN, TSJDF, Corregidores, caja 32A, exp. 29, ff. 3–3v and 5–5v; AGN, Civil, vol. 1059, exp. 4, ff. 3–3v; Pizzigoni, *Testaments of Toluca*, 33.

parties agreed to the sale of land in Milpa Alta. It included the Spanish word "para." (By contrast, the first time "para" appeared in a Toluca testament was over a century earlier, in 1692).[50] While the inclusion of a preposition indicates extensive Spanish linguistic influences, at the same time, though, it may not have been all that out of the ordinary: it appeared in a formulaic phrase common to legal documents: "para [la] camara de su magestad" (to his majesty's exchequer). Notably, the document was issued by Milpa Alta's cabildo, which is to say by precisely by those individuals most likely to be conversant with Spanish administrative and legal conventions.[51]

If not in government documents, the few other stage 3 borrowings can be found in sources dealing with financial matters. A 1772 accounting document written in Nahuatl that pertained to Bartolomé Francisco – and that was included in a lawsuit along with Bartolomé's testament – provided details of payments for the rental of a parcel of tribute land, with the proceeds having been assigned to the church. In the yearly accounting of the rentals, the author of the document used the Spanish word *porque* (because, in this context). While the rental document contained several loanwords, including "boelta" (*vuelta,* here referring either to a reimbursement or to an amount that was overdue), the accompanying testament did not.[52] Financial arrangements again provide the context for another set of stage 3 borrowings in a set of documents pertaining to don Gabriel Melchor in 1715. Three such borrowings appear in the sources. One of the documents was a certification by the local cabildo of don Gabriel's testament. It listed his loans, debts, and other obligations. The certification included the preposition *desde* (since).[53] The two others, from the accompanying testament itself, were verbs that had been assimilated into Nahuatl conventions for verb endings, in this case *desquitaroa* and *cobraroa* (respectively, "to compensate or pay back" and "to collect"). The first verb, with emphasis added, appeared in the statement "Ca ye sexiuh-pha oquimotoquili ypan xihuitl de 1714 anos Ca ye opeuh yn Cuenta, Ca ytla OhuaSic y matlactli xihuitl ca yoquidesquitaro yn tomin" ("He has already sowed it one year, in the year of 1714, when the account began, and when it reaches ten years the money will have been paid off"). The second instance, with *cobraroa,* appears in the following sentence:

Yhua niquitohua ca ome cortinas, oquihuicac prenda cohuetero, Ca ysica quimo-quixtilis yn D.ⁿ Juan Lorenso ca ypanpatzinco ca quimotlahuiquililia, Ca yhuaxcatzin

[50] Pizzigoni, *Testaments of Toluca.*   [51] AGN Tierras, vol. 2426, exp. 13, ff. 6–6v.
[52] AGN, Tierras, vol. 2669, exp. 7, ff. 2 and 3–3v (the latter being the testament).
[53] AGN, Tierras, vol. 1905, exp. 8, f. 7.

yn S,tos, yntlacamo ca yca hui [gostissia ?] qui**cobraros**que y nopilhuan, y nehuatl ca ninomaquixtitiuh, camo tlei nicnohuiquililia, y noermano D.ⁿ J.ⁿ lorenso.

And I say that soon don Juan Lorenzo is to redeem the curtains that the firework-maker took in hock, because he owes him, and they are the property of the saints. If he doesn't, my children are to collect them by legal procedures. As I redeem myself [before God?], I owe nothing to my brother don Juan Lorenzo.

The documents from which these examples are taken were from Tlahuac and not Xochimilco. As a result, they belonged to a different writing tradition.[54]

Even so, the loanwords in don Gabriel's testament had one thing in common with those from Xochimilco, namely, the high incidence of Spanish loanwords that had to do with economic relationships. These included such examples as pesos, of course, but also censo, obraje, bill of sale, concierto, *caja* (lockbox), and salary. In a similar vein, a notarial contract by Xochimilco's council officers referred to a "cotador" or *contador* (bookkeeper).[55] To these terms can be added others, such as *surco* (furrow, for a chinampa) and *huerta* (orchard or irrigated land). One distinctive use of loanwords that suggests more pervasive Hispanic influences can be seen in a title to land awarded to Antonio Bernabe by the cabildo officers of Tecomitl in 1720. Reflecting the ongoing utility of usufruct arrangements, the document identified the land as "tlali de buen comun," which is to say communal land. Interestingly, the councilmen opted for this phrasing in place of an equivalent Nahuatl term like *altepetlalli*.[56] Another unusual instance of borrowing from Spanish can be found in a petition from San Miguel Topilejo in 1768. The authors invoked the legal concept of custom, or *costumbre* (in this case rendered in the plural as "costobreyes").[57]

Political contexts such as this help explain the adoption of other specific terms. A Nahuatl election report for Xochimilco in 1692 unsurprisingly includes the word "ylecsio." Even less surprising are the appearance of the following terms in a petition – "recago" (as in *rezago*), "pleyto," "anparador," *corte*, and "probisio Real" – given that it was written by the delinquent governor, don Diego Juárez, in 1650, when he faced a lawsuit filed with the high court over tribute arrears that had to do with the contravention of a royal order.[58] Alternatively, and as one would expect, loanwords were borrowed for religious objects or concepts, such

---

[54] AGN, Tierras, vol. 1905, exp. 8, ff. 4–4v.   [55] AGNM, Xochimilco, vol. 1, ff. 43–43v.
[56] AGN, Tierras vol 2327 exp 10, f. 1.
[57] AGN, Criminal, vol. 24, 1a tramite, ff. 50–50v.
[58] AGN, Hospital de Jesús, vol. 325, exp. 5, ff. 8–9.

as *altartzin* (as in altar, here with a reverential ending), "bigiliya" (vigil), and "retapitos" (retablos). A list of church expenses, written by a fiscal of the church in Santiago Tepalcatlalpan in 1680 used the Spanish noun when referring to the church's organ. Beyond matters of religion, politics, and economics, other technical terms that appeared as loanwords in the sources included "mayestro" (*maestro*; in this case, as a title for a man), *esquina* (corner), *paila* (a metal pan), and *partera* (midwife).[59]

The overwhelming majority of late colonial loanwords, then, were nouns, just as one would expect to find in much older documents. We can see a further instance of the stable quality of Xochimilco's Nahuatl in the preference of the Xochimilca for using Nahuatl terms that could, in theory, be used interchangeably with common Spanish equivalents. In 1631, for instance, doña María Juana continued the tradition of referring to a document, and a notarial one at that, as *amatl* from the old Nahuatl term for paper.[60] The same word was chosen by another high-ranking member of the nobility: in 1588 the elder don Martín Cerón y Alvarado continued to use the term *amatl* even as he referred to his testament as an *escritura*.[61] In the eighteenth century, while Nahuas continued to use the term *amatl* they now sometimes did so alongside other, more specific identifications of the sources, as with the phrase "amatl carta de venta" in two 1729 bills of sale.[62]

Other Nahuatl terms also proved enduring even when there were loanwords that could serve as common equivalents. Some of these terms had to do with pastoralism. Thus we see *tecpancalli* being used to mean an enclosure specifically for livestock, which is to say a corral. Interestingly, the governor don Hipólito Bautista de Alvarado, who also held the office of interpreter, used tecpancalli in his Spanish translation of a Nahuatl document (i.e., as a Nahuatl loanword into Spanish).[63] Such terminology was likely to be found in communities up in the montes, where there were numerous livestock ranches. In 1673, Diego López opted to use the old

[59] UNAM, Biblioteca Nacional, Fondo Reservado, Archivo Franciscano, Caja 112, exp. 1531, ff. 4–5v; AGN, Civil, vol. 2215, exp. 1, f. 11; AGN, TSJDF, Corregidores, caja 31B, exp. 62, f. 7; AGN, Civil, vol. 1059, exp. 4, ff. 3–3v; AGN, Tierras, vol. 2327, exp. 10, ff. 6–7v; AGN, Tierras, vol. 2427, exp. 5, f. 2; AGN, Tierras, vol. 2427, exp. 10, f. 6; AGN, Tierras, vol. 2429, exp. 3, ff. 14–15; AGN, TSJDF, Corregidores, caja 31B, exp. 63, f. 3; AGN, Vínculos y Mayorazgos, vol. 279, exp. 1, ff. 12–13v; AGN, Vínculos y Mayorazgos, vol. 279, exp. 1, ff. 19–21v. For the church organ, see AGN, Criminal, vol. 233, exp. 18, ff. 279–280 and 283–284.
[60] UNAM, Fondo Reservado, Archivo Franciscano, caja 112, exp. 1531, ff. 4–5v.
[61] AGN, Vínculos y Mayorazgos, vol. 279, exp. 1, ff. 6–7v.
[62] AGN, Tierras, vol. 2669, exp. 10, ff. 4 and 7v.
[63] AGN, TSJDF, Corregidores, caja 31B, exp. 63, f. 4 (the Nahuatl original is on f. 3).

Nahuatl term *cuacuahueque* for cattle even though bulls, oxen, and cows were all originally foreign animals for which Spanish terms were widespread (and that had been in New Spain for 150 years at that point).[64] The surprising presence of the archaic term for cattle shows that the cultural persistence of older Nahuatl was not simply confined to the lake areas of Xochimilco, where one would expect to find a fainter influence of outsiders given their aquatic orientation and the continuation of chinampa cultivation as an indigenous specialty. Intriguingly, though, the same degree of continuity with older Nahuatl forms – and the corresponding absence of stage 3 phenomena – was also to be found in upland areas. These included such altepetl as San Miguel Topilejo, San Pedro Atocpan, San Pablo Oztotepec, and Santa María de la Asunción Milpa Alta.

In the eighteenth century these communities produced a good number of Nahuatl documents, all of which exhibited the same pronounced retention of earlier Nahuatl forms. Few of them likewise contained stage 3 linguistic changes. Presumably two demographic and environmental factors explain these patterns of continuity: for one thing, the communities were pretty remote; for another, there were few resources there and, as we have seen, land was not especially suitable for intensive cultivation. As a result, pastoralism and pulque production were the predominant economic activities, and the extensive nature of livestock ranching would not have been conducive to the formation of populous, dense communities of outsiders among local residents. According to the 1778 census, San Pablo (presumably Oztotepec) had 869 Native inhabitants, of whom sixteen were Spaniards and twenty-three were mestizos. Milpa Alta, a large town, had 2,548 inhabitants of whom less than 1 percent (a mere twenty-one individuals) were Spaniards. San Pedro Atocpan, with 1,592 residents, and Topilejo, with 774, did not have a single Spanish or casta resident, at least not officially.[65]

COMMUNITIES, SCRIBES, AND LOCAL DOCUMENTARY TRADITIONS

In place of the usual stage 3 characteristics, the Nahuatl sources from Xochimilco – both upland and lacustrine – exhibited other manifestations of linguistic change. These changes took several forms. The most conspicuous were those changes that had to do with orthography and

---

[64] AGN, Tierras, vol. 1750, exp. 1, ff. 37–37v.

[65] AGN, Padrones, vol. 29, f. 3v (258 alternative foliation).

handwriting. The neat, regular script of the early colonial period gradually morphed into less consistent, more idiosyncratic writing, often with larger and less evenly sized letters. This process was slow. The 1673 testament of Diego López, for instance, closely resembled the clear, consistent script of the early seventeenth century. It was only in the eighteenth century that such changes in writing style took hold, as with a land title from Tecomitl in 1720, and they did so especially in that century's second half.[66] Alternative spellings of words also came into being, as did greater variation in the spelling of words, at times with inconsistencies appearing in a single document. In 1768, for instance, a petition from San Miguel Topilejo rendered the name of the community as both "San Miguel tonpilego" and "sa miguel topolegu."[67]

Also prominent were changes in the expressive richness of the language. This trend took several forms. During the seventeenth century, the elevated, polite discourse of the nobility went into decline and disappeared. In its place were the more frequent additions of reverential endings to words, typically with -*tzin* or -*tzintli*, as with separate instances in which Nahuas wrote the word "testamentotzin" for "testament."[68] In addition, the sources tended to become less eloquent and had fewer embellishments. This last change can be seen most clearly in the formulaic statements found in standardized documents such as testaments, which previously had typically followed long-established conventions set down by Molina and early Nahua scribes like Martín Pauper de Monte Alegre and Mateo Ceverino de Arellano. All of this is to suggest that some of the most substantial changes in Nahuatl writing took place under internal stimuli rather than the external ones stemming from encounters with outsiders. As such, they likely reflected greater autonomy of local communities in training scribes and maintaining their own documentary traditions.

The changes can also be seen in terms of deviations from the stylistic conventions of well-established writing traditions of major centers. Xochimilco, with its distinctive and deep-seated writing tradition, proved either less susceptible to change or – to view the issue from another angle – the changes were less rapid and substantial there than elsewhere. For this

---

[66] AGN, Tierras, vol. 2327, exp. 10, f. 1. For another example, see vol. 1750, exp. 1, ff. 37–37v.

[67] AGN, Criminal, vol. 24, 1a tramite, ff. 50–50v.

[68] See the example of "testamentotzin" in a bill of sale from 1729 as well as another legal document referring to a testament from Xochimilco in 1765, AGN, Tierras, vol. 2669, exp. 10, f. 7v, and vol. 2670, exp. 2, ff. 10–10v.

reason, the 1715 testament of don Gabriel Melchor, set down Tlahuac – where there may have been a less robust writing tradition – contained several stage 3 loanwords as well as significant changes in orthography even though the handwriting remained neat and regular, apart from the inconsistent capitalizations. Another example of this was a greater use of the letter "s," including, at times, its repetition, as with "ssihuapilli" (*cihuapilli*, or "noblewoman, lady").[69]

These changes were minor in comparison with other communities that lacked strong scribal tradition. Tlahuac, after all, was home to a significant religious center, with a Dominican friary. This religious influence also applied to outlying communities in Xochimilco's jurisdiction, where parish seats were founded, including Milpa Alta (in the 1560s), San Antonio Tecomitl (1581), San Gregorio Atlapulco (by 1600), and Santa María Tepepan (1646). Tellingly, it would seem, Tolyahualco did not have a friary, and the village only gained jurisdictional separation from the city of Xochimilco in the late seventeenth century, by which time a strong writing tradition may not have had enough time to develop.[70] If this were to have been the case, it would explain why Juana Martina's 1693 testament was full of deviations from the sources produced elsewhere in Xochimilco's juridiction. Some of the differences in this testament may also have stemmed from the possibility that two scribes had set down Juana's last wishes. The handwriting of the recto side of the folio was very messy; halfway down the verso folio, a second, neater script took over, before reverting, at the end, to the original hand. (Only one notary was named). Beyond the issue of handwriting however, the scribe (or scribes) tended to omit entire syllables, often rendering the vocabulary unclear and the grammar less intelligible. These quirks can be identified through the departures from conventional phrasing, as with "ma mochiti ca" apparently being a shortened version of the phrase "ma mochintin quimatican" ("let all know that") and "atzitl" being a substitute for *amatzintli* (the word *amatl*, for "paper," with a reverential suffix). Additionally, the scribe – if not the testator – skipped over many of the common opening statements found in wills, referring only briefly to the trinity before stating that God shall render judgment on her and stating that, "Now if I die in the coming time, he is likewise to come take me."[71]

[69] AGN, Tierras, vol. 1905, exp. 8, ff. 4–4v and 7.

[70] AGN, Indios, vol. 30, exp. 13, ff. 9–9v; exp. 165, ff. 157v–158, and exp. 182, ff. 170v–171v.

[71] AGN, Tierras, vol. 2427, exp. 6, ff. 3–3v.

In Xochimilco as elsewhere in central Mexico the tendency to pass quickly over the typical preamble and either simplify or omit formulaic phrases became hallmarks of eighteenth-century sources. María Sebastiana's 1702 testament omitted the standard statement about being sound of mind and, unusually, set down her requests for masses to ease her soul through purgatory only at the end of the testament, rather than as one of its first provisions. Were it not for these variations on the standard format of the document, her testament would have had much in common with its sixteenth-century predecessors, although the scribe did use some unusual orthography, as with "notlasotaxin dios" instead of "notlaçotatzin dios" (my precious father, God) and "tlalmile" in place of *tlalmilli* (cultivated fields).[72] A similar tendency to leave out some formulas can be seen in other testaments, as with Micaela Isabel's 1746 will, which opened with "Jesus, Mary, and Joseph" – but with no mention of the trinity – before identifying the testator and then quickly stating, "God is exercising his justice and love on me; if I die, I place my spirit and soul entirely in his hands. As to my earthly body, I am to lie buried at the feet of my precious father San Miguel." The swift, abbreviated movement through the opening statement, in this case, might be explained by the overall brevity of the document. It was not even 200 words in length.[73]

Other testaments' preambles were even more terse. Miguel Vicente, in 1712, left out the customary phrases about being sound of mind and of returning to the earth from whence he came. The scribe skipped these phrases despite (or perhaps because) the testament was lengthy, covering some two and a half manuscript folios. Even more brief was don Marcos Antonio, of Tepepan, who dove straight into his first bequest when setting down his 1735 testament. He completely skipped the usual formulas. Santiago de la Cruz likewise left out much from his will, set down a year later, and some of the text kept by the scribe seems to have been garbled. The orthography, moreover, was unusual, with "tasmento" in place of *testamento* (and no apparent abbreviation mark). Manuela Francisca's 1795 testament was likewise direct, stating briefly that she was sick, that her body was made of earth, as God had created it, and that she was now awaiting death.[74] It should be noted, however, that the trend toward simplification and brevity was not universal. In 1769, Josef Nicólas's testament remained quite elaborate. He was especially forthcoming

---

[72] AGN, Tierras, vol. 1179, exp. 1, ff. 3–3v.   [73] AGN, Tierras, vol. 1863, exp. 2, f. 4.
[74] AGN, TSJDF, Corregidores, caja 31B, exp. 81, ff. 1–2; AGN Tierras, vol. 2669, exp. 7, f. 8; AGN, Tierras, vol. 2427, exp. 10, f. 6; AGN, TSJDF, Corregidores, caja 31B, exp. 35, ff. 1–1v.

about his soul passing through purgatory as well as his devotions to the saints.[75]

At times it appeared less as though the notary sought to omit phrases than that he was unfamiliar with them. Rosa María's testament of 1769 was quite unusual. The scribe seems to have been unacquainted with the typical statements. He left some of them out entirely, repeated others, and deviated from the usual sequence of the introduction: "Truly my earthly body is very sick, but my soul is very sound; but my earthly body is very sick. If God effaces me in the coming time, I place my spirit and soul very entirely in his hands, for it was redeemed by him with his precious blood. No one at all can hide from death; when God has effaced me, I place my spirit and soul very entirely in his hands." The conclusion was no less distinctive: "The memorandum of testament of me the sick person named Rosa María has ended. My sick person's statement is to be carried out and executed. May it thus be done."[76]

Aside from departures from the old conventional wording of testaments, in the eighteenth century the scribes' writing and orthography changed significantly, which points to further deviations from notarial conformity.[77] Some of these alterations were trivial. Matheo Francisco's 1707 testament, set down in Tolyahualco, stood out from others of its time by having conspicuously large letters. This gradually became something of a trend over the eighteenth century. In another example, Bartolomé Francisco's will was written in large, uneven, and messy letters, and, similarly, the scribe who set down doña Petrona Antonia's will, in 1759, wrote in distinctively large and thick script. The scribe also used an unconventional abbreviation for Francisco, writing it "fran#co" (with a kind of angled pound sign), rather than just as "franco." Other orthographic variations were more significant. Doña María Pascuala's testament formed part of a couple of distinct patterns. The first involved using the letter z in place of s or c and ç. The other involved substituting the letter e, at the end of nouns, for the old i. Thus we read "tlale" for land and "tlalmile" for cultivated land (in place of *tlalli* and *tlalmilli*). This variant spelling applied to Nahuatl nouns ending in *-lli* as well as *-tli*. As such, "ichtacatzintle" replaced *ichtacatzintli* while "caltzintle" departed from the conventional *caltzintli* (a small house). Such alternative orthography

---

[75] AGN, Tierras, vol. 2327, exp. 10, ff. 6–7v.

[76] AGN, Tierras, vol. 2669, exp. 9, ff. 8–8v.

[77] The term *notarial conformity* is from Melton-Villanueva, *The Aztecs at Independence*, 93.

may have reflected speech patterns, not least because they can be seen in documentation across the entirety of the eighteenth century.[78]

Whereas some orthographical variations were straightforward and readily comprehensible, others pose a greater challenge to comprehension. Rosa María's 1769 testament, which contained the repetitive and unconventional formulaic phrases, also had a number of orthographic idiosyncrasies. The notary created no little confusion by reducing -*tl* and -*ll* spellings to just a single -*l*, thereby making it difficult, at times, to distinguish between words and to identify the discrete nouns that were merged within agglomerative clusters. Making matters worse, the scribe also reversed himself, at times adding -*tl* to a single -*l*, even doing so with Spanish loanwords. Thus, with random capitalization, the word "tlanoBel" is hard to decipher as the Spanish, *la noble*. The document is full of other orthographic inconsistencies. In place of the standard "tz" combination he used an "s," which can create confusion with different sounds. The scribe, moreover, added extra vowels within and after consonants, such as "neche" for *nech*-, "teche" for *tech*-. The additional vowel becomes more troublesome when it is added to words like *manic* (to be spread out, to be located), such that "maniquic" is actually manic with an additional *i* appended to it, which in turn required that the original, final *c* be converted to *qui*. The additional final c is a further quirk of the notary's style, one that is hard to figure out. The same confusion appears in the phrase "noconnehuic," which is *noconeuh* along with the additional *i* and *c* (noconeuh being the possessive form of *conetl*, or "child"). It is worth noting here that Rosa María's testament was produced in Xochimilco itself and not an outlying settlement in the jurisdiction. It was also written by a noble, don Antonio de Santa María, who served as a church notary.[79]

His identity might provide a clue about the origins of these changes in eighteenth-century documentary production. Those individuals who were writing the testaments increasingly seem to have been the church notaries rather than the municipal scribes serving on the Nahua cabildo. The surviving testaments point to this gradual shift in authorship over time. In the sixteenth century, for instance, six testaments were written by the escribanos of the town council, as opposed to just the one by the notary of the church (for one other, the scribe's identity is unknown). This stands in

---

[78] AGN, Tierras, vol. 2427, exp. 6, f. 1; vol. 2429, exp. 3, ff. 14–15 and 21–21v; vol. 2669, exp. 7, ff. 2 and 3–3v; AGN, Civil, vol. 1059, exp. 4, ff. 3–3v; AGN, Tierras, vol. 1179, exp. 1, ff. 3–3v and AGN, TSJDF, Corregidores, caja 31B, exp. 35, ff. 1–1v.

[79] AGN, Tierras, vol. 2669, exp. 9, ff. 8–8v.

contrast to the period after 1750 when church notaries wrote four out of five testaments. Making the contrast even more vivid, between 1650 and 1795, only one of fourteen testaments was set down by someone who explicitly identified himself as a municipal scribe. Furthermore, in only two of the instances in which someone serving on the cabildo set down a testament after 1600, the author was not a formal tlacuilo; rather, it was don Diego Juárez, the last member of the ruling dynasty to serve as governor and in other administrative capacities.[80] His identity as a member of the Nahua upper class is also pertinent; such individuals were more likely to be literate, especially given their close associations with Franciscan friars, and as individuals with direct experience in government service, they would have necessarily been familiar with documentary and legal conventions. Literacy, of course, was an essential requirement of municipal leadership.

The social status of the scribes also changed over time. Initially, in the sixteenth century, not one of the eight testaments was authored by someone with the honorific title "don." In other words, none of the scribes were members of the upper echelon of Nahua society. That pattern shifted in the seventeenth century such that four of the ten testaments were written by someone identified as a "don." The pattern continued in the eighteenth century, although it was less pronounced then: individuals identified as a "don" wrote five of twenty-two testaments. What all this means is that, over time, those who wrote the last wills and testaments were increasingly likely to be church notaries and members of the upper nobility. What remains unknown is how they learned to read and write, who taught them, and how far their education was rooted in experience with the model testaments of the sixteenth century. One wonders if the changes in the documents also arose, indirectly, from the ongoing controversies within the church about the instruction of Native peoples in Spanish or their own languages, as well as the process of secularization taking place in the late eighteenth century.[81] Perhaps it is reasonable to assume that, as the decades passed, the documents increasingly diverged from their earlier

---

[80] UNAM, Fondo Reservado, Archivo Franciscano, caja 112, exp. 1531, ff. 4–5v. The analysis here and in the next paragraph is based on the testaments cited in this chapter and elsewhere in the book.

[81] Mark Z. Christensen, *Nahua and Maya Catholicisms: Texts and Religion in Colonial Central Mexico and Yucatan* (Stanford: Stanford University Press, 2013), 16, 66, 80; Matthew D. O'Hara, *A Flock Divided: Race, Religion, and Politics in Mexico, 1749–1857* (Durham: Duke University Press, 2010); William B. Taylor, *Magistrates of the Sacred: Priests and Parishioners in Eighteenth-Century Mexico* (Stanford: Stanford University Press, 1996); D. A. Brading, *Church and State in Bourbon Mexico: The Diocese of Michoacán, 1749–1810* (New York: Cambridge University Press, 1994).

equivalents because the individuals writing them were less likely to have been the municipal tlacuilos of old. Either way, a key trend seems quite clear: whereas in the sixteenth century documentary production had been closely intertwined with colonial institutions and their representatives, as with Molina's model testament and Mateo Ceverino de Arellano's variation of it, by the second half of the colonial period, Xochimilco's Nahuatl had become less regular, less consistent, and arguably more independent and distinct. As part of this process, writing styles may have become specific either to the communities in which the sources were produced or, perhaps, to the scribes who wrote them. Put another way, there may have been a significant degree of local creativity on the part of the notaries, as Miriam Melton-Villanueva has suggested for scribal traditions in altepetl near Metepec.[82] In this regard, the identities, backgrounds, and educational experiences of key intermediaries in scribal traditions may have played a vital role in changes in Nahua culture, much as Mark Christensen has found for the fiscales and maestros who wrote unpublished, unofficial religious texts.[83]

In spite of the possibility that local writing traditions may have influenced the phrasing and orthography of Xochimilco's documents, other changes became common if not consistent over time. The Spanish loanword *solar*, or house plot, increasingly appeared as "xolal," a phenomenon that was seen elsewhere in Mexico. The new spelling emerged in the eighteenth century and appeared in at least half a dozen documents from Xochimilco, although in one instance it was spelled "xolali."[84] Changes in the sources also extended to inconsistent spellings. Sometimes, as with xolali, they were minor and insignificant. On other occasions, though, they could be quite different from the older style. If "notlasotaxin," or "our beloved father" (with the reverential ending), can be distinguished immediately from *notlaçotatzin*, "notatxi" proves more problematic (both "xolali" and "notatxi" appear in the same testament).[85] Other examples were no less tricky. Doña María Pascuala had two complementary testaments set down for her – with the second functioning like a codicil – and this latter document contained the almost unfathomable "nipoi" in place of *nipohui* (for the verb *pohui*, "to count or belong"). Another pair of testaments, from the

[82] Melton-Villanueva, *The Aztecs at Independence*, 91.

[83] Christensen, *Nahua and Maya Catholicisms*, 84–88.

[84] AGN, Tierras, vol. 2429, exp. 3, ff. 14–15, AGN, Civil, vol. 1059, exp. 4, ff. 3–3v, AGN, Tierras, vol. 1832, exp. 1, ff. 22–23, AGN, Tierras, vol. 2327, exp. 10, ff. 6–7v, AGN, TSJDF, Corregidores, caja 31B, exp. 81, ff. 1–2, and, for the exceptional spelling, AGN, Tierras, vol. 1179, exp. 1, ff. 6–6v.

[85] AGN, Tierras, vol. 1179, exp. 1, ff. 6–6v.

late 1780s in San Gregorio Atlapulco, are particularly hard to decipher. The greatest trouble stems from the interchangeable use of the letters l, c, and t. Other irregularities included changes in letter sequence – hence "anme" for "amen" – and other variations, such as "neguatlli" for *nehuatl* and "yngua" for *yhuan* ("and," "along with," "with"). The scribe was also inconsistent, especially in substituting the letters *u* and *o* such that in one place he writes the loanwords *nomemoria testamento* as "nomemura notestanmeto," while in another they become "numemuria notesanmetu." If these words are readily understood, on its own, "anlanpullon" was not. Thankfully its context in the document reveals it to have been Atlapulco, the name of the town.[86]

Pronunciation, as one would expect, explains the majority of the variations in orthography. One example comes to us from a petition by the fiscal of the church in San Miguel Topilejo, "don crispobal des satiagu," who also wrote "satisimo sancram" (with an abbreviation for "sacramento"). Instead of omitting letters, some scribes used the letters t and d interchangeably, thereby producing "deutitipa sata ana" for the place name Teotitipan Santa Ana. In this manner Dominica appeared as "tominica" while God was referred to as "hueytlatocatzi Rey noesdro senior" (with noesdro for *nuestro*).[87] In another example from Tecomitl, which itself was set down as "Thecomic," the scribe for the cabildo referred to a "don thoMingo."[88] Similarly, in a bill of sale from 1667, we see "desdico" for *testigo* as well as the memorable variant spelling "pefrerno" for *febrero* (February).[89] Beyond this eccentricity, to judge from other examples, Nahuatl pronunciation had not changed dramatically by the eighteenth century insofar as it still remained quite distinct from Spanish. At least, this would appear to have been the case with such words as "repoblica" (*república*), "ni.pehualdia" (*nicpehualtia*), "partolome" (*Bartolomé*), and "cioda" (for *ciudad*), to give just a few of the more immediately recognizable examples.[90] One common sign of Spanish

---

[86] AGN, Tierras, vol. 2429, exp. 3, ff. 14–15 and 21–21v; AGN, Tierras, vo. 2327, exp. 1, ff. 14–14v and 15v.

[87] AGN, Criminal, vol. 24, 1a tramite, ff. 50–50v. The letter *g* might be swapped for a *c*, as with "dieco de la cruz," while elsewhere Baltasar appeared as "Bartesal." AGN, Tierras, vol. 1832, exp. 1, ff. 22–23 and AGN, Tierras, vol. 1863, exp. 2, ff. 2–2v. Don Diego de San Pedro's testament had "tesdamedo" and "nehuatl nodoca" and "tlaçoDatzin" in it, AGN, Tierras, vol. 2427 exp. 5, f. 2.

[88] See also the "alhuasil mayor" in the land title, AGN, Tierras, vol. 2327, exp. 10, f. 1.

[89] AGN, TSJDF, Corregidores, caja 31A, exp. 2, f. 3.

[90] AGN, Tierras, vol. 1179, exp. 1, ff. 6–6v, AGN, Tierras, vol. 1832, exp. 1, ff. 22–23, AGN, Tierras, vol. 2327, exp. 1, ff. 14–15v and 18–19, AGN, Tierras, vol. 2269, exp. 7, f. 8, and AGN, TSJDF, Corregidores, caja 31B, exp. 80, ff. 1–1v.

influence, at least orthographically, could be seen in the use of the double *ll* as a *y* sound, as in "lleguatzin" for *yehuatzin* (the third person; he, she, it, they) and Mollotlan for the toponym Moyotlan.[91]

On a couple of occasions, the eccentricities of some scribes' writing make their documents appear to be unique. The 1783 testament of Miguel Francisco has particularly unconventional orthography. Most striking, though, is the scribe's handwriting. Unlike any other writing produced in Xochimilco's jurisdiction, the text is pretty much illegible, and the angular strokes for the letters appear to be exceptional. While Pascual Gregorio was the altepetl's formal scribe, such was the distinctiveness of his hand that one wonders where he was trained and by whom.[92]

Testaments such as this suggest a considerable degree of autonomy enjoyed by Nahuas in producing documents for consumption within their own communities. The community-oriented writing traditions are well known for generating a particular kind of documentary genre, the community histories called *títulos primordiales*, or "primordial titles." Several such documents were produced in Xochimilco. Intriguingly, one of the testaments to be preserved in the archives, which was separated from other community sources with which it would have belonged, was at once a título and a testament. In 1715, the Nahuas of a tlaxilacalli within Xochimilco named Santissima Trinidad Tlalnahuac initiated litigation against the residents of a separate, outlying village beyond the city over the rights to two parcels of land. As part of the lawsuit, the litigants presented a copy of a testament, set down more than forty years earlier, in 1672, by Francisca María. The testament appears on a darkened piece of maguey paper and was written in a neat hand, one that looks entirely in keeping with the writing of the late seventeenth century. Moreover, the document contained no obvious anachronisms, and the Nahuatl was consistent with the age – the opening statements were brief, with the tlacuilo having skipped over much of the usual formulaic phrasing, and there were some distinctive features, such as swearing on the cross and the testator asking the lords and the rulers to forgive her for her sins – but none of the language seems to have been out of the ordinary. The document stated that Francisca, as a single woman with no offspring or heirs, elected to bequeath her land to the lords and rulers of the community with the proviso that they ensure it be used and cultivated

---

[91] AGN, TSJDF, Corregidores, caja 32A, exp. 29, ff. 3–3v and 5–5v and AGN, TSJDF, Corregidores, caja 31B, exp. 62, f. 7. See also AGN, Tierras, vol. 2327, exp. 10, ff. 6–7v.
[92] AGN, TSJDF, Corregidores, caja 32B, exp. 72, f. 3.

so as to support religious festivals for Corpus Christi, Easter, and the titular fiesta of the community, which in Nahuatl was termed the *alte-peylhuitl*, or the altepetl holiday (or saint's day).

Accordingly, after Francisca's demise, the lands passed into the posses-sion of the community. The document now became part of the altepetl's collection of papers. As a result, the testament was either copied or modified: set down on maguey paper, the testament is striking for having been surrounded by a border consisting of two parallel lines, much as one might find in a land título.[93] And, to remove any remaining uncertainty about the type of document it was, at the bottom of the page appears a label, "titulo de ss^{ma} trinidad," one that reveals the testament to have been converted, after being put into effect, into a land title. The tailoring of this document by the community likely reflects its autonomous scribal and archival tradition even as the hybrid quality of the source – as a título and a testament – likewise reflects a merging of different documentary genres for local needs. Together they reveal, as do the wider corpus of late colonial testaments, the evolving but still vital tradition of writing within local communities.[94]

CONCLUSION

Written forms of Nahuatl expression in Xochimilco had both distinctive, local qualities and a resilient character. Certain kinds of orthography, figures of speech, and vocabulary reflected local patterns, some of which were regional while others were potentially related to the communities where the sources were produced. As with the documents from several altepetl near Metepec, which Miriam Melton-Villanueva examined, com-munities in and around the southern lakes may have developed their own particular notarial styles even as scribes themselves elaborated their own customs.[95] The deviations away from older conventions and models of testaments, including the wording of formulaic phrases, as well as changes in handwriting and orthography, are hard to account for. They may have derived from other cultural shifts, or departures in the identities of those who drafted the documents. Church notaries increasingly seemed to be the

---

[93] Several primordial titles survive for communities in the jurisdiction in AGN, Tierras, vol. 3032, exp. 3 and 4. For Santa María de la Asunción Milpa Alta, see ff. 207r–213r, 220r–227v; Santa Marta, ff. 202r–206v; San Andrés Mixquic, ff. 3 213r–216r; and Los Reyes, near San Juan Temamatla, ff. 276r–277v.

[94] AGN TSJDF, Corregidores, caja 31B, exp. 63, f. 3.

[95] Melton-Villanueva, *The Aztecs at Independence*, 97.

ones who set down testators' last wishes in the late colonial period, rather than the scribes of the cabildo. Alternatively, perhaps changes in education account for the shifts, as with the church equivocating about whether to encourage bilingualism, which became a significant source of controversy in the eighteenth century, in particular.[96]

Additionally, the changes may have arisen out of material conditions or the frequency and extent to which Nahuas encountered and engaged with non-Native peoples. If material circumstances did matter then such changes as took place to the lake area's ecology and economy may not have had an effect on documentary production until later. If this were the case, it would prove difficult to trace the evolution of linguistic change into the nineteenth century for the simple reason that the writing of Nahuatl sources went into sharp decline after Independence.[97] The changes that can be observed in the Nahuatl sources, then, had enigmatic origins. But what remains clear is that the Nahuatl in Xochimilco did not undergo substantial alteration after the mid-sixteenth century, at least when it came to loanwords. Apart from a few exceptional cases, the sources remained solidly rooted in the second stage of linguistic change identified by James Lockhart. It would seem reasonable to suppose that continuities in the landscape and in the area's ecological autonomy had a great bearing on the persistence of Xochimilco's indigenous cultural heritage.

---

[96] Taylor, *Magistrates of the Sacred*, 95–96, 337–340.
[97] For an analysis of nineteenth-century sources, see Melton-Villanueva, *The Aztecs at Independence*.

Conclusion

As the native-language sources suggest, the history of Xochimilco and the chinampa districts still exhibited a great deal of continuity at the end of the colonial period. The area's residents were predominantly Nahuas, and they retained their demographic superiority by a wide margin over non-Native peoples. The Nahuas still spoke Nahuatl, of course, and they continued to bequeath chinampas, grain bins, and other indigenous items to their heirs in documents set down in their own language. The Nahuas resided in tlax-illacalli, those subunits of the altepetl which, itself, remained intact (as did the civil and ecclesiastical jurisdictions that relied on it). The Nahuas' communities were still located in the same, broadly recognizable landscape, one that stretched from the lakes to the sierras. Unlike Lakes Zumpango and Xaltocan to the north of the Basin of Mexico – which had essentially dried up – Lakes Xochimilco and Chalco were still deeply lacustrine environments (devastatingly so, at times of flooding). Much of the water management program persisted, including the dams and embankments and the hydraulic compartments as well as the ancient causeways of Mexicalzingo and Tlahuac, the latter having been renovated in the late eighteenth century. As geographers have noted, the chinampas and the engineering works had contributed to the making of a palimpsest landscape, one made up of accumulated layers of additions and modifications of engineering works.[1] A great deal of landesque capital underpinned the ongoing viability of the modified landscape.

Just as the area's ecology persisted so too did its economic foundations. Farmers still constructed and cultivated their bountiful aquatic gardens.

---

[1] Luna Golya, "Modeling the Aztec Agricultural Waterscape of Lake Xochimilco," 165.

Fewer chinampas may have been kept under communal ownership but a good many Nahuas remained smallholders. Some even maintained substantial landholdings that underpinned their status as members of the Nahua nobility. Reflecting old patterns of dispersed holdings, their properties often included land in the montes, as with don Hipólito and don Joseph Bautista de Alvarado, who alternated as governors of Xochimilco in the late seventeenth century and whose grandchildren, in the 1760s, still maintained their honorific titles and sizable estate.[2] Beyond landed wealth, a majority of the population continued to be employed in specialized trades, of which there were a wide variety, from fishermen and the makers of canoes and furniture to carpenters and stone masons. Local marketplaces did brisk trade, and merchants and artisans engaged in commercial exchanges, near and far, that relied on canoe transportation. There thus remained in Xochimilco, unlike many other places, a strong degree of social differentiation within the indigenous community.[3]

These continuities owed much to the enduring ecological autonomy of the chinampa districts. Just as the environment and its resources survived so Nahuas retained control of them. This autonomy also goes some way toward explaining why relatively few non-Native peoples made Xochimilco and other lakeside communities their homes, especially in comparison with other altepetl of the region. If non-Native peoples did secure access to lacustrine or piedmont resources, they often did so on terms set by the Nahua community. Thus Xochimilco rented out communally held property – its swamps, pastures, quarry, and the hacienda of Teuhtli, and other lands – to generate income for the community. Given their demographic preponderance, Nahuas faced fewer daily cross-cultural interactions and exchanges than did their fellow Native peoples elsewhere. The infrequent references to non-Native peoples in Nahuatl testaments found a counterpart in the comparative absence of Hispanic influences in the native-language sources themselves, which remained conspicuously rooted in the second stage of linguistic change.

The changes in Nahuatl that did take place in the latter half of the eighteenth century reflected the strength of community attachments. Nahuas' identity continued to be closely connected to their local associations. If anything, their micropatriotism might have deepened over time,

---

[2] AGN, Tierras, vol. 2670, exp. 1.
[3] Tetzcoco has been identified as the one other altepetl that retained a strong oficio tradition in the Basin of Mexico. Gibson, *The Aztecs under Spanish Rule*, 351.

as shown by the particularly local characteristics of their written language and the success of some previously subordinate communities in securing their jurisdictional independence. Institutions, particularly the church and the cabildo, remained foci of the community, and political constituencies remained strong, as shown in the concerted efforts of Xochimilco's cabildo, together with its alcaldes from smaller communities in its jurisdiction, to oppose the intrusions of lake-area haciendas in the early years of the nineteenth century.[4] Notably, by 1789, the ranks of the cabildo's officers had expanded to include thirteen alcaldes in addition to those from the altepetl's three constituent districts, thereby providing greater representation for those in outlying communities in the jurisdiction.[5]

At the same time, though, the contrasts between Xochimilco at the dawn and the twilight of the colonial period were vivid. The Xochimilca had suffered epidemic diseases and catastrophic demographic decline such that by 1800 the population was a fraction of its original size (perhaps just a quarter). During that time, Xochimilco became far more ethnically diverse, particularly with the gradual settling of Spaniards and the growth in the population of people of mixed ancestries. The city went from being an entirely Native American community – primarily consisting of Nahuas but also Otomí and, possibly, other groups – to one in which a quarter of the population in the urban, nucleated core, and a smaller proportion in the surrounding countryside, were individuals of mixed and non-Native ancestries. In addition, Spaniards brought with them new systems of government and introduced new civil authorities into the altepetl.[6] Of these novelties, the Nahuas made full use of the municipal council to preserve what they could of earlier political preferences and to defend their interests. And when pressed by circumstance, colonial demands, or the interference of unwanted intruders, the Nahuas turned to the legal system, having become, in the process, conversant with the conventions of the law and highly adept at using them. The Franciscans established a strong presence in the city, and Nahuas, as elsewhere, fashioned their own, local version of Catholicism. A strong cult of the saints, for instance, was a characteristic of late colonial Nahuatl testaments.

In spite of the survival of the lakes, the environment had changed significantly over the three centuries. At the time of the Spanish–Mexica

---

[4] AGN, Desagüe, vol. 43, exp. 5.

[5] Gibson, *The Aztecs*, 190, 515n138; AGN, Civil, vol. 1344, exp. 1 and 2; see also AGN, Tierras, vol. 1631, exp. 1.

[6] Cline, "A Cacicazgo in the Seventeenth-Century," 265–266.

War, the Aztec Empire had presided over the conversion of the majority of the southern lakes into the vast chinampa zone. Chinampas filled what previously had been the flowing waters of the lakes, even in the deepest parts furthest from the lakeshores. So numerous had the islands been in the lake that they constituted as much as half its entire surface area. The thousands of chinampas had been cultivated intensively to meet the dietary needs and preferences – toward cereals and vegetables, but not much meat – of tens of thousands of people. Thanks also to their abundant harvests, which continued long into the colonial period, the Native communities of the lake areas had been central to generating large tribute revenues for the government while also continuing to provision the capital. The extensive, large-scale water management system had served to make the region so very productive even as it protected Mexico Tenochtitlan from inundation.

After the Spanish–Mexica War significant changes set in. The chinampas furthest from the shores were washed away following breaches of causeways and dams. In their place were free-flowing waters. Sections of the lakes became watery enough that sizable waves, when the winds were up, could capsize canoes. In the late sixteenth century, localized flooding occasionally ruined harvests, damaged or destroyed chinampas, and disrupted daily life, at times bringing dislocation and hardship. But such floods, caused though they were by the extreme variations in climate during the Little Ice Age, remained infrequent. Some of the chinampas that did not get destroyed in flooding became vacant because of population loss, and with fewer farmers, Nahuas left more of the islands alone so that they could gather reeds and straw in place of crops. Alternatively, Nahuas turned to raising livestock on the chinampas.

To these alterations in land use other modifications were made to the watery landscape. Some of the former chinampa districts reverted to swamps. Others were converted into pastures which pushed further into the lakes from the shores, particularly when the owners of rural estates sought to expand their holdings. By the eighteenth century, with the growing market for meat, hides, and leather in Mexico City, intensive horticultural farming increasingly vied with extensive agriculture, primarily pastoralism, which had previously been confined to the upland areas. While Nahua communities continued to provide valuable tribute income to the government, haciendas began to replace them as the primary source of sustenance for the capital. The revitalized hydraulic engineering works continued to serve as flood defenses for Mexico City, but the government now also sought to protect haciendas from inundation. As the haciendas spread beyond the shores, the volume of the lakes decreased. Floods stemming from high levels of rainfall and from the smaller capacity of the lakes seem to have become more frequent, severe, and widespread. Geographers have observed that population recovery, alterations to land use with the rise of haciendas, and changes in climate during the late colonial period combined to create what Georgina Endfield termed "landscape instability." In this scenario, communities had less resilience when they faced adverse conditions. If this instability characterized the "little drought age" in parts of western and northern Mexico, in the southern lake areas its counterpart came in the form of too much water.[7] The lakeside communities also became more vulnerable to the risks of flooding at times when there were climate extremes, as in the aftermath of the Tambora eruption of 1815. That vulnerability was exacerbated by the encroachment of haciendas into the lake waters and by the policies of the colonial administration, which came to favor the interests of haciendas.

The extent to which Xochimilco enjoyed some degree of ecological autonomy shifted over the course of the colonial period. Under Aztec rule, the southern lakes had been carefully modified, monitored, and managed. The demise of the Aztec imperial state upended this and ushered in a greater degree of independence for the chinampa districts from ecological supervision. The Spanish government was, at least in the early years, largely uninterested in intervening in the southern lake environment. By default, then, the management of the southern lakes' hydrology reverted to lake-area communities. Unless labor demands dictated otherwise, Nahua cabildos could deploy their citizens to repair engineering works and clear canals on their own. Even when laborers were scarce and the government eager to recruit as many of them as it could for alternative projects, Nahuas were able to divert workers to their own water management projects. Only in the 1740s did agents of the Bourbon administration seek to assert control over the southern lakes' hydrology more frequently and insistently. This they did by revitalizing the old infrastructure and by requiring that canals be kept clear of impediments to the flow of water. Their interventions, resolute though they were, remained conservative in outlook. Bourbon-era reformers tended to distrust innovations to the hydraulic works: numerous inspections sought to identify recent changes

---

[7] Endfield, "Climate and Crisis in Eighteenth Century Mexico," 99–125; Endfield and O'Hara, "Degradation, Drought, and Dissent," 402–419; Endfield and O'Hara, "Conflicts over Water," 255–272; Endfield et al., "Conflict and Cooperation," 221–247; Swan, "Mexico in the Little Ice Age," 633–648.

to them so that they could be removed or reversed. In a parallel to the pre-contact past, much of the late colonial engineering works thus ended up resurrecting those constructions, like the causeway dividing Lakes Xochimilco and Chalco at Tlahuac, that dated back to Aztec times. Now, though, the return to old, pre-contact practices marked an erosion of Nahua communities' ecological autonomy.

The advance of haciendas into the lakes only added to the trend of reduced independence for Native communities in the management of their lacustrine resources. The aquatic buffer that had provided such essential protection against colonial intrusion became more porous. When appeals to the government for protection against the haciendas failed, that buffer began to disappear altogether, especially when haciendas positioned themselves as allies in the preservation of the capital's interests. The argument advanced by several hacendados (or at least their representatives) was that hacienda lands in the lake had to be kept dry so as to ensure the ample supply of meat and wheat to Mexico City; conversely, allowing water to penetrate and saturate their lake-area lands represented (and heightened) the same threat of flooding faced by the capital.

The fact that hacendados increasingly came to be high-ranking figures in the establishment surely reinforced the sense of alignment between government and hacienda interests. A few hacendados had long been members of the elite, as with don José Olmedo y Luján, the peninsular Spaniard whose commercial interests in the seventeenth century extended around the Atlantic world. But now, in the late eighteenth century, hacendados were more likely to be members of the merchant guild, the capital's administrative institutions, the ecclesiastical hierarchy or, in the case of the Marqués de San Miguel de Arauyo y Santa Olaya, the titled nobility. Vera Candiani has noted that, as a motive for pursuing the desagüe project, members of the Spanish upper class sought to separate water and earth and to fix them as distinct natural elements. Doing so would enable the landowners to consolidate and expand their interests.[8] In Xochimilco, the same underlying motivations applied. But there, where drainage remained unfeasible, the solution for Spaniards lay in fashioning drained pastures out of the lake. This goal came to dominate economic and ecological relationships between hacendados, desagüe authorities, and lakeside communities, to the detriment of Nahua residents.

---

[8] Candiani, *Dreaming of Dry Land*, 291.

Changing class relations also affected the Nahua community internally. At the outset of the colonial era, the upper echelon of Nahua society had consisted of the dynastic rulers and their lineages alongside a few other families of similar, superior social status (although their members did not serve as tlatoque). Below this exclusive rank were a greater number of lesser nobles. The nobility's position and authority rested on several foundations, not the least of which was the wealth generated by commoners and dependent laborers who worked communal lands, including chinampas, that had been set aside for the nobility. Over time these reciprocal relationships – in which commoners worked land in return for rights of citizenship – began to break down. To a certain extent, the desire for commoners to escape these exactions reflected the increased pressures of demographic decline. But demographic decline affected these relationships in a second way. The Nahua nobility's numbers likewise collapsed. In place of the old Nahua hierarchy, a new single-tiered and multiethnic upper class came into being. The new elite was defined by wealth, as in the past, but now its wealth was founded less on the combined control of subordinate laborers and access to community lands than it was by ownership of private property. The political legitimacy of the new leaders ceased to rest so firmly on lineage. Instead, esteemed ancestry was replaced by expectations that leaders be good stewards of community resources and honest, competent managers of municipal finances.

Ecological autonomy and changes to demography help us to identify the timing of historical changes. Changes to the landscape occurred immediately in the aftermath of the Spanish–Mexica War. So too did demographic decline. But whereas the landscape remained more or less the same for the next two centuries, demographic upheaval continued unabated into the mid-seventeenth century, after which time further changes followed with the rise of a Spanish community. With population collapse and demographic and ethnic reconstitution, the first two centuries of the colonial era witnessed further related changes, among them the passing of the old order of the tlatoque, the collapse of traditional bases of authority, and the acute dislocations in the political economy of the chinampa districts. By the turn of the eighteenth century, though, Xochimilco's landscape and ecological autonomy, which reinforced one another, had proved resilient. That continuity came to an in the eighteenth century when haciendas increasingly intruded into the lakes.

Beyond revealing patterns of ethnohistorical change and offering a periodization for them, the combined methodology of the New Philology and environmental history also enables us to discern the processes involved in those patterns of change. Here the twin facets of environmental history, landscape and demography, come together and to the fore. Whereas much of the treatment offered in the book has involved disaggregating the two for analytical purposes, ultimately the two were deeply intertwined. Demographic decline made an indelible mark on the landscape: in the centuries leading up to the arrival of Europeans, the population size of the region had increased as chinampa cultivation expanded; thereafter, demographic collapse meant that chinampas fell vacant; intensive horticulture gave way, in part, to extensive farming practices, from livestock ranching to the gathering of reeds and straw; this trend advanced with further demographic decline and the conversion of some of the swamps and chinampas into pastures; as those pastures pushed into the lakes, the reduced volume of the lakes contributed to more frequent and severe flooding, which in turn reduced the ecological autonomy that had previously shielded Xochimilco from disruption. Now, the lake area's landscape was less stable. This instability coincided with political instability on the eve of Mexico's Independence.

On July 5, 1817, a Spanish official for the jurisdiction of Xochimilco embarked from the lakeshore in a large canoe. He accompanied officials of the desagüe project and, responding to complaints by Xochimilco and other Nahua communities about haciendas being the cause of ongoing flooding, they conducted an inspection of the damage to the lake areas. They passed through channels that merged with the royal canal and entered the waters where innumerable chinampas had been submerged. Taking in the view of the destruction, the crown's legal agent and the local official for Xochimilco confirmed that the chinampas numbered in their thousands, and that the fruits of their harvests had consisted of flowers and foodstuffs, including corn, which had been the main source of subsistence for the local residents. The flooding over the previous four years had brought them "the greatest misery." Later in the tour of inspection, the authorities traveled the three leagues by canoe to San Gregorio Atlapulco. They again noted the inundation of the chinampas and remarked that the lost harvests contributed to rising food prices in the capital. So bad was the flooding, they further noted, that it was hard to identify the shoreline. The shallows near the shore made for difficult passage in the canoe. One of the desagüe officials remarked that while they were worried about capsizing, their greatest fear was of the insurgents, who were known to be in the area. If the insurgents had come to the shore when the officials were there, he admitted, "we would certainly have been lost."[9]

Three years later, the Nahuas of Tlahuac also worried about their survival. Again facing ruinous floods, they appealed once more to the tottering viceregal administration for help. They concluded their petition with a powerful lament. They stated that their pueblo was flooded to such an extent that their distressed sighs were all they had left to persuade the authorities to help them. They added that their experience of the rising waters, which continued to increase year on year, was one of anguish at the private interests – meaning the haciendas – that will bring "ruin to this capital and to our hearts, which sink in distress at the end of our lives."[10]

---

[9] AGN, Desagüe, vol. 43, exp. 5, f. 7v. The rest of the inspection can be found on ff. 6v–11.
[10] "Nuestro pueblo está anegado en tan sumo grado que nuestros afligidos suspiros suplen las voces que nos faltan para persuadirlo; y creemos con experiencia que la elevacion que las aguas tienen, y que sigue tomando de año en año la laguna por angustiar su vaso la conveniencia y el interes privado, vendrá á servir de ruina á esta capital, y á nuestros corazones naufragar en angustias de terminar nuestras vidas." AGN, Tierras, vol. 3708, f. 4v.

Glossary

(N: Nahuatl, S: Spanish)

Acalli (N). Canoe, literally "water-house"

Acalotli (N, acalote as a loanword in S). Canal

Acequia (S). Canal

Acequia real (S). Main (royal) canal from Chalco Atenco to Mexico City

Adelantado (S). A military leader authorized by the crown to explore or conquer territory, also a royal governor in charge of a province

Ahuejotes (S, from N). Water willows, often planted to reinforce the sides of chinampas

Albacea (S). Executor of a testament

Albarradón (S). Dike (*see also* tlaltenamitl)

Alcalde (S). Judge or cabildo member

Alcalde mayor (S). Magistrate; Spanish official in charge of a district

Alguacil (S). Constable

Alhóndiga (S). Grain market and storehouse

Almácigo (S, from Arabic). Seedbed nurseries, made on rafts in chinampa cultivation

Almud (S). A measurement of one-twelfth of a fanega

Altepetl (N). Nahua ethnic state; the essential sovereign, sociopolitical unit of central Mexico

Altepetlalli (N). Land of the altepetl

Amatl (N). Paper, document

Amparo (S). A protective judicial order

Atoctlalli (N). Irrigated land, which could be synonymous with chinampa

Audiencia (S). Court and governing body under the viceroy and its jurisdiction

Barrio (S). A subdivision of a town or neighborhood, equivalent to a calpolli or tlaxilacalli

Bordo (S). Barrier or small dam to hold back water

Braza (S). Unit of measure equal to a fathom

Caballería (S). A land grant of moderate size, approximately 105 acres

Cabecera (S). Head town

Cabildo (S). A municipal council

Cacica (S, from Arawak). A female Native American ruler or high-ranking noblewoman (*see also* cacique)

Cacicazgo (S, based on cacique). An entailed, indigenous estate

Cacique (S, from Arawak). A Native American ruler

Caja de comunidad (S). Community chest or treasury

Callalli (N). Agricultural land belonging to a household and associated with its residence

Calpixqui (N). Tribute collector

Calpollalli (N). Land of the calpolli

Calpolli (N). A subdivision of an altepetl (*see also* barrio and tlaxilacalli)

Calque. A loan translation, i.e., a translation of a foreign idiom using native-language vocabulary

Calzada (S). Raised road or causeway; often functioned as a dike and also had openings to allow for the passage of canoes

Camellón (S). An artificial, raised garden plot of land built up in shallow water (*see also* chinampa and chinamitl)

Camino real (S). Royal road

Canícula (S). A brief dry spell in the otherwise wet summer season

Capellanía (S). Chantry or chaplaincy

Carga (S). A load, usually of two bushels

Carnicería (S). Slaughterhouse or meat market

Casa de comunidad (S). The building for the municipal government (*also* casa real)

Casta (S). An individual of mixed racial ancestry

Castizo (S). An individual of mixed Spanish and mestizo ancestry

Cédula (S). Royal order

Césped (S). Bed of vegetation made from aquatic plants used in the cultivation of chinampas; also, turf

Chalupa (S). Small canoe

Chapines (S). Blocks of mud with a hole inside them for planting seeds; used in cultivation of chinampas

Chinamitl (N). Meaning enclosure, an artificial, raised garden plot of land built up in shallow water (*see also* camellón and chinampa)

Chinampa (S). An artificial, raised garden plot of land built up in shallow water (*see also* camellón and chinamitl)

Chinampaneca (N). The people of the chinampas (*also* chinampatlaca)

Chinantlalli (N). Alternative term for chinampa

Ciénega (S). Marsh or swamp (literally a place full of mud or silt); in the eighteenth century, also a pasture in the lakes

Cihuapilli (N). Noblewoman, lady

Cimiento (S). The foundation for a chinampa

Ciudad (S). City

Coatequitl (N). Rotational labor draft for the altepetl

Cocolitzli (N). Literally "sickness" or "pest," possibly typhus or a kind of hemorrhagic fever

Cofradía (S). A confraternity or lay religious brotherhood

Compuerta (S). Sluicegate

Concierto (S). Legally binding agreement, often for property

Congregación (S). Congregation or resettlement of scattered populations

Convento (S). Monastery

Corregidor (S). The Spanish officer in charge of a corregimiento

Corregimiento (S). A royal jurisdiction; the office, institution, or jurisdiction of the corregidor

Cuacuahueque (N). Cattle

Derrama (S). An unauthorized or additional tribute

Desagüe (S). Drainage, often used to refer to the project to drain the Basin of Mexico's lakes

Dobla (S). Seasonal draft labor (repartimiento) for agriculture, heavier workload than the sencilla

Doctrina (S). Doctrine, parish jurisdiction

Don/doña (S). Spanish honorific titles, like "Sir" and "Lady" in English

Ducado (S). Unit of currency, ducat

Embarcadero (S). Wharf, dock, or pier

Encomendero (S). An individual with the encomienda rights to indigenous labor and tribute

Encomienda (S). Grant of Native American tribute and labor and the jurisdiction of that grant

Escribano (S). Notary

Estancia (S). Farm or community subordinate to an altepetl

Estancia de ganado mayor (S). Ranch for cattle

Estancia de ganado menor (S). Ranch for sheep or goats

Fanega (S). Unit of dry measure, about 1.5 bushels

Fiscal (S). Civil functionary, church steward, or prosecutor

Gobernador (S). Governor

Hacendado (S). Hacienda owner

Hacienda (S). Large, landed estate

Huerta (S). Orchard or irrigated land

Huipil (N). Woman's shirt

Huiyametl (N). Spruce or hemlock trees, used to make canoes

Juez (S). Judge

Justicia (S). Justice, or a judge

Labrador (S). Farmer

Laguna (S). Lake

Lagunilla (S). Small lake, pond, or pool

Macehualli, pl. macehualtin (N). Indigenous commoner (*also* macehuales in Spanish)

Maguey (S). Agave, source of the drink pulque and used to make fibers for various purposes

Maravedí (S). Monetary unit; thirty-four maravedís typically equaled one real

Marqués (S). Marquis, often refers to Fernando Cortés

Marquesado (S). Marquisate, often refers to the estate of Fernando Cortés and his heirs

Matlaltotonqui (N). Typhus (*see also* tabardillo)

Matlazahuatl (N). A widespread illness or epidemic, possibly typhus or hemorrhagic fever; sometimes synonymous with cocoliztli

Mayorazgo (S). Entail

Mayordomo (S). Majordomo, custodian, or confraternity officer

Mecatl (N). A cord or rope, used a unit of measure for the area of land

Medida (S). Measure

Merced (S). Grant, usually of land

Merino (S). Town officer

Mestizaje (S). The process of biological or cultural mixing

Mestizo/a (S). An individual of Spanish and indigenous ancestry

Milpa (S, from N). Plot of land or cornfield

Monte (S). Hillside, upland area, sometimes with scrub, brush, or forest lands

Mulato/a (S). An individual of mixed Spanish and African ancestry

Nahuatlato (N). Translator (literally "Nahuatl speaker")

Nehuitzan (N). A unit of measure for chinampas and irrigated land, equivalent to a quahuitl

Obraje (S). Workshop, often for manufacturing textiles

Oficiales (S). Officers, skilled workers

Oficio (S). Office, trade, craft specialization

Oidor (S). Audiencia judge

Parcialidad (S). Large section of a town

Parroquia (S). Parish

Parte (S). Part or portion of a town

Pasto (S). Pasture

Patrimonio (S). Private estate

Patronato Real (S). Royal authority in ecclesiastical affairs

Pedregal (S). A rocky area near Coyoacan formed from the lava of a volcanic eruption

Peso (S). Monetary unit of eight reales or tomines

Pillalli (N). Land of a noble

Pilli, pl. pipiltin (N). Nahua noble (*see also* principal)

Pochtecatl, pl. pochteca (N). Merchant

Pósito (S). Municipal storehouse

Potrero (S). Paddock

Principal (S). Native American noble (*see also* pilli)

Pueblo (S). Town

Pulque (N). Alcoholic beverage fermented from maguey

Quahuitl (N). "Stick," standard unit for measuring land, usually seven to ten feet in length (*see also* nehuitzan)

Quechpozahualiztli (N). Mumps

Rancho (S). Ranch or small town

Real (S). Monetary unit, one-eighth of a peso

Regatón (S). Middleman, reseller, or speculator

Regidor (S). Municipal councilman

Repartimiento (S). Mandatory draft labor, also sometimes the forced sale of goods

Repartimiento de tierras (S). Land redistribution

Sarampión (S). Measles

Sencilla (S). Seasonal draft labor (repartimiento) for agriculture, lighter workload than the dobla

Señorío (S). Lordship, i.e., the land and estate of a lord

Subdelegado (S). Late colonial officer in charge of a district, replacing the corregidor and alcalde mayor

Suerte (S). Plot of land

Sujeto (S). Subject or subordinate community

Tabardillo (S). Typhus (*see also* matlaltotonqui)

Tameme (N). Native American porter or carrier

Tecpan (N). Native American noble palace

Tecpancalli (N). Corral, enclosure

Teniente (S). Deputy or assistant

Tepetate (S, from N). Hardpan, infertile soils

Tepixqui, pl. tepixque (N). Minor official of the calpolli

Tepuzque (S, from N). Coins or coinage, from the Nahuatl tepoztli, meaning metal

Tequimilli (N). Tribute field

Tequitl (N). Tax or labor service

Tequitlalli (N). Tribute land

Tequitlato (N). Overseer of tribute or labor service

Tercio (S). One-third, or a third of a year, referring to tribute payment schedules

Términos (S). Boundaries or limits

Terrazguerro (S). Dependent laborer who worked for a noble

Teuctli (N). Lord

Tianquiz (S, from the Nahuatl tianquiztli). Marketplace

Tierra (S). Land

Tierra baldía (S). Vacant or public land, also known as tierra realenga

Tierra caliente (S). Hot, tropical lowlands

Tierra firme (S). Mainland (as distinct from chinampa lands)

Tilmati (N). Man's cloak; cloth generally (tilma in Spanish)

Títulos primordiales (S). Primordial titles, or community histories

Tlacuilo (N). Scribe, writer, or painter

Tlalcohualli (N). A category of land tenure for private ownership

Tlalhuehuetque (N). Land elders

Tlalli (N). Land

Tlalmilli (N). Cultivated field

Tlaltenamitl (N). Dike (*see* albarradón)

Tlatoani, pl. tlatoque (N). Dynastic ruler

Tlatocatlalli (N). Land of the tlatoani

Tlaxilacalli (N). A calpolli/barrio; also, in Xochimilco, one of the three subdivisions of the altepetl, each with its own tlatoani (*see also* tlayacatl)

Tlayacatl (N). A subunit of an altepetl; in Xochimilco, one of the three subdivisions of the altepetl, each with its own tlatoani (*see* tlaxilacalli)

Tomín (S). Monetary unit, one-eighth of a peso (as with a real), a term in Nahuatl for coin, cash, or money generally

Topile (N). Constable or other community officer; someone who holds a staff of office

Trajinero (S). Middleman or carrier; can refer to canoeist

Tributo (S). Tribute

Vaquero (S). Cowboy or cattle guard

Vara (S). Staff of office; also a unit of measure (about thirty-three inches in length)

Vecino (S). Citizen or property-owning resident of a town

Visita (S). Church or community administered by nonresident clergy; also an official inspection

Visitador (S). Inspector

Yonta (S). a yoke, or unit of measure, derived from the amount of a land a yoke of oxen could typically plow in a day; typically used for holdings in upland areas and not chinampas

Zacatl (N). Straw, lake reeds, fodder

Zahuatl (N). Smallpox, although it might also have referred to measles or different intensities of the same disease

Zanja (S). Drainage ditch

Zoquimaitl (N). A pole with a bag on its end for scooping mud and constructing chinampas

Bibliography

ARCHIVES

Archivo General de la Nación (AGN), Mexico City

Alcaldes Mayores
Archivo Histórico de Hacienda, Temporalidades
Bienes Nacionales
Civil
Criminal
Desagüe
Genealogía [microfilm]
General de Parte
Historia
Hospital de Jesús
Indiferente Virreinal
Indios
Inquisición
Intestados
Matrimonios
Ordenanzas
Reales Cédulas Duplicadas
Tierras
Tribunal Superior de Justicia del Distrito Federal (TSJDF)
Vínculos y Mayorazgos

Archivo General de las Indias (AGI), Seville

Indiferente
Justicia

Mapas y Planos
Audiencia de México
Patronato

Archivo General de Notarías del Departamento del Distrito Federal (AGNM), Mexico City

Sección Juzgados de Primera Instancia, Serie Xochimilco
Notary 4, Hernando Arauz, vol. 9

Archivo Histórico Nacional, Madrid

Diversos Colecciones

Instituto Nacional de Antropología e Historia (INAH), Archivo Histórico, Mexico City

Fondo Franciscano

The Latin American Library (LAL), Tulane University, New Orleans

Viceregal and Ecclesiastical Mexican Collection

Library of Congress, Washington, DC

Krauss Collection

The Newberry Library, Chicago

Ayer Collection

Universidad Nacional Autónoma de México (UNAM), Biblioteca Nacional, Mexico City

Fondo Reservado: Archivo Franciscano

PUBLISHED PRIMARY SOURCES

Acosta, José de. *Natural and Moral History of the Indies.* Jane E. Mangan, trans., and Frances M. López-Morillas, ed. Durham: Duke University Press, 2002.

Actas de Cabildo del Ayuntamiento de la ciudad de Mexico, vol. 27: Actas Antiguas de cabildo. Ignacio Bejarano, comp. Mexico City: A. Carranza y Comp. Impresores, 1908.

Alva Ixtlilxochitl, Fernando de. *The Native Conquistador: Alva Ixtlilxochitl's Account of the Conquest of New Spain*. Amber Brian, Bradley Benton, and Pablo García Loaeza, trans. and eds. University Park: The Pennsylvania State University Press, 2015.

Obras históricas. Edmundo O'Gorman, ed. Mexico City: Universidad Nacional Autónoma de México, Instituto de Investigaciones Históricas, 1975.

Alzate y Ramírez, Joseph Antonio de. "Memoria sobre agricultura," *Gacetas de literatura de México*. Vol. 2. 382–399. Puebla: reimpresa en la oficina del Hospital de S. Pedro, 1831.

Anderson, Arthur J. O., Frances Berdan, and James Lockhart, eds. *Beyond the Codices: The Nahua View of Colonial Mexico*. Berkeley: University of California Press/UCLA Latin American Center, 1976.

The Badianus Manuscript (Codex Barberini, Latin 241) Vatican Library: An Aztec Herbal of 1552. Emily Walcott Emmart, ed. and trans. Baltimore: The Johns Hopkins University Press, 1940.

Benavente, Toribio de (Motolinia). *Motolinia's History of the Indians of New Spain*. Francis Borgia Steck, trans. Washington, DC: Academy of American Franciscan History, 1951.

Cartas del licenciado Jerónimo Valderrama y otros documentos sobre su visita al gobierno de Nueva Espana, 1563–1565. France V. Scholes and Eleanor B. Adams, eds. Mexico City: J. Porrúa, 1961.

Cepeda, Fernando de. *Relación vniversal legitima, y verdadera del sitio en qve esta fvndada la muy noble, insigne, y muy leal ciudad de México. cabeça de las provincias de toda la Nueva España*. Mexico City: Imprenta de Francisco Salbago, 1637.

Chimalpahin Quauhtlehuanitzin, don Domingo de San Antón Muñón. *Chimalpahin's Conquest: A Nahua Historian's Rewriting of Francisco López de Gómara's La conquista de México*. Susan Schroeder, Anne J. Cruz, Cristián Roa-de-la-Carrera, and David E. Tavárez, ed. and trans. Stanford: Stanford University Press, 2010.

Annals of His Time. James Lockhart, Susan Schroeder, and Doris Namala, eds. and trans. Stanford: Stanford University Press, 2006.

Codex Chimalpahin: Society and Politics in Mexico Tenochtitlan, Tlatelolco, Texcoco, Culhuacan, and Other Nahua Altepetl in Central Mexico. 2 vols. Arthur J. O. Anderson and Susan Schroeder, eds. and trans. Norman: University of Oklahoma Press, 1997.

Códice Cozcatzin. Ana Rita Valero de García Lascuráin and Rafael Tena, eds. Mexico City: Instituto Nacional de Antropología e Historia, 1994.

Códice Osuna. Facsimile ed. Luis Chávez Orozco, ed. Mexico City: Ediciones del Instituto Indigenista Interamericano, 1947.

Colección de documentos inéditos, relativos al descubrimiento, conquista y organización de las antiguas posesiones españolas de ultramar. Vol. 22. Madrid: Tipografía de Archivos, I. Olózaga, 1929.

Colección de documentos inéditos, relativos al descubrimiento, conquista y colonización de las posesiones españolas en América y Oceanía, sacados, en su mayor parte, del Real Archivo de Indias. Vols. 2, 8, 13, and 41. Madrid: Imprenta Española, Torija, 1864.

Cortés, Hernán. *Letters from Mexico.* Anthony Pagden, ed. and trans. New Haven: Yale University Press, 1986.

Cartas y documentos. Mario Hernández Sánchez-Borbón, ed. Mexico City: J. Porrúa, 1963.

Covarrubias Orozco, Sebastián de. *Tesoro de la lengua castellana o española.* Madrid: Editorial Castalia, 1995.

Díaz del Castillo, Bernal. *Historia verdadera de la conquista de la Nueva España.* José Antonio Borbón Rodríguez, ed. Mexico City: El Colegio de México, 2005.

The Discovery and Conquest of Mexico, 1517–1521. A. P. Maudslay, trans. New York: Farrar, Strauss, and Cudahy, 1956.

Documents pour servir à l'histoire du Méxique. Paris: E. Leroux, 1891.

Durán, Diego. *Historia de las indias de Nueva España e islas de la tierra firme.* 2 vols. Mexico City: J. Porrúa, 1984.

El libro de las tasaciones de pueblos de la Nueva España, Siglo XVI. Mexico City: Archivo General de la Nación, 1952.

Ixtlilxochitl, don Fernando de Alva. *Obras históricas.* 2 vols. Edmundo O'Gorman, ed. Mexico City: Universidad Nacional Autónoma de México, Instituto de Investigaciones Históricas, 1975–1977.

Karttunen, Frances, and James Lockhart, eds. *Nahuatl in the Middle Years: Language Contact Phenomena in Texts of the Colonial Period.* Berkeley: University of California Press, 1976.

López de Gómara, Francisco. *Historia de la conquista de México.* Mexico City: Editorial Pedro Robredo, 1943.

Moderación de doctrinas de la Real Corona administradas por las ordenes mendicantes, 1623. France V. Scholes and Eleanor B. Adams, eds. Mexico City: J. Porrúa, 1959.

Molina, Alonso de. Facsimile ed. *Vocabulario en lengua castellana y mexicana y mexicana y castellana.* Mexico City: J. Porrúa, 2001.

Ojea, Hernando. *Libro tercero de la Historia religiosa de la prouincia de México de la Orden de Sto. Domingo.* Mexico City: Museo Nacional de México, 1897.

Real Academía Española. Facsimile ed. *Diccionario de autoridades.* Madrid: Editorial Gredos, 1990.

Restall, Matthew, Lisa Sousa, and Kevin Terraciano, eds. *Mesoamerican Voices: Native-Language Writings from Colonial Mexico, Oaxaca, Yucatan, and Guatemala.* New York: Cambridge University Press, 2005.

Sahagún, Bernardino de. *Florentine Codex: General History of the Things of New Spain.* 13 vols. Charles E. Dibble and Arthur J. O. Anderson, eds. and trans. Santa Fe: School of American Research/University of Utah, 1970–1982.

Sobre el modo de tributar los indios de Nueva España a Su Majestad, 1561–1564. France V. Scholes and Eleanor B. Adams, eds. Mexico City: J. Porrúa, 1958.

Torquemada, Juan de. *Monarquía indiana.* 3 vols. Mexico City: J. Porrúa, 1969.

Vetancurt, Agustín de. *Teatro mexicano.* Mexico City: J. Porrúa, 1971.

Villaseñor y Sánchez, José Antonio de. *Theatro americano*. Mexico City: Editora Nacional, 1952.

SECONDARY SOURCES

Acuna-Soto, Rodolfo, David W. Stahle, Malcolm K. Cleaveland, and Matthew D. Therrell. "Megadrought and Megadeath in 16th Century Mexico." *Emerging Infectious Diseases*, vol. 8, no. 4 (2002): 360–362.

Acuna-Soto, Rodolfo, David W. Stahle, Matthew D. Therrell, Richard D. Griffin, and Malcolm K. Cleaveland. "When Half the Population Died: The Epidemic of Hemorrhagic Fevers of 1576 in Mexico." *FEMS Microbiology Letters*, vol. 240, no. 1 (2004): 1–5.

Alchon, Suzanne A. *A Pest in the Land: New World Epidemics in a Global Perspective*. Albuquerque: University of New Mexico Press, 2003.

Altman, Ida. *Emigrants and Society: Extremadura and America in the Sixteenth Century*. Berkeley: University of California Press, 1989.

Altman, Ida, and James Lockhart, eds. *Provinces of Early Mexico: Variants of Spanish American Regional Evolution*. Los Angeles: UCLA Latin American Center Publications, 1976.

Amith, Jonathan D. *The Möbius Strip: A Spatial History of Colonial Society in Guerrero, Mexico*. Stanford: Stanford University Press, 2005.

Arco, Lee J., and Elliot M. Abrams. "An Essay on Energetics: The Construction of the Aztec Chinampa System." *Antiquity*, vol. 80, no. 310 (2006): 906–918.

Armillas, Pedro. "Gardens on Swamps." *Science*, vol. 174, no. 4010 (1971): 653–661.

Artís Espriu, Gloria. *Regatones y maquileros. El mercado de trigo en la ciudad de México (siglo XVIII)*. Mexico City: El Centro de Investigaciones y Estudios Superiores en Antropología Social, Ediciones de la Casa Chata, 1986.

Avila López, Raul. *Chinampas de Iztapalapa, D. F.* Mexico City: Instituto Nacional de Antropología e Historia, 1991.

Bennassar, Bartolomé. *Valladolid au siècle d'or, une ville de Castille et sa campagne au XVIe siècle*. Paris: La Haye, Mouton et Cie, 1967.

Benton, Bradley. *The Lords of Tetzcoco: The Transformation of Indigenous Rule in Postconquest Central Mexico*. New York: Cambridge University Press, 2019.

Berdan, Frances. *The Aztecs of Central Mexico: An Imperial Society*. New York: Harcourt Brace Jovanovich, 1982.

Boone, Elizabeth Hill. *Stories in Red and Black: Pictorial Histories of the Aztecs and Mixtecs*. Austin: University of Texas Press, 2000.

Borah, Woodrow. *Justice by Insurance: The General Indian Court of Colonial Mexico and the Legal Aides of the Half-Real*. Berkeley: University of California Press, 1983.

Borah, Woodrow, and Sherburne F. Cook. *The Population of the Mixteca Alta, 1520–1960, Ibero-Americana*, no. 50. Berkeley: University of California Press, 1968.

The Aboriginal Population of Central Mexico on the Eve of the Spanish Conquest, Ibero-Americana, no. 45. Berkeley: University of California Press, 1963.

The Indian Population of Central Mexico, 1531–1610. Ibero-Americana 44. Berkeley: University of California Press, 1960.

The Population of Central Mexico in 1548: An Analysis of the Suma de visitas de pueblos, Ibero-Americana, no. 43. Berkeley: University of California Press, 1960.

Price Trends of Some Basic Commodities in Central Mexico, 1531–1570, Ibero-Americana, no. 40. Berkeley: University of California Press, 1958.

Borejsza, Aleksander. "Village and Field Abandonment in Post-conquest Tlaxcala: A Geoarchaeological Perspective." *Anthropocene*, vol. 3 (2013): 9–23.

Boyer, Richard. *La gran inundación: Vida y sociedad en México, 1629–1638.* Mexico City: Secretaria de Educación Pública, 1975.

Brading, David A. *Church and State in Bourbon Mexico: The Diocese of Michoacán, 1749–1810.* New York: Cambridge University Press, 1994.

Haciendas and Ranchos in the Mexican Bajío: León, 1700–1860. Cambridge: Cambridge University Press, 1978.

Miners and Merchants in Bourbon Mexico, 1763–1810. New York: Cambridge University Press, 1971.

Braudel, Fernand. *The Mediterranean and the Mediterranean World in the Age of Philip II.* 2 vols. Sian Reynolds, trans. New York: Harper and Row, 1966.

Burkhart, Louise M. *Nahua-Christian Moral Dialogue in Sixteenth-Century Mexico.* Tucson: University of Arizona Press, 1989.

Burns, Jordan N., Rodolfo Acuna-Soto, and David W. Stahle. "Drought and Epidemic Typhus, Central Mexico, 1655–1918." *Emerging Infectious Diseases*, vol. 20, no. 3 (2014): 442–447.

Burns, Kathryn. "Notaries, Truth, and Consequences." *The American Historical Review*, vol. 110, no. 2 (April 2005): 350–379.

Colonial Habits: Convents and the Spiritual Economy of Cuzco, Peru. Durham: Duke University Press, 1999.

Butzer, Karl W. "Cattle and Sheep from Old to New Spain: Historical Antecedents." *Annals of the Association of American Geographers*, vol. 78, no. 1 (1988): 29–56.

Butzer, Karl W., and E. K. Butzer. "Transfer of the Mediterranean Livestock Economy to New Spain: Adaptation and Ecological Consequences." In B. L. Turner, ed., *Global Land Use Change: A Perspective from the Columbian Encounter.* 151–193. Madrid: Consejo Superior de Investigaciones Científicas, 1995.

Butzer, Karl W., and E. K. Butzer. "The 'Natural' Vegetation of the Mexican Bajío: Archival Documentation of a 16th-Century Savanna Environment." *Quaternary International*, 43/44 (1997): 161–172.

Calnek, Edward E. "Settlement Pattern and Chinampa Agriculture at Tenochtitlan." *American Antiquity*, vol. 37, no. 1 (1972): 104–115.

Candiani, Vera. *Dreaming of Dry Land: Environmental Transformation in Colonial Mexico City.* Stanford: Stanford University Press, 2014.

"The Desagüe Reconsidered: Environmental Dimensions of Class Conflict in Colonial Mexico." *Hispanic American Historical Review*, vol. 92, no. 1 (2012): 5–39.

Cañizares-Esguerra, Jorge. "Introduction." In Daniela Bleichmar, Paula De Vos, and Kristin Huffine, eds., *Science in the Spanish and Portuguese Empires, 1500–1800.* 1–5. Stanford: Stanford University Press, 2009.

Nature, Empire, and Nation: Explorations in the History of Science in the Iberian World. Stanford: Stanford University Press, 2006.

How to Write the History of the New World: History, Epistomologies, and Identities in the Eighteenth-Century Atlantic World. Stanford: Stanford University Press, 2002.

Carballal Staedtler, Margarita, and María Flores Hernández. "Hydraulic Features of the Mexico-Texcoco Lakes during the Postclassic Period." In L. J. Lucero and B. W. Fash, eds., *Precolumbian Water Management.* Tucson: The University of Arizona Press, 2006, 155–170.

"Las calzadas prehispanicas de la isla de México." *Arqueologia*, vol. 1 (1989): 71–80.

Carrasco, Pedro. "Los señores de Xochimilco en 1548." *Tlalocan*, no. 7 (1977): 229–265.

Castañeda de la Paz, María. "Central Mexican Indigenous Coats of Arms and the Conquest of Mesoamerica." *Ethnohistory*, vol. 56, no. 1 (Winter 2009): 125–161.

"Un plano de tierras en el *Códice Cozcatzin*: Adaptaciones y transformaciones de la cartografía prehispánica." *Anales de Antropología* (Instituto de Investigaciones Antropológicas, Universidad Nacional Autónoma de México), vol. 40. no. 2 (2006): 41–73.

Chance, John K. *Race and Class in Colonial Oaxaca.* Stanford: Stanford University Press, 1978.

Chance, John K., and William B. Taylor. "Estate and Class in a Colonial City: Oaxaca in 1792." *Comparative Studies in Society and History*, vol. 19, no. 4, (1977): 454–487.

Chardon, Roland. "The Elusive Spanish League: A Problem of Measurement in Sixteenth-Century New Spain." *Hispanic American Historical Review*, vol. 60, no. 2. (1980): 294–302.

Chevalier, François. *La formation des grandes domains au Mexique, terre et société aux XVIe– XVIIe siècles.* Paris: Université de Paris, 1952.

Christensen, Mark Z. *Nahua and Maya Catholicisms: Texts and Religion in Colonial Central Mexico and Yucatan.* Stanford: Stanford University Press, 2013.

Chuchiak, John F., IV. "Forgotten Allies: The Origins and Roles of Native Mesoamerican Auxiliaries and Indios Conquistadores in the Conquest of Yucatan, 1526–1550." In Laura E. Matthew and Michel R. Oudijk, eds., *Indian Conquistadors: Indigenous Allies in the Conquest of Mesoamerica.* 175–225. Norman: University of Oklahoma Press, 2007.

Clark, Fiona. "'Read All About It': Science, Translation, Adaptation, and Confrontation in the *Gazeta de Literatura de México*, 1788–1795." In Daniela Bleichmar, Paula De Vos, and Kristin Huffine, eds., *Science in the Spanish and Portuguese Empires, 1500–1800.* 147–177. Stanford University Press, 2009.

Cline, S. L., ed. and trans. *The Book of Tributes: Early Sixteenth-Century Nahuatl Censuses from Morelos*. Los Angeles: UCLA Latin American Center Publications and the University of California, 1993.

"A Cacicazgo in the Seventeenth Century: The Case of Xochimilco." In H. R. Harvey, ed., *Land and Politics in the Valley of Mexico: A Two-Thousand Year Perspective*. 265–274. Albuquerque: University of New Mexico Press, 1991.

Colonial Culhuacan, 1580–1600: A Social History of an Aztec Town. Albuquerque: University of New Mexico Press, 1986.

Coe, Michael D. "The Chinampas of Mexico." *Scientific American*, vol. 121, no. 1 (1964): 90–98.

Connell, William F. *After Moctezuma: Indigenous Politics and Self-Government in Mexico City, 1524–1730*. Norman: University of Oklahoma Press, 2011.

Conway, Richard. "Rural Indians and Technological Innovation, from the Chinampas of Xochimilco and Beyond." In *Oxford Research Encyclopedia of Latin American History*. Oxford: Oxford University Press, 2018.

"The Environmental History of Colonial Mexico." *History Compass*, vol. 15, no. 7 (2017).

"Spaniards in the Nahua City of Xochimilco: Colonial Society and Cultural Change in Central Mexico, 1650–1725." *The Americas*, vol. 71, no. 1 (2014): 9–35.

"Lakes, Canoes, and the Aquatic Communities of Xochimilco and Chalco, New Spain." *Ethnohistory*, vol. 59, no. 3 (2012): 541–568.

Cook, Noble David. *Born to Die: Disease and New World Conquest, 1492–1650*. Cambridge: Cambridge University Press, 1998.

Cook, Noble David, and W. George Lovell, eds. *"Secret Judgments of God": Old World Disease in Colonial Spanish America*. Norman: University of Oklahoma Press, 1992.

Cook, Sherburne F. *Soil Erosion and Population in Central Mexico*. Berkeley: University of California Press, 1949.

The Historical Demography and Ecology of the Teotlalpan. Berkeley: University of California Press, 1949.

Cook, Sherburne F., and Woodrow Borah. *Essays in Population History*. 3 vols. Berkeley: University of California Press, 1971–1979.

Cope, R. Douglas. *The Limits of Racial Domination: Plebeian Society in Colonial Mexico City, 1660–1720*. Madison: University of Wisconsin Press, 1994.

Crewe, Ryan. "Building in the Shadow of Death: Monastery Construction and the Politics of Community Reconstitution in Sixteenth-Century Mexico." *The Americas*, vol. 75, no. 3 (2018): 489–523.

Crosby, Alfred W. *Ecological Imperialism: The Biological Expansion of Europe, 900–1900*. New York: Cambridge University Press, 1986.

The Columbian Exchange: Biological and Cultural Consequences of 1492. Westport: Greenwood, 1972.

Cuenya Mateos, Miguel Ángel. *Puebla de los Ángeles en tiempos de una peste colonial: Una mirada en torno al matlazahuatl de 1737*. Puebla: Benemérita Universidad Autónoma de Puebla, 1999.

Daniels, John D. "The Indian Population of North America in 1492." *William and Mary Quarterly*, vol. 49, no. 2 (1992): 298–320.

Deeds, Susan M. *Defiance and Deference in Mexico's Colonial North: Indians under Spanish Rule in Nueva Vizcaya*. Austin: University of Texas Press, 2003.

Denevan, William M. *The Native Population of the Americas in 1492*. Madison: University of Wisconsin Press, 1976.

Derby, Lauren. "Bringing the Animals Back In: Writing Quadrupeds into the Environmental History of Latin America and the Caribbean." *History Compass*, vol. 9, no. 8 (2011): 602–621.

Doolittle, William E. *Canal Irrigation in Prehistoric Mexico: The Sequence of Technological Change*. Austin: University of Texas Press, 1990.

"Agricultural Change as an Incremental Process." *Annals of the Association of American Geographers*, vol. 74, no. 1 (1984): 124–137.

Drelichman, Mauricio, and Hans-Joachim Voth. *Lending to the Borrower from Hell: Debt, Taxes, and Default in the Age of Philip II*. Princeton: Princeton University Press, 2014.

Durán, Juan Manuel, Martín Sánchez, and Antonio Escobar, eds. *El agua en la historia de México*. Guadalajara: Universidad de Guadalajara, 2005.

Dusenberry, William H. "The Regulation of Meat Supply in Sixteenth-Century Mexico City." *Hispanic American Historical Review*, vol. 28, no. 1 (1948): 38–52.

Elliott, J. H. *Imperial Spain, 1469–1716*. New York: Penguin, 1990.

Endfield, Georgina H. *Climate and Society in Colonial Mexico: A Study in Vulnerability*. London: Blackwell, 2008.

Endfield, Georgina H., and Sarah L. O'Hara. "Degradation, Drought, and Dissent: An Environmental History of Colonial Michoacan, West Central Mexico." *Annals of the Association of American Geographers*, vol. 89, no. 3 (1999): 402–419.

"Conflicts over Water in 'the Little Drought Age' in Central México." *Environment and History*, vol. 3, no. 3 (1997): 255–272.

Endfield, Georgina H., Isabel Fernández Tejedo, and Sarah L. O'Hara. "Conflict and Cooperation: Water, Floods, and Social Response in Colonial Guanajuato, Mexico." *Environmental History*, vol. 9, no. 2 (2004): 221–247.

Ethridge, Robbie, and Sheri M. Shuck-Hall, eds. *Mapping the Mississippian Shatter Zone: The Colonial Indian Slave Trade and Regional Instability in the American South*. Lincoln: University of Nebraska Press, 2009.

Evans, Susan Toby. *Ancient Mexico and Central America*. New York: Thames and Hudson, 2013.

Ezcurra, Exequiel. *De las chinampas a la megapolis: El medio ambiente en la cuenca de México*. Mexico City: Fondo de Cultural Económica, 1991.

Few, Martha, and Zeb Tortorici, eds. *Centering Animals in Latin American History*. Durham: Duke University Press, 2013.

Florescano, Enrique. *Breve historia de la sequía en México*. Mexico City: CONACULTA, 2000.

Estructuras y problemas agrarios de México, 1500–1821. Mexico City: Secretaría de Educación Pública, 1971.

Precios del maíz y crisis agrícolas en México, 1708–1810. Mexico City: El Colegio de México, 1969.

Fraser, Valerie. *The Architecture of Conquest: Building in the Viceroyalty of Peru, 1535–1635.* New York: Cambridge University Press, 2009.

Frederick, Charles D. "Chinampa Cultivation in the Basin of Mexico: Observations on the Evolution of Form and Function." In Tina L. Thurston and Christopher T. Fisher, eds., *Seeking a Richer Harvest: The Archaeology of Subsistence, Intensification, Innovation, and Change.* 117–124. New York: Springer Science + Business Media, 2007.

García Acosta, Virginia, Juan Manuel Pérez Zevallos, and América Molina de Villar, eds. *Desastres agrícolas en México: Catálogo histórico, vol. I: Época prehispánica y colonial, 958–1822.* Mexico City: Fondo de Cultura Económica, 2003.

García de León, Antonio. *Tierra adentro, mar en fuera: El Puerto de Veracruz y su litoral a Sotavento, 1519–1821.* Mexico City: Fondo de Cultura Económica, Universidad Veracruzana, and Secretaría de Educación del Estado de Veracruz, 2011.

García Sanchez, Magdalena A. "El modo de vida lacustre en el valle de México, ¿mestizaje o proceso de aculturación?" In Enrique Florescano and Virginia García Acosta, eds., *Mestizajes tecnológicos y cambios culturales en México.* 21–90. Mexico City: El Centro de Investigaciones y Estudios Superiores en Antropología Social, 2004.

Gardiner, C. Harvey. *Naval Power in the Conquest of Mexico.* Austin: University of Texas Press, 1956.

Gerhard, Peter. *A Guide to the Historical Geography of New Spain.* Rev. ed. Norman: University of Oklahoma Press, 1993.

Gibson, Charles. *The Aztecs under Spanish Rule: A History of the Indians of the Valley of Mexico, 1519–1810.* Stanford: Stanford University Press, 1964.

"Rotation of Alcaldes in the Indian Cabildo of Mexico City." *The Hispanic American Historical Review*, vol. 33, No. 2. (May, 1953): 212–223.

Tlaxcala in the Sixteenth Century. Stanford: Stanford University Press, 1952.

Glave Testino, Luis Miguel. *Trajinantes: caminos indígenas en la sociedad colonial, siglos XVI/XVII.* Lima: Instituto de Apoyo Agrario, 1989.

Glick, Thomas F. *Irrigation and Society in Medieval Valencia.* Cambridge: Harvard University Press, 1970.

González Aparicio, Luis. *Plano reconstructivo de la región de Tenochtitlan.* Mexico City: Instituto Nacional de Antropología e Historia, 1973.

Goubert, Pierre. *Beauvais et le Beauvaisis de 1600 à 1730: contribution à l'histoire sociale de la France du XVIIe siècle.* Paris: Editions de l'Ecole des hautes études en sciences sociales, 1982.

Gruzinski, Serge. *Las cuatro partes del mundo: Historia de una mundialización.* Mexico City: Fondo de Cultura Económica, 2010.

Haring, C. H. *The Spanish Empire in America.* New York: Harcourt Brace Jovanovich, 1975.

Haskett, Robert. *Indigenous Rulers: An Ethnohistory of Town Government in Colonial Cuernavaca.* Albuquerque: University of New Mexico Press, 1991.

Hassig, Ross. *Mexico and the Spanish Conquest.* London: Longman, 1994.

Trade, Tribute, and Transportation: The Sixteenth-Century Political Economy of the Valley of Mexico. Norman: University of Oklahoma Press, 1985.

Henige, David P. *Numbers from Nowhere: The American Indian Contact Population Debate.* Norman: University of Oklahoma Press, 1998.

Hernández, Lucina, ed. *Historia ambiental de la ganadería en México.* Xalapa: Instituto de Ecologia, 2001.

Hoberman, Louisa Schell. "Technological Change in a Traditional Society." *Technology and Culture*, vol. 21, no. 3 (1980): 386–407.

Hoberman, Louisa Schell, and Susan Migden Socolow, eds. *The Countryside in Colonial Latin America.* Albuquerque: University of New Mexico Press, 1996.

Hodge, Mary G. "Lord and Lordship in the Valley of Mexico: The Politics of Aztec Provincial Administration." In H. R. Harvey, ed., *Land and Politics in the Valley of Mexico: A Two Thousand Year Perspective.* 113–139. Albuquerque: University of New Mexico Press, 1991.

Horn, Rebecca. "Testaments and Trade: Interethnic Ties among Petty Traders in Central Mexico (Coyoacan, 1550–1620)." In Susan Kellogg and Matthew Restall, eds., *Dead Giveaways: Indigenous Testaments of Colonial Mesoamerica and the Andes.* 59–83. Salt Lake City: The University of Utah Press, 1998.

Postconquest Coyoacan: Nahua-Spanish Relations in Central Mexico, 1519–1650. Stanford: Stanford University Press, 1997.

Jordan, Terry G. *North American Cattle-Ranching Frontiers: Origins, Diffusion, and Differentiation.* Albuquerque: University of New Mexico Press, 1993.

Kaplan, Steven L. *Bread, Politics and Political Economy in the Reign of Louis XV.* The Hague: Martinus Nijhoff, 1976.

Karttunen, Frances. *An Analytical Dictionary of Nahuatl.* Austin: University of Texas Press, 1983.

Kellogg, Susan. *Weaving the Past: A History of Latin America's Indigenous Women from the Prehispanic Period to the Present.* New York: Oxford University Press, 2005.

Law and the Transformation of Aztec Culture, 1500–1700. Norman: University of Oklahoma Press, 1995.

"Aztec Inheritance in Sixteenth-Century Mexico City: Colonial Patterns, Prehispanic Influences." *Ethnohistory.* vol. 33, No. 3 (Summer, 1986): 313–330.

Kirchoff, P. "Mesoamerica: Its Geographic Limits, Ethnic Composition, and Cultural Characteristics." In Sol Tax, ed., *Heritage of Conquest.* 17–30. Glencoe: The Free Press, 1962.

Lakomäki, Sami. *Gathering Together: The Shawnee People through Diaspora and Nationhood, 1600–1870.* New Haven: Yale University Press, 2014.

Lee, Raymond L. "Grain Legislation in Colonial Mexico, 1575–1585." *Hispanic American Historical Review*, vol. 27, No. 4 (1947): 647–660.

Leonard, Irving A. *Books of the Brave: Being an Account of Books and of Men in the Spanish Conquest and Settlement of the Sixteenth-Century New World.* Berkeley: University of California Press, 1992.

Lewis, Laura A. *Hall of Mirrors: Power, Witchcraft, and Caste in Colonial Mexico.* Durham: Duke University Press, 2003.

Licate, Jack A. *Creation of a Mexican Landscape: Territorial Organization and Settlement in the Eastern Puebla Basin, 1520–1605.* Chicago: Department of Geography, University of Chicago, 1981.

Lipman, Andrew. *The Saltwater Frontier: Indians and the Contest for the American Coast.* New Haven: Yale University Press, 2017.

Lipsett-Rivera, Sonya. *To Defend Our Water with the Blood of Our Veins: The Struggle for Resources in Colonial Puebla.* Albuquerque: University of New Mexico Press, 1999.

Livi-Bacci, Massimo. *Conquest: The Destruction of the American Indios.* Cambridge: Polity Press, 2008.

"The Depopulation of Hispanic America after the Conquest." *Population and Development Review,* vol. 32, no. 2 (2006): 199–232.

Lockhart, James. *Nahuatl as Written: Lessons in Older Written Nahuatl, with Copious Examples and Texts.* Stanford and Los Angeles: Stanford University Press and UCLA Latin American Center Publications, 2001.

The Nahuas after the Conquest: A Social and Cultural History of the Indians of Central Mexico, Sixteenth through Eighteenth Century. Stanford: Stanford University Press, 1992.

Nahuas and Spaniards: Postconquest Central Mexican History and Philology. Stanford and Los Angeles: Stanford University Press and UCLA Latin American Center Publications, 1991.

The Men of Cajamarca: A Social and Biographical Study of the First Conquerors of Peru. Austin: The University of Texas Press, 1972.

"Encomienda and Hacienda: The Evolution of the Great Estate in the Spanish Indies." *The Hispanic American Historical Review.* vol. 49, no. 3 (Aug., 1969): 411–429.

Spanish Peru, 1532–1560: A Colonial Society. Madison: The University of Wisconsin Press, 1968.

Lockhart, James, and Stuart Schwartz. *Early Latin America: A History of Colonial Spanish America and Brazil.* New York: Cambridge University Press, 1983.

López Austin, Alfredo. *Textos de medicina Nahuatl.* Mexico City: Universidad Autónoma de México, 1975.

Lorenzo, José Luís, ed. *Materiales para la arqueología de Teotihuacan.* Mexico City: Instituto Nacional de Antropología e Historia, 1968.

Loreto López, Rosalva. *Una vista de ojos a una ciudad novohispana: La Puebla de los Ángeles en el siglo XVIII.* Puebla: CONACYT, Instituto de Ciencias Sociales y Humanidades, Alfonso Vélez Pliego de la Benemérita Universidad Autónoma de Puebla, 2008.

Lovell, W. George, Henry F. Dobyns, William M. Denevan, William I. Woods, and Charles C. Mann. "1491: In Search of Native America." *Journal of the Southwest,* vol. 46, no. 3 (2004): 441–461.

Luna Golya, Gregory. "Modeling the Aztec Agricultural Waterscape of Lake Xochimilco: A GIS Analysis of Lakebed Chinampas and Settlement." PhD dissertation, Pennsylvania State University, 2014.

Lynch, John. "The Institutional Framework of Colonial Spanish America." *Journal of Latin American Studies*, vol. 24 (1992): 69–92.

MacLeod, Murdo J. *Spanish Central America: A Socioeconomic History, 1520–1720*. Reissued ed. Austin: University of Texas Press, 2008.

"Some Thoughts on the Pax Colonial, Colonial Violence, and Perceptions of Both." In Susan Schroeder, ed., *Native Resistance and the Pax Colonial in New Spain*. 129–142. Lincoln: University of Nebraska Press, 1998.

Malvido, Elsa, and Carlos Viesca. "La epidemia de cocoliztli de 1576." *Historias*, vol. 11 (1985): 27–33.

Mangan, Jane A. *Trading Roles: Gender, Ethnicity, and the Urban Economy in Colonial Potosí*. Durham: Duke University Press, 2005.

Mann, Charles C. *1491: New Revelations of the Americas before Columbus*. New York: Alfred A. Knopf, 2005.

Martin, Cheryl English. *Rural Society in Colonial Morelos*. Albuquerque: University of New Mexico Press, 1985.

Martin, Norman F. *Los vagabundos en la Nueva España, siglo XVI*. Mexico City: Editorial Jus, 1957.

Martinez-Serna, Gabriel. "Jesuit Missionaries, Indian Polities, and Environmental Transformation in the Lagoon March of Northeastern New Spain." *Journal of Early American History*, vol. 3, no. 2–3 (2013): 207–234.

Mathes, W. M. "To Save a City: The Desagüe of Mexico-Huehuetoca, 1607." *The Americas*, vol. 26, no. 4 (1970): 419–438.

Melton-Villanueva, Miriam. *The Aztecs at Independence: Nahua Culture Makers in Central Mexico, 1799–1832*. Tucson: University of Arizona Press, 2016.

Melton-Villanueva, Miriam, and Caterina Pizzigoni. "Late Nahuatl Testaments from the Toluca Valley: Native-Language Ethnohistory in the Mexican Independence Period." *Ethnohistory*, vol. 55, no. 4 (2008): 361–391.

Melville, Elinor G. K. *A Plague of Sheep: Environmental Consequences of the Conquest of Mexico*. New York: Cambridge University Press, 1994.

Meyer, Michael C. *Water in the Hispanic Southwest: A Social and Legal History, 1550–1850*. Tucson: University of Arizona Press, 1996.

Meyer, Michael C., William L. Sherman, and Susan M. Deeds. *The Course of Mexican History*, 9th ed. New York: Oxford University Press, 2011.

Mijares Ramírez, Ivonne. *Escribanos y escrituras públicas en el siglo XVI: El caso de la Ciudad de México*. Mexico City: Universidad Nacional Autónoma de México, 1997.

Mestizo alimentario: El abasto de la ciudad de México en el siglo XVI. Mexico City: Universidad Nacional Autónoma de México, 1993.

Miller, Shawn. *An Environmental History of Latin America*. New York: Cambridge University Press, 2007.

Miranda, José. *El tributo indígena en la Nueva España durante el siglo XVI*. Mexico City: Fondo de Cultura Económica, El Colegio de México, 1952.

Morehart, Christopher T. "Mapping Ancient Chinampa Landscapes in the Basin of Mexico: A Remote Sensing and GIS Approach." *Journal of Archaeological Science*, vol. 39 (2012): 2541–2551.

Morehart, Christopher T., and Daniel T. A. Eisenberg. "Prosperity, Power, and Change: Modeling Maize at Postclassic Xaltocan, Mexico." *Journal of Anthropological Archaeology*, vol. 29 (2010): 94–112.

Moreno García, Heriberto. *Haciendas de tierra y agua en la antigua ciénega de Chapala*. Michoacan: El Colegio de Michoacán, 1989.

Mörner, Magnus. "The Spanish American Hacienda: A Survey of Recent Research and Debate." *Hispanic American Historical Review*, vol. 53, no. 2 (1973): 183–216.

Mundy, Barbara E. *The Death of Aztec Tenochtitlan, the Life of Mexico City*. Austin: University of Texas Press, 2015.

Musset, Alain. "El siglo de oro del desagüe de México, 1607–1691." In *Obras hidrálicas en América colonial*. 53–65. Madrid: Centro de Estudios Históricos de Obras Públicas y Urbanismo, 1993.

De l'eau vive à l'eau morte: enjeux techniques et culturels dans la vallée de Mexico (XVIe–XIXe s). Paris: Éditions Recherche sur les Civilisations, 1991.

Nash, Linda. "Beyond Virgin Soils: Disease as Environmental History." In Andrew C. Isenberg, ed., *The Oxford Handbook of Environmental History*. 76–107. New York: Oxford University Press, 2014.

Nesvig, Martin A., ed. *Local Religion in Colonial Mexico*. Albuquerque: University of New Mexico Press, 2006.

Neukom, Raphael, Joelle Gergis, David J. Karoly et al. "Inter-Hemispheric Temperature Variability over the Past Millennium." *Nature Climate Change*, vol. 4, no. 5 (2014): 362–367.

O'Callaghan, Joseph F. *A History of Medieval Spain*. Ithaca: Cornell University Press, 1975.

Offner, Jerome A. *Law and Politics in Aztec Texcoco*. New York: Cambridge University Press, 1983.

O'Hara, Matthew D. *A Flock Divided: Race, Religion, and Politics in Mexico, 1749–1857*. Durham: Duke University Press, 2010.

Oslender, Ulrich. *The Geographies of Social Movements: Afro-Colombian Mobilization and the Aquatic Space*. Durham: Duke University Press, 2016.

Oudijk, Michel R., and María Castañeda de la Paz. "Un testamento pictográfico de Xochimilco." *Revista Española de Antropología Americana*, vol. 36, no. 2 (2006): 111–123.

Oudijk, Michel R., and Laura Matthew, eds. *Indian Conquistadors: Indigenous Allies in the Conquest of Mesoamerica*. Norman: University of Oklahoma Press, 2007.

Outerbridge, Thomas. "The Disappearing Chinampas of Xochimilco." *The Ecologist*, vol. 17, no. 2/3 (1987): 76–83.

Ouweneel, Arij. *Shadows over Anáhuac: An Ecological Interpretation of Crisis and Development in Central Mexico, 1770–1810*. Albuquerque: University of New Mexico Press, 1996.

Owensby, Brian P. *Empire of Law and Indian Justice in Colonial Mexico*. Stanford: Stanford University Press, 2008.

Palerm, Ángel. *Agua y agricultura: Ángel Palerm, la discusión con Karl Wittfogel sobre el modo asiático de producción y la construcción de un modelo para el estudio de Mesoamérica*. Mexico City: Universidad Iberoamericana and Agencia Española de Cooperación Internacional, Dirección General de Relaciones Culturales y Científicas, 2007.

Obras hidráulicas prehispánicas en el sistema lacustre del Valle de México. Mexico City: Instituto Nacional de Antropología e Historia, 1973.

Parker, Geoffrey. *Global Crisis: War, Climate Change and Catastrophe in the Seventeenth Century*. New Haven: Yale University Press, 2014.

Parsons, Jeffrey R. "The Role of Chinampa Agriculture in the Food Supply of Aztec Tenochtitlan." In Charles E. Cleland, ed., *Cultural Change and Continuity: Essays in Honor of James Bennett Griffin*. 233–257. New York: Academic Press 1976.

Parsons, Jeffrey R., Mary H. Parsons, Virginia Popper, and Mary Taft. "Chinampa Agriculture and Aztec Urbanization in the Valley of Mexico." in I. S. Farrington, ed., *Prehistoric Intensive Agriculture*. 49–96. Oxford: British Archaeological Reports, 1985.

Pérez Zevallos, Juan Manuel. *Xochimilco Ayer*. 3 vols. Mexico City: Instituto Mora, Gobierno del Distrito Federal, Delegación Xochimilco, 2002–2003.

"El Gobierno Indígena de Xochimilco (Siglo XVI)." *Historia Mexicana*, vol. 33, no. 4 (1984): 445–462.

Pérez Zevallos, Juan Manuel, and Luis Reyes García, eds. *La fundación de San Luis Tlaxialtemalco según los títulos primordiales de San Gregorio Atlapulco, 1519–1606*. Mexico City: Instituto Mora, 2003.

Phelan, John Leddy. *The Kingdom of Quito in the Seventeenth Century: Bureaucratic Politics in the Spanish Empire*. Madison: University of Wisconsin Press, 1967.

Pilcher, Jeffrey M. *The Sausage Rebellion: Public Health, Private Enterprise, and Meat in Mexico City, 1890–1917*. Albuquerque: University of New Mexico Press, 2006.

Pizzigoni, Caterina. *The Life Within: Local Indigenous Society in Mexico's Toluca Valley, 1650–1800*. Stanford: Stanford University Press, 2012.

Testaments of Toluca. Stanford: Stanford University Press, 2007.

Polushin, Michael A. "Bureaucratic Conquest, Bureaucratic Culture: Town and Office in Chiapas, 1780–1832." PhD dissertation, Tulane University, 1999.

Prem, Hanns J. "Disease Outbreaks in Central Mexico during the Sixteenth Century." In Noble David Cook and W. George Lovell, eds., *"Secret Judgments of God": Old World Disease in Colonial Spanish America*. 38–42. Norman: University of Oklahoma Press, 1991.

Radding, Cynthia. "The Children of Mayahuel: Agaves, Human Cultures, and Desert Landscapes in Northern Mexico." *Environmental History*, vol. 17, no. 1 (2012): 84–115.

Landscapes of Power and Identity: Comparative Histories in the Sonoran Desert and the Forests of Amazonia from Colony to Republic. Durham: Duke University Press, 2005.

Wandering Peoples: Colonialism, Ethnic Spaces, and Ecological Frontiers in Northwestern Mexico, 1700–1850. Durham: Duke University Press, 1997.

Ramos, Rebeca, Ludka de Gortari Krauss, and Juan Manuel Pérez-Zevallos. *Xochimilco en el siglo XVI.* Mexico City: El Centro de Investigaciones y Estudios Superiores en Antropología Social, Cuadernos de la Casa Chata, 1981.

Restall, Matthew. *When Montezuma Met Cortés: The True Story of the Meeting That Changed History.* New York: Ecco, 2018.

"The New Conquest History." *History Compass,* vol. 10, no. 2 (2012): 151–160.

"A History of the New Philology and the New Philology in History." *Latin American Research Review,* vol. 38, no. 1 (2003): 113–134.

The Maya World: Yucatec Culture and Society, 1550–1850. Stanford: Stanford University Press, 1997.

Restall, Matthew, and Kris Lane. *Latin America in Colonial Times.* New York: Cambridge University Press, 2012.

Reyes García, Luis. "Genealogía de doña Francisca de Guzmán, Xochimilco 1610." *Tlalocan,* vol. 7 (1977): 31–35.

Ringrose, David R. *Madrid and the Spanish Economy, 1560–1850.* Berkeley: University of California Press, 1983.

"Transportation and Economic Stagnation in Eighteenth-Century Castile." *Journal of Economic History,* vol. 28, no. 1 (1968): 51–79.

Rojas Rabiela, Teresa. *La cosecha del agua en la Cuenca de México.* Mexico City: Centro de Investigaciones y Estudios Superiores en Antropología Social, 1998.

ed. *Presente, pasado y futuro de las chinampas.* Mexico City: Centro de Investigaciones y Estudios Superiores en Antroplogía Social, 1995.

ed. *La agricultura chinampera: Compilación histórica.* Mexico City: Universidad Autónoma Chapingo, 1993.

"Ecological and Agricultural Changes in the Chinampas of Xochimilco-Chalco." In H. R. Harvey, ed., *Land and Politics in the Valley of Mexico: A Two Thousand Year Perspective.* 275–290. Albuquerque: University of New Mexico Press, 1991.

Las siembras de ayer: La agricultura indígena del siglo XVI. Mexico City: Centro de Investigaciones y Estudios Superiores en Antroplogía Social, 1988.

"Aspectos tecnológicos de las obras hydráulicas coloniales." In T. Rojas Rabiela, R. Strauss, and J. Lameiras, eds. *Nuevas noticias sobre las obras hidráulicas prehispánicas y coloniales en el Valley de México.* 44–55. Mexico City: Instituto Nacional de Antropología e Historia, 1974.

Rojas Rabiela, Teresa, and Juan Manuel Pérez-Zevallos. *Indice de documentos para la historica del antiguo señorío de Xochimilco.* Mexico City: El Centro de Investigaciones y Estudios Superiores en Antropología Social, Cuadernos de la Casa Chata, 1981.

Rojas Rabiela, Teresa, Elsa Leticia Rea López, and Constantino Medina Lima, eds. *Vidas y bienes olvidados: Testamentos indígenas novohispanos.* 4 vols. Mexico City: Centro de Investigaciones y Estudios Superiores en Antropología Social, Consejo Nacional de Ciencia y Tecnología, 1999–2002.

Rojas Rabiela, Teresa, R. Strauss, and J. Lameiras, eds. *Nuevas noticias sobre las obras hidráulicas prehispánicas y coloniales en el Valle de México.* Mexico City: Instituto Nacional de Antropología e Historia, 1974.

Roller, Heather F. *Amazonian Routes: Indigenous Mobility and Colonial Communities in Northern Brazil.* Stanford: Stanford University Press, 2014.

Romero Frizzi, María de los Ángeles. *Economía y vida de los españoles en la Mixteca Alta: 1519–1720.* Mexico City: Instituto Nacional de Antropología e Historia, 1990.

Ruiz Medrano, Ethelia. *Gobierno y sociedad en Nueva España: Segunda Audiencia y Antonio de Mendoza.* Mexico City: El Colegio de Michoacán y el Gobierno del Estado de Michoacán, 1991.

Sanders, William T., Jeffrey R. Parsons, and Robert S. Santley. *The Basin of Mexico: Ecological Processes in the Evolution of a Civilization.* New York: Academic Press, 1979.

Sauer, Carl O. *Colima of New Spain in the Sixteenth Century.* Berkeley: University of California Press, 1948.

The Aboriginal Population of Northwestern Mexico. Berkeley: University of California Press, 1935.

Schilling, Elisabeth. "Los 'jardines flotantes' de Xochimilco. Una selección." In Teresa Rojas Rabiela, ed., *La agricultura chinampera: Compilación histórica.* 77–109. Mexico City: Universidad Autónoma Chapingo, 1993.

Schroeder, Susan. ed., *Native Resistance and the Pax Colonial in New Spain.* Lincoln: University of Nebraska Press, 1998.

"The Noblewomen of Chalco." *Estudios de Cultura Náhuatl,* vol. 22 (1992): 45–86.

Chimalpahin and the Kingdoms of Chalco. Tucson: University of Arizona Press, 1991.

Schroeder, Susan, and Stafford Poole, eds. *Religion in New Spain.* Albuquerque: University of New Mexico Press, 2007.

Schroeder, Susan, Stephanie Wood, and Robert Haskett, eds. *Indian Women in Early Mexico.* Norman: University of Oklahoma Press, 1997.

Schwaller, Robert C. *Géneros de Gente in Early Colonial Mexico: Defining Racial Difference.* Norman: University of Oklahoma Press, 2016.

"The Importance of Mestizos and Mulatos as Bilingual Intermediaries in Sixteenth- Century New Spain." *Ethnohistory,* vol. 59, no. 4 (2012): 713–738.

Schwartz, Stuart B., and Frank Salomon. "New Peoples and New Kinds of People: Adaptation, Adjustment, and Ethnogenesis in South American Indigenous Societies (Colonial Era)." in Stuart B. Schwartz and Frank Salomon, eds., *The Cambridge History of Native Peoples of the Americas.* 443–502. New York: Cambridge University Press, 1999.

Scott, James C. *The Art of Not Being Governed: An Anarchist History of Upland Southeast Asia.* New Haven: Yale University Press, 2009.

Sempat Assadourian, Carlos. "La despoblación indigena en Perú y Nueva España durante el siglo XVI y la formación de la economía colonial." *Historia Mexicana,* vol. 38, no. 3 (1989): 419–453.

Sherman, William L. "A Conqueror's Wealth: Notes on the Estate of Don Pedro de Alvarado." *The Americas,* vol. 26 (1969): 199–213.

Simpson, Lesley Byrd. *Exploitation of Land in Central Mexico in the Sixteenth Century.* Berkeley: University of California Press, 1952.

Skopyk, Bradley. *Colonial Cataclysms: Climate, Landscape, and Memory in Mexico's Little Ice Age.* Tucson: University of Arizona Press, 2020.

"Rivers of God, Rivers of Empire: Climate Extremes, Environmental Transformation and Agroecology in Colonial Mexico." *Environment and History*, vol. 23, no. 4 (2017): 491–522.

"Undercurrents of Conquest: The Shifting Terrain of Indigenous Agriculture in Colonial Tlaxcala, Mexico." PhD dissertation, York University, 2010.

Sluyter, Andrew. *Black Ranching Frontiers: African Cattle Herders of the Atlantic World, 1500–1900.* New Haven: Yale University Press, 2012.

"Recentism in Environmental History on Latin America." *Environmental History*, vol. 10, no. 1 (2005): 91–93.

Colonialism and Landscape: Postcolonial Theory and Applications. Lanham: Rowman and Littlefield, 2002.

"From Archive to Map to Pastoral Landscape: A Spatial Perspective on the Livestock Ecology of Sixteenth-Century New Spain." *Environmental History*, vol. 3, no. 4 (1998): 508–528.

Smith, Earle C., and Paul Tolstoy. "Vegetation and Man in the Basin of Mexico." *Economic Botany*, vol. 35, no. 4 (1981): 415–433.

Sousa, Lisa. *The Woman Who Turned into a Jaguar and Other Narratives of Native Women in Archives of Colonial Mexico.* Stanford: Stanford University Press, 2017.

Soustelle, Jacques. *Daily Life of the Aztecs on the Eve of the Spanish Conquest.* Patrick O'Brien, trans. Stanford: Stanford University Press, 1961.

Spores, Ronald. *The Mixtecs in Ancient and Colonial Times.* Norman: University of Oklahoma Press, 1984.

Stahle, David W., Edward R. Cook, Dorian J. Burnette et al. "The Mexican Drought Atlas: Tree-Ring Reconstructions of the Soil Moisture Balance during the Late Pre-Hispanic, Colonial, and Modern Eras." *Quaternary Science Reviews*, vol. 149 (2016): 34–60.

Studnicki-Gizbert, Daviken, and David Schecter. "The Environmental Dynamics of a Colonial Fuel-Rush: Silver Mining and Deforestation in New Spain, 1522 to 1810." *Environmental History*, vol. 15, no. 1 (2010): 94–119.

Suárez Argüello, Clara Elena. *Camino real y carrera larga: La arriería en la Nueva España durante el siglo XVIII.* Mexico City: El Centro de Investigaciones y Estudios Superiores en Antropología Social, 1997.

Swan, Susan L. "Drought and Mexico's Struggle for Independence." *Environmental Review*, vol. 6, no. 1 (1982): 54–62.

"Mexico in the Little Ice Age." *Journal of Interdisciplinary History*, vol. 11, no. 4 (1981): 633–648.

Taylor, William B. *Magistrates of the Sacred: Priests and Parishioners in Eighteenth-Century Mexico.* Stanford: Stanford University Press, 1996.

Drinking, Homicide, and Rebellion in Colonial Mexican Villages. Stanford: Stanford University Press, 1979.

Landlord and Peasant in Colonial Oaxaca. Stanford: Stanford University Press, 1972.

Terraciano, Kevin. *The Mixtecs of Colonial Oaxaca: Ñudzahui History, Sixteenth through Eighteenth Centuries.* Stanford: Stanford University Press, 2001.

Tolstoy, Paul. "Settlement and Population Trends in the Basin of Mexico (Ixtapaluca and Zacatenco Phases)." *Journal of Field Archaeology*, vol. 2, no. 4 (1975): 331–349.

Tolstoy, Paul, Suzanne K. Fish, Martin W. Boksenbaum, and Kathryn Blair Vaughn. "Early Sedentary Communities of the Basin of Mexico." *Journal of Field Archaeology*, vol. 4, no. 1 (1977): 91–106.

Tortolero Villaseñor, Alejandro, ed. *Tierra, agua y bosques: Historia y medio ambiente en el México central.* Mexico City: SEMCA, Instituto de Investigaciones Dr. José María Luis Mora, Universidad de Guadalajara, 1996.

Townsend, Camilla. *Annals of Native America: How the Nahuas of Colonial Mexico Kept Their History Alive.* New York: Oxford University Press, 2019.

ed. and trans. *Here in This Year: Seventeenth-Century Nahuatl Annals of the Tlaxcala-Puebla Valley.* Stanford: Stanford University Press, 2010.

Tutino, John M. *Making a New World: Founding Capitalism in the Bajío and Spanish North America.* Durham: Duke University Press, 2011.

"The Revolutionary Capacity of Rural Communities: Ecological Autonomy and Its Demise." In Elisa Servín, Leticia Reina, and John Tutino, eds., *Cycles of Conflict, Centuries of Change: Crisis, Reform, and Revolution in Mexico.* 211–268. Durham: Duke University Press, 2007.

From Insurrection to Revolution in Mexico: Social Bases of Agrarian Violence, 1750-1940. Princeton: Princeton University Press, 1989.

"Creole Mexico: Spanish Elites, Haciendas, and Indian Towns, 1750–1810." PhD dissertation, University of Texas at Austin, 1976.

"Hacienda Social Relations in Mexico: The Chalco Region in the Era of Independence." *Hispanic American Historical Review*, vol. 55, no. 3 (1975): 496–528.

Vågene, Åshild J., et al. "Salmonella Enterica Genomes from Victims of a Major Sixteenth- Century Epidemic in Mexico." *Nature Ecology and Evolution*, vol. 2, no. 3 (2018): 520–528.

Van Young, Eric. "Two Decades of Anglophone Historical Writing on Colonial Mexico: Continuity and Change since 1980." *Mexican Studies/Estudios Mexicanos*, vol. 20, no. 2 (2004): 275–326.

The Other Rebellion: Popular Violence, Ideology, and the Mexican Struggle for Independence, 1810–1821. Stanford: Stanford University Press, 2001.

"The New Cultural History Comes to Old Mexico." *Hispanic American Historical Review*, vol. 79, no. 2 (1999): 211–247.

"Mexican Rural History since Chevalier: The Historiography of the Colonial Hacienda." *Latin American Research Review*, vol. 18, no. 3 (1983): 5–61.

Hacienda and Market in Eighteenth-Century Mexico: The Rural Economy of the Guadalajara Region, 1675–1820. Berkeley: University of California Press, 1981.

Vassberg, David E. *The Village and the Outside World in Golden Age Castile: Mobility and Migration in Everyday Rural Life.* New York: Cambridge University Press, 1996.

Land and Society in Golden Age Castile. New York: Cambridge University Press, 1984.

Viqueira Albán, Juan Pedro, and Tadashi Obara-Saeki. *El arte de contar tributarios: Provincia de Chiapas, 1560–1821*. Mexico City: El Colegio de México, 2017.

Vitz, Matthew. *A City on a Lake: Urban Political Ecology and the Growth of Mexico City*. Durham: Duke University Press, 2018.

Vries, Jan de. *The Dutch Rural Economy in the Golden Age, 1500–1700*. New Haven: Yale University Press, 1974.

White, Richard. *The Middle Ground: Indians, Empires, and Republics in the Great Lakes Region, 1650–1815*. New York: Cambridge University Press, 2010.

White, Sam. *A Cold Welcome: The Little Ice Age and Europe's Encounter with North America*. Cambridge: Harvard University Press, 2017.

Whitmore, Thomas M. *Disease and Death in Early Colonial Mexico: Simulating Amerindian Depopulation*. Boulder: Westview Press, 1992.

"A Simulation of Sixteenth Century Population Collapse in the Basin of Mexico." *Annals of the Association of American Geographers*, vol. 81, no. 4 (1991): 464–487.

Wilken, Gene C. "A Note on Buoyancy and Other Dubious Characteristics of the 'Floating' Chinampas of Mexico." In I. S. Farrington, ed., *Prehistoric Intensive Agriculture in the Tropics*, vol. 1. 31–48. Oxford: British Archaeological Reports, 1985.

Wittfogel, Karl. *Oriental Despotism: A Comparative Study of Total Power*. New Haven: Yale University Press, 1957.

"Developmental Aspects of Hydraulic Societies." In J. Steward, ed., *Irrigation Civilizations: A Comparative Study – A Symposium on Method and Result in Cross- Cultural Regularities*. 28–42. Washington, DC: Pan American Union Social Science Monographs 1, 1955.

Wolf, Eric R. "The Vicissitudes of the Closed Corporate Peasant Community." *American Ethnologist*, vol. 13, no. 2 (May, 1986): 325–329.

"Closed Corporate Peasant Communities.in Mesoamerica and Central Java." *Southwestern Journal of Anthropology*, vol. 13, no. 1 (Spring, 1957): 1–18.

Wood, Stephanie. "Corporate Adjustments in Colonial Mexican Indian Towns: Toluca Region, 1550–1810." PhD dissertation, University of California, Los Angeles, 1984.

Yannakakis, Yanna. *The Art of Being In-Between: Native Intermediaries, Indian Identity, and Local Rule in Colonial Oaxaca*. Durham: Duke University Press, 2008.

Yun Casalilla, Bartolomé. *Sobre la transición al capitalismo en Castilla: Economía y sociedad en Tierra de Campos, 1500–1830*. Valladolid: Junta de Castilla y León, Consejería de Educación y Cultura, 1987.

Zavala, Silvio A. *Estudios acerca de la historia del trabajo en México*. Mexico City: El Colegio de México, Centro de Estudios Históricos, 1988.

El servicio personal de los indios en la Nueva España. Mexico City: Colegio de México, Centro de Estudios Históricos, Colegio Nacional, 1984.

ed. *Ordenanzas del trabajo, siglos XVI y XVII*. Mexico City: Editorial Elede, 1947.

Index

Other Books in the Series (continued from page ii)